HANDBOOK OF GLOBAL RESEARCH AND PRACTICE IN CORRUPTION

Handbook of Global Research and Practice in Corruption

Edited by

Adam Graycar

Australian National University, Canberra, Australia

Russell G. Smith

Australian Institute of Criminology, Canberra, Australia

Edward Elgar

Cheltenham, UK • Northampton, MA, USA

Published by
Edward Elgar Publishing Limited
The Lypiatts
15 Lansdown Road
Cheltenham
Glos GL50 2JA
UK

Edward Elgar Publishing, Inc.
William Pratt House
9 Dewey Court
Northampton
Massachusetts 01060
USA

A catalogue record for this book
is available from the British Library

Library of Congress Control Number: 2011931004

FSC
www.fsc.org
MIX
Paper from
responsible sources
FSC® C018575

ISBN 978 1 84980 501 8 (cased)

Typeset by Servis Filmsetting Ltd, Stockport, Cheshire
Printed and bound by MPG Books Group, UK

Contents

Contributors

Editors

Adam Graycar is Professor of Public Policy at the Australian National University (ANU), where he is also Dean of the Australian National Institute for Public Policy and Director of the Research School of Social Sciences. In 2010 he established the Transnational Research Institute on Corruption at the ANU. From 1994 to 2003 he was Director of the Australian Institute of Criminology, a Federal Government research agency. He has had long experience both in government and in academia. He has held academic posts in Australia and in the United States, and has worked internationally across several spheres.

Russell G. Smith has qualifications in law, psychology and criminology from the University of Melbourne and a Ph.D. from King's College London. He practised as a lawyer before becoming a lecturer in criminology at the University of Melbourne. He then took up a position at the Australian Institute of Criminology, where he is now Principal Criminologist and head of the Global Economic and Electronic Crime Program. He has published extensively on aspects of computer crime, fraud control, and professional regulation and is currently President of the Australian and New Zealand Society of Criminology.

Contributors

Jay S. Albanese is a criminologist and Professor in the Wilder School of Government and Public Affairs at Virginia Commonwealth University. He served as Chief of the International Center at the National Institute of Justice from 2002–2006. Recent books include: *Organized Crime in Our Times* (2011), *Transnational Crime and the 21st Century* (2011), and *Professional Ethics in Criminal Justice: Being Ethical When No One is Looking* (2011).

Shreya Basu is a Research Fellow at the Lee Kuan Yew School of Public Policy (National University of Singapore). Her current research focuses on governance and anti-corruption reforms in developing countries. In her previous appointment as an analyst at Ernst & Young India she participated in advisory and assessment projects for private sector corporations on corruption-related laws, regulations and standards.

Linda Courtenay Botterill is Professor in Australian Public Policy at the University of Canberra. Her field of expertise is Australian politics and public policy with a focus on rural policy and politics. Her work in this area builds on nearly 15 years as a public policy practitioner in the Australian Public Service, as a policy officer in two industry associations and as an adviser in the Office of the Minister for Primary Industries and Energy. Her work is focused on the policy development process with a particular interest in the role of values in the policy process and how these values become embodied in institutional structures.

J. Edgardo Campos is Governance Adviser for Bangladesh at the World Bank. Before joining the bank he was an Assistant Professor of Public Policy and Management at the Wharton School of the University of Pennsylvania. He has co-authored three books and numerous papers on issues pertaining to political economy, governance and corruption. In 1997, Campos and his co-author were awarded the Charles Levine Prize for the best book on comparative politics.

David Chaikin is an Associate Professor in Business Law at the University of Sydney Business School, and a practising attorney. David has been a Senior Assistant Secretary and Head of the International Criminal Law Enforcement and Security Branch of the Australian Attorney-General's Department, and a Senior Legal Officer with the London-based diplomatic body, the Commonwealth Secretariat. He is an advisor to governments and multinational corporations in the Asia/Pacific region. His publications include *Corruption and Money Laundering: A Symbiotic Relationship* (2009); *Money Laundering, Tax Evasion and Tax Havens* (2009); and *A Critical Examination of How Contract Law is Used by Financial Institutions Operating in Multiple Jurisdictions* (2010).

Duncan Chappell, a lawyer and criminologist, is currently an Adjunct Professor in the Faculty of Law at the University of Sydney, and an Adjunct Professor in the School of Criminology at Simon Fraser University in British Columbia, Canada. A former Director of the Australian Institute of Criminology and former Deputy President of the Commonwealth Administrative Appeals Tribunal, he has also held senior academic posts in Australia, Canada and the United States. His recent research and publishing activities include art crime and the illicit traffic of cultural objects.

Dr Cindy Davids is a Senior Lecturer in the School of Law at Deakin University in Melbourne, Australia. Her interdisciplinary legal research expertise encompasses legal regulation and professional misconduct, professional and public sector ethics, anti-corruption, and police accountability. Dr Davids has been the Chief Investigator on a number of significant collaborations with organisations such as the Australian Federal Police, the Victorian Ombudsman, and Victoria Police. Her book *Conflict of Interest in Policing* was published in 2008.

Inez Dussuyer is Principal Investigation Officer at the Victorian Ombudsman. She has conducted a number of investigations in this role since 2005. Prior to that Inez held a number of positions in the Victorian Department of Justice, including Project Manager for the Victorian Implementation Review of the Recommendations from the Royal Commission Into Aboriginal Deaths In Custody and Assistant Director (Research) at Crime Prevention Victoria. She is a criminologist and has worked in academic institutions in Canada, France and Australia.

Lisa Ann Elges is a human rights lawyer specializing in criminal law and governance issues. For 12 years, she has studied and worked in Japan, later serving as legal advisor and programme manager with the Asia Crime Prevention Foundation in conjunction with the UN Asia and Far East Institute from the Prevention of Crime and Treatment of Offenders. She joined the TI Asia Pacific Department in 2000 where she most recently developed the Forest Governance Integrity Programme. She now manages the Climate Governance Programme at TI while pursuing her Ph.D. at the Environment and Policy Research Institute of the Frei Universitaet in Berlin.

Marcus Felson is Professor of Criminal Justice at Texas State University. He is author of *Crime and Nature* (2006) as well as *Crime and Everyday Life* (2010), and co-author (with Ronald V. Clarke) of *Opportunity Makes the Thief* (1998). He has authored 'A theory of co-offending' (Crime Prevention Studies, Volume 15, 2003) and 'Redesigning hell: preventing crime and disorder at the port authority bus terminal' (Crime Prevention Studies, Volume 6, 1996, *Preventing Mass Transit Crime*). Professor Felson is the originator of the routine-activity approach to crime rate analysis and has lectured in more than 20 countries on that topic.

Scott A. Fritzen, Vice-Dean (Academic Affairs) and Associate Professor at the Lee Kuan Yew School of Public Policy (National University of Singapore), specializes in the analysis of governance reform and capacity strengthening in developing countries. His current research focuses on the comparative analysis of anti-corruption strategies, public sector decentralization and social policy reforms in Southeast Asia. His Master in Public Affairs and Urban and Regional Planning degree and Ph.D. in Public Affairs are both from the Woodrow Wilson School of Public and International Affairs, Princeton University.

Larissa Gray is a lawyer by background currently working in the Financial Market Integrity Unit of the World Bank on AML/CFT and related issues, including the Stolen Asset Recovery Initiative. She has been at the Bank since 2008 and has authored four publications: *Stolen Asset Recovery: A Good Practices Guide to Non-Conviction Based Asset Forfeiture* (2008); *Politically Exposed Persons: A Guide for the Banking Sector* (2009); *Asset Recovery Handbook* (2011) and *Barriers to Asset Recovery Study* (in press). Prior to joining the World Bank, she was a criminal prosecutor in Canada.

Rose Gill Hearn has been Commissioner of the New York City Department of Investigation since inception of the Bloomberg Administration in 2002 and is the longest serving DOI Commissioner. Under the Commissioner's leadership, DOI has established new corruption prevention and remediation initiatives; achieved record-high arrest numbers; and hosted the first New York City National Watchdog Conference. Gill Hearn contributed to the book *Local Integrity Systems: World Cities Fighting Corruption and Safeguarding Integrity* (2008) and *Public Integrity*, a journal on ethics and leadership. Prior to her appointment as Commissioner, Gill Hearn was an Assistant United States Attorney in the Southern District of New York.

Finn Heinrich is Programme Manager, Research Department, Transparency International Secretariat, Germany. Finn Heinrich is co-ordinating TI's research activities, with a focus on anti-corruption assessment tools, in particular the National Integrity System Assessment programme. Prior to joining TI in August 2008, he was the Director of Programs at the international civil society network CIVICUS: World Alliance for Citizen Participation. Finn holds a Ph.D. in Political Science from Fern Universität Hagen (Germany) and a master's degree in Social Sciences from University of Mannheim and has published several articles and books on civil society and governance issues.

Robin Hodess is Group Director, Research & Knowledge, Transparency International Secretariat, USA, and was appointed Group Director of Research and Knowledge at TI in January 2011. Her previous roles at TI include Director of Policy and Research and Chief Editor of the Global Corruption Report. She came to TI and Berlin from New York, where she had developed a programme on economic globalisation, 'Justice and the World Economy,' for the Carnegie Council on Ethics and International Affairs. Prior to this, she taught media and politics at the Free University Berlin and Leipzig University.

Penny Jorna has a Bachelor of Arts in Psychology and Graduate Certificate in Criminology both from Charles Sturt University, and a Masters in Criminology from the University of Sydney. She has undertaken market research and taught English in South Korea as well as working for publishing companies and the Australian Government Department of Defence. She is currently a Research Officer in the Global Economic and Electronic Crime Program at the Australian Institute of Criminology.

Matti Joutsen is Director of International Affairs at the Ministry of Justice of Finland. He has worked as a criminologist at the National Research Institute of Legal Policy at the Ministry of Justice (1974–1981) and as Senior Researcher and subsequently as Director of the European Institute for Crime Prevention and Control, affiliated with the United Nations (1981–2000). He has been an expert to the United Nations, the Council of Europe and the European Union on, among others, issues relating to corruption. He headed the delegation of Finland in the drafting of the United Nations Convention against Transnational Organized Crime (UNTOC) and the United Nations Convention against Corruption (UNCAC).

Louis de Koker is a Professor of Law at Deakin University, Australia, and a Visiting Professor at the University of Johannesburg, South Africa. He holds various degrees in law, including a doctorate and a master's degree in corporate law from the University of the Free State, South Africa, and a master's degree from St John's College, Cambridge. Prior to joining Deakin University he was the director of the Centre for the Study of Economic Crime at the University of Johannesburg. His research focuses on money laundering control in developing countries. As a consultant to the various international bodies, including the Financial Market Integrity Unit of the World Bank. he has advised various governments on financial crime risk assessment and appropriate regulation.

Peter Larmour is Professor of Public Administration and Policy at the University of the South Pacific in Suva, Fiji. His book *Interpreting Corruption: Culture and Politics in the Pacific Islands* is due out from the University of Hawaii Press in January 2012. He co-edited *Governments NGOS and Anti Corruption: the New Integrity Warriors* (Routledge 2009) with Barry Hindess and Luis de Sousa. He teaches an annual course on 'Corruption and Anti-Corruption' with the New South Wales Independent Commission Against Corruption at the Australian National University.

William B. Magrath is Lead Natural Resource Economist in the South Asia Agriculture Unit of the World Bank, where he is responsible for economic and sector studies and investments in forestry and natural resources management and the World Bank's work on environment and natural resource law enforcement. He is the lead author of *Timber Theft Prevention: Introduction to Security for Forest Managers* (2007) and studies on natural resource accounting, common property management and soil conservation. He has graduate degrees from the University of Michigan.

Bryane Michael has over 12 years of experience in anti-corruption. He has served as an advisor to some of the largest governments – including the governments of Russia, Turkey, Bulgaria, Ukraine, Bolivia and others and a number of international agencies (EU, UNDP OECD, OSCE, World Bank, and others). He spent much of his professional life at the World Bank and later OECD before returning to academia. His academic background includes a recent Adjunct Professorship at Columbia University, several years as a non-resident fellow at the Stockholm School of Economics, almost 10 years of teaching at Oxford University and graduate work in economics at Harvard and Oxford.

Shaun Moss is the Regional Procurement Manager for the East Asia and Pacific Region of the World Bank. He spent six years working in the Europe and Central Asia Region, where he led the Bank's work on public procurement reform in several countries. Before joining the Bank in 1999, Mr. Moss was a director of a leading UK consulting firm specializing in procurement.

Richard Mulgan is Emeritus Professor of Government in the Crawford School of Economics and Government at the Australian National University, Canberra. His most recent book *Holding Power to Account* (2003) explores the various dimensions of accountability. His research interests include Greek political theory, accountability and public management.

Stephen Mumford is the Director of Investigations at the Victorian Ombudsman (VO). In this role he manages major investigations and systemic reviews, with many matters culminating in reports tabled in Parliament. Several of these investigations have arisen from disclosures made to the Ombudsman using the provisions of the Whistleblowers Protection Act 2001. He has 11 years' experience at VO, initially as a senior investigator and then managing the Ombudsman's complaint-handling functions. Prior to joining the VO, Stephen worked as a practitioner and a manager in a variety of community services settings

Gregory P. Noone is a member of the Public International Law and Policy Group (PILPG), a nonprofit organization that provides free legal assistance to developing states and substate entities involved in conflicts. He also teaches international law and politics at West Virginia University and is an Adjunct Professor of Law at Roger Williams University School of Law and Case Western Reserve University. He appears regularly as a commentator on international and national television and radio.

Nicole Leeper Piquero is a Professor in the Criminology Program at the University of Texas at Dallas and currently serves as a Trustee-at-Large on the Academy of Criminal Justice Sciences Executive Board. She received her Ph.D. in Criminology and Criminal Justice from the University of Maryland. Her research focus includes the study of white-collar and corporate crimes, criminological theory, as well as gender and crime.

Kenneth Polk joined the Criminology Department, University of Melbourne in 1985. He received his BA at San Diego State, MA at Northwestern, and Ph.D. at UCLA (all in sociology). He was previously Professor of Sociology at the University of Oregon. A major focus of recent research has been on violence and homicide, but he also has examined issues of crime prevention, juvenile justice and white collar crime. He is a leading authority on art crime.

Francesca Recanatini is a Senior Public Sector Specialist in the Public Sector Governance anchor (PRMPS) of the World Bank. She leads the Anti-corruption Thematic Group providing advice and guidance on anti-corruption preventive work and institutions of accountability. She also co-ordinates the work on governance and anti-corruption diagnostic tools and indicators in sectors and in fragile countries and the work on Anti-Corruption Authorities. Before joining the World Bank, she worked at the IRIS Center at the University of Maryland focusing on institutional reforms in transition economies.

Grant Schubert holds a Bachelor of Laws with First Class Honours from Victoria University, Melbourne. In 2009 he completed a clerkship in the Criminal Justice Division of the Australian Government Attorney-General's Department. He graduated from the Leo Cussen Institute, Melbourne, in 2010, and was admitted as an officer of the Victorian Supreme Court. In the same year, Grant undertook an academic research position in the School of Law at Deakin University, during which the research for his joint chapter in this volume was undertaken. He is presently a Legal Officer with the Commonwealth Director of Public Prosecutions.

Ian Scott is Visiting Professor at the City University of Hong Kong and Emeritus Professor and Fellow of the Asia Research Centre at Murdoch University in Perth, Australia. He taught at the University of Hong Kong between 1976 and 1995 and was Chair Professor of the Department of Politics and Public Administration between 1990 and 1995. Between 1995 and 2002, he was Chair Professor of Government and Politics at Murdoch University. His latest book is *The Public Sector in Hong Kong* (2010).

Dina Siegel is Professor of Criminology at Utrecht University in the Netherlands. She received her Ph.D. in cultural anthropology from the VU University, Amsterdam. She has published on the Russian mafia, human trafficking, crime in the diamond sector, XTC industry, underground banking, and the role of women in criminal organizations. Her most recent publications include: *The Mazzel Ritual: Customs, Culture and Crime in the Diamond Trade* (2009) and *Organized Crime: Culture, Markets and Policies* (2007).

Glenn Sullivan is a Director at the Victorian Ombudsman's (VO) office having joined in 2007 after a long career in complaint resolution at the Transport Accident Commission. He has been responsible for leading several major whistleblower investigations at the VO's office. Glenn has represented the VO's office and provided input to an interdepartmental committee responsible for reviewing the Whistleblowers Protection Act 2001. He has also conducted VO training sessions for public sector staff in whistleblowing and complaint handling. He is the co-author of Ombudsman Victoria's Good Practice Guide to complaint handling for Victorian Public Sector Agencies.

John Wanna is the Sir John Bunting Chair of Public Administration (ANZSOG) at the Australian National Institute for Public Policy at the Australian National University, Canberra. His latest books include *Comparing Westminster* (2009), *The Reality of Budget Reform in OECD Nations* (2010) and *Policy in Action* (2010). His interests include public management, executive politics, budgeting and public finance.

Glenn T. Ware is Chief Investigative Counselor with the World Bank's Department of Institutional Integrity, where he supervises fraud and corruption investigations. Before joining the Bank, he served as Managing Director of Diligence, a global risk management and consulting firm. He has published many scholarly articles on anticorruption and global governance. He holds a law degree from Harvard Law School.

PART I

CONTEXTUALISING CORRUPTION

1 Research and practice in corruption: an introduction

Adam Graycar and Russell G. Smith

Corruption has been a feature of human behaviour since the beginning of time. It has been part of the structure of human relationships, and very much bound into the way people live with each other and distribute status and power. While some say that patronage and rent-seeking have lubricated social relationships, there is sufficient evidence to show that it is the poorest who are hurt when this behaviour is institutionalized. It is even more distressing when the behaviour is unpredictable, irregular, and random.

International trade has been a feature of human behaviour for millennia. But in recent centuries new transport mechanisms and new technologies have made for economic interdependence. Compounded by digital technologies which move money around the world at the speed of light, and global business moguls who seek advantage opportunistically and capriciously, corruption takes on a new dimension. Political instability has also taken on a cross-national dimension, and it is often fuelled by, and in turn fuels corruption.

Corruption has great significance for society and its governance. While the level of corruption varies among countries, the impacts of corruption disproportionally affect the poorest and most vulnerable in any society. When it is pervasive, corruption weakens economic growth and undermines the rule of law for *every nation,* and invariably deters investment. In rich countries corruption pushes taxes to higher levels than they need to be, and services are of lesser quality than they might be.

This book is an edited collection of new, original research and policy analysis dealing with the most important concepts and empirical research in corruption and its prevention. Its focus is international and transnational. It provides a critical analysis of the key areas of current research interest in corruption and its control and also outlines a potential research agenda for the future. It has a research rather than a practitioner focus, and seeks to provide a single source-book of current research and discussion on topical and critical aspects of foreign corrupt practices globally.

Corruption manifests itself in many ways and at different levels. Corrupt behaviour causes outrage to victims and those who value civil society; it impedes good government and administrative practice. In 2008 the World Economic Forum (2008) estimated that corruption accounts for about 5 per cent of global GDP (about US $2.6 trillion) and furthermore it is estimated that every year around $1 trillion is paid in bribes and $40 billion is looted by corrupt political leaders

Corruption poses threats to principles of democracy, justice and the economy. It affects all countries regardless of their level of development. Nevertheless, some countries experience corruption more than others, and of course some places have more corruption than others. There is a widespread but still non-random distribution of corruption in societies, and thus a challenging field of study for scholars from various disciplines with the ongoing arguments about a uniform definition and measurement of corruption and, importantly, the limited effect of scholarly work in this area.

The academic literature on corruption is often focused on big picture examples of corruption: studies of whole regimes and studies of nation states (Larmour & Barcham, 2006; Chang & Chu, 2008; Transparency International, 2009a), studies of economic development on a grand scale (Stapenhurst & Kpundeh, 1999; Levy & Kpundeh, 2004), and studies of the rule of law (Licht et al., 2007; Uslaner, 2008). There are global league tables of corruption (Transparency International, 2009b); there are indexes of bribe paying (Transparency International, 2008a); there are studies of corruption in whole sectors such as in water (Transparency International, 2008b), health (Transparency International, 2006), climate change (Transparency International, 2010). There are studies of situations such as the context and operations of corrupt subsidy frauds (Passas & Nelken, 1993); there are studies of victims of corrupt behaviour (Hunt, 2007) whether they be food aid recipients (Deshingkar et al., 2005; Radelet, 2006), victims of shoddy construction (Green, 2005), or banking victims (Passas, 1996 and 1997).

There is a very diverse literature on corruption and a great deal of this is bound within disciplinary categories. In the political science literature Heidenheimer and Johnston (2008) have edited a thousand-page volume that covers definitions and perceptions, modernization and development, political processes and comparisons across time and place, as well as specific studies of activities in Africa and Asia, studies in authoritarian regimes and liberal democracies, and also processes in political parties and political campaigns. The themes here focus on distortions of process and the corrupt manipulation of systems structured for the benefit of many that are hijacked for the advantage of the few. Studies of political corruption help us understand the institutions and processes that allocate power and achieve or distort the attainment of well-intentioned and articulated political goals.

Johnston (2005) takes the analysis further in his book *Syndromes of Corruption* where he documents, with strong data, how groups exchange wealth and power and do so in the shadow of the strengths and weaknesses of the state. By identifying 'influence markets', 'elite cartels', 'oligarchs and clans' and 'official moguls' he shows how reform can be applied, building on the evidence of operations of these syndromes in different political environments

From the seminal work of Susan Rose-Ackerman (1975) on the economics of corruption to more recent comprehensive analyses of corruption, economists have examined corruption in virtually every aspect of macroeconomic and microeconomic behaviour and in the allocation, distribution and delivery of goods and services. Aidt (2003), for example, covers issues such as incentives, rents, welfare effects, institutional capacity and self-reinforcing corruption, while Khan and Sundaram (2000) have a focus on the specifics of corruption in economic development. The World Bank (http://www.worldbank.org/) has focused on development issues and has a massive literature on corruption measurement and control (Kaufman et al., 2006) and governance options (Kaufman, 2005). The World Bank Institute (www.worldbank.org/wbi), a research unit within the World Bank, currently undertakes economic analyses of seven topics: climate change; growth and crisis; governance; fragile and conflict-affected states; health systems; public–private partnerships; and urban studies. Rose-Ackerman (1999) weaves many threads together by examining the economic impact of corruption and how high level officials manipulate political power and civil service processes, especially in the development context.

Historians have documented ancient and recent manifestations of the phenomenon. Anthropologists have studied gifts, bribes and patronage in different cultures, while lawyers have written extensively on the rule of law and the jurisprudence surrounding corruption. International agencies such as the United Nations, the World Bank, Transparency International and a host of NGOs have made extensive studies of corruption and gone the extra step to propose positive responses to its control. However, many of these reports focus on whole countries or are at a very high level of abstraction.

Specific works such as Quah's (2003) *Controlling Corruption in Asia*, and Larmour and Wolanin's (2001) *Corruption and Anti-Corruption* propose practical institutional responses. Passas (1998) has written about how transnational organized crime has fuelled corruption and how illegal markets have been manipulated by criminal operators, thus weakening social control. Numerous specific studies focus on preventing and controlling economic crime (Grabosky, 2001), money laundering (Levi et al., 2007), and building organizational integrity (Boardman & Klum, 2001).

Anechiarico and Jacobs (1996) issue a note of caution and argue that the pursuit of absolute integrity, the proliferation of mechanisms to root out corruption, can sometimes be counter-productive and make it much more difficult to govern.

To begin with, nearly everyone has views about what activities and behaviours are corrupt; – but in many respects corruption is like an elephant – it's easier to identify than it is to describe! Definitions abound – most commonly the Transparency International (2010) definition 'the abuse of entrusted power for private gain'. Also useful is Robert Klitgaard's (1991) formula C = M+D-A (corruption equals monopoly plus discretion minus accountability). This provides a basis for shaping culture and work activities.

The measurement of corruption has always been problematic due to several reasons such as the hidden nature of corruption, the lack of consensus on the definition of corruption and, last but not least, the multifaceted nature of corruption. Still in general, activities that involve bribery and graft, extortion, kickbacks, misappropriation theft and fraud by virtue of one's position, self-dealing, patronage, abuse of discretion, creating or exploiting conflict of interest, nepotism, clientelism and favouritism, as well as political manipulation are all generally agreed to constitute corrupt behaviour. These various corrupt behaviours occur in different activities and different sectors of all societies. Most commonly these apply in:

- buying things (procurement processes, issuing contracts etc.);
- appointing personnel;
- delivering programmes or services;
- making things (road construction, major capital works, housing developments etc.);
- controlling activities (licensing/regulation/issuing of permits etc.); and
- many forms of administration (justice mostly, but also health, environmental services, etc.).

As can be understood from this classification every sector that delivers services to the public is vulnerable, and different societies may be expected to have vastly different experiences. And again this is the case in both rich countries and poor countries. Despite this fact a great deal of the literature on corruption focuses on poor countries and sets admirable strategies that develop means and methods for:

- criminalization, investigation, prosecution, sanctions;
- the workings of anti-corruption agencies;

- structural reform (civil service, legislature, judiciary etc.); and
- capacity building (education, strengthening integrity, mobilization of the public etc.).

Rich countries generally have these controls in place and yet there are still many examples of petty and serious corruption (minor incidents, scandals, and state capture) even where there is legislation and enforcement, structural integrity and a vigilant press. Implementation of these uniform strategies does not always yield successful results as corruption can take many forms with regard to its nature, focus, and scope. Therefore as McCusker (2006) states, with our background of inoperative and/or disintegrated controls, every anti-corruption strategy should focus on the sophisticated relationship between the initiators, participants and targets of the corrupt act.

Analysis of corruption, and strategies to prevent and or control corruption activities can take place on a sector-by-sector basis. We can study economic institutions and global trade; we could examine international conflict and the trade in weapons. We know that justice systems that unfairly deny the rule of law have severe consequences as well as international implications. Much the same can be said of corruption in agriculture, energy and resources and environmental and climate change matters. The nation state used to be the main unit for analysis, but this is clearly no longer the case. Corruption has global impacts, and while much legislation is limited by national borders, nefarious activities cross borders with impunity, and law enforcement is often severely constrained by jurisdictional limits.

Through rigorous analysis and theoretical foundations, this book provides a multi-disciplinary and international account of corruption and its control from the perspectives of public policy, criminal law and criminology, as well as considering principles of prevention and control of corruption in both the public and private sectors across the globe. We include research and analysis from countries representing all continents, thus providing a unique opportunity to examine how legal and policy responses have been created to deal with the problems of corruption that arise not only in new and developing economies, but also in Western democratic regions that, despite their best efforts, continue to fall prey to corrupt practice in government and business.

This book has a tri-partite structure that begins with a review of corruption in its historical perspective and a comparative analysis of research into corruption which has developed, globally over time, particularly since 1990 when there has been increased awareness of the relevance of corruption to economic and social development. Consideration is then given to the global dynamics of corruption control and the work conducted at the World Bank in which the design and implementation of governance and anti-corruption reforms are based on micro-data and greater ownership of the diagnostic process by individual countries.

Part II explores corruption as it occurs in practice in varying sectors, markets and jurisdictions. In relation to public sector activities, the risks of corruption that arise in government procurement are presented and solutions given for minimizing such risks, especially for the largest economies. A case study is then presented of how the sanctions against Iraq in the Oil For Food programme were circumvented. There are lessons for governments in how to avoid procurement-related corruption in global aid programmes.

Turning to the major environmental challenges facing the 21st century, evidence is presented of how corruption has arisen in connection with major environmental change programmes globally. Some of the governance challenges within climate finance flows are considered and suggestions made for overcoming such challenges through enhanced safeguards and measures to ensure better transparency, accountability and integrity. One environmental approach, Reducing Carbon Emissions from Deforestation and Forest Degradation (REDD+), is examined and consideration given to the more general risks of corruption that have arisen in connection with the forestry industry.

In relation to the business world, we examine the relationship between corruption and financial crime and, in particular, how fraud and financial crime are facilitated by corrupt practices, including opportunities for corruption created by the global financial crisis and government stimulus payments. The ways in which corruption can be facilitated through the use of international financial transactions is explored in a chapter which examines the presence of corrupt practices involving offshore financial centres. A specific case study is also provided of corruption in the global diamond trade and another chapter reviews the many corrupt practices that have arisen in connection with the global trade in art and antiquities. Part II concludes with an analysis of how information and communications technologies have not only facilitated conventional corrupt practices, but created new opportunities for corruption within the information technology industry itself.

Part III explores the avenues that exist for corruption to be prevented and controlled and provides illustrations of some of the more successful developments in a variety of countries. It begins by exploring how preventive measures can best be monitored and evaluated, and how monitoring progress in the fight against corruption takes place in multi-project, multi-stakeholder organizations. It then describes the international normative approaches that have been taken to the control of corruption, especially the United Nations Convention Against Corruption and then examines some of the specific legislative responses that countries have used to prevent corrupt conduct and, more particularly, to follow the financial proceeds of corrupt conduct. An example is provided of how one anti-corruption measure, the OECD's Convention against Bribery, has been implemented in the United States, the United Kingdom and Australia.

Consideration is also given to how the global anti-money laundering regime and the laws that enable the confiscation of the proceeds of crime and criminally-derived assets can be used in the fight against global corruption. One particular issue that is explored concerns the question of whether an activist regulatory stance can overcome legislative problems in preventive anti-corruption agencies such as those present in Montenegro. A case study of one of the world's first, and most successful anti-corruption agencies is then presented with an examination of Hong Kong's Independent Commission Against Corruption, and how this has evolved over time.

Part III then turns to an analysis of how cultures of integrity can be promoted within both the public and private sectors, and also how educational measures can be used to minimize risks of corruption occurring. Of course, it is apparent that raising awareness of corruption requires systems and procedures to be created that enable individuals who become aware of illegality to report it in the public interest. We examine a number of innovative approaches to whistleblowing in Australia, in this regard. Finally, we end with an examination of the methods and politics of performance measurement in anti-corruption agencies and the extent to which performance indicators affect institutional survival.

REFERENCES

Aidt, T. (2003), 'Economic analysis of corruption: a survey', *Economic Journal*, **113**(491), 632–52.

Anechiarico, F. and J. Jacobs (1996), *The Pursuit of Absolute Integrity: How Corruption Control makes Government Ineffective*, Chicago: University of Chicago Press.

Boardman, C. and V. Klum (2001), 'Building organisational integrity', in P. Larmour & N. Wolanin (eds), *Corruption and Anti-corruption*, Canberra: Asia Pacific Press, 82–96.

Chang, E. and Y. Chu (2008), 'Corruption and trust: exceptionalism in asian democracies?, *The Journal of Politics*, **68**(2), 259–71.

Deshingkar, P., C. Johnson & J. Farrington (2005), 'State transfers to the poor and back: The case of the food-for-work program in India', *World Development* **33**(4), 575–91.

Grabosky, P. (2001) 'The prevention and control of economic crime', in P. Larmour & N. Wolanin (eds), *Corruption and Anti-corruption*, Canberra: Asia Pacific Press, 146–58.

Green, P. (2005) 'Disaster by design: corruption, construction and catastrophe', *British Journal of Criminology*, **45**(4), 528.

Heidenheimer, A. and M. Johnston (eds), (2008), *Political Corruption: Concepts & Contexts*, New Brunswick, N.J.: Transaction Publishers.
Hunt, J. (2007), 'How corruption hits people when they are down', *Journal of Development Economics*, **84**(2), 574–89.
Johnston, M. (2005), *Syndromes of Corruption: Wealth, Power, and Democracy*, New York: Cambridge University Press.
Kaufmann, D. (2005), 'Back to basics – 10 myths about governance and corruption', *Finance and Development – English Edition*, **42**(3), 41–3.
Kaufmann, D., A. Kraay, A. & M. Mastruzzi (2006), 'Measuring corruption: myths and realities', Washington, D.C.: World Bank Institute.
Khan, M. and J. Sundaram (2000), *Rents, Rent-seeking and Economic Development: Theory and Evidence in Asia*, Cambridge: Cambridge University Press.
Klitgaard, R. (1991), *Controlling Corruption*, Berkeley, California: University of California Press.
Larmour, P. and M. Barcham (2006), 'National integrity systems in small Pacific island states, *Public Administration and Development*, **26**(2), 173–84.
Larmour, P. and N. Wolanin (eds), (2001), *Corruption and Anti-corruption*, Canberra: Asia Pacific Press.
Levi, M., M. Dakolias and T. Greenberg (2007), 'Money laundering and corruption', in J. Campos & S. Pradhan (eds), *The Many Faces of Corruption: Tracking Vulnerabilities at the Sector Level*, Washington: World Bank, 389–426.
Levy, B. and S. Kpundeh (2004), *Building State Capacity in Africa: New Approaches, Emerging Lessons*, Washington, D.C.: World Bank Publications.
Licht, A., C. Goldschmidt and S. Schwartz (2007) 'Culture rules: the foundations of the rule of law and other norms of governance, *Journal of Comparative Economics*, **35**(4), 659–88.
McCusker, R. (2006), *Review of anti-corruption strategies*, Technical and Background Paper No. 23, Canberra: Australian Institute of Criminology.
Passas, N. (1996), 'The genesis of the BCCI scandal', *Journal of Law and Society*, 57–72.
Passas, N. (1997) 'The mirror of global evils: A review essay on the BCCI affair', *Trends in Organized Crime*, **2**(3), 49–49.
Passas, N. (1998), 'Structural analysis of corruption: the role of criminogenic asymmetries, *Transnational Organized Crime*, **4**(1), 14.
Passas, N. and D. Nelken (1993), 'The thin line between legitimate and criminal enterprises: subsidy frauds in the European Community', *Crime, Law and Social Change*, **19**(3), 223–43.
Quah, J. S. T. (2003), *Curbing Corruption in Asia: A Comparative Study of Six Countries*, Singapore: Marshall Cavendish Academic.
Radelet, S. (2006), 'A primer on foreign aid', Washington DC: Center for Global Development.
Rose-Ackerman, S. (1975), 'The economics of corruption, *Journal of Public Economics*, **4**(2), 187–203.
Rose-Ackerman, S. (1999), *Corruption and Government: Causes, Consequences and Reform*, Cambridge: Cambridge University Press.
Stapenhurst, R. and S. Kpundeh (1999), *Curbing Corruption: Toward a Model for Building National Integrity*, Washington, D.C.: World Bank Publications.
Transparency International (2006), *Global Corruption Report 2006: Corruption and Health*, Berlin: Transparency International.
Transparency International (2008a), *Bribe Payers Index 2008*, Berlin: Transparency International.
Transparency International (2008b), *Global Corruption Report 2008: Corruption in the Water Sector*, Berlin: Transparency International.
Transparency International (2009a), *National Integrity Systems – Country Studies Egypt, Lebanon, Morocco, Palestine*, Berlin: Transparency International.
Transparency International (2009b), *Corruption Perception Index*, Berlin, http://www.transparency.org/policy_research/surveys_indices/cpi/2009/cpi_2009_table.

Transparency International (2010), 'Frequently asked Questions about Corruption', available at: http://www.transparency.org/news_room/faq/corruption_faq (accessed 2 July 2010).
Transparency International (2010), *Global Corruption Report 2010: Climate Change*, Berlin: Transparency International.
Uslaner, E. (2008), *Corruption, Inequality, and the Rule of Law: the Bulging Pocket Makes the Easy Life*, Cambridge, New York: Cambridge University Press.
World Economic Forum (2008), 'Clean Business Is Good Business: The Business Case Against Corruption', available at: http://www.weforum.org/pdf/paci/BusinessCaseAgainstCorruption.pdf. (accessed 7 March 2009).

2 Corruption in the broad sweep of history

Marcus Felson

Corruption is a product of the interplay between (a) primary human imperatives and (b) an economic and social system trying to control and channel those imperatives. Primary human imperatives include both looking after one's personal interests and meeting social commitments to friends and relatives. A strong tension is inherent between these primary human imperatives and the larger economic and social system. That tension is strongest with the modern form of economic organization. Hence corruption, despite its ancient presence, becomes especially relevant in a modern world. Although corruption becomes especially an issue as developing nations move towards a modern world, we should not assume that the tension will go away once they are developed.

Those aware of Max Weber (1947 [1904]) will immediately recognize the origins of the current argument in his description and analysis of the broad sweep of economic and social history. Weber was perhaps the greatest historical theorist of economic and social life. On the one hand, he gathered vast detail as he studied and described each society. On the other hand, Weber summarized those details within a very general analytical framework. Each society has a prevalent authority system that governs its behaviour, and that authority system is central for understanding it. Weber synthesized information about the broad sweep of economic and social history with three authority systems: (a) traditional, (b) patrimonial, and (c) rational-legal. This chapter explains his general categories, then shows why they help us to understand and conceptualize corruption.

Within a traditional system, individuals are constrained by the rules and mores of society, but those constraints do not stand between primary human imperatives and productivity. Thus a traditional hunting and gathering society follows the teachings of the past and the social ties of kinship, whether or not these lead to greater efficiency. Traditional systems often apply in agrarian societies with small village life, and are not oriented towards a modern society. However, traditional systems may persist into a modern era. A prime example of a traditional system is the interplay of the Hindu religion and the economy in India. Each economic role is largely defined by caste and hence by tradition, within minimal economic flexibility and little regard to efficiency. Within a traditional system, many economic behaviours that we might regard as corrupt from an outside viewpoint are actually part of the rules. Thus assigning jobs by caste and village is intrinsic to the way of life, and should not be viewed as corrupt behaviour as a matter of personal deviance, except when those collective obligations are circumvented.

The patrimonial system is very distinct from the traditional system because of its reliance on personal rule. In this system the ruler does not distinguish between personal and public life, treating state resources and decisions as his personal affair. The agents of the ruler act in his name and on his behalf. It is still possible for those agents to be corrupt only in the sense that they cheat the ruler of his due. If the ruler's agents mistreat the citizens, they are acting within the rules of the system – so long as they send the proceeds back to the ruler and do not take more than their allotted share. This is quite evident in the history of tax farmers whose job was to demand tribute and payments from the provinces. They would be perceived as corrupt to us today, but they were not corrupt in the terms of their system, unless they hid the proceeds from the ruler in their own selfish interest. Examples of patrimony range from Roman emperors to President Ferdinand Marcos in the Philippines and Colonel Khadaffi in Libya – reflecting extension of authority beyond a local area. This leads us to ask whether such power has been established by force or by normative authority, or some combination. But regardless of the answer to that question, extracting resources from the population is intrinsic to the system, not a violation of it.

The rational-legal system of economic and social organization has an entirely different set of expectations from the traditional and patrimonial systems. The rational-legal system is closely related to Weber's textbook concept of 'formal organization' and bureaucracy – a word he uses in positive terms. Under this system, all persons follow rules and fit into formal roles that are separate from the personal, family, and friendship interests of their incumbents. The rulers and role incumbents are substitutable, so that a formal organization persists over time, pursuing goals beyond the individual. This impersonality includes hiring based on competence and certification, and promotion based on ability and productivity. The role incumbents must follow rules, and must be oriented towards goal achievement beyond themselves. They are also supposed to treat each client equally, according to the rules, ignoring personal ties and predilections. Thus modern life conflicts fundamentally with primary human imperatives. Bureaucracy in Weber's terms is like a machine, since it separates personal interests (including family and friend commitments) from larger interests, facilitating the latter. Yet this form of economic and social organization only emerged in the past 200 years or less in Europe, and in most of the world did not really begin to spread until after 1950. In many parts of the world, the rational-legal form is only beginning to emerge. The distinction between persons and positions is difficult to accept fully in any era, which helps explain why it was so late to arrive.

Of course, Weber's concept of rational formal organization is an ideal type. It describes the official position of many modern societies; but that does not mean that everybody follows those rules all of the time. Indeed, a rational-legal system creates a fundamental tension in society, because it is only natural for each person to take care of oneself and one's family and friends, even in violation of general rules and roles. Thus the rational-legal system is almost directly in conflict with primary human imperatives – which do not go away simply because society no longer welcomes them as much as before. Indeed, corruption has much greater potential in the rational-legal system than in the traditional or patrimonial systems of economic and social organization. The levels of corruption possible in a rational-legal system far exceed anything possible in the traditional system, which provides more local controls and hardly expects people to abandon their personal ties while engaging in productive work. The corruption in a modern system also exceeds the corruption of the patrimonial system, within which one must cheat the ruler in order to be corrupt, but the ruler and his agents extracting from everybody else is part and parcel of that economic and social system.

The corruption potential of a rational-legal system is dramatically greater mainly because that system conflicts with basic human tendencies. If human beings are both selfish and social, then the modern form conflicts with each. It conflicts with the selfish tendencies because each individual has something to gain from evading less pleasant role assignments or taking resources beyond entitlement. It conflicts with social tendencies because each individual feels commitments to friends, family, and those with less social distance and wants to help them more than strangers. Hence treating everybody alike under the rules is unnatural for real people.

Given its conflict with human selfishness and human sociability, the rational-legal system should have died an early death. Yet it survives and spreads for a simple reason: this strange and hardly human form of social and economic organization is extremely productive in material terms. It makes more cars. It processes more customers and clients. It shortens the lines and puts a chicken in every pot. And so the least human of social and economic systems is also the most productive. Thus our selfish and social interests are torn between the immediate gains from violating the rules and the more general gains from following them. The best individual solution is to break the rules yourself but get everybody else to follow them, yielding a productive society as a whole that you can then exploit. However, if too many people do that then the productivity of the whole system declines and the rational-legal system becomes a figment of imagination.

Imaginary rational-legal systems are all too common. In a way the real lesson of the 2000 Presidential election and the case of *Gore vs Bush* in Florida is the corruption and mismanagement of state and local governments in the United States.[1] In Weber's terms, each occupational role is assigned to a specialist, with overlapping roles minimized. Those familiar with corruption issues will immediately recognize this as a flaw, for the lack of overlap makes it easier for one person to corrupt the system and avoid discovery. In contrast, overlapping makes it possible for someone else to check, or more generally for people to check on another.

Weber relied too much on the power of the normative system to keep each incumbent performing properly. Here we turn to another great theorist, James Madison (1787), whose famous Federalist Paper Number 10 explained the need for a system of checks and balances. Although Madison was considering legislative matters, his general principle was that individuals are corruptible (in the broad sense), but that their selfish and personal interests can be used to counter one another.

The theory of checks and balances may be the essential general theory of corruption control. In both government and business, checks and balances are employed to protect responsible decisions and actions. Rival political parties, parliamentary question periods, a free press, regulatory agencies, free competition in the marketplace, overlapping roles, auditors and accountants – each of these is a special example of the general rule that checks and balances are needed to prevent personal and social interests from impairing efficiency and productivity. Thus Madison sought to reconcile primary human imperatives with the requirement that everyone has a fair shake.

Modern corruption has to do with positions, and modern organization creates lots of positions demanding that people suppress their selfish interests. In the era of traditional and patrimonial authority, corruption was limited and modern corruption did not exist (although a more primitive and limited form of corruption did apply, even then). When organization is poorly designed and managed, we can expect corruption as a result; but we can also expect various organizational goals to be poorly achieved. In fighting corruption, we must always remember what we are asking of people: to set aside personal interests and personal ties and to follow rules for the greater *impersonal* good. But we must also understand that we can never completely win the war against corruption, nor can we give it up.

We can never win it because primary human imperatives always outweigh impersonal goals. We can never give up the struggle because our modern prosperity depends on containing these personal and social goals while on the job. But if we don't contain it, it grows and takes over. Like housekeeping, no vacuum sweeper works permanently but the failure to vacuum lets a home get dirtier and dirtier.

Yet corruption cannot be controlled by assuming that people can be trained in ethics alone, since it is impossible to talk people out of being people. But it is possible to train people to supervise one another and hence to provide a system of checks and balances. Such a system works best when criminalization and punishment work only at the extreme, when the system operates on a normal basis without getting to that point. Control depends on designing more secure systems, efficient supervision, and effective checks and balances. As technology takes new forms, it brings new opportunities for corruption and hence demands new checking and balancing. With the march of technology, more and more value is intangible – contained in electronic data that are not easily watched with the naked eye. But systems can be designed to keep track of electronic data, too, thus interfering with the opportunities for corruption. As society becomes more complex in technology, corrupt practices can more easily escape notice, at least for a while. But in time we learn to use technology to reduce the complexity of supervision and thence to create methods for managing, checking, and balancing so that formal organization keeps personal and social needs under a reasonable degree of containment. An organization must find simplicity and accountability to avoid corruption. That means overcoming organizational and technical complexity with new forms of simple checks and balances. When that is achieved, modern society can achieve simple monitoring while requiring complex conspiring, and corruption will diminish. Developing nations face the same principles but at an earlier stage, with formal organization replacing family and patrimonial systems in places not yet ready for that to happen. But, of course, no place is fully ready to give up its personal and social tendencies, ands so the work of reducing corruption is never complete.

NOTE

1. In reality, elements of traditional and patrimonial society remain in a modern world, including the United States. However, these mixes are most evident in societies presently undergoing major transitions towards modernity.

REFERENCES

Madison, James, (1787), 'Federalist Paper Number Ten', available online at http://thomas.loc.gov/home/histdox/fed_10.html (accessed March 24, 2011.)

Weber, Max, (1947) [1904)], *The Theory of Social and Economic Organization* (originally, *Wirtschaft und Gesellschaft*), translated by A. M. Henderson and Talcott Parsons), Glencoe, IL: Free Press.

3 Measuring corruption

Finn Heinrich and Robin Hodess

INTRODUCTION

Corruption, defined as 'the abuse of entrusted power for private gain',[1] is not a recent phenomenon. The study of corruption, however, its frequency and forms, causes and consequences, has expanded dramatically in the past 15 years. Why is this so? Since the 1990s, there has been a growing awareness of the relevance of corruption to economic and social development – and this has gone hand in hand with emergence of empirical research on corruption. The growing evidence on corruption and its impact has in turn increased interest in corruption among policymakers, development practitioners and academics alike.

The focus on corruption research has ranged from questions of definition, to measurement, to the analysis of the relationship between corruption and relevant social, political and economic phenomena, such as human rights, media freedom, democracy, economic development, social inequality, foreign investment and the like (Lambsdorff, 2005; Treisman, 2007; Pellegrini & Gerlagh, 2008). More evidence, and a growing awareness of the need to measure and understand corruption, has led to a vastly more sophisticated set of tools and approaches to assessing corruption. With the emergence of these new methods, it is important to take stock of results: research has overwhelmingly proved the hypothesis that corruption has a negative impact on people and on markets. Corruption, research shows, regardless of method, is a negative sum game.

This chapter provides an overview of recent developments in the field of measuring corruption. In line with the overall policy-oriented focus of the handbook, it focuses on those tools and methodological approaches that have emerged from both academic research and anti-corruption practitioners as they aim to provide data which is useful for policy. Other methods for analysing corruption, such as in-depth case studies, socio-psychological tests of corrupt behaviour, institutionalist approaches to explaining corruption, or anthropological inquiries into cultures of corruption, offer rich detail and cutting-edge theoretical models but are of more limited utility for policy. They therefore remain outside the scope of our review.

STUDYING CORRUPTION: METHODS ON THE ROAD TO UNDERSTANDING

Corruption is by definition a clandestine activity, making it hard to measure. This has led researchers to seek proxies, most often now understood as perceptions of corruption, and to establish the presence of antidotes, those factors most likely to prevent corruption from occurring. Here, the 'inputs' of transparency, accountability and integrity and other elements of good governance have come to be seen as key factors in preventing the 'output' of corruption. Clearly, the rise of these concepts, which is reflected in Figure 3.1, is closely related to the ascendance of the good governance agenda in development policy over the last decade.

As a contribution to advancing knowledge on corruption and good governance, a first generation of corruption-measurement tools emerged in the 1990s, which gave us the big picture about corruption, measuring corruption at aggregate level. A second generation then offered more actionable indicators, providing assessments that better pointed to patterns of corruption and corruption risk. Now a third generation of corruption measurement tools has come to the fore. These offer us targeted, bottom-up, actor-focused and locally-owned findings about corruption and its causes – and they make the explanation of corruption both richer and more specific, but also more complicated.

Similar reviews of the methodologies for evaluating corruption have been undertaken over the past half-decade (Kalniņš, 2005; Heller, 2009; UNDP, 2008). On the whole, these earlier reviews addressed the issues of cross-country comparisons, input vs. output dimensions of corruption and aggregate vs actionable indicators. In short, they include both first- and

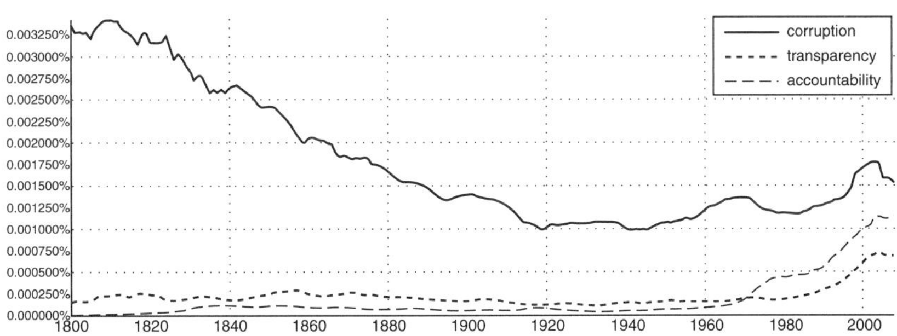

Source: Zinnbauer, 2011

Figure 3.1 Frequency of words 'corruption', 'accountability' and 'transparency' in English books

second-generation corruption-research methods. In our work as anti-corruption practitioners, we have noticed a trend towards a new generation of tools, which we feel is important to recognize as a distinct category of corruption measurement. This new or third generation of corruption measurement tools often focus on a single country, use highly disaggregated indicators, mixed-method research designs and other innovative features.[2]

Ultimately, a mix of corruption measurement methodologies is required so that researchers of many stripes can engage in the field, and policy-makers can have a diverse array of data and analysis at their disposal with which to make more informed decisions about how to apply resources to prevent and redress corruption. Civil society activists working to address corruption can also benefit from the methodological mix, by using high-level rankings to create peer pressure, cross-country evaluations to distil best practices and complex participatory assessments to engage with other anti-corruption actors on joint diagnosis and action.

FIRST GENERATION MEASUREMENT TOOLS: PUTTING CORRUPTION ON THE MAP

Following in the footsteps of the launch of the UN's Human Development Index in 1990, the 1990s saw a proliferation of similar cross-country indices. These indices focused on a range of political, social and economic issues, such as democracy, peace, or women's empowerment, and their main purpose was to raise awareness about an issue among policy-makers. By ranking countries, such indices stimulated (re)action by governments of those countries that ranked poorly. Headline indices also provided insight for donors, investors and concerned citizens about the relative standing of their country of interest versus others.

Assessments of corruption were part of this trend. Here, TI's Corruption Perception Index (CPI) and the World Bank's Governance Indicators (WBGI), which includes a 'Control of Corruption' dimension, are the two most noteworthy examples. The CPI and WBGI, which started in 1994 and 1996 respectively, rely on largely the same methodological approach of using existing cross-national data sources, such as expert ratings, public opinion polls and surveys among business people, to generate a composite indicator of the extent of perceived corruption in a country. By combining a large number of individual sources, these aggregate measures limit the potential measurement error and bias in any one of them, particularly since these measures rely on broad perception-based indicators. Ultimately, these indicators quantify a generalised 'corruption syndrome', measuring as they do a country's overall perceived corruption levels via a single score.

Perception-based corruption indices have received significant scrutiny and a fair share of criticism, with concerns ranging from their lack of conceptual precision (Oman & Arndt, 2006), lack of transparency of data (de Maria, 2008), the problematic validity of underlying data sources, choices about aggregation and weighting (Hawken & Munck, 2011), potential interdependence of sources (Knack, 2006), to their sole reliance of perception-based measures (Andersson & Heywood, 2009).

Despite these criticisms, the CPI and WBGI have been important for putting corruption on the agenda of both global policymakers and the social science research community alike (Lambsdorff, 2006). The CPI's most relevant impact has been to press governments and their partners towards concrete anti-corruption reforms by highlighting the seriousness of the 'corruption challenge' for their country. The WBGI's specific contribution has been to offer a multi-dimensional view of governance, allowing the comparison of a country's perceived levels of corruption to other areas of governance (e.g. the extent to which its citizens have a voice in public affairs). In addition, the WBGI indicator offers a measure of corruption which is comparable over time and can therefore be used to identify countries which have improved or respectively deteriorated in their control of corruption.

SECOND GENERATION CORRUPTION MEASUREMENT TOOLS: BENCHMARKING ACROSS TIME AND SPACE

In the early 2000s, when the fight against corruption – as part of the larger good governance agenda – had been firmly established as a priority for both the public and private sector, new measures were required which helped to benchmark progress over time as well as to enable comparisons with peers. At the same time, these new measurement methods aimed to better understand how corruption works and what could be done to stop it.

Two main types of 'second generation' tools were developed to address these concerns. One set of new tools sought to go beyond perception-based expert measures to examine the actual experience of people exposed to corruption. While facing a number of measurement challenges, such as recall effects and social desirability issues, such 'victimization surveys' were able to reveal the overall extent of bribery, and were often representative at country level. Further, with appropriate stratification, they could be used to look at the extent of bribery in terms of income level and gender of the bribe-payer. Such surveys were generally conducted as public opinion polls, but there are also examples of specialized 'exit polls' at hospitals as well as business surveys.[3]

Prominent examples are the International Crime Victim Survey (ICVS)[4] and Transparency International's Global Corruption Barometer.[5] The ICVS is co-ordinated by the Dutch Ministry of Justice in conjunction with the United Nations Inter-regional Crime and Justice Research Institute (UNICRI). It includes questions on the respondent's experience with a range of crimes, including corruption. More than 70 countries were surveyed in the latest round of surveys in 2004/5. The ICVS is implemented at non-regular intervals. TI's Global Corruption Barometer examines the views and experiences of citizens with regard to a range of corruption issues, from satisfaction with government efforts to fight corruption, willingness to report corruption, and frequency of bribery as experienced across a range of public services. The Global Corruption Barometer is based on a public opinion survey that is implemented in approximately 60–80 countries on a bi-annual basis. Both of these tools not only enable corruption experience to be assessed, but provide ample data for comparisons across time and space.

The second set of tools focuses on integrity, transparency and accountability issues as they assess anti-corruption systems, standards and practices of countries, i.e. the 'inputs' of the corruption equation. These tools have resulted in the emergence of a large and still-growing ensemble of disaggregated indicators,[6] which unpack the corruption syndrome into a number of key components that are viewed as critical as a bulwark against corruption (e.g. budget processes, public financial management, integrity mechanisms, business practices). The focus of second generation tools is on assessing the extent to which anti-corruption provisions and practices exist, that is, whether the appropriate inputs, such as a transparent budget process, a strong anti-corruption system and solid financial management practices, are in place to prevent corruption from occurring. These tools usually examine both the existing legal framework (that is, what is on the books, in terms of law or regulation) as well as how the framework is implemented in practice

Examples include the Global Integrity Index,[7] the Open Budget Index,[8] Public Expenditure and Financial Accountability Framework (PEFA) and the Promoting Revenue Transparency Companies Report. The Global Integrity Index, which started in 2004, uses more than 300 indicators to examine the most relevant aspects of a country's anti-corruption system, both in law as well as in practice. The indicators include quantitative scores (which are summarized in a number of key dimensions and an overall rating for the country), as well as brief qualitative comments by an in-country expert. Data is currently available for 104 mainly developing and transitioning countries. More recently, Global Integrity has begun to adapt the tool to subnational as well as sectoral contexts. The Open Budget Index,[9] available since 2006, surveys countries' budget practices with regard to their transparency and accountability. It is based on a detailed questionnaire administered by in-country civil society organizations and researchers in close to 100 countries. It has shown that installing a transparent budget process can be achieved by a dedicated government rather quickly and with limited capacity and resource requirements, as the example of top-performing South Africa and much-improving Mongolia and Liberia indicate.

Co-ordinated by the World Bank, the Public Expenditure and Financial Accountability Framework (PEFA) is another example of a tool that assesses a component of the corruption prevention system, examining the performance of the public budgeting and accounting systems throughout the entire budget cycle via a range of indicators. Data is collected by World Bank teams in collaboration with experts from the government being assessed. The PEFA framework is rolled out on an ongoing basis at country level, with no attempt to standardize data collection across countries. As a consequence, there are no comparative reports on the PEFA results.[10] As a final example of this approach to business practices, Transparency International's Promoting Revenue Transparency Companies Report,[11] with two editions thus far (2008 and 2011), analyses more than 40 of the world's major oil and gas companies according to the extent of their reporting on organizational and financial matters, their country by country reporting, as well as the scope of their anti-corruption programmes.

WHAT DOES THE LEAP MEAN? LOOKING AT FIRST AND SECOND GENERATION TOOLS TOGETHER

Second generation corruption measurement tools make it possible to investigate the extent to which people's experiences align with their perceptions as well as with the perceptions of the experts. In other words, they enable us to test the reliability of first-generation corruption-measurement tools. The results are mixed, but generally positive.

The question of how expert perceptions of corruption, people's experiences with bribery and the anti-corruption measures of a country aligned, was crucial for establishing the validity of each of these indicators as well as for understanding the inter-linkages among various forms of corruption

Table 3.1 How do different corruption measures correlate?

	CPI	GII
GCB	–.65** (83)	–.56** (54)
CPI	1.00	.64** (78)

Note: Pearson's R; N in brackets.

Source: Transparency International: CPI 2010a and GCB 2010; Global Integrity: GII data is for most recent year available.

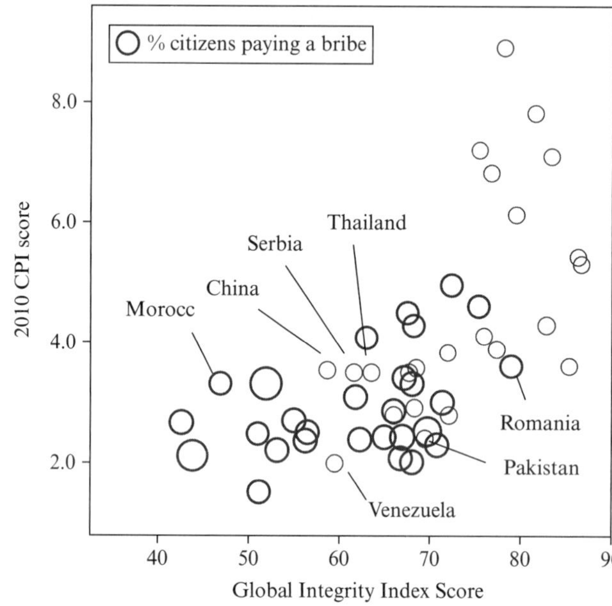

Figure 3.2 Corruption perceptions, corruption experiences and anti-corruption safeguards

and between them and a government's anti-corruption efforts. In Table 3.1 we report the most recent results from the key perception indicator (CPI 2010), experience measure (GCB 2010) and input measure (Global Integrity Index, GII).

The results indicate overall strong correlations among these measures, although they are far from perfect. Figure 3.2 depicts the country scores on the CPI and Global Integrity Index with the size of each 'country circle' indicating the percentage of citizens who paid a bribe for a public service over the last 12 months, taken from the GCB. Whereas the countries in the upper right-hand corner (i.e. countries with low levels of perceived corruption and strong anti-corruption systems) are also 'low bribery' countries, the situation at the bottom left of the figure (i.e. high levels of perceived corruption, weak anti-corruption systems) is less straightforward. Here, we find not only countries with a high percentage of reported bribery, but also countries where bribery is much less common than their high levels of perceived corruption and rather weak integrity systems would suggest, such as Venezuela, Morocco and China. Similarly, Pakistan and Romania exhibit more bribery than one would expect based on the relative strength of their anti-corruption systems.

On the whole, whereas for high CPI scores, i.e. rather 'clean' countries, the results of the different measures correlate highly, this holds true to a lesser extent for countries with medium or low CPI scores. Here, one finds a number of outliers and anomalies, indicating that the 'corruption syndrome' comes in more shapes and forms than the 'no corruption syndrome'.

In addition, the emergence of second generation tools and their findings has allowed us to establish that experience of corruption is less common than one would expect when looking at perception-based data (Mishler & Rose, 2008; Olken, 2009). This does not call into question the relevance of corruption perception measures, not least since perceptions matter as they often serve to guide actual behaviour. However, the limitation of perception-based assessments should be acknowledged more clearly by their users – particularly in the policy community – and experience-based data should be seen as a crucial complement in advancing the collective knowledge on corruption.

A common limitation of first and second generations of corruption measurement tools has been the focus on either corruption or its antidote: integrity, accountability and transparency. Very few of these measurement tools combined both aspects, which was a challenge taken up by the next generation of tools.

THIRD GENERATION TOOLS: ASSESSING SPECIFIC CORRUPTION RISKS

While second generation tools have continued to expand over recent years, a new wave in corruption measurement is made up of a set of tools which focuses on capturing corruption risks within the context of a specific local setting. Many of these tools grew out of the findings of second generation research, meaning results of corruption measurement research pointed to a particular risk or vulnerability which merited further analysis. The key purpose of third generation tools is to provide a comprehensive and nuanced assessment of a corruption issue in a specific context, while the generation of comparative data across contexts is much less of a concern (Kaufmann & Kraay, 2008, p. 25).

While these third generation tools feature different methodological approaches and have different content foci, they generally share the following underlying features:

- *Country ownership*: in response to the first and second generation measurement tools, which were largely owned by institutions operating at the international level, the third generation tools place a premium on country ownership, which should encompass the development of the research tool, its implementation, analysis and usage (OECD, 2008).
- *Participatory approaches*: since these approaches are often implemented with a specific policy or advocacy goal in mind, these measurement tools tend to rely on highly participatory approaches to collecting, validating and interpreting the evidence in the form of multi-stakeholder advisory groups, stakeholder surveys, validation workshops, or even user-generated data, such as community scorecards.
- *Process focus*: while most first and second generation tools focus on relatively static indicators, the third generation tools place an emphasis on examining the relevant actors and the ways they interact with each other in a given institutional setting.[12] This allows for tracking dynamics and processes within a given corruption system. In turn, identifying such processes deepens the understanding of how corruption works and what needs to be done about it.
- *Triangulation of data types*: recognizing that, in the process of analysing specific corruption risks, different actors might have different but equally important perspectives to bring to the table, such approaches rely on various information sources which are often brought together via a process of triangulation. Public opinion surveys, key informant interviews, legal reviews, surveys of public sector officials or firms, and an analysis of official records are often combined to elucidate the complex ways in which actors and institutions interact with each other in a given governance context. This means that third generation indicators enable the rather rigid boundaries of 'corruption vs anti-corruption' research focus to be increasingly transcended. For example, there is trend in public service delivery assessments of combining user's experiences

with corruption with an analysis of the governance system of the respective sector.[13].

- *Evidence-based advocacy intervention*: whereas first and second generation tools usually simply present their findings, the third generation tools are often applied within the context of a larger evidence-based advocacy context. In other words, the generation of the evidence by the respective tool is not the purpose in itself, but is the first step in a larger process to generate, interpret and use data to influence policy (Court & Young, 2006).

Given the sheer number of these tools, whose genesis is often in their second generation 'parents', makes it difficult to select examples. Rather than give a systematic overview of this new generation of measurements, we've decided to identify and present the main types of third generation tools based on the primary 'unit of analysis'.

Main Types of Third Generation Tools Based on Primary 'Unit of Analysis'

Institutions

Based on the understanding that corruption requires holistic systems of closely intertwined governance institutions, which practice and promote integrity, several approaches seek to analyse the performance of these 'integrity systems', either at national level (Transparency International, 2010a; Head et al., 2008) or increasingly also at local level (Huberts et al., 2008; Transparencia Venezuela, 2004; Jachev & Bowser, 2008; CIET social audit).[14] At national level, the focus on institutions assesses the respective roles of the main governance institutions vis-à-vis each other. At local level, this often involves the use of a comparative benchmarking approach to generate impetus among municipalities to strengthen their performance.

Laws and policies

As a consequence of the growing national and international attention to fighting corruption, a wide array of anti-corruption legislation and policies have been established. These range from comprehensive national anti-corruption strategies, to anti-corruption reforms agreed with regional bodies[15] to fully-fledged international conventions, such as the United Nations Convention Against Corruption[16] or the OECD Anti-Bribery Convention.[17] Here, self-assessments as well as independent monitoring tools have been developed to assist governments and civil society in tracking progress in implementing laws, regulation and policies.

Subsystems and processes

Further corruption risk areas that have been the subject of third generation tools comprise subsystems and processes within the overall governance system. Here, specific attention has been paid to measuring those areas that are particularly prone to corruption risk. For the first such area, political financing, Transparency International developed a tool to assess the extent of transparency of political funding, which has since been adapted to both Southeast Asia, Sub-Saharan African and the Western Balkan context (Transparency International, 2007). In public procurement, the OECD has developed indicators which can be used by governments or external actors to assess procurement systems against international best practice standards (OECD, 2010). Finally, a subsystem often believed crucial to measuring the extent of corruption is that of public financial management. Here, Public Expenditure Tracking Surveys have become a widely used approach to trace any 'leakage' in financial flows from origin to final output (Reinikka & Svensson, 2003; Savedoff, 2008).

Sectors

Yet another approach to unpacking corruption risks is related to sector-specific tools. Here, one needs to distinguish between tools applied in three kinds of sectors. The first are *broad societal sectors*, that is, public sector, civil society sector and the business sector, where either broad sectoral assessments (for example, the World Bank's Doing Business programme)[18] or comparative assessments of individual entities prevail (for example Transparency International 2009, One World Trust's Global Accountability Report,[19] TI Colombia's Public Sector Index programme).[20] The second type of sector is that of frontline *public service delivery sectors*, such as education or health, where the focus is often on corruption at the interface between public servants and users of these services (Chaudhury et al., 2006; Transparency International, 2010b). The third category focuses on other *sectors at the interface of public and private actors*, such as forestry (Kishor and Rosenbaum, 2003), land management (Burns et al., 2010) or transport (World Bank, 2009).

As their common features indicate, the implementation of third-generation corruption measurement tools is a significantly more complex undertaking than the application of the various indices of the first and second generation of tools. As the breadth of tools mentioned above indicates, third-generation research requires local capacity as well as an enabling political context, including a space for independent civil society, a certain degree of political will and a somewhat open system of public policymaking. Where these conditions are present, such tools can have a strong impact on bridging the gap between corruption research and policy. However, where these conditions are absent, implementation of such participatory multi-stakeholder approaches is likely to – at best – yield solid information without any policy uptake, and at worst jeopardize the credibility of the approach itself, as the ruling elites capture and 'corrupt' it.

CONCLUSION: CORRUPTION MEASUREMENT – LOOKING FORWARD

The presentation of the three generations of corruption measurement highlights the continuously evolving set of methodological approaches to measuring corruption. The generations complement each other in terms of purpose, outputs, target group, and approaches. Table 3.2 summarizes the key features of the three generations of measurement tools.

Table 3.2 Key features of measurement tool generations

	Composite indicators (1st generation)	*Comparative meso-level assessments (2nd generation)*	*Country specific multi-method assessments (3rd generation)*
Primary purpose	Awareness-raising, naming & shaming	Benchmarking across time & space	Diagnosis, recommendation & policy/advocacy
Main output	Single ranking	Multiple rankings; comparative reports	In-depth corruption or governance assessment
Level of aggregation	High	Medium	Low
Data	Expert perceptions	Expert assessments or experiential surveys	Multiple data sources; focus on triangulation
Primary unit of analysis	Country	Governance system	institution, sector, policy, subsystem
Main target group	Senior government, international business leaders, media	International donors, business sectors	Donors in-country, local civil society, public officials,
Ownership	International institution	International institution, in co-operation with country partners	Country stakeholders, with technical support from international institution

Given the evolution of methodologies over the last 15 or so years, it is fair to conclude that the field of applied corruption research has become extremely innovative, wide in coverage, and better able to drill down into the black box of corruption. This all bodes well for research that is context specific and suited to understanding policy interventions, especially in their localized application.

After a decade and a half of moving from aggregate towards more and more disaggregated data, however, a certain reversal of this trend might also be called for. Rather than a further dissection of corrupt transactions, the next research frontier might well lie in aggregating the many scattered stand-alone tools and approaches – by country, sector or other aggregation principle. The most pressing measurement gap may no longer be about how to best capture a specific context, but rather the opposite: how to ensure that lessons are learned that have some meaning beyond this specific context. Given the immense growth in applied research on corruption, investing research into the synthesis and integration of findings and approaches, e.g. by using systematic reviews, is likely to substantially further our collective knowledge.

While donor agencies (one of the main supporters of corruption research, particularly that carried out by civil society) may be supportive of such meta-studies and reviews, recent funding trends are not auspicious. The focus in funding for governance currently lies in measuring results and achieving value for money for donor interventions. This translates into an ever-growing pressure for practitioners to monitor, evaluate and thereby prove the impact of their work – a demand, which, if it is also able to advance collective knowledge on anti-corruption interventions, is very welcome.

Given that many of the measurement tools presented here are closely linked to the aid system (via aid funding or direct ownership by a donor), this trend among donors is likely to have a profound impact on what will be measured in terms of corruption – and what will not. For example, the current focus of third generation tools on process tracing and in-depth analysis, which comes somewhat at the expense of quantifiable indicators, is likely to be short-lived and could actually be reversed. While from an anti-corruption policy perspective there are still many gap in terms of our understanding of complex corruption systems (for example in the form of policy or state capture, patronage, and other hidden power dynamics), the fact that these phenomena eschew easy quantifications is likely to place them at the bottom of most donor grant shortlists. Donors increasingly seem to want 'a simple problem with a simple solution' (Eyben, 2010). Corruption clearly does not fit the bill. There are no silver bullets for measuring corruption.

The next era of corruption researchers have a distinct challenge. How to advance the field – to study more accurately the hidden transactions that comprise corruption – while at the same time synthesizing the multitude of data already gathered. The real challenge therein, with all methods we have covered and with those to come, is to create a better understanding of corruption and its drivers, as well as the solutions that work to stop it. While these are not small tasks, one aspect leaves us particularly optimistic: a new generation of researchers is breaking new ground and picking up corruption as a substantial new area of study across a number of disciplines. The growing diversification of methods and approaches to studying corruption will create more noise in the field, making simple explanations moot. They will also serve as a powerful impetus to draw conclusions about corruption – its whys and wherefores – from many angles and approaches. Anything less will probably continue to be inadequate to the challenge.

NOTES

1. http://www.transparency.org/about_us
2. The present article draws on preliminary work undertaken within the context of Transparency International's GATEway project, which seeks to take stock of the proliferating field of (anti-) corruption measurement tools and to assist researchers and practitioners in finding and using tools which are appropriate for their specific purpose. For more information, please visit www.transparency.org/gateway.
3. See, for example, the Business Environment and Enterprise Performance Surveys, available at http://www.ebrd.com/pages/research/economics/data/beeps.shtml
4. http://en.wikipedia.org/wiki/International_Crime_Victims_Survey
5. http://www.transparency.org/policy_research/surveys_indices/gcb
6. www.agidata.org
7. www.globalintegrity.org
8. www.internationalbudget.org
9. www.internationalbudget.org
10. The PEFA indicator data can be found at https://www.agidata.org/. For an external comparative analysis of PEFA indicator data, see di Renzio, 2009.
11. http://www.transparency.org/policy_research/surveys_indices/promoting_revenue_transparency
12. This is linked to the growing popularity of political economy approaches (Unsworth, 2007; Fritz et al., 2009).
13. See, for example, http://www.transparency.org/regional_pages/africa_middle_east/transparency_in_public_service_delivery
14. http://www.ciet.org/en/method/social-audits/
15. For example in the context of EC (pre-) accession negotiations (OSI-EUMAP 2002) or in form of the African Peer Review Mechanism (http://www.aprm-international.org/).
16. http://www.uncaccoalition.org/en/uncac-review.html
17. http://www.transparency.org/global_priorities/international_conventions/projects_conventions/oecd_convention
18. http://www.doingbusiness.org/
19. http://www.oneworldtrust.org/index.php?option=com_content&view=article&id=75&Itemid=143

20. http://www.transparenciacolombia.org.co/Publicaciones/ÍndicedeTransparenciadelas EntidadesPúblicas/tabid/195/Default.aspx

BIBLIOGRAPHY

Andersson, S. and P.M. Heywood (2009), 'The politics of perception: use and abuse of Transparency International's approach to measuring corruption', *Political Studies*, **57**, 746–67.

Burns, T., K. Deininger, H. Selod and K. Dalrymple (2010), 'Implementing the land governance assessment framework', FIG Congress 2010 Facing the Challenges - Building the Capacity, Sydney, Australia, 11–16 April.

Chaudhury, N., J. Hammer, M. Kremer, K. Muralidharan and F.H. Rogers (2006), 'Missing in action: teacher and health worker absence in developing countries', *Journal of Economic Perspectives*, **20**(1), 91–116.

Court, J. and J. Young (2006), 'Bridging research and policy in international development: an analytical and practical framework', *Development in Practice*, **16**(1), 85–90.

de Maria, W. (2008), 'Measurements and markets: deconstructing the corruption perception index', *International Journal of Public Sector Administration*, **21**(7), 777–97.

di Renzio, P. (2009), 'Taking stock: what do PEFA assessments tell us about PFM systems across countries?', ODI Working Paper 302.

Eyben, R. (2010), 'The big push back (and push forward)', Report from the Big Push Back meeting, Institute for Development Studies, 22 September.

Fritz, V., K. Kaiser and B. Levy (2009), *Problem-Driven Governance and Political-Economy Analysis*, Washington, DC: World Bank.

Hawken, A. and G.L. Munck (2011), 'Does the evaluator make a difference? measurement validity in corruption research', Committee on Concepts & Methods Working Paper Series No. 48, March.

Head, B.W., A.J. Brown and C. Connors (eds) (2008), *Promoting Integrity: Evaluating and Improving Public Institutions*, Aldershot, UK: Ashgate Publishing.

Heller, N. (2009), 'Defining and measuring corruption: where have we come from, where are we now, and what matters for the future?', in R.I. Rotberg (ed.), *Corruption, Global Security, World Order*, Baltimore, US: Brookings Institution Press, pp. 47–66.

Huberts, L., F. Anechiarico and F. Six (eds) (2008), *Local Integrity Systems. World Cities Fighting Corruption and Safeguarding Integrity*, The Hague: BJU Legal Publishers.

Jachev, Z. and D. Bowser (2008), *Methodology: For Measuring the Index of Responsibility, Transparency and Accountability (RTA) at Local Level*, Skopje, Macedonia: UNDP.

Kalniņš, V. (2005), 'Assessing trends in corruption and impact of anti-corruption measures', Discussion Paper, Anti-Corruption Network for Transition Economies, 6th General Meeting, Istanbul, Turkey, 30–31 May.

Kaufmann, D. and A. Kraay (2008), 'Governance indicators: where are we, where should we be going?', *World Bank Research Observer*, **23**(1), 1–30.

Kishor, N.M. and K.L. Rosenbaum (2003), 'Indicators to monitor progress of forest law enforcement and governance initiatives to control illegal practices in the forest sector', *International Forestry Rev.*, **5**(3), 211–218.

Knack, S. (2006), 'Measuring corruption in Eastern Europe and Central Asia: a critique of the cross-country indicators', World Bank Policy Research Working Paper 3968.

Lambsdorff J. (2005), 'Consequences and causes of corruption: what do we know from a cross-section of countries?', Discussion Paper of the Economics Department, Passau University, No. 34-05, May.

Lambsdorff J. (2006), 'Measuring corruption – the validity and precision of subjective indicators (CPI)' in C. Sampford et al. (eds), *Measuring Corruption*, Aldershot, UK: Ashgate, 81–100.

Mishler, W. and R. Rose (2008), 'Seeing is not always believing: measuring corruption perceptions and experiences', Paper Prepared for the Elections, Public Opinion and Parties 2008 Annual Conference, University of Manchester, UK, 12–14 September.

OECD (2008), 'Donor approaches to governance assessments', Concept Paper and Agenda Annotations, OECD/DAC GOVNET Conference on Governance Assessment and Aid Effectiveness, London, 20–21 February.

OECD (2010), 'Methodology for assessing procurement systems (Maps) February 2010', available at http://www.oecd.org/dataoecd/50/33/45181522.pdf (accessed 11 March 2011).

Olken. B. (2009), 'Corruption perceptions vs. corruption reality', *Journal of Public Economics*, **93**(7–8), 950–64.

Oman, C.P. and C. Arndt (2006), *Uses and Abuses of Governance Indicators*, Paris: Development Centre of the OECD.

OSI-EUMAP (2002), *Monitoring the EU Accession Process: Corruption and Anti-Corruption Policy*, Budapest: OSI.

Pellegrini, L. and R. Gerlagh (2008), 'Causes of corruption: a survey of cross-country analyses and extended results', *Economics of Governance*, **9**(3), 245–63.

Razafindrakoto, M. and F. Roubaud (2010), 'Are international databases on corruption reliable? A comparison of expert opinion surveys and household surveys in Sub-Saharan Africa', *World Development*, **38**(8), 1057–69.

Reinikka, R. and J. Svensson (2003), 'Survey techniques to measure and explain corruption', World Bank Working Paper 3071.

Savedoff, W. (2008), *Public Expenditure Tracking Surveys: Planning, Implementation and Uses*, Washington DC: World Bank.

Transparency International (2007), *CRINIS Report: Money in Politics – Everyone's Concern*, Berlin: Transparency International & The Carter Center.

Transparency International (2009), *Transparency in Reporting on Anti-Corruption: A Report on Corporate Practices*, Berlin: Transparency International.

Transparency International (2010a) 'National Integrity System Assessment Toolkit', available at http://www.transparency.org/content/download/49651/794092/NIS+toolkit.pdf (accessed 12 March 2011).

Transparency International (2010b), *Africa Education Watch. Good Governance Lessons for Primary Education*, Berlin: Transparency International.

Transparencia Venezuela (2004), 'Sistema de Evaluación de la Transparencia en la Gestión Municipal en Venezuela', *Manual de aplicación del Sistema de Evaluación*.

Treisman, D. (2007), 'What have we learned about the causes of corruption from ten years of cross-national empirical research?', *Annual Review of Political Science*, **10**, 211–44.

UNDP (2008), *A Users' Guide to Measuring Corruption*, UNDP Oslo Governance Centre.

Unsworth, S. (2007), 'Re-thinking governance to fight corruption', *U4 Brief No. 7*, CMI.

World Bank (2009), *Deterring Corruption and Improving Governance in Road Construction and Maintenance*, Washington, DC: World Bank.

Zinnbauer, D. (2011), 'Fighting corruption in 1811 and 2011 – what's new?', available at http://blog.transparency.org/2011/02/18/fighting-corruption-in-1811-and-2011-whats-new/ (accessed 14 March 2011).

4 Assessing corruption at the country level

Francesca Recanatini

INTRODUCTION

Over the past ten years researchers have increasingly focused on the link between poor governance, corruption and economic growth. The cross-country evidence has shown how poor governance and corruption can be harmful for the standard of living and the distribution of income of citizens, reducing income per capita and literacy, while increasing infant mortality. Further, poor governance distorts public expenditure and increases poverty, reducing investment efficiency.[1] These initial results have posed two challenges for practitioners and policymakers:

(i) to move beyond anecdotal evidence to a systematic approach for measuring governance and corruption and their determinants; and
(ii) to use data and rigorous analysis to support institutional reforms at the country level to curb corruption and improve governance.

Governance and corruption are however multi-dimensional phenomena that can affect different sectors and groups of citizens in a country. Their complexity and multi-sectoral breadth have translated into different methods to define and measure them, leading to a sizeable amount of quite dissimilar information and data. Moreover, the initial research focus on the causes of corruption and poor governance has led to a mushrooming of cross-country indicators. This has posed some difficult tradeoffs for policymakers. Research objectives have often called for comparability and standardization across countries, while effective reform design requires highly disaggregated and country specific data that are comparable over time for monitoring purposes.

This chapter proposes an alternative approach to the design and implementation of governance and anti-corruption reforms based on micro-data and greater ownership of the diagnostic process. The (causal) link between corruption and institutional factors is still not fully understood and policymakers and practitioners have struggled to translate broad recommendations that have emerged from cross-country analysis (for example, greater transparency and accountability) into concrete and specific policy reforms applicable at the country level. In some cases, political economy challenges at the implementation stages have led to the partial implementation of the proposed reforms. In other cases, the country did not have the system and/or the capacity to identify policy priorities, failing to design the most effective reform policy.

Building on these considerations and given the limitations of what can be achieved with cross-country, aggregated data, practitioners have concentrated their efforts on developing alternative approaches that can better inform policymakers at the country level, while promoting ownership of the reform process. In particular, a team of practitioners at the World Bank has developed an approach to governance and anti-corruption assessment and reform that uses multiple surveys to collect highly dis-aggregated data and a participatory process to policy design. The participatory approach used – to finalize the instruments for the data collection, to validate the results; and to draft policy recommendations – creates the foundation for greater ownership and sustainability of the reform process at the country level.

Key components of this country-specific diagnostic assessment are:

(i) focus on institutions and institutional factors, rather than individuals;
(ii) emphasis on experiential rather than perception data;
(iii) application of a multi-pronged approach, gathering data from more than one type of respondent;
(iv) employment of local NGOs and specialists in the data-gathering process, capitalizing on and strengthening local knowledge and expertise; and
(v) active involvement of the government, civil society and business representatives at different stages of the implementation process.

This approach has been implemented in about 15 countries and has empowered governments to develop their own governance and anti-corruption strategies based on more objective, micro-level data and a participatory model. The data collected have also allowed practitioners to go beyond a generic concept of corruption by unbundling different types of corruption and identifying more appropriate policy measures.

While in many cases it is premature to evaluate the impact of this alternative approach, some interesting by-products have already emerged. A few countries (Paraguay and Mozambique) have mobilized resources and used on their own the same approach for a second round of assessment. In a couple of cases the country has chosen to institutionalize part of this assessment, integrating it in their regular data collection implemented by the National Statistical Agency. Finally, the newly available data has allowed researchers to further our understanding of the link between institutional factors and different types of corruption, and of the impact of poor governance and corruption on citizens.

The rest of this chapter is organized as follows. Section 2 briefly describes the analytical framework behind this alternative approach, while section 3 summarizes the approach used. Section 4 focuses on the factors that may promote ownership and sustainability of the reform process at the country level, while section 5 is devoted to building the gap between analysis and policy-making by illustrating how to use this type of micro-level data for policy advice. This overview does not intend to be comprehensive of all the topics that could be explored. Instead, it provides a number of illustrations of what can be analysed. In the final section of the chapter some of the limitations of this approach are discussed and possible directions for future work.

THE ANALYTICAL FRAMEWORK

As emphasized above, this approach aims to address two of the fundamental challenges policymakers faced when trying to curb corruption and improve governance: (i) to obtain the most relevant type of information to identify priorities for reform; and (ii) to create the conditions for sustaining the reform process over time. The choice of tools and the breadth of the stakeholders involved in the implementation process are the cornerstone of this approach.

To better understand the logic behind this approach, and how it can potentially be adapted to new challenges (sector-specific governance and anti-corruption assessment, for example), an analytical framework is introduced that comprises four, broadly defined pillars that can be used to design a methodology to assess governance and corruption (Figure 4.1):

(i) the ***conceptual dimension***, which helps define the object of the assessment;
(ii) the ***empirical tools and the sample*** used for the assessment;
(iii) the ***process*** by which the assessment is implemented; and
(iv) the ***type of analysis and use*** of the data collected, including policy action.

The first pillar focuses on the analytical concepts that should be taken into account at the beginning of the design work. The clear definition of the objective and variable(s) to study is the first step of any rigorous assessment.[2] Only when this definition is clear, practitioners can proceed to develop the empirical tools for the subsequent field work.

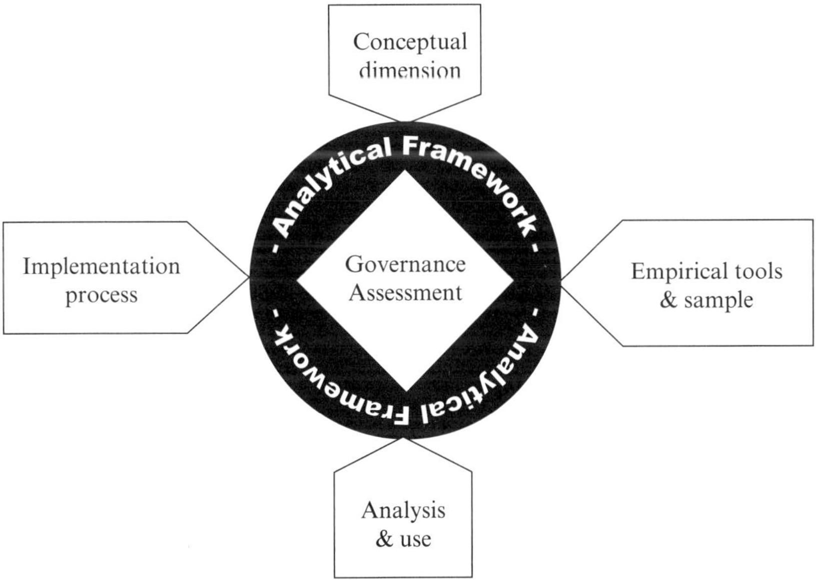

Figure 4.1 Measuring governance – the inputs

The second pillar comprises the specific characteristics of both the tools and the field work. The empirical instruments can take many different forms and use different statistical approaches, leading to significantly different types of data on corruption and governance. Based on the definition of the final objective, practitioners may choose different approaches and tools.

The 'implementation' pillar focuses on the process through which the tools are designed and implemented, and the data are analysed. This dimension, often overlooked, can affect greatly the type and number of outcomes of a governance assessment (see Box 4.1 for an illustration). For the purpose of capacity building and sustainable monitoring, for example, the implementation process should be fully participatory and should promote partnerships between civil society and the government. If the assessment process is not 'owned' by a broad range of stakeholders, it will not be sustained over time nor will its findings feed back into the policymaking process. Research objectives and cross-country monitoring, on the other hand, do not need to rely on such fully participatory process for data collection, and require instead comparable tools and samples for a meaningful analysis.

The final pillar of an assessment is the analysis of the information collected and its use. Key at this stage is the choice of technique that can

BOX 4.1 DIFFERENT OBJECTIVES, DIFFERENT CHOICES

Sierra Leone Governance and Anti-Corruption (GAC) Assessment

The GAC Assessment in Sierra Leone responded to the demand for action on governance received from the former Minister of Presidential Affairs, Mr. Momodu Koroma, on behalf of the President (February 27, 2002). This initiative, in collaboration with DFID, focused on capacity through long-term partnerships between civil society and government and in-depth diagnostics of the quality of governance. To foster collaboration among local stakeholders and successful implementation of the GAC, the government established a Steering Committee (SC), comprising the Governance Reform Secretariat (GRS), representatives from the Vice-President Office, the Anti-Corruption Committee, the civil society, the media, the Central Statistical Agency and donors (DFID, UNDP, EU, WB). The SC focused on designing and implementing three diagnostic surveys (to public officials, households and business people) to assess

Corruption Perception Index (CPI) by Transparency International

The Transparency International CPI is a composite annual index that comprises information from business people and analysts about their perception of corruption within a country. First introduced in 1995, the CPI attempts to measure how corruption affects a country's business life. It aims to raise public awareness on corruption and to add pressure to governments to address this issue. In 2003, the CPI included data for 133 countries from 17 different surveys, produced by 13 independent institutions. The CPI includes all countries for which at least three sources are available. All the sources for the CPI's calculations apply an homogenous definition of corruption: 'the misuse of public power for private gains'. Each source uses its own scaling system. The data is then standardized to determine each country's mean value using a two-step procedure. The final result is an index for each country institutional weaknesses and strengths in the country. The surveys were completed in 2003 by a local firm with the technical assistance of the WB. A widely disseminated report summarized the results and provided the SC with key information for the design of a National Governance Strategy. The Strategy was presented and discussed at a National Workshop in early 2005. http://www.worldbank.org/wbi/governance/sierraleone/index.html

that takes values between 0 (highly corrupt) and 10 (clean). When using the CPI, comparisons from year to year should be based on scores and not a country's rank because the rank might change due to the addition or subtraction of new countries to the sample. Although changes in the CPI score might indicate a change in the rating, it also reflects a change in methodology or number of sources available. http://www.transparency.org/

allow practitioners to separate 'noise' from 'true information' and aggregate meaningfully the data available.[3] Aggregation, if possible, should be carried out without unnecessary loss of information. Thus, it is important to carefully select the method and level of aggregation appropriate for the task at hand.[4] The final use of the resulting information is also critical and will inform the practitioner's choice about the other dimensions of the assessment.

In sum, to measure governance is the product of the choices made along each of these four dimensions. The approach presented in this chapter focuses on the quality of governance and the extent of corruption[5] and aims at developing and implementing a reform policy. Thus, it comprises tools that allow the collection of experiential micro-level data and the active involvement of government and civil society for the implementation of the assessment.

Clearly, choices relative to each pillar are influenced by the purpose of the assessment and lead to significantly different types of information. Furthermore, these choices can lead to additional types of outcomes in the process, since knowledge and information are not the only outcome of governance assessments (Figure 4.2).

Consider, for example, the case of the assessment in Sierra Leone, described in Box 4.1. The main purpose of this exercise was to gather data for policy design. The creation of the Steering Committee and the close collaboration between local stakeholders and international experts

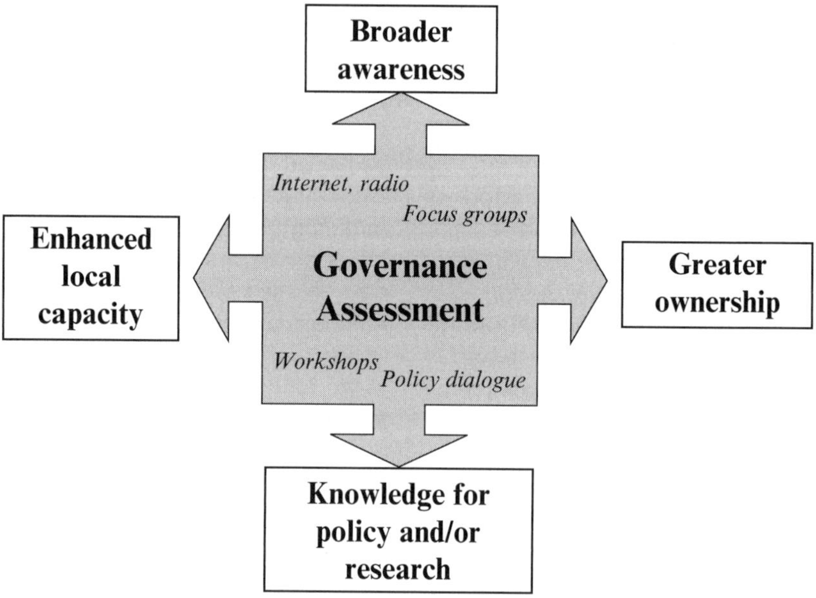

Figure 4.2 Measuring governance – possible outcomes

for the data collection and analysis, ensured in addition the transfer of skills and capacity at the local level. It further promoted dialogue between civil society and the government, and built a broader consensus for policy reform within the government. Moreover, the use of the media (radio and newspapers) and local workshops for the dissemination of the results of the assessment increased awareness in the country about the issues and the challenges ahead. The reform implementation still faced significant challenges but the participatory approach used help to mitigate these challenges. Next, the main features of the approach and the tools used are discussed.

THE APPROACH – A BRIEF DESCRIPTION

As emphasized at the beginning, the limitations of single-source, cross-country data have pushed policymakers and practitioners to develop an alternative approach that can be used for the design of specific reform policies at the country level. As a result, the World Bank has designed a more comprehensive approach focused on micro-level data collected from a multiplicity of stakeholders.[6] The instruments used as part of this approach are detailed, country-specific surveys of thousands of households, business people and public officials. These tools are designed to provide the basis of technical discussions for policymakers and civil society for policy formulation, complementing the traditional sources such as experts' opinions or case-study analysis. The surveys utilize experience-based (rather than 'opinions') type of questions, reducing the element of perceptive subjectivity. Because of their focus on experiences, these surveys can lead to a non-political debate on concrete reforms to improve governance. Furthermore, the combined surveys of households, business people and public officials permit triangulation and consistency checks of the results.

The responses of public officials to very specific questions on the quality of governance and the extent of corruption in their own agencies are especially useful and can make a difference in persuading political establishments to take difficult reform decisions. The analysis developed with this approach can also help build consensus among key stakeholders, who are encouraged to make use of the results to promote a constructive debate on institutional reform for better governance. In addition, the surveys can be used to establish quantitative benchmarks for subsequently monitoring the success of institutional reforms already underway, and, if necessary, to redirect them to concentrate efforts on priority areas.

The design and implementation of these surveys allow a variety of objectives to be achieved:

(i) identify the different forms of corruption present in the country;
(ii) measure economic and social costs of poor governance and corruption;
(iii) provide information on the country's underlying institutional structure;
(iv) foster learning through the close collaboration between external experts and local counterparts;
(v) promote long-term, sustainable partnerships between government and civil society; and
(vi) obtain an initial benchmark of public sector performance and extent of corruption.

The rationale behind each survey is the following

- *Public Officials Survey*. This survey gathers information of public organizations and their practices from the point of view of their own employees. Public official responses can reveal crucial information about the structure of incentives and actual degree of enforcement within their own agency, the existence and use of accountability mechanisms, the quality of rules and procedures, the degree of transparency of budget and employment decisions, and the overall quality of management.

- *Business Survey*. This survey focuses on the business environment, with special emphasis on the effects of public sector governance and corruption on private sector development. It examines the firms' roles as users of public services, subject to regulations and rules for licences and permits. Special attention is given to the functioning and effectiveness of the judicial system.
- *Household Survey*. Citizens are targeted in their roles as users of public services, and clients for licences and permits, with special focus on health care and education. The survey focuses on the quality of and the accessibility to public services, the experience that citizens have with inappropriate procedures and behaviour, the information available on basic rights and accountability mechanisms.

These in-depth diagnostic surveys and the associated action plans have been completed in several countries in partnership with bilateral agencies and NGOs. For a list of the countries and to review the resulting reports, please visit: http://agidata. Next, the challenge of implementing anti-corruption reforms is discussed, focusing in particular, on the potential role that active participation of different stakeholders – as used in this approach – can have in addressing this issue.

OWNERSHIP AND SUSTAINABILITY OF THE REFORM PROCESS

To design a reform aimed at improving governance and curbing corruption is only the first step. The reform needs to be implemented and progresses need to be monitored over time. Implementation and monitoring require sustained effort and support, often over the medium-long term. A large literature exists on such challenge and the political economy of reforms.[7] This issue is especially relevant for governance and anti-corruption reforms, which often aim to alter significantly the distribution of rents and power within a country.

Field experience in several countries suggests that building coalitions early on between civil society and government is an important element to promote ownership of the reform process and ensure its sustainability. Establishing channels through which civil society and government can demand greater accountability from each other promotes a citizen-government dynamic that can substantially strengthen the implementation of governance and anti-corruption reforms. The ownership of the reform process can be further reinforced by actively disseminating the results of the assessment via broad-based workshops and jointly drafting the policy reforms.

This empirical observation is supported by recent political economy studies. The political economy literature[8] has increasingly focused on understanding the factors affecting the 'demand' and the 'supply' for changes and reforms. In the long run, the main factors triggering demand for (institutional) reforms appear to be learning and the accumulation of knowledge (North, 1990). On the supply side, instead, this literature emphasizes the challenge posed by special interest groups and societal interests in the design and implementation of policies that can lead to collective action problems. A few solutions have been suggested to address these issues:[9] the empowerment of the beneficiaries of the reforms; the promotion of coalition building and the active participation of the relevant stakeholders in the policy process; the role of public information campaign and knowledge dissemination on the reforms; and the focus on the existing incentive structures rather than organizations and people.

The country-specific diagnostic approach presented in this chapter tries to translate into practice the intuitions of economists and political scientists: focus on incentives and active participation are the key elements to promote demand for reforms and ensure that these reforms are implemented. In practice, this often implies that the design and implementation of reforms rely on broad-based participation, involving all government branches, civil society, financial sector institutions, and the business community. Such broad participation can be ensured and sustained through the creation of institutionalized partnerships between the government and local NGOs. These partnerships encourage a more integrated and collaborative debate between government and civil society stakeholders over the policy making process. In addition, a fully participatory approach adopted from beginning to end paired with rigorous data collection and analysis promotes a wider sense of ownership of the process and the resulting policy, guaranteeing a true integration of the results into policymaking and greater long-term monitoring capacity.

The emphasis on sustainability and capacity building is another novel element of this approach. In contrast to other types of assessment, the data collection and analysis are carried out locally. This promotes capacity building at the local level, which is especially relevant for the sustainability of the reforms. The ability to monitor on a regular basis governance and corruption is a priority for developing countries that aim to strengthen the effectiveness of their government. This monitoring activity requires a multi-disciplinary national capacity, both human and institutional, which is weak in many developing countries, and which this type of approach can help foster.

The use of empirical and diagnostic tools as a means to build local capacity is not a novel approach. Living Standards Measurement Surveys (LSMS) by the World Bank have been employed in many countries to build national capacity to analyze social policy.[10] The evidence suggests that building analytical capacity requires explicit planning, significant time and money, open access to data and strong support from policymakers. The experiences of countries such as Bolivia, Georgia, and Latvia show how it is possible to successfully progress from diagnostics to concrete, participatory action plans, while improving local analytical and policy capacity in the process.[11] Next are offered some illustrations of the use of the data for policy purpose.

ANALYSIS AND USE OF THE DATA

In-depth diagnostic surveys can be especially useful for policy purposes. The specificity of the information and its focus on experiences rather than perceptions permit an in-depth assessment of the quality of governance across the major institutions, providing a detailed map of institutional weaknesses and strengths. This helps identify specific priority areas for reform, facilitating the policy design at the country and local level. In this Section we discuss a few illustrations prepared with the data collected using this three-survey approach. The individual country reports, with a much richer discussion and analysis, are available at http://agidata

The surveys begin investigating the level of trust of citizens with respect to various public agencies. Trust of citizens is a fundamental condition of any legitimate government. However, as Figure 4.3 demonstrates for public institutions in Guatemala, only a small percentage of citizens in this country believe that public agencies are honest. This lack of trust is consistent among different groups of citizens – households, business people and public officials, in this case – suggesting the severity of the problem.

The level of honesty and trust in public institutions is closely related to the extent of corruption perceived by the citizens and its impact on the economy of the country. In many countries, the majority of respondents identify corruption as a top socio-economic challenge and regard it as one of the most serious obstacles to business development. The survey instruments provide various measures of corrupt behavior. To illustrate general perceptions of respondents we present in Figure 4.4 the answers of

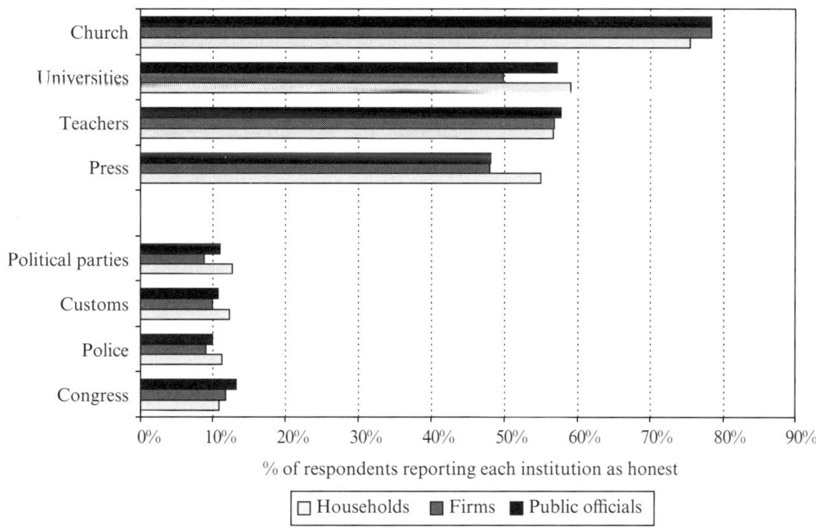

Figure 4.3 Honesty and institutions (as reported by households, firms and public officials, Guatemala, 2004)

households and public officials from Sierra Leone to the question which is the most serious problem (among a given list). Even though the perceptions may not reflect actual levels of corruption, the responses are consistent across different categories of respondents, showing that the population overwhelmingly sees corruption as a major problem.

The detailed survey data make it possible to go beyond the one-dimensional analysis of the problem, offering insights on institutional factors that may exacerbate the governance problem faced by the country. A common factor, emerging frequently both from the survey data and the subsequent focus group discussion, is the limited knowledge citizens have about corruption-reporting mechanisms. In Madagascar, for example, less than one-eighth of the population confessed to know how to report corruption. This clearly reduces the accountability of public officials. Moreover, the survey data highlights a significant difference between common citizens and public officials on knowledge and use of corruption-reporting mechanisms, since citizens more often lack this knowledge. This gap in knowledge can be easily addressed and can help create a strong external oversight mechanism.

Knowledge of the corruption reporting system is, however, only the first part in establishing an effective oversight mechanism. The system needs also to be accessible and safe. Public officials report that the systems to report corruption in their country are flawed across several dimensions.

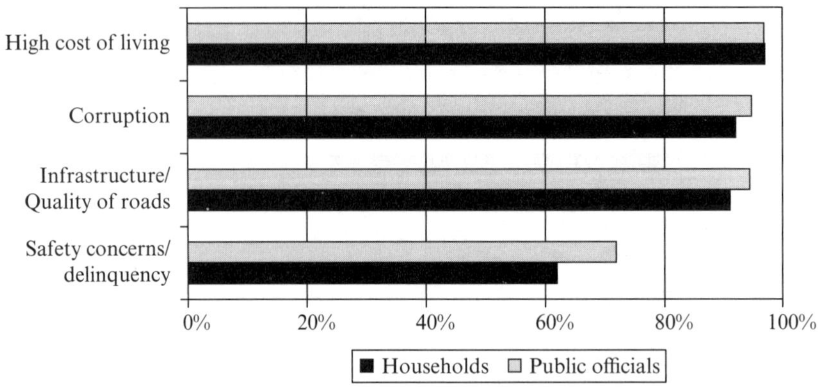

Figure 4.4 Corruption – one of the most important challenges, Sierra Leone, 2004 (% of respondents reporting that these are very serious problems)

In particular, on average more than half of public officials interviewed in selected Latin American countries say that reporting corruption is complicated, unsafe, and that the mechanisms to report are politicized. The evidence also shows that the majority of users who paid a bribe were either urged to pay by public officials or felt obliged to do so because they believe it is the appropriate way to obtain a service.

The Many Faces of Corruption

One of the critical advantages of in-depth surveys is the ability for practitioners to unbundle corruption in its different forms: (i) administrative corruption (for example bribes to obtain public services); (ii) corruption in public procurement (for example bribes to obtain public contracts); (iii) nepotism and purchase of positions in public agencies; (iv) diversion of public funds and embezzlement of assets; (v) state capture and influence peddling. The general outlook on several types of corrupt behavior in public administration, corruption in public procurement, and provision of public services as viewed by different categories of respondents is presented in Figure 4.5.

The data evaluate general levels of corruption in the public sector by examining the responses of firm managers and public officials across eight countries, as well as to single out the most harmful types of corruption. Each country faces a serious governance challenge. However, the most endemic type of corruption is different in each one. Petty corruption is extremely serious in Guinea and Sierra Leone, as well as corruption in

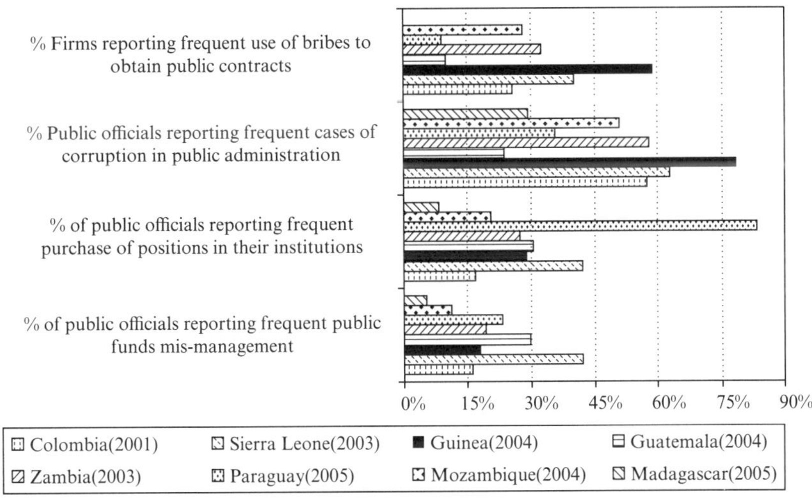

Figure 4.5 Extent of corruption, selected countries, 2003–2005

public procurement, as reported by firms. On the other hand, nepotism and purchase of public positions, viewed as leading to more bribery because of the potential rents associated with a public position, are more frequent in Paraguay.

One of the key functions of public agencies is delivery of services to citizens. Bribery, however, can limit access of the poor to public services, imposing additional regressive tax on users, and, as demonstrated later, reduces incentives to provide services of high quality. In countries like Sierra Leone and Guinea this is a mammoth challenge. Countries like Mozambique, Zambia and Colombia are also facing a serious challenge. But the detailed information summarized in Figure 4.5 suggests that one common approach may not be the most effective solution and that each country will need to prioritize which form of corruption to address first.

However, public agencies are not all equally tainted with corruption. There is a significant heterogeneity within the government. As the surveys focus on public agencies rather than on individual respondents, it becomes possible to explore this heterogeneity by stratifying responses. Researchers can, therefore, focus on alternative types of corruption as reported by public officials employed in different public agencies. Consider, for example, the case of Honduras. Municipal agencies face a greater challenge than other state agencies in terms of awarding public contracts and mismanagement of public funds. On the other hand, the judiciary struggles to deliver public services. This information emphasizes that public officials working in different agencies observed different levels and types of corruption. Such

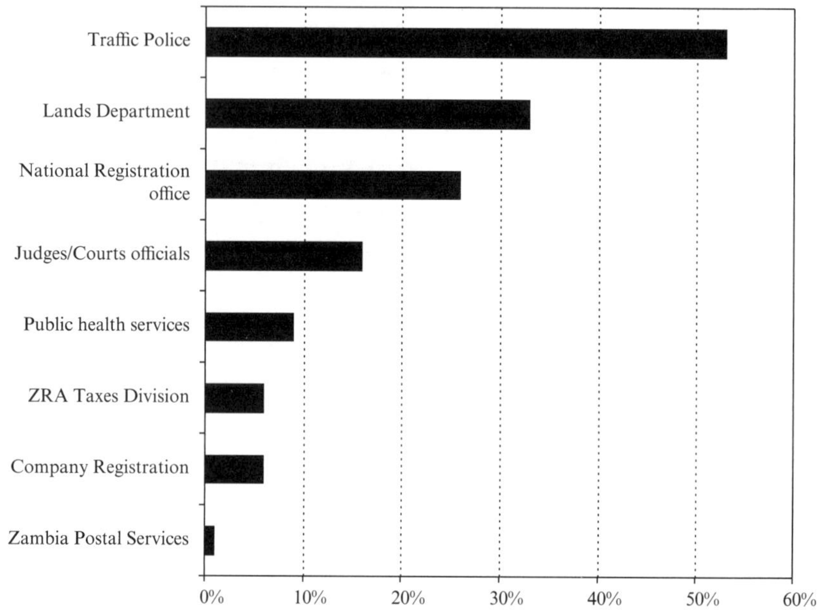

Note: The frequency was calculated for those users who contacted the agency seeking attention.

Figure 4.6 Frequency of bribes (as reported by managers, Zambia, 2003)

breakdowns across various dimensions can provide invaluable information on the institutional development of a country, especially when considering or evaluating the results of a decentralization process.

Firm managers can provide additional information relevant for policy design on corruption in public services in their role of users of public services. Though managers in all the countries report that bribery in provision of public services occurs frequently, not all services are affected equally. The surveys we implement allow us to identify the services for which bribery is more frequent. Figure 4.6 reports managers' responses for different public services in Zambia. The complete list of public services consists of 18 items. The surveys also provide information on the level of satisfaction with a service, the incidence of bribe extortion from public officials, and the amount of bribes paid for each service. Figure 4.6 highlights that business people, who frequently use services where rent-seeking practices are common, systematically incur additional costs equivalent to an implicit tax. In the case of Zambia, this is especially true for dealings with traffic police, the Land Department and the National Registration Office.

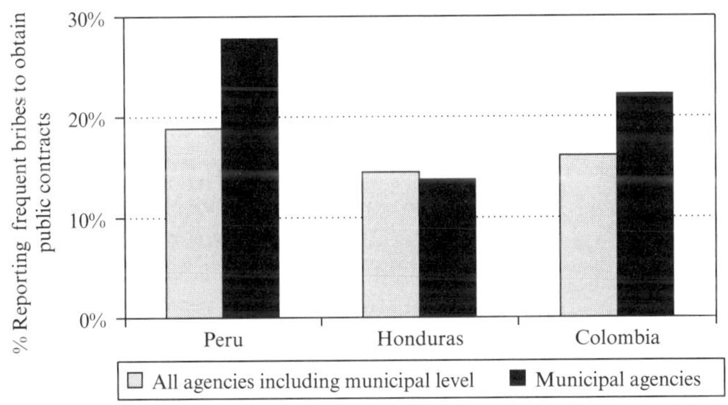

Figure 4.7 *Public officials at different levels of government report different levels of corruption: bribes to obtain public contracts (as reported by public officials, 2001)*

The experiences of firms with bribery are not limited to public services. Corruption distorts regulatory environment, and enterprises are forced to pay to be able to continue to operate their business. This type of bribery can take different forms: payments to facilitate judiciary procedures, obtaining contracts with state entities, updating tributary situation, and processing various licenses and permits. Each form of corruption highlights a precise institutional weakness that could be addressed by an appropriate policy change. Firm managers report that the process of obtaining various permits and contracts with state agencies, as well as judiciary procedures are the public transactions that most often require a bribe to be completed.

Rent-seeking behavior of public officials becomes especially harmful if, in exchange for a bribe, firms receive public contracts. As the amount of kickbacks is on average between 10 to 20 per cent of the contract awarded, the practice is often not only considered as a large-scale case of corruption, but also the one that distorts efficient allocation of resources. The survey permits us to identify the agencies, the level of government, and the regions where bribes to obtain public contracts are more pervasive. By exposing direct experiences of public officials in different government agencies, Figure 4.7 shows that local agencies are more susceptible to such type of corruption. Experiences from public officials offer another illustration of intra-agency aspects of corrupt practices. Candid responses of public servants with information on institution and location, where the interview took place, make it possible to track the regional and institutional patterns of corruption. As in procurement, municipal agencies are often crippled by embezzlement in many countries.

The capture of state by powerful private interests can jeopardize significantly the social and economic development of entire countries. To detect the signs of 'grand' corruption the survey distinguishes several key governmental agencies, whose decisions could influence the legal environment. These include the Parliament, officials of the Government and municipal authorities, various regulatory agencies, higher judiciary authorities, and the Central Bank. This type of corruption came first to the attention of policymakers in the wake of the transition process, especially in countries such as Russia and Ukraine. More work and research has been done since then, using especially the data from firm level surveys, across many countries. The evidence collected through these diagnostic surveys in Latin American countries offer an illustration that State Capture is not a problem limited to transition economies. More than half of public officials in Peru, for example, believe that interest groups have the ability to and do influence legislature, judiciary, local authorities, high-level officials and regulatory agencies.

Sometimes, 'State Capture' is disguised as legitimate political contributions from private firms and citizens to a political movement or a party. In this connection, of interest are the extent of such practices and the perceptions of respondents about gains received from such donations. The survey of enterprises asks business people if in their opinion private firms benefit from providing a financial political contribution to a candidate. The results for three Latin American countries show that a significant proportion of managers in Colombia and Honduras believe that political contributions are frequent and that private firms benefit from contributions they made.

The survey data can also help to shed light on the institutional environment, which shapes the behavior of public officials in personnel and budget administration. By using the evidence from three countries in Latin America on the decision-making process within agencies, we illustrate how detailed information can help to focus on institutionalized practices of governance in the public sector. For example, public officials report that the decision-making process in public agencies is politicized and based on private connections leading, therefore, to inefficient outcomes in the administration of public resources (Figure 4.8). This type of information is critical for policymakers to design the most effective policy response.

Costs of Mis-governance and Corruption

The growing body of empirical research has emphasized the key role of poor governance and corruption in lowering the standards of living and worsening the distribution of income among citizens (Kaufmann, 2000).

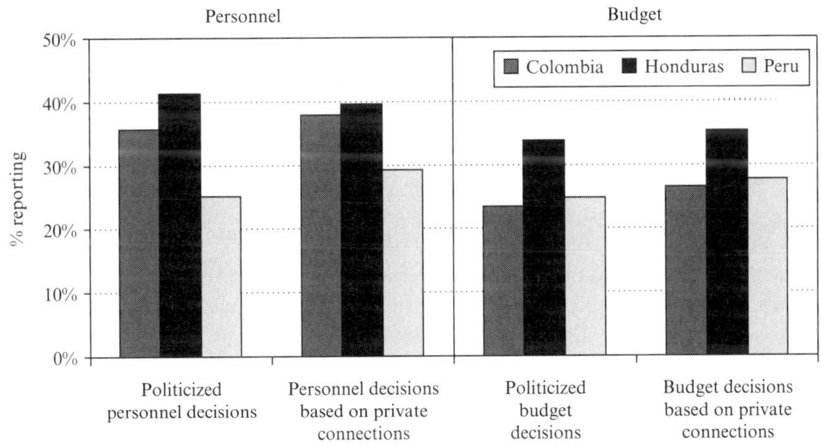

Figure 4.8 How are personnel and budget decisions made in public agencies? (as reported by public officials, selected countries, 2001)

The channels through which corruption influence development include detrimental effects on poor, lower investment and growth, lower quality and accessibility of public services, such as health care and education. To illustrate the importance of data on governance in this context we provide examples of the link between poor governance and economic outcomes.

There are several mechanisms through which corruption influences the well-being of poor citizens. First, corruption contributes to discrimination of people in terms of access to public services. By examining cross-country evidence from the surveys of users, we conclude that the costs of corruption, in addition to the cost of illegal payments, materialize in a number of users who give up applying for a service as they cannot afford a bribe. This negatively influences social development because poor citizens are restricted from using basic services such as health care and education. The user survey includes a list of public services that citizens decided not to use because of different reasons, among others – high extra official payments. In Zambia, for example, more than 20 per cent of households reported they were discouraged because of corruption and decided not to seek a service, though needed, with the Revenue Authority and health services.

There is also abundant evidence that corruption affect the poorer citizens disproportionately. If an amount of bribe is measured relative to income it turns out that the costs of corruption are not even across all categories of citizens. The empirical evidence from several countries in our sample (Sierra Leone, Honduras, Paraguay, Peru, Ecuador and Zambia) suggests that for the majority of public services corruption penalizes excessively the poorer and more vulnerable citizens, acting as a regressive tax on users of public services. That is, the low income users pay the relatively higher bribes to obtain any public service.

Quality and Accessibility of Public Services

The costs of poor governance materialize not only in revenue losses and additional taxes on citizens. Poor governance also results in problems with public service provision and accessibility. That is why the measures of quality and accessibility of public services to users are important indicators of the general performance of the public sector as well as each institution in particular. The data from surveys of public officials in various countries suggest that in many agencies as few as half of respondents report that public services provided by their organization are accessible to the poor. In such countries as Cambodia, Paraguay and Bolivia, on average, only about 50 per cent of public officials indicate that services are accessible to the poor.

A further dimension of public sector performance is the quality of services provided by each individual public agency. Consider, for example, the case of Zambia. The survey data provides a general outlook on the quality of public services from the point of view of households and business people. The Zambia Commercial Bank and the Postal Service rank quite high in term of quality of the service provided. Agencies such as the Pension Office, the Traffic Police and the Public Health Services, instead, are consistently rated quite low in term of quality by both households and business people.

Another way to approach the problem of quality is to look at it in connection with bribery. We combine the data from the public official survey in Peru into the indices of service quality and bribery aggregated by agency. Figure 4.9 shows the scatter plot of service quality versus bribery, where each point represents an agency. As indicated, there is significant negative correlation between bribery and service quality, suggesting that paying a bribe will not guarantee a better quality. In addition, this evidence suggests that the quality of public services varies not only across countries but even to the larger extent across agencies, with some institutions exhibiting greater effectiveness than others. At the same time, because bribery does not result in higher quality of service, lower income users are penalized even further.

The survey included a number of questions that measure various aspects of service provision. These aspects include public officials' evaluations of prices, quantity, and formality of rules that regulate service provision. Using these measures, we can have a better understanding of the quality

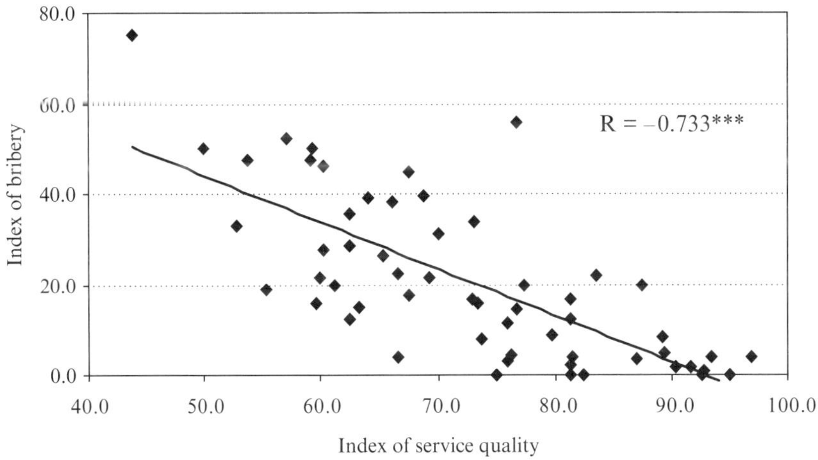

Note: Each dot on the graph represents data aggregated for one public agency. Indices of bribery and service quality rate the agency's quality of service and level of bribery on the scale from 0 to 100. The equation of the fitted regression line is: $Y = 95.2 - 1.02{*}X$

Figure 4.9 Indices of service quality and bribery (based on public officials' responses, Peru, 2001)

and the cost of public services. This information together with the data on agencies can help to define vulnerable institutions and suggest priorities for policymakers. Additionally, it is known that the quality of regulations as measured by simplicity, clarity, stability and strict implementation of rules is an important determinant of institutional performance. The survey to public officials employs several questions that capture the quality of the regulatory framework in personnel, budget and service management. One of these questions measures the formality of rules in service provision. In several of the countries included in our sample, more than 20 per cent of public officials report that public service in their institution is provided according to informal and non-written rules.

Focusing on Special Areas: Health Care and Judiciary

The in-country detailed diagnostic surveys can be easily adapted to local conditions and needs, for example, to include a group of questions or a special section to study particular sectors, where corruption is known to have the most detrimental effects on development, or which play an important role in shaping regulatory environment, such as judiciary branch of power.

As mentioned before, high bribes restrict access to public services for the poor. The phenomenon is particularly pernicious if it is observed in such essential service as health care. In the case of Peru, Romania and Zambia, for example, corruption indeed hinders access to health care. In addition, often the percentage of those not using medical services because of high bribes, as in Romania, is much lower among high-income earners than among low-income respondents.

Developing countries often suffer from the lack of strong law enforcement. The judiciary is frequently overrun with corruption and fails to address the basic needs of citizens. The lack of credibility about the effectiveness and fairness of the judiciary system discourages households from using the formal judiciary system and leads to a wide use of alternative conflict-resolution mechanisms, which is the sign of a weak judiciary. The survey data indicate that in Peru about 30 per cent of respondents who had to resolve a dispute during two past years used some alternative mechanism, instead of the formal judicial system – the fact that clearly shows the deficiency of the judiciary in that country.

Country-Specific Indices of Public Sector Performance – A Brief Description

The country-specific survey data described in the previous section can be used for in-depth analysis at the agency-level. The data collected provide a wide range of information about governance, corruption and service delivery across key, pre-selected institutions within a country, based on public officials' responses. These data can be analyzed to evaluate the quality of governance across agencies to identify both weak institutions (in need of reform) and strong institutions (examples of good governance), and to unbundle corruption in its various forms – such as administrative corruption, state capture, corruption related to procurement, theft of goods and public resources, purchase of licenses and regulations.

This agency-level analysis follows the approach introduced by Kaufmann, Mehrez and Gurgur (2002) for Bolivia using similar survey data. Their approach minimizes respondents' bias and measurement error due to individual differences in perceptions using a factor analysis technique. Intuitively, this technique permits us to summarize individual public official's responses by the institution where the respondent works. The outcome of this procedure is a set of governance indices for each public institution of the country analysed. This information can be further aggregated by the location of the institution. This attempts to capture the idea of geographical differences in quality of governance and corruption, and to exploit possible variations for similar agencies.

To construct the indices for the analysis, the individual responses are first rescaled and synthesized into agency indices using a factor analysis technique. In particular, all questions about individual perceptions, which can be scaled from 1 to 7 (or 1 to 5) in the original survey, are rescaled from 0 to 100, in order to facilitate percentage interpretation (0 always meaning the lowest level of quality of governance, corruption, access or service performance). Several variables are then constructed with the objective of capturing different aspects of the quality of governance, the presence of corruption within the institutions and the access and availability of public services provided to the citizens.

The resulting agency-specific indices can be calculated by country, by region and by city, depending on the information available and the objective of the analysis. Tables 4.1 and 4.2 provide the definitions of the governance and corruption indicators that can be constructed.

This approach is a powerful policy tool to evaluate the performance of different state agencies and to design targeted, more effective policies. Table 4.3 shows, for example, the performance of agencies and Ministries in Sierra Leone along a few, selected governance dimensions. At the same time, because of the increasing number of countries that have completed diagnostic surveys, these indices can be used to compare the performance of similar institutions across different countries, complementing and deepening the insights obtained by using aggregate indicators.

These indicators have been useful to improve our understanding of the impact and the potential causes of corruption at the country level. Kaufmann, Montoriol and Recanatini (2008) analyse the link between governance and service delivery. The paper explores first which household characteristics may affect the decision to seek public services. Higher education and age are associated with higher probability of being discouraged when seeking a public service. Trust in state institutions decreases the probability of being discouraged, while knowledge of mechanisms to report corruption and extent of social network increase it, suggesting that households may rely on substitutes through networks. The paper then complements the household analysis with a supply-side analysis using the data from public officials and the corresponding agency-level indicators discussed above. The econometric analysis suggests that corruption reduces the supply of services, while voice mechanisms and clarity of the public agency's mission increase it.

The use of these agency-specific indicators for within- and cross-country analysis highlights ways for governance improvements in underperforming institutions and supports the hypothesis that priorities for reform are not the same across countries or across public agencies within the same country. Recanatini, Prati and Tabellini (2005) focus instead

Table 4.1 Definition of agency-specific governance indicators

Governance variable	Definition
Access to the poor	Access by poor citizens to the public service provided by the institution, as reported by public officials. High numbers imply greater levels of access.
Audit mechanisims	Percent of cases where the decisions on personnel, budget and service management are subject to external and/or internal audits.
Enforcement of rules	Frequency with which rules/guidelines/regulations in the personnel, budget and service management are strictly monitored and enforced.
Meritocracy	Frequency with which decisions on personnel management issues are based on professional experience/merit/performance or education levels.
Mission	Index determining the degree of understanding of agency's objective and own tasks and responsibilities by public officials within the institution.
Openness	Frequency with which rules/guidelines/regulations in the personnel, budget and service management are announced and opened to the internal of the institution.
Politicization	Percent of cases where the decisions on personnel, budget and service management are subject to political interference and influence.
Quality of rules	Frequency with which rules/guidelines/regulations in the personnel, budget and service management are formally written, simple, clear, not adding too many administrative steps.
Resources	Percent of cases where physical, financial and human capital resources of the agency are adequate.
Transparency	Percent of cases where the decisions on personnel, budget and service management are done transparently.
Voice	An index representing the existence of consumer feedback and complaint mechanisms available to service users.
Wage satisfaction	Percent of employees very satisfied or somewhat satisfied with their wages and benefits.

on agency-specific factors that may affect corruption in ten developing countries. The sources of the data are the surveys described in this chapter, focused on employees working inside each public agency, as well as customers of the agency (households or firms). The authors find that corruption is influenced by two kinds of variables. On the demand side, corruption is more prevalent among agencies that provide services to firms. On the supply side, the internal organization of the agency is a

Table 4.2 Definition of corruption indices

Index	Definition
Overall corruption index	Corruption index comprising four type of corruption: bribery over regulatory/legal decisions, bribery over public contracts, corruption in personnel management and corruption in budget management.
Corruption in personnel management	Corruption index representing the percentage of cases where decisions on personnel management are based on unofficial payments (job purchase).
Corruption in budget management	Corruption index representing the frequency within the institution of irregularities/diversion of funds or any other type of budget abuse.

major determinant of corruption. Three features of the organization are systematically associated with less corruption: having decisions regularly audited by external or internal auditors; maintaining open and transparent procedures; and basing personnel decisions on criteria of merit and professional competence. Moreover, the procedure for appointing the head of the agency also matters. Agencies whose head is popularly elected are systematically more corrupt and adopt worse internal organizations.

CONCLUSIONS

Over the past decades, policymakers have increasingly faced the challenge of designing and implementing an effective reform to improve governance and curb corruption. For a reform to be effective, policymakers need to have the most relevant type of information to identify priorities and to create the conditions for sustaining the reform process over time, since these often aim at altering significantly the distribution of rents and power within a country. This chapter proposes an alternative approach to policy design based on country-specific, micro-level data and the active participation of citizens in the design and implementation of the reform in an attempt to address these challenges.

This approach has been adapted and used in about 18 countries around the world and a few lessons have emerged. Country-specific assessments should be viewed as complementary to cross-country aggregate indicators and should be used together to obtain a more comprehensive picture of the state of governance and corruption in a country, as a few countries have begun doing. The active participation of citizens in the design and implementation of the governance reform does create

Table 4.3 Governance indicators by institution, Sierra Leone

	Audit	Enforcement of rules	Transperency	Citizen voice	Wage satisfaction	Overall corruption
Presidential affairs	52	74	55	59	17	29
Ministry of Finance	57	68	54	60	25	22
Quasi-independent institutions	69	85	63	78	32	46
Ministry of Trade and Industry	64	84	59	63	19	32
Ministry of Internal Affairs	60	76	61	76	0	33
Ministry of Energy and Power and NPA	72	92	61	69	25	39
Ministry of Foreign Affairs & International Cooperation	50		54	50	30	28
Ministry of Development & Economic Planning	54	72	57	58	25	47
Ministry of Social Welfare, Gender & Children's Affairs	59	71	56	58	13	33
Ministry of Health & Sanitation	54	71	55	65	21	36
Ministry of Information and Broadcasting	55	68	51	60	18	20
Ministry of Education, Science and Technology	54	69	55	67	26	32
Ministry of Youth and Sports	56	76	52	72	25	14
Ministry of Labour and Industrial Relations	61	71	56	64	25	28
Ministry of Agriculture and Food Security	60	69	58	66	16	39
Ministry of Local Government & Municipal and district councils	58	72	57	63	15	33

Ministry of Transport & Communications	64	77	57	66	31	25
Ministry of Works and Public Maintenance	53	67	53	68	5	14
Ministry of Lands, Housing & Country Planning			57	56	13	34
Ministry of Mineral Resources	60	67	55	55	21	16
House of Parliament	54	53	59	50	13	28
Office of the Attorney General, Minister of Justice and Director of Public Prosecutor	60	75	55	67	25	22
Traffic Police and Road Transport Authority	41	74	54	63	34	36
Supreme Courts	64	78	56	72	43	25
Local Courts	61	68	53	77	36	34
SALWACO/GVWC and SIERRATEL	56	73	57	58	35	30
SALPOST	61	66	54	60	28	39
Port Authority	53	66	54	59	42	37
SL National Tourist Board and SL Standards Bureau	44		49	51	63	63
Police and Prisons	59	68	53	66	25	33
Post-conflict institutions	60	71	54	64	44	26
WHOLE COUNTRY	58	71	55	66	25	32

greater local capacity and stronger ownership, which in turn can ensure sustainability of reform process. Moreover, the greater ownership of the design and implementation of reforms has led to the (south-south) exchange of knowledge and the creation of interesting partnerships between countries. The highly disaggregated data have also furthered the research agenda on the determinants and the impact of poor governance and corruption.

On the other hand, this approach requires a significant amount of time and resources to be implemented, making it difficult to use in emergency situations or when resources are scarce. It can also be extremely challenging for the implementing unit to co-ordinate successfully many different actors, especially the international ones. Finally, this approach can be jeopardized by unforeseen political changes happening at the country level, as we have observed in a few countries. This risk can be mitigated by the involvement of international NGOs and the donor community to support the reform process.

NOTES

1. Kaufmann (2000); Knack S. and J. Anderson (1999); Gupta S., H. Davoodi, and R. Alonso-Terme (1998); Mauro (1995); Tanzi and Davoodi (1997); World Bank (2004); Svensson (2005).
2. Munck and Verkuilen (2002) introduce a general framework for the design of instruments to study complex and multi-facet variables, including important steps of conceptualization, measurement and final aggregation of data.
3. A variety of techniques has been recently developed in development and labor economics using multi-source survey data and mix of qualitative and quantitative data. An excellent reference for household survey data is Deaton (1997).
4. A few examples are worth mentioning. Kaufmann, Kraay and Zoido-Lobaton (KKZ) (1999b) uses the method of unobserved components to produce six cross-country governance indicators. Others apply factor analysis technique to distill regional and/or agency-specific information from survey data (Kaufmann, Mehrez and Gurgur, 2002; Kaufmann, Monteriol, Recanatini, 2008).
5. For the purpose of this chapter, governance is defined as '*the process, institutions and customs through which the function of governing is carried out*' (Kaufmann et al. 1999a), while *corruption* is defined as '*the use of the power of public office for personal gain*'. The definition of corruption includes all (and only) activities in which 'public officials, bureaucrats, legislators and politicians use powers delegated to them by the public to further their own economic interests at the expense of the public good', (Jain, 2001). This definition embraces many different forms of corruption from administrative corruption to 'state capture' – when powerful groups buy influence and shape the laws to their benefit.
6. See Kaufmann, Pradhan and Ryterman (1998) for the description of the original approach and implementation in Latvia, Georgia and Albania.
7. See Drazen, (2002) and Burki & Perry (1998) for a review of the literature.
8. Among the others, see Bardhan (1997), North (1990), and Olson (1965).
9. See Johnston and Kpundeh (2004) and Gonzales de Asis (2000).
10. Blank and Grosh (1999) provides a detail review of the experience of five countries in

terms of four aspects of capacity building – training, technical assistance, research and recruitment.

11. In Bolivia, civil service and procurement reform are being emphasized, while in Latvia, tax and customs reform have become priority items on the national agenda. In cities such as Campo Elias, Venezuela, and Ternopyl, Ukraine, the combination of the evidence from a recent governance survey and collective action by civil society is leading to improvements in local government effectiveness, a greater 'voice' for citizens in government decisions, improved government accountability to citizens, and better provision of public services.

BIBLIOGRAPHY

Ades, A. and R. Di Tella (1999), 'Rents, competition and corruption', *American Economic Review*, **89**(4), 982–93.

Alesina, Alberto (1999), 'Do corrupt government receive less foreign aid?', *NBER Working Paper Series*, **7108**(May).

Bardhan, P. (1997), 'Corruption and development', *Journal of Economic Literature*, **35**(3), 1320–46.

Bearse, P., G. Glomm and E. Janeba (2000), 'Why poor countries rely mostly on redistribution in-kind', *Journal of Public Economics*, **75**(March).

Blank, L. and M. Grosh (1999), 'Using household surveys to build analytical capacity', *The World Bank Research Observer*, **14**(2).

Broadman, H. and Recanatini, F. (2002), 'Seeds of corruption', *MOCT-MOST, Economics of Planning*, March 2002.

Burki, S. and G. Perry (1998), *Beyond the Washington Consensus: Institutions Matter*, Washington DC: World Bank.

Deaton, A. (1997), *The Analysis of Household Surveys: A Microeconometric Approach to Economic Development Policy*, Washington DC: John Hopkins/World Bank.

Drazen, A. (2000), *Political Economy in Macroeconomics*, Princeton: Princeton University Press.

Fisman, R. and R. Gatti (2002), 'Decentralization and corruption: evidence across countries', *Journal of Public Economics*, **83**.

Friedman, E., S. Johnson, D. Kaufmann and P. Zoido-Lobaton (2000), 'Dodging the grabbing hand: the determinants of unofficial activity in 69 countries', *Journal of Public Economics*, **76**, 459–93.

Gonzales de Asis, M. (2000), 'Reducing corruption: lessons from Venezuela', *PREM Notes* **39**, May, Washington DC: The World Bank.

Gupta, S., H. Davoodi and R. Alonso-Terme (1998), 'Does corruption affect income inequality and poverty?', *IMF Working Paper*, WP/98/76, IMF.

Hunt, J. (2005), 'Why are some public officials more corrupt than others?', *NBER Working Paper Series*, No. 11595 (August).

Hunt, J. and S. Laszlo (2005), 'Bribery: who pays? who refuse? what are the payoffs?', *NBER Working Paper Series*, No. 11635 (September).

Jain, A. (2001), 'Corruption: a review', *Journal of Economic Surveys*, **15**(1), 71–121.

Johnson, S., D. Kaufmann, J. McMillan and C. Woodruff (2000), 'Why do firms hide? Bribes and unofficial activity after communism', *Journal of Public Economics*, **76**, 495–520

Johnston, M. and S. Kpundeh (2004), 'Building a clean machine: anti-corruption coalitions and sustainable reform', *World Bank Policy Research Working Paper*, **3466** (December).

Kaufmann, D. (2005), 'Back to basics: 10 myths about governance and corruption', *Finance and Development*, September, **42**(3), IMF.

Kaufmann, D. (2000), 'Governance and anti-corruption', in Vinod Thomas (ed.), *The Quality of Growth*, Washington DC: The World Bank.

Kaufmann, D., A. Kraay and P. Zoido-Lobaton (1999a), 'Governance matters', *World Bank PRD Working Paper* No. **2196**.
Kaufmann, D., A. Kraay and P. Zoido-Lobaton (1999b), 'Aggregating governance indicators', *World Bank PRD Working Paper* No. **2195**.
Kaufmann, D., G. Mehrez and T. Gurgur (2002), 'Voice or public sector management?', mimeo, Washington DC: The World Bank, (May).
Kaufmann, D., J. Montoriol and F. Recanatini (2008), 'How does bribery affect public service delivery? Micro-evidence from service users and public officials in Peru', *World Bank Policy Research Working Paper*, No. **4492**, Washington:The World Bank.
Kaufmann, D., S. Pradhan and R. Ryterman (1998), 'New frontiers in diagnosing and combating corruption', PREM Note No. 7, Washington DC: World Bank.
Knack, Stephen and J. Anderson (1999) 'Is "good governance" progressive? Institutions, inequality, and poverty reduction', paper presented at the 1999 Annual Meeting of the American Political Science Association, Atlanta, Georgia.
Kpundeh, S., (1999), *Curbing Corruption: Toward a Model for Building National Integrity*, Washington DC: Economic Development Institute, The World Bank.
Lui, F. (1985), 'An equilibrium queuing model of bribery', *Journal of Political Economy*, **93**(4).
Mauro, P. (1995), 'Corruption and Growth', *Quarterly Journal of Economics* (August).
Munck, G. and J. Verkuilen (2002), 'Conceptualizing and measuring democracy: evaluating alternative indices', *Comparative Political Studies*, **35**(1).
North, D. (1990), *Institutions, Institutional Change and Economic Performance*, Cambridge: Cambridge University Press.
Olson, M. (1965), *The Logic of Collective Action*, Harvard Economic Studies.
Recanatini, F., A. Prati and G. Tabellini (2005), 'Why are some public agencies less corrupt than others? Lessons for institutional reform from survey data', mimeo, Washington DC: World Bank.
Svensson, J. (2005), 'Eight questions about corruption', *Journal of Economic Perspectives*, **19**(3), 19–42.
Svensson, J. (2003), 'Who must pay bribes and how much?', *Quarterly Journal of Economics*, **118**(1), 207–230.
Tanzi, V. and H. Davoodi (1997), 'Corruption, public investment and growth', *IMF Working Papers*, WP/97/139.
Treisman, Daniel (2000), 'The causes of corruption: a cross-national study', *Journal of Public Economics*, **76** (June).
World Bank (2004), *Making Services Work for the Poor*, World Development Report, 2004, Washington DC: World Bank.

PART II

CORRUPTION IN PRACTICE

5 Corruption in procurement*

Glenn T. Ware, Shaun Moss, J. Edgardo Campos and Gregory P. Noone[1]

INTRODUCTION

Corruption is a worldwide scourge that afflicts both developed and developing countries alike and which requires constant attention by many sectors of society if it is to be kept in check. It has its most damaging impact, however, on those weakened systems that have the least capability to prevent, detect, and stop its debilitating effects.[2] The African Union estimates that approximately one quarter (or US$148 billion) of Africa's gross domestic product is 'lost to corruption each year'.[3] In Kenya alone, international donors estimate that since 2002, nearly one billion dollars has been stolen as a result of corruption.[4] In Asia, the Asian Development Bank (ADB) reports that in one Asian country, approximately US$48B may have been lost to corruption over a 20-year period.[5] And, in Latin America, the Inter-American Development Bank (IADB) estimates that about 10 per cent of GDP is on average lost to corruption annually.[6]

This social pandemic has been pervasive in public procurement. It distorts public finance, impairing the delivery of public services, such as the building of schools, the provision and quality of medical care and, ultimately, retarding efforts to reduce poverty. Globally, Transparency International estimates that at least US$400 billion per year is lost to bribery and corruption in public procurement, increasing government costs by about 20 to 25 per cent.[7] In Asia, the ADB has noted that several countries have paid 20 to 100 per cent more for goods and services than they would have had to otherwise.[8] And, in Uganda, it is estimated that approximately $107 million is lost annually to corruption, mostly through public procurement.[9]

Public procurement is particularly susceptible to corruption because of the high value of funds involved, which usually account for between 10 and 20 per cent of a country's Gross Domestic Product (GDP)[10] and because of the expenditure profile of public procurement programmes. In contrast with the other major components of a country's public expenditure, public procurement usually involves a relatively low volume of high-value transactions (typically a few hundred procurement transactions conducted annually by each public institution, the most valuable of which may involve millions of dollars). By contrast, for example, expenditures on public-sector salaries, invariably involve a much higher volume of low-value transactions, each of which is less attractive to potentially corrupt public officials.

The susceptibility of public procurement to corruption is further exacerbated by the relatively high degree of discretion which public officials, politicians and parliamentarians typically have over public procurement programmes, in comparison with other areas of public expenditure. For example, in a typical annual public investment planning cycle, parliamentarians usually get to decide, through their influence over and voting on public expenditure bills, which roads get funded from the public purse and in which locations. There is invariably a strong incentive for such parliamentarians to promote 'pork barrel' projects in their own constituencies to stimulate economic activity and thus bolstering their chances of re-election. Likewise, in the implementation of public investments, it is typically a senior civil servant who gets to decide, often under pressure from those same parliamentarians, which contractor wins the contract to build the publicly-funded road, even under circumstances where a competitive tender is conducted. By contrast, other large chunks of public expenditures such as salaries and public debt are paid directly to recipients based on set rules and involve very little discretion. The corruption risks inherent in this scenario tend to be elevated in developing countries, where the legislative, regulatory and institutional frameworks put in place to curtail the discretionary aspects of public procurement tend to be weaker than those in the West.

Given the amounts of money at stake, public procurement is often typified by cut-throat competition between bidding companies, which rely heavily on public contracts for their survival. The dependency of private-sector companies on public-sector business is often disproportionately greater in developing countries, where public procurement may amount to more than 20 per cent of GDP, where the state is the largest economic actor, and where the private sector may be relatively under-developed. The juxtaposition of high volumes of expenditure, excessive and unbridled discretion afforded to public officials, and the presence of dependent private-sector contractors often creates a ready market for corruption in public procurement.

The causes and impact of corruption vary from country to country. Generally, the less capacity a country has to prevent, detect, and punish corruption, through checks and balances, controls, and monitoring and more broadly to enforce laws and regulations, the greater the likelihood of corruption. Most experts agree that the monopoly of power, wide discretion, weak accountability, and the absence or deficit of transparency magnify opportunities for corruption.[11] These pathologies (deviations/abnormalities/vulnerabilities) are anchored in a distorted incentive system that entices individuals, often including very capable ones, and institutions, both public and private, to engage in corrupt activities.

Just like a computer hacker that can intrude into a computer system at many points in the network, so too can corrupt actors intrude into a procurement procedure at many points along the procurement chain. One of the most sophisticated and developed procurement systems in the world is that of the United States federal government. Guided by many laws and regulations, as well as monitored by administrative and legislative bodies, it handles the massive U.S. defence and executive agencies' budgets.[12] Nevertheless, numerous incidents of corruption still occur annually. One of the most recent cases is that of a senior U.S. Department of Defense (DOD) acquisition official, who pleaded guilty to criminal conspiracy relating to involvement with Boeing, a major defence contractor. The official admitted to secretly arranging a job with Boeing at the same time she was acting in her governmental capacity in negotiating a US$23 billion-dollar acquisition by the U.S. Air Force from Boeing.[13] The sheer magnitude of the funds at stake and the relative ease with which the criminal conduct occurred indicates that even the most advanced procurement systems are prone to control breakdown, particularly when the controls rely on human judgements. For its part, Boeing accepted responsibility for the misdeed, agreed to pay over US$600 million dollars in fines and fired its Chief Financial Officer, who had agreed to the deal with DOD official.[14]

To control corruption in public procurement, it is imperative for one to understand how public procurement procedures operate and which methods may be effective in reducing corruption risks. This chapter explores how corruption attacks public procurement, identifies 'red flags' that may indicate the operation of corruption schemes, and examines potential vulnerabilities that exist along the procurement chain. The chapter also discusses various instruments that can be helpful in preventing corruption in public procurement. It concludes with a discussion of comprehensive vulnerability assessments as a new, potentially promising *ex ante* instrument to reduce the risk of corruption in public procurement.

THE AIM OF PUBLIC PROCUREMENT

To be effective, public procurement must be responsive to the demands of its stakeholders – the public, the government, and the private sector. A country's public procurement system must provide the required inputs to the delivery of public services – typically, goods, civil works and services – at low cost and with appropriate levels of quality. To achieve this objective, most public procurement systems attempt to emulate the operation of the market, mostly by requiring the conduct of competitive tendering procedures for major acquisitions, except in exceptional circumstances (see, for instance, the case of emergency procurement in Appendix A). A truly competitive process enables the country to effectively utilize public funds, whether from domestic revenues, foreign aid, or loans which are critical for developing good infrastructure, promoting human capital, reducing poverty, and enhancing economic growth. The key principles governing a competitive public procurement system include:[15]

- *Rules-based*: countries should have a clear and adequate legal and regulatory framework in place to guide public procurement. The laws, regulations, policies, and implementing rules must promote fairness (and be seen as fair to all potential bidders) and thus discourage discrimination (primarily between national and international companies) and favouritism: the equal treatment of bidders in the public procurement process promotes greater certainty and *predictability* in the awarding of contracts which is essential to fostering healthy *competition*.
- *Competition*: a public procurement system should encourage competition in the bidding out of government contracts. In most cases, competition results in better quality and lower cost, both of which are key desired outcomes of a well-functioning system. There will be special circumstances when alternative modes may yield better results. The rules and regulations should be clear on what instances such alternatives may be adopted and should limit discretion in deciding when to adopt them.
- *Transparency*: the public procurement process should imbue confidence among the public that the government will provide legitimate services for citizens rather than increase private wealth of government officials and/or narrow private interests. The easiest way to accomplish this objective is to ensure transparency in decision making throughout the entire procurement process, that is, to show that it is using tax payers monies responsibly. Transparency 'refers to the ability of all interested participants to know and understand the actual means and processes by which contracts are awarded and managed. This requires the release, as a minimum, of information sufficient to allow the average participant to know how the system is intended to work, as well as how it is actually functioning'.[16]

- *Accountability*: public officials should be held responsible for the proper implementation of rules and regulations governing public procurement and should accordingly be held accountable for procurement decisions which they make. Accountability requires that there be a credible sanctioning system for violations of the rules, consistent with due process. This implies the adoption of adequate internal controls and audit procedures as well as a complaints system for bidders to challenge decisions in addition to appropriate administrative and judicial review bodies that have the authority to impose corrective measures and remedies.
- *Economy*: a key part of the implicit social contract between the government and the citizenry is that the government will spend taxes prudently and effectively. For public procurement, this means the government should procure goods, works, and services at a reasonable cost and with reasonably good quality, that is, obtain good value for money.
- *Efficiency*: time is money and time wasted is money lost. Rules and procedures should thus encourage the completion of the procurement process within a reasonable length of time as well as the timely delivery/implementation of the goods, services, and works procured.

CORRUPTING PUBLIC PROCUREMENT

In public procurement, corruption schemes often occur in similar form, shape, nature and anatomical structure worldwide.[17] This section examines some of the most common corruption schemes that occur in public procurement, with a particular emphasis on procurement in the developmental context, and identifies corresponding red flags that could indicate the operation of a particular scheme.[18]

Bribes or 'kickbacks' are one of the most common features of corruption schemes in public procurement.[19] A kickback typically occurs when a company that wins a public contract 'kicks back' a bribe to the government official(s) who influenced the award of the contract (either voluntarily or under duress) to that company. Generally, the kickback is a percentage of the value of the contract and, in highly corrupt environments, it becomes an added cost that all bidders must take into consideration when bidding on public contracts, which makes it all the more insidious.[20] Kickbacks are paid by bidders both to buy influence over the procurement decision-making process and to solicit direct and immediate rewards.[21] For example, an urban transport project in Africa, costing more than $100 million, was cancelled after systemic corruption was discovered by investigators working for an international financial institution. The officials involved in the scheme used their control over the procurement process to extract bribes from contractors who were willing to participate both in the project and the corruption scheme.

Scheme 1: Kickback Brokers – Agents and Local Representatives

Kickback brokers appear in various forms – a local agent, representative, or joint venture partner in the purchaser's country. A local representative is often necessary when an international company wants to do business in a country where they do not have a local office or ongoing business operations. Local representatives or 'business development agents', as they are often called, are a common feature of international trade and are utilized by many large companies which operate in foreign markets, including in developing countries.[22] Typically, a business will retain the services of an agent to market, distribute or resell their goods, products and services. Because of their expertise, local knowledge and connections, using a local agent has become a proven way for companies to enter new markets.

In the development context, local agents are also used to assist companies bidding on public contracts. The local agent typically represents the foreign company locally, obtains the bidding documents, submits the required financial and technical bid and attends all meetings relating to the procurement, including pre-bid meetings and public bid opening meetings. By using a local agent, the foreign company obviates the need to maintain a permanent presence in the purchaser's country. In corrupt transactions, the local agent is compensated for 'capturing' the contract for the foreign bidder by exerting influence on the local public officials, including by agreeing and paying kickbacks to them. Success fees may be built into the agency agreement between the multinational company and the local agent, which has the effect of providing the local agent with a powerful incentive to be as aggressive as possible to assist the foreign bidder in winning the contract.

This incentive structure is a fertile breeding ground for corruption. It has become all too common for local agents to share a portion of their success fee with the officials who are awarding the contract. These fees can range from a few percentage points to a significant percentage of the contract value. The ability of the purchasing government to detect these illicit transactions is often constrained by the fact that the agency agreement between the foreign company and the agent appears legitimate and customary.[23] In fact, the agent may be nothing more than a legalized conduit for money to flow between a foreign bidder and those in government responsible for awarding the contract.[24] In other cases, a multinational company may hire a local agent to help it win government contracts and, while the multinational company may not specifically authorize the local agent to pay bribes, it is prepared to turn a blind eye to the business methods, including bribe-paying, which the local agent has to employ to win the contract. In such cases, the multinational company may use the local agent to keep itself at arm's length from corrupt practices, which is a particular consideration of multinational firms registered in countries with legislation which prohibits and penalizes bribing foreign officials. In still other circumstances, a multinational company may hire a local agent for legitimate marketing purposes and may be unaware of the fact that the local agent is engaging in corrupt practices to help it win a given contract.

In a recent case involving a U.S. manufacturing company, the company retained as its local agent a company owned by the son of a prominent government official to assist the U.S. company in winning state-funded contracts in the local agent's country. The relationship of the local agent to government officials was not known to the U.S. company at the time they hired the local agent, nor was the U.S. company aware that its local agent was sharing its fee with government officials responsible for awarding the contract. Indeed, the local agent did not reveal the fee-splitting arrangement with its U.S.-based principal. The scheme was, nevertheless, detected by the U.S. firm as a result of a robust internal compliance programme that spotted a red flag regarding the agent's relationship with government officials. A resultant forensic examination led the company to dismiss the local agent.[25]

In the procurement process, project overseers should be aware of typical red flags that may signal kickback-related problems including:

- Improper bidder selection. For example, repeated contract awards by sole sourcing of a single supplier without competition, often at higher than market prices;
- Involvement of an unnecessary middleman or local agent in a public contract, where the local agent adds no obvious value to the performance of the contract;
- Procurement officials who accept inappropriate gratuities, such as expensive meals or gifts, from bidders or their local agents;
- Unexplained or conspicuous wealth of government officials who are responsible for overseeing or implementing public procurement, particularly in countries where public-sector salaries are low;
- Certain government officials have a widely-known reputation in the local community for demanding or accepting bribes;

- Under-delivery or poor performance of a public contract by a favoured contractor, followed by recurrent contract awards to the same contractor;
- Former government officials acting as suppliers to a public-sector institution of a project for which they were previously responsible or as a local agent of a foreign company bidding on contracts awarded by that institution or project;
- Close personal relationship, including family ties between suppliers or local agents and government officials with authority over public procurement.

Scheme 2: Bid Rigging

Bid rigging occurs when a competitive public tender, which has as its purpose open and fair competition between all interested bidders, is manipulated in such a way as to pre-determine the outcome of the tender in favour of a pre-selected bidder.[26] In some cases, this manipulation takes places among some or all of the bidders participating in the tender without the knowledge of the public officials responsible for conducting the tender; in others, those public officials actively participate in the manipulation, sometime with the willing collaboration of some or all of the bidders or, at other times, by coercing some or all of the bidders to participate in the bid-rigging scheme.[27]

Bid rigging can take subtle forms.[28] For example, specific requirements can be written into certain sections of the bidding documents, such as the technical specifications or the qualification requirements, so that only a particular product will meet the specification and bids offering other competitor products will be rejected on grounds of technical non-responsiveness, or that a particular bidder will qualify to be awarded the contract and bids submitted by other bidders will be rejected on the grounds that those bidders are unqualified. In a recent investigation of an educational book project, the specifications contained in the bidding documents were found to have required unnecessarily specialized paper for use in the printing of the books and only one bidder – the favoured bidder – had access to that paper.[29] Alternatively, a favoured bidder may be given inside information, not made available to all other bidders, which enables the favoured bidder to enter the lowest-priced bid. In another variation, the public officials responsible for conducting the public tender may give the favoured bidder access to the bidding documents before they are formally disseminated, so that the favoured bidder has more time than other bidders to prepare his bid. By way of typology, the following four common bid rigging schemes have been identified by enforcement officials engaged in investigating fraud and corruption in public procurement:

Bid suppression
One or more competitors agree not to bid or are coerced by one of the bidders or, in some cases, by a public official, into not bidding, or withdrawing a previously submitted bid, so that a designated bidder will win. In return, the non-bidder may receive a subcontract to the winning bidder or a payoff for not bidding.

Complementary bidding
Co-conspirators submit token bids which are intentionally high or which intentionally fail to meet all of the requirements of the tender, in order to allow a favoured bidder to win. Complementary bids are designed to give the appearance of real competition in a public tender.

Bid rotation
Co-conspirators submit bids but, by agreement, take turns being the low bidder on a series of related contracts. In a recent series of tenders for civil works to rehabilitate rural roads in four remote provinces of a small Asian country, it was found that a group of four local contractors had pre-arranged to rotate the contract awards between them. Given the rural location of the works, the four companies were well known to each other and, because of the remoteness of the location of the works and the small value of the contracts, contractors from other provinces were not interested in competing for the contracts. These circumstances facilitated the rotation of the bids between the conspirator firms.

Customer or market allocation
Co-conspirators agree to divide up customers or geographic areas. The result is that the co-conspirators will not bid against each other or will submit only complementary bids when a solicitation for bids is made by a customer or in an area not assigned to them. This scheme is most commonly found in the service sector and may involve quoted prices for services as opposed to bids.[30]

'Low balling'
In this case, the designated company submits the lowest bid with the understanding of the public official responsible for awarding the contract that, once awarded, the contract will subsequently be amended and the contract price increased to enable the winning bidder to complete the work and to inflate his profit margin, part of which may be shared with

the public official. A corollary but related feature is the abuse of the 'change orders' process. In such instances, the favored bidder 'low balls' his bid with the understanding or expectation that he can eventually make up for their low bid by submitting change orders to the contract, which are then approved by the involved public official. The change orders materially change the contract price. In a recent construction project, a contractor was able to increase the price of its contract by submitting change orders, which were approved by acquisition officials, on the basis that a site inspection conducted subsequent to the contractor's starting work revealed unexpected ground conditions not foreseen in the specification contained in the bidding documents. The acquisition officials approved the change order in exchange for a facilitation payment.[31]

Common indicators of bid rigging identified by leading enforcement officials are:

- Identical bids submitted by different bidders either with respect to individual line items in the bids, or to the total bid prices;
- All bids submitted are substantially higher than the procuring entity's cost estimate of the contract, or substantially higher than comparable bids submitted by the same bidders for similar works or in other areas;
- A winning bidder subcontracts performance of part of the contracted works to one or more losing bidders with or without the client's knowledge;
- There is indication of a physical alteration of one or more bids, particularly at the last minute or after submission;
- The prices quoted by some bidders for particular line items are substantially higher than the prices quoted by other bidders for the same items and bear no relation to cost; this is a common technique for hiding excessive profits within a winning bid, which is subsequently used to pay bribes to the awarding public official;
- The range of bid prices shows a wide gap between the winner and all other bidders: this may be an indicator that all bidders other than the winning one have been given instructions to price their bids above a certain pre-determined price;
- The bid prices of all bidders vary from one another by the same increment, for example winning bid price plus 1 per cent, plus 2 per cent etc.;
- A bidder submits different bid prices for the same line item on different contracts that are tenders close together in time;
- There is physical evidence of collusion in the bids submitted, such

as different bidders submitting bids with the same handwriting, or in the same type of envelope, or containing the same mathematical or spelling errors, or with the same contact information, such as telephone or fax numbers;
- Qualified bidders do not bid, especially if they initially took steps to bid, such as applying to pre-qualify; this may be a sign that they have been coerced by the procuring entity not to bid or have been induced by another bidder not to bid;
- When a contract is re-bid, for example because all the bids submitted in the original tender were unacceptable, the prices of the bids submitted in the re-bid result in the same ranking order of the bidders or some bidders fail to submit bids in the re-bid;
- Also in re-bidding, there are significant increases in the prices of bids submitted by most bidders over the prices which they previously submitted, when there has been no commensurate increase in the cost of the same items;
- Prices mysteriously drop when a new bidder begins participating in public tenders, which may indicate that bidders were colluding among themselves to keep prices artificially high, in the absence of competition from a bidder who had not been part of the collusion scheme.[32]

It should be noted that bid rigging is not unique to developing economies, but a vulnerability of all procurement systems. For example, in a case in New York, 11 public school officials were arrested for receiving kickbacks and arranging bid rigging on maintenance contracts for public schools.[33] The officials would fake competition by requiring the selected bidder to provide phony bids from other potential bidders, in order to meet bidding rules which required the submission of at least three competitive bids as a condition of the tender being considered valid.[34] The kickbacks received by the public officials amounted to 10 per cent of the contract price.[35]

Scheme 3: Use of Front or Shell Companies

Corrupt public officials commonly use front or shell companies, generally in conjunction with other schemes, such as kickbacks, to disguise their illegal influence over the award of public contracts, for which the same public officials are formally responsible. Using a front company enables the corrupt public official to rig the tender and, commonly, to exert coercive influence over other, genuine bidders, in order to ensure that his front company wins the contract and he enjoys the resultant, illegal private

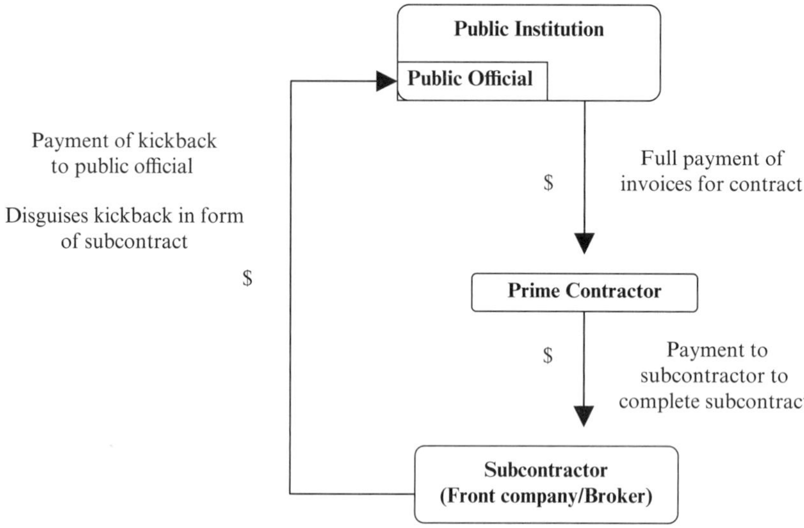

Figure 5.1 *Front company appears as a subcontractor but functions as a broker or intermediary*

gain. Frequently, the corrupt public official has no intention that his front company will actually implement the contract which it wins, with the result that contract performance is negligible or non-existent. The resulting impact is that the quality of the goods, services or works provided is generally very poor – a typical trick is that old, used or refurbished equipment is supplied to the public procuring entity under the contract – and, in some cases, the goods or services may not be delivered at all.

Alternatively, a front company may appear as a subcontractor to a prime contractor and actually function as a broker or intermediary between the prime contractor and the corrupt public official. In this way the subcontract disguises the kickback paid by the prime contractor to the public official, while no real performance is rendered to the public procuring entity under the subcontract. While the prime contractor may be coerced into agreeing to participate in such a scheme, it is often the case that the corrupt public official who demands the bribe may also have control over the payment of the prime contractor's invoices; the public officials provides a benefit to the prime contractor by ensuring that its invoices are paid promptly and in full, with dispute, thus enabling the prime contractor to funnel the bribe through the subcontract to the public official (Figure 5.1).

Money can be easily disguised in subcontractor shell company arrangements that provide a mechanism to launder money or move it offshore.

In a case investigated by one of the authors, a West African company was acting as an intermediary for a West African public official. In order to disguise and launder the kickback, the front company acted as a subcontractor to the bribe-paying prime contractor, a prominent European company. The subcontracting front company invoiced the prime contractor for 'technical data' amounting to 30 per cent of the contract value. The subcontractor was later discovered to be passing money to public procurement officials. The prime contractor paid the invoice but did not receive any 'technical data' in return for the payment. When questioned why they paid, executives of the European company replied that 'this is the way business is done here' and shrugged off further questions by investigators.

Front companies can be stacked up in layers to hide the true identity of the ultimate recipient of a kickback. Stacking front companies makes detection of the ultimate beneficiary extremely difficult. The task of detecting true ownership is made even more difficult when the front company or companies are created in so-called 'secrecy jurisdictions' that may cloak company ownership with privacy rules.[36]

A recent report by the U.S. Government Accounting Office noted the significance of shell companies in facilitating criminal activity: 'Law enforcement officials and other reports indicate that shell companies have become popular tools for facilitating criminal activity, particularly money laundering'.[37]

Perhaps the starkest example of the pervasive use of front companies is the well-publicized U.N. 'Oil-for-Food' investigation conducted by the Volcker Commission. Former high-ranking Iraqi officials created scores of front companies to steal funds for the regime's own use, instead of the humanitarian use for which the funds under the program were intended.[38] The front companies were used for procuring weapons, funding the Intelligence Service, and otherwise supporting the former regime, thus depriving Iraqi citizens of much-needed humanitarian services.[39]

In many developing countries, legitimate companies owned by prominent families, some of whose members may include serving government officials and have ownership interests in the companies, are awarded contracts to provide legitimate services to the government.[40] Often, the ownership of these companies is general public knowledge and the award of contracts is not necessarily done in secret.[41] Because of their high-level connections, these official-owned enterprises have the power to divert public resources to projects that may not actually be in the public interest.[42] In a case investigated by one of the authors, a project director on an urban transport project had awarded several contracts to a consulting company, of which he was the listed principal owner. Even more startling, no attempt had been made to hide the ownership of the consulting company and no government overseers of the project had ever checked to ensure that contracts were not let in this fashion.[43]

Some of the red flags that indicate the existence of shell or front companies include:

- Previously unknown companies, with no track record of implementing government contracts, serving as subcontractors to foreign or local prime contractors on a project;
- A subcontractor company is registered in a secrecy jurisdiction;
- Payments are made against invoices to accounts held by companies registered in a secrecy jurisdiction;
- The subcontractor company has an opaque ownership structure;
- The owners of the subcontractor company are listed as law firms or as incorporation agents, rather than as named individuals; this form of listing may be used to hide the identity of the individuals who benefit financially from the company's business operations;
- The subcontractor company lacks visible corporate facilities, such as a headquarters building;
- The point of contact provided by the subcontractor company is a personal residence or an answering service;
- Companies winning sizeable or recurrent government contracts have opaque ownership structures;
- Family members of senior government officials hold ownership or management roles in companies which win government contracts;
- Recurrent appearances of government officials at company headquarters.

Other Schemes[44]

Though kickback schemes are the primary vehicles through which corruption is perpetrated in public procurement, there are other schemes that do not involve kickbacks but, nevertheless, result in the manipulation of public procurement for private gain.

Misrepresentation of facts

Public officials may simply misrepresent facts, in order to subvert public procurement procedures and steal money from the government. Public officials may collude with a favoured bidder in order to enable that bidder to win a contract resulting from a public tender which it would otherwise not have won, had the rules of the tender been correctly applied.

In a recent public tender in an Asian country, the chairman of a bid evaluation committee in a government ministry colluded with a corrupt bidder

Table 5.1 Prices of bids as originally submitted

Bidder	Bid price			Bid security amount	2% of bid price required
	Lot 1	Lot 2	Total		
Bidder A	$81 176	$91 168	$172 344	$3446.88	2.00%
Bidder B	$100 105	$112 056	$212 161	$4300.00	2.03%
Bidder C	$ –	$148 540	$148 540	$3000.00	2.02%
Bidder D	$58 120	$163 907	$222 027	$4441.00	2.00%

Table 5.2 Bid evaluation report as submitted for government approval

Bidder	Bid price			Bid security amount	as % of bid price
	Lot 1	Lot 2	Total		
Bidder B	$100 105	$112 056	$212 161	$4300.00	2.03%
Bidder A	$81 176	$147 168	$228 344	$3446.88	1.51%
Bidder C	$ –	$148 540	$148 540	$3000.00	2.02%
Bidder D	$58 120	$163 907	$222 027	$4441.00	2.00%

Amount of Public Funds
Stolen: $56 000

to steal US$56,000 in public funds in the award of a public contract for the supply of equipment in two lots, by allowing the bidder to withdraw the bid that it had originally submitted by the bid submission deadline and to replace it with a high-priced bid, to which the contract was then awarded.

In Tables 5.1 and 5.2 above, the corrupt bidder is Bidder A. The price of the bid originally submitted by the bid submission deadline for Lot 2 was US$91,168 (Table 5.1). In the evaluation of bids, the bid evaluation committee found that the bid submitted by Bidder B for Lot 2 was technically non-responsive, as the equipment offered by Bidder B failed to meet the requirements of the technical specifications in the bidding documents. As a result, Bidder B's bid for Lot 2 was correctly rejected. This created a price difference between Bidder A's bid price for Lot 2 and the price of the next-ranked bid, submitted by Bidder C, of US$57,372 (US$148,540 less US$91,168). The chairman of the bid evaluation committee spotted the opportunity presented by this situation, approached Bidder A and conspired with that company to allow him to withdraw his original bid for Lot 2, which was priced at US$91,168, and, a few days after the deadline for the submission of bids, allowed Bidder A to submit a new, fraudulent bid, priced at US$147,168. The report on the bid evaluation process (Table 5.2), which was submitted to the government for its approval, made no mention of the Bidder A's US$91,168 bid but recorded only that Bidder A had submitted a bid priced at US$147,168. The corrupt public official attempted to conceal his fraud by failing to keep written records of the bid opening meeting, at which the bidders' prices were read out, including Bidder A's US$91,168 price. By this fraud, the public official managed to defraud the government of US$56,000 on a US$91,168 bid.

In this case, there was a telling red flag, which the government failed to spot. The bidding documents required that each bid should be accompanied by a bid security in an amount equal to 2 per cent of the bidder's total bid price for Lot 1 and Lot 2. The total price of Bidder A's bids, as originally submitted, was US$172,344 and the bid correctly contained a bid security in the amount of US$3,446.88. The amount of the bid security was correctly recorded in the bid evaluation report, which was prepared by the bid evaluation committee and reviewed and cleared by the government. However, given Bidder A's falsified bid price for Lot 2, Bidder A's falsified total bid price was US$228,344, which would have required a bid security in the amount of US$4,566.88 (2 per cent of US$228,344), not one of US$3,446.88. Unfortunately, the government's reviewing authority failed to spot this red flag in the bid evaluation report and approved the award of contract for Lot 2 to Bidder A at a price of US$147,168, thereby allowing the corrupt public official and Bidder A to complete their fraud. It was only later, when one of the other bidders complained, that the government authorities detected the fraud.

Red flags which may indicate misrepresentation of facts include:

- the procuring entity fails to keep written minutes of the public bid opening meeting;
- the minutes of the public bid opening are not signed in their original form by all the members of the bid opening committee or by the representatives of the bidders who attended the public bid opening;
- there is a time delay between the public bid opening and the dissemination of the minutes of the bid opening to all the bidders;
- the procuring entity fails to keep adequate written records of the procurement process, such as a written report on the bid evaluation process, minutes of the bid opening meeting, copies of the bids submitted or copies of correspondence with the bidders;
- the bids submitted contain written corrections, deletions or interlineations, which alter key information contained in the bid, such as prices or the bid validity period (it may be impossible to tell whether such revisions to a bid were made before or after the bid was submitted).

CORRUPTION VULNERABILITIES OF THE PROCUREMENT SYSTEM

Procurement-related corruption is perpetrated in a variety of ways, as discussed in the previous section and, very often, corruption schemes are interrelated and used in a complementary manner which reinforce the effectiveness of each scheme and makes them more difficult to combat. While the risk of corruption can be reduced by a well-designed and well-regulated system, no public procurement system is totally corruption-proof. Like a computer software programme, it may contain structural holes, gaps or weaknesses, which allow corruption to seep into the procurement process.[45] A procurement system has numerous portals or entry points, each having a 'responsive control adjustment'[46] that seeks to secure it from attack, much like a patch on a software programme that ostensibly closes a particular entry point to a hacker. The holes may be unintentional, or in their worst form, trap doors designed by corrupt officials to create vulnerabilities for their later exploitation.

In order to minimize the risk of corruption, government leaders should examine their procurement system for potential vulnerabilities.[47] To this end, an overview of the system *is* instructive. Below, various phases of the procurement process are presented and for each phase, possible vulnerabilities are identified. Indicators of corruption risks, corresponding to the vulnerabilities, are also presented. These indicators have been drawn from the extensive experience of the World Bank in preventing, detecting, combating and investigating corruption in its projects. The Bank has conducted numerous such investigations and from this experience has identified 'yellow flags' or early warning signals to watch for throughout a project's cycle.[48] Many of these flags have appeared in several investigations regardless of country or sector.

Procurement can generally be viewed in four phases:

1) Project identification and design;
2) Advertising, prequalification, bid document preparation, and submission of bids;
3) Bid evaluation, post-qualification and award of contract; and,
4) Contract performance, administration and supervision.[49]

For each phase, possible vulnerabilities that may be susceptible to corruption are listed. Identifying these vulnerabilities permits the formulation of remedial measures and control mechanisms that strengthen the procurement system and reduce the risk of corruption.[50]

Project Identification and Design

This phase includes the selection of projects as well as the identification of funding sources for the project. The preliminary phase is critical for setting the tone for the subsequent phases. In a number of countries, projects face the challenge of political influence; for example, the selection of roads projects is often heavily influenced by politicians, who use their approval authority over the annual agency budgets to pressure the procuring entity – typically the Ministry of Public Works or Ministry of Transport – to insert their favoured projects into the Ministry's budget proposal. Road projects are thus identified and selected less on the basis of the public's transportation needs and more on the basis of political expediency: the projects serve as a source of campaign financing. This distortion at the outset of a project may set up a dynamic that leads to bid rigging or collusion in later phases.[51] Budgetary insertions guarantee that there will be funding for the project; bid rigging or collusion guarantee that the expected diversion of funds to political and other unintended uses is realized.

The following are 'yellow flags' that merit further investigation before proceeding to the next phase:

- The project selection and approval process lacks clear, objective criteria for selecting projects.
- In the case of physical works: (i) selected locations are not based on a demonstrated public need; (ii) the component parts of the project are too numerous and small to avail of potential economics of scale economies.
- The Government does not have sufficient capacity to monitor decentralized units which are responsible for conducting the procurement.
- The procurement plan relies too heavily on local competitive bidding, so that contracts to be tendered will not be tendered internationally.
- There is no affirmative anti-corruption control plan built into the project design.
- Cost estimates are inconsistent with market rates.
- Least-cost solutions have not been considered.

Advertising, Prequalification, Bidding Document Preparation, and Submission of Bids

This phase begins when a need has been identified and the responsible public institution decides that a public procurement contract is necessary to achieve the desired outcome. Multiple yellow flags exist which apply to this phase.

Advertising

The widespread, public advertisement of an invitation to bid for public contracts is an essential element of transparency and an indispensable measure, which is needed to alert interested bidders of an opportunity to bid on a public contract. Not only should the invitation to bid be widely publicized, it should be disseminated in sufficient time ahead of the deadline for submission of bids to give potential bidders adequate time to obtain the bidding documents and prepare and submit their bids. Widespread public advertising is one of the key components of the competitive tendering process and is essential to maximizing competition and, therefore, to undermining would-be cartels or other bid-rigging schemes, as the colluding bidders have no way of telling which other bidders intend to bid. The participation of bidders from outside the collusive scheme is key to disrupting the scheme's operation, which is why colluding bidders often try to limit the public advertisement of invitations to bids or to ensure that tenders are not advertised at all.

Yellow flags in this phase may include:

- an invitation to bid on a public contract awarded by competitive tendering is not advertised;
- an invitation to bid is advertised but only on a restricted basis; for example, a provincial government tender is advertised only within that province and not throughout the country;
- an invitation to bid on a high-value contract, which is likely to be of interest to foreign bidders, is advertised only in the procuring country's local or national press, not internationally;
- an invitation to bid is advertised in only one newspaper and, even then, in only one print run of that newspaper, the number of copies of which is limited and sell out rapidly;
- an advertisement of an invitation to bid does not include all the information which a potential bidder needs in order to decide whether or not to bid and to obtain the bidding document, such as the name and address of the official or organization from which the bidding documents may be obtained or the deadline for submission of bids;
- an advertisement of an invitation contains all the required information but the tender is conducted in a manner which is inconsistent with the published information; for example, the location of the office where bids are required to be submitted is changed at the last minute and not all bidders are notified of the change;
- an invitation to bid is published with a very short notification period; for example the deadline for submission of bids falls due only 3 or 4 days after the first publication of the invitation to bid;
- an invitation to bid is advertised on the procuring entity's public

website but access to the website is controlled by a password requirement or is otherwise restricted.

Prequalification

For high-value or technically complex public contracts, it is common for the procuring entry to apply prequalification of bidders to ensure that only those qualified bidders, that have the necessary experience, capability and resources to perform the contract successfully, are allowed to bid on the contract. Bidders must meet certain contract-specific qualification requirements in order to be prequalified to bid. This stage is designed to screen out frivolous, unreliable, or unqualified firms. However, it may also be used as a device to favour a small subset of bidders or to screen out other qualified bidders.

Yellow flags applicable to this stage may include:

- the invitation to prequalify is insufficiently advertised (see advertising yellow flags, above);
- Inadequate time given for preparing and submitting prequalification applications;
- prequalification requirements are stated in vague or unclear terms or are unrelated to the contract to be awarded;
- prequalification documents require applicants to submit voluminous administrative documentation in multiple copies and the absence of a single document results in the rejection of a firm's application;
- Applicants are required to be pre-registered, on a government-approved register, before being allowed to apply to prequalify;
- The prequalification requirements bear no relation to the performance requirements of the contract; for example, for a construction contract estimated to cost US$10 million, to be constructed over a period of two years, applicants are required to have access to cash equal to US$15 million, whereas a much lower level of cash flow would be adequate to perform the contract satisfactorily;
- The prequalification requirements cannot be met by any applicant; for example, prequalification documents for the construction of a dam in an Asian country required applicants to have built two dams of similar size in the past five years but no dam had been built in the country in more than a decade;
- The method of evaluation of applicants' qualifications is not stated in the prequalification documents or the method to be used is subjective, such as being based on an arbitrary merit points system;
- Bidders are pre-qualified for certain contracts but subsequently fail to bid for all contracts for which they have been pre-qualified (see Box 5.1 below).

BOX 5.1 PRE-QUALIFICATION – WHAT COULD GO WRONG?

A provincial government in an Asian country carried out pre-qualification of bidders to bid on two contracts for the construction of urban roads. Contract No. 1 had an official cost estimate of US$11 621 500, while Contract No. 2 was estimated to cost US$12 000 000. During prequalification, eight bidders applied to pre-qualify and six of them, Bidders A through F, were pre-qualified to bid for both contracts. When bids were submitted, it turned out that, for each of the two contracts, only three of the six pre-qualified bidders had purchased the bidding documents and submitted bids, even though all six pre-qualified bidders had been pre-qualified to bid for both contracts. The bid evaluation report indicated the following bids were submitted bids and the following bid prices:

Contract No. 1

Name of Bidder	Read-out Price US$	Read-out Discount US$	Final Read-Out Price US$
Bidder A	12 549 756	0	12 549 756
Bidder B	12 401 759	0	12 401 759
Bidder C	15 190 019	3 568 528	11 621 499

Contract No. 2

Name of Bidder	Read-out Price US$	Read-out Discount US$	Final Read-Out Price US$
Bidder D	13 933 488	0	13 933 488
Bidder E	13 795 146	0	13 795 146
Bidder F	12 008 765	0	12 008 765

The procuring entity recommended to award Contract No. 1 to the lowest evaluated bidder, Bidder C, at a contract price of US$11 621 499, which was US$1 lower than the official cost estimate for the contract, and to award Contract No. 2 to Bidder F at a contract price of US$12 008 765.

Yellow Flags in this prequalification:

- While all six firms applied to pre-qualify to bid for two contracts and were successfully pre-qualified to bid for both contracts, each applicant purchased the bidding documents for and bid for only one of the two contracts. This is a clear indicator that either the pre-qualified firms colluded to reduce competition for each contract, or perhaps even to rig the tender and determine the winning bidder in advance or that the procuring entity coerced each of the six pre-qualified firms into bidding for only one contract.
- The price discount offered by Bidder C for Contract No.1 results in that bidder's bid moving from the highest-priced bid to the lowest-priced bid, at a bid price that is within US$1 of the official cost estimate for the contract. This is an indicator that the procuring entity had informed Bidder C of the official cost estimate before it submitted its bid. It may also indicate that the three bidders for Contract No. 1 colluded to arrange the award of the contract to Bidder C or that either the procuring entity or Bidder C or perhaps both of them, had coerced Bidders A and B into allowing Bidder C to win Contract No. 1.
- The discount offered by Bidder C for Contract No. 1 is dubious and may be fraudulent. It is also possible that, if Bidders A and B were not involved in collusion, this discount may not have been included in Bidder C's bid when it was originally submitted nor read out at the public bid opening, but that the procuring entity allowed Bidder C to introduce the discount after the submission and opening of bids, thereby changing the ranking of the bids, once the prices of the bids submitted by Bidder A and Bidder B were known.

Preparation of bidding documents

The bidding documents for a particular contract perform several essential functions, including defining the rules by which bidders should abide when preparing and submitting their bids, defining the technical requirements of the procurement, including the technical specifications of the goods to be procured, and defining the criteria which will be used to evaluate the bids and decide on the winning bidder. Bidding documents usually comprise standard sections, such as instructions to bidders and general conditions of contract, and contract-specific sections, which vary according to the contract being tendered. In the absence of appropriate checks and balances, bidding documents may be manipulated to favour a few bidders or a single bidder or manufacturer.

Yellow flags in bidding documents may include:

- Contracts for similar or related goods or works are not packaged together into a single bidding document but are split into several separate tenders, each covered by a separate bidding document. This may be an indicator of splitting of contracts to prevent interest by foreign bidders or by large companies, thus allowing small, often local companies to minimize competition or to rig the tenders among themselves;
- The fee charged to potential bidders to obtain the bidding documents is excessive, by comparison with the value of the goods to be procured; for example, a procuring entity proposed to charge a fee of US$5,000 for a bidding document to procure goods estimated to cost US$200,000. The bidding document fee was excessive and probably intended to deter certain bidders, particularly small companies, from purchasing the bidding documents;
- the procuring entity issues bidding documents in a form other than that of the standard bidding documents approved for official use; this may enable the procuring entity to use arbitrary evaluation criteria or to avoid imposing standard contract conditions on favoured bidders, thereby harming the public interest;
- Technical specifications in bidding documents contain brand names or are based on a single manufacturer's products, thus limiting competition to that manufacturer or its authorized distributors and discriminating against other manufacturers' products;
- Bidding documents do not provide bidders with clear instructions on how they should prepare their bids or how they should structure their bid prices;
- Bidding documents fail to disclose to the bidders the criteria to be used to evaluate their bids and how those criteria will be applied to identify the winning bid.

Submission of bids

As discussed earlier, the bidding process itself may involve collusion among bidders with or without the participation of government officials; inside information may be sold so that a few select companies are able to cheat the process. Bidders in collusion may also agree among themselves that certain bids will be won by a designated company and that contracts are shared among members of the cartel. See Box 5.2.

BOX 5.2 DIRTY TRICKS AT PUBLIC BID OPENINGS

The public opening of the bids submitted in response to a public tender, at which representatives of all bidders are entitled to attend to witness their bids being opened and the prices publicly read out, is an indispensable element of transparency in public procurement. Nevertheless, it is one of the phases of the procurement process that is most frequently targeted by corrupt public officials and bidders to try to undermine the integrity of the procurement process.

When conducting a public opening of bids for the supply of computer equipment to a government department of a Central Asian country, the Chairman of the bid opening committee had entered into a corrupt relationship with one of the bidders, Bidder D in the example below.

Bidder	Bid Prices as Read Out (US$)	Bid Prices as Written in Bids (US$)
Bidder A	$2 450 650	$2 450 650
Bidder B	$2 226 730	$2 226 730
Bidder C	$2 725 000	$2 725 000
Bidder D	$2 190 525	$2 583 760

In the conduct of a public opening, bids are required to be opened in random order and, to facilitate this, bidders are required to submit their bids in unmarked envelopes, so that no one attending the meeting can tell which envelope contains which bidder's bid. However, the Chairman of the bid opening committee had prearranged with Bidder D that, while he would submit his bid in an unmarked envelope as required, he would cut off a small section of the corner of the envelope, to enable him to identify Bidder D's bid before opening the envelopes.

While conducting the public opening of the bids, the Chairman made sure that he first read out the prices of Bidders A, B and C and left Bidder D's bid until last, by which time the other three bidders' prices were known to him and to everyone else attending the meeting; they had been written on a board on prominent display in the meeting room. When he opened Bidder D's bid, he immediately said that it was priced higher than those of Bidders A and B and that it would, therefore, be unlikely to win the contract award. So, instead of reading out Bidder D's price as written in the bid (US$2 583 760), the Chairman read out a fictitious price of US$2 190 525, which was lower than the prices of the other three bidders. The representatives of Bidders A, B and C did not notice anything wrong with the process, as neither they nor anyone else attending the meeting could see that the Chairman had not read out the price of Bidder D's bid as it was written in the bid. Bidder D's representative at the public bid opening, who was complicit in the fraud, noted down the new, fictitious price of his bid and, a few hours after the conclusion of the bid-opening proceedings, was allowed by the Chairman to alter his Bid Form to indicate the read-out price of US$2 190 525 and to substitute his bid security with one which matched the lower bid price.

'Yellow flags' may include:

- One or more favoured bidders are informed of the procuring entity's cost estimate for the contract, while other bidders are not;
- The procuring entity fails to provide clarification of the bidding documents, as sought by bidders or circulates the clarification only to one or more favoured bidders;
- There is a delay in time between the deadline for submission of bids and the public bid opening;
- The locations for submission of bids and bid opening or the location of one or both events is switched at the last minute and not all bidders are informed of the switch;
- Certain bidders or groups of bidders are prevented from submitting their bids; for example, in a tender for a high-value provincial construction contract in a small country in South-Eastern Europe, a cartel of bidders from the province where the works were to be constructed placed armed gunmen outside the provincial government office where the bids were to be submitted on the date of the deadline for bid submission, in order forcibly to prevent bidders from the capital city, where most of the country's construction companies were based, and other provinces from submitting their bids;
- Bids are submitted and accepted after the bid submission deadline;
- Bids are not opened in public;

- The procuring entity fails to keep accurate minutes of pre-bid meetings, including questions and answers, and to distribute them promptly to all bidders;
- Price discounts in one or more bids are not read out at the public bid opening, but are subsequently evaluated, altering the ranking of the bids;
- The procuring entity fails to provide secure storage of bids submitted before the deadline, leaving such bids at risk of being prematurely opened and information about their prices being shared with competitor bidders.

Bid Evaluation

The evaluation of bids is the most important phase of a public procurement procedure, as it is at this juncture that the procuring entity makes the decision as to which of the competing bidders will be awarded the contract. The reliability, integrity and transparency of this key step in the process depends mainly on how clearly the bid evaluation criteria were originally expressed in the bidding documents and on whether those criteria are faithfully applied in making the award decision.

Not all evaluation systems are created equal and some types of evaluation systems are particularly prone to exploitation by corrupt public and/or the bidders who influence them, because of the excessive discretion which they afford those public officials in the contract award decision-making process. While price is the most widely-used evaluation criterion in public procurement, other, non-price criteria are also commonly applied; these may include the delivery time, payment schedule, the operating costs of the equipment, efficiency, the compatibility of the equipment offered with existing equipment owned and operated by the procuring entity, the availability of after-sales service and spare parts, training, safety, environmental impact.

The extent to which these non-price evaluation criteria are quantified and expressed in monetary terms in bid evaluation – as they are for instance required to be under the World Bank's Procurement Guidelines – often largely dictates the extent to which the evaluation process is prone to undue or corrupt influence. The most vulnerable evaluation systems are those which convert evaluation criteria – sometimes, inexplicably, even price itself – into notional points, which are then awarded to each bid by one or more evaluators based on his or her own subjective assessment of the worth of the bid against each criterion. Under such evaluation systems, there is often no right or wrong answer in the decision-making process, as the winning bid is simply the one which is accorded the most points;

in such a situation, the decision is wide open to corrupt influence and it becomes all but impossible to hold the evaluators accountable for the correctness of their decision.

Post-qualification

In some countries, the pre-qualification process has been streamlined in order to foster greater competition. With an e-procurement system, this takes the form of an electronic supplier registry where firms interested in bidding on government contracts must submit electronically documents that are typically required during pre-qualification and attest to their qualifications. The information is then stored in the registry and retrieved when a firm has bid on a contract. Once the 'winning bidder' has been selected, its qualifications to perform the contract, including in particular those submitted to the supplier registry, are subjected to evaluation, that is, 'post-qualification'. Otherwise, it is declared 'disqualified' and the firm with the next best bid is selected for post-qualification.

Depending on the post-qualification criteria and decision-making arrangements, the most qualified and cost-effective bidder may be prevented from receiving the award. When the best bidder fails to win the award, price of delivery increases, quality decreases and the destructive consequences of corruption take shape. 'Yellow flags' in this phase are numerous and provide many signals for the possible occurrence of corruption. These are presented in Box 5.3 below.

Contract Performance, Administration, and Supervision

This phase begins immediately after the contract is awarded and the contractor/vendor is then 'on the clock' and expected to make progress in fulfilling the terms and conditions of the contract. It includes the management of the contract by the procuring entity, in particular the monitoring of proper implementation. The monitoring procedures must be established in advance and should include complete documentation and accurate records to ensure accountability that the money is being used as specified in the contract, as well as default procedures. Numerous vulnerabilities exist during the performance of the contract itself as well as the oversight during the performance.

A common problem in many developing countries is that accounting systems are weak, which further undermines the public procurement process. Weak accounting permits financial irregularities to go undetected as well as illicit conduct to occur (for example often 'ghost names' of fictitious personnel populate the payroll).[52]

BOX 5.3 MONITORING BID EVALUATION – EARLY WARNING INDICATORS

Unreasonable delays in evaluating the bids and selecting the winner.

The evaluators use evaluation criteria other than those which were specified in the bidding documents.

The evaluators use the same criteria as were specified in the bidding documents but apply them in a manner other than was stipulated in the bidding documents.

Bid evaluation committee members do not have the technical expertise necessary to evaluate bids correctly.

The bidding process is controlled by a small number of persons in the procuring entity.

A high-level public official or politician, senior to the members of the evaluation committee, intervenes in the process and the ranking of bids changes as a result.

Two or more versions of the bid evaluation report are circulating within the bid evaluation committee, each recommending award of the contract to a different bidder, and factors within the evaluation committee are lobbying for their version to prevail.

Qualified bidders drop out voluntarily as the bidding process progresses such that only one firm is left at the post-qualification stage.

High number of complaints about the bid process and evaluation received from losing bidders, especially when lower-priced bids are declared non-responsive.

Complaints received from bidders during evaluation include a high degree of specificity about the evaluation process, including details of other bidders' bids, indicating that members of the evaluation committee are feeding confidential information to their preferred bidder.

The same bidder repeatedly wins similar types of contracts.

The prices of all but one of the bids submitted are close to each other and significantly above the purchaser's cost estimate, while the remaining bid is significantly lower in price than all the others and close to the cost estimate.

Similarities between competing bids (for example format of bid, typeface, identical unit prices, identical spelling, grammatical and/or arithmetic errors, photocopied documents).

Bid securities are acquired by competing bidders from the same financial institution.

Bid securities submitted by several bidders bear the same date of issue and/or sequential serial numbers.

A bidder lists multiple addresses.

Unit prices in competing bids vary inconsistently by amounts greater than 100 per cent.

Unit prices in competing bids are identical.

Bidders propose identical items, for example the same make and model (may indicate the specification was based on a single product).

Common ownership of competing bidders.

The Bid Evaluation Report has been revised or re-issued.

An arithmetic check of the bid(s) is not performed or results in a bidder being favoured inappropriately.

An evaluated bidder should have been disqualified based on the information submitted in their bid.

The lowest bidder is disqualified and the explanation, if any, provided is weak.

Seeking clarification is used as to disguise financial negotiations with the winning bidder.

Vested interests are identified among members of bid-evaluation committee.

Falsification of curricula vitae in consultant services proposals.

Unreasonable delays in negotiating and executing the contract.

Contract is not in conformity with bid documents (for example specification and quantities).

Contractor's name differs between Contract and Bid Evaluation Report.

Contract amount is different than amount in Bid Evaluation Report allowed under Bank.

Contract includes allowances for variations which are not part of the bidding documents.

Subcontracting requirements are imposed.

Rigorous system for handling contract variations and evaluating claims not defined in the contract.

Staff involved in contract award decisions become involved in contract supervision (award and supervision are with the same procuring entity).

Monitoring the contract and work completed is important for controlling corruption. A contract that is not properly and frequently monitored leaves opportunity for individuals to siphon money without completing the necessary work, or providing the quality of work expected. It is essential to conduct forensic spot checks to ensure the work is being completed in accordance with the contract. However, if the forensic spot checks are completed in a predictable and routine manner, opportunity still exists for the contractor to disguise illegal activity. 'Yellow flags' for this phase are presented in Box 5.4 below.

Broader Governance Concerns

There are three critical, overarching factors that underpin the procurement system and which may engender and/or heighten possible risks of corruption throughout the procurement chain: budget management, personnel management, and staff capacity. Chapter eight deals with the first. The second and third are discussed in a number of the sector chapters but are worth highlighting in the context of procurement.

In many developing countries, civil service reform has proven to be a major challenge and the experience of donors to date on providing assistance for such efforts has not been very encouraging.[53] Recruitment, promotion, and assignments are typically not very well defined and, even if there are clear rules, they tend to be overridden by political concerns. Performance is rarely the measure by which promotions are based. These conditions provide fertile ground for patronage and nepotism to emerge. And over time, an internal market for civil service jobs is created where the 'price' of a position is derived from the potential corruption returns that it can generate for the office holder. In the area of procurement, this could imply the 'purchase' of positions for district engineers, internal auditors, external auditors, and so on, which would then contribute to the pursuit of corrupt deals.[54]

To target corruption specifically within the procurement system, introducing reform for the entire civil service is often the much-needed starting point. A well-functioning procurement system, with lower incentives for corruption, is typically achieved through methods that foster accountability, establish true market conditions within the civil service system to allow governments to develop competitive and skilled employers, inculcation of a code of ethics that promotes the value of public goods more than private interests,[55] appropriate compensation schemes to maintain capacity,[56] and establish public independence of public procurement officials to alleviate pressure from high-ranking political officials so they can make balanced decisions based on merit and the proper application of procurement regulations.

BOX 5.4 TRACKING CONTRACT ADMINISTRATION – 'YELLOW FLAGS'

Contract specifications or scope of work altered after contract awarded.

Site inspection indicates that work performed was not in accordance with the technical specifications (below-specification civil works, goods and services are accepted).

Site inspection indicates that project completion is less than that certified or that a completed project is not operational.

Goods or services not being used, or being used for purposes inconsistent with intended purposes.

Wrong quantities of goods and materials are delivered.

Delays in the delivery of goods or services in any part of the contract implementation process.

Substitution of nominated consultant staff with less qualified and inexperienced personnel.

Frequent changes in key staff of PMU/PIU.

Changes in PIU/PMU responsible for post-procurement verifications.

Lack of, or low level, oversight of the physical works.

Absence or insufficient verification of scope of work and physical inspections.

Site diaries and meeting minutes are not maintained.

Written instructions are not given to contractors; instructions given to contractors, particularly to alter the contract, are given orally and not recorded in writing.

Incomplete records in PIU/PMU – significant number of missing documents.

High frequency of Change Orders to the contract.

'As-built' drawings are photocopies of technical specifications in the bidding documents.

The detailed drawings, 'as-built' drawings, back-up data sheets contain errors or repetitive entries.

Failure to pay progress payments and invoices on a timely basis.

Excessive number of signatures required to approve progress payments.

Evaluation of contractors' performance not recorded.

Costs overruns are inadequately explained or justified.

Customer/client dissatisfaction with completed facilities.

Staff capacity is another issue that requires attention but often is ignored in the context of anticorruption. Where staff lack training and experience in procurement, auditing, accounting, reporting, and so on, the procurement process will be inefficient and possibly confusing (and thus opaque). This too creates pressure for corruption, for example bribes being paid by contractors to get the agency to release payments. Increasing both initial and on-the job training on procurement rules and mechanisms for both public personnel and the private sector engaged in procurement is extremely important to sustaining a well-functioning procurement system. Policy officials should be required to continually review programs and undergo and provide training when the need arises.[57] Training should include, among others, techniques for identifying suspicious patterns of corrupt procurement practices.[58] With adequate training and well-defined objectives both efficiency and accountability are enhanced.

TOOLS AND REMEDIES

Tackling corruption in procurement requires a multifaceted approach that extends beyond controls and attacks the problem from many different angles. This section explores several promising measures that can help reduce corruption in public procurement. These measures can be classified broadly into two categories, supply side interventions and demand side mechanisms, and typically address problems of monitoring, reporting, and enforcement. The former include interventions that governments can adopt to improve internal processes and the latter mechanisms designed to complement and/or strengthen these interventions.

Supply Side Interventions

E-procurement

Perhaps one of the most promising recent innovations in the area of public procurement is the use of information communication technologies (ICT). Given an appropriate and supportive legal and regulatory framework, adequate training of staff, and sufficient support from the political leadership, ICT solutions in the procurement field (so called 'E-procurement') can increase competition, enhance transparency, reduce administrative costs,[59] and improve government efficiency, and in the process control corruption in public procurement.[60] For instance, the introduction of an e-public tender board where all advertisements (alternatively referred to as invitations to bid) have to be posted greatly reduces the incidence of collusion. Field investigations of the World

Bank into corruption in its projects suggest that, in some countries, firms have developed a 'round robin' system in which each takes turns as the 'winning bidder'. For any given contract, the 'winning bidder' agrees to share part of the rent premium with the others in return for their cooperation to 'bid higher' or withdraw midway through the bidding process. But for collusion to work, the number of firms with express intent to bid on a contract needs to be restricted. The larger the number of firms, the smaller the side payments that the 'winning bidder' can offer, and thus the less the incentive of the other potential bidders to buy in. A common tactic to limit participation has been to restrict advertising. In one case that the authors were made aware of, firms and public works officials in a particular municipality connived with the regional newspaper to produce two editions of its daily for a period of two weeks, an early edition and the regular edition.[61] The advertisement for municipal contracts would be placed in the early edition and the firms would purchase all of these copies. This actually met the legal requirement that an invitation to bid must be placed in a newspaper with at least regional circulation for a period of two weeks. But, with this scheme, no one other than the colluding firms were made aware of the contract. An electronic public tender board counteracts schemes of this sort and expands the potential number of bidders for any given contract and thus reduces the risk of corruption through collusion.

Several countries have adopted an e-procurement system primarily to cut down on costs and generate savings for the government and their experience suggests that e-procurement can indeed lead to substantial savings and, by implication, reduce corruption. These include among others Chile, Korea, and Mexico. Box 5.5 below summarizes the efforts of these countries.

It is important to emphasize, however, that the adoption of ICT can improve performance and reduce corruption only if systemic weaknesses or problems are addressed adequately. First, laws and regulations governing procurement have to be simplified. Among the benefits of the application of IT is to increase transparency and improve time efficiency. If the laws and regulations are complex these benefits are marginalized. Second, management systems have to be streamlined in ways that enhance transparency, accountability, and efficiency and procurement staff need to have adequate training. Third, implementation rules and practices for procurement have to be standardized; for example, standard bid documents, uniform rules for advertising. Fourth, procurement officials have to acquire a more business orientation in managing the procurement process; for example, efficiency in inventory management, fairness in contract management. And fifth, adequate oversight mechanisms

BOX 5.5 THE POTENTIAL BENEFITS OF A WELL FUNCTIONING E-PROCUREMENT SYSTEM

The Republic of South Korea[62]

The Republic of Korea introduced e-procurement in the late 1990s primarily to enhance transparency and reduce human contact between government officials and private firms bidding on government contracts. Procurement regulations were streamlined and a new ICT-based system was introduced as the anchor for these new regulations. Prior to this reform, both government and suppliers were engaged in time-consuming and convoluted processes. There was no consistency in supplier information across agencies and many were involved in pre-arranged bidding practices.

The new system has served as a focal point for more than 30 procurement-related external agencies to obtain information and gain access to over 420000 standardized products, documents, and expedited payments. Online access has allowed suppliers to pre-qualify, in addition to being able to retrieve all the relevant information on the bidding process, including comparative assessments across agencies. The wide availability of relevant information and the increased number of participating bidders has most likely mitigated the risks of collusion and bid rigging. Specifically, e-procurement has led to a decrease in procurement staff and speedier conduct of disbursements/payments. In 2002, the system counted over 25,000 public agencies and 87,000 companies involved in conducting close to $20 billion worth of transactions. And, due to improved efficiency, the government has saved over $2.5 billion.

Mexico[63]

With an estimated 25 per cent of the public budget directed towards procurement expenditures in the 1990s, the Mexican government felt compelled to address inefficiency and corruption in public procurement: high surcharges were incorporated by bidders to compensate for these costs. CompraNet, the Mexican e-procurement system, was borne out of this recognition.

Over 250 federal agencies and municipalities have conducted $25 billion worth in transactions through CompraNet. Administrative costs have decreased by 20 per cent due to the reduction in both paperwork and previously required face-to-face interaction. And, because the invitations to bid, awards, and payments are published online, interested firms and the general public, particularly concerned civil society groups, can now easily view procurement records 'on demand,' which has increased transparency, competition, and accountability. For example, the so-called 'Towelgate' scandal that marred the Presidential Palace was instigated by online information on CompraNet's transactions that revealed large discrepancies in the value of towels.

Chile

Through the Public Procurement System Strategic Plan, the Government of Chile streamlined the regulations on public procurement, establishing standard rules and an online national information system.[64] Chile's Public Purchasing Law required that all public procurement services be conducted through this system. ChileCompra established an electronic, interactive marketplace for suppliers and buyers to initiate and complete their transactions in one central location, accessible to several government institutions. This led to the standardization of all documents relevant to public procurement process which were made available online and to the creation of a registry for all participating bidding companies.[65]

In 2001, the public procurement market in Chile was valued at close to $7 billion a year, with 10 per cent of the Gross National ttProduct allocated to public procurement expenditures. The introduction of ChileCompra has allowed more users to participate in the public procurement process (thereby increasing competition), reduced the transaction time of a bid cycle, and led to a more cost-effective way of doing business for the government. The efficiency gains, compounded with the decrease in the cost of procurement advertisements have contributed to savings of over $70 million annually for the government.[66]

have to be put in place.[67] E-procurement can be an effective a tool for reducing corruption. But it must be complemented by these institutional reforms.

Forensic audits

An appropriately structured e-procurement system improves the monitoring and reporting capabilities of government and thus oversight of the procurement process. Oversight can be strengthened through the conduct of random forensic audits. Audits are a routine control in the public procurement process. However, most audits focus on process controls and do not sufficiently 'drill down' to determine the beneficial use of the funds. Accordingly, routine audits should be conducted but contain forensic features built into their terms of reference. These forensic features drive auditors to 'look behind the paper' and verify, for example, the authenticity of invoices submitted by contracts, verify that material noted on the invoices has been delivered, installed or built and also may include site visits to determine if contractors actually exist or are shell enterprises. Random selection puts potential fraudsters on guard and reduces their expected gain (and thus their incentives to perpetrate corruption).

Selective sanctioning: leveraging investigative and enforcement capacity

Reporting and auditing are critical to identifying corrupt transactions and to increasing the risk of detection. In turn, effective enforcement increases the 'risk of punishment'.[68] This begins with independent investigators who have authority to affect present and future contracts. There must be a system in place that can competently receive a complaint, conduct an investigation, pursue a prosecution, provide for mechanisms for adjudication/convictions, and devise remedies.

This system, however, is not always available given the fact that not all countries have the capacity to undertake the required efforts. Therefore it becomes all the more important that international financial institutions such as the World Bank, the Inter-American Development Bank, the European Bank for Reconstruction and Development, create and maintain robust, independent and credible investigative capacity. Because these institutions receive overwhelming numbers of complaints, heads of their investigative unit can select cases for investigation and sanctioning that can then be leveraged to the maximum extent possible. By publicly sanctioning a carefully selected group of cases (multi-sector, large and small companies) and deliver maximum sanction, an asymmetrical deterrent impact can cause companies to take preventive action to reduce the likelihood of corruption in their operations.

Voluntary disclosure programmes[69]

To complement sanctions, IFIs (International Financial Institutions) can also institute 'voluntary disclosure programme', which would allow contractors to self-report fraud and corruption in their operations. 'In exchange for a complete, timely, and truthful disclosure' an agreement would be made 'not to debar the contractor from eligibility' for future business contracts.[70]

Obtaining co-operation from parties involved in illicit behaviour in exchange for immunity or reduced sanctions has obtained growing popularity because of the asymmetrical advantage given to law enforcement officials by having an insider provide a detailed map of the proceedings. The practice of reducing sanctions in exchange for disclosure has increasingly been codified in many legal systems around the world. Among the countries providing some form of leniency for cooperating parties include, France,[71] the United States,[72] Pakistan,[73] Poland,[74] Argentina,[75] Brazil,[76] Italy,[77] and Kosovo.[78] The United Nations Convention Against Corruption (which has been signed by 140 states and ratified by more than 45 states) has entered into force, and also provides a powerful precedent by specifically encouraging states to consider implementing programmes which provide incentives for insiders to illicit activity to make disclosures to law enforcement agencies.[79]

Demand Side Mechanisms

External monitoring

In contrast to the use of investigators, which implies that a crime may have been committed, is the use of monitors. Monitors are able to closely scrutinize the procurement process from the beginning and thus can help prevent the occurrence of corruption. 'Independent Compliance Monitors' are new emerging critical players serving oversight functions for controlling fraud and corruption.[80] The use of monitors in the procurement process has increased even in the United States. The U.S. Department of Defense and Securities and Exchange Commission (SEC) use monitors to observe the performance of contractors who have had employees engaged in wrongful or corrupt conduct.[81] In developing countries, innovative approaches suggest that this may be a promising avenue for restraining corruption despite weak enforcement.

In countries where corruption is rife in public procurement, civil society groups can be useful external allies in combating corruption. This can be done by identifying and matching appropriate civil society groups to the different phases of the procurement chain. An example of such a mapping is given in Appendix C for the case of a Roads project.

Transparency International's Integrity Pact illustrates the potential of engaging civil society in monitoring the procurement process. In the 1990s, Transparency International (TI) introduced the Integrity Pact (IP) as a tool to curtail the incentive for corruption in public procurement by committing governments and bidders to an agreement guaranteeing both parties specific rights and obligations. The Integrity Pact (IP) serves as a contract that requires that neither the government nor the bidders would engage in corruption by pledging not to 'pay, offer, demand or accept bribes, or collude with competitors to obtain a contract, or while carrying it out'. A third-party monitor is engaged to oversee the proper implementation of the mutual agreement. In essence, the IP was designed as a credible commitment device that could assure both bidders and the government that no one is 'playing games' and the process is truly without bias.

The level of success of the IP is determined by the stage of the procurement process in which it is introduced. Ideally, implementation of the IP should commence in the planning stage and cover the design, construction, installation or operation of assets, in addition to the pre-selection of bidders, bidding and contracting proper. By beginning with feasibility and preparatory stage, the IP can enter at the most relevant stage of the process with the selection of contractors/suppliers/licences and exit at the final stage of the process when the main activities have been implemented, thereby ensuring a strong and consistent presence throughout the entire process.

The IP levels the playing field by assuring companies that their competitors are not participating in bribery – it solves a co-ordination problem. The government benefits from the IP not only by fostering transparency and mitigating corruption in procurement but also by establishing a more cost-efficient procurement process that benefits the government financially and the country economically. Currently the TI Integrity Pact is being used in more than 14 countries. Successful cases in which the Integrity Pact was implemented in its entirety include Argentina and Colombia.[82] (Box 5.6.)

Reporting and access to information

The role of the media, as well as local and international nongovernmental organizations (NGOs), is also critical in monitoring and exposing corruption. Reporters and journalists should be educated on the public procurement process so that they can better understand where potential problems may lie as well as spot them when they appear. In this context, complementary national legislation should include a 'freedom of information' Act which would allow the citizenry, watchdog groups and the media to see who are getting contracts, what are the terms and what is

BOX 5.6 USING IP IN PUBLIC PROCUREMENT OF GARBAGE COLLECTION SERVICES IN ARGENTINA

In 2000, the Municipality of Moron implemented the IP in their bidding process for garbage collection service, valued at $48 million. This specific IP was developed from recommendations and input from the 2000 International Workshop on Integrity Pacts in Bogota, Colombia and the latest IP used in Colombia. All four pre-qualified bidders signed the IP, thereby committing themselves to the requirements set forth in the pact to ensure the procurement process would avoid the incentive for corruption. TI's National Chapter in Argentina, Poder Cuidadono, served as the monitor of the IP throughout the bid evaluation, award decision process, and implementation of the contract. Violations to the contract would lead to the application of sanctions in the amount of 10 per cent with the prospect of also being blacklisted for five years. A hearing to discuss the bidding document and terms of the contract brought more than 500 people together to provide an opportunity to modify or amend any of the documents. Following the hearing an internet website published the final bidding documents. In addition to the steps and rationale leading up to the final document, ultimately the awarded contract was valued at $32 million and thereby resulted in substantial savings.

the value of the contracts.[83] The ability of published findings which result in negative publicity for corrupt individuals and companies cannot be underestimated.[84]

The power of information though is partly a function of how well it is understood by the general public. Making a new law available to the public may not be enough because it may not be easily comprehensible. NGOs can play an important role in this regard. In the Philippines for instance, Procurement Watch Inc. (PWI) was born out of the need to educate civil society organizations, the media, politicians, government officials, and the general public on the virtues of a well-functioning procurement system, including in particular curbing corruption, and on the implications of a proposed overhaul of procurement legislation. In order to galvanize support for the passage of a new omnibus law on public procurement, it was necessary to make different groups understand the rationale for and the basic workings and implications of the proposed law, a critical requisite for addressing the problem of collective action.[85] Upon passage of the law, PWI began conducting training workshops for NGOs interested in monitoring public bidding in their respective regions, for media, and for small and medium-sized enterprises interested in bidding on government contracts. PWI has opted to specialize on the issue of procurement, particularly on tackling corruption in this area. Its experience suggests that, to promote reforms in public procurement, it may be critical for some NGOs in other developing countries to undertake a similar role.

Information sharing and collective action

Several IFIs have created investigation units designed to ferret out both internal and external fraud and corruption. However, the IFIs do not share their information nor do they engage in collective sanctioning. IFIs should be encouraged to co-operate in an information-sharing programme that could be centred in a 'Transnational Corruption Information Sharing Center' (TCISC).[86] The TCISC could process information that would be useful in business/loan decisions, investigations, and assistance with national law enforcement efforts. The shared information would also be useful in collective action that could be imposed on corrupt regimes, corporations, and individuals. Both activities would face considerable bureaucratic and political obstacles. Institutions may claim that the sanctioning action by another institution is politically motivated and fail to take collective action. Or, one institution may be reluctant to rely on the investigative findings of other institutions out of concern for lack of integrity or thoroughness in the investigative process. This process could be managed, however, if information was widely shared among IFIs and the institutions retained the right 'to autonomously review the findings of other institutions and make independent determinations'; these collective actions could deter some of the greatest offenders in illicit procurement schemes.[87]

Norms and conventions: addressing cross-border corruption

The evolving international trends in minimizing corruption and fraud in the public procurement process includes harmonization of norms, standards, practices and vocabulary – all of which help foster greater transparency and predictability in the procurement process. Model procurement regulations and codes such as the United Nations Commission on International Trade Law (UNCITRAL) and the American Bar Association's assist in the standardization of this field.[88] Another critical piece to this effort is the continued emergence of regional and international conventions. Four international anti-corruption conventions include scores of nations committed to fighting corruption: the Organization of

American States (OAS) Inter-American Convention Against Corruption, the Organization of Economic Cooperation and Development (OECD) Convention on Combating Bribery of Foreign Officials in International Business Transactions, the Council of Europe's Criminal Law Convention on Corruption and the aforementioned and recently ratified United Nations Convention Against Corruption (UNCAC).[89] An added benefit of participation in multilateral conventions, as research indicates, is that countries who are 'more open to the international economy and participate more broadly in international organization (such as the IMF, OECD, UN and World Bank) tend to have lower levels of perceived corruption'.[90]

CONCLUSION: WHERE TO NEXT?

Environmental impact assessments were introduced in the 1980s and in the initial stages there were those that argued that these would impair project progress, be too costly, and retard development. Today, however, environmental impact assessments are a fact of life in large public works projects.

The newest and most innovative idea in the field of fraud and corruption prevention is the Corruption Vulnerability Assessment (CVA). Like an environmental impact assessments, a CVA can be conducted prior to the onset of large developmental projects involving public procurement. A CVA is an intelligence-driven assessment that would determine the likelihood of corruption occurring in a planned project. It would examine the environment in a particular country in terms of corruption vulnerabilities that might put funds at risk prior to the onset of distribution. Upon its completion, project designers and international financial institutions would have more information upon which to take graduated measures to ensure that public money is used for the intended purposes. For example, if government officials or their families have widespread holdings in private companies, a mandatory financial disclosure programme can be installed to ensure that officials do not steer contracts to their own business entities. If project monitors are active in a project, the results of the CVA will provide critical information for the monitor to use in tailoring their monitoring protocol.

Briefly, the CVA would contain the following elements:

- *Environmental and Country Risk (ECR):* the ECR would assess the country environment in relation to corrupt practices. Are bribes necessary to obtain contracts, licences and permits – if so, what are the methodologies and schemes most commonly employed? Are conflicts of interest between government officials and businesses common? What is the status of anti-corruption programmes at the national, state and local level? Does the government have the capacity to uncover, detect and prosecute corruption at the highest level of government?

- *Systems and Control Review:* the systems and control review assesses what anti-corruption measures are in place to prevent corruption from occurring within a given project. Are auditors trained to spot indicators of corruption? Are the government officials who manage the project required to make financial disclosure of their assets and outside ownership interests? Are appropriate hotlines established for reporting corruption by both government watchdogs and civil society? Are companies bidding on the project required to maintain corporate governance and compliance programmes? Are investigative assets available to follow up on allegations of fraud and corruption?
- *Human Factors:* this component examines reputations, associations, activities and ethics of individuals running the projects. Do they have undisclosed liabilities or questionable financial reporting? Do project officials have existing allegations of corruption or do they have a reputation for obtaining bribes in their official capacity?

By obtaining comprehensive information on the likelihood of corruption, the methods likely to be employed and the actors who will participate before the distribution of funds, advance control measures could be uniquely and specifically employed to ensure public funds are less susceptible to corruption.

Flowing from the CVA, project supervisors, MDB fiduciary staff and auditors and monitors should conduct routine *enhanced due diligence* throughout the project cycle. Enhanced due diligence would mean that project overseers would scan the environment throughout the project cycle based on the litany of red and yellow flags noted previously. To conduct enhanced due diligence, widespread training of fiduciary staff needs to occur to ensure that they are aware of corruption risks and able to spot early warning indicators throughout the project cycle to mitigate corruption risk. By having a control framework where all fiduciary staff are part of the anti-corruption control, the risk of detection will increase the likelihood of reducing corruption

Corruption in public procurement presents one of the most vexing social problems confronting governments. It weakens economies, creates entrenched cynicism among civil society, and in some cases threatens the very governments which permit illegal schemes to continue unabated. To address this, it is necessary to establish a clear and adequate legal and regulatory framework. But this is hardly sufficient. Laws and regulations need to be enforced and extra and consistent vigilance exercised by all corners of society.[91]

There is, however, hope as corruption in public procurement manifests itself in recurring patterns of illicit behaviour that present opportunities for intervention. This chapter has attempted to explore the common anatomy and vulnerabilities that occur in the public procurement process. By raising awareness of these vulnerabilities across disciplines, new approaches and methodologies for successful control interventions can be studied, implemented and evaluated to determine what can be done to mitigate the effects of corruption. Certainly the intelligent application of information and communications technology, that is, e-procurement systems, holds some promise in resolving some of these concerns. Today, there is a heightened sense of urgency in addressing one of the most serious obstacles to development effectiveness. Hopefully this chapter has provided an impetus to further the dialogue among and efforts of various stakeholders.

APPENDIX A: THE SPECIAL CASE OF EMERGENCY PROCUREMENT: A JUSTIFIED EXCEPTION OR AN AVENUE FOR CORRUPTION?[92]

In times of an emergency or in a post-conflict environment, the need to speed funds to a region is great and thus excessive controls can have a negative impact on necessary and immediate relief. Accordingly, an elaborate procurement system which can be mapped for vulnerabilities may not be practicable in emergency procurements. In emergency procurement such as post-disaster or post-conflict, a balance is needed so as not to excessively control distribution at the front end of the control regime so that the money flows quickly. Yet a system of checks must still be in place. In situations brought upon by natural or manmade disasters when the front-end distribution controls are slacked in order to speed distribution, continuous monitoring is essential and back-end enforcement becomes even more important.

Following the devastating tsunami in the Pacific there have been many accusations of corruption on several different levels. Such cases include diverting food from victims to shopkeepers to be sold, or to officials' homes. Other reports describe military personnel stopping incoming aid trucks and charging a tax to bring in supplies.[93] Yet another case involved local officials taking a cut of employees' wages in exchange for referring them to employers for work.[94] The corruption extends beyond officials; in some locations people have registered themselves in two or three different areas as victims, in an attempt to receive two or three times the return on what they lost.[95] People take advantage of disasters much like a computer hacker will take advantage of an unprotected computer network.

One of the more serious cases of corruption in Aceh, Indonesia was a result of taking shortcuts in the building of homeless shelters for the victims of the tsunami disaster. The shelters were long wooden barracks, and in an attempt to save money on the structure, which would house 500,000 people, the contractor did not attach the wood to the concrete foundation. The concrete used for the foundation contained more sand (and less concrete) than is safe, and it was also made too shallow. The end result is the contractor stealing money in order to enrich himself, or perhaps to pay off government officials – or both; while the citizens are relegated to unsafe housing and are victimized again.[96]

In 2005, a group of experts went to Indonesia to study ways to reduce corruption in Tsunami Relief Operations. This group identified a number of risks associated with corruption in post-disaster situations. They include:

- Extreme urgency during the relief phase, with priority on saving lives;
- Logistical difficulties in getting assistance to people in need;
- Massive inflows of funds from various providers, overwhelming recipient governments' ability to manage procurement and finance functions;
- Disruption of administrative systems and control measures at local levels;
- Lack of co-ordination of responsibilities, with some donors insisting on managing funds and procurement themselves;
- Disruption of normal markets for goods and services;
- Special rules and incentives of aid providers for post-disaster assistance;
- Inexperience of aid providers with local conditions.

Some suggestions for managing these increased risks include systematic and transparent needs assessment procedures; integration of affected people into assessment and decision-making processes; specific management systems to assess and sort all assistance delivered and offered, and to match this to assessed need; donor co-ordination to agree on common procurement approaches and guidelines; channels for reporting suspicions of corruption.[97]

In the United States, after Hurricane Katrina ripped the Gulf Coast thousands of people were displaced. The American Red Cross in an effort to help as many people as possible quickly distributed cash to affected individuals and families who requested such assistance. Unfortunately, false claims were filed as part of an illicit scheme to steal relief money.[98] A lack of controls and safeguards invites intrusion and often that intrusion is designed to reap financial rewards.

Accordingly, even in developed countries like the United States – a natural disaster provides tremendous opportunity for those with the incentive, opportunity, rationalization and capability to be corrupt. But unlike less-developed countries, the U.S. has tremendous back-end capacity to detect and prosecute fraudsters who have taken advantage of a slack control environment.[99] In developing countries, the lack of front-end prevention and control and back-end enforcement provides a virtual breeding ground for corruption.

The experience of the tsunami in Asia and the hurricane in the United States clearly demonstrates that there is no working model yet in place that can prevent corruption from invading emergency relief.

APPENDIX B: RELATED CORRUPTION SCHEME

Embezzlement

This scheme involves government officials stealing from projects by a variety of means, some as straightforward as writing cheques to themselves or their family members. The payments are made typically with fraudulent invoices or by having ghost employees on the payroll. At times the siphoned funds are used to finance buildings and structures that are never used by the public but instead are diverted to government officials for their personal use.

Misuse of Public Assets

Because of the broad (and often times unchecked) discretion that many officials have and the resources at their disposal, governmental officials are often found using official vehicles, planes, computers, credit cards, and facilities for their own gain or gain of their political party or personal interest group. These cases run from small misuse of office computer equipment to misuse of aircraft for private events and functions. In one case investigated by the authors, a government-owned jet aircraft was taken for personal use at a cost to taxpayers in the hundreds of thousands of dollars by mischaracterizing the flight as an 'overland navigation training flight' in the aircraft logbook and the official authorization government airlift request. Still in other cases, government officials may abuse their position by structuring projects that favour their personal interests. For example, for an urban transport project, government officials may ensure that roads are built or bus stops are placed in areas that favour businesses they own or that favour their families' interests.

In a number of development projects, investigators discovered misuse of project vehicles and theft of petrol as commonplace.[100] While seemingly insignificant, the absence of a vehicle from a roads project may prevent governmental inspectors from travelling to a road to inspect the progress of corruption. This resultant lack of oversight creates further vulnerabilities in the control architecture and permits more theft.

Red flags of this type of abuse include among others:

- Official vehicles being used for personal errands;
- Intermingling of government assets and personnel (e.g. computer, support staff) with personal matters;
- Consumption of government officials at higher rates then justified by government business;

- Appearance of governmental assets at personal residences;
- Overtime payments to expense for personal errands;
- Known reputation for abuse of assets;
- Appointment of friends, relatives and even spouses to government positions; and,
- Unjustified consulting studies.

APPENDIX C: MAPPING EXTERNAL MONITORS TO THE VALUE CHAIN: AN EXAMPLE FOR THE ROADS SECTOR

Procurement Phase	Possible External Monitors
Preliminary: Project Design and Selection	(1) Universities with engineering schools. Student monitoring groups formed to vet/comment on selection and design/ estimates. This could be part of a practicum program prior to graduation (2) Contractors Association, if reputable (3) Association of Civil Engineers, if reputable
Initial Phase	
Bid document preparation	
Advertising Pre-qualification	NGO with focus on anticorruption and preferably with some expertise in procurement, e.g. local TI chapter, religious organization. Observer status in bids and awards committee
Selection of the Winning Bidder	
Bid Evaluation Post qualification	NGO with focus on anticorruption and preferably with some expertise in procurement, e.g. local TI chapter, religious organization. Observer status in bids and awards committee
Performance Phase	
Disbursements/payments	Association of CPAs. Training may be needed to conduct forensic audits. Audits done randomly.
Project completion	(1) Universities with engineering schools. Student monitoring groups formed to vet/ comment on selection and design/estimates. This could be part of a practicum program prior to graduation (2) Contractors Association, if reputable (3) Association of Civil Engineers, if reputable

NOTES

* This chapter was originally published as Chapter 9 of the publication, *The Many Faces of Corruption: Tracking Vulnerabilities at the Sector Level* (J. Edgardo and Sanjay Pradhan (eds)), Washington, DC: The World Bank. It is reproduced here with permission of the World Bank. The International Bank for Reconstruction and Development, The World Bank, is the source and copyright holder of the data used.

1. This chapter could not have been completed without the efforts of Nisha Narayanan who provided invaluable, just-in-time research assistance and Dr Diane Noone who provided advice and inputs on legal and investigative aspects.
2. See Transparency International, *Global Corruption Report 2006*, available at http://www.globalcorruptionreport.org/download.html#download.
3. Thachuk, K. (2005), 'Corruption and international security,' *SAIS Review* (Winter-Spring) **XXV**(1): 143152, 149.
4. Wax, E. (2005), 'Kenya is buffeted by graft scandals,' *The Washington Post*, February 13, A21.
5. Asian Development Bank (1998).
6. Mora (2004).
7. http://www.transparency.org/global_priorities/public_contracting
8. Asian Development Bank (1998).
9. Muguzi, Henry, Newsletter 3/2005 August: Northern Uganda, http://www.ms.dk/sw9301.asp
10. In the European Union, the total value of public procurement (the purchases of goods, services and public works by governments and public utilities) was €1,500 billion or about 16 per cent of the EU's GDP in 2002. See EU Public Procurement website at http://ec.europa.eu/internal_market/publicprocurement/index_en.htm
11. See for instance Klitgaard (1988), Rose-Ackerman (1978) and (1999).
12. Federal Acquisition Regulation at http://www.arnet.gov/far/. In addition, the Defense Contract Audit Agency has over 4,500 staff designated to audit the massive defense procurement system on top of the thousands of inspectors general that exist at the defense and service agency level, https://www.jagcnet.army.mil/JAGCNETInternet/Homepages/AC/ArmyFraud.nsf/(JAGCNetDocID)/86DABEE8FC6CC4DA8525703F005519E9/$FILE/ISS%20Compliance%20Agreement.pdf
13. Merle, R. and Markon, J. (2004), 'Ex-Pentagon official admits job deal,' *The Washington Post,* April 21, A1. See also Merle, R. (2004), 'Long fall for Pentagon star: Druyun doled out favors by the millions,' *The Washington Post,* November 14, A1.
14. Overby, P. (2006), 'Boeing moves forward after government fine,' National Public Radio's Morning Edition, May 16, found at http://www.npr.org/templates/story/story.php?storyId=5407530
15. For an excellent and more extensive discussion of these principles, see Burton (2005) and Wittig (2005). Both are OECD publications.
16. Wittig (2005), p. 111
17. Ware, G.T. and G.P. Noone (2005), 'The anatomy of transnational corruption', *International Affairs Review* (Fall) **14**(2), 29–52, p. 31. These are mechanisms designed to generate kickbacks or divert procurement funds to private use.
18. The red flags listed in this chapter came from a variety of sources, including the authors fieldwork, lessons provided by leading transnational investigators such as W. Michael Kramer, and a variety of publications, see e.g. http://www.bhutanaudit.gov.bt/contents/papers/asosai-pakistan/Overview%20of%20Fraud%20and%20Corruption%20Detection%20Process.pdf; http://www.srac.gpg.gov.za/Anti-corruption%20booklet.pdf; and http://www.wmkramer.com/1basics.html
19. Ware, G.T. and G.P. Noone (2005), 'The anatomy of transnational corruption', *International Affairs Review* (Fall) **14**(2), 29–52, pp. 33–34.
20. The authors have uncovered elaborate 'commission sharing agreements' between joint

venture multinational companies, allocating kickback amounts among the partners based on the percentage of interest in the company.

21. Independent Inquiry Committee into The United Nations Oil-For-Food Programme, Paul A. Volcker, Chairman. Third Interim Report, August 8, 2005. Found at http://www.iic-offp.org/documents/Third%20Interim%20Report.pdf
22. One of the authors has been retained by a large company to ensure that its four hundred agents conducting business overseas are not engaged in corruption in violation of the U.S. Foreign Corrupt Practices Act of 1977, Pub.L. No 95-213, 91 Stat 1494, (as amended in 1988 and 1998).
23. U.S. contractors conducting business with agents overseas are increasingly conducting due diligence investigations of their prospective foreign agents to determine if they have a reputation or known practice of paying bribes to obtain contracts for the companies they represent.
24. The Titan case has been one of the most significant cases of corruption involving an agent as Titan received the largest FCPA fine in history to date. See *Securities and Exchange Commission v. The Titan Corporation,* Civil Action No. 05-0411 (U.S.D.C., D.D.C., filed March 1, 2005) (requiring Titan to pay over $28 million in civil and criminal fines for violating the FCPA by funneling, through intermediaries, inappropriate payments to government officials in Benin and several Asian countries).
25. Id. at n. 1.
26. Not all kickback schemes however involve bid rigging. Because of the prevalence of bribery, it is increasingly possible to have a completely transparent bidding process with the winning bidder paying a bribe after contract signing. In such situations, the need for a bribe is well understood by all the bidders and their pricing reflects these fees.
27. In a recent case in Africa, forensic investigators found minutes of a meeting between government officials deciding who would win certain consulting contracts on a mega-million road construction project months before the bids were actually opened.
28. Rose-Ackerman (1978) writes that competition among service providers would reduce corruption.
29. Id. at n. 1.
30. See 'Preventing and detecting bid rigging, price fixing, and market allocation in post-disaster rebuilding projects: an antitrust primer for agents and procurement officials' by the U.S Department of Justice. Found at http://www.usdoj.gov/atr/public/guidelines/disaster_primer.htm.
31. Internal documents.
32. See 'Preventing and detecting bid rigging, price fixing, and market allocation in post-disaster rebuilding projects: an antitrust primer for agents and procurement officials' by the U.S Department of Justice. Found at http://www.usdoj.gov/atr/public/guidelines/disaster_primer.htm.

    See also a thoughtful analysis on detecting bid rigging as a result of charges filed in Sweden for suspected bid rigging on road contracts. Jakobsson, M. (June 2004). 'Bid-rigging in Swedish procurement auctions' found at http://www.joensuu.fi/taloustieteet/ott/scandale/tarto/papers/Maria%20Jakobsson.pdf.
33. 'Eleven school custodians arrested for kickback and bid rigging scheme,' Office of New York State Attorney General Eliot Spitzer Press Release, December 11, 2001. Found at http://www.oag.state.ny.us/press/2001/dec/dec11b_01.html.
34. *Id.*
35. *Id.*
36. Secrecy jurisdictions are countries with very lax business registration requirements, bank regulations, and tax requirements.
37. U.S. Government Accounting Office Report 06-376, April 2006, 'Company formations: minimal ownership information is collected,' pp. 30–31.
38. The report includes the use of front companies and kickbacks in the UN Oil-For-Food Programme. See Independent Inquiry Committee into The United Nations Oil-For-Food Programme, Paul A. Volcker, Chairman. Manipulation of the Oil-For-Food

Programme by the Iraqi Regime, October 27, 2005. Found at http://www.iic-offp.org/documents/IIC%20Final%20Report%2027Oct2005.pdf.
39. See 'U.S. identifies front companies for Saddam Hussein regime,' press release from The Office Of Public Affairs, U.S. Department of the Treasury, Washington, D.C., April 15, 2004. Found at http://www.cpa-iraq.org/transcripts/20040415_front_companies.html
40. As opposed to a front company which is generally not a legitimate or ongoing concern.
41. In cases uncovered by the authors, the companies were registered corporations with government officials listed as directors, shareholders, or officers of the corporation.
42. For an interesting analysis and discussion of the front companies of cronies, children, and relatives of the late Ferdinand Marcos, and the impunity with which these companies were used to extract rents, see Manapat (1991).
43. Id. at n. 1.
44. There are other corruption schemes which are not directly linked to procurement but likewise involve fraudulent use of public funds. See Appendix B.
45. See Mitchell, L.E. (2005), 'Symposium: corporate misbehavior by elite decision-makers symposium: perspectives from law and social psychology: structural holes, CEOs, and informational monopolies – The missing link in corporate governance' *70 Brooklyn L. Rev. 1313* (Summer) pp. 1320–1344. 'Structural holes' exist in procurement systems because the procurement process is made up of a network of people and where there are multiple networks linked together the resulting holes are often exploited for personal advantage/gain.
46. A responsive control adjustment is the affirmative act of closing system vulnerabilities, e.g. loopholes.
47. Thachuk, K. (2005), 'Corruption and international security,' *SAIS Review* (Winter-Spring) **XXV**(1): 143152, 146–149. Thachuk discusses the vulnerabilities of the justice system, trade and financial sectors, and security forces. With the latter, Thachuk asserts that 'criminal and terrorist groups depend on unimpeded cross-border movements, and so border guards, customs officers, and immigration personnel are notable targets of corruption'. By way of example, Thachuk cites the Beslan school massacre, the bombing of a Moscow metro station and bus stop, and the two Russian airliners 'destroyed mid-flight by female suicide bombers who bribed their way onto the planes'.
48. Major investigations take the form of Fiduciary Reviews and are conducted by the Bank's internal investigation unit, the Department of Institutional Integrity. USAID has also developed a similar indicator base. See Fraud Indicators, Office of the Inspector General Investigations, USAID, http://www.usaid.gov/oig/hotline/fraud_awareness_handbook_052201.pdf
49. The vulnerabilities identified in this chapter come principally from the Forensic Services Unit of the World Bank's Department of Institutional Integrity.
50. An assessment of the total number of vulnerabilities within the system can provide a metric that reflects the overall risk of corruption in the conduct of bidding and the implementation of government contracts.
51. See Chapter 5 on Transport and the Roads Sector in this volume.
52. Werlin, H.H. (2005), 'Corruption and Foreign Aid in Africa', *Orbis* **49**, 517–527, 521.
53. See Nunberg (1997) and Manning (2004).
54. See for example, Trepte, Peter (2005).
55. See Odhiambo and Kamau (2003)
56. Executive Summary 'Fighting Corruption and Promoting Integrity in Public Procurement', OECD 2005, at p. 12
57. Burton, Robert A. (2005), 'Improving integrity in public procurement: the role of transparency and accountability'. Fighting Corruption and Promoting Public Integrity in Public Procurement, OECD, 28.
58. Sacerdoti, Giorgio (2005), 'Forum workshop on identifying risks in the bidding process to prevent and sanction', Fighting Corruption and Promoting Public Integrity in Public Procurement, OECD, 153-160

59. See http://www.idea-knowledge.gov.uk/idk/core/page.do?pageId=82701.
60. For an extensive discussion of the potential impact of e-procurement on curbing corruption, see World Bank (2006). In a recent report commissioned by the OECD, South Korea's use of e-procurement provides encouraging news on the value of e-procurement platforms. See http://www.nibr.no/content/download/3663/17219/file/OECD-rapport+2005-+aase.pdf.
61. Interview with a senior official of the Public Work's Ministry.
62. 'Korea's move to e-procurement' PREMnotes. Number 90, July 2004, World Bank. See http://siteresources.worldbank.org/INTPEAM/Resources/premnote90.pdf
63. Kossick, Robert, 'Best practice profile: CompraNet' May 10, 2004. See http://www.undp.org/surf-panama/egov/docs/programme_activities/bpractices/e-procurement_in_mexico-compranet.pdf
64. Republic of Chile – Country Procurement Assessment Report, Report #28914-CL, LAC, World Bank, August 2004.
65. ChileCompra Strategic Plan 2002–2004 Public Procurement System, see www.chilecompra.cl.
66. Government procurement over the Internet, IDB, October 20, 2004 and World Telecommunication/ICT Development Report 2006, International Telecommunications Union.
67. For a more detailed discussions, see World Bank (2006a).
68. Some scholars suggest that there are three distinct policy approaches that can be employed against corruption: status quo (e.g. no additional resources for detection or punishment); individual level deterrence (e.g. increase resources for better detection and punishment); and, alter the 'structural conditions relevant to corruption' (e.g. reduce bureaucratic inefficiency; make legislation more congruent with social demands). See Nas, T.F., A.C. Price, C.T. Weber (1986), 'A policy-oriented theory of corruption', *American Political Science Review,* (March) **80**(1): 116.
69. The legal research on the existence of global disclosure programs was provided by Ms. Pascale Dubois, Senior Counsel, The World Bank Group.
70. Ware, G.T. and G.P. Noone (2005), 'The anatomy of transnational corruption', *International Affairs Review* (Fall) **14**(2), 42–3.
71. In France, for certain offences, the French Criminal Procedure Code (*Code de Procédure Pénale)* allows the district prosecutor to implement alternative proceedings, called a *composition*, instead of a criminal prosecution. The defendant can avoid formal criminal proceedings altogether in exchange for an admission of guilt and the fulfillment of special conditions (i.e. paying a fine or performing community service). See C. PR. PÉN. Arts. 41-1 to -3 (2004) (Fr.).
72. In the United States, several agencies, including the Environmental Protection Agency, the Department of Justice Antitrust Division, the Securities and Exchange Commission, and the Department of Health and Human Services utilize voluntary disclosure programmes. See Environmental Protection Agency, Incentives for Self-Policing: Discovery, Disclosure, Correction and Prevention of Violations, 60 Fed. Reg. 66706 (Dec. 22, 1995); see also Anne K. Bingaman, Assistant Attorney General, Remarks Before the Antitrust Section of the American Bar Association (Aug. 10, 1993), *reprinted in* 6 Department of Justice Manual Section 7-2A.470 at 7-244.315 (1995); see generally Report of the Securities and Exchange Commission on Questionable and Illegal Corporate Payments and Practices (submitted to the Senate Banking, Housing and urban Affairs Committee May 12, 1976); *In re Sealed Case,* 676 F.2d 793 (D.C. Cir. 1982); and see generally Richard A. Feinstein and Jonathan L. Diesenhaus, *Unmasking Health Care Fraud and Abuse*, Legal times (July 17, 1995).
73. Pakistan's National Accountability Bureau Ordinance offers full or conditional pardons to persons who make full and true disclosures of their violations and provide the names of persons involved in the corrupt schemes. It also provides violators with potential amnesty from incarceration if they admit to their corrupt practices and return the assets or gains acquired through the corrupt practices. See National Accountability Bureau

Ordinance, Pakistan Ordinance No. XVIII of 1999, §§ 25, 25A, and 26, as amended by Pakistan Ordinance Nos. XIX of 1999 and IV of 2000.

74. To fight organized crime, Poland utilizes the *świadek koronny*, or crown witness, law in which a criminal who testifies against his or her accomplices receives immunity, as well as identity protection if he or she risks retaliation. See *Ustawa z dnia 25 czerwca 1997 r. o świadku koronnym.*
75. Argentina fights drug trafficking crimes by either reducing the punishment or dismissing the case against a person who helps authorities to uncover the identity of other wrongdoers or identify other drug shipments. See paragraph 29 ter of Law Nr. 23.737. Argentina also permits the reduction of penalties for a wrongdoer who provides the state with information leading to the location of a kidnapping victim. See paragraph 41 ter of Law Nr. 25.742.
76. Brazil's leniency programme encourages voluntary communication of information on anti-competitive practices by guaranteeing the informant immunity from punishment as long as the Ministry of Justice had no knowledge about the illicit practice prior to the informant's disclosure. See Brazilian Antitrust Law, Law 10.149/2000 of Dec. 21, 2000.
77. Italy's '*pentiti*' laws offer immunity from prosecution and/or reductions of penalties and witness protection to co-operating persons who provide information regarding subversion of the democratic order by violent means, terrorist activities, mafia-type organizations, kidnapping, drug trafficking, and smuggling. See, e.g., Law No. 304 of May 29, 1982; Law N. 15 of Feb. 15, 1980; Law N. 34 of Feb. 18, 1987; Decree-Law No. 8/91; Law No. 45/01; Decree-Law No. 8 of Jan. 15, 1991; and Law. No. 45 of Feb. 15, 2001.
78. Prosecutors in the United Nations-led interim civil administration of Kosovo may request full immunity from prosecution if a judge determines that a suspect or defendant will give evidence that is likely to prevent further criminal acts or lead to the successful prosecution of another suspect. See UNMIK Regulation No. 2001/21, on Co-operative Witnesses (Sept. 20, 2001); UNMIK Regulation No. 2003/26, Provisional Criminal Procedure Code of Kosovo, Arts. 298-303 (July 6, 2003).
79. Article 37(3) of the UN Convention Against Corruption, which entered into force in December 2005, provides: 'Each State Party shall consider providing for the possibility, in accordance with fundamental principals of its domestic law, of granting immunity from prosecution to a person who provides substantial cooperation in the investigation or prosecution of an offense established in accordance with this Convention.'
80. See e.g. Homer E. Moyer, Jr. (2005), *Corporate Counsel-Law Firms, Voluntary Disclosure, Independent Compliance Monitors and Other FCPA Enforcement Issues*, Metropolitan Corporate Counsel (June), cited at http://www.metrocorpcounsel.com/current.php?artType=view&artMonth= June&artYear= 2005&EntryNo=3063
81. Zucker, J.S. (2004), 'The Boeing suspension: has increased consolidation tied the Department of Defense's Hands?' (April) The Army Lawyer, found at https://www.jagcnet.army.mil/JAGCNETInternet/Homepages/AC/ArmyFraud.nsf/(JAGC NetDocID)/86DABEE8FC6CC4DA8525703F005519E9/$FILE/The%20Boeing%20 Suspension.pdf
82. Status Report on 'The integrity pact: the concept, the model, and present applications' Transparency International, December 3, 2002. pp. 27–30.
83. The United Kingdom recently enacted such legislation and the United States has similar legislation: http://www.epic.org/open_gov/foia/us_foia_act.html as do numerous other nations, see http://www.freedominfo.org/.
84. See for instance the impact of lifestyle checks conducted by the Philippine Center for Investigative Journalism (http://www.pcij.org/stories/2003/bir.html).
85. Campos, J. E. and J. Syquia, J. (2006), 'Managing the Politics of Reform: Overhauling the Legal Infrastructure of Public Procurement in the Philippines', monograph, Washington, D.C. The World Bank.
86. Ware, G.T. and G.P. Noone (2005), 'The anatomy of transnational corruption', *International Affairs Review* (Fall) **14** (2): 40.

87. Ibid., 42.
88. See UNCITRAL website for Model Law on Procurement of Goods, Construction and Services with Guide to Enactment. Found at http://www.uncitral.org/uncitral/en/uncitral_texts/procurement_infrastructure/1994Model.html; See also http://www.abanet.org/.
89. The Organization of American States (OAS) Inter-American Convention Against Corruption, Treaty Doc. No. 105-39; the Organization of Economic Cooperation and Development (OECD) Convention on Combating Bribery of Foreign Officials in International Business Transactions, Treaty Doc. No. 105-43, 1997 U.S.T. Lexis 105; and the Council of Europe, Criminal Law Convention on Corruption, ETS no. 173., entered into force July 1, 2002. United Nations Convention Against Corruption (UNCAC), U.N. Doc A/58/422 (adopted Oct. 31, 2003), entered into force December 15, 2005.
90. Sandholtz, W. and Gray, M. (2005). *International Determinants of National Corruption Levels*, Transparency International, Global Corruption Report 2005, p. 269, available at http://www.globalcorruptionreport.org/download.html#download
91. Soreide (2003) notes in a survey of firms in the OECD that 'as many as 55% of the respondents did not think that tender rules could prevent corruption. Fifteen per cent said that tender rules do function as an obstacle, while only six per cent considered tender rules to be an *efficient* obstacle to corruption'.
92. The research and writing of this appendix was provided by Benjamin M. Cox.
93. Batha, E., 'Corruption and aid,' *Reuters*. (November 9, 2005) Found at http://www.alertnet.org/thefacts/reliefresources/11315551833.htm.
94. Harvey, R., 'Corruption challenge for Aceh aid,' *BBC News* (May 31, 2005). Found at http://newsvote.bbc.co.uk/mpapps/pagetools/print/news.bbc.co.uk/2/hi/asia-pacific/4583557.stm.
95. See the International NGO Forum on Indonesian Development (March 23, 2005). Found at http://www.infid.be/aceh_combating_corruption.htm.
96. See the International NGO Forum on Indonesian Development (March 23, 2005). Found at http://www.infid.be/aceh_combating_corruption.htm.
97. See ADB/OECD/TI. 'Curbing corruption in Tsunami Relief Operations', Proceedings of the Jakarta Expert Meeting. 7–8 April 2005. Manila: Asian Development Bank, p. 51.
98. 'Dozens indicted in alleged Katrina scam: Red Cross contract workers accused of filing false claims' reported by CNN and found at http://www.cnn.com/2005/LAW/12/28/katrina.fraud/index.html.
99. Yen, H., 'GAO probes Katrina credit card bills: audits examine purchases by federal workers for abuse, overpayment', *The Washington Post*. (December 27, 2005), A23. See also http://www.cnn.com/2005/LAW/12/28/katrina.fraud/index.html.
100. Internal documents.

BIBLIOGRAPHY

Articles and Books

Asian Development Bank (1998), *AntiCorruption: Policies and Strategies*, Manila, Philippines: Asian Development Bank.

Batha, E. (2005), 'Corruption and aid', *Reuters*, (November 9). Found at http://www.alertnet.org/thefacts/reliefresources/11315551833.htm.

Burton, Robert A. (2005), 'Improving integrity in public procurement: the role of transparency and accountability', in *Fighting Corruption and Promoting Integrity in Public Procurement*, Paris: OECD, pp. 23–8.

Campos, J. E. and Syquia, J. (2006), *Managing the Politics of Reform: Overhauling the Legal Infrastructure of Public Procurement in the Philippines*, monograph, Washington, DC: The World Bank.
Easton, T. (2005), 'The hidden wealth of the poor: a survey of microfinance', *The Economist*, (November 5), 58.
Harvey, R. (2005), 'Corruption challenge for Aceh aid,' *BBC News*. (May 31). Found at http://newsvote.bbc.co.uk/mpapps/pagetools/print/news.bbc.co.uk/2/hi/asia-pacific/4583557.stm.
Jakobsson, M. (2004), 'Bid-rigging in Swedish procurement auctions' (June). Found at http://www.joensuu.fi/taloustieteet/ott/scandale/tarto/papers/Maria%20Jakobsson.pdf.
Klitgaard, R. (1988), *Controlling Corruption*, Berkeley: University of California Press.
Lederer, E.M. (2004), *Russia, China, Britain Rally to Back Annan*, The Associated Press, December 3.
Manapat, Ricardo (1991), *Some Are Smarter Than Others: The History of Marcos' Crony Capitalism*, New York: Aletheia Publications.
Manning, Nick and Neil Parison (2004), *International Public Administration Reform*, Washington, DC: The World Bank.
Merle, R. and J. Markon (2004), 'Ex-Pentagon official admits job deal', *The Washington Post*, (April 21), A1.
Merle, R. (2004), 'Long fall for Pentagon star: Druyun doled out favors by the millions', *The Washington Post* (November 1), A1.
Mitchell, L.E. (2005), 'Symposium: corporate misbehavior by elite decision-makers symposium: perspectives from law and social psychology: structural holes, CEOs, and informational monopolies – the missing link in corporate governance', *Brooklyn L. Rev.* **70**(1313) (Summer).
Mora, Jose Eduardo (2004), 'Central America: the high cost of corruption' Inter Press Service, http://www.worldrevolution.org/article/1624.
Nas, T.F., A.C. Price and C.T. Weber (1986), 'A policy-oriented theory of corruption', *American Political Science Review*, **80**(1), 107–119.
Nunberg, Barbara (1997), 'Rethinking Civil Service reform: an agenda for smart government', Poverty and Social Policy Working Paper, Washington, DC: World Bank.
Odhiambo, Walter and Paul Kamau (2003), 'Public procurement: lessons from Kenya, Tanzania, and Uganda', Paris: OECD Development Centre,Working Paper No. 208. Found at http://www.u4.no/document/literature/Odhiambo-public-procuremnt-Tz-Ug-Ky.pdf
Overby, P. (2006), 'Boeing moves forward after government fine,' National Public Radio's Morning Edition, May 16, found at http://www.npr.org/templates/story/story.php?storyId=5407530
Paine, L., R. Deshpande, J.D. Margolis and K.E. Bettcher (2005), 'Up to code: does your company's conduct meet world-class standards?', *Harvard Business Review*, December, **83**(12).
Rose-Ackerman, S. (1978), *Corruption: A Study in Political Economy*, New York: Academic Press.
Rose-Ackerman, S. (1999), *Corruption and Government: Causes, Consequences, and Reform*, Cambridge: Cambridge University Press.
Sandholtz, W. and M. Gray (2005), *International Determinants of National Corruption Levels*, Transparency International, Global Corruption Report 2005, found at http://www.globalcorruptionreport.org/download.html#download
Soreide, Tina (2006), 'Procurement procedures and the size of firms in infrastructure contracts,' Paper prepared for the World Bank ABCDE Conference, Tokyo: May 29–30.
Stone, R.W. (2004), 'The Political economy of IMF lending in Africa', *American Political Science Review*, **98**(4), 577–91.
Thachuk, K. (2005), 'Corruption and international security', *SAIS Review*,Winter-Spring, **XXV**(1), 143–52.

Trepte, Peter (2005), 'Transparency and accountability as tools for promoting integrity and preventing corruption in procurement: possibilities and limitations', Paris: OECD.
Uslaner, E. M. (2005), *Trust and Corruption*, Transparency International, Global Corruption Report 2005, found at http://www.globalcorruptionreport.org/download.html#download
Ware, G.T. and G.P. Noone (2005), 'The anatomy of transnational corruption', *International Affairs Review*, **14**(2), 29–52.
Wax, E. (2005), 'Kenya is buffeted by graft scandals', *The Washington Post*, February 13, A21.
Werlin, H.H. (2005), 'Corruption and foreign aid in Africa', *Orbis*, Summer, **49**, 517–27.
Wittig, Wayne A. (2005), 'Linking islands of integrity to promote good governance in public procurement: issues for consideration' in *Fighting Corruption and Promoting Integrity in Public Procurement*, Paris: OECD, pp. 109–114.
World Bank, 2006(a), *Corruption vs. Technology in Public Procurement*, forthcoming.
World Bank, 2006(b), *Note on a strategy for improving public procurement performance in Andhra Pradesh*, unpublished document, South Asia Region (SAR).
Yen, H. (2005), 'GAO probes Katrina credit card bills: audits examine purchases by federal workers for abuse, overpayment', *The Washington Post*, December 27, A23.
Zucker, J.S. (2004), 'The Boeing suspension: has increased consolidation tied the Department of Defense's hands?', April, The Army Lawyer, found at https://www.jagcnet.army.mil/JAGCNETInternet/Homepages/AC/ArmyFraud.nsf/(JAGCNetDocID)/86DABEE8FC6CC4DA8525703F005519E9/$FILE/The%20Boeing%20Suspension.pdf

Documents

'Best practices in combating corruption' OSCE Office of the Coordinator for Economic and Environmental Activities. Found at http://www.osce.org/item/13568.html.
'Eleven school custodians arrested for kickback and bid rigging scheme,' Office of New York State Attorney General Eliot Spitzer Press Release, December 11, 2001. Found at http://www.oag.state.ny.us/press/2001/dec/dec11b_01.html.
The Executive Office of the President Office of Management and Budget Memorandum for Heads of Departments and Agencies dated April 16, 2002, found at http://www.dot.gov/ost/m60/correspond/ofpp041602.htm.
Independent Inquiry Committee into The United Nations Oil-For-Food Programme, Paul A. Volcker, Chairman. Third Interim Report, August 8, 2005, found at http://www.iic-offp.org/documents/Third%20Interim%20Report.pdf
Independent Inquiry Committee into The United Nations Oil-For-Food Programme,
Paul A. Volcker, Chairman. Manipulation of the Oil-For-Food Programme by the Iraqi Regime, October 27, 2005, found at http://www.iic-offp.org/documents/IIC%20Final%20Report%2027Oct2005.pdf.
Mainstreaming Anti-Corruption Activities in World Bank Assistance (Washington, D.C.: World Bank Report No. 29620, (2004).
'Preventing and detecting bid rigging, price fixing, and market allocation in post-disaster rebuilding projects: an antitrust primer for agents and procurement officials' by the U.S. Department of Justice. Found at http://www.usdoj.gov/atr/public/guidelines/disaster_primer.htm.
Status Report on 'The integrity pact: the concept, the model, and present applications' Transparency International, December 3, 2002.
Transparency International, *Global Corruption Report 2006*, found at http://www.globalcorruptionreport.org/download.html#download.
UNCITRAL website for Model Law on Procurement of Goods, Construction and Services with Guide to Enactment. Found at http://www.uncitral.org/uncitral/en/uncitral_texts/procurement_infrastructure/1994 Model.html

U.S. Foreign Corrupt Practices Act of 1977, Pub.L. No 95-213, 91 Stat 1494, (as amended in 1988 and 1998).
U.S. Government Accounting Office Report 06-376, April 2006, 'Company formations: minimal ownership information is collected'.

6 Circumventing sanctions against Iraq in the Oil-for-Food programme

Linda Courtenay Botterill

In her introduction to a recent book on corruption in international business, Eicher (2009a, p. 2) notes that 'not all illegal behaviour is corrupt, and not all corrupt behaviour is illegal'. There is also a fine distinction between the unethical and the corrupt. This chapter discusses a case which highlights this definitional blurring. In 2005, the Australian monopoly grain exporter AWB Limited was identified in a UN inquiry as the worst offender in circumventing the very complex Oil-for-Food sanctions regime that had been put in place against the Iraqi regime of Saddam Hussein. Cooperation with Iraq's requests to bypass sanctions was confined to a small group of company employees who went to considerable lengths to disguise their activities. The Australian legal system did not consider AWB Limited to have broken any Australian law, so in this sense the company did not operate illegally. The events described below became a national scandal and were largely regarded as unethical. However, the principal actors were arguably not corrupt as there is no evidence they profited personally from their activities and, until the kickbacks became public, there was no principal–agent problem as the company was not disadvantaged. When the events became public though the consequences for AWB Limited were profound.

The revelation of AWB Limited's involvement in sanctions-busting activities was a major political scandal in Australia and seemed to threaten to bring down key Cabinet Ministers as suggestions, never proved, were raised that the Government had been aware of AWB Limited's activities and had chosen to turn a blind eye. Following the revelations of the UN inquiry, the Australian Government instituted its own inquiry, led by Commissioner the Honourable Terence Cole, into the involvement of Australian companies in the Oil-for-Food scandal. This served to keep the issue on the front page of major daily newspapers for the best part of a year. While the behaviour of some officials at the UN was clearly corrupt (Meyer and Califano, 2006), there is a question over whether the activities of AWB Limited were, or simply constituted normal business practice. The Australian Inquiry and subsequent court cases examining AWB Limited's activities either found that no Australian laws had been broken or that there was insufficient evidence to bring cases against senior company officials.

While clearly an example of dubious ethical behaviour, the AWB Limited case raises some interesting issues relating to the imposition of economic sanctions in international relations and their enforcement at domestic level. National governments commit to implement sanctions in order to put pressure on the receiving nation to behave or cease to behave in a particular way. However, the cost of those sanctions is borne by private actors – companies and individuals whose activities the sanctions seek to constrain. Barber (1979, p. 377) has pointed to this problem with sanctions implementation, arguing that 'While sanctions are decided by government, compliance is required at all levels – individuals, firms, financial organisations – and the greatest compliance is demanded of those who have to pay the highest price'. In many cases, nations fail to take comprehensive monitoring and enforcement action within their borders to ensure the sanctions are effective. This was the case in Australia during the Oil-for-Food programme and raises the question as to whether companies that acted contrary to the sanctions, but not illegally under Australia law, were acting corruptly.

This chapter is set out as follows. It describes the UN sanctions against Iraq and how they evolved into the highly complex Oil-for-Food programme. It then seeks to put AWB Limited's activities into the context of major institutional changes occurring in the Australian wheat industry in the 1990s. Much of the analysis of the AWB scandal to date (for example, Bartos, 2006; Overington, 2007) has been ahistorical and has not considered the complexity either of the sanctions regime or the international grains market. It has also neglected the issue of the lack of regulatory structures within Australia to monitor and enforce sanctions. The chapter then describes the 'gaming' of the sanctions by Iraq and AWB Limited's involvement and considers the problems inherent within sanctions themselves as an instrument of international policy and the incentives and opportunities they create for both the receiving nation and companies trading with them to find mechanisms and exploit loopholes for bypassing the arrangements. It finishes by seeking to unpack the debate around AWB Limited's activities, which moved from consideration of possible business corruption to one of political scandal.

THE SANCTIONS AGAINST IRAQ AND THE DEVELOPMENT OF THE OIL-FOR-FOOD PROGRAMME

Sanctions were first imposed against Iraq by the UN Security Council in 1990, following that country's invasion of Kuwait (Security Council

Resolution 661). Resolution 661 sought to prevent the import of goods by member states from Iraq or Kuwait, the prevention of the export of goods to Iraq or Kuwait and the prevention of the extension of credit or other financial or economic resources to Iraq or Kuwait. Australia signed up immediately, announcing an embargo on oil imports from Iraq and Kuwait, a ban on the sale of defence-related equipment to Iraq and restrictions on financial transactions (Evans 1990). This latter restriction impacted immediately on the Australian grains industry. The monopoly wheat exporter, then the statutory Australian Wheat Board[1], was left with outstanding contracts for nearly $400 million worth of grain, as well as being owed the bulk of $US630 million of Iraqi debt to Australian exporters. (Shovelan, 1990) The Iraqi market was an important one for Australia, accounting for 12 per cent of Australia's export wheat trade at the time the sanctions were announced. (AWB Limited undated, p. 5) Following the announcement of the sanctions, the grains industry's peak body, the Grains Council of Australia (GCA) arranged an emergency delegation to the Prime Minister, seeking assurances that Australia's grain growers were not going to bear the financial burden of the nation's commitment to the UN resolution. The sanctions were a major issue for the industry and debate over appropriate compensation for growers for the loss of the market and non-payment of Iraqi debt continued as late as 2005. (Senate Rural and Regional Affairs and Transport References Committee, 2005)

Over the course of September and October 1990, further sanctions were authorized by the UN Security Council against Iraq (Resolutions 662, 664, 665, 666, 667, 669, 670, 674 and 677), covering issues such as the treatment of third-country nationals and the use of 'human shields'; calling for the release of hostages; calling on Iraq to respond to international demands; and reminding the international community of its obligations under Resolution 661. In November 1990, the Security Council adopted Resolution 678 authorizing the use of force against Iraq. A coalition led by the United States commenced an air campaign on 15 January 1991, followed by a ground campaign on 24 February which was ended by a 'formal framework for a permanent cease-fire', adopted by the Security Council as Resolution 686 on 2 March 1991 (Malone, 2006, pp. 68–73). As illustrated by the range of issues covered by the Resolutions of 1990 and 1991, the sanctions regime shifted its focus over time and became increasingly demanding on Saddam Hussein's regime in terms of the behaviours it was trying to influence. Initially set up to persuade Iraq to leave Kuwait, later Resolutions sought Iraq's disarmament as a condition for lifting sanctions.

Throughout the development of the sanctions regime, there had been concern about their humanitarian impact. A '661 Committee' was established early on to authorize the export of humanitarian assistance to Iraq in the form of medical supplies and foodstuffs. Resolution 687 in November 1990 amended the sanctions to allow for the cash sales of foodstuffs to Iraq; however, the ban on credit sales remained in place. The concessions provided by Resolution 687 proved inadequate in addressing the humanitarian impact of the sanctions and in August 1992 the Security Council adopted Resolution 706, which set out the parameters of the programme that was to become Oil-for-Food.

In her consideration of the ethics of sanctions enforcement, Damrosch (1994, p. 65) writes that:

> the normative basis for the Iraqi sanctions programme is to enforce the prohibition on aggression and to ensure that Iraq, which attacked one neighbor (Iran) in 1980 and another (Kuwait) in 1990, is deterred from further violations. Additionally, maintenance of sanctions through 1993 and beyond remains normatively justified to the extent that the sanctions continue to serve the objectives of denying to Iraq the capacity to threaten peace and security, especially through weapons of mass destruction.

Damrosch's analysis gives considerable weight to Iraq's possible development of weapons of mass destruction as providing sufficient ethical justification for the prolonged use of sanctions even 'where the brunt falls on the civilian population rather than the actual wrongdoers'. (Damrosch, 1994, p. 57) The implementation of the Oil-for-Food programme is evidence, however, that the international community itself was not comfortable with persisting with sanctions that resulted in major humanitarian distress.

The implementation of the Oil-for-Food programme took some time as Iraq initially rejected the terms of the arrangement. This is perhaps not surprising as the proposed scheme was the most comprehensive sanctions arrangement ever put forward by the UN and constituted an 'unprecedented exercise of international jurisdiction over the internal affairs of a sovereign state'. (Doxey, 1996, p. 37) The arrangement would see the Security Council effectively 'controlling a sovereign state's revenues and directing its expenditures'. (Malone, 2006, p. 116) Finally, in April 1996, the international community made a 'rare concession to Baghdad' (Malone, 2006, p. 117) by giving Iraq responsibility for the distribution of goods under the proposed Oil-for-Food programme. The Iraqi Government agreed to the Distribution Plan for Iraq and signed a Memorandum of Understanding with the UN and the Oil-for-Food programme came into effect in May 1996.

In a nutshell, the Oil-for-Food programme was designed to provide Iraq with the wherewithal to purchase food and other humanitarian goods with the proceeds of sales of its oil, which were allowed to recommence under the programme. In order to ensure that the oil revenue was only spent on approved purchases, an escrow account was set up into which proceeds from the oil sales were deposited, and out of which suppliers of approved humanitarian goods would be paid. This complex arrangement, which was later described as 'destined for corruption' (Meyer and Califano, 2006, p. 1), also included a system of inspections of humanitarian imports and of oil shipments.

Wheat was an approved import into Iraq and the Australian Wheat Board was quick to act, announcing that it was 'the first western grain merchant back into Iraq following the lifting of the UN embargo on oil sales'. (Australian Wheat Board, 1996) In announcing its return to the market, the Board explained:

> We've maintained close contact with Iraq, potentially one of our largest wheat importers in the Middle East. The Iraqis have continued to buy wheat for cash from us and we're anxious to resume normal business with them as soon as possible. (Australian Wheat Board, 1996)

THE EVOLUTION OF WHEAT MARKETING ARRANGEMENTS IN AUSTRALIA

An important element in the story of the involvement of AWB Limited in the Oil-for-Food scandal was the significant changes to the institutional arrangements for wheat marketing in Australia taking place contemporaneously with the Oil-for-Food programme. A statutory Australian Wheat Board had been in place, after a couple of temporary war-time arrangements, since 1948. It was the centrepiece of a wheat-stabilization scheme, based in broadly agrarian ideas of collective marketing and protecting wheatgrowers from the vagaries of the market. Dunsdorfs (1956, p. 296) lists the principles underpinning the scheme as '(a) Price Guarantee. (b) Home Consumption Price. (c) Stabilization fund. (d) Wheat Board'. The wheat crop was 'pooled' to spread marketing risks across growers and the Wheat Board was granted a monopoly on the marketing of wheat in both the domestic and export market. As a statutory authority, the Australian Wheat Board was an agency of government, its employees were public servants and the Board was a source of advice for the government on the international grain trade.

These arrangements lasted relatively unchanged for 40 years, in spite of the overall deregulation of Australian agricultural support from the 1970s onwards. The export monopoly, also known as the 'single desk' was something of an article of faith for Australia's National Party, a point which was of some significance when the Oil-for-Food scandal broke in Australia. The 1950s and 1960s was a period of entrenchment of the wheat marketing arrangements (Cockfield and Botterill, 2007) as the *Wheat Stabilization Act 1948* was renewed on a regular basis, with little change to the nature of the support offered to growers. From 1969 onwards, there were incremental changes to wheat marketing policy, which gradually exposed growers to market signals.

The first significant change to the arrangements occurred in 1989 with the deregulation of the domestic wheat market. This occurred against the wishes of the grains industry and led to the initiation of a strategic planning process by the grains industry's peak body, the Grains Council of Australia. The planning process, originally intended to look at wheat marketing 'from paddock to plate, including [. . .] institutional arrangements, past strengths and weaknesses, and requirements for the future' (Hooke, 1993, p. 39), quickly became focused on the future role and structure of the Australian Wheat Board and its export monopoly. By the late 1990s the industry had agreed a model of wheat marketing which saw the privatization of the Australian Wheat Board and it transition to AWB Limited, which was transferred to grower ownership but retained the export monopoly. The company was listed on the Australian Stock Exchange in 2001. This institutional transformation was also the culmination of an important values shift among employees of the organisation. The pre-1989 Board had been a 'marketer as distinct from a trader'. (Ryan, 1984, p. 124) Once it was competing on the domestic market, the Board needed skills in risk management and employees who operated as traders on the domestic market. The traders faced a different set of incentives from the marketers who had been driven by a collective notion of delivering outcomes for growers. The new breed of employees were more driven by their personal ambition to succeed within the organization and this shift in the internal culture of the organization accelerated after the privatization occurred. (Botterill, forthcoming) This values shift set the scene for the company's activities in Iraq as the approach changed from a focus on 'doing it for the growers' to '*get that deal*. Get the best possible price!' (Overington, 2007, p. 79, original emphasis)

The privatization of the Australian Wheat Board and the creation of AWB Limited was occurring at the same time as the Oil-for-Food programme was being developed and implemented. The decision by the Grains Council to support privatization of the Australian Wheat Board and Iraq's agreement to the Distribution Plan that gave effect to the Oil for Food (OFF) Programme occurred within weeks of each other. This timing clearly created some confusion among commentators when the bypassing of sanctions came to light, as they had difficulty distinguishing between the government entity, the Australian Wheat Board, and the privatized AWB Limited.

The international grain trade is notoriously opaque. It is dominated by a handful of private companies who keep their cards close to their chest. The trade is very secretive and the price of grain at any point in time is far from transparent. Having relied on the old statutory Wheat Board to advise it on the international wheat trade for decades, the Department of Foreign Affairs and Trade (DFAT) had not developed the expertise internally to scrutinize in any detail the contracts it was forwarding to the UN under the Oil-for-Food programme. As a monopoly trader, the company also had a monopoly on expertise.

THE DEVELOPMENT AND 'GAMING' OF THE OIL-FOR-FOOD PROGRAMME

A state on the receiving end of economic sanctions has two broad choices: comply with the requirements of the international community or find a strategy for living with the sanctions. Galtung (1967) identifies three approaches that resistant states can adopt if they pursue the latter course: adaptation to sacrifice, restructuring the economy in response to changed circumstances and smuggling. Under these circumstances defeating the sanctions becomes 'a major national activity'. (Barber, 1979, p. 377) Iraq chose not to comply with the demands of the international community and developed a series of strategies for extracting hard currency from companies with which it was doing business, contrary to the intentions of the sanctions regime.

Before describing the mechanisms that Iraq employed, and with which AWB Limited cooperated, it is worth noting that the literature on economic sanctions generally agrees that sanctions do not work in achieving their goals. (Barber, 1979, p. 384) The longer the sanctions last, the less likely the target state is to comply with international demands. (Doxey, 1996, p. 104; Renwick, 1981, p. 87) The nature of the Oil-for-Food programme gave Iraq the opportunity it needed to find ways around the arrangements. Doxey (1996, p. 106) points out that 'Far-reaching exemptions undermine the effectiveness of the sanctions' and the Oil-for-Food programme was in essence a very complicated set of exceptions.

Iraq employed a range of strategies to bypass the sanctions, the most lucrative of which was oil smuggling which generated a massive \$11.8 billion (Malone, 2006, pp. 129–130) during the course of the programme. The 'gaming' of the humanitarian programme also generated significant hard currency – a further \$1.8 billion, of which more than 14 per cent was courtesy of the Australian wheat exporter AWB Limited. (Volcker et al, 2005, p. 262)

The first tactic which Iraq introduced in 1999 to exploit the humanitarian programme was to impose various charges on imports of humanitarian goods. Meyer and Califano (2006, p. 112) note that by late 2000, 'almost no prospective suppliers of goods to Iraq would see their bids approved by the Iraq ministries without agreeing to pay a kickback'. In the case of AWB Limited, this was payable as an 'inland transportation fee' to a Jordanian company, Alia for General Transportation and Trade, which was 49 per cent owned by the Iraqi government. The fee was initially $US10-12 per tonne which the AWB recovered from the escrow account by building it into the contract price for the wheat. Alia did not actually provide any transport services on behalf of AWB Limited; the arrangement was clearly a mechanism for funnelling hard currency to the Iraqi government. The second mechanism was a 10 per cent after-sales service fee added to all contracts from November 2000, collected through the inland transport mechanism and in addition to the inland transportation fee. This raised the transport fee to $US44.50 per tonne. (Cole, 2006, p. 113)

Evidence before the Cole inquiry set up by the Australian government suggests that the actions bypassing the sanctions were undertaken by a small group of employees within AWB Limited who went to considerable lengths to hide their activities from their colleagues. As evidenced by emails tendered to the inquiry, they were clearly aware that their actions were in all probability in breach of sanctions. It appears that the AWB Limited Board was uninformed about much of the activity and areas of the company beyond the International Sales and Marketing Division were similarly unaware. When suspicions were aroused and questions were raised, assurances were given that the conduct of the Iraq trade had UN approval. (Botterill, 2007, p. 10)

AWB Limited is not the first grain company to bypass sanctions in pursuit of its business interests. Conrad (1990, p. 118) notes that 'the major grain trading companies are in a position at times to operate against the interests and without the knowledge of American and other governments'. He cites both US sanctions against the Soviet Union in 1980 and international action against Rhodesia between 1968 and 1975 as occasions on which the grain trade appeared to operate contrary to sanctions agreements. In the case of Rhodesia, he argues (1990, p. 118) that 'governments proved unable to control the activities of these large grain traders, or even confirm exactly what was taking place and how'. This does not excuse AWB Limited but does highlight the challenges of sanctions implementation involving large, international trading companies whose business interests are seriously jeopardised by sanctions.

UNPACKING THE SCANDAL

Understanding the AWB Limited scandal requires consideration at several levels. This section examines these different dimensions of the story and attempts to draw some conclusions about the ethics of the situation. Was it a case of corruption or simply normal business practice that became embroiled in scandal because of the peculiar nature of the privatization process and the residual involvement of government in monitoring the export monopoly that it had granted the company?

The foundations of the story lie in the behaviour of the company, or more specifically some of its employees, in bypassing the UN sanctions regime. The facts that emerged during the Cole inquiry are clear. Employees of AWB Limited complied with requests to implement procedures in the sale of wheat which facilitated the payment of millions of dollars of kickbacks to Saddam Hussein's regime. These kickbacks bypassed the sanctions put in place by the international community and agreed by the Australian government. The sanctions evasion appears to have been the work of a small group of individuals within AWB Limited who concealed their activities from their colleagues and, probably, from the AWB Limited Board and senior management.

Corruption is difficult to define and, as noted above, Eicher makes the important point that there is often confusion between corruption and legality (Eicher, 2009a, p. 2). She distinguishes between public and private corruption and, in the case of the latter, argues that corruption occurs when the individual places their own interests above those of the company. For the purposes of her edited book, she defines corruption as 'any act where a trust between the principal, the one whose interests are supposed to be protected, is violated by the agent, the one who is supposed to be protecting the principal's interests'. (Eicher 2009a, p. 4) This definition suggests that the employees of AWB Limited were not operating corruptly. There is no evidence that they personally profited from the kickback schemes.

Identifying the principals in this case is slightly complicated by the unconventional share structure of the privatized AWB Limited. Reflecting the agrarian collectivist origins of the wheat marketing arrangements, the privatized entity had a dual share structure which privileged growers over other shareholders. Each wheatgrower, as defined in the company's constitution, received one Class A share. These shareholders elected the majority of the members of the board of AWB Limited but received no dividends. Class B shares were allocated proportionally on the basis of grower holdings in a Wheat Industry Fund which had been accumulated from grower levies since 1989. Class B shareholders elected the minority of

AWB Limited board members and had a right to receive dividends. Class B shares became fully tradeable on the Australian Stock Exchange when AWB Limited listed on 22 August 2001. During the Parliamentary debate over the privatization legislation, Wilson Tuckey MP made the obvious point about the dual class share structure: 'The problem is that the proposal is to create a company that is run by its customers but which seeks over time to attract non-customer share capital. This creates a massive conflict of interest'. (Tuckey, 1997, p. 9138) He went on to point out that:

> . . .the question arises of investors being interested in shares when the directors' main interest is in returns to their customers. Is the AMP going to go and buy a lot of my farmers' shares. . .? Are they going to buy their shares and say, 'This is a great investment. The directors do not want to make a profit. They want to return all the money to their customers, the wheat producers'. (Tuckey, 1997, p. 9139)

This arrangement meant that there were two potential 'principals' involved. The first, the A class shareholders, were the grain growers whose interest was to maximize returns on the sale of wheat. From their perspective, the bypassing of the UN sanctions was unproblematic; they subscribed to the normal business practice argument. In 2008 Mr Jock Munro, a wheat grower from NSW, told a Senate Inquiry into wheat export marketing arrangements that:

> We all know what really happened with the Cole inquiry and the Iraq oil for food business. It was all about getting food to the starving Iraqi people, and of course there had to be a kickback paid to Saddam Hussein—everybody knows that; it was just that we got caught up in the mess. (Senate Rural and Regional Affairs and Transport Committee, 2008, RRA&T, 13)

The other principals in the equation were the non-grower B-class shareholders, who were badly impacted by the drop in the company's share price when the scandal came to light; although it could be argued that the agents were still acting in their interests while the kickbacks remained secret and the company was making a strong profit. In the short-term, the agents did act to maximize returns to the company's shareholders and no laws were broken while they achieved this goal. In the long term, however, the kickbacks scandal cost the company its export monopoly and saw the share price plunge. During the Cole Inquiry, the shareholders also suffered. As Eicher argues, 'There are efficiency losses from the poor morale of a company besieged by bad press during a corruption scandal'. (Eicher, 2009b, p. 46) At the time of writing, AWB Limited is subject to two competing takeover bids and the price on offer is much lower than the share price the company enjoyed in the early days of privatization.

One step removed from the actual sanctions-busting activity itself is the issue of accountability. Because AWB Limited was in the privileged position of holding an effective legislated export monopoly, the Australian government could not avoid being drawn into the scandal. The coincidence of the timing of the privatization and the implementation of Oil-for-Food had several consequences, as did the privatized company's decision to retain the name AWB Limited. With respect to the former, and as noted above, the privatization greatly diminished, if not completely removed, government access to expertise about the international grain market. Much of the debate around DFAT's failure to pick up the kickbacks centred on officers on the Middle East desk who did not detect the inflation of the wheat price to recover the transportation fees being paid to Iraq. The international grain trade is far from transparent and it is unreasonable to expect that middle-ranking public servants would be able quickly to acquire the expertise to unravel the intricacies of the wheat contracts they were scrutinizing. The Department of Foreign Affairs and Trade (DFAT), in retrospect naively, relied on the UN's processes for examining the wheat contracts. They may also have had a misplaced faith that AWB Limited's employees, who only recently had been public servants and colleagues, would remain 'bound by public service procedures and expectations of integrity'. (Mulgan, 2009, p. 341) A further consideration is that the privatization of the Australian Wheat Board was not a high-profile privatization beyond the relatively closed agricultural policy community. The debate surrounding privatization took several years and the actual privatization itself took place in two stages with the passage of legislation in 1997 and then in 1998. AWB Limited employees ceased to be public servants in 1997, but it is unlikely that DFAT staff were aware of the details of the transition arrangements within AWB Limited.

The second, apparently trivial, issue associated with the privatization and the scandal, was the company name. As the Australian Wheat Board, the former statutory authority was frequently referred to by the acronym, AWB. The adoption by the privatized company of the name AWB Limited meant that the transition from statutory authority to private company was not immediately obvious to anyone without a detailed knowledge of wheat marketing arrangements. Clearly the new company wanted to benefit from the strong reputation that the Australian Wheat Board had among growers and its international customers, but the decision to use this name greatly confused much of the commentary at the time of the Cole Inquiry. Even the Minister for Foreign Affairs, Alexander Downer, slipped up in his terminology, referring to the 'Australian Wheat Board' when speaking of AWB Limited during the Cole Inquiry. The government's entanglement with the scandal was clearly linked to this confusion about the company's status.

Apart from the privatization process removing the government from access to expertise about the operation of the international grain market and confusing the issue as to whether AWB Limited was a government entity or a private company, there was a further issue for the government. The retention of the export monopoly by the privatized entity meant that the government had some interest in the operation of the company. However, the oversight structure it had in place in the form of the Wheat Export Authority was very limited in its powers (Botterill and McNaughton, 2009). The peculiar nature of the privatization confused the issue of accountability for AWB Limited's behaviour and opened the way for the issue to become a political scandal through suggestions that government departments and Cabinet Ministers should have known, and probably did know, about AWB Limited's sanctions evasion. The central question in the scandal became who was accountable and for what? (Mulgan, 2009). Mulgan (2009, p. 342) concludes that 'DFAT certainly failed in its duty to monitor compliance by Australian companies'. He goes on to suggest (2009, p. 342) that:

> The AWB affair not only provides an example of DFAT's failure to hold a company accountable for respecting a UN sanctions regime, but also highlights weaknesses in the capacity of Australian political institutions to hold government departments to account.

The linkage between the government and AWB Limited's actions, however uncertain and confused, opened the way for the Opposition to turn the issue into a political scandal and, incidentally, provided a major boost to the career of Kevin Rudd. As Tiffen (1999, p. 21) argues, 'Over the past two decades, scandals have almost become the common currency of partisan politics as righteousness, revenge and political efficacy all pointed in the same direction'. AWB Limited's payments of kickbacks to Saddam Hussein's regime provided the opposition Labor Party with a useful weapon against a fourth-term Howard government. Because of some very poor tactics by the company (Botterill, 2007) in its dealings with the Cole Inquiry, what should have been a three-month inquiry dragged on for close to a year, providing the opposition with daily material to use to attack the Howard government and its most senior ministers. According to Tiffen (1999, p. 23):

> Business corruption only rarely graduates to the ranks of general public scandal. However, sometimes it is so predatory or on such a grand scale that it becomes a broader political issue, because of the institutional and policy inadequacies that permitted it, or because it has been abetted or protected by political connections.

The AWB Limited scandal appears to meet all these criteria. AWB Limited was the worst offender in bypassing the sanctions in the humanitarian component of Oil-for-Food. There were clear institutional failures because DFAT and the WEA either did not have, or failed to use their expertise and monitoring powers to uncover the sanctions-busting activities. The privatization process which left a monopoly in the hands of a private company increasingly appeared to be a policy failure. Finally, the National Party, which was a partner in the governing Coalition, had strong connections with many of the key players at AWB Limited and had long been a supporter of the export monopoly, providing sufficient prima facie evidence for the opposition of political involvement in covering up AWB Limited's activities.

The final element for consideration in analysing the AWB Limited scandal is the consequences for the company, and at this point the consideration of whether the activities constituted corruption is probably moot as the outcome for the company was devastating. The company was disgraced by the scandal and a number of its employees became a laughing stock during the Cole Inquiry as they attempted to defend the apparently indefensible and engaged in semantic debates which wasted time and heightened the impression that the company's behaviour had been, at best, of dubious ethics. As I have reported elsewhere (Botterill, 2007, p. 11),

> There were also some extraordinary exchanges with AWB witnesses that caused laughter from the public gallery and frustration on the part of the Commissioner. When Mr Charles Stott gave evidence, Counsel for AWB asked the Commissioner to 'ask those who are laughing to desist from laughing. This is not a matter for laughing' (Transcript, p. 2497). After a lengthy exchange between Mr Stott and Mr Agius on the Tigris matter and whether the wheat shipment in 1996 had been a donation, the Commissioner observed 'It's a loan, for heaven's sake' (Transcript, p. 2212). On another occasion, Mr Agius was moved to ask 'How is business done at the AWB if nobody reads their emails, . . .?' (Transcript, p. 2859).

Following the Inquiry, the government gave the industry an ultimatum – set up an alternative company structure or face the loss of the export monopoly. Although the National Party continued to argue strongly for the retention of the single desk, its Liberal Party coalition partner was not as keen. The Prime Minister, John Howard, told the Parliament in May 2007:

> If growers are not able to establish the new entity by 1 March next year, the government will propose other marketing arrangements for wheat exports. Let me make this clear to the House. The options available would include further deregulation of the wheat export market. (Howard, 2007, p. 2)

The election of the Labor government in November 2007 marked the end for the monopoly with the new Minister for Agriculture, Fisheries and Forestry announcing that the government would be removing the arrangements which privileged AWB Limited. (Burke 2008) Legislation effecting this change was passed in 2008.

LESSONS FROM THE SCANDAL

The primary lesson for government arising from this episode relates to the implementation of economic sanctions. Mulgan (2009, p. 345) argues that 'Overall then, a number of accountability failures by government agencies can be identified in the AWB affair, both internationally within the UN Secretariat and domestically within DFAT and the WEA. All fell short in their obligations to monitor the activities of companies trading with Iraq under the OFFP'. Nations differ in their enthusiasm for actually implementing the sanctions to which they commit. Sanctions are not costless to the 'sending' nation and, as noted at the beginning of this chapter, are generally borne by private actors. For a company like AWB Limited, the potential loss of a large, important export market was of great concern and, as subsequently borne out by the Cole Inquiry and the failed attempts to prosecute AWB Limited executives, bypassing the sanctions was not illegal. The company ended up paying a high price for its involvement in the kickback arrangements through the loss of its export monopoly but that was arguably a quirk of the particular company and its rather peculiar structure post-privatization. Had the company not been the beneficiary of a legislated benefit in the form of the monopoly, it is arguable that there would have been fewer major consequences. This suggests that the type of sanctions-busting activities engaged in by AWB Limited would happen again in the future unless countries who sign up to sanctions are prepared to implement domestic legislation giving their commitment domestic force.

Perhaps unrelated to the issue of corruption but certainly pertinent to this story, is the process of privatizing a powerful monopoly. The process which led to the establishment of AWB Limited was quite different from the other privatizations that took place in Australian in the 1980s and 1990s. The debate took place in the relatively closed rural policy community and without reference to the government agencies normally involved in a policy change of this magnitude. (Aulich and Botterill, 2007.) By leaving the monopoly with the company, the government became entangled in its business dealings and guilty by association of bypassing a UN sanctions regime. The government opened itself up to political attack, in spite of seeking to limit the damage by setting up a very limited inquiry and resisting a broader Senate Inquiry.

The employees of AWB Limited who were complicit with Iraq's request to bypass the sanctions do not appear to have benefited personally from their activities. As agents of the company, they arguably served the interests of shareholders until such time as the kickbacks became public. Although not illegal, bypassing sanctions to which the Australian government was committed was ethically questionable and served to undermine international attempts to change the behaviour of what was largely seen as a pariah state.

NOTE

1. The Australian Wheat Board was established in 1948 and, as explained below was privatized as AWB Limited in the late 1990s. To avoid confusion, this chapter uses the term 'Australian Wheat Board' when referring to the statutory entity and 'AWB Limited' when referring to the privatized company.

REFERENCES

Aulich, C. and L. Botterill (2007), 'A very peculiar privatisation: the end of the statutory Australian Wheat Board', Australasian Political Studies Association Conference Monash University, 24–26 September.

Australian Wheat Board (1996), 'AWB off the mark in Iraq', AWB Grain Statement, 22 May 1996.

AWB Limited (undated), 'Submission to Senate Rural and Regional Affairs and Transport Reference Committee', Inquiry into 'compensation arrangements after writing off of the Iraqi wheat debt'.

Barber, J. (1979), 'Economic sanctions as a policy instrument', *International Affairs*, **55**(3), 367–84.

Bartos, S. (2006), *Against the Grain: The AWB Scandal and Why It Happened*, Sydney: UNSW Press.

Botterill, L. and A. McNaughton (2009), 'At the intersection of international and municipal law : the case of Commissioner Cole and the Wheat Export Authority' in J. Farrall and K. Rubenstein (eds), *Sanctions, Accountability and Governance in a Globalised World,* Cambridge: Cambridge University Press, 239–59.

Botterill, L.C. (2007), 'Doing it for the growers in Iraq?: The AWB, Oil-for-Food and the Cole Inquiry', *Australian Journal of Public Administration*, **66**(1), 4–12.

Botterill, L.C. (forthcoming), 'Life and death of an institution: the case of collective wheat marketing in Australia ', *Public Administration.*

Burke, T., the Hon MP (2008), 'Government takes next steps to end wheat monopoly', Media Release by the Minister for Agriculture, Fisheries and Forestry DAFF08/006B, 6 February, 2008.

Cockfield, G. and L.C. Botterill (2007), 'Deregulating Australia's wheat trade: from the Australian Wheat Board to AWB Limited', *Public Policy*, **2**(1), 44–57.

Cole, T.R., the Honourable AO RFD QC (2006), *Report of the Inquiry into certain Australian companies in relation to the UN Oil-for-Food Programme* Volume 3: Sales, allegations and inquiries January 2001 – December 2005 Canberra, Commonwealth of Australia.

Conrad, J.A. (1990), *The Entrepreneurial State: Market Structure and State Trading in Wheat*, Ann Arbor, Michigan: UMI Dissertation Information Service.

Damrosch, L.F. (1994), 'The collective enforcement of international norms through economic sanctions', *Ethics and International Affairs*, **8**, 59–75.

Doxey, M.P. (1996), *International Sanctions in Contemporary Perspective*, Basingstoke, UK: Macmillan Press Ltd.

Dunsdorfs, E. (1956), *The Australian Wheat-Growing Industry 1788–1948*, Melbourne: The University Press.

Eicher, S. (2009a), 'Introduction: what corruption is and why it matters' in S. Eicher (ed.) *Corruption in International Business: The Challenge of Cultural and Legal Diversity*, Burlington, VT: Gower, pp. 1–14.

Eicher, S. (2009b), 'When shareholders lose (or win) through corruption' in S Eicher (ed.) *Corruption in International Business: The Challenge of Cultural and Legal Diversity*, Burlington, VT: Gower, pp. 31–46.

Evans, G., the Hon QC MP ((1990) 'Australian sanctions against Iraq', Minister for Foreign Affairs and Trade News Release, 6 August, 1990.

Galtung, J. (1967), 'On the effects of international economic sanctions: with examples from the case of Rhodesia', *World Politics*, **19**(3), 378–416.

Hooke, M. (1993), 'The Australian Grains Industry: planning for the future', *Agricultural Science*, **6**(1), 39–45.

Howard, J., the Hon MP (2007) *Questions Without Notice: Wheat*, House of Representatives Hansard, 22 May 2007.

Malone, D.M. (2006), *The International Struggle Over Iraq: Politics in the UN Security Council 1980–2005*, New York: Oxford University Press.

Meyer, J.A. and M.G. Califano (2006), *Good Intentions Corrupted: The Oil-for-Food Scandal and the Threat to the U.N.*, New York: Public Affairs.

Mulgan, R. (2009), 'AWB and oil for food: some issues of accountability' in J. Farrall and K. Rubenstein (eds), *Sanctions, Accountability and Governance in a Globalised World*, Cambridge: Cambridge University Press, pp. 334–351.

Overington, C. (2007), *Kickback: Inside the Australian Wheat Board Scandal*, Crows Nest, NSW: Allen & Unwin.

Renwick, R. (1981), *Economic Sanctions*, Cambridge, Mass.: Harvard University Centre for International Affairs.

Ryan, T.J. (1984), 'Wheat Marketing', *Review of Marketing and Agricultural Economics*, **52**(1), 117–128.

Senate Rural and Regional Affairs and Transport Committee (2008), *Reference: Wheat Export Marketing Bill 2008 and Wheat Export Marketing (Repeal and Consequential Amendments) Bill 2008 [Exposure drafts]* Official Committee Hansard, 22 April 2008 Canberra, Official Hansard Report, http://www.aph.gov.au/hansard/senate/commttee/S10724.pdf.

Senate Rural and Regional Affairs and Transport References Committee (2005), *Iraqi Wheat Debt – Repayments for Wheat Growers*, Canberra: AGPS.

Shovelan, J. (1990) *AM Program*, ABC Radio, 8 August 1990.

Tiffen, R. (1999), *Scandals – Media, Politics and Corruption in Contemporary Australia*, Sydney: UNSW Press.

Tuckey, W., MP (1997) *Wheat Marketing Amendment Bill 1997: Second Reading Debate* House of Representatives Hansard, 2 October 1997.

Volcker, P.A., R.J. Goldstone and M. Pieth (2005) *Manipulation of the Oil-for-Food Programme by the Iraqi Regime*, Independent Inquiry Committee into the United Nations Oil-for-Food Programme, http://www.iic-offp.org/documents/IIC%20Final%20Report%2027Oct2005.pdf 27 October 2005.

7 Identifying corruption risks in public climate finance governance

Lisa Ann Elges

Climate change is probably one of the most serious challenges our and future generations face. Global greenhouse gas emissions have been rising and a strong body of scientific evidence shows that there are likely to be severe consequences for the global climate if they are not reduced. Governments and multilateral organizations have pledged substantial sums of 'public climate finance' to mitigate impacts on the global climate and to adapt to the consequences of climate change. In order to safeguard these investments, it is important to ensure exemplary governance in their administration. Weak governance of public climate finance will compromise transparency and accountability in their disbursement. This opens the door to corrupted decision making, which risks a misallocation of funds and threatens the legitimacy of global efforts to work toward the global public good of a stable climate.

Addressing climate change means taking decisive action *to adapt* to present and forecasted climatic impacts (adaptation) and *to mitigate* those impacts by reducing greenhouse gas (GHG) emissions (mitigation). According to the International Panel on Climate Change (IPCC: 4th Assessment Report: Climate Change, 2007) global emissions need to at least peak if not decline by 2015 in order to 'limit global mean temperature increases to 2–2.4°C above the pre-industrial level, and to be around 50 per cent of current levels by 2050'. In 2009, at the Global Climate Summit in Copenhagen, an Accord was struck to keep temperature increases at or below 2°C. The recent climate meeting in Cancun underscored this commitment as well as the need to generate 'new and additional' sources of public and private finance to achieve climate goals.

GOVERNANCE CHALLENGES AND CORRUPTION RISKS

The governance challenges and potential risks in climate finance derive from (1) the volume of money needed and being spent to adapt to and to mitigate climate change; (2) the complexity of the climate finance architecture through which that money is delivered, and (3) weaknesses in the transparency, accountability and integrity of those institutions involved in deciding how climate finance is spent and actually spending it. The combination of these factors heightens the risk that climate finance may be lost to corruption.

This chapter discusses some governance challenges within climate finance flows and suggests ways to overcome these challenges through enhanced safeguards against corruption and measures to improve transparency, accountability and integrity. It provides an overview of the global climate financing arrangements currently in place or planned – to give a sense of the sheer volumes and complexity of money being committed to climate change. The chapter then discusses generally the challenges and corruption risks associated with climate finance and decision-making processes around how, where and for what the money may be spent, illustrated by two examples concerning the UN Framework Convention on Climate Change (UNFCCC) Adaptation Fund, and the Climate Investment Funds (multilateral donor trust funds under the multilateral development banks). The concluding section suggests some options to better address the identified risks to ensure more effective, transparent and accountable climate financing.

COMPLEX GLOBAL CLIMATE FINANCING ARRANGEMENTS

Sources and Volumes of Money

The sums involved in addressing climate change are huge. The UN Framework Convention on Climate Change (UNFCCC) estimates the actual costs for mitigation alone to be between US$210–230 billion and approximately half of that for adaptation by 2030.[1] So far, governments of the OECD countries[2] have agreed to raise up to US$100 billion new climate money annually from public and private sources by 2020.[3] In the short-term, they also agreed to contribute up to US$30 billion in 'fast-track finance' between 2010 and 2012 to fund both adaptation and mitigation actions. To date 17 countries have submitted pledges, with Japan the largest contributor (US$15 billion) followed by the European Union (US$10.5 billion) and the United States (US$3 billion).[4]

Generally speaking, global climate finance flows are channelled through three modalities: (1) global funds established under the UN organizations such as the UNFCCC and the UN Development Programme (UNDP), (2) multilateral donor trust funds established by the multi-lateral Development Banks (MDBs), and (3) direct bilateral funding arrangements between a donor and recipient countries. Through these arrangements developed countries contribute public money to support adaptation and mitigation actions in developing countries.

The text in Box 7.1 illustrates the complex web of climate funding sources, many of which have overlapping objectives. The growing complexity of the climate finance landscape with its patchwork of 'new and additional' funding sources – from donations and loans, from the public and private sectors, and from market and non-market sources – makes it increasingly difficult to assess whether the money is being well spent or not. Aside from bilateral fast-start finance commitments, no less than eight multilateral/global funds have been established or operationalized with an expected expenditure volume of US$8.5 billion alone since 2008 – most of which is public money.

CLIMATE FINANCE GOVERNANCE CHALLENGES

Within the current climate financing framework where large sums of money are distributed through multiple channels, deciding on how that money should be spent and holding its spenders accountable for their decisions are key governance challenges. Good decision-making appears to be frustrated by (a) a general lack of clarity of the climate financing terms – on what basis climate finance ought to be spent; and (b) insufficient requirements to ensure transparency, accountability and integrity in the institutional and operational policies of climate financing and financed actors. Good governance is further confounded by confused chains of accountability with a myriad of different actors involved subject to different rules for monitoring, reporting and verifying climate finance decisions and expenditures. With such deficiencies in transparency, accountability and integrity, risks of corruption are likely to exist, particularly where there are high perceptions of corruption in specific countries and commercial sectors.

Increased efforts to ensure transparent and accountable governance around the allocation, delivery and use of climate finance are needed. Transparency International's Global Corruption Report on Climate Change explores shortfalls and attenuate corruption risks in climate governance. The current precautions do not appear robust enough to ensure against the abuse of 'entrusted power for private gain' in climate financing decisions. Without sufficient integrity and anti-corruption safeguards and public oversight, corrupt behaviour is likely to undermine

BOX 7.1 OVERVIEW OF THE CLIMATE FINANCE ARCHITECTURE

UNFCCC Funds

Under the UNFCCC, the Global Environmental Facility (GEF) operates the GEF Trust Fund,[5] the Least Developed Countries Fund (LDCF), and the Special Climate Change Fund (SCCF). All three funds are financed by contributions from donor countries and administered by implementing agencies, mainly UNDP and UNEP, occasionally the World Bank.

The GEF Trust Fund climate focal area received US$1.02 billion for the period 2006–2010 from 32 countries and has earmarked US$1.36 billion for 2010–2014. The Fund provides both grants and concessional loans for adaptation and mitigation projects in the areas of renewable energy, energy efficiency, new low-GHG energy technologies, sustainable transportation, adaptation and developing country support for submitting National Communications under UNFCCC obligations.[6]

The LDCF supports developing countries to prepare National Adaptation Action Plans (NAPAs). As of May 2010, total pledged contributions amounted to US$221 459 413[7] and as of November 2010, 45 countries had submitted NAPAs to the UNFCCC Secretariat[8] – each costing at or approximate to the maximum amount available, US$200,000[9].

Aiming to implement 'long-term adaptation measures that increase the climate resilience of national development sectors', the SCCF supports primarily adaptation and technology transfer projects which are 'additional' or taken on because of climate change and not a traditional development-type project. So far, the Fund has earned pledges to the tune of US$150 million and has approved 28 projects costing a little over US$97 million.

Also under the governance of the UNFCCC COP is the Adaptation Fund (AF). The AF provides grants for adaptation projects in developing countries[10]. It differs from the above Funds in that it is financed by a 2 per cent levy on the sale of certified emissions reductions (CERs = carbon credits) from Clean Development Mechanism (CDM) project activities and donor contributions. To date, the fund has generated a total commitment of US$216 152 698 of which US$130 570000 is revenue from carbon credit sales and the rest as donor contributions. In September 2010, the Adaptation Fund Board approved the Funds' first two projects in Senegal (direct access) and in Honduras (UNDP).

Multilateral Development Bank Funds

Outside of the UN system, the Climate Investment Funds (CIFs) were established in 2008–2009 as multilateral donor trust funds to support low-carbon and climate-resilient development through scaled-up financing. CIFs are channelled through the African Development Bank (AfDB), Asian Development Bank (ADB), European Bank for Reconstruction and Development (EBRD), Inter-American Development Bank (IADB), and World Bank Group (WBG). The CIFs include the Clean Technology Fund (CTF, est. 2008), The Forest Investment Programme (FIP), the Scaling-up Renewable Energy in Low-Income Countries Pilot Programme (SREP) and the Pilot Programme of Climate Resilience (PPCR). To date, the CIFs tally at close to USD $6.2 billion involving pledged contributions as follows:

CIFs	Total	Grants (millions)	Loans (millions)	Capital (millions)
CTF	4 400 000 000	2791	892	722
FIP	515 500 000	403		112.5
SREP	300 000 000	227.6		82.4
PPCR	972 000 000	614		358
Total	6 187 500 000	4035.6	892	1274.9

The objectives and specific actions funded vary with each CIF. The CTF aims primarily to provide incentives for low carbon and GHG emissions mitigating projects and technology deployment and transfer. By November 2010, 15 CTF projects were approved in Egypt (1)[11] , Mexico (4)[12], Philippines(1)[13], South Africa (2)[14] , Thailand (2)[15], Turkey (3)[16], Ukraine(1)[17] and Vietnam(1)[18] totalling US$880 million.[19]

Designed to support REDD (Reduced Emissions from Deforestation and Degradation) project preparatory actions and project investments (to address and overcome causes of forest loss and land degradation), the FIP as of July 2010 has selected pilot projects in Brazil, Burkina Faso, Democratic Republic of Congo, Ghana, Indonesia, Mexico, Laos and Peru.

The SREP supports investments (by overcoming investment barriers) in lowincome countries for energy efficiency, renewable energy and access to modern sustainable energy. Six pilot projects in Ethiopia, Honduras, Kenya, Maldives, Mali and Nepal have so far been selected.

PPRC is designed to provide programmatic finance for national climate resilient national development plans consistent with NAPAs and in complement to other sources of adaptation finance. Pilot projects have been selected in nine countries (Bangladesh, Bolivia, Cambodia, Mozambique, Nepal, Niger, Tajikistan, Yemen and Zambia) and in two regions: the Caribbean (Dominican Republic, Grenada, Haiti, Jamaica, Saint Lucia, Saint Vincent and the Grenadines) and the Pacific (PNG, Samoa and Tonga).

UNDP and World Bank Forest Funds

Outside of the CIFs and the UNFCCC system are two additional funds: the Forest Carbon Partnership Facility Programme (FCPF) operated by the World Bank and the UN REDD programme administered by UNDP in coordination with UNEP and the FAO. The FCPF houses a 'Readiness Fund' to assist countries in developing national REDD strategies and programmes to assess and monitor forest-based emissions reductions. The FCPF also establishes a 'Carbon Finance Mechanism' to pay countries for emissions reductions achieved through REDD. To date, the FCPF has sequestered pledges of US$152.7 million for the Readiness Fund and US$152.67 million and US$68.6 million for the Carbon Fund (not yet in operation). The Readiness Fund has committed US$44.6 million to country projects and US$23.6 to 'associated country services'.

Similar to the FCPF, the UN-REDD programme supports the capacity of national governments to prepare and implement national REDD strategies with the involvement of all stakeholders. As of November 2010, pledged contributions were US$106.5 million from Norway (US$84.4 million), Spain (US$20.2 million) and Denmark (US$8.07 million). Budgets at close to US$76.5 million have been approved for 2 global and 8 country projects in Bolivia, Democratic Republic of Congo (DRC), Indonesia, Panama, Papua New Guinea, Tanzania, Vietnam and Zambia.

Other Funds

In addition to these, there are a number of other multilateral and bilateral climate funds including Japan's Hatoyama initiative[20] with a portfolio of US$15 billion. Climate Finance Options, a web-based information portal on climate financing, operated by UNDP and the World Bank, lists no less than 46 climate financing public and private sources for both adaptation and mitigation projects.[21]

Long-term Climate Finance

Following from decisions reached at the Cancun Climate Summit, a new global Green Climate Fund is to be set up to channel climate finance over the longer term. While some initial agreements appear to have been reached regarding how that fund would be governed and – over the next year(s) designed,[22] clarity on how it would be financed, what it would finance and its relationship with existing climate funds and financing arrangements is lacking. Although and presumably, the fund would house 'new sources of finance'.

Despite all the climate billions being committed and already or soon to be spent, it has been clear from the onset that climate finance must be generated from both public and private sources: Tax payer money from rich industrialized countries alone is not enough to fund the transformational changes needed for industrial, energy and transportation sectors to move toward low or zero carbon economies. Nor is it enough to cover efforts to increase climate resilience or the predictable losses caused by climate-induced extreme weather events, flooding, droughts, and sea level rise.

A number of the MDB- and GEF-operated global climate funds aim to increase public–private blended finance or co-financing schemes to provide incentives for low carbon and sustainable investments. These often involve non-concessional and concessional loans and/or grants. Climate Finance Options, a web-based information portal on climate financing, operated by

UNDP and the World Bank, lists no less than 46 climate financing sources for both adaptation and mitigation projects, including those mentioned above.

Aside from these initiatives, additional emerging and important sources of climate finance are market and non-market mechanisms. In November 2010, the High Level Advisory Group (HLAG) on Climate Finance convened under the auspices of the UN Secretary-General, published an influential report[23] which aimed to identify 'practical proposals on how to significantly scale up long-term financing for mitigation and adaptation strategies in developing countries from various public and private sources, and how best to deliver it'. The Report discusses various options non-market mechanisms such as taxing transportation (aviation and maritime) and financial transactions, and reallocating fossil fuel subsidies. It also proposes that carbon markets can create revenue (a source of climate finance) through levies placed on inframarginal rents gained through a climate change mitigation projects.[24]

In this context, another significant outcome of the Cancun climate meetings was to consider the establishment of one or more (new) market-based and non-market-based mechanisms to promote and enhance the cost-effectiveness of mitigation actions. This would include ensuring voluntary participation, supported by the promotion of fair and equitable access, complementing support for Nationally Appropriate Mitigation Actions (NAMAs),[25] stimulating mitigation across the economy, safeguarding environmental integrity, ensuring a net GHG decrease and/or avoidance, supplementing domestic mitigation efforts in UNFCCC Annex 1 countries and ensuring good governance, robust market functioning and regulation.[26]

Already in place is the international carbon market which has developed from UNFCCC Annex I Parties GHG emissions reductions commitments and the institution regional market instruments and the Clean Development Mechanism (CDM) and Joint Implementation (JI) under the Kyoto Protocol. The World Bank estimated the total allowance market in 2009 at US$122 billion, dominated by the EU ETS; and the project-based market to be about US$3.3 billion, dominated by CDM while the voluntary carbon market represented a volume of US$338 million in 2009.[27]

climate-financed actions by decreasing cost-effectiveness, output quality, sustainable development and overall climate benefits.

TRANSPARENCY, ACCOUNTABILITY AND INTEGRITY IN DECISION-MAKING PROCESSES

Opportunities for corruption may exist in the decision-making processes at both global and national levels regarding how, for what and to whom climate finance is apportioned.

Climate finance requires increased transparency to assure that it is in fact 'new and additional' and that it is not being 'double-counted' as development aid money.

Fast-start finance (introduced above) accounts for most 'new and additional' financial contributions. Under the 2009 Copenhagen Accord[28] and following its 'endorsement' at the 16th Sessions of the UNFCCC Conference of States Parties in Cancun in December 2010,[29] developed countries known as Annex 1 countries[30] commit to contributing up to USD$ 30 billion between 2010 and 2012. That money is to be 'new and additional'[31] and used equally for adaptation and mitigation actions.[32] So far, Climate Funds Update reports that US$29.7 billion have been pledged. However, owing to lack of transparency about the terms of intended contributions, the modalities for spending, the purposes (adaptation or mitigation) and the money sources (new and additional basis) are difficult to assess.[33]

From a governance perspective, whether or not climate finance is 'new and additional' is important: if development aid resources are reallocated as climate finance, then important development objectives may be sacrificed – unless there is a clear understanding of what overlap may exist between the two programmes. If development aid is repackaged as 'new and additional' climate finance, or even if climate finance is reported as development aid, this could amount to double accounting – demonstrating a lack of integrity in public financial allocations.

Climate finance requires increased transparency to assure that decisions taken are subject to public scrutiny and oversight.

National and local decision-making involves similar questions including how priority adaptation and mitigation needs are determined, which government agencies, sectors, regions and/or communities should be responsible for and benefit from incoming climate finance and on what basis.

Poor climate finance decisions can result from the complexity of the task, aggravated by a number of reasons including lack of sufficient technical, financial or scientific capacity or knowledge. This weakness is generally appreciated within the UNFCCC climate change negotiations where capacity building and knowledge sharing are priority areas of action. But even with good technical know-how, decisions are not easy. While most climate funds provide sets of criteria to help decision makers, the criteria themselves are often unclear. 'Vulnerability' and 'urgency', for example, remain highly subjective terms, which are generally understood but have not and probably will not achieve a global consensus on user-definition or application.[34]

Poor decisions *may* also be influenced by bribery, conflicts of interest, kick-backs and other forms of 'abuse of entrusted power for private gain'. This *could* result in the skewing of climate benefits for preferred countries or groups within countries. If there are perceptions that climate-funding schemes are unfair, unjust and untrustworthy, this can erode institutional legitimacy. From a financial perspective, project cost effectiveness and quality would be reduced, sometimes substantially.

Good climate finance governance would demand that decision-making processes should be as transparent as possible. Transparency enables third parties to assess and monitor what and how decisions have been taken and strengthens the legitimacy of the decisions and their makers. So far, analyses of global climate funds[35] show that there is not sufficient transparency, as discussed below.

Adaptation Fund: Need for Increased Transparency in Accreditation Procedures

The Adaptation Fund (AF) under the Kyoto Protocol of the UNFCCC has been applauded for good governance. It is seen as a useful model for how climate finance could be pooled and delivered in the long term. But even the AF faces a number of transparency challenges, which may impact its success in delivering climate finance. The AF, for example, enables developing countries to receive funding support through two channels: direct access and via Multinational Implementing Entities (MIEs) such as UNDP and UNEP. In the direct access model, a National Implementing Entity (NIE) must first be accredited to receive and administer climate finance.[36] An NIE must be a 'national legal entity' and meet specified fiduciary standards concerning financial management and integrity, institutional capacity and transparency and self-investigative powers. These requirements are outlined by the AF Operational and Policy Guidelines (AF OPGs). An NIE must also be officially nominated and endorsed by the government of the developing country which it represents. As of February 2011, three NIEs have been accredited in Jamaica,[37] Senegal[38] and Uruguay.[39] While the criteria for accrediting these NIEs are elaborated in Annex 2 of the AF OPGs, information or documentation regarding the actual review and assessment of the AF Accreditation Panel of each NIE is not publicly available. The same is true regarding MIEs. The fact that no outsider to the accreditation processes can see what fiduciary standards were used to ascertain whether a NIE or MIE should be accredited raises concerns.

This information is important. It reveals what standards or systems are in place to ensure the successful implementation and cost effectiveness of actual project proposals which NIEs may submit pursuant to their accreditation. The first NIE project approved by the AF is to take place in Senegal. The proposal document is available on the AF website. While the proposal includes the project objectives and actions, it omits reference to anti-corruption safeguards to be employed in project implementation. It does describe a mechanism to ensure transparency in project sub-contracting and procurement, but the NIE itself is charged with investigating and penalizing misconduct.[40] This raises concerns of whether or not the NIE could be subject to conflicts of interest.[41] The basis for the concerns rests rather with the AF's own criteria for NIE fiduciary standards, which focus on responsive and investigatory capacities for financial mismanagement, fraud and corruption but not preventative ones.[42]

Climate Investment Funds: Need for Increased Transparency in Decision-making Processes

Like the Adaptation Fund, the Climate Investment Funds (CIFs) (see Box 7.1 above) are viewed as a model for climate financing because of their innovative governance structure, which enables civil society observer participation and consultation. Even if the CIFs have generally been criticized for functioning as a parallel source of climate finance outside the UNFCCC process, they have made significant advances in terms of good governance policy. Many civil society observers view their role as periphery, often saying that their interventions are permitted but not 'heard' or taken up in any concrete way.[43] The CIF disclosure policy (approved May 2009) provides for an 'information document' concerning 'proposed programmes and projects' to be made public at least two weeks prior to a decision on the funding of the proposal. Yet there is no guarantee that all project or investment-plan information will be disclosed if the CIF deems that there are 'justifiable reasons' for non-disclosure.[44] Once projects have been approved, as in the case of most projects under the Clean Technology Fund, the terms and concessionality of the grants or loans are not disclosed, not explained or simply unknown.[45] Because the CIFs are funded by voluntary contributions of public finance from developed countries, the apparent limited disclosure practice regarding how and on what terms the money is being spent prevents effective oversight by national institutions such as ministries of finance, national accounting offices or tax payer interest groups.

The CIF decision-making process regarding the eligibility and selection of countries and projects also raises some concerns. Under the Scaling-Up Renewable Energy Programme (SREP) for instance, a Sub-Committee decides which countries are selected as pilot countries. In the first selection round, that decision rested on a report of an Expert Group (EG) of six individuals[46] who were chosen by the Sub-Committee according to agreed criteria.[47] The EG reviewed background country information and expressions of interest (EOI) submitted by 32 interested governments. The governments were invited to submit EOIs on the basis of eligibility assessed by the CIF Administrative Unit,[48] through the country offices of the Multilateral Development Banks (MDBs).

Based on its review according to the pilot country selection criteria (determined by the Sub-Committee), the EG submitted a report in June 2010 in which it recommended six pilot countries (Ethiopia, Honduras, Kenya, Maldives, Mali, and Mongolia) and three alternative countries (Armenia, Liberia and Nepal).[49] At its June 2010 meeting, the Sub-Committee decided, based on the one delegation's insistence that LDCs should account for half the pilot countries, Mongolia[50] would be replaced by Nepal. The decision did not provide sufficient clarity as to why the other chosen non-LDC countries should not be replaced, nor did it allow for debate on whether the LDC requirement should apply at all.[51] Further, the EG report did not provide an evaluation of EOIs submitted by other governments – as the EG's terms of reference did not require it to do so. Some Committee members argued that such information is necessary for the CIFs to build trust among their constituencies and to enable developing countries to submit approvable EOIs and project proposals. The follow-up Sub-Committee meeting in November 2010 concluded that such information may be shared through bilateral channels but is not likely to be publicly disclosed.[52]

The SREP example thus raises concerns as to how decisions are taken to determine pilot countries for a future spending on projects amounting in total public spending of US$300 000. Further, whether or not those decisions can be challenged by developing countries and what appeal process may apply is still unclear.

CORRUPTION RISKS: IF OR WHEN THE MONEY DISAPPEARS?

The newness of climate finance offers little basis for assessing what has gone wrong to date.[53] This is more of a probability question. In many countries where climate finance is to be delivered levels of corruption are perceived as high as evidenced in TI's Corruption Perception Index.[54] Further, TI's Briber Payers Index shows that commercial sectors likely to be involved in climate adaptation and mitigation projects, that is, construction, public works, land and property development, mining, oil and gas, and electricity are considered prone to being influenced by corruption and in some cases, state capture.[55] These surveys suggest a relatively high probability of at least some climate finance being lost to corruption – *if* appropriate safeguards and systems of governance are not in place or supported enough to enable the absorption and spending of climate money. This is not a reason to reconsider climate finance funding in these countries, rather it underscores the need for strong and practical anti-corruption safeguards.

In a worst-case scenario, if a significant amount of climate project funding were corrupted, what would happen? As stated above, the complexity of the structure coupled with unclear rules on transparency and accountability, suggests that assigning responsibility or fault may be difficult, if not impossible. Taking preventative measures to ensure against corruption risks becomes all the more important until more clarity on governance frameworks exists.

Some Preventative Measures

Demanding greater transparency, accountability and integrity on the part of climate finance decision makers and their institutions is a positive step to reducing corruption risks. Civil society plays an important role in this effort. Objective, research-based advocacy and innovative media can help encourage constructive changes in current climate finance policies and practices.

On another very practical level, most climate finance expenditures will involve public procurement or contracting of services or goods to achieve an adaptation or mitigation action. Transparency International's Minimum Standards for Public Contracting (See Box 7.2 below) provide a framework for preventing and reducing corruption based on clear rules, transparency, and effective control and auditing procedures throughout the contracting process. These are a helpful tool for governments, businesses, civil society, monitors and the media to measure whether a

BOX 7.2 TRANSPARENCY INTERNATIONAL'S MINIMUM STANDARDS FOR PUBLIC CONTRACTING

Public procurement authorities should:

- Implement a code of conduct that commits the contracting authority and its employees to a strict anti-corruption policy. The policy should take into account possible conflicts of interest and provide mechanisms for reporting corruption and protecting whistleblowers.
- Allow a company to tender only if it has implemented a code of conduct that commits the company and its employees to a strict anti-corruption policy.
- Maintain a blacklist of companies for which there is sufficient evidence of their involvement in corrupt activities; alternatively, adopt a blacklist prepared by an appropriate international institution. Debar blacklisted companies from tendering for the authority's projects for a specified period of time.
- Ensure that all contracts between the authority and its contractors, suppliers and service providers require the parties to comply with strict anti-corruption policies. This may best be achieved by requiring the use of a project integrity pact during both tender and project execution, committing the authority and bidding companies to refrain from bribery.
- Ensure that public contracts above a low threshold are subject to open competitive bidding. Exceptions must be limited and clear justification given.
- Provide all bidders, and preferably also the general public, with easy access to information about:
  - activities carried out prior to initiating the contracting process
  - tender opportunities
  - selection criteria
  - the evaluation process
  - the award decision and its justification
  - the terms and conditions of the contract and any amendments
  - the implementation of the contract

  - the role of intermediaries and agents
  - dispute-settlement mechanisms and procedures.
- Limit confidentiality to legally protected information.
- Make available to the public equivalent information on direct contracting or limited bidding processes.
- Ensure that no bidder is given access to privileged information at any stage of the contracting process, especially information relating to the selection process.
- Allow bidders sufficient time for bid preparation and for prequalification requirements when these apply. Allow a reasonable amount of time between publication of the contract award decision and the signing of the contract, in order to give an aggrieved competitor the opportunity to challenge the award decision.
- Ensure that contract 'change' orders that alter the price or description of work beyond a cumulative threshold (for example, 15 per cent of contract value) are monitored at a high level, preferably by the decision-making body that awarded the contract.
- Ensure that internal and external control and auditing bodies are independent and functioning effectively, and that their reports are accessible to the public. Any unreasonable delays in project execution should trigger additional control activities.
- Separate key functions to ensure that responsibility for demand assessment, preparation, selection, contracting, supervision and control of a project is assigned to separate bodies.
- Apply standard office safeguards, such as the use of committees at decision-making points and rotation of staff in sensitive positions. Staff responsible for procurement processes should be well trained and adequately remunerated.
- Promote the participation of civil society organizations as independent monitors of both the tender and execution of projects.

contracting system provides minimum transparency assurances. Applying these standards in a way consistent with local laws and procedures could enhance the cost-effectiveness and overall quality of adaptation or mitigation project delivery. Beyond these standards, TI has also developed a useful tool called an 'Integrity Pact'[56] aimed at preventing corruption in public contracting.

> The pact is essentially an agreement between a government or government department (at the national, sub-national or local level) and all bidders for a public contract. It stipulates rights and obligations to the effect that neither side will: pay, offer, demand or accept bribes; collude with competitors to obtain the contract; or engage in such abuses while executing the contract.
>
> TI has seen the pact tried and tested over ten years in hundreds of contracts in over 15 countries. What makes it a unique tool is the introduction of an independent monitoring system under the leadership of civil society, which ensures increased accountability of public resources.

CONCLUSION

Good governance in climate finance is important to enhance equitable, efficient and effective adaptation and mitigation projects and programmes across the globe. This means enabling or enhancing transparency, accountability and integrity in climate finance delivery and decision-making processes. Given the newness of climate finance, known cases of corruption remain few and the potential loss of climate finance to corruption an estimate of probability and risk. In this context, much can be learned from experiences in development aid delivery. While better governance can ensure better climate financing results, applying such requirements as conditionality for climate finance could delay the desired and urgent benefits for climate change adaptation and mitigation. But climate finance is also seen as a vehicle to promote transformational changes for better governance. It is therefore important that both global and national climate finance governance systems strive for the highest levels of transparency, accountability and integrity now and in the longer term.

Preventing corruption in climate finance can involve efforts to ensure that decisions taken to allocate and spend funds are transparent and that decision-makers are legally bound to perform with integrity and not to engage in corrupt behaviour. Clear rules and compliance measures regarding climate expenditures can facilitate greater integrity, transparency and accountability on the part of money givers and takers. Independent public oversight bodies may be enabled, engaged and/or strengthened to monitor decision-making, investigate allegations of misconduct and impose sanctions or penalties as appropriate and in accordance with the law. Developing the capacities of concerned or affected non-governmental actor groups to take part in and/or be consulted on climate finance decisions, to monitor climate financing processes and to call into question wrongful actions may constitute an important component of an overall anti-corruption strategy.

NOTES

1. FCCC/TP/2008/7, 26 November 2008, 'Investment and financial flows to address climate change: an update.'
2. States Parties to the UN Convention on Climate Change, listed in Annex I of the Treaty.
3. Draft decision -/CP.16: 'Outcome of the work of the Ad Hoc Working Group on long-term Cooperative Action under the Convention' December 2010.
4. See http://www.climatefundsupdate.org/fast-start-finance
5. Including support for vulnerability and adaptation assessments as part of national communications.
6. http://www.climatefundsupdate.org/listing/gef-trust-fund
7. http://www.climatefundsupdate.org/listing/least-developed-countries-fund
8. http://unfccc.int/cooperation_support/least_developed_countries_portal/submitted_napas/items/4585.php
9. http://www.thegef.org/gef/sites/thegef.org/files/documents/C.27.9%20Status%20Report%20on%20the%20Climate%20Change%20Funds.pdf
10. Parties to the Kyoto Protocol.
11. IBRD's Egypt Wind Power Development Project costing USD$150 million implemented by IBRD with Egyptian Electricity Transmission Company (EETC).
12. Mexico's Urban Transport Transformation Program at USD$ 200 million implemented by IBRD and Banco Nacional de Obras (BANOBRAS); Mexico's private Sector Wind Development (Sub Project-IFC's EDF La Ventosa) at US$15.6 million implemented by IFC with Electrica del Valle de Mexico (EVM) -subsidiary of EdF and IDB (CTF money managed by IFC); Mexico Efficient Lighting and Appliances at US$50 million implemented by IBRD with National Financiera (NAFIN). Oversight by Secretaria de Energia; Mexico Renewable Energy Plan at US$53 million implemented by IBD.
13. Renewable Energy Accelerator Program (REAP) at US$20 million implemented by IFC.
14. South Africa Energy Efficiency Program at US$15 million implemented by AfDB+IFC and the South Africa Sustainable Energy Acceleration Program at US$85 million implemented by AfDB+IFC.
15. Sustainable Energy Finance Program at US$30 million and the Thailand Renewable Energy Accelerator Program at US$40.00 million, both implemented by IFC.
16. Turkey Private Sector Sustainable Energy Financing Facility (TurSEFF) at US$50 million implemented by EBRD, Implemented through Akbank, Denizbank, Garanti, and Vakıfbank; Turkey's Commercializing Sustainable Energy Finance Program at US$22 million implemented by IFC and EBRD joint initiative; and Turkey's Private Sector Renewable Energy and Energy Efficiency Project at USD$100 million implemented by IBRD, Türkiye Sınai Kalkınma Bankası A.Ş. (TKSB), and Turkiye Kalkinma Bankasi, Guarantor: Republic of Turkey.
17. Ukraine Renewables Direct Lending Facility at US$27.8 million implemented by EBRD.
18. Sustainable Energy Finance Program (V-SEF) at US$30.8 million implemented by IFC.
19. http://www.climateinvestmentfunds.org/cif/node/2
20. http://www.climatefundsupdate.org/listing/hatoyama-Initiative
21. http://www.climatefinanceoptions.org/cfo/index.php
22. Draft decision -/CP.16: Outcome of the work of the Ad Hoc Working Group on

long-term Cooperative Action under the Convention, paras 102–112. http://unfccc.int/files/meetings/cop_16/application/pdf/cop16_lca.pdf
23. Report of the Secretary-General's High-level Advisory Group on Climate Change Financing, 5 November 2010, see http://www.un.org/wcm/webdav/site/climatechange/shared/Documents/AGF_reports/AGF_Final_Report.pdf
24. Inframarginal rents (IMR) refer to the difference between the cost of a project (e.g. valued at $15/CO2t) in relation to the amount of emissions reductions achieved and the market value of the emissions reductions (e.g. $25/CO2t). A profit or IMR of $10 would be gained. Transactions costs (e.g. $3) , taxes (e.g. $2) and other costs involved would then be subtracted, leaving a net profit for one or many project developers, investors and/or other key participant. The proposal rests on the assumption that there is a stable market price at $25/CO2t. Its viability would also depend on the weight of transaction costs – which may or may not include facilitation payments or corruption.
25. See The Bali Action Plan, para 1(b)ii (2007), http://unfccc.int/files/meetings/cop_13/application/pdf/cp_bali_action.pdfhttp://unfccc.int/files/meetings/cop_13/application/pdf/cp_bali_action.pdf
26. Section D (paras 80 – 85), see http://unfccc.int/files/meetings/cop_16/application/pdf/cop16_lca.pdf
27. Kossoye, A. & Ambrosi, P. 2010. World Bank Report: State and Trends of the Carbon Market 2010. Accessed 30 August 2010 from URL: www.worldbank.org
28. http://unfccc.int/resource/docs/2009/cop15/eng/l07.pdf
29. Draft decision -/CP.16: Outcome of the work of the Ad Hoc Working Group on long-term Cooperative Action under the Convention, S.IV(A)(1), see http://unfccc.int/files/meetings/cop_16/application/pdf/cop16_lca.pdf
30. Parties to the UNFCCC listed under Annex I of that Convention, see http://unfccc.int/parties_and_observers/parties/annex_i/items/2774.php
31. A global consensus on what 'new and additional' means has yet to be achieved. The intention of the term is that climate finance should not be a reallocation of development aid.
32. Copenhagen accord, para. 8, Infra n. 5.
33. See WRI: Summary of Developed Country Fast-Start Climate Finance Pledges at http://pdf.wri.org/climate_finance_pledges_2010-11-24.pdf; see also: http://www.climatefundsupdate.org/fast-start-finance
34. See Olmos, Santiago. 'Vulnerability and Adaptation to Climate Change: Concepts, Issues, Assessment Methods'. Climate Change Knowledge Network, July 2001; See also, Füssel, Hans-Martin. 'Review and quantitative analysis of indices of climate change exposure, adaptive capacity, sensitivity, and impacts' – Development and Climate Change, Background Note to the World Development Report 2010. Potsdam Institute for Climate Impact Research (PIK), Germany
35. Not much information is available regarding national climate finance decision-making experiences given in most cases the money simply has not yet arrived or national funds are still under-construction.
36. Adaptation Fund Board: Operational Policies And Guidelines For Parties To Access Resources From The Adaptation Fund, paras 27–8. See http://www.adaptation-fund.org/system/files/file/AFB_Operational%20Policies%20and%20Guidelines.pdf
37. Planning Institute of Jamaica: see http://www.pioj.gov.jm/
38. Centre de Suivi Ecologique: see http://www.cse.sn
39. Agencia Nacional de Investigacion e Innovacion: see www.anii.org.uy
40. Senegal's NIE Proposal: Adaptation To Coastal Erosion In Vulnerable Areas: Sanctions for the faults committed by applicants or contractors, p. 50. See http://www.adaptation-fund.org/system/files/SENEGAL_Adapation%20project_full_28%20oct%202010_0.pdf
41. In such cases, the institution of a third part, public oversight mechanism to investigate and review allegations of misconduct avoids conflict of interest questions for implementing bodies.

42. Illustrative Means of Verification: (1) Demonstration of capacity and procedures to deal with financial mismanagement and other forms of malpractice; (2) Evidence of an objective investigation function for allegations of fraud and corruption.
43. http://www.climateinvestmentfunds.org/cif/sites/climateinvestmentfunds.org/files/Review_of_Practices_NGO-CSO_Particiaption_Final.pdf
44. Note on Disclosure of Documents Prepared for Purposes of the Climate Investment Funds. See http://www.climateinvestmentfunds.org/cif/sites/climateinvestmentfunds.org/files/Note%20on%20disclosure%20of%20Documents%20-%20may%202009.pdf
45. Nakhooda, Smita. The Clean Technology Fund: Insights for Development and Climate Finance, WRI, March 2010. See http://pdf.wri.org/working_papers/clean_technology_fund.pdf
46. http://www.climateinvestmentfunds.org/cif/sites/climateinvestmentfunds.org/files/EXPERT_Group%20members_051110.docx
47. http://www.climateinvestmentfunds.org/cif/sites/climateinvestmentfunds.org/files/Criteria_for_selecting_Experts_032610_KEY_Document.pdf
48. http://www.climateinvestmentfunds.org/cif/Administrative_Unit
49. http://www.climateinvestmentfunds.org/cif/sites/climateinvestmentfunds.org/files/SREP%204%20Report%20of%20the%20SREP%20Expert%20Group%20June%202010_final.pdf
50. Apparently, the government of Mongolia has written a letter to the CIF Administrative Unit regarding the pilot country selection which is published on the CIF website but following the link leads only to a blank uploaded document. See http://www.climateinvestmentfunds.org/cif/workingdocuments/1960. The same results are seen with a similar letter by the government of Djibouti.
51. Pilot country eligibility criteria had been determined by the sub-committee following its March 2010 meeting which requires low-income status but not LDC status. See http://www.climateinvestmentfunds.org/cif/workingdocuments/1960. The same results are seen with a similar letter by the government of Djibouti.
52. Summary of the co-chairs meeting of the SREP sub-committee November 8, 2010, para.12. See http://www.climateinvestmentfunds.org/cif/sites/climateinvestmentfunds.org/files/SREP%20Co_chairs%20summary_Novemberber_2010_010411.pdf
53. It has been reported that in one country where US$200,000 received via the LDCF to prepare a NAPA (National Adaptation Action Plan), the government outsourced the study to a private institution for US$25,000. The account of the remaining US$175,000 was not made public and it is not clear what was reported to the LDCF.
54. http://www.transparency.org/policy_research/surveys_indices/cpi/2010/results
55. http://www.transparency.org/news_room/latest_news/press_releases/2008/bpi_2008_en
56. http://www.transparency.org/global_priorities/public_contracting/integrity_pacts

8 Corruption in REDD+ schemes: a framework for analysis

Peter Larmour

REDD – reducing carbon emissions from deforestation and forest degradation – promises to be a cheap and effective way of reducing the amount of carbon in the atmosphere. First proposed by the governments of PNG and Costa Rica in 2005, it has been gaining international favour, particularly after the Copenhagen Conference. REDD+ includes other measures to enhance forest carbon stocks. One REDD mechanism – payment for Environment Services (PES) – envisages paying governments or landowners for not cutting down trees (Angelsen, 2009; Howes, 2009 for PNG).

The idea of REDD+ is simple to explain, but it also seems simple to cheat. The international rules are still unclear and – being international – will be hard to enforce. Once in place, the complexity of REDD+ regulations will create its own opportunities for corruption. Markets in carbon credits already provide opportunities for speculation by 'carbon cowboys' (Filer, 2010). The huge flows of money envisaged are attractive to criminals. In any case, forestry has a poor track record for illegality, including corruption. Some of the countries signing up for REDD have poor reputations for corruption in government.

There is a small but growing literature on corruption risks in REDD schemes, often starting from the experience of illegal logging (Tacconi et al., 2009; Brown, 2010; Bofin et al., 2011). Transparency International's upcoming Global Corruption Report will focus on climate change. This chapter proposes a framework summarizing types of diagnoses and cures for corruption and applies it to REDD+[1]. First, to set the scene, it identifies some similarities and differences between the literature on corruption and the literature on REDD.

THE TWO WORLDS OF ANTI-CORRUPTION AND REDD+

First, solutions to deforestation and corruption often seem to lie outside the scope of the problems they address. Thus Angelsen concludes 'broad societal policies and non-forestry policies play a critical role' in deforestation

(2009, p. 137). These could include agriculture or tax policy. Similarly Daniel Kauffman (2005) has argued 'you don't fight corruption by fighting corruption'. It is often more effective to work indirectly, by public sector reform. Even more broadly, just as there is a 'forestry transition' there may be a 'corruption transition' (Grundlach and Paldam, 2008). As countries become richer they become less corrupt: and the causal flow is from income to corruption rather than the other way round. While we can't afford to just let it happen, policy and institutional design should at least go with the grain of these broader social forces.

Second, both make distinctions between developing and developed countries, and are caught up in questions of historical justice, blame and responsibility (Bulkeley and Newell, 2010, pp. 35–53). The UN Framework Convention on Climate Change has different rules for developed countries (so called Annex 1) and developing countries (non-Annex 1) countries. The latter complain that they are being penalized for a problem caused by the former. In the world of anti corruption, Transparency International's (TI) Corruption Perceptions Index shows rich countries to be less corrupt than poor ones, but its Bribe Payers Index shows rich country companies bribing officials in poorer countries. Rapidly industrializing countries like China or Brazil can play victim and perpetrator of climate change and corruption.

Third, both anti-corruption and REDD face problems of translation between levels of government: international, national and domestic. In REDD it is translation from international agreements to action at national and local levels. An unresolved issue is whether REDD payments should be made to national or local governments, or direct to landowners. Corruption control, by contrast has traditionally been a national concern, albeit imperfectly carried out by the police and courts (with some international co-operation through Interpol). TI initially planned to operate only at the international level, dealing with corruption in international business (De Sousa, Larmour and Hindess, 2009). It has been particularly successful in getting international financial institutions like the World Bank to take corruption seriously. But it was quickly persuaded it would lack credibility unless it created national 'chapters' (which in turn typically generate quite local projects).

These three levels are different moral and legal orders, as well as political ones. We are not surprised if nation states follow their own perceived interests, and bend international rules to their own interests. Carried out by individuals at national and local level, such opportunism and hypocrisy looks more like 'corruption'. There may also be differences in values between national elites and local people. Transparency International's focus group research in PNG, for example, finds local people forgiving of corruption by their peers (seen as 'doing it tough' in difficult conditions), while at the same time deeply suspicious of elite misbehaviour (Walton, 2009).[2]

Fourth, both literatures have a practical intent. Their authors are interested in the phenomena of deforestation and corruption, but they want to do something about it (REDD+ and anti-corruption). In the anti-corruption world Robert Klitgaard wrote against the fatalism of earlier arguments that nothing much could be done about the problem. His 1988 book *Controlling Corruption* provided an analytic framework and concrete examples of successful efforts. The contributors to a World Bank volume (Campos and Pradhan, 2007) use his formula 'Corruption = Monopoly + Discretion – Accountability' to identify risks in various sectors of government activity, including in forestry. Similarly, climate change think tanks nudge their researchers towards practical implications and non-pessimistic conclusions. Neither literature sees a tension between theory and practice.

Fifth, the dominant international framework for thinking about both corruption and deforestation has been broadly institutionalist. It emphasizes the choices individuals make within long established 'rules of the game'. Arid Angelsen's work on REDD (for example 2009) generally follows this approach. Susan Rose Ackerman's work (1978, 1999) is particularly influential in the world of anti-corruption (she was also a sometime adviser to the World Bank). This approach is attentive to the paradoxes of government intervention, in concepts such as moral hazard and misaligned or perverse incentives. Its ideas about 'principals' and 'agents' underlay the aborted efforts to reform UK legislation in 2003. It is productively applied to corruption in REDD in Brown (2010), acknowledging Rose- Ackerman's influence. Brown identifies three areas in which corruption is likely to emerge in REDD:

(i) *Manipulating Baselines*. Governments and project promoters perversely 'stand to gain from expanding deforestation in anticipation of the REDD start date to open the greatest wedge from which to gain future credits' (Brown, 2010, p. 261). Brown points out that corrupt officials could argue that they are acting in the national interest in so doing.
(ii) *Doublecounting*, particularly if the future REDD regime allows both national and project level schemes.
(iii) *Verification*, local level officials could be bribed to report that promised reductions in deforestation had taken place when in fact they had not.

To counter these risks Brown proposes design changes and better enforcement (ibid. 263–266). Governments should try to set national baselines over large clearly defined areas, reducing reliance on smaller projects that are less easy to monitor and more easy to double count. They should involve local communities, NGOs and international organizations in monitoring, and draw on international technical assistance. Annex 1 (that is, developed countries) should do more to discourage their own nationals from abetting corruption in developing countries, particularly the US Foreign Corrupt Practices Act, and the OECD convention on Combating Bribery of Public Officials.

In this chapter I want to take a slightly different tack, starting from corruption, and putting the institutional approach into a broader context, with greater emphasis with individual psychology (on the one hand), and broader political concerns (on the other).

Definitions and Types

Whereas the proponents of REDD are inventing new concepts (and acronyms) the writers on 'corruption' are dealing with a long-standing phenomenon about which there are many different academic and popular views. The cost, of course, is that the REDD debate is hard for outsiders to follow, heavy with acronyms, and its principles hard to communicate to those who are supposed to implement it.

'Corruption' – in English at least – is an ancient word, often bandied about and saturated with moralism. The cost of its familiarity is loss of precision, and more moralism than may be warranted. For example, it may be relatively easier to mobilize the population of a country against 'corruption' than it is to mobilize them against 'deforestation'. Everyone is against corruption, though when you look more closely they may have different things in mind. Fewer see the point of avoiding deforestation.

Activists often get impatient with arguments about definition (preferring to get on with fighting the problem). Government officials typically have to run with the definitions available in the national law. The definition of corruption as 'use of public office for private gain' has become the international standard. Brown's sophisticated institutionalist account adopts it without question (2010, p. 237; p. 242). It reflects long-standing liberal suspicions of government (for example, as expressed in Angelsen's 2009 evaluation of the risk in various REDD+ architectures). But it only takes us so far. Its focus on public office can overlook corruption within the private sector or NGOs (both important actors in REDD+). It can also miss corruption that doesn't involve personal enrichment – for example corruption on behalf of family, clan, region or political party (or, perhaps, nation in the international arena where global standards are set). Some of this has been called 'noble cause' corruption.

A political scientist, Mark Warren (2004) argues that the public/private preoccupation is somewhat out of date. It fitted eighteenth-century concerns to protect individual liberties against absolute states. But it has nothing particular to say about democracy and the fact that there are other sources of power in complex modern societies: big corporations and the media, for example. He argues that an overarching meta-norm of democracy is inclusion of those affected by decisions, and he proposes a new definition of corruption as 'duplicitous exclusion'. For example, a job that is supposed to be open to everyone is in fact given to the person that bribes the selectors; or a tender open to all is settled among friends. Warren's definition points to the moral quality of hypocrisy that we find offensive in corruption: officials espouse one (inclusive) value, but practice the other (exclusive). This definition would cover weak or incomplete local consultation processes over REDD+ schemes, as well as such high-level exclusions as the choice of companies to carrying out verification under a Clean Development Mechanism (Shapiro 2010).

Different types of corruption may also impact differently on REDD. The standard distinction made is between petty and grand corruption. The former is small payments made in exchange for services that should have been provided for free. It is often visible and socially accepted (because of low salaries) even if formally illegal. The second is the more secretive, illegal, grand corruption of minister and senior officials, accepting bribes for bending the rules towards the giver. The World Bank and its work on oil revenues have popularized a third term 'policy corruption' whereby leaders change the law to suit their own business interests. It is, by definition, not illegal.

Each type is likely to be present in the world of REDD+, and each requires a different kind of treatment. Small, socially accepted payments may be rife on the forestry frontier, where poorly paid inspectors may rely on the co-operation of people they are supposed to regulate. Grand corruption is more likely over the award of timber concessions (or agriculture concessions which have an indirect effect on the profitability of deforestation). Policy corruption comes in the design of REDD+ schemes, or broader land-use schemes so that they can be tailored to ministers' personal or political interests (Tacconi, Downs and Larmour, 2009). In his study of institutional breakdown in timber booms, Ross (2001) makes a similar distinction between rent seeking (grand corruption, breaking the law) and rent seizing (policy corruption, changing the law, for example the law protecting forests). The personal interest there may be financial (ministers own timber companies, especially in PNG) or political (the votes of farmers keen to clear forests are important to Ross's argument).

While government agencies, private firms and the links between them,

Table 8.1 Causes of and cures for corruption

	Diagnosis	Cure
Behavioural	Bad people	Character, virtue, training
Structural	Bad systems	Public sector reform
Political	Abuse of power	Checks and balances

are the traditional focus of anti-corruption, the institutional world of REDD is more ethically complicated. It includes NGOs, professional law and accounting firms, universities and think tanks. They may be complacent about corruption risks among themselves, in for example recruitment, consultancy and publication. Conflicts of interest are rife (Shapiro, 2010). Loosely defined professional norms may be inadequate to the risks posed by REDD+.

Diagnoses and Cures

Corruption is often described as a 'cancer'. Running with this medical metaphor, we could also ask if it were more like a virus, pointing to issues of infection and resistance. But if it is a virus it might be less treatable. Or is it something you have to live with, or may grow out of (as the transition arguments suggest)? In each case the diagnosis suggests the cure. However, the history of medicine shows that diagnoses and cures are often only loosely connected. Folk remedies persist without much theoretical justification. Some old cures may also work against a new disease. Some popular remedies may do more harm than good.

Table 8.1 sets out a highly simplified summary of diagnoses and cures for corruption. Tables 8.2, 8.3 and 8.4 drill down within it. and speculate how these diagnoses and cures might be relevant to REDD. The risks of corruption may lie in the agencies administering REDD+, including international organizations, the private sector and NGOS. They may also involve the promoters of projects, private loggers, or the owners of land brought under REDD+.

In a third column of Tables 8.2 to 8.4, I have tried to focus on risks and issues that are REDD specific. However, as we have seen, effective cures may be much broader in scope: for example (in PES) involving corruption in government payment systems, or (in REDD+) corruption in agricultural land use.

Table 8.1 identifies three types of theory about corruption: behavioural (or individual); structural (or organizational); and political (including political economy).[3] The oldest argument about corruption, going back

Table 8.2 Behavioural diagnoses and cures

Behavioural theory	Diagnosis	Cure	REDD-specific
Expectancy	Corruption is a calculated choice Actors will calculate chances of shirking or gaming or cheating	Raise perceived chances of detection; reduce perceived costs of compliance; appeal to alternative altruistic motives	Make compliance easy as well as punishing deviance. Make inspection highly visible. Encourage non-financial motives for conservation as well
Equity	Corruption is justified by perceived unfairness in work or society	Reduce – or better justify – perceived inequalities	Take on 'big fish'. Focus initial efforts on relatively equal regions. Reduce wage differentials between international and national organisations
Acceptance	Corruption is the way we do things here: everyone does it	Improve induction, role modelling, staff turnover, role models	Use new rather than historically corrupt agencies. Improve HR practices like induction and training. Invoke community sanctions in local projects

to ancient China, is whether it is caused by 'bad systems' or 'bad people' (Alatas, 1968). There is also a long-standing sense that politics is – perhaps necessarily – corrupt, and relationships between government and business are particularly risky in a mixed economy.

There are subtypes of each general theory set out in Tables 8.2 to 8.4. For example, economic theories tend to assume that individual choices are rational. So does a strand of criminology. But individuals are also concerned with equity and fairness, and some research (Uslaner, 2008) suggests that perceptions of corruption may increase with inequality, through lack of trust.

A confused organizational structure, with unclear or overlapping lines of accountability creates conflicts of interest and provides opportunities for corruption. Viewing work as a process rather than hierarchy identifies choke points at which corrupt payments may be extracted (queues

Table 8.3 Structural diagnoses and cures

Structural theory	Diagnosis	Cure	REDD-specific
Firm structure	Corruption = monopoly + discretion – acccountability	Increase competition; reduce discretion; overlap jurisdictions to allow choice	Distrust monopolistic government funds. Pay attention to local monopolies of verification and approval
Internal organization	Confusion and overlap create opportunities for corruption, particularly by long-serving 'resident experts' within organisations	Simplify; reduce conflicts of interest; separate monitoring from approval and payment; rotate staff	Complexity will increase risks
Work process	Opportunities for corruption occur at different points in process	Sector-by-sector analysis; identify choke points; adopt Sarbanes-Oxley accounting standards.	Monitor flows of cash as well as carbon. Learn from abuse in other national payment systems, like welfare

are particularly vulnerable), (Campos and Pradhan, 2007). In the USA, the Sarbanes Oxley accounting standards require firms to conduct an assessment of their own distinctive internal fraud risks.

Political theories tend to identify power as the villain, and the classic constitutional answer – embodied in the US constitution – is the idea of checks and balances, and mutual oversight, so that the system is better than the individuals in it. Of course as Warren (2004) points out there are now more sources of power than the government. Constitutional checks and balances may be particularly weak in NGOs and international organizations, where a sense of mission, or of powerlessness or of professionalism may make members complacent about (for example) conflicts of interest, recruitment or payment practices.

The next column identifies where these principles apply specifically or distinctively to REDD. In some ways REDD policies will be subject to the same risks as any other government policies, and the same general

Table 8.4 Political diagnoses and cures

Political theory	Diagnosis	Cure	REDD-specific
Constitutional	Corruption is abuse of powert	Checks and balances, independent offices, inspect the inspectors	Link REDD to existing National Integrity System. Extend checks and balances to international actors, firms and NGOS. Inspect the inspectors
Democratic	Corruption is duplicitous exclusion	Open processes, opportunities for appeal, transparency	Advertisement for jobs and contracts in REDD Participatory consultation with landowners and loggers.
Government/ business relations	Governments must anticipate and respond to business needs in mixed economies	Regulate but don't ban lobbying, post separation employment etc.	Design REDD to include loggers. Provide REDD-related local employment. Show revenue benefits to local governments

principles should apply to them. That is why general assessments of a country's governance environment, as carried out in Bofin et al. (2011) are relevant whatever specific form REDD may take. But REDD may pose distinctive or extreme risks and dilemmas, perhaps it takes place in remote areas, or involves particularly corrupt agencies (for example forestry), or because it involves cash payment.

For REDD Table 8.2 suggests inspection and verification regimes, for money as well as carbon, need to be highly visible if they are going to deter rational choices to act corruptly. Schemes may do better in countries or regions that are relatively more equal. Low salaries are often cited as an excuse for petty corruption, but Uslaner (2008) suggests that salary differentials may matter too (including, in a donor-driven world, differentials between international and local pay scales). To the extent that behaviour is driven by a desire for social acceptance, REDD's proponents should try to avoid agencies which have a reputation for corruption (perhaps forestry departments) and try to implement REDD+ through new agencies, or those (perhaps Ministries of Finance) with cleaner reputations. In any case they should pay attention to how new recruits are inducted into REDD+ agencies, and their informal organizational cultures. Kaufman's public administration classic, *The Forest Ranger* (1960) describes how the US Forest Service created an *espirit de corps* amongst its officials, protecting them from the inevitable local pressures they faced working in isolated locations.

In the structural terms of Table 8.3, the arguments about the risk of monopolies support market – rather than fund-based approaches to PES. Within funds, surpluses may be siphoned off in legal but extravagant salaries allowances, car loans, cheap mortgages and so on, for employees, board members and their cronies. It may also be necessary to break down spatial monopolies created during decentralization, which may concentrate PES project approval, verification and payments in a few hands.

The risk of long-established staff capitalizing on their inside knowledge of confused administrative systems can be reduced by rotating staff, and insisting that they take leave due to them (so that their replacements can see what they have been up to). Choke points are different between sectors and work process. Sarbanes Oxley accounting rules require that firms look at their own internal controls, recognising that different firms may face different risks (Coenan, 2008, pp. 192–199).

In PES there may be conflicts of interest if a single official is involved in approval, verification and payment for the environmental services provided. It is easy to imagine corrupt complicity between the promoters of a scheme and the officials approving, verifying and paying for it: ghost schemes, for example. The intangibility of the service compounds the difficulty, as does the remoteness of the locations in which projects may take place, making them hard to inspect. Remedies suggested by Skutsch et al. (2009) include community monitoring, and paying local people for the act of measurement itself rather than hard-to-measure reductions in emissions.

The political theories suggest integration with existing systems of checks and balances (where they exist, for example in the judiciary, or ombudsman system), and the creation of systems of checks and balances in international organisations and NGOs dealing with REDD+. The guards need guarding too.

The theory of government-business relations is more controversial and counterintuitive, but derives from the insight that – in a mixed economy – the private sector carries out what in some ways are 'public' functions: providing jobs, and producing taxable revenue. In a socialist economy these tasks were carried out by public enterprises (Jessop 1990). A capitalist economy cedes initiative to the private sector and politicians who want to get elected on the strength of jobs and public services must anticipate private sector needs. They need to know what these needs are. Their deference to capital is structural, rather than a result of ideological sympathy, or campaign contributions. Hence the political-economic value of lobbying, revolving doors and even campaign contributions, even though they have overtones of corruption. They need to be regulated, rather than driven underground.

CONCLUSIONS

Both REDD and anti-corruption are prospective. REDD is still being designed and – all we have is pilot projects (Sills at al., 2009) and government efforts at 'readiness' (Bofin et al., 2011). Empirically, there is much to be learned from earlier similar schemes to protect the environment: corruption in protected areas, or conservation funds. Brown draws lessons for REDD from the Clean Development Mechanism (2010, pp. 244–252). Barr et al. draw lessons from Indonesia Reforestation Fund (2009).

The anti corruption literature is prospective for different reasons. There has been plenty of corruption in the past, but it has often been invisible. Occasionally it erupts in a scandal, and is investigated by a commission of inquiry. Otherwise anti-corruption reformers tend to put their efforts into prevention of future corruption, through improved systems, selection and training. For an NGO like Transparency International, prevention is also more prudent than chasing prominent but dangerous individuals who have been shown to be corrupt in the past.

NOTES

1. The paper on which this chapter is based was produced as part of Australia Research Council Grant with Drs Luca Tacconi, Frank Jotzo and Emma Aisbett, and doctoral students Fiona Downs and Patrick Doupe. The framework was developed with collaborators in the NSW Independent Commission Against Corruption, particularly Dr Robert Waldersee, Dr Michael Nest and Alexandra Mills (though none of them is responsible for the use I am putting it to here). I am also grateful to CIFOR for funding my participation in a panel on 'Following the Money' at the 14th International Anti Corruption Conference in Bangkok, in November 2010. I am also grateful for comments from Crawford School colleagues at a research workshop in December 2010.
2. Anglesen (2009) talks in terms of the 3 Es (Efficiency, Effectiveness, and Equity), and it may be (as an empirical matter) that there is a difference in the relative weight given to these values between different REDD+ actors, and at different levels of government. Appeals to these ethical principles may also become highly politicized and opportunistic. For example, 'compensation' is an important equity principle in REDD (owners being compensated for lost opportunities) and, for example, in PNG it is a highly valued

principle of conflict resolution. However, there is also a PNG history of inflated compensation claims and more recent examples of corrupt government layers getting a slice of claims they settle out of court.

3. Whereas institutional theories distinguish individuals from institutions, in the tables I have introduced a third term 'politics'. While it is sensible to talk about political institutions (Parliament elections etc.), the word institution suggests a normative consensus that cannot be taken for granted (Stoker, 2006, pp. 5–7), particularly in developing counties. 'Politics' points to the processes of bargaining and confrontation that take place when values are not shared, and to the issue of power, and its abuse, which is important in understanding corruption. Dealing with politics explicitly within the table (rather than leaving it disruptively outside) helps to suggest cures.

BIBLIOGRAPHY

Alatas, S. (1968), *The Sociology of Corruption*, Singapore: D. Moore Press.

Angelsen, A. (ed.) (2009), *Realising REDD+: National Strategy and Policy Options*, Bogor: CIFOR.

Barr, C., A. Dermawan, H. Purnomo and H. Komarudin (2009), 'Readiness for REDD: Financial Governance and lessons from Indonesia's Reforestation Fund (RF)', *CIFOR Infobriefs*, **20**(November), Bogor: CIFOR.

Bauhr, M. (2009), 'Corruption in the Carbon Market: International Organizations, Transparency and the Clash of Values', Working Paper Series, **15**, University of Gothenberg: The Quality of Government Institute.

Bofin, P., M. du Preez, A. Standing and A. Williams (2011), 'REDD Integrity: Addressing governance and corruption challenges in schemes for reducing emissions from deforestation and forest degradation (REDD)', U4 Report February, 1 CHR, Michelsen Institute and U4 Anti-Corruption Resource Centre.

Brown, M. (2010), 'Limiting corrupt incentives in a global REDD regime', *Ecology Law Quarterly*, **37**, 237–68.

Bulkeley, H. and P. Newell (2010), *Governing Climate Change*, Global Institutions Series, Abingdon: Routledge.

Campos, E. and S. Pradhan (2007), *The Many Faces of Corruption: Tracking Vulnerabilities at Sectoral Level*, Washington: The World Bank.

Coenan, T. (2008), *Essentials of Corporate Fraud*, New Jersey: Wiley and Sons.

De Sousa, L., P. Larmour and B. Hindess (eds) (2009), *Governments, NGOs and Anti-Corruption: the New Integrity Warriors*, London: Routledge.

Doig, A. (1995), 'Good government and sustainable anti-corruption strategies: a role for independent anti-corruption agencies?', *Public Administration and Development*, **15**, 151–65.

Filer, C. (2010), 'The carbon cult in Papua New Guinea', Paper presented to the forests of Oceania Working Session, Association for Social Anthropology in Oceania.

Grundlach E. and M. Paldam (2008), 'The transition of corruption: from poverty to honesty', Working Paper No. 1411, Durstenbrook: Kiel Institute for the World Economy.

Howes, S. (2009), 'Cheap but not easy: the reduction of greenhouse gas emissions from deforestation and forest degradation in Papua New Guinea', *Pacific Economic Bulletin*, **24**(1), 130–43.

Huther, J. and A. Shah (2000), 'Anti corruption policies and programs: a framework for analysis', Working Paper, Washington: The World Bank.

Jessop, M. (1990), *State theory: Putting the Capitalist State in its Place*, Philadelphia: Penn State Press.

Kaufman, H. (1960), *The Forest Ranger: A Study in Administrative Behavior*, Washington: Resources for the Future Press.

Kaufmann, D. (2005), 'Back to basics: 10 myths about governance and corruption', *Finance and Development*, **42**(3).
Klitgaard, R. (1988) *Controlling Corruption*, Berkeley: University of California Press.
Klitgaard, R. (1997), 'Cleaning up and reinvigorating the civil service', *Public Administration and Development*, **17**, 487–509.
Rose-Ackerman, S. (1978), *Corruption: a Study of Political Economy*, New York: Academic Press.
Rose-Ackerman, S. (1999), *Corruption and Government: Causes Consequences and Reform*, Cambridge and New York: Cambridge University Press.
Ross, M. (2001), *Timber Booms and Institutional Breakdown in South East Asia*, Cambridge: Cambridge University Press.
Sills, E., E. Madeira, W. Sunderlin and S. Wertz-Kanounnikoff (2009), 'The evolving landscape of REDD+ projects' in A. Angelsen (ed.), *Realising REDD+: National Strategy and Policy Options*, Bogor: Centre for International Forestry Research, 265–80.
Spector, B., M. Johnston and P. Dininio (2005), 'Learning across cases: trends in anti-corruption strategies', in B. Spector (ed.), *Fighting Corruption in Developing Countries: Strategies and Analysis*, Bloomfield: Kumarian.
Shapiro, M. (2010), 'Conning the climate', *Harpers Magazine*, 31–9.
Skutsch, M., P. Laake, E. Zahabu, B. Karky and P. Phartiyal (2009), 'Community monitoring in REDD+' in A. Angelsen (ed.), *Realising REDD+: National Strategy and Policy Options*, Bogor: CIFOR, 101–112.
Stoker, G. (2006), *Why Politics Matters: Making Democracy Work*, Basingstoke: Palgrave Macmillan.
Tacconi, L., F. Downs and P. Larmour (2009), 'Anti-corruption policies in the forest sector and REDD+', in A. Angelsen (ed.), *Realising REDD+: National Strategy and Policy Options*, Bogor: CIFOR, 163–74.
Uslaner, E. (2008) *Corruption, Inequality and the Rule of Law*, Cambridge: Cambridge University Press.
Walton, G. (2009), 'Rural peoples' perceptions of corruption in Papua New Guinea', Port Moresby: Transparency International (PNG) (March).
Warren, M. (2004), 'What does corruption mean in a democracy', *American Journal of Political Science*, **48**(2), 328–43.

9 Corruption and crime in forestry[1]

William B. Magrath

1. INTRODUCTION

One of the most profound and far-reaching environmental changes of the last 50 years was the loss of around 25 per cent of the world's forest area. Concentrated in the tropics, but also involving forests in temperate and boreal areas, deforestation is having global consequences which science and policymakers are still just beginning to recognize. These include an untold loss of biological and genetic diversity with potentially long-term consequences for agriculture and food security and for medicine and human health; a contribution of perhaps one-fifth of the atmospheric load of greenhouse gases that contribute to global warming and climate change; disruption to the lives and livelihoods of many of mankind's most marginalized and disenfranchised cultures and people; and loss of habitat for thousands of species of plants and animals. Going along with deforestation, the forestry sector in the developing world falls short in contributing as it should to social and economic development. Public forest revenues seldom achieve reasonable targets; growth and employment in forest-based industry is frequently distorted and inefficient; the quality of forest science and technology lags badly behind that of other agricultural and natural resource sectors. Remarkably these problems persist; concerted international development assistance efforts, years of international negotiations and consultations and dedicated efforts by countless activists and civil society organizations, have not succeeded in protecting forest resources. Understanding the failure of forestry to thrive is therefore a pressing environmental policy research problem and one that has attracted growing attention.

One of the most important, and surprisingly relatively recent, insights in the forest policy literature and policy discourse is that much of the weakness of forestry is literally, as well as figuratively, a crime. Virtually every country in the world has established land-use plans, forest management programmes and policies, timber taxation and revenue systems and other legal instruments to protect forests and related resources and to provide for managed, controlled and legitimate forest exploitation. It is being increasingly recognized and openly acknowledged that, along with the benign forces that help to drive loss of forest cover, corruption and crime come together in forestry and are together prime drivers of deforestation and the general failure of forestry. The duality of crime and corruption is a particularly important characteristic of the forestry sector: persistent crime on the scale to be observed in the forestry sector cannot occur and be sustained without corruption as an enabler and, in the same way, corruption arises and persists because criminal gains are sufficient to support both bribers and bribe takers.

This chapter selectively reviews some key recent findings about crime and corruption in developing country forestry. Section 2 describes forestry as a special case of the more general problem of the 'resource curse'. The notion of the resource curse refers to the observation that countries seemingly well-endowed with valuable natural resources tend to perform poorly in comparison with less well-endowed countries. Along with other contributors, corruption is an important ingredient to the resource curse problem. As will be discussed, among the consequences of corruption in forestry is the economically inefficient land use and erosion of forestry institutions' technical ability to effectively regulate forest use. Furthermore, a key implication of this is that solutions to crime and corruption will need to arise from outside the forestry sector as traditionally conceived. Paradoxically, however, sustained progress against forest crime and corruption requires technical progress within the forestry sector. Section 3 concludes by discussing principles for the situational prevention of illegal logging at the forest management unit level and by reviewing the key policy and research recommendations emerging from research on forest corruption and crime in developing countries. The balance of this introduction reviews evidence on the significance and nature of the problem.

Forest crime, including illicit activities like illegal logging, illegal occupation of forest land, woodlands arson, wildlife poaching, and encroachment, on both public and private forests and corruption, is rampant worldwide. It is particularly troubling in developing countries, where illegal logging in public lands alone causes estimated losses in assets and revenue in excess of US$10 billion annually – more than eight times the total official development assistance dedicated to the sustainable management of forests. As much as US$5 billion is lost annually to governments due to evaded taxes and royalties, on legally sanctioned logging. Within developing countries, one billion extremely poor people depend upon forests for part of their livelihoods, and as many as 350 million people living in and around forests are heavily dependent on them for their livelihood and security. These vulnerable groups are at risk from illegal logging and removals of timber and non-timber products from the forests. Moreover, violations of protected areas boundaries threaten the conservation of forest resources and biodiversity. Legitimate forest enterprises are subjected to unfair competition through price undercutting and discouraged from making socially and environmentally responsible investments in the sector.

Illegal logging distorts the marketplace and legitimate forest enterprises are subjected to unfair competition through price undercutting and discouraged from making socially and environmentally responsible investments into the sector. An analysis for the US estimates that domestic roundwood prices would be 2 to 4 per cent higher if 'suspicious' wood production were eliminated. In the absence of competition from illegal producers, the US would be able to increase its exports of wood products by about US$460 million per year. Illegal forest operations can be linked to conflicts and wars.

Estimating the extent of illegal logging and trade in illegal timber and timber products presents a number of problems, and regardless of the definitions and methodology used, the exact magnitude cannot be known with certainty. Speculation about illegal activity can, nevertheless, be examined in a rigorous fashion using a number of well-accepted tools and methods. Discrepancies in wood supply-demand balances, import-export statistics, price trends, revenue realization, forest cover change estimates, and other 'red flags' are all faulty, in one way or another, indicators and measures of illegal logging. Available data, however, are sufficient to illustrate the magnitude of the problem. Table 9.1 provides estimates of illegal logging as a percentage of total wood harvest in 17 countries. Illegal logging in these countries is believed to range from 10 to 15 per cent of total harvest in North-West Russia to up to 80 per cent of total harvest in Bolivia and Peru and 90 per cent in Cambodia.

In an in-depth, multi-country study of illegal logging, Seneca Creek Associates (2004) found that the value of suspicious wood products worldwide may be as high as US$23 billion. Of the total of illegal timber, the study estimates that about US$5 billion enters world trade (Table 9.2), representing as much as 10 per cent of the value of global trade of primary wood products. The study also estimates that 12 per cent of global softwood roundwood exports and as much as 17 per cent of global hardwood roundwood exports are of suspicious origin. Less than 4 per cent of global trade in softwood lumber and plywood originates with timber of suspicious origin, but as much as 23 per cent of hardwood lumber exports, and 30 per cent of hardwood plywood exports might be considered suspicious. Economic analysis suggests that this illegal material depresses world wood prices by 7 to 16 per cent on average.

There is a range of other illicit activities associated with timber harvesting and trade, beyond cutting trees where and when it is proscribed. Such

Table 9.1 Indicative estimates of illegal logging in selected countries (various years)

Country	% of total production	(000) Cubic meters
Bolivia	80	465
Brazil	20–47	33 620–79 000
Cambodia	90	900
Cameroon	50	1605
Colombia	42	1365
Ecuador	70	950
Gabon	70	2520
Ghana	60	725
Indonesia	70–80	7825–8945
Laos	45	310
Malaysia	Up to 35	Up to 7210
Myanmar	50	1940
Papua New Guinea	70	2100
Peru	80	1510
Russia	10–15 (North-West) 50 (Far East)	23 290
Thailand	40	15
Vietnam	20–40	500–1000

Sources: Savcor Indufor Oy (2004), FAO (2006) and European Forest Institute (2005).

Table 9.2 Global volume and value of suspicious wood products

	Volume (000 m^3)	Value (US$ million)
Production		
Roundwood	130 994	12 053
Lumber	25 236	6917
Plywood	9957	3535
Sub-total		**22 505**
Imports		
Roundwood	19 973	1624
Lumber	5780	1477
Plywood	5125	1820
Sub-total		**4921**
Exports		
Roundwood	17 967	1231
Lumber	6928	1846
Plywood	5237	1718
Sub-total		**4795**

Source: Adapted from Seneca Creek Associates (2004).

associated activities include irregular timber sales, corruption in the award of concessions and service contracting; evasion of taxes, royalties and other fees by enterprises or by communities or private forest owners; circumvention of labor laws; and unauthorized wood processing. Corruption and other financial crime often involve money laundering, adding another dimension to the constellation of what should be considered forest crime. Other important forest-related crimes that cannot be discussed here due to lack of space include illegal hunting and wildlife trade, wildland arson, and encroachment and illegal forest clearance.

2. THE NATURAL RESOURCE CURSE

Natural resource wealth, it would seem, ought to provide a growth advantage to a developing country, and should certainly not retard development. Nevertheless, numerous studies have found a distinct and strong negative correlation between resource wealth and growth. The apparently paradoxical observation that development seems to lag in many countries well-endowed with natural resources, although primarily arising from consideration of oil and mineral-rich countries, provides a potential link between the problems of illegal logging and corruption.

Explanations of the resource curse include a variety of mechanisms such as 'rentier effects' and (anti) 'modernization effects' (Ross, 2001),[2] the 'Dutch disease' and others. The rentier effect occurs in states where national budgets based on revenues from the export of natural resources allow governments to mollify dissent (buy off critics through lavish infrastructure projects or outright graft), avoid accountability pressures (because taxes are low), and repress opposition movements, independent business groups, and civil society organizations. This links to the argument that states dependent on natural resources also tend to thwart secular modernization pressures – for example higher levels of urbanization, education, and occupational specialization – because budget revenues are derived from a small workforce that deploys sophisticated technical skills that can only be acquired abroad (oil is largely extracted by foreign, not domestic, firms).

Damania, Deacon and Bulte (2005) expand on these concepts, and Ross (2001) and Kishor and Damania (2007) specifically focus on the forestry sector. Ross develops a distinction between 'rent seeking' and 'rent seizing' and argues that an additional dimension of the resource curse that affects forestry are forces that are unleashed to lead to erosion of the capacity of forestry agencies to enforce controls on resource use. Kishor and Damania (2007) assert that 'corruption in the forest sector is . . . contagious and weakens governance through other segments of the economy'.

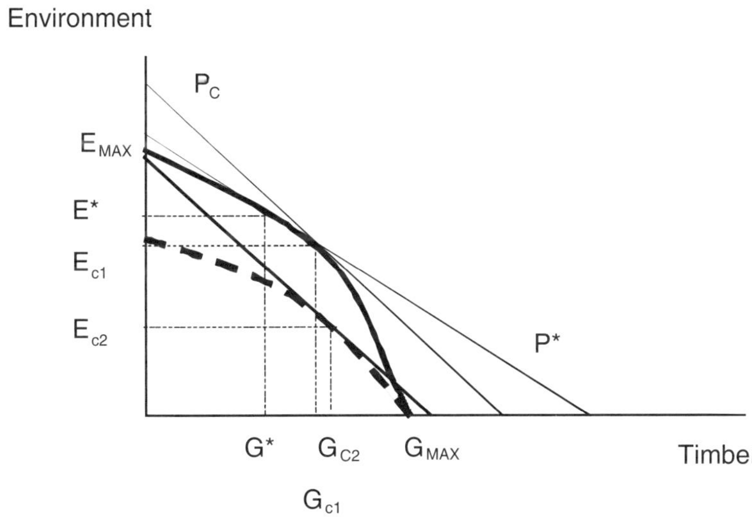

Figure 9.1 *Static and dynamic institutional erosion*

Dauvergne (2001) argues that strategic bargains and compromises between loggers and their sociopolitical allies dilute and deflect environmental reforms, particularly informal networks of loggers, private, state officials (politicians, bureaucrats, and military officers), societal powerbrokers, and other corporate executives (firms along the trade chain, including affiliates and financiers). The aggregate effect he says is to steer reforms toward the formal rules of governance – international agreements, public corporate language and, state policies – and away from the informal elements – the expected and accepted norms that arise from webs of state-business alliances. This strengthens formal rules but allows an erosion of actual performance producing a widening gap between the rules/rhetoric and actual norms/practices on the ground.

One suggestion in the 'resource curse' literature (Ross, 2001; Kishor and Damania, 2007) is that a consequence of corruption for forestry and natural resource management agencies could be erosion of institutional capacity. This is an important observation because a primary focus of development assistance to forestry agencies is precisely the development of institutional capacity, and if corruption is both widespread and a factor that by itself degrades capacity, the likely success of development efforts is obviously called into question.

Figure 9.1 illustrates how institutional erosion could occur. A given forested landscape has some potential for production of both unpriced environmental goods and services and of timber. Over the relevant range, increasing environmental output requires a sacrifice of timber output and vice versa. The convex curve E_{MAX} G_{MAX} represents the feasible maximum combinations of environmental and timber production that can be generated under the control of a regulatory agency. A regulatory entity operating in the social interest will evaluate the tradeoff between environmental impacts and production of timber and would seek to guide production to G*, E* where the social value of the marginal sacrifice of environmental quality equates with the social value of the marginal gain of timber (denoted by the slope of the price line P^*).

Now consider regulation with corruption. Timber interests will through bribes, political influence and other measures lead the agency to regulate against a lower valuation of the tradeoff between timber and environmental quality (P_C). In the first instance, this will lead to production at G_{ci}, E_{ci}, a socially excessive amount of timber and lower than socially optimal environmental quality.

The overproduction of timber and the under production of environmental quality by a corrupt agency is an intuitive result, but it is not the end of the resource curse analysis of institutional erosion. The dynamic effect is shown in Figure 9.1 as a downward pivot of the production possibilities frontier from E_{MAX} G_{MAX} to one such as that shown by the dotted line. As a result of these dynamics, the sector will always produce less environmental quality but impacts on timber output are ambiguous. As suggested by Ross (2001), over time, as stakeholders in the agency respond to the priorities implied by the corrupt opportunities and preferences, there is not just a shift along the production surface, but also to a decline in the capacity of the agency to deliver environmental quality. This decline in capacity is asymmetric with respect to the ability of the agency to achieve environmental and commodity outputs. For example, in a corrupt agency environment, facilities and equipment dedicated to water quality monitoring will be neglected, but capacity related to timber harvest scheduling, for example, would be retained. A similar and perhaps more potent impact would be felt through impact on the motivation of staff whether directly corrupt or not, who will observe differential opportunities for career development and satisfaction. Individuals with personal interest and dedication to environment will either leave the agency or not be attracted to it in the first place.

Analysis of multi-country case studies, such as Ross's review of experience in Malaysia, the Philippines and Indonesia seem to support the notion of institutional erosion. In all these countries, the capacity of forestry agencies seems to have declined over periods in which corruption and state capture has been significant. This institutional erosion is one of the more insidious results of corruption in natural resource sectors and from a policy response perspective one of the most troublesome. As discussed in Section 3, responding to crime and corruption in forestry requires institutions capable of performing relatively complex technical tasks and conducting transactions to a reasonable commercial standard. With forestry agencies subject to erosion from within due to the resource curse, governments and development agencies are confronted with a race between the forces on institutional erosion and their ability to develop skills and capacity.

Land Allocation Effects of Collusive and Non-collusive Corruption in Forestry

Before developing on those issues, it is useful to consider the ways in which different types of corruption can affect deforestation, usually considered the most important measure of forestry performance. Among the most important considerations about corruption, as it affects any sector, are its impacts on resource allocation, prices and the distribution of economic surplus. Much of the public sector corruption that receives attention stems from the ability of officials to manipulate the provision of services, authorization or other goods or services. Prototypically the corrupt official will demand a bribe or other inducement from the potential public service client. While there are numerous typologies and classifications of kinds of corruption, in the case of the forestry sector it is particularly useful to reflect on the differing implications of two contrasting classes of corruption; collusive and non-collusive corruption.[3] The distinction between the two is based on degree of joint interest between and among the bribe payer and the bribe taker. Collusive corruption occurs when both the official and the provider of the corrupt payment together gain from the corrupt transaction. When a forestry official permits a logger to exceed an environmentally sustainable harvest limit, or to breach some other harvest rule, they are colluding for mutual gain. A forestry official demanding a bribe from a logger for allowing the logger to proceed with an otherwise legal and sustainable operation is an example of non-collusive corruption. Non-collusive corruption in forestry is frequently seen in what are usually termed petty corruption cases, such as demands for bribes at road checkpoints.

Non-collusive corruption is essentially a matter of distribution of economic surplus via quasi-monopoly power. Non-collusive corruption in forestry tends to be a tax on logging and will, as illustrated below, tend to reduce deforestation. Significantly, the gain in the case of collusive corruption in forestry will come at the public's expense in the form of environmental degradation or excessive resource depletion, and is the principal

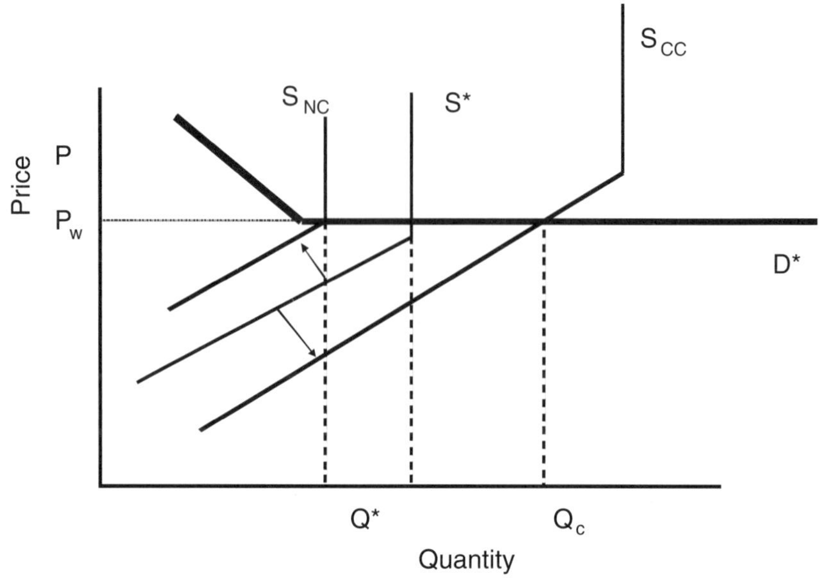

Figure 9.2 Collusive and non-collusive corruption

way in which forestry and natural resource-based corruption is distinct from corruption in most other settings. Cases of collusive corruption in forestry would often be termed examples of state capture.

Figure 9.2 shows how collusive and non-collusive corruption differ in driving outcomes in a timber and forestry land market. The supply of timber from a region without corruption is shown as S*. In typical forestry economics fashion, S* rises as a function of increasing marginal cost of access and extraction until reaching a sustainable harvest constraint at Q* at which point the supply curve turns vertical. For simplicity, Figure 9.2 illustrates a situation where high value local demand is satisfied and marginal price is set by a perfectly elastic world price. As usual, the area above the supply curve and below the demand curve represent social surplus and the area below the supply curve bounded by the equilibrium quantity indicate social costs, in this case costs of operations and the user and environmental cost of harvesting standing timber. At Q*, the assumed annual allowable cut, user cost is zero because it equates to the optimal time to harvest. To the right of Q* user costs are positive and increasing with Q.

Non-collusive corruption is shown in Figure 9.2 as an upward shift of the Supply curve from S* to S_{NC}. This is the sort of corruption that occurs when an inspector threatens to withhold an otherwise legitimate permit, and is non-collusive in the sense that the interests of the corrupt official and the client are not aligned. The corrupt official gains, the provider of the corrupt payment loses and this is effectively a tax on logging. From an environmental perspective, non-collusive corruption can be considered desirable, and possibly even appealing.

Collusive corruption, by contrast, is illustrated by the shift from S* to S_{CC}. This would occur when a forestry official uses their authority to license logging in excess of the sustainable volume. The collusion of the official and the logger is leading to excessive logging and imposing costs on society in the form of excessive depletion and environmental damage.

That corruption can lead to either increases or decreases in logging and deforestation is often not recognized in discussions of forest policy, but it is a critical observation. While corruption in forestry and other natural resource sectors may be non-collusive, collusive corruption is probably of greater interest and of special policy significance.

3. SITUATIONAL CRIME PREVENTION TECHNIQUES IN FORESTRY

While much recent forestry literature and debate focuses on governance and corruption themes, relatively little has made a specific bridge to the literature on crime and criminology. As suggested above, corruption occurs in forestry largely to permit illegal activity and much of the illegal activity of real policy concern is undertaken with corruption as a prime modality. The *prevention, detection, suppression and restoration* framework provides a practical organizing framework for both diagnostics and policy prescriptions (Figure 9.3). Detection, suppression and recovery from illegal logging and forestry corruption involve special issues and techniques that are beyond the scope of this chapter.[4]

Modern criminological theory proposes three general causes of crime: *structural, psychological* and *situational*. So-called structural causes of

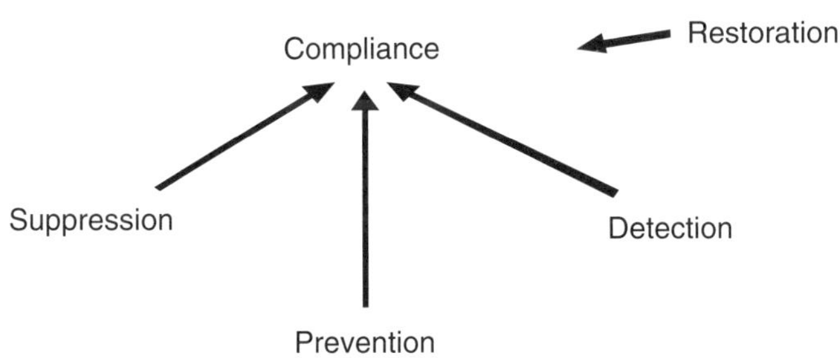

Figure 9.3 Operational components of a forest law enforcement regime

crime are those that derive from the ways in which societies are organized and structured. Economic disparities between rich and poor, gaps between urban and rural populations, between powerful and disenfranchized groups or between racial and ethnic groups are the kinds of structural features of a society that can contribute to crime. In the discussions on forestry, one of the most frequently cited root causes of deforestation is poverty. However, it needs to be recognized that poverty-driven illegality may also be due to unclear property rights or mismatch between customary and formal institutionalized rights; not criminal intent per se.

Differentials in power can also contribute to crime. In the case of forestry, it is often noted that rich and powerful elites are able to exploit their positions and privileges to take advantage of valuable natural resources. Greed-based crime can involve corruption or can be carried out through agents, operatives or contractors. There can obviously be close connection between the issues of overall governance and those that influence the ways that the distribution of power in a society can contribute to crime and corruption. Whatever the specific socio-structural causes of crime in any particular setting, the essential preventive response is social change. Poverty reduction through rural and agricultural development, job creation policies and programmes, provisions of social services and forms of support to disadvantaged groups and communities may be justified on their own merits. But they can also be justified as a partial response to forest crimes, just as they are justified in many countries as part of a response to urban crime and violence.

Studies of illegal logging at the local scale are limited in number, and while each case is unique, together they show the relevance of socio-political factors to the occurrence of illegal logging on a large scale. Casson and Obidinski (2002) discuss the changing dynamics of the 'illegal' logging sector in the two districts of Berau, East Kalimantan and Kotawaringin Timur, Central Kalimantan in a way that parallels Dauvergne. They show that 'illegal' logging is not a simple case of criminality, but a complex economic and political system involving multiple stakeholders. McCarthy (2000) describes illegal logging in south Aceh in similar terms. Based on research from 1996–1999, he examines the institutional arrangements associated with illegal logging, explores how logging networks emerge, how they operate, and how they respond to economic and political changes as well as interventions by outside conservation agencies. He shows how political, economic and social exchanges have emerged around illegal logging, creating institutionalized relationships that operate contrary to formal state legal norms. Extra-legal logging generates revenue for local networks and the district budget and offers impoverished villagers viable survival strategies while endangering the forest. McElwee (2004) discusses illegal logging in Vietnam in similar terms. While the state

Table 9.3 Examples of situational crime prevention techniques

Increasing effort	*Increasing risks*	*Reducing reward*
Target hardening	Entry/exit screening	Target removal
Access control	Formal surveillance	Property identification
Deflecting offenders	Employee surveillance	Removing inducements
Controlling means	Natural surveillance	Rule-setting

Source: Based on Pease (1997).

continues to blame local people for illegal logging and attendant deforestation, she shows that perceived criminal and corrupt actions by the government have significantly contributed to the problem. She describes that the way local people speak of 'illegal loggers' explain their actions in terms of social justice, poverty alleviation, and local control, rather than in the state's terms of 'illegality'.

While structural and psychological theories of crime may explain some crimes, neither can explain nor help prevent all crimes. In any case, neither provides much guidance or advice to the forest manager. In contrast, *circumstantial* or *situational theories* of crime generally posit that crime is opportunistic and can occur when the environment permits. Situational crime prevention has been defined as: 'a pre-emptive approach that relies not on improving society or its institutions, but simply on reducing opportunities for crime' (Clarke, 1992). Many of the generic crime prevention techniques listed in Table 9.3 can be concretely applied in forestry, and many are within the scope of control of forest managers. Measures to increase effort, which include target hardening and access control, directly raise the costs of crime by making it physically more difficult. Examples include stronger gates and locks and higher fences. These measures could include even more exacting and demanding processes that make crime more costly and difficult.

Situational crime prevention at the Forestry Management Unit (FMU) level is discussed at length by Magrath et al. (2007) who highlighted four basic dimensions of FMU-level crime prevention practices:

- Attention to the extent to which basic forest management planning decisions, such as compartment and coupe layout, road development, harvest scheduling and choice of silvicultural system are made in recognition of their impacts on and connections to threats and vulnerabilities.
- Effort exerted to implement *access controls* to manage entry and exit to and from the FMU and to limit the presence of potential criminal

threats while permitting access to legitimate users. These can range from physical barriers, to signage systems, to surveillance and patrols.

- Adoption of timber transaction processes and controls, with appropriate separation of financial management responsibilities from physical resource custody, chain-of-custody hardware and software systems, accounting controls and related systems to minimize risks of fraud and corruption.
- Integrated security planning, training and assignment of management and functional responsibilities for resource protection.

Magrath et al. (2007) also discussed ways in which public policies and forest-use contractual arrangements can promote or hinder adoption of enhanced security practices at the FMU level. These include whether forest concession fee and royalty arrangements indemnify managers from losses due to theft versus obligating concessionaires to pay for all removals whether by the concession or by illegal third parties; whether security performance is explicitly factored into concession renewal decisions; and whether concession contracts and forest management planning regulations specifically require preparation of written security plans.

Policy and Operational Recommendations

Public policies that promote good governance generally, and good forestry more particularly, should be the starting point for reforms to promote a proactive approach to timber and timber land security. Timber theft prevention needs to build on a fundamentally sound approach to resource management. Similarly, the issues related to fraud prevention in timber transactions are best approached on the basis of fundamentally sound commercial practices in the conduct of timber sales. Building on these general frameworks, there are many possibilities, including options discussed below, to shape public policies to support asset security in forestry by shifting the incentives that drive resource allocation and behavior by managers and resource users.

Incorporate security in design of tenures and licences

Much of the world's forest land, especially areas with commercial timber potential, are owned and managed by government agencies. However, one of the most significant trends underway in forestry globally is the restructuring of forest and forest land tenure arrangements.

For instance, in much of South Asia, recognition that local communities can have strong interest in resource protection and can be better positioned than government agencies to control illegal grazing and firewood collection has been an important driver behind the expansion of social and community forestry. In contrast, in Indonesia, decentralization of control over forest resources was done with no attention to security implications – with disastrous consequences.

While resource protection implications have been implicit in some forest tenure reform discussions, they have not received the attention they deserve. Simply put, forest resources should not be placed under the control of those unable to provide for their security and protection. This principle should be applied to public agencies as well as to private and community entities. In a broad range of circumstances, putting a premium on forest protection could be expected to favour decentralized and community-oriented tenures.

Consider security performance in licence award and renewal

An extension of the principle of integrating consideration of security in the design of tenure systems should be to incorporate security in the determination of individual award and renewal decisions. Corporate histories or 'track records' in relation to protection performance should be explicit criteria in the evaluation of bids and applications for forest concessions and logging licences. International firms should be required to provide documentation of their security performance in other jurisdictions in which they operate, and their claims should be verified with the relevant authorities. Concessionaires and licensees also should be evaluated regularly on their resource protection performance and on the quality of their prevention planning. Furthermore, satisfactory performance should be a condition for extension or renewal.

Require standards and security planning

The planning and operational control obligations that governments place on private forestry operations vary and often could be criticized as excessively onerous and arcane. However, when timber theft is pervasive and persistent, governments should require concessionaires and licensees to prepare and submit for approval timber theft prevention or comparable security plans. Introduction of this kind of requirement could be on the same basis as are the plans required for infrastructure, harvesting, environmental impact, or other more conventional topics. This would be within the existing jurisdiction and discretion of virtually any Minister of Forestry.

Deduct illegal harvest from AAC (Annual Allowable Cut) and include in royalty and fee assessments

Governments should not indemnify concessionaires and licensees from the results of poor security performance. Especially in the case of long-term forest management concessions arrangements, in which resource protection is or ought to be a specific obligation, resources lost due to illegal activities, whether caused by the concessionaire or by others, should be deducted from the concessionaire's authorized harvest volume. Where contracts permit, in certain circumstances, concessionaires also should be held liable for royalties, fees and other charges on resources lost due to illegal activity.

Emerging Research Priorities

What also quickly becomes apparent from the study of corruption and crime in forestry is that the forestry sector, perhaps like many other sectors, encompasses the full range of human frailties, weaknesses and susceptibilities to greed and avarice. The explicit study of crime and corruption in forestry is a relatively new field. As is inevitable in any inquiry into illicit activities, data and information is limited and any claim or representation needs to be looked at with suspicion and doubt. In forestry, data problems are probably even more severe than in many other areas for several reasons. Forests themselves are highly diverse and difficult to measure and describe in an easy to understand and standardized manner. Answering even seemingly basic questions, such as 'how much forest does a country have?' can become an incredibly complicated matter of varied definitions, criteria, data and interpretation. Still, several key themes deserving priority for policy research emerge:

Sectorally targeted versus general governance reforms. Forestry-related corruption seldom occurs in isolation and often appears to be of similar magnitude and consequence as corruption across the economy and as in other economically important sectors. The unanswered strategic question that this poses is whether forestry, or for that matter any other sector-specific entry point either is, or under some conditions could be, desirable or particularly promising for governance reforms.

Criminal justice sanctions versus compatible incentives. An important message from the institutional economics literature is that institutional innovations are much more likely to succeed and persist when the motivations of actors are aligned. The extent to which, however, there is scope for incentive compatible innovations in dealing with forestry corruption is as yet unclear. Where conditions permit there is probably large scope for design of systems that distribute rights to forest resources in ways that insulate from corruption risks. More problematic are situations where forest sector structures, such as tenure, fiscal systems, regulatory arrangements and trade and industry patterns have been instituted on the basis of prior forms of rent capture, such as in Cambodia, Papua New Guinea,

Indonesia and the Solomon Islands. To the extent that systems with pathological features are ensconced, the scope for incentive compatible reforms may be more limited. In such cases, it may be necessary to resort to mechanisms that confront opposing motivations and incentives, such as criminal prosecutions. Further, from among the possible legal alternatives that might be available, such as prosecution under forestry, corruption, money laundering or other criminal provisions, there is little analysis on which to base a strategy.

Pathways to reform. One finding from the literature review is the commonality of natural resource corruption in a wide range of countries, including very significant levels of corruption during earlier phases of development in what are today developed countries with reasonable natural resource governance. Allegations of corruption and forest crime were, for example, driving forces in the Progressive Era reforms in the United States that included establishment of the US Forest Service. Similar experiences have been noted in other countries. Less well understood are the processes by which reform occurred, and there is very limited analysis of the transferability of experience to today's developing countries.

Professionalism and ethics. So far during the study, most emphasis has been placed on economic and policy constructs, and limited attention has been given to cultural and ethical aspects as they may change and evolve and affect forestry corruption and reform prospects. The particular professional culture of forestry may, in addition, present special consideration, either supportive or constraining, in respect of anti-corruption. More work is needed to consider and understand these aspects so that options related to education, development of training in ethics can be considered and integrated into forestry curricula, in-service training and staff selection and promotion criteria.

Connections between technical, managerial and oversight mechanisms. Efforts to develop technical forestry practice have often failed in corrupt environments and are sometimes dismissed as unworkable precisely because of the capture of forestry practice by corrupt elements. Work on timber theft prevention, however, suggests that internal and external controls can be critical instruments for addressing corruption and fraud in timber transactions. An important lesson from this work is that standardized, consistent and high-quality technical and commercial practices are needed to permit the detection of misfeasance in timber transactions. As a practical matter, without predictability in respect of what is normal and legitimate, identification of illegal or corrupt becomes impossible. This implies that, at least under some circumstances, development of technical methods and procedures can be an important good governance approach. Reconciling the apparent potential to improve technical practice with the risk of merely embellishing fundamentally compromised systems is an important issue needing further review.

Going further, emerging work on transparency, extractive industries transparency and on independent forest monitoring, suggest that in addition to the established concepts on internal and external controls, provisions may be appropriate in forestry and other natural resource settings for what could be termed *public controls*. These would be built around the public disclosure of information on resource management transactions and results, with an expectation that public scrutiny and political processes would help provide discipline that would detect and deter corruption. While the value of transparency and information disclosure is well accepted, information disclosure by itself may not be sufficient. In particular, there is a need to explore the parallel for public controls of internal and external controls that generally operate on the basis of being triggered by 'red flags' that signal deviations from some expectations of normal. It may be that for public controls to operate effectively, in addition to mere disclosure of results, there is a need for disclosure of plans and expectations against which the attentive public(s) may compare and contrast the performance of forestry agencies. If this is borne out, it would carry forward additional implications for the value and governance significance of investments in technical and managerial aspects of forestry.

NOTES

1. William B. Magrath, Lead Natural Resource Economist, South Asia Region, Sustainable Development Department. Much of the research summarized in this chapter is the result of an Australia Agency for International Development (Ausaid) sponsored study by the World Bank on the Links between Forestry and Corruption in East Asia and the Pacific. The opinions expressed herein are those of the author and should not be ascribed to the World Bank or Ausaid.
2. This discussion draws heavily on Isham, and others 2002.
3. I am in debt to Naaz Barma for calling my attention to this distinction.
4. For an overview see, Magrath (2010).

BIBLIOGRAPHY

Akella, Anita Sundari and James B. Cannon (2004), *Strengthening the Weakest Links: Strategies for Improving the Enforcement of Environmental Laws Globally*, Washington DC: Conservation International.

Arvis , Jean-Francois and Ronald E. Berenbeim (2003), *Fighting Corruption in East Asia: Solutions from the Private Sector*, Washington, DC: World Bank Publications.

Bhargava, Vinay and Emil Bolongaita (eds) (2004), *Challenging Corruption in Asia: Case Studies and a Framework for Action*, Washington DC: World Bank.

Biderman, A.D. and A.J. Resiss Jr (1967) 'On exploring the "dark figure" of crime', *Annals*, (November), 1–15. Quoted in W.G. Skogan (1977), 'Dimensions of the dark figure of unreported crime', *Crime and Deliquency*, **1**, 41–50.
Bryett, K. and P. Osborne (2000), 'Criminal prosecution: procedure and practice: international perspectives', *Research Report* 16. Belfast, Northern Ireland Office, Statistics and Research Branch, Criminal Justice Policy Division (available at http://www.irishtimes.com/newspaper/special/2000/justice/16.pdf).
Casson, Anne and Krystof Obidzinski , (2002), 'From New Order to regional autonomy: shifting dynamics of "illegal logging" in Kalimantan, Indonesia', *World Development*, **30**(12), 2133–251.
Chomitz, Kenneth (2006), *At Loggerheads? Agricultural Ezpansion, Poverty Reduction and Environment in the Tropical Forests*, Washington DC: The World Bank.
Clarke, R.V. and J. Eck (2003), *Become a Problem Solving Crime Analyst*, Cullompton, UK: Willan Publishing.
Clarke, R. (1992), *Situational Crime Prevention: Successful Case Studies*, New York: Harrow and Heston.
Colchester et al. (2006), *Justice in the Forest: Rural Livelihoods and Forest Law Enforcement*, Bogor, Indonesia: CIFOR.
Cornish, D.B. and R.V. Clarke (2003), 'Opportunities, precipitators and criminal decisions', in *Theory for Practice in Situational Crime Prevention, Crime Prevention Studies*, Vol 16. Monsey, NY: Criminal Justice Press, available at www.popcenter.org
Damania, R., R. Deacon and E. Bulte (2005), 'Resource abundance, poverty and development: an empirical assessment', *World Development*, **3**, 1029–54.
Dauvergne, Peter (2001), *Loggers and Degradation in the Asia-Pacific: Corporations and Environmental Management*, Cambridge: Cambridge University Press.
European Forest Institute (2005), *Impact of the Reduction of Illegal Logging in European Russia on the EU and European Russia Foreign Sector Trade*, Joensuu, Finland: European Forest Institute.
FAO (2005), *Best Practices for Improving Law Compliance in the Forest Sector*, Rome: FAO.
Global Witness (2005), *A Guide to Independent Forest Monitoring*, London: Global Witness.
Global Witness (2007), *Cambodia's family trees – illegal logging and the stripping of public assets by Cambodia's elite*, available at http://www.globalwitness.org/library/cambodias-family-trees.
Greenberg, T.S., L.M. Samuel, W. Grant and L. Gray (2009), *Stolen asset recovery a good practices guide for non-conviction based asset forfeiture*, Washington, DC: World Bank.
Hughes, G. (1998), *Understanding Crime Prevention: Social Control, Risk and Late Modernity*, Buckingham, UK: Open University Press.
Isham, J., M. Woolcock, L. Pritchett, and G. Busby (2002), 'The varieties of rentier experience: how natural resource endowments affect the political economy of economic growth', unpublished mimeo, 8 January.
Johnson, S. (2002), 'Documenting the undocumented', *ITTO Tropical Forest Update*, **12**(1), 6–9.
Kishor, Nalin and Richard Damania (2007) 'Crime and justice in the Garden of Eden: improving governance and reducing corruption in the forestry sector', in Edgardo Campos and Sanjay Pradhan (eds), *The Many Faces of Corruption: Tracking Vulnerabilities at the Sector Level*, Washington, DC: The World Bank, April, pp. 91–116.
McCarthy, John F. (2000), '"Wild Logging": the rise and fall of logging networks and biodiversity conservation projects on Sumatra's rainforest frontier', CIFOR Occasional Paper 31 (October), Bogor, Indonesia: Center for International Forestry Research.
McCusker, Rob (2006) 'Review of anti-corruption strategies', Technical Background Paper No. 23, Australian Government, Australian Institute of Criminology.
McElwee, Pamela (2004), 'You say illegal, I say legal: the relationship between "illegal" logging and poverty, land tenure and forest use rights in Vietnam', *Journal of Sustainable Forestry*, **19**(1/2/3), 97–135.
Magrath, W. B. (2010), 'Assessing and benchmarking national FLEG systems', in Michael J. Pescott, Patrick B. Durst and Robin Leslie (eds), *Forest Law Enforcement and Governance:*

Progress in Asia and the Pacific, Food and Agriculture Organization of the United Nations, Bangkok: RAP Publication.
Magrath, W.B., R.L. Grandalski, G.L., Stuckey, G.B. Vikanes and G.R. Wilkinson (2007), 'Timber theft prevention: introduction to security for forest managers', East Asia and Pacific Region Sustainable Development Discussion Paper. East Asia and Pacific Region Sustainable Development Department.
National Crime Prevention Institute (2001), *Understanding Crime Prevention*, 2nd edn, Woburn, MA: Butterworth Heinemann.
Savcor Indufor Oy (2004), Impact Assessment of the EU Action Plan for Forest Law Enforcement, Governance and Trade (FLEGT), Helsinki: Savcor Indufor Oy.
Pease, K. (1997), 'Crime prevention', in M. Maguire, R. Morgan and R. Reiner (eds), *The Oxford Handbook on Criminology*, Oxford: Oxford University Press.
Pescott, Michael J., Patrick B. Durst and Robin N. Leslie (2010), *Forest Law Enforcement and Governance: Progress in Asia and the Pacific, Food and Agriculture Organization of the United Nations*, RAP Publication: Bangkok.
Pyne, S. (2009), 'The hand on the torch: a survey of woods arson', Paper prepared for the World Bank, Washington DC: World Bank.
Quah, Jon S.T.. 'Best Practices for Curbing Corruption in Asia'. The Governance Brief, Issue 11-2004. Governance and Regional Cooperation Division. Regional and Sustainable Development Department. ADB, Manila, Philippines: Asian Development Bank.
Quah, Jon S.T. (2006), 'Curbing Asian corruption: an impossible dream?', *Current History*, **105**(690), April, 176–79.
Ross M, (2001), *Timber Booms and Institutional Breakdown in Southeast Asia*, Cambridge: Cambridge University Press, series on Political Economy of Institutions and Decisions.
Seneca Creek Associates (2004), *'Illegal' Logging and Global Wood Markets: the Competitive Impacts on the US Wood Products Industry*, Washington, DC: American Forest and Paper Association.
Setiano, Bambang and Y. Husein (2005), 'Fighting forest crime and promoting prudent banking for sustainable forest management', CIFOR Occasional Paper No. 44, Bogor: CIFOR.
Shah, Anwar (2006), 'Corruption and Decentralized Public Governance', World Bank Policy Research Working Paper 3824, January, Washington, DC: World Bank.
Spector, Bertram I. (ed.) (2005), *Fighting Corruption in Developing Countries*, Bloomfield CT: Kumarian Press.
Shea, J. (1940), 'Our pappies burned the woods', *American Forests*, **46**(April), 159–62, 174. Discussed in S. Pyne (2009).
World Bank (1999), 'Assessing political commitment to fighting corruption', PREM notes, **29**, (September), Washington DC: World Bank.
World Bank (2000), *Anticorruption in Transition: A Contribution to the Policy Debate*, Washington DC: World Bank.
World Bank (2005), *FIU Workbook 2005*, World Bank Capacity Enhancement Program, Washington DC: World Bank.
World Bank (2007), *Strengthening World Bank Group Engagement on Governance and Anticorruption*, Washington DC: World Bank.
World Bank, (2009), 'Roots for good forest outcomes: an analytical framework for governance reforms', Report No. 49572-GLB, Washington: DC, the World Bank, Agriculture and Rural Development Department.
World Bank & UN Office on Drugs and Crime (UNODC) (2009a), *Income and asset Declarations: Tools and Trade-offs*, Washington, DC: World Bank.
World Bank & UNODC (2009b), *Stolen Asset Recovery Management of Returned Assets: Policy Considerations*, Washington DC: World Bank.
World Wildlife Fund and World Bank (WWF and WB) (2007), *Management effectiveness tracking tool: reporting progress at protected areas sites*, Second edition, available at: http://assets.panda.org/downloads/mett2_final_version_july_2007.pdf

10 The relationship between corruption and financial crime

Nicole Leeper Piquero and Jay S. Albanese

INTRODUCTION

The term corruption, much like the phrase white-collar crime,[1] is apt to bring a stereotypical image of the offender to mind. In the case of corruption, that person is most often thought to be an individual who holds a political office, while the image of a white-collar offender usually brings to mind a wealthy high-powered business executive.[2] At first glance, these two concepts seem to operate in two different worlds – where one concerns the public sector and the other the private sector. The two actually have much in common and in fact could be thought of as two sides to the same coin. The purpose of this chapter is to highlight the similarities between the two areas of study and to demonstrate that scholars working in both traditions face similar hurdles in advancing their respective research agendas.

This chapter will focus on three major areas where the two fields of study, corruption and white-collar crime, share similarities. First, a definitional dilemma plagues both areas of inquiry. Much as when Justice Stewart expressed in a 1964 US Supreme Court decision (*Jacobellis v. Ohio*) regarding defining obscenity, 'I know it when I see it', the same sentiment could be expressed by scholars who study either or both white-collar crime and corruption. Everyone knows what it is when they see it but are hard pressed to be able to precisely define the respective concepts. Second, both concepts, perhaps due to the lack of a consensus definition, are difficult constructs to operationalize and measure. Both are steeped in a tradition of relying upon qualitative case studies to illustrate the malfeasances to be examined but face significant challenges when trying to find quantitative means of measurement. Third, understanding how the public perceives the issues of corruption and white-collar crime are important areas of study in both strands of research (Treisman, 2000; Schoepfer, Carmichael & Piquero, 2007; Piquero, Carmichael & Piquero, 2008; Holtfreter et al., 2008; Olken, 2009). Public perceptions of crime are important to understand because they indicate not only an important aspect about normative culture but also shed light on formal social controls (Stylianou, 2003).

DEFINITIONAL DILEMMAS

Scholars studying both corruption and white-collar crime must first overcome the lack of a definitive definition for their respective topics of inquiry. This is usually accomplished by scholars indicating at the outset which definition they will use in their research project; but this is still not an easy task because the topics these scholars are studying are often not clearly defined by criminal statutes and even in some cases the terms (for example, corruption and white-collar crime) themselves are not found in existing penal codes (Geis, 2002). Deriving a consensus definition of corruption appears to be somewhat easier than compromising on a definition of white-collar crime. This could perhaps be attributed to the fact that corruption could be viewed as a special form of white-collar crime (Zimring & Johnson, 2005), or that corruption refers to a more specific kind of behaviour, whereas white-collar crime encompasses a broader range of behaviours.

So, where does that leave the field with respect to an agreed-upon appropriate definition and conceptualization of corruption? Treisman (2000, p. 399) defines corruption as 'the misuse of public office for private gain'. Transparency International (www.transparency.org) defines it in their Corruption Perceptions Index (CPI) as 'the abuse of public office for private gain'. Nye (1967, p. 419) provides the most detailed definition to include 'behavior which deviates from the formal duties of a public role because of private-regarding (personal, close family, private clique) pecuniary or status gains; or violates rules against the exercise of certain types of private-regarding influence'. Finally, Zimring and Johnson (2005, p. 796) define corruption more broadly as 'the illegal use of power for personal gain'.

Each of the above definitions of corruption emphasizes two interrelated themes. The first component usually focuses upon the offender's position or job and the associated power that comes along with such a position. The second part involves using the position and the ensuing power in order to procure something of value to the individual. Definitions of corruption can vary with regard to the scope of who should be included; some will limit corruption to the acts of public officials (political corruption) while others will broaden the definition to include those who are not office holders but still have some degree of power (business corruption) such as businessmen and businesswomen (Gardiner, 2002).

Other definitional dilemmas concern the actual behaviours to be included in the conceptualization and operationalization of corrupt behaviour. Nye (1967, p. 419) delineates corruption to include: 'bribery (use of a reward to pervert the judgement of a person in a position of trust), nepotism (bestowal of patronage by reason of ascriptive relationship rather than merit); and misappropriation (illegal appropriation of public resources for private-regarding issues)'. While most agree that bribery constitutes corruption, there is still the issue of which part of the act is to be focused on – the taking of the bribe or the person offering the bribe. Zimring and Johnson (2005, p. 796) argue that 'corruption is by definition an act of a person who either has the economic power to bribe another or the power to provide a favor for the bribe'. In other words, both the giver and the taker have some sort of power that can be used to get what they want.

The final corruption definition issue to be addressed concerns the legal definition of what is defined as corrupt. Most criminal statutes do not define corruption per se but rather focus upon particular acts that would constitute corrupt behaviour. For example, corruption is not a crime in the US penal code but bribery, graft, and conflicts of interest are clearly defined (in Title 18, Chapter 5). In addition, the US penal code defines these crimes of corruption in broad terms. These specific acts, bribery, graft, and conflicts of interest, are applied not only to those who hold a public office, but are also extended to include those individuals in finance institutions as well as those in sporting contests. Additionally, definitions of what constitutes corrupt behaviour will vary across different jurisdictions and, in particular, across countries. What legally constitutes corruption in one country may be perfectly legal and acceptable in another. Thus, various definitions across the different jurisdictions makes cross-national research challenging (see Piquero & Piquero, 2006).

The definitional issue has been found to be more problematic and at times hampering for those who study white-collar crime (see Helkamp, Ball & Townsend, 1996 for a more detailed review). The definitional conundrum surrounding white-collar crime can be traced back to the origins of the term. Sutherland introduced the term 'white-collar crime' during his 1939 Presidential address at the annual meeting of the American Sociological Society and then expanded upon his initial thoughts and presented data in his book, *White Collar Crime*, which clarified and expanded his previous arguments (see Geis, 2002 for a more detailed review). Sutherland (1983, p. 7) noted that white-collar crime may be approximately defined as 'a crime committed by a person of respectability and high social status in the course of his occupation' and further elaborated that the 'concept is not intended to be definitive, but merely to call attention to crimes not ordinarily included within the scope of criminology'.

Most white-collar crime scholars refer to Sutherland's definition as an offender-based definition of white-collar crime. Offender-based definitions emphasize the high social status, power, and respectability of the actor as essential characteristics of white-collar crime (Benson & Simpson, 2009,

p. 9). Others prefer to use an offence-based definition of white-collar crime that is based upon the nature of the illegal act and more in line with criminal statutes (Benson & Simpson, 2009). Edelhertz (1970) offered the following offence-based definition of white-collar crime: 'an illegal act or series of illegal acts committed by non-physical means and by concealment or guile to obtain money or property, to avoid the payment or loss of money or property, or to obtain business or personal advantage'.

Regardless if one prefers an offender-based definition in lieu of an offence-based definition of white-collar crime, corruption falls squarely within the purview of white-collar crime scholarship. Sutherland's earliest offender-based definition of white-collar crime certainly includes corrupt behaviours because both include the status of the offender and the occupational opportunity to offend. As Geis (2002, p. 42) notes, even despite Sutherland's inability to clearly define a definition of white-collar crime, what he clearly was focusing on and drawing attention to were 'people who used positions of prestige and power to violate the law'. This is the precise focus of attention of corruption scholarship.

An offence-based definition of white-collar crime also incorporates corruption. In fact, Edelhertz (1970) identified four categories of white-collar crime with one specific category (Abuses of Trust) where corruption clearly fits. His categories included (Edelhertz, 1970, pp. 19–20):

1. Personal Crimes: crimes by persons operating on an individual, ad hoc basis, for personal gain in a nonbusiness context.
2. Abuses of Trust: crimes in the course of their occupations by those operating inside businesses, government, or other establishments, or in a professional capacity, in violation of their duty of loyalty and fidelity to employer or client.
3. Business Crimes: crimes incidental to and in furtherance of business operations, but not the central purpose of such business operations.
4. Con Games: white-collar crime as a business, or as the central activity of the business.

On the other hand, another definition of white collar crime includes three categories of conduct: crimes of fraud (embezzlement, extortion, forgery, and fraud), crimes against public administration (bribery, obstruction of justice, official misconduct, and perjury), and regulatory offences (administrative, environmental, labour and manufacturing violations, and unfair trade practices) (Albanese, 1995). Clearly, corruption is a definitional component of some, but not all, of these offences, suggesting that corruption can be considered as part of the larger area of white collar crime. For example, embezzlement, fraud, and crimes against public administration are often carried out by public officials or private business persons for *personal profit or benefit*. On the other hand, bribery and extortion involves a corrupt exchange between public officials and private citizens or business, which *benefits both parties*. Therefore, it can be seen that corruption is generally of two broad types: misuse of public office or abuse of power for private gain (Albanese, 2011).

Even more recent definitions of white-collar crime encompass the key components that allow corruption to be easily considered a special type of white-collar crime. For example, Reiss and Biderman (1980, p. 11) defined white-collar crimes as 'violations of law in which penalties are attached that involve the use of a violator's position of economic power, influence, or trust in the legitimate economic or political institutional order for the purpose of illegal gain or to commit an illegal act for personal or organizational gain'. Shapiro (1990, p. 350) prefers a definition of white-collar crime that focuses on violations of trust by noting that 'the violation and manipulation of the norms of trust – of disclosure, disinterestedness, and role competence – represent the modus operandi of white-collar crime'. As such, these forms of stealing would include misappropriation, self-dealing, corruption, and role-conflict.

All in all, scholars working in both the corruption area and the broader area of white-collar crime must contend with a variety of definitional issues including what and who the law defines as criminal. What both strands of scholarship share in common is that they are dealing with crimes of the powerful – that is, people who have either the economic power to pay for what they want or the power to provide the favour in the first place (Zimring & Johnson, 2005). Both strands of research are interested in learning about and understanding the behaviour of individuals who use and abuse their trusted positions (whether they are public officials or individuals who hold other forms of power, such as police officers or businesspersons) in order to advance their own personal interests.

ISSUES OF MEASUREMENT

Given the definitional problems associated with the terms 'corruption' and 'white-collar crimes', it should come as no surprise that scholars have encountered problems with respect to how to operationalize and measure these concepts. The measurement challenges faced by these scholars are not unlike those faced by other social scientists, those who try to quantify socially defined constructs, but the challenges are magnified because of the hidden nature of these offences and the ability of those engaging in these actions to hide or disguise their behaviours.

The measurement of conventional forms of crime (for example, robbery, rape, larceny) has received considerably more attention than has the measurement of either white-collar crime or corruption. In order to gain a sense of how much crime exists, criminologists have relied upon both objective and subjective measurement strategies. Objective measures of crime refer to what is officially reported to criminal justice agencies. Whether measured as rates of arrest, prosecution or conviction, these strategies are not without their limitations. The dark figure of crime (or the crimes not known to the police) and issues of system bias (for example, police departments or prosecutors will selectively enforce some statutes over others) have always hampered the use of official measures of crime. The use of official measures of crime to identify corruption and white-collar crime face additional obstacles beginning with the lack of a consensus definition and extending to the crime types themselves – they are crimes that tend to be well-hidden, have a diffuse victimization, and are engaged in by those very people who should be monitoring and preventing their execution.

Subjective measures of crime rely upon surveying a sample of respondents to ask about their own experiences with crime as either the offender (self-report surveys) or the victim (victimization surveys). All self-report survey strategies must contend with finding an appropriate sample from which the results can be generalized. As such, finding variation in the dependent variable (that is, crime or victimization) requires large (usually) national samples from which generalizations can be made. While the use of self-report surveys has not been particularly useful in trying to measure corruption or white-collar crime, in large part because these are not incidents that offenders are likely to self-report, the use of victimization surveys has been a more fruitful approach in trying to understand how much white-collar crime and corruption exists. Most white-collar crime victimization surveys specifically focus on incidents of fraud (see Levi, 2001; Kane & Wall, 2006; Schoepfer & Piquero, 2009 for more detailed reviews) while corruption is typically operationalized as bribery. For example, the International Crime Victim Survey (ICVS) conducted by the United Nations Office on Drugs and Crime asks individuals from a variety of different nations whether or not any 'government official, for instance a customs officer, a police officer, or inspector in your country' asked or expected the respondent to pay a bribe for his or her services in the past year (van Dijk, van Kesterent & Smit, 2008). While victim surveys have been used to assess both corruption and white-collar crime – specifically fraud, the principle method of measuring these concepts has been by means of methods that assess public perceptions (reviewed in the section below) about how serious of an issue they believe the specific acts to be.

Finally, one additional form of data collection that has been quite successful in the study of both corruption and white-collar crime is the use of a case study approach. Case studies have an important role to play because in all fields of enquiry, such as health, environment, and crime, formerly 'hidden' problems are almost always discovered and their nature documented through a careful examination of individual cases (Kazdin 2011). Individual cases are responsible for 'discovering' the conduct and provoking further, more systematic research, into its true extent. Indeed, the basis for subsequent efforts to identify key measurable variables and correlates for larger studies are always rooted in the findings of case studies. Problems that were poorly understood a generation ago (for example, breast cancer, prostate cancer, mercury poisoning, and white collar crime) are now much better understood, due to an accumulation of case studies which provided the understanding and parameters for wider research efforts which followed.

Case studies are of many types; they can be restricted to a single case, but more often they examine a specific jurisdiction, sub-category of conduct, or small samples. Single-case studies can be useful for laying out the parameters of a poorly understood phenomenon from a health disaster to questionable political fund-raising (de Azavedo and Pereira, 2010; Liddick, 2001; Mishra et al., 2009). Other kinds of case studies examine a group of known cases to identify similarities and differences. These kinds of research efforts have been very fruitful in both the natural and social sciences where representative samples are difficult, or far too costly, to collect (MacLin, 2010; Qaydi, 2010). Finally, larger case studies examine all known cases in a particular jurisdiction. While these studies are not comprehensive, they often represent all that can be known within cost constraints, and their results, although not definitive, are often the best available. These findings are commonly used to form the basis for public policy decisions on a variety of important issues including parole release, tourist behaviour, and context of corrupt conduct (Andersson, 2008; Hipp and Yates, 2009; Klein and Osleeb, 2010).

Case study research generally suffers because the samples used may not be generalizable. However, the inability to gather representative samples easily or cost-effectively make reliance on case-study research in white-collar crime and corruption a necessity. Increasingly, there are examples of case-study research being used to inform public policy on white-collar crime and corruption, not because the level of knowledge is sufficient, but because the investment in developing more systematic knowledge on these difficult-to-measure issues is simply not forthcoming (Hill, 2010; Maljevic et al., 2008; United Nations Office on Drugs and Crime, 2010).

UNDERSTANDING PUBLIC PERCEPTIONS

Public perceptions of crime and punishment have been a much researched area in criminology and criminal justice (Roberts & Stalans, 1997; Stylianou, 2003), with fewer studies focusing on white-collar crime perceptions, and even fewer on corruption perceptions. In general, this line of research tends to ask respondents, usually via phone or in-person surveys, how they perceive and/or view certain crimes, their seriousness, and how they believe each should be punished. The notion underlying this area of research is not only to understand what and why the public perceives about crime (that is, which crime types are deemed as 'serious') but to also gain an understanding of what the public believes should be done about it. Knowing such information should then provide useful data for policy-maker s in deciding which issues to be addressed first and suggest potential courses of action to curb its continuation.

Within the corruption area, one of the most commonly used measures of public perceptions can be found in the Corruptions Perception Index (CPI). The CPI is a measure developed by Transparency International (www.transparency.org) which uses an aggregate indicator that combines different sources to rank order countries around the globe (and has done so since 1995) according to the 'degree to which corruption is perceived to exist among public officials and politicians'. Much like earlier-reviewed definitions regarding corruption, Transparency International defines corruption as 'the abuse of entrusted power for private gain'. Countries are ranked on a scale from 0 (indicating the country is highly corrupt) to 10 (indicating that the country is highly clean), using 13 different data sources. These data sources are often surveys of those likely to have exposure, such as business owners, and those conducting business in multiple countries. The 2010 report examined 178 countries and found that nearly three quarters of them scored below a five on the scale (Transparency International, 2010) including, for example, Sudan which scored 1.6, Russia 2.1, and China 3.5 (the US scored 7.1 while Australia scored 8.7). Another measure is the Bribe Payers Index (BPI) which rates the likelihood that companies will pay bribes when they do business abroad. The data for the BPI comes from interviews with 2700 private-sector leaders in 22 countries. Conducted by Gallup International, the BPI is a perception index of experienced business persons focusing exclusively on corrupt practices in international business (Bribe Payers Index, 2008).

Measures of public perceptions of white-collar crime have followed the tradition of scholarship that examines ranking crime in terms of how serious it is perceived to be. Sellin and Wolfgang (1964) conducted the first study that examined public perceptions of crime seriousness and found remarkable consistency across the seriousness ratings, especially as they related to violent crimes. Criminologists have continued to rank public perceptions of crime seriousness over the years but with more refined measurement strategies (Stylianou, 2003) and with the inclusion of different varieties of white-collar crime (Rossi et al., 1974; Wolfgang et al., 1985). Results rather consistently show that Americans perceive white-collar crimes to be as serious, if not more serious than, street crimes (Cullen et al., 1983, 1985; Holtfreter et al., 2008; Kane & Wall, 2006; Piquero, Carmichael & Piquero, 2008; Rosenmerkel, 2001; Schoepfer, Carmichael & Piquero, 2007).

Although surveys of public perceptions have yielded important preliminary findings, caution must still be exercised when interpreting and extrapolating from these sets of studies. The biggest drawback to these kinds of surveys is that that data are not drawn from direct knowledge or experience of a crime but rather based upon opinions and beliefs regarding the crime in question (Treisman, 2007). As such they reveal nothing about the prevalence of crime types but do offer insights into societal views regarding citizens presumed beliefs about the nature of crime. Additionally, these surveys must also overcome issues regarding response bias (as some individuals may provide socially desirable responses), question interpretation (absent an operational definition, the crime in question may connote different things to different people; this is especially true with regards to corruption and white-collar crimes), and question probing (the more specific the question, the more different the perception has been found to be, see Unnever & Cullen, 2005).

CONCLUSION: DIRECTIONS FOR FUTURE RESEARCH

This chapter has reviewed three themes, definitional issues, measurement concerns, and public perceptions, that each relate to both the study of corruption and white-collar crime. While each respective area of research has forged its own research agenda and has amassed its own body of scholarship, the similarities across the research areas illustrate how important these topics are for future research and suggest that scholars working in each area could teach and learn from one another. With regard to the definitional dilemma, white-collar crime research could learn much from corruption researchers in ways to manage and overcome a lack of consensus regarding the definition of the term in question. For example, one way around the definitional issue is to focus on identifying the specific types of behaviours and actions that comprise the term of interest (Langseth,

2006). Corruption, for example, has narrowly focused on bribery as the quintessential way to measure the larger concept of corruption. On the other hand, white-collar crime scholarship has stumbled in terms of developing a unified research agenda. With white-collar scholars continually running on the definitional treadmill, the area of research is fractured such that scholars working in this area may or may not be studying the same phenomenon. Scholars relying on offence-based definitions of white-collar crime are inching closer to the corruption model but still have a way to go.

All social scientists whether working from criminology, sociology, economics, or political science backgrounds, must all contend with measurement error. Given that the dependent variables are all socially constructed concepts, the best approaches to capturing these phenomena are the ones that look to multiple sources or use a triangulation method to capture the crimes of interest. While crime is typically measured by means of official statistics (those crimes known to criminal justice agencies), self-report studies, and victimization surveys, these methods of measurement do not capture crimes that are by their very nature hidden and deceitful. For example, scholars have illustrated how official measures of white-collar crime (specifically fraud and forgery) are not appropriate indicators (Steffensmeier, 1989).

Finally, public perceptions research has proliferated in both the study of corruption and of white-collar crime; yet, much more work still needs to be done. Corruption research has tended to focus narrowly on assessing perceptions of public officials, business persons, and politicians taking and making bribes, while white-collar crime research has focused more broadly on assessing the seriousness of a list of different white-collar crimes and their associated punishments when compared to street crimes. Additionally, public perception surveys regarding corruption have typically been examined cross-nationally, while the white-collar crime research has primarily focused on American samples. Both bodies of literature could borrow from the other. For example, corruption researchers could focus more on collecting representative samples from businesses, or residential samples from particular nations, and ask respondents about a variety of different types of corruption (including local political corruption and corrupt business practices) as well as associated punishments for each of the acts, while white-collar crime researchers could work towards better cross-national samples.

In closing, there are several areas that corruption research should pay attention to and build upon. Scholars need to be cautious of and avoid the definitional dilemma that white-collar crime scholars fell into. It is crucial to move past the definitional issues and focus squarely on ways to operationalize and expand the measurement of corruption. To date, most of the attention has focused on political corruption, but there is a pressing need to develop, apply, and extend self-report measures of corruption to some of the other many domains of society that also must deal with corrupt practices and behaviours. For example, corruption research needs to be further explored and fleshed out in areas such as athletics, military, and campaign contributions. Research is being conducted in many of these areas but without a concerted effort by all scholars interested in these wrongdoings. The point being stressed here is that corruption exists in many aspects of life and it is a virtual certainty that most people will have been a victim of some sort of corrupt practice at some point in their lives. All these forms of victimization need to be explored.

There is also a need to consider and measure corruption at different units of analysis (i.e., individuals, organizations, jurisdictions). One particularly useful example comes from Sherman's (1978) seminal study of corruption in the police profession, and in particular his more objective-based measure of corruption. Specifically, instead of measuring the frequency of corrupt acts, Sherman (1978, p. 188, emphasis in original) measured 'changes over time in the quantity of *organization* generally present in corruption activities'. Of course, such data are limited with respect to record-keeping differences, operational distinctions within and across jurisdictions over time, but these forms of official corruption measures would provide a counter-point to self-report measures.

More generally, there is a need to bring a more multi-disciplinary and multi-level theoretical approach to the study of corruption. To date, there are rudimentary understandings of why corruption exists at the organizational or macro level, and what individual and situational factors are related to corrupt behaviour (Treisman, 2007). The research efforts that should spring forth with respect to the study of corruption should strongly consider, as is common within white-collar crime research, how individuals act in certain situational and organizational contexts. Thus, perspectives that recognize and exploit micro- and macro-level processes would be ideal and preferred to those that rely upon only macro-level explanations. In one fascinating case study example, Vaughan (1996) studied the decision-making processes of NASA in order to better understand what led to the space shuttle Challenger disaster. She found that professional, organizational, and individual factors all interacted to provide what appeared to be normative behaviours within NASA. Soon thereafter, Simpson and her colleagues (1998) took Vaughan's approach one step further in an analysis of corporate crime decision-making and found support for a combined model that yielded support for both individual and situational/contextual characteristics to simultaneously influence offenders' decisions to engage in corporate illegality. These types of approaches (micro-macro understandings) could and should be utilized in future corruption research in order to better understand the context of individuals' beliefs regarding normative behaviours.

Returning to the parallel highlighted at the outset, this chapter closes by cautioning scholars to be careful so as not to get trapped in the definitional issues of corruption as this can virtually stall any efforts at studying the problem. Instead, it is recommended that researchers double-up their efforts and start measuring corruption, at all levels of analysis, in order to gain a better understanding of the phenomenon, to include its patterning, correlates, and causes. After all, as Lord Kelvin reminds us 'When you cannot measure, your knowledge is meager and unsatisfactory'.

NOTES

1. The terms white-collar crime and finance crime are often used interchangeably along with numerous other synonyms (see Friedrichs, 2010 for a review). The term white-collar crime will be used throughout this chapter.
2. The image of a business executive as a deviant pays homage to the origins of the label of white-collar criminal offered by Sutherland (1983). This is commonly regarded as an offender-based definition and will be juxtaposed with an offence-based definition later in the chapter.

REFERENCES

Albanese, J.S. (1995), *White Collar Crime in America*, Upper Saddle River, NJ: Prentice Hall.

Albanese, J.S. (2011), *Transnational Crime and the 21st Century: Criminal Enterprise, Corruption, Opportunity*, New York: Oxford University Press.

Andersson, S. (2008), 'Studying the risk of corruption in the least corrupt countries'. *Public Integrity*, **10**, 193–214.

Benson, M.L. and S.S. Simpson (2009), *White-Collar Crime: An Opportunity Perspective*, New York, NY: Routledge.

Bribe Payers Index (2008), *2008 Bribe Payers Index*. Berlin: Transparency International, http://www.transparency.org/policy_research/surveys_indices/bpi/bpi_2008.

Cullen, F.T., G.A. Clark, B.G. Link, R.A. Mathers, J.E. Niedospial and M. Sheahan (1985), 'Dissecting white-collar crime: offence type and punitiveness', *International Journal of Comparative and Applied Criminal Justice*, **9**, 15–28.

Cullen, F.T., G.A. Clark, R.A. Mathers and J.B. Cullen (1983), 'Public support for punishing white-collar crime: blaming the victim revisited?', *Journal of Criminal Justice*, **11**, 481–93.

de Azevedo, A.M.M. and N.M. Pereira (2010), 'Environmental regulation and innovation in high-pollution industries: a case study in a Brazilian refinery', *International Journal of Technology Management & Sustainable Development*, **9**, 133–48.

Edelhertz, H. (1970), *The Nature, Impact and Prosecution of White Collar Crime*, Washington, DC: US Government Printing Office.

Friedrichs, D.O. (2010), *Trusted Criminals*, Fourth Edition, Belmont, CA: Thomson-Wadsworth.

Gardiner, J. (2002), 'Defining corruption', in A.J. Heidenheimer and M. Johnston (eds), *Political Corruption: Concepts and Contexts*, New Brunswick, NJ: Transaction Publishers, pp. 25–40.

Geis, G. (2002), 'White-collar crime', in G.W. Potter (ed.), *Controversies in White-Collar Crime*, Cincinnati, OH: Anderson, pp. 37–52.

Helmkamp, J., R. Ball and K. Townsend (eds) (1996), *Definitional Dilemma: Can and Should there be a Universal Definition of White Collar Crime?*, Morgantown, WV: National White Collar Crime Center.

Hill, D. (2010), 'A critical mass of corruption: why some football leagues have more match-fixing than others', *International Journal of Sports Marketing & Sponsorship*, **11**, 221–35.

Hipp, J.R. and D.K. Yates (2009), 'Do returning parolees affect neighborhood crime?: a case study of Sacramento', *Criminology*, **47**, 619–56.

Holtfreter, K., S. Van Slyke, J. Bratton and M. Gertz (2008), 'Public perceptions of white-collar crime punishment', *Journal of Criminal Justice*, **36**, 50–60.

Kane, J. and A. Wall (2006), *The 2005 National Public Survey on White Collar Crime*, Fairmont, WV: National White Collar Crime Center.

Kazdin, A.E. (2011), *Single-case Research Designs: Methods for Clinical and Applied Settings*, New York: Oxford University Press.

Klein, Y.L. and J. Osleeb, (2010), 'Determinants of coastal tourism: a case study of Florida Beach Counties', *Journal of Coastal Research*, **26**, 1149–56.

Langseth, P. (2006), 'Measuring corruption', in C. Sampford, A. Shacklock, C. Connors and F. Galtung (eds), *Measuring Corruption*, Burlington, VT: Ashgate Publishing, pp. 7–44.

Levi, M. (2001), 'White-collar crime victimization', in N. Shover and J.P. Wright (eds), *Crimes of Privilege: Readings in White-Collar Crime*, New York: Oxford University Press, pp. 67–74.

Liddick, D. (2001), 'Political fund-raising, patron-client relations, and organized criminality: two case studies', *Journal of Contemporary Criminal Justice*, **17**, 346–58.

MacLin, O.H., R. Tapscott and M. Kimberly-MacLin (2010), 'Face recognition in context: a case study of tips on a call-in crime TV show', *North American Journal of Psychology*, **12**, 459–68.

Maljević, A., D. Datzer, E. Muratbegović and M. Budimlić, (2008), 'Professional police in Bosnia and Herzegovina: case study – police corruption', *European Journal of Crime, Criminal Law & Criminal Justice*, **16**, 209–224.

Mishra, P.K., R.M. Samarth, N. Pathak, S.K. Jain, S. Banerjee and K.K. Maudar, (2009), 'Bhopal gas tragedy: review of clinical and experimental findings after 25 Years', *International Journal of Occupational Medicine & Environmental Health*, July, 193–202.

Nye, J.S. (1967, 'Corruption and political development: a cost-benefit analysis', *American Political Science Review*, **61**(2), 417–27.

Olken, B.A. (2009), 'Corruption perceptions vs. corruption reality', *Journal of Public Economics*, **93**, 950–64.

Piquero, N.L., S. Carmichael and A.R. Piquero, (2008), 'Assessing the perceived seriousness of white-collar and street crimes', *Crime and Delinquency*, **54**, 291–312.

Piquero, N.L. and A.R. Piquero (2006), 'Democracy and intellectual property: examining trajectories of software piracy', *ANNALS, AAPSS*, **605**, 104–127.

Qaydi, S.A. (2010), 'Industrial solid waste management in the United Arab Emirate rural areas: case study the Northern Emirates', *International Journal of Academic Research*, **2**, 58–64.

Reiss, A.J. Jr. and A. Biderman (1990), *Data Sources on White-Collar Law-Breaking*, Washington, DC: National Institute of Justice.

Roberts, J.V. and L. Stalans (1997), *Public Opinion, Crime and Criminal Justice*, Boulder, Co: Westview Press.

Rosenmerkel, S.P. (2001), 'Wrongfulness and harmfulness as components of seriousness of white-collar offenses', *Journal of Contemporary Criminal Justice*, **17**, 308–327.

Rossi, P.H., R. White, C.E. Bose and R.E. Berk (1974), 'The seriousness of crimes: A normative structure and individual differences', *American Sociological Review*, **39**, 224–37.

Schoepfer, A., S. Carmichael and N.L. Piquero (2007), 'Do perceptions of punishment vary between white-collar and street crimes?', *Journal of Criminal Justice*, **35**, 151–63.

Schoepfer, A and N.L. Piquero (2009), Studying the correlates of fraud victimization, *Journal of Criminal Justice*, **37**, 209–215.
Sellin, T. and M. Wolfgang (1964), *The Measurement of Delinquency*, Montclair, NJ: Smith Patterson.
Shaprio, S. (1990), 'Collaring the crime, not the criminal: reconsidering the concept of white-collar crime', *American Sociological Review*, **55**, 346–65.
Sherman, L.W. (1978), *Scandal and Reform: Controlling Police Corruption*, Berkeley, CA: University of California Press.
Simpson, S.S., R. Paternoster and N.L. Piquero (1998), Exploring the micro-macro link in corporate crime research', *Research in the Sociology of Organizations*, **15**, 35–68.
Steffensmeier, D. (1989), 'On the causes of white-collar crime: an assessment of Hirschi and Gottfredson's claims', *Criminology*, **27**, 345–58.
Stylianou, S. (2003), 'Measuring crime seriousness perceptions: what have we learned and what else do we want to know', *Journal of Criminal Justice*, **31**, 37–56.
Sutherland, E. (1983), *White-Collar Crime: The Uncut Version*, New Haven: Yale University Press.
Transparency International, (2010), *Corruption Perceptions Index, 2010*, Berlin, Germany: Transparency International.
Treisman, D. (2000), The causes of corruption: a cross-national study', *Journal of Public Economics*, **76**, 399–457.
Treisman, D. (2007), 'What have we learned about the causes of corruption from ten years of cross-national empirical research?', *American Review of Political Science*, **10**, 211–244.
United Nations Office on Drugs and Crime, (2010), *Crime and Instability: Case Studies of Transnational Threats*, Vienna: UNODC, available at http://www.unodc.org/documents/data-and-analysis/Studies/Crime_and_instability_2010_final_26march.pdf.
Unnever, J.D. and F.T. Cullen (2005), 'Executing the innocent and support for capital punishment: implications for public policy', *Criminology & Public Policy*, **4**, 3–37.
Van Dijk, J.J.M., J.N. van Kesteren and P. Smit (2008), *Criminal Victimisation in International Perspective, Key Findings From the 2004–2005 ICVS and EU ICS*, The Hague: Boom Legal Publishers.
Vaughan, D. (1996), *The Challenger Launch Decision*, Chicago, IL: University of Chicago Press.
Wolfgang, M., R. Figlio, P. Tracy and S. Singer (1985), *The National Survey of Crime Severity*, Washington, DC: US Government Printing Office.
Zimring, F.E. and D.T. Johnson (2005), 'On the comparative study of corruption', *British Journal of Criminology*, **45**, 793–809.

11 Corrupt practices involving offshore financial centres

David Chaikin

INTRODUCTION

This chapter explores the relationship between offshore financial centres (OFCs) and international criminal activity. The first part examines the phenomenon of OFCs and canvasses three important research issues: whether OFCs are more susceptible vehicles for transnational crimes, whether OFCs have been captured by onshore financial institutions and professionals, and whether there is any meaningful difference between OFCs and tax havens. The next section outlines the legitimate uses of OFCs, pointing out that a lack of information about OFCs makes it difficult to provide an objective judgement of their licit and illicit role in international commerce.

From a criminological perspective, the hallmark of OFCs is their lack of transparency, which is generally regarded as a major obstacle to the prevention and investigation of transnational crimes, including corruption. The secrecy structures of OFCs are not only based on their banking and financial secrecy laws, but also and perhaps more importantly on the widespread use of international business companies (IBCs). However, many of the secrecy features of IBCs, such as nominee ownership, corporate directors and bearer share are also found in onshore jurisdictions, raising the question of whether a lack of transparency is an exclusive problem of OFCs.

The role of OFCs in providing corrupt facilities is illustrated by the literature and practical cases concerning organized crime, money laundering, shell bank fraud, grand corruption, illicit capital flight and international tax evasion. More recently, the Global Financial Crisis has raised the question as to whether OFCs have contributed to international financial instability because of their hosting of largely unregulated hedge funds and private equity firms. The response of the international policy making community and law enforcement to OFCs is then explained.

There is a detailed case study of the Stanford International Bank offshore ponzi[1] scheme, with an analysis of the relationship between offshore and onshore regulation. One of the major lessons that may be drawn from this case is that regulatory enforcement of offshore vehicles needs to be improved, and that onshore regulators must ensure that onshore players do not exploit the 'offshore spaces' so as to facilitate corrupt practices.

OFFSHORE FINANCIAL CENTRES

The term OFC originated in the early 1980s and was initially viewed as a less pejorative term than tax havens. Over time, OFC became the favourite nomenclature of powerful international policy making bodies, such as the International Monetary Fund (IMF), the Financial Stability Forum (FSF), the Financial Action Task Force (FATF), and the Organisation of Economic Co-operation and Development (OECD), but national jurisdictions tended to stick to the phrase tax haven (Sharman & Gordon, 2009, pp. 78–95; Palan, Murphy & Chavagneux, 2010).

There is no internationally accepted definition of an OFC because different international policy bodies have emphasized different aspects of OFCs based on their own agendas and perspectives. This in turn has resulted in competing lists of jurisdictions that are classified as OFCs. The definition of OFC that I will use in this chapter is one promulgated by the IMF in 2003 (International Monetary Fund, 2003):

> Countries or jurisdictions with financial centres that contain financial institutions that deal primarily with non residents and/or in foreign currency on a scale out of proportion to the size of the host economy. Non resident-owned or -controlled institutions play a significant role within the centre. The institutions in the centre may well gain from tax benefits not available to those outside the centre.

This definition excludes International Financial Centres (IFCs) such as London, which dominates the Euromarket, New York which hosts US government-approved International Banking Facilities, as well as the Japanese Offshore Market, albeit that these facilities are designed to attract non-residents' transactions and investments.

There are a series of research questions that are important in understanding the relationship between OFCs and corruption. Are financial institutions in OFCs that deal largely with non-residents more susceptible vehicles for criminal activity? That is, given that OFCs have been created to avoid onshore regulatory or tax requirements (Palan, Murphy & Chavagneux, 2010, p. 124), does this mean that OFCs are more likely to be used by onshore criminals? There is no sound empirical data to assist in answering this question. However, international policy making bodies have assumed that OFCs may facilitate more risky economic activity if there is an absence of or low levels of regulation. The additional assumption that is made is that OFCs lack incentives to police licensed entities which cater exclusively to non-residents, thereby making them more attractive to criminals in other jurisdictions.

A related research theme is the relationship between offshore and onshore. It has been argued that some OFCs have been captured by onshore (non-resident) institutions and professionals, resulting in offshore regulation that is designed to avoid regulatory obligations in the onshore environment. According to this view, powerful and sophisticated professionals (lawyers, accountants, and bankers) have captured tax haven jurisdictions and have the wherewithal to move their operations between havens (Tax Justice Network UK, 2008, pp. 158, 170; Palan, Murphy & Chavagneux, 2010, pp. 12–14, 100–104). This is linked to an earlier idea that many of the OFCS have commercialized their sovereignty by enabling third parties to influence the drafting of laws which favoured non-resident tax payers (Palan 2003). Whether this is the case or not is difficult to prove, but there is no question that offshore legislation has been specifically designed and marketed to meet the needs of onshore investors, who have included criminals. The implication of this analysis is that merely targeting OFCs for increased regulation is unlikely to be successful unless it is accompanied by new regulatory and enforcement measures against powerful onshore clients, professionals and players.

There is also a debate concerning the concept of offshore and its relationship to national tax havens (Robinson, 1998, p. 395). The prominent non-governmental organization, Tax Justice Network, argues that it is an error to treat OFCs as tax havens, albeit that they are part of the offshore economy. Accordingly, tax havens are specific and identifiable geographical jurisdictions which 'create legislation designed to assist persons – real or legal – to avoid the regulatory obligations imposed upon them in the place where they undertake the substance of their economic transactions' (Tax Justice Network UK, 2008, pp. 10, 22–24). In contrast, OFCs are the 'commercial communities hosted by tax havens which exploit the structures that can be created using the tax haven's legislation for the benefit of those residents elsewhere' (Tax Justice Network UK, 2008, pp. 10–11, 25–27).

LEGITIMATE USES OF OFCS

A major challenge in examining OFCs is the lack of adequate information concerning their role in the international financial system (International Monetary Fund, 2000, p. 20). Hilton McCann (2006) in his book on

Offshore Finance has argued that the absence of knowledge of the role and risks of OFCs has clouded an objective analysis of OFCs. It is also difficult to understand the significance of illicit and corrupt characteristics of OFCs, without a sophisticated knowledge of their legitimate functions in international commerce.

The Financial Stability Forum has identified the following legitimate functions of OFCs (Financial Stability Forum, 2000, p. 10):

> Maximization of profits by international companies through low tax regimes;
> Securitization of financial products issued by international companies through special purpose vehicles;
> Asset protection by individuals and companies;
> Income tax minimization and avoidance of investment disclosure by investors;
> Minimization of tax and avoidance of regulatory requirements by financial institutions' affiliates in OFCs;
> Minimization of tax of customers of financial institutions; and
> Accumulation of reserves by insurance companies in low tax regimes.

It may be questioned whether some of these functions are 'legitimate' or ethical, for example the avoidance of tax and regulatory requirements in offshore jurisdictions. The issue of legitimacy has been tied to the question of transparency. There is a widespread belief among law enforcement that OFCs provide opportunities for concealing illegal transactions, including money laundering, corruption and other financial crimes. It is the lack of transparency of OFCs that has been the major issue for onshore governments (Picciotto, 2007). The secrecy features of OFCs have created problems in detecting, investigating and prosecuting financial crime, as well as the confiscation of the proceeds of crime and the recovery of tax evasion monies.

SECRECY STRUCTURES OF OFCS

Banking and financial secrecy have become a hallmark of OFCs. In most OFCs[2] specific secrecy legislation has been enacted based on the Swiss model so as to protect the privacy of customers in relation to their financial affairs (Antoine, 2002; Chaikin, 2005b). Legislation-based bank secrecy is treated seriously in OFCs where violations may be punished by criminal fines and/or imprisonment. In many jurisdictions the statutory right of secrecy has been bestowed not only on financial institutions, but also on providers of financial services, trust companies and international business companies (Antoine, 2005, pp. 98–100).

International business companies (IBCs) are companies established in an OFC that are not permitted to engage in business with residents and are generally not subject to any local taxes. There is a range of offshore corporate forms, including companies limited by shares, companies limited by guarantee, hybrid companies, companies with unlimited duration, limited duration companies, limited liability companies, cell companies and not-for-profit companies (Siemens, 2010, pp. 44–55). Each of these types of offshore companies have features that are attractive to both legitimate investors and criminals.

It is estimated that there are 2 million IBCs, with the largest producer being British Virgin Island (800 000), Hong Kong (500 000) and Panama (370 000) (Palan, Murphy & Chavagneux, 2010, p. 57). Where one or more entities in an OFC are utilized in a transaction, additional layers of secrecy may be created. For example, if an offshore trust is managed by an IBC that acts as a trustee of an offshore trust then the secrecy obligations applicable to trusts and IBCs may be invoked.

IBCs are frequently criticized for their inherent secrecy, for example, permitting nominee ownership of shares, nominee and corporate directors, and bearer share facilities, as well as a lack of public record of accounts (Palan, Murphy & Chavagneux, 2010, pp. 85–6). However, with the exception of bearer shares, most of these so-called secrecy features are also available to private companies in common law jurisdictions. For example, public disclosure of beneficial ownership of shares in private companies has never been a corporate law requirement in countries such as Australia, England and the United States (Chaikin, 2005a, pp. 208–33; Chaikin, 2006, pp. 141–60).

The most objectionable secrecy feature of OFCs has been the facility of bearer shares, whereby ownership of shares may be transferred by mere delivery, thereby facilitating anonymous ownership. However, it is not only OFCs that allow bearer shares: most continental European jurisdictions have allowed bearer shares.[3] Under pressure from the FATF and OECD, nearly all OFCs have immobilized bearer shares by requiring that all bearer share certificates be placed into custody with an authorized or registered custodian.[4] The registered custodian is subject to express regulation concerning knowing its client and the beneficial owner: it cannot accept a deposit of bearer shares unless it is informed of the beneficial owner of the shares and the identity of those persons who have relevant interests in those shares.

IBCs have sometimes been described as 'sham' corporations because they do not have a physical presence in the local jurisdiction, or are deemed not to be managed and controlled by that jurisdiction for taxation purposes, or that they are in some other way misleading from a taxation perspective (Palan, Murphy & Chavagneux, 2010, p. 13). It is also suggested that the place of incorporation of the company or corporate form may be misleading in that contrary to its appearance it is not regulated and taxed by the offshore jurisdiction. This criticism is apposite not only to traditional OFCs, but also jurisdictions such as the state of Delaware in the United States. For example, Delaware's limited liability companies (LLCs) are attractive to non-US citizens and non-US residents because they have an automatic reputational advantage of US legitimacy with significant tax advantages.[5] At the same time, Delaware's LLCs do not provide beneficial ownership information to the state registrar and have privacy protection similar to corporations found in OFCs (US Government Accountability Office, 2006, p. 2).

The FATF has stated that there are two criteria indicating excessive secrecy in national laws and enforcement (Financial Action Task Force (FATF), 2007, p. 8):

> Secrecy provisions which can be invoked against, but not lifted by competent administrative authorities in the context of enquiries concerning money laundering; and
> Secrecy provisions which can be invoked against, but not lifted by judicial authorities in criminal investigations related to money laundering.

Given that money laundering offences relate to predicate crimes, such as drug trafficking, fraud and increasingly also bribery and corruption, excessive secrecy may be applicable to the investigation of corruption-type offences.

Although some OFCs have permitted absolute bank secrecy, the vast majority of OFCs have allowed bank secrecy to be set aside in relation to domestic criminal investigations. Over time and as a result of external pressure, most of the OFCs have amended their legislation so as to permit international co-operation in combating corruption and corruption-like offences. This has meant that secrecy laws may not be invoked as a ground for challenging a request for mutual assistance in a criminal case of money laundering, and more recently corruption.[6]

CORRUPT USE OF OFCS

Organized Crime and Money Laundering

In 1998 a UN-sponsored study of secrecy identified the vulnerability of OFCs to organized crime (Blum, Levi, Naylor & Williams, 1998, p. 7):

> Criminal organizations are making wide use of the opportunities offered by financial havens and offshore centres to launder criminal assets, thereby

> creating roadblocks to criminal investigations. Financial havens offer an extensive array of facilities to foreign investors who are unwilling to disclose the origin of their assets.

Similarly government and academic studies have suggested that the lack of transparency of OFCs through banking, corporate, tax and other commercial legislation is the single most important obstacle to international law and tax enforcement (Blum, Levi, Naylor & Williams, 1998, pp. 17–18; US Senate Permanent Subcommittee on Investigations Minority Staff, 2010). The fundamental tenet of these studies is that it is the anonymity of facilities offered by OFCs that is extremely attractive not only to organised criminal groups who seek to launder the proceeds of their criminal activities, but also to High Net Worth Individuals (HNWIs) and multinational corporations that aim to evade or aggressively avoid tax obligations.

Rodney Gallagher, a former financial services adviser to the British Government in relation to the British Crown dependencies in the Caribbean, has testified that the OFCs role in money laundering should not be overemphasized (US House of Representatives Subcommittee on Oversight and Investigations Committee on International Relations Hearing, 2006). Gallagher argued that OFCs' role was secondary to International Financial Centres (IFCs), in regard to money laundering. According to Gallagher, whereas illicit monies are frequently sourced from large developed countries and placed initially in onshore banks (placement), the illicit monies are then moved through small offshore jurisdictions (layering stage) and eventually end up in rich developed onshore IFCs, such as New York, London or Zurich (integration). The implication of Gallagher's argument is that since illicit monies are most likely to be detected at the placement stage of money laundering, greater attention must be focused on the initial deposits of monies in onshore banks.

This is not to ignore the importance of OFCs in illicit activities. The IMF has expressed concern with OFCs compliance with the FATF 40+9 Recommendations for AML/CTF, in particular the low level of general compliance in core areas such as 'customer identification, the monitoring of transactions, and international cooperation' (International Monetary Fund 2008b: 8). Indeed, the FATF expressed its disapproval of OFCs when it launched its blacklisting programme, which mainly targeted offshore jurisdictions (Sharman, 2009, pp. 573–596). However, OFCs have made significant changes to their legal and regulatory systems, so that today OFCs compliance with AML standards 'is generally comparable to that of non-OFC jurisdictions' (International Monetary Fund, 2008a; International Monetary Fund, 2008b). Whereas more economically powerful OFCs such as the Cayman Islands and Jersey have a good report card, small Pacific jurisdictions such as Vanuatu and Nauru have a relatively low level of compliance, frequently due to their lack of access to sufficient governmental resources (Sharman & Mistry, 2008).

Offshore Shell Bank Fraud

A shell bank is a bank incorporated in a jurisdiction which does not require the bank to have a physical presence and where it has no affiliation with a regulated financial services group (Basel Committee on Banking Supervision, 2003, p. 1). Shell banks have been a phenomena of the offshore world. They were originally created in small islands in the Caribbean (for example, Anguilla, Turks and Caicos, Antigua/Barbuda) and later spread to jurisdictions in the South Pacific (for example, Nauru and Vanuatu). The banking laws of those countries allowed the creation of special bank licences whereby an IBC registered under local laws could describe itself as a bank, if it paid a licence fee to the government.

Offshore shell banks, which are also known as paper banks, suitcase banks and brass plate banks, are inherently fraudulent vehicles (Shockey, 1990; US Senate Permanent Subcommittee on Investigations Minority Staff, 2001; Hitt, 2000). With little if any capital, no place of business and none of the usual characteristics of an actual bank, shell banks became the poster boy of advanced fee frauds and money laundering during the 1990s. Frequently, shell banks falsely claimed they have assets of millions if not billions of dollars. The modus operandi of shell banks was simple in facilitating frauds and other financial crimes. A shell bank may issue certificates of deposit to investors without the financial means to repay the investment, issue false bank statements to provide credibility to fraudulent tax schemes, or make phony loans or inflate balance sheets of worthless companies. Shell banks have also been used for money laundering, tax evasion and prime bank instrument fraud (Walters, 1995; Securities and Exchange Commission, 2010a).

Offshore shell banks have two features that are of general significance for OFCs. First, shell banks are not subject to adequate regulation by the government of the OFC that issues the licence. Since they have no physical staff or permanent employees, it is extremely difficult if not impossible for bank regulators to 'monitor bank activities, inspect records and question bank personnel' (US Senate Permanent Subcommittee on Investigations Minority Staff, 2001, p. 9). Typically, the owners or controllers of shell banks are unknown, so that the opportunities for using the bank to commit fraud or engage in money laundering are significant. Second, the licence of a shell bank will be subject to a condition that it does not carry out any banking business locally or carry out transactions in the local currency. Consequently, there is little incentive for the licensing jurisdiction to regulate shell banks.

At one time shell banks could be found in most offshore jurisdictions, but the larger OFCs, such as the Cayman Islands and Bahamas, stopped issuing licences for shell banks in the late 1990s. A landmark US Senate report on correspondent banking and money laundering, coupled with the Bank of New York scandal of 1999 paved the way for the abolition of shell banks. However, it was only after 9/11 that shell banks were shut out of a large part of the world's financial system. Under the Patriot Act, US banks have been prohibited from providing correspondent banking facilities to shell banks, or to foreign banks which provided such facilities to shell banks.[7] As a result of the US correspondent banking rules and the creation of new AML standards, the laws of many countries have been amended so as to ban their banks from operating correspondent bank accounts for shell banks and requiring increased due diligence in their correspondent bank relationships.

Most offshore jurisdictions have abolished shell bank licences, and it may be expected in the not-too-distant future that no country will permit the licensing of such fraudulent entities. The issue then is whether offshore banks that are not shell banks pose higher criminal risks to the international financial system compared with onshore banks. A US Senate report in 2001 concluded that offshore banks per se impose higher criminal risks because offshore regulators have neither the incentive nor resources to properly regulate them.[8] Similarly the FATF has taken the position that inadequate licensing and supervision of offshore banks provides a conduit for money laundering (FATF, 2007).

Grand Corruption

The misuse of offshore jurisdictions to launder the proceeds of grand corruption is well documented (Chaikin, 2005c, pp. 27–46; Winer, 2006). For example, a corrupt procurement officer at the United Nations hid $1 million in an offshore bank in Antigua as part of the laundering of the proceeds of the monies generated from the UN arms-for-oil scandal (Chaikin, 2005c, pp. 27–46; Winer, 2006). IBCs have featured in many political corruption scandals, including Sani Abacha of Nigeria, Benazhir Bhutto of Pakistan and the political elite in Kazakhstan. In each of these cases, the Swiss bank deposits were held in the names of IBCs secretly controlled by or for the benefit of allegedly corrupt politicians. The existence of the IBCs created an added layer of secrecy, which prevented or delayed identifying the beneficial owner.

Corrupt Politically Exposed Persons (PEPs) have exploited both OFCs and major International Financial Centres (IFCs) in transferring illicit monies from their home jurisdictions (Chaikin, 2010, pp. 1–4). For example, the former Chilean President, Augusto Jose Ramon Pinochet Ugarte, used various versions of his name, three Chilean passports (with different names, photographs and signatures), various aliases, names of family members, his personal assistant, accounts in the name of offshore front companies (including BVI companies controlled by his Chilean lawyer) and Chilean military officers to open up bank accounts in Argentina, Bahamas, Cayman Islands, Chile, Gibraltar, Spain, Switzerland, the United Kingdom and the United States.

Many of the Politically Exposed Persons (PEP) corruption cases demonstrate the misuse of multinational banks based and regulated in IFCs in moving illicit corrupt monies through both OFCs and IFCs (Chaikin & Sharman, 2007). For example, Vladimiro Illich Lenin Montesinos Torres, former Presidential Advisor and Chief of the Peruvian National Intelligence Service under President Alberto Fujimori, created a network of corruption that spread into every sector of the country-executive, legislative branch, judiciary, political parties, local government, military, private sector, media and civil society (Jorge, 2008, pp. 111–2; Chaikin & Sharman, 2009, pp. 141–4). The proceeds of arms-related corruption were laundered through Switzerland, the United States, Luxembourg, Cayman Islands, Panama and Mexico. The Peruvian government recovered about $174 million, including $77 million from Switzerland, $20 million from the United States, and $33 million from the Cayman Islands (World Bank and United Nations Office on Drugs and Crime, 2007, pp. 19–20; Jorge, 2008, pp. 115–23; Chaikin & Sharman, 2009, p. 141).

Illicit Capital Flight

Capital flight is the legal or illegal movement of funds from countries seeking refuge from currency restrictions, depreciation of currency and/or confiscation of assets, and political or economic instability. Capital flight is not a new phenomenon: the Protestant Huguenots in 17th century France and the German Jews during the 1930s exported capital to escape religious and racial persecution.

A distinction may be drawn between illicit and licit capital flight. Illicit capital flight may be defined as an 'unauthorised transfer of capital if the form of foreign exchange, banknotes or securities from a country that forbids or restricts such transfer abroad by its residents (Swiss Bankers Association, 2008; Chaikin, 2005b). Some commentators describe illicit flight capital as largely undocumented tax evasion, in effect a 'flight to secrecy' (Chaikin, 2005b, p. 105). It has been estimated that annual illicit capital outflows (which would include illicit capital flight and international dirty money transfers) may be between $1 to $1.6 trillion (Baker, 2005, p. 23).

The significant point is that illicit capital flows from developing countries to richer developed countries, which may be IFCs and/or OFCs. The impact on development is huge, given that illicit capital flight dwarfs overseas aid: 'at best overseas aid replaces 20 per cent of illicit capital flight' (Palan, Murphy & Chavagneux, 2010, p. 174). The forms of illicit money flows (fraudulent transfer pricing, criminal money laundering, and cross-border corruption payments) are facilitated by the existence of secrecy laws and practices in OFCs (Palan, Murphy & Chavagneux, 2010, pp. 174–5; International Task Force, 2007).

International Tax Evasion

Professor Ronen Palan in his co-authored book, *Tax Havens: How Globalization Really Works*, has argued that international tax evasion is the key underlying feature of globalization as it affects wealthy individuals and multinational enterprises. Here there is a link between corruption and tax evasion. Given that corrupt actors will not disclose their illicit income to national tax authorities, corruption ultimately will lead to tax evasion and/or tax fraud. Although Palan considers that OFCs are a major facilitator of corruption, money laundering and other financial crimes, it is tax evasion that makes tax havens 'one of the most important instruments in the contemporary, globalized financial system' (Palan, Murphy & Chavagneux, 2010, pp. 4, 237). That is, tax havens are not mere marginal players in international business: they are central players 'to the world of finance, to the world of business of managing the monetary resources of an organization, country or individuals' (Palan, Murphy & Chavagneux, 2010, p. 4).

The major challenge posed by OFCs is the difficulty of national tax agencies obtaining information from OFCs showing that a taxpayer may be engaged in tax fraud and/or evasion (Chaikin, 2009). Previously OFCs did not co-operate in tax cases except in very limited circumstances, such as where there was clear evidence of tax fraud. The most significant development in this area has been the endorsement by major onshore and offshore financial centres of the OECD tax information exchange standard. Within a very short period of time, hundreds of bilateral tax information exchange agreements (TIEAs) have been entered into. It is too early to determine whether TIEAs will be effective in combating international tax crimes; however, they are a major step in international co-operation, which will result in OFCs being subject to greater scrutiny in relation to their role in illicit tax activities

Financial Crises and Systemic Instability

In 2000 the Financial Stability Forum Working Group found that OFCs had not been a 'major causal factor in the creation of systemic financial problems', such as those arising in the Asian Financial Crisis (Financial Stability Board, 2000). However, the report which identified 42 jurisdictions as OFCs, expressed concern that some OFCs may in the future contribute to financial instability because of their failure to comply with international standards relating to money laundering, securities and related financial services, prudential banking and/or insurance standards. These standards have been created by the Financial Action Task Force (FATF), the International Organisation of Securities Commissions (IOSC), the Basel Committee on Banking Supervision (Basel Committee), and the International Association of Insurance Supervision (IAIS) respectively. Subsequently, the IMF implemented an OFC Programme to assess the compliance levels of OFCs with the key international standards. The latest IMF reviews suggest that compliance by OFCs is generally as high as other jurisdictions (International Monetary Fund, 2008b).

However, OFCs have been blamed for facilitating the fraudulent and corrupt accounting practices associated with major corporate collapses, such as Parmalat and Enron (Tavakoli, 2008, pp. 42–4, 104–7). The use of non-transparent special purpose vehicles in OFCs has allowed secretive hedge funds and private equity firms to engage in massive speculation and regulatory avoidance, resulting in major pressures on the global financial system. The umpire is still out as to whether and how OFCs contributed to the Global Financial Crisis, in particular whether they 'exacerbate[d] existing tensions and problems in the financial system . . . [or] . . . add[ed] a distinct layer of instability to the financial system' (Palan, Murphy & Chavagneux, 2010, p. 162; Mann, 2009).

OFFSHORE BANK FRAUD AND CORRUPTION CASE STUDY

The relationship between offshore bank fraud and corruption is illustrated by a case that the US Securities and Exchange Commission (SEC) and Department of Justice have brought against the offshore bank Stanford International Bank (SIB) and its founder Sir Robert Allen Stanford (Stanford). In 2009 the SEC accused Stanford of running an $8.2 billion ponzi scheme whereby investors deposited monies with the Antiguan-based SIB, and in return received certificates of deposit guaranteeing substantial returns. The ponzi scheme operated for more than 17 years, with later investors being paid out from earlier investors. The inducement was that investors were offered above-market returns on what was presented as a conservative investment strategy.

The history of this SIB case shows a symbiosis between offshore and onshore actors. In 1985 Sir Allen Stanford, the brains behind the alleged ponzi fraud, created a shell bank called Guardian International Bank in the British Crown dependency of Montserrat, which attracted adverse interest by British regulatory authorities. In 1990 Stanford moved the bank's principal location to Antigua, another British dependency, and changed its name to Stanford International Bank Limited (SIB). To get rid of the 'shell bank taint', Stanford organized SIB so that it had a physical office in Antigua and local employees who provided limited services, such as keeping account records, sending out client statements, and processing credit card bills for certain clients. Despite claims to the contrary, SIB could not be considered to be a shell bank or a sham entity. However, the Antiguan employees have been described as 'passive' and 'marginalized' and it has been alleged that the independent auditor of SIB conducted audits without obtaining any source records of the investment funds, such records being located outside Antigua (*Receiver's Response to the Antiguan Liquidators' December 3 Supplemental Brief*, 2009, pp. 9–11). Indeed, nearly all of the management and financial operations of the Stanford group, including the Antiguan bank, were carried out in Sir Allen Stanford's offices in the United States (*Receiver's Response to the Antiguan Liquidators' December 3 Supplemental Brief*, 2009, pp. 9–11). Bank employees in Antigua had no authority or function in selling certificates of deposit or in handling the investment activities of SIB. Instead, US-based employees of the Stanford Group controlled the actual sales, deposits and investments. Further, the investors did not actually pay for their certificates of deposit by transmitting funds to the SIB in Antigua, but sent the monies to onshore banks in the United States, Canada and Europe. Four onshore banks have been accused of facilitating the ponzi fraud by acting as conduits to pay off earlier investors, and transmitting investors' funds to Sir Allen Stanford and his onshore companies (Cohn, 2009).[9] From this it may be argued that the US, Canadian and European connections are very significant, and that the connection to Antigua were merely a façade to prevent discovery of the fraud.

This case also illustrates the importance of the relationship between offshore and onshore regulation in preventing corrupt or fraudulent practices. It is fortunate that the SEC Office of Inspector General has produced a detailed 150-page report on the regulatory deficiencies of the SEC in tackling this offshore ponzi scheme and that there are extensive civil and criminal filings in the United States, as well as United Kingdom liquidation and receivership rulings pertaining to this case. An examination of this primary material, coupled with secondary news sources, provides insights into the relationship of onshore and offshore regulation.

According to the SEC Office of Inspector General's (OIG) report, SEC investigators in Texas were 'aware since 1997 that Allen Stanford was likely to be operating a Ponzi scheme', having come to that conclusion a mere two years after Stanford Group Company (SGC), Stanford's investment adviser, registered with the SEC in 1995 (Securities and Exchange Commission Office of Inspector General, 2010, p. 16). Despite four examinations by local SEC auditors, a number of complaints made by foreign investors to the SEC, and anonymous whistle-blowing by several ex-employees of Stanford, no enforcement action was taken by the SEC until 2009, following the exposure of the unrelated Bernie Madoff ponzi scam.

How did the Stanford ponzi scandal last for so long? Why did the SEC not nip the ponzi scam in the bud, thereby preventing billions of dollars of investors' losses? Is the Stanford case an illustration of an absence of regulation? In answering these questions, what is the relevance of the offshore dimension in facilitating the alleged fraud? At first glance the case seems surprising since the US SEC Enforcement Division is famous for its highly skilled and aggressive investigatory skills, with a track record of enforcement that is the envy of securities regulators throughout the world (Chen, 2010; Lake, 2010). One plausible explanation is that the SEC like any government agency is largely risk adverse and did not place priority in investigating an alleged offshore ponzi scam which had not yet run its full course during the stock market boom. Further, there appears to have been no complaint made by any American investor, of being defrauded by the offshore bank whilst the ponzi scheme was in operation, even though more than 37 per cent of the sales of certificates of deposit were issued to US citizens (*Receiver's Response to the Antiguan Liquidators' December 3 Supplemental Brief*, 2009, p. 6). There was thus no US constituency or US politician pressing the SEC to investigate. The OIG report notes that the suspected ponzi scam did not fit within the priorities of the SEC at this time that were geared to combating accounting frauds involving professionals (Securities and Exchange Commission Office of Inspector General 2010b, pp. 26, 128–9). There were major bureaucratic hurdles in getting the SEC head office in Washington DC to listen to a regional SEC office's concerns of a suspected offshore fraud that might not even be securities-related. Further, the OIG report found that there was an enforcement culture in the SEC which rewarded employees based on the number of cases that were dealt with, rather than the seriousness of the case (Securities and Exchange Commission Office of Inspector General, 2010b, pp. 122–4). It appears that the Stanford/SIG case was viewed as too difficult and too costly because it involved a foreign bank secrecy jurisdiction, with little perceived benefit in launching an extensive international investigation (Securities and Exchange Commission Office of Inspector General, 2010b, p. 39). All these factors suggest that the offshore factor was highly relevant – lack of onshore victim complainants, low priorities for offshore fraud investigations, costs and difficulties in cracking foreign bank secrecy – in preventing any comprehensive, properly resourced investigation being launched.

This is not to discount the influence of onshore factors in perpetuating the alleged fraud. The Stanford Group, which was affiliated with the Antiguan bank and hundreds of related companies, was a US-registered investment adviser and broker-dealer, with clearing functions through the then prestigious Wall-Street firm, Bear Stevens. This provided the mask of a regulated US corporation. Indeed, the ability of Stanford to sell through a US-based broker dealer gave it 'an imprimatur of legitimacy to foreign investors' from Europe, Latin and South America. There were other onshore reputational factors, such as the role of the Hong Kong and Shanghai Bank in providing correspondent banking facilities for the Antiguan bank, thereby lending its considerable prestige to the offshore investment (Stanford Victims Coalition European Group, 2010).

The OIG report investigated whether any corrupt or improper influence had affected the SEC investigation. The OIG, after questioning relevant government officials, concluded that the failure of the SEC Fort Worth Office to pursue enforcement action was not due to 'any improper professional, social or financial relationship on the part of any former or current SEC employee' (Securities and Exchange Commission Office of Inspector General, 2010b, p. 149).[10] This conclusion was reached despite the fact that there was a glowing endorsement of Sir Allen Stanford by the former US President George W Bush, and that the former senior enforcement counsel of the SEC in the Forth Worth Office had sought to represent Allen Stanford in proceedings brought by the SEC in circumstances where that counsel had been previously involved in the SEC investigation of Stanford and his companies. Moreover, during the relevant period Allen Stanford and related corporate entities 'donated $1.9 million in political contributions to over 90 politicians, political action committees and congressional committees' in the United States (*Receiver's Interim Report Regarding Status of Receivership, Asset Collection and Ongoing Activities*, 2010, p. 8). The effect of these political gifts is not clear; however, the US receiver of the Stanford Group is trying to recover these gifts which were allegedly sourced through funds from defrauded investors.

Although the SEC has been cleared of any impropriety, foreign regulators have not escaped accusations of corruption. The US Department of Justice has brought criminal charges against the former administrator and Chief Executive Officer of Antigua's Financial Services Regulatory Commission (FSRC), in addition to its criminal case against Sir Allen Stanford.[11] This is an extraterritorial claim by US authorities, in that they are seeking to punish a foreign regulator who it is alleged did not exercise sufficient diligence over Stanford International Bank (SIB), which has no physical presence in the United States. In particular, the Department of Justice prosecutors have charged Leroy King with aiding and abetting securities fraud by accepting thousands of dollars of alleged bribes so as to ignore the ponzi scheme.[12] It is alleged that King ensured that there were no proper audits and examinations of SIB's books and records, including its investment portfolio, that King provided Sir Allen Stanford with access to the FSRC's confidential regulatory files, including the SEC's requests to the FSRC for information about Stanford's operations, and that King allowed Stanford 'to essentially dictate the FSRC's responses to the SEC's information requests' (Securities and Exchange Commission, 2009). If these charges are sustained, it would provide a massive blow to the integrity of offshore financial regulation.

There was more subtle questionable behaviour, including the purchase of political influence in Antigua. Allen Stanford ingratiated himself with the Antiguan government, which rewarded him with Antiguan citizenship and a recommendation for a knighthood. Stanford companies were one of the most significant employers in Antigua, a British Crown dependency of 80000 people in the Caribbean. SIB lent the Antiguan government $80 million, and financed other projects of benefit to Antigua (*Receiver's Interim Report Regarding Status of Receivership, Asset Collection and Ongoing Activities*, 2010). The absence of adequate Antiguan government regulation of SIB may be attributed not only to Stanford's political influence in Antigua, but also the lack of incentive to regulate an offshore bank. SIB as an IBC was prohibited by Antiguan law from offering banking services to Antiguan residents. The regulatory motivation to protect depositors and investors (who were foreign) or to maintain high prudential standards for the purpose of financial stability was sadly missing in the SIB matter.

CONCLUSIONS

What then is the significance of OFCs in relation to the problem of corruption. There are two characteristics of OFCs that have facilitated corrupt practices. First, OFCs have relied on excessive bank and corporate secrecy as a business model to obtain and maintain an onshore clientele. This has allowed OFCs to earn substantial fees from corrupt onshore clients. Until relatively recently, offshore secrecy has been a significant obstacle to the prevention and investigation of financial crimes, as well as the recovery of the proceeds of corruption. In the past 10 years, the OECD and the FATF and more recently G20 have sought to address the problem of secrecy by demanding changes to laws in OFCs. Although it would be premature to claim that financial secrecy is no longer an obstacle to combating financial crimes, major revisions in OFCs' regulations means that a lack of transparency in OFCs is no longer a distinctive characteristic of OFCs. Second, OFCs have licensed banks, corporations and other financial structures and instruments that have not been subject to adequate regulation which has resulted in abusive financial activities. Although certain facilities are no longer available in OFCs, such as shell banks or anonymous bearer shares, there is still a problem that OFCs lack economic incentives to regulate licensed entities that are exclusively aimed at non-residents.

The range of corrupt and illicit activities in OFCs and the case study of Stanford International Bank show a symbiosis between offshore and onshore actors. It would seem that the function of the 'offshore space' may to provide jurisdictional hurdles to the discovery of illicit conduct but that the nerve centre of criminality may be located onshore. The implication of this is that not only must there be an improvement of regulatory enforcement of offshore vehicles, but that onshore regulators must ensure that onshore players do not exploit the offshore space so as to facilitate fraud, money laundering or corruption. Further research is required to properly understand the full ramifications of the offshore/onshore relationship so that policymakers, regulators and law enforcement can apply appropriate strategies to deal with abusive financial conduct.

NOTES

1. A ponzi scam is an investment fraud that pays initial investors huge returns from monies contributed by new investors. Such scams ultimately collapse because the so-called returns are fictitious and merely a device to lure unsuspecting investors (Securities and Exchange Commission 2011).
2. Not all OFCs have statutory-based bank secrecy, let alone excessive secrecy. For example, OFCs such as Jersey, Guernsey, Isle of Man and Bermuda, have common law bank-customer confidentiality, but do not have any legislation creating bank secrecy.
3. Some European countries, such as Belgium, have abolished bearer securities, so as to remove the anonymity that has facilitated organized crime and tax fraud (Serebriakoff 2007).

4. See for example, *Business Companies Act 2004* ss 67-76 (British Virgin Islands), *International Companies Amendment Act 2008* (Samoa).
5. Under US law, Delaware's LLCs are not subject to US taxation if they do not carry on business in the United States and where they are owned and managed by non-US citizens and non-US residents (Winston 2009: 24–26).
6. See UN General Assembly, *United Nations Convention Against Corruption*, 31 October 2003, A/58/422 ('UNCAC') art 48, par 7, art 31 par 7 and art 40.
7. See 31 USC §5318(j), *Uniting and Strengthening America by Providing Appropriate Tools Required to Intercept and Obstruct Terrorism Act of 2001* (United States of America) ('Patriot Act'). See also Chaikin (2010), 34–68.
8. US Senate Permanent Subcommittee on Investigations Minority Staff (2001) estimated in 1999 that there were 4,000 licensed offshore banks which control nearly $5 trillion in assets.
9. The suit names as defendants, Toronto Dominion Bank of Canada, Trustmark National Bank of Mississippi, the Bank of Houston, London-based HSBC Bank, and the Swiss private banking division of France's Societe Generale.
10. The report recommended at pp. 150–151 a number of changes that the SEC should enact to improve the effectiveness of the decision making process in its Enforcement Division.
11. See Allen Stanford indictment, *United States v. Robert Allen Stanford et al.*, Court Docket Number: H-09-342, before US District Judge David Hittner. The trial which was scheduled for 2011 has been indefinitely postponed after the Judge found Stanford unfit to stand trial because of his drug addiction.
12. Ibid. See paragraphs 38, 45–49, 52–63, 65–66, 69–74, 79–80, 85, 88 and 91.

REFERENCES

Allen Stanford indictment (2009), *United States v. Robert Allen Stanford et al*, Court Docket Number: H-09-342.

Anti Money Laundering and Counter Terrorist Financing Act 2006 (Australia) ('AMLCTF').

Antoine, R. (2002), *Confidentiality in Offshore Financial Law*, Oxford: Oxford University Press.

Antoine, R. (2005), *Trusts and Related Tax Issues in Offshore Financial Law*, Oxford: Oxford University Press.

Baker, R. (2005), *Capitalism's Achilles Heel: Dirty Money and How to Renew the Free-Market System*, London: John Wiley and Sons.

Basel Committee on Banking Supervision (2003), Bank for International Settlements, *Shell banks and Booking Offices*, Basel, Switzerland: Bank for International Settlements.

Blum, J.A., M. Levi, T. Naylor & P. Williams (1998), *Financial Havens, Banking Secrecy and Money Laundering*, United Nations Office for Drug Control and Crime Prevention, Vienna: United Nations Office for Drug Control and Crime Prevention.

Business Companies Act 2004 (British Virgin Islands)

Chaikin, D. (2005a), 'Nominee shareholders: Legal, commercial and risk aspects', *Australian Journal of Corporate Law*, **18**(3), 288–303.

Chaikin, D. (2005b), 'Policy and fiscal effects of Swiss Bank secrecy', *Revenue Law Journal*, **15**(1), 90–110.

Chaikin, D. (2005c), 'Policy and legal obstacles in recovering dictator's plunder', *Bond Law Review*, **17**(2), 27–46.

Chaikin, D. (2006), 'Penetrating Foreign Nominees: A failure of strategic regulation', *Australian Journal of Corporate Law*, **19**(2), 141–60.

Chaikin, D. (2009), 'Tax havens: An Australian perspective', in D. Chaikin (ed.), *Money Laundering, Tax Evasion and Tax Havens*, North Melbourne: Australian Scholarly Publishing, pp. 96–108.

Chaikin D. (2010a), 'A critical examination of how contract law is used by financial institutions operating in multiple jurisdictions', *Melbourne University Law Review*, **34**(1), 34–68.
Chaikin, D. (2010b), 'International anti-money laundering laws: Improving external accountability of political leaders', U4 Anti Corruption Resources Centre Briefing Paper, August 2010, **4**(1), Bergen, Norway: U4 Anti-Corruption Resources Centre.
Chaikin, D. and J.C. Sharman (2007) *Final APG/FATF Anti-Corruption/AML/CFT Research Paper*, FATF/PLEN(2007)37, Paris, France.
Chaikin, D. and J.C. Sharman (2009), *Corruption and Money Laundering: A Symbiotic Relationship*, New York: Palgrave.
Chen, M. (2010), 'Senators probe inaction against Stanford', *Houston Chronicle*, http://www.chron.com/disp/story.mpl/business/7213620.html, accessed 3 March 2011.
Cohn, S. (2009), 'Stanford investors sue five banks tied to alleged scam', *CNBC*, 24 August, viewed 28 February 2011, http://www.cnbc.com/id/32540057/Stanford_Investors_Sue_Five_Banks_Tied_to_Alleged_Scam.
Financial Action Task Force (FATF) (2007), *Annual Review of Non-Cooperative Countries and Territories 2006-2007*, Eight Non-Cooperative Countries and Territories Review, Paris: Financial Action Task Force.
Financial Stability Forum (2000), *Report of the Working Group on Offshore Centres*, Basel, Switzerland: Financial Stability Forum.
Hitt, J. (2000), 'The billion-dollar shack', *New York Times*, http://www.nytimes.com/2000/12/10/magazine/the-billion-dollar-shack.html?ref=nauru, accessed 3 March 2011.
International Companies Amendment Act 2008 (Samoa).
International Monetary Fund (2000), *Offshore Financial Centres: The Role of the IMF*, Washington DC: International Monetary Fund.
International Monetary Fund (2003), *External Debt Statistics: Guide for Compilers and Users – Appendix III, Glossary*, Washington DC: International Monetary Fund.
International Monetary Fund (2008a), 'IMF Executive Board integrates the Offshore Financial Center Assessment Program with the FSAP', *Public Information Notice* (PIN) No. 08/82, Washington DC: International Monetary Fund.
International Monetary Fund (2008b), *Offshore Financial Centers: Report on the Assessment Program and Proposal for Integration with the Financial Sector Assessment Program*, Washington DC: International Monetary Fund.
International Task Force (2007), *Illicit Financial Flows and Capital Flight*, The Royal Ministry of Foreign Affairs, Norway: Briefing paper for the first meeting of the Task Force, Oslow, Norway: International Task Force.
Jorge, G. (2008) 'The Peruvian efforts to recover proceeds from Montesinos's criminal network of corruption' in M. Pieth, (ed.), *Recovering Stolen Assets*, Bern: Peter Lang 111–134.
Lake, A. (2010), 'The SEC's case against Sir Robert Allen Stanford – a case study in investigative and enforcement failure', *Federal Criminal Defense Blog*, webblog, viewed 28 February 2011, http://www.federalcriminaldefenseblog.com/2010/04/articles/securities-and-exchange-commis/the-secs-case-against-sir-robert-allen-stanford-a-case-study-in-investigative-and-enforcement-failure/.
Mann, N. (2009), 'Offshore Finance Centres are to blame for crisis, says Pope', *This is Guernsey*, http://www.thisisguernsey.com/2008/12/09/offshore-finance-centres-are-to-blame-for-crisis-says-pope/, accessed 3 March 2011.
McCann, H. (2006), *Offshore Finance*, Cambridge: Cambridge University Press.
Palan, R. (2003), *The Offshore World: Sovereign Markets, Virtual Places, and Nomad Millionaires*, Ithaca: Cornell University Press.
Palan, R., Murphy, R. & Chavagneux, C. (2010), *Tax Havens: How Globalization Really Works*, Ithaca: Cornell University Press.
Picciotto, S. (2007), 'Tackling tax havens and "Offshore" Finance', Paper presented at a seminar on Money Laundering, Tax Evasion and Financial Regulation, Transnational Institute, Amsterdam, 12–13 June.

Receiver's Interim Report Regarding Status of Receivership, Asset Collection and Ongoing Activities (2010), *Securities and Exchange Commission v Stanford International Bank, Ltd et al*, 3-09-CV-0298-N.
Receiver's Response to the Antiguan Liquidators' December 3 Supplemental Brief (2009), *In re Stanford International Bank, Ltd. Debtor in a Foreign Proceeding*, 3-09-CV-0721-N.
Robinson, J. (1998), *The Laundrymen*, London: Simon & Schuster.
Securities and Exchange Commission (2009), 'SEC charges two accountants and Antiguan regulator for roles in Stanford Ponzi Scheme', SEC Press Release No 2009-140, viewed 28 February 2011, http://www.sec.gov/news/press/2009/2009-140.htm.
Securities and Exchange Commission (2010a), *How Prime Bank Frauds Work*, 28 February 2011, http://www.sec.gov/divisions/enforce/primebank/howtheywork.shtml
Securities and Exchange Commission Office of Inspector General (2010b), *Investigation of the SEC's Response to Concerns Regarding Robert Allen Stanford's Alleged Ponzi Scheme*, Case No. OIG-526.
Securities and Exchange Commission (2011), *Ponzi Scams: Frequently Asked Questions*, available at http://www.sec.gov/answers/ponzi.htm
Serebriakoff, A. (2007), *Abolition of Bearer Shares in Belgium*, KBL Private Bank Luxembourg, http://www.kbl.lu/wps/portal/internet/p_LuxTitresPorteur?WCM_GLOBAL_CONTEXT=&LANG=en, accessed 3 March 2011.
Sharman, J.C. (2009), 'The bark is the bite: international organizations and blacklisting', *Review of International Political Economy*, **16**, 573.
Sharman, J.C. and R. Gordon (2009), 'International Financial Centres, tax havens and money laundering,' in D. Chaikin (ed.), *Money Laundering, Tax Evasion and Tax Havens*, Melbourne: Australian Scholarly Publishing, pp. 78–95.
Sharman, J.C. and P.S. Mistry (2008), *Considering the Consequences: The Development Implications of Initiatives on Taxation, Anti-Money Laundering and Combating the Financing of Terrorism*, London: Commonwealth Secretariat.
Shockey, J. (1990), *Offshore Shell Banks*, paper presented at the Annual Symposium on International Economic Crime, Jesus College, University of Cambridge.
Siemens, E. (2010), *Offshore Company Law*, Geneva: Academy & Finance.
Stanford Victims Coalition European Group (2010), 'The Role of HSBC in the Stanford Bank Fraud', *Stanford's Forgotten Victims*, webblog, viewed 28 February 2011, http://stanfordsforgottenvictims.blogspot.com/2010/09/role-of-hsbc-in-stanford-bank-fraud.html.
Swiss Bankers Association (2008), *Due Diligence Agreement* (CDB 08), Basel, Switzerland: Swiss Bankers Association.
Swiss Federal Act on Banks and Savings Banks 1934 (Switzerland)
Tavakoli, J.M. (2008), *Structured Finance and Collateralized Debt Obligations*, New York: John Wiley & Sons.
Tax Justice Network UK (2008), *Tax Havens Creating Turmoil*, evidence submitted to the UK Treasury Committee of the House of Commons.
US Government Accountability Office (2006), *Company Formations Minimal Ownership Information is Collected and Available*, Report to the US Senate Permanent Subcommittee on Investigations, Committee on Homeland Security and Government Affairs, Washington DC: United States Government Printer.
US House of Representatives Subcommittee on Oversight and Investigations Committee on International Relations Hearing (2006), *Offshore Banking, Corruption and Terrorism*, Washington DC: United States Government Printer.
US Senate Permanent Subcommittee on Investigations Minority Staff (2001), United States Senate, *Report on Correspondent Banking: A Gateway of Money Laundering*, Washington DC: United States Government Printer.
US Senate Permanent Subcommittee on Investigations Minority Staff (2010), United States Senate, *Report on Tax Haven Banks and US Tax Compliance*, Washington DC: United States Government Printer.
UN General Assembly, *United Nations Convention Against Corruption*, 31 October 2003, A/58/422 ('UNCAC').

Uniting and Strengthening America by Providing Appropriate Tools Required to Intercept and Obstruct Terrorism Act of 2001 (United States of America) ('Patriot Act').
Walters, A. (1995), *A Practical Guide to Identifying Advance Fee & Prime Bank Instrument Fraud*, London: Sweet & Maxwell.
Winer, J.M. (2006), Evidence given to the Hearing before the Subcommittee on Oversight and Investigations of the Committee on International Relations, *Offshore Banking, Corruption and the War on Terrorism*, United States House of Representatives.
Winston, R L. (2009) *The Future of Tax Havens and Recent Brazilian Anti-tax Avoidance Measures*, Paper presented to the Brazilian-American Chamber of Commerce, New York City, NY, July 7.
World Bank and United Nations Office on Drugs and Crime, (2007) *Stolen Asset Recovery (StAR) Initiative: Challenges, Opportunities, and Action Plan*, Washington DC.

12 Corruption and the global diamond trade

Dina Siegel

INTRODUCTION

For many generations the social world of diamond traders was considered as secretive and isolated. Emphasizing the value of their product, but also trying to protect themselves from the risks outside, diamond traders around the world created their own organization, their own rules and codes of behavior, argot and rituals, in which they shared the common values and norms, but also applied social control and justice mechanisms. Trade diasporas in general, and diamond traders in particular, proved the great importance of these mechanisms in the course of history. This guaranteed their survival in a hostile society and their relative independence from local authorities. They based their activities on trust and intense interpersonal relationships, they established worldwide networks, markets and institutions and later they also introduced advanced technology and increased their co-operation with state agencies.

The most rapid and significant changes in the diamond trade took place at the end of the 20th and the beginning of the 21st century, which shocked the generations-long traditions and internal dynamics. One of the processes was the shift in the symbolism of a diamond. While diamonds have symbolized love, passion and wealth since antiquity, in the last years of the 20th century an attempt was made to change the meaning of diamonds into a symbol of war, cruelty and misery. An example of this shift is the so-called 'blood diamonds'. The negative image of the diamond trade in general and in particular in regard to these 'blood diamonds' was based on alleged activities of diamond traders such as facilitating and financing civil wars in several African countries and smuggling and laundering diamonds from conflict areas and corruption.

In most publications on corruption the issue of diamonds is restricted to 'conflict diamonds'. In this chapter I will analyse two different kinds of corruption in the global diamond trade, namely corruption in production countries and corruption as part of organized crime activities.

Some economic sectors are considered more vulnerable to crime and corruption than others: in Western Europe and the United States, the construction sector, cafés, restaurants and hotels, the music sector, the waste disposal sector; in the Benelux countries specifically, the meat production sector; and in Eastern Europe, cars, flowers, art and liquor are associated with illegal and often organized crime activities (Vander Beken, 2004). The diamond sector was often mentioned during my study as one of such 'criminal branches', which was discovered by organized crime in the 1990s.

This chapter will focus specifically on corruption in the global diamond industry in the turbulent period at the end of the 1990s and the early 2000s. It is based on data collected during my fieldwork study of the diamond trade in different settings between 2001 and 2006 (Siegel, 2008; Siegel, 2009).

Although I will use the term 'corruption' for practical purposes, I will show how a Western understanding of corruption does not explain (or suit) the situation in diamond-producing countries and how this concept is used (and misused) in a Western political context.

THE DIAMOND PIPELINE AND THE CRIMINAL ACQUISITION OF DIAMONDS

The diamond pipeline depicts the movements of diamonds from the mine to the shops and consists of different phases. Several attempts were made to identify the vulnerability of the diamond industry to illicit activities, including corruption (Tailby, 2002; Vander Beken, 2004). It is possible to follow these vulnerabilities at each phase of the diamond pipeline, from production to retail.

Production and Rough Trade

The first step of mining is excavation of a pit into the pipe, the so-called 'open-pit' process. There are also other categories of mines: underground, alluvial, undersea and coastal. The diamond mines are usually located many miles from villages or small towns, often in impenetrable jungles. In Africa, each of the many small mines is officially controlled by licensees, who in turn often work for investors supplying the equipment and other facilities. According to a Global Witness report, however, '. . . many diggers, supporters and dealers are not licensed and therefore operate outside official oversight'.[1]

When diamonds are found, either by individuals or by licensees who collect them from different diggers, they are usually brought to the open markets in nearby villages to small-scale diamond dealers for sale. The offices of these local dealers vary from small market shops with a scale, a fan and a sheet of white paper for identification of the diamond's colour, to modern offices behind barbed wire, with surveillance cameras and bodyguards. Small to middle-sized traders have different methods of selling. They can sell rough diamonds to middlemen, who either sell on to larger dealers, or directly to the owners of polishing factories. They can also sell by tender but then they may face the risk that there will be not enough buyers, or that there will be swings in the market. Tenders are also held only in a very limited number of locations.[2] Large local producers sell the greater part of their production to the Central Selling Organization (CSO) of De Beers, and usually a small portion, called 'windows' (5–20 per cent) independently.

The trade ritual in the local diamond centres in production countries is similar to the practices among diamantairs in Antwerp, Ramat Gan or Mumbai. The price of a diamond is never spoken aloud, but written down; sometimes the small piece of paper goes back and forth many times before an agreement is reached. When there is no agreement, the buyers approach other dealers. The competition is intense from both sides. The estimations of my informants were that the profits of small-scale dealers are large; on a very successful day a dealer may earn \$150 000–\$200 000. When there is no luck, most of the dealers still have other businesses: from selling shoes or electronics to cafés and restaurants. Luxury cars, richly furnished villas, two to four wives wearing expensive clothes and jewels – these are the indications of their wealth. In Congo there are many dealers who also function as priests. They even set up their own churches, inside which they make their deals.

Most illicit opportunities are to be found at this first stage of production (mining) and rough trade. At the production level, illegal mining, individual or organized theft from legitimate mines, in addition to smuggling and theft during transport are possible. During the trade in rough diamonds in local centres, illicit trade, robberies of traders, stone substitution, valuation fraud, mixing illegally mined stones with legitimate goods, manipulation of provenance can all take place (Tailby, 2002, p. 2), as well as theft during transit.

Certification

The next step from the local town is to the capitals, where the necessary procedures are initiated to get a certificate. This takes place in the better districts of the African capitals, where mostly foreign diamond firms have their main offices. The diamonds either come from their own local offices in provincial towns or directly from individual sellers (local small dealers).

The first examination and sorting of stones takes place here. There is much suspicion and control at this stage. The pockets of sorters' trousers are sewn shut to exclude the possibility of theft and there are multiple controls at the entrance of the offices.

After examination and sorting, certificates of origin are granted.[3] The packages with diamonds are sealed and transferred to international airports to be flown to the cutting and polishing centres. Officially, African state governments control the production of diamonds. However the activities of mine officials, who are supposed to monitor and evaluate the performance of miners, licensees, dealers and exporters, are often not conducted according to the written regulations. In most cases, these officials are unskilled, underpaid and possess no technical or logistic support. Under these conditions direct deals with the illicit dealers and smugglers present perhaps the better option.[4] The state officials lose control over the entire sector because they cannot influence the behaviour of the miners and middlemen.[5]

In African diamond-producing countries, the access of specific officials to certificates, a scarce and sought-after commodity, presents a vulnerable link in the chain. The control system in these countries is often presented as the weakest point in diamond production, since in most diamond-producing countries there is a competition-based diamond buying system, which involves a large number of official, but also unofficial, offices and individuals. In such a system no central registration and monitoring is possible.[6] The major actors are diamond middlemen who buy diamonds from diggers and miners. With the right connections, good gifts and a bit of luck it is not difficult to avoid all kinds of bureaucratic procedures, to get certificates and to transfer diamonds to Europe.

For the diamond organization, however, this control system (or to be more precise: the lack of control) is a blessing, because it allows for more influence on the transport of rough diamonds from producing countries to Europe. The organization is also able to control possible competition from the side of individuals or small groups of dealers who try to do business outside the registered diamond networks. This information is important for the control of illicit activities and the creation of the diamond industry's own legality. The relevant officials in the production countries are used for this purpose. Gifts received by officials from diamond traders vary from rough diamonds to other items and money. The value of a gift is dependent on different aspects, such as the required efficiency (how quickly the procedure can be completed) and the importance of a deal (how large is a parcel, the origin of rough, etc.). These gifts can include TVs or DVD players, mobile telephones and even cars. Gift-giving to local officials is taken for granted in this context; nobody views it as an abnormal process, but as part of a negotiation process, a culture of hospitality, or family obligations. In societies where family links are strong and based on clearly defined moral codes these social norms are very powerful. The diamond industry can easily manipulate these habits and rituals, and gain its power and control by playing the local rules of the game.

Corruption in Diamond Institutions

The next step is the processing centres. Transforming unattractive, mainly gray and dull rough diamonds into the beautiful shining stone we recognize from advertisements and jewellers' shop windows is a very precise process, in which millions of workers are involved. The most important countries where diamonds are cut, polished and processed into jewels are India, Belgium, Israel and the USA, while China, Thailand and Dubai are becoming more and more important competitors.

The processing factories vary from one country to another in size, working conditions, and use of technology: from air-conditioned rooms with computers and advanced equipment to small and badly lit rooms, crowded with sweating workers, who use only loupe and wheel. Many factories are traditional family businesses, though in Belgium and Israel the work is not done at home, while in India houses are specially designed for the business. There, in the 1980s, the processing took place in one or two rooms at the front side on the ground floor, while the actual living quarters were at the back of the house or on the second floor (Legrand, 1985, pp. 244–45). In India, whole families dedicate their life and work to the diamond business (Kuriyan, 2002, pp. 1–2). The Indian centre of diamond processing is in Gujarat, in the cities of Surat, Bhavnagar and Bhuj (Kuriyan, 2002, p. 3). Another world centre of the trade in gems and diamonds is Bangkok. With the huge boom of the Thai economy in the 1980s the presence of (mainly Jewish) diamond traders has grown as well.

At the level of the cutting and polishing process and the trade in polished diamonds, illicit activities and theft, as well as the trading of illicit stones in the legitimate market, child labour and exploitation can happen. Last but not least, at the wholesale level there is a great danger of illicit sales and theft from manufacturers and consumers.[7]

According to representatives of the diamond industry, one quarter of the diamonds on sale in South Africa, for example, could be 'conflict diamonds', which means diamonds mined in regions riddled by civil war and ethnic conflicts. The issue of 'conflict diamonds' was introduced by several NGOs at the end of the 20th century, and led to the Kimberley Process through a United Nations Resolution in 2003. The Kimberley Process has 49 members representing 75 countries and requires governments to certify that shipments of rough and uncut diamonds are not being used in conflict areas to finance local wars and violence. Despite the Kimberley Process, different NGO reports testify that diamonds from conflict areas are still being smuggled and processed in legal diamond institutions.

In addition to 'conflict diamonds', there is also the problem of synthetic diamonds sold as authentic ones, or sold without certification. Recent reports show that there is a growing number of people who discover that their diamonds are not authentic or of lower quality than mentioned in the official certificate.[8] It appears that in the grading process and the laboratory systems of the diamond industry there is a lack of control and plenty of opportunities for fraud.

In 2005 a big scandal erupted at the Gemological Institute of America, the services of which are used by thousands of diamond traders. It is difficult to determine the origin of diamonds. Diamonds are homogeneous stones, they look the same, and above all they also look like cubic zirconium, rock crystal, white topaz and some other minerals. Inexperienced consumers may even buy pieces of glass instead of diamonds. In order to prove and guarantee the quality of diamonds and to convince customers that they are buying a real diamond there are certificates of authenticity, provided by the Gemological Institute of America.[9] In the 1990s –2000s, the GIA grading reports[10] became a routine for diamond traders and the opinion of GIA specialists was usually highly respected and valued among diamantairs around the world. In 2005, however, two counterfeit GIA Diamond Grading reports were discovered in Antwerp. In the course of the investigation it appeared that in 1995 the GIA top managers had already heard about the possibility of fraud and bribery. One of such practices even led to a lawsuit in 2002, when one diamantair accused the GIA of collaborating with a group of diamantairs to value diamonds higher than their worth and inventing a complex 'fraudulent scheme' to hide their real value. When the diamantair tried to sell the evaluated diamond to his client, the stone was returned to him after the client conducted his own investigation. There were more cases, similar to this, especially in the period between 2002–2005,[11] most of which did not lead to lawsuits.

An internal GIA investigation took place in 2005, as a result of which four employees were fired. However, neither their names, nor the names of the traders who bribed them for falsified certificates were disclosed, nor the extent of damage. For the diamond community, which is used to naming and shaming procedures this was quite a difficult situation. In an emotional message on his website, a leading diamond traders wrote: 'The lesson is simple. If we publicly ruin someone's reputation, the potential monetary loss is so great that it just does not pay to bribe, i.e. deterrence. If we don't ruin the reputations of bribers, they will continue to operate and eventually beat the GIA into the ground'.[12] For the decision-makers of the solution, pacification of the conflict for the sake of preserving the reputation of the institute was more important than the disagreement inside the community.

Corruption at the State Level

Weak governments and lack of control in Central Africa led to the development of the informal diamond economy, which allows hundreds of thousands of miners and middlemen to survive, but also attracts criminal organizations and government officials, as well as different rebel groups (Dietrich 2002). According to Global Witness: 'law enforcement authorities lack training, funding and expertise to tackle the illicit diamond trade; governments lack the political will to govern the diamond industry; and there is little regional coordination to stop illicit trading'.[13]

In countries where 'conflict diamonds' originate, governments have little influence on the situation at the local mines and even at their own borders to monitor the diamond export. According to the NGOs there is a lack of commitment, such as in the Democratic Republic of Congo and in Angola.[14] However, there is a difference between commitment to international agreements such as the Kimberley Process, and commitment to indigenous groups involved in a process of negotiation. In this case, it is often forgotten that it was not the Kimberley Process that ended civil wars and ethnic conflicts, but internal peace-making mechanisms and local negotiation processes. It would therefore be too simple to view corruption as a negative phenomenon if it can facilitate peaceful negotiations through personal and informal processes.

The high level of corruption in countries like Angola and Sierra Leone is often mentioned as one of the reasons for the failure of the Kimberley Process. In my view, the real reason does not lie in corruption as a social phenomenon, but in our Western interpretation of this age-old way of life in most African societies. The resulting irresponsible and insensitive pressure and policy-making could very well be the real reasons behind the failure of the Kimberley Process. The question is whether the term corruption should even be applied to societies where 'greasing the wheel' is a way of life, and the only way to survive.

CORRUPTION OR A WAY OF LIFE?

While in the West 'corruption' is a widely accepted term designating the abuse of public office for private gain (Alatas, 1990; Rose-Ackerman,

1996), it has another meaning in the non-Western world, which it is more difficult to identify (Tanzi, 1995). Here, corruption is 'socially embedded in "logics" of negotiation, gift-giving, solidarity, predatory authority and redistributive accumulation' (Oliver de Sardan, 1999, pp. 25). I subscribe to the anthropological approach to 'corruption' as a Western concept which tries to separate between public and private while ignoring the reality of face-to-face communities that are based on the exchange of gifts, on patronage, and strong kinship links. The academic literature provides a wide range of evidence about such societies and interrelationships. Therefore, what in the Western world is considered corrupt and illegal appears to be viewed as moral and normal in other contexts. Anthropological research proves that 'what is termed "corruption" from an outsider's (or "etic") perspective, is often linked to a code of values and behavior that is widely known and accepted from an insider's (or "emic") perspective; people know how the system of favours works and how to work it – even if they are reluctant to admit this publicly' (Shore and Haller, 2005, p 12). What is called corruption in the West can also be viewed as gift-giving and social networking. Gift-giving, often described as bribery, is the most important aspect of analysis of so-called corruption practices. To label gift-giving as 'bribery' is to make too fast, too stereotypic and too irresponsible judgement. Gifts and their exchange between parties is an old, established phenomenon, described in classical anthropological studies as a basis for correct relationships and balanced reciprocity (Evans-Pritchard, 1940; Malinowski, 1961). The kula exchange ring among the Trobriand Islanders, studied by Malinowski, always consisted of a circle – a gift and its counter-gift (Malinowski, 1961). More than a ritual this was a symbolic expression of safe guarantee between potential rivals. This exchange involved thousands of people from different groups, and regulated their relationships. Oliver de Sardan describes the meaning of 'little gifts' in African societies as thanks for services rendered. 'This "kola nut" is not a fixed or negotiated price of remuneration, nor is it a brokerage commission; it is above all a moral duty' (1999, p. 38). In Niger, a gift is brought to the customary chief when one greets him to assure his goodwill in the future (p. 39).

In many cultures, gift-giving is a dominant social custom which includes codes of behavior, moral values and expectations, showing respect, mutual rights and obligations and strengthening relationships, based on reciprocity and reconciliation of self-respect and definition of one's position inside the society (De Bary, 1991, pp. 3, 4). It is so accepted that nobody views it as an abnormal process, but as part of the hospitality culture and even national pride. In some cultures refusing gifts is a token of bad manners, rejection, unrespectable attitude and even direct hostility, and refraining from giving gifts is even 'a risk of attracting misfortune' (Oliver de Sardan, 1999, p. 40). 'To refuse a favor to a "recommended" person generates shame. To refuse a gift in return for help generates shame' (Oliver de Sardan, 1999, p. 46). And 'shame is, in the majority of African cultures, a powerful means of social control' (ibid). In addition, gifts often do not even provide economic advantages, but regulate debts and duty relationships (see also Marx, 1974, p. 213).

The dilemma can develop when the moral obligations and social habits, connected to shame and social obligations are confronted with the Western morality of non-corruption. Two socio-cultural logics are becoming clear: what is considered to be corrupt in Europe is not necessarily the same in Africa. In societies where family links are strong and based on clearly defined moral codes, one cannot expect that the public employee will apply other principles in his public dealings. As some authors predict, 'centuries-old and widely accepted social norms will often prove more powerful as guides to behavior than new and often imported rules based on arm's length, impersonal, and universal principles' (Tanzi, 1995, p. 25).

The superiority of the West with its paternalistic and moralistic strain is manifested here. 'The West exchanged the old racist coinage for a new currency. "Uncivilized" became "underdeveloped". "Savage peoples" became the "third world"' (Easterley, 2007, p. 21). Gift-iving is now considered bribery and corruption.

Another possible perception of what in Western society is called corruption, is worldwide existing patronage relations. According to Boissevain, patronage is 'the complex of relations between those who use their influence, social position or some other attributes to assist and protect others and those whom they so help and protect' (1989, p. 307). This system is to be found in many other societies (See, Waterbury, 1989).

Some societies and political regimes could not even survive without corruption. According to Waterbury, in Morocco, corruption is 'a planned, cultivated, and vital element in assuring the survival of a regime' (1989, p. 340). This was even truer in the case of Soviet Russia. In the USSR, according to Rosner, 'secrecy, corruption, theft and cover-ups are constant factors in day-to-day activity' (Rosner, 1986, p. 127). The Soviet people developed a perception according to which 'the moderate exploitation of power for individual interests improves the quality of life. . .' (Shlapentoch, 1989, p. 218). Corruption came to be considered normal and unavoidable and the only way to survive (Simis, 1982; Ledeneva, 1998; Siegel, 2005).

Doing a favour can vary from clear rules of the game, based on informal exchange or social links, and positions of the two parties in exercising power and manipulation. A good example of the latter is a classic study by the anthropologist Frederick Bailey, who did ethnographic research in a rural East Indian village in the 1950s. He found that the local population viewed the agents of the local government as 'a collection of individuals who could be manipulated, one way or another, into doing a favor' (1994, p. 32). From other research it appears that in West Bengal, 'particular contacts and general networks may be maintained and cultivated with a strategic consideration also' (Ruud, 2000, p. 277). These personal contacts allow plenty of possibilities to solve problems and obtain economic benefits. 'Networks are explicitly employed as a strategy to cope with the bureaucracy' (p. 281).

In other words, when discussing the 'problem of corruption' in, for instance, diamond producing African countries, generalizations and superficial conclusions must be avoided. Tradition, cultural codes and existing relationships and networks must be carefully analysed. Patronage and clientelism have their own morality, at least in the perception of the local people (Shore and Haller 2005, p. 12). Therefore, focusing on corruption as a problem in the 'developing world prevents us from understanding that these are practices developed within a fully mature normative system of no less moral validity than any other normative system' (Ruud, 2000, p. 271).

CORRUPTION AND ORGANIZED CRIME

The meaning of corruption is different when it is linked to organized crime in the West. Tailby identified four criminal strategies in diamond-related criminal activities (2002, p. 2). Firstly, criminals become employed by a mine with the purpose of stealing diamonds, once 'inside'; secondly, miners or other diamond industry employees are approached by criminal organizations resulting in theft (at different stages of the diamond pipeline); thirdly, theft takes place during transit between main points in the pipeline; and fourthly, criminal groups trade in illicit diamonds in different war regions. In the abovementioned strategies the importance of criminal networks and corruption is emphasized.

Since the beginning of the 1990s, the diamond sector in Antwerp has been confronted with the rising interest of organized crime groups in the context of smuggling, money laundering, organized robberies and fraudulent activities. The risk is that organized crime will be able to penetrate the semi-autonomous sector of diamond traders, or the possibility that insiders will get an offer 'they cannot refuse' and become partners in crime. Diamond-related crimes may be either local or transnational, varying from spectacular robberies from prestigious museums and exhibitions, to smuggling through complex schemes from Sierra Leone to Antwerp. There are various criminal organizations involved in illicit diamond activities.

The phenomenon of smuggling from diamond mines mentioned earlier could perhaps be explained by the extreme poverty and poor chances for the local population. When an individual smuggles diamonds found in a mine, a miner hopes to improve his personal situation and that of his family, to survive physically and to continue his expectation of an improved life. Smuggling can also be viewed as an economic guarantee or investment, when people migrate from one country to another. There is, however, also another kind of smuggling. African couriers, who work for large crime groups, or individual smugglers, who work independently are often arrested in different European sea- and airports. The methods of smuggling vary from sticking stones on different parts of the body, to swallowing them or hiding them in double-bottom suitcases. The couriers usually arrive legally, with a tourist or business visa, but they often stay much longer than legally allowed. A few hotels in the diamond neighborhood of Antwerp became meeting places for these couriers, who often know each other, or who make their first contacts with 'friends of friends', as appeared during my fieldwork. This phenomenon developed as a result of the Kimberley Process, when 'conflict diamonds' were being smuggled through other, non-conflict countries and 'overseas territories' (Weyzig, 2004, p. 62) into the markets where they could be mixed with non-conflict diamonds. Some scholars even called the introduction of the Kimberley certificates a perfect system to launder conflict diamonds (Peleman, 2002). Very often, however, the rough diamonds from Sierra Leone, Angola, and other 'problematic' countries simply appear in the diamond market in Europe. The Kimberley Process did not study in-depth the mechanism of the illegal diamond trade. The non-registered smuggled diamonds were not even mentioned as a possibility and therefore did not appear in the Kimberley agreement (ibid.). The smuggling networks of diamonds from Angola, however, are mentioned in other reports. These networks include Belgian diamond companies, which provide false certificates of origin, such as of Zambia – a country where there are no conflicts, but also no diamonds. There are also cases when Antwerp diamantairs send their own couriers to African countries for smuggling activities. One can conclude that indirectly the Kimberley Process created new forms of organized crime activities.

During my fieldwork I discovered that informal contacts between the officially registered diamond traders and the so-called pseudo-diamantairs (self-appointed diamantairs) and non-registered brokers were taking place, despite the assertions of many diamantairs that the sector is hermetically closed to any dubious figures. Business remained business and brokers connect not only among the respectable diamond dealers, but also among the diamantairs and those, who offer a good price for good stones. The certificate of origin, which purports to prevent smuggling, thus became an effective instrument to create an illusion that the consumer will not buy a 'blood diamond', that she is safe from being accused of co-operation with evil regimes and the murder of innocent children. Such a guarantee provides a feeling of control, responsibility, political correctness and security. This illusion is, on the other hand important for trust and good business in the diamond sector.

The smuggling of 'conflict diamonds' became an issue in connection with several Indian diamond traders. In January 2007 Belgian police raided a diamond district in Antwerp, closing 20 diamond firms.[15] The raid was allegedly connected to the Monstrey investigation, which started in October 2005.[16] Monstrey Worldwide Services, a shipping firm, was accused of fraud, which took the form of 'black trade', when legally imported diamonds were fictively exported abroad, but in reality remained in Antwerp. The profits were not indicated, the VAT-imposition was not paid and the account books were falsified.[17] More than 150 diamond companies were involved in this fraud, which was estimated by Belgian federal police to be more than 100 million euros.

The Great Robbery

The Antwerp Diamond Center became the site of a $118 million robbery on 16 February 2003. No less than 123 safes at the Grunberger diamond office building were robbed. Investigators have tried to figure out how the thieves managed to break into one of the world's most secure vaults, with the conclusion that it could happen only with assistance from inside the community of diamantairs; that the thieves avoided security in the building and the door was not forced; later it appeared that they copied keys and replaced videocassettes. They allegedly possessed security passes and knew the exact position of the cameras. All these cameras, alarms, 24-hour security guards on every entrance and exit and cameras in the vault could not prevent the robbery.[18]

The 'professionalism' of the thieves, as the police put it, was evident from the way the alarm system was manipulated: it appeared to function normally, but nothing was registered. Apparently, the videocassettes were replaced with blank tapes. The selection of the stones was also well planned: rough or half cut stones, which are more difficult to sell, were not taken.

The Max Fisher Bank

Fouad Abbas settled in 1986 in Antwerp, where he established his company TTS Diamonds. He also owned diamond businesses in Bombay, Geneva, London and Tel Aviv and a diamond mine in Guinea. In 1986, Abbas came in contact with two Dutch hash dealers. The role of Abbas was to co-ordinate between the Dutch drugs organizations and Asian (mainly Pakistani) criminal groups in shipments of hashish.

Abbas was introduced to one of the employees of the Max Fischer private bank in Antwerp, whose clients were mainly Belgian diamantairs. In this bank he opened several coded African accounts. The employee agreed to transfer through these accounts large cash deposits to different banks in the world. The agreement between Abbas and the employee was that above regular bank commission the latter would also receive a 'personal commission', which he could put in his own pocket. In return no questions on the origin of the money would be asked. In addition, Dutch guilders, the proceeds of the deals in hash in the Netherlands, were converted to US dollars and transferred to different off-shore locations in the world, which Abbas invested in real estate. Through this bank, Abbas transferred more than 48 million Dutch guilders in the period 1989–1992 (Schaap, 1999, p. 70). During this time, Abbas laundered billions of Belgian francs, the proceeds of drugs money through his TTS Diamonds firm.[19]

In 1995, the Max Fischer bank went bankrupt. It appeared that Abbas was not the only client of the Max Fischer Bank who was involved in illegal activities and illicit transactions. During the investigation it came out that hundreds of clients opened accounts using fictitious names and did not pay taxes nor repay levies on moveable property tax.[20] The conclusion of the researchers was that for six years the bank falsified its annual account reports in order to obscure its internal money-laundering activities.[21]

Diamonds and Mafia

Another case of organized crime activities and corruption happened in November 2007 in the United States, when David Gross, a former Nassau County Court Judge, was sentenced for laundering $400 000 in cash and stolen diamonds while working for the Genovese mafia family.[22] Gross worked as a lawyer for an insurance company and was elected to the bench in 1999. He had contacts with several members of the Genovese family, one of the most powerful criminal organizations in the United States, with a rich history connected to the names of Lucky Luciano, who joined the family after arranging the murder of Joe Masseria, Frank Costello, Vito Genovese, and other famous gangsters.

Gross co-operated with this group to launder more than $400 000 dollars in stolen jewels. He was caught in 2005, when negotiating with an undercover FBI agent, who presented himself as a trafficker in stolen African diamonds. In the course of the investigation it appeared that Gross laundered thousands of dollars made in stolen jewels through a restaurant in Long Island.[23] He received a share of the laundering commission, ranging from 15 to 20 per cent.

The above cases are in no way an exception. The 'upperworld' is no less involved in diamond-related crimes than the underworld. Much illegal activity takes place among the diamantairs themselves, but the main threat comes from professional criminals outside their community. The diamond industry has always been aware of external threats and has tried to protect itself by strong internal cohesion and by shielding itself from the outside world. Over the last few years, however, a series of criminal events have brought to light the vulnerability of the sector. The changing economic reality has led to the introduction of new players on the global market and to increased competition on a world level (Vander Beken, 2004, p. 111). The market was opened up when several links in the diamond processing chain were moved to low-wage countries. But more importantly, as a result of growing mobility and increased international flows of goods and money, the opportunities for crime have increased as well.

Organized crime seems to be very interested in diamonds; it manifests itself not only in large diamond cities, such as Antwerp, Dubai or New York, but stones stolen from Sierra Leone, Liberia or Russia could be anywhere, from the shabby houses of local priests in Monrovia to the display cases of large stores in Amsterdam and Rio de Janeiro. Whether these are 'conflict diamonds', or 'peacefully smuggled or stolen' diamonds, criminals make huge profits. Corruption facilitates these diamond-related activities.

CONCLUSION

In this chapter an attempt is made to show different meanings of corruption in regard to the diamond industry. While gift-giving, personal favours, clientelism and patronage are the normal way of life in production countries, in the Western world corruption is strongly associated with crime in general and organized crime in particular. It is difficult and probably futile to force change on age-old cultural practices and ways of thinking. Only the process of westernization and economic development will be able to have an impact on these types of social relations.

On the other hand, when corruption serves organized crime activities it must be combated by law enforcement like any other serious crime. I doubt whether prevention of corruption in the diamond world can work, given the historically proven seductive nature of these precious stones.

NOTES

1. 'Making it Work', Washington DC: Global Witness and Partnership Africa Canada, 2004, p. 17.
2. Such as in Cape Town and Johannesburg, where tenders are held by TrnasHex, or in Luanda by Endiama.
3. This certificate system became even more complex after the Kimberley Process.
4. Diamond Industry Annual Review, 2004.
5. Ibid.
6. *Global Witness*, 2001, Can Controls Work? A Review of the Angolan Diamond Control System. Briefing Document, December.
7. At the more sophisticated end of the spectrum we find theft from exhibitions and museums, which are mainly conducted in the context of organized crime.
8. Using forensics to root out corruption in the diamond industry, 15 May, 2010, on: www.diamondtopics.com
9. Other major gemological centres are the International Gemological Institute (IGI) and The European Gemological Laboratory (EGL). There are dozens of small labs all around the world.
10. In addition to the Rapaport price reports.
11. Rapaport News, 9-11-2005, on: http://www.diamonds.net/news/newsitems.asp?num=13638&type=all&topic=all&sear
12. Rapaport, M., GIA's Bribery Scandal, 4-11-2005, on: http://www.diamonds.net/new/newsitem.asp?num=13569
13. 'Making it Work', Washington DC: Global Witness and Partnership Africa Canada, 2004:17.
14. Ibid:17, 18.
15. Rapaport News on: http://www.diamond.net/news/NewsItem.aspx?ArticleID=16659
16. In the course of this investigation, an Indian diamantair died during a police raid in December 2006.
17. Belgische Senaat Handelingen, Thursday, 9 November 2006, on: https://www.senate.be
18. The *Guardian*, February 19, 2003; Rapaport News, February 17, 2003: http://www.diamonds.net/news; CNN. com, February 28, 2003: http://edition.cnn.com/2003/WORLD?europe/02/27/belgium.diamonds.ap/
19. *De Standaard*. November 16, 2001; *Het Nieuwsblad*, November 16, 2001; *De Financieel-Economische Tijd*, November 16, 2001.
20. *De Financieel-Economische Tijd*, August 7, 1998; *De Financieel-Economische Tijd*, April 3, 2001.
21. *De Financieel-Economische Tijd*, April 3, 2001.
22. Department of Justice, FBI New York Division, Press Release, at: http://newyork.fbi.gov/dojpresserl/pressrel07/moneylaundering071307.htm
23. Rapaport News, on: www.diamonds.net

BIBLIOGRAPHY

Alatas, S. (1990), *Corruption: Its Nature, Causes and Function*, Aldershot, Brookfield, USA, Hong Kong, Singapore, Sydney: Avebury.

Bailey, F. (1994), *The Witch-hunt, or, The Triumph of Morality*, Ithaca, NY, Cornell University Press.

Bary, de W. (1991), *Learning for One's Self. Essay on the Individual in Confucian Thought*, Lincolnwood, Il: Colombia University Press.

Boissevain, J. (1989), 'Patronage in Sicily' in, Heidenheimer, A. M. Johnston and V. LeVine (eds), *Political Corruption. A Handbook*, New Brunswick (USA) and Oxford (UK): Transaction Publishers.

Campbell, J. (1989), 'Village Friendship and Patronage' in, Heidenheimer, A. M. Johnston and V. LeVine (eds), *Political Corruption. A Handbook*, New Brunswick (USA) and Oxford (UK): Transaction Publishers.

Dietrich, C. (2002), *Hard Currency: The Criminalized Diamond Economy of the Democratic Republic of the Congo and its Neighbours*, Partnership Africa Canada, IPIS, June.

Easterly, W. (2007), *The White Man's Burden*, Oxford: Oxford University Press.

Evans-Pritchard, E. (1940), *The Nuer*, Oxford: The Clarendon Press.

Kuriyan, V. (2002), 'No Problems Here: Success, Complacency and Suspicion in the Indian Diamond Industry', *The Diamonds and Human Security Project*, Partnership Africa Canada.

Ledeneva, A. (1998), *Russia's Economy of Favours. Blat, Networking and Informal Exchange*, Cambridge: Cambridge University Press.

Legrand, J. (1980), *Diamant: Mythe, Magie en Werkelijkheid*, Brussel/Amsterdam: Elsevier.

Malinowski, B. (1961), *Argonauts of the Western Pacific*, New York: Dutton.

Marx, E. (1974), *Bedouin of the Negev*, Tel-Aviv: Reshafim (in Hebrew).

Naylor, R. (1998), 'The Rise of the Modern Arms Black Market and the Fall of Supply-Side Control' in, *Transnational Organized Crime*, **22**.

Oliver de Sardan, J. 1999, 'A Moral Economy of Corruption in Africa? in: *The Journal of Modern African Studies*, **37**(1), 25–52.

Peleman, J. (2002), 'Conflictdiamanten – gezien vanuit Afrika' in, *Tijdschrift voor Criminologie*, **4**(44), 358–66.

Rose-Ackerman, S. (1996), 'Democracy and "grand" corruption', in: *International Social Science Journal*, **48**(3).

Rosner, L. (1986), *The Soviet Way of Crime*, Massachusetts: Bergin & Garvey Publishers.

Ruud, A. (2000), *Corruption as Everyday Practice. The Public-Private Divide in Local Indian Society*, in: Forum for Development Studies, **2**, Norwegian Association for Development, Norway: Routledge.

Schaap, C. (1999), *Heling Getoetst – Studie naar het Witwassen van Geld en de Strafbaarstelling door Middel van de Hellingsbepalingen*, Deventer: Gouda Quint.

Shlapentoch, V. (1989), *Public and Private Life of the Soviet People*. Oxford, New York: Oxford University Press.

Shore, C. and D. Haller (2005), *Corruption. Anthropological Perspective*, London: Pluto Press.

Siegel, D. (2005), *Russische Bizniz*. Amsterdam: Meulenhoff.

Siegel, D. (2008), 'Diamonds and Organized Crime. The case of Antwerp', in D. Siegel and H. Nelen (eds), *Organized Crime. Culture, Markets and Policies*, Dordrecht: Springer.

Siegel, D. (2009), *The Mazzel Ritual, Culture, Customs and Crime in the Diamond Trade*, New York: Springer.

Simis, K. (1982), *USSR: The Corrupted Society*, New York: Simon and Schuster.

Tailby, R. (2002), 'The illicit market in diamonds', *Trends & Issues in Crime and Criminal Justice*, No. 218, Australian Institute of Criminology. January. *Developments*, **32**(4), December.

Vander Beken, T., L. Cuyvers, B. De Ruyver, M. Defruytier and J. Hansens (2004),

Kwetsbaarheid voor Georganiseerde Criminaliteit. Een Gevalstudie van de Diamantsector. Gent: Academia Press.

Waterbury, J. (1989), 'Endemic and Planned Corruption in a Monarchical Regime' in, Heidenheimer, A., M. Johnston and V. LeVine (eds), *Political Corruption. A Handbook*, New Brunswick USA and Oxford UK: Transaction Publishers.

Weyzig, F. (2004), The Kimberly Process Certification Scheme one year after: state of affairs in the European Union, Fatal Transactions, SOMO, NIZA.

Wood, B. and J. Pelemans (1999), *The Arms Fixers – Controlling the Brokers and Shipping Agents*, Oslo: NISAT.

13 Corrupt practices in the global trade in art and antiquities

Duncan Chappell[1] *and Kenneth Polk*[2]

INTRODUCTION: THE 'GHIYA CONSPIRACY'

In June 2003, following an intensive undercover operation, Indian police in the city of Jaipur raided the home of a wealthy businessman, Vaman Narayan Ghiya. A search of the house revealed a set of secret cupboards in which were concealed hundreds of colour photographs of ancient Indian sculptures. The sculptures, many hacked away crudely from temple walls and with missing limbs or heads, were displayed haphazardly near the sites from which they had been removed. The police also discovered a large number of auction catalogues from Sotheby's and Christies, the international auction houses located in London and New York (Keefe, 2007; Watson, 1998).

Based on these discoveries, as well as further finds across the country of hordes of looted artefacts hidden at various properties owned by Ghiya, the police concluded that they had uncovered a sophisticated antiquities trafficking operation with links to auction houses and private collectors in Europe and North America. Their subsequent interrogation of Ghiya confirmed this suspicion.

Ghiya admitted to heading an international business which had conducted its activities without disruption over three decades, illegally exporting thousands of plundered antiquities to overseas buyers using an elaborate laundering process. Most of the goods were shipped through a free trade zone established in Geneva, Switzerland, where Ghiya maintained three shell corporations. These companies would trade objects between themselves to establish a false provenance for the artefacts before forwarding them on to auction houses, dealers and collectors who could claim the antiquities came from Swiss rather than Indian sources. Many of those involved in this elaborate scheme were fully cognisant of its deceptive qualities and willingly participated in it, while others chose to ignore or question the provenance of the artefacts they received. Ghiya was usually paid through dummy bank accounts, repatriating funds through *hawala,* a paperless and virtually untraceable remittance system widely used in India (Keefe, 2007; Watson, 1998).

There is no doubt that Ghiya could not have achieved this long-standing and successful trafficking operation without the assistance provided by many individuals, ranging from those involved in the original theft of artefacts to the middlemen who facilitated their transportation, first to points in India controlled by Ghiya and then overseas to their ultimate destinations. There were also strong but unsubstantiated suspicions that Ghiya's nefarious activities had been protected through a range of high-level political and allied governmental connections he had established in India.

Officials responsible for protecting the thousands of archaeological sites, museums and other locations scattered across India from which the items were taken, as well as those involved in inspecting shipments prepared for export, were either bribed to turn a blind eye to this activity, or duped into believing that the items being exported were fakes rather than original artefacts whose unlicensed removal from the country is prohibited. India, like many antiquities-rich countries, has for many years had in place strict laws regulating the export of items which form a part of its cultural heritage. Under the provisions of the Indian Antiquities and Art Treasures Act 1972 all antiquities not less than 100 years of age must be registered with the Central Government, while any export of such an item requires a Central Government, permit (International Foundation for Art Research, 2010).

The 'Ghiya Conspiracy', as it has been termed, provides a graphic illustration of the way in which corrupt practices at many levels facilitate the continuing operation of a lucrative international market in art and antiquities, which is in large part reliant upon the illicit transfer of artefacts from less wealthy source nations like India, to the rich countries of the West where demand is greatest. In the balance of this chapter we seek to describe the nature and scope of this market, and the corrupt practices upon which it depends, based in part upon research that we have conducted in the region of Southeast Asia. We also consider the effectiveness of contemporary efforts to curb this market, including the associated corruption. In speaking of corruption, and corrupt practices, we are guided in general by the definitions offered of such terms by Transparency International (TI). According to TI the operational definition of corruption is the 'abuse of entrusted power for private gain', and a distinction is made between 'according to rule' corruption and 'against the rule' corruption:

> Facilitation payments, where a bribe is paid to receive preferential treatment for something that the bribe receiver is required to do by law, constitute the former. The latter, on the other hand, is a bribe paid to obtain services the bribe receiver is prohibited from providing. (TI, 2009)

RESEARCH LIMITATIONS

We should begin by recognizing that study of the illicit traffic in cultural heritage material at large, especially in Asia, is at a much earlier, and therefore cruder, level of development than studies of such illicit markets as those involving drugs or the trade in humans. This is not because the traffic itself is new. In fact, one could easily argue that the plunder of antiquities pre-dates such problems as the current issues with illicit drugs since it extends back through the centuries. The tombs of the Egyptian pharaohs were often plundered almost as soon as they had been sealed. In China, a catalogue of what were even by then ancient bronzes appeared as early as 1092, and a similar catalogue of the antiquities collection of the Song court was published in 1123 (Debaine-Francfort, 1999, p. 15). No 'grand tour' was complete without the learned gentleman returning home with various plundered trinkets to demonstrate his intimate acquaintance with Greek and Roman culture.

What is remarkable is that the commentary on the plunder of cultural heritage has been so slow to evolve, and that there has been almost no major research grant money devoted to its study, or to an examination of the corruption so necessary for the success of this traffic. Our work, for example, has been done almost exclusively out of our own resources. This is a major issue when it is recognized that the traffic itself is truly multi-national and transnational in scope. There are many different countries that yield up, however unwillingly, cultural material for the market. The chains involved from initial plunder to ultimate sale are lengthy and extend potentially across many national boundaries. Those involved represent many different languages and cultural backgrounds, languages and backgrounds that these investigators do not speak and are ignorant of.

Further, we are not helped in any way by the existing criminal justice system in terms of knowledge or even data. Virtually all art crime, including cultural heritage crime, like most corrupt practices, belong to the well-known 'dark figure' of crime, that is, they reside outside of the reach of current crime statistics. Numbers of estimates have been made of the value of the annual market in trafficked antiquities, ranging from USD $300 million to $6 billion (Atwood, 2004, p. 221). The market has also been said to rank behind only the trade in drugs and arms in the scale of its illicit trafficking (Charney, 2009). Estimates like these, and especially those comparing the relative size of all such trafficking activities, must be viewed with great caution since they are based on the flimsiest of empirical data and analysis.

Some interesting attempts have been made to examine the link between the illicit market in cultural heritage property and the level of corruption prevailing in a given society. Thus Fisman and Wei (2009) have examined customs data in source and destination countries involved in this market. Taking advantage of different reporting incentives regarding smuggled artefacts between these countries, they have been able to generate a measure of illicit trafficking in these goods from US customs import records and the purportedly identical trade as recorded by customs authorities in exporting countries. Their findings show a reporting gap which is highly correlated with the corruption level of the exporting nation, as measured by the World Bank's composite corruption indices (Kaufman et al., 2006). This work offers a promising framework for studying both corruption and the illicit market in cultural heritage property, but it is at this stage still very much an emerging rather than fully developed approach.

FEATURES OF THE ILLICIT TRAFFIC IN ANTIQUITIES

Our previous research (see, for example, Alder & Polk 2005; Alder, Chappell & Polk 2009) into the traffic in antiquities, mostly focused on Southeast Asia, suggests that there are many similarities with other forms of illicit markets. (see also Mackenzie, 2005). Like most of these other markets (for a description, see Chawla and Pietschmann, 2005), the antiquities traffic has a strong international component. The demand from purchasers is the basic economic force which drives the market (and the consequent destruction of sites), and a significant component of that demand is found in such market centres as London, New York, Paris, Brussels or Amsterdam, among others. Particularly, but not uniquely, in Asia there is as well a strong domestic and regional demand for these objects which, as we shall see, complicates how we look at the control issue.

Given the international reach, the trade must contend with the problem that the movement of material out of the country of origin is illegal. Virtually all of the nations which supply the antiquities markets have put in place strong legal prohibitions against the removal of such material from the country of origin. In turn, this tends to generate two problems common to illegal markets. One, smuggling operations are required given that export is illegal, and these often involve complexities imposed by the nature of the goods being transported. In the case of some of the Cambodian and Chinese stone objects, which often are quite large and exceptionally heavy, both the size and weight issues complicate the movement process. Huge crates, and the equipment necessary to move them, are expensive, and not easily either hidden or disguised. Two, if there is to be consistent and repeated movement of material across national boundaries, assurance of the success of the endeavours can be improved through the corruption of public officials. Both of these problems are addressed through the natural development of forms of organized social activity that we are likely to term 'organized crime'. There certainly is evidence in terms of the movement of these large objects through China, Cambodia and Thailand of some level of corrupt organization that resembles what is seen elsewhere in terms of organized crime.

Complicating all of this is the problem common to illicit markets that there are actually many different kinds of cultural objects and markets rather than just one 'antiquities market'. One of our earliest informants, for example, was a dealer in jade objects from China. These items are actually quite small, and a relatively large 'volume' of material can be carried easily on the person. In this case, there is no need for the complication of an 'organization' to assure a constant supply of material since a dealer can obtain a reasonable supply of material on a single trip, carrying a large inventory on the person. Similarly, we have found that dealers in Chinese ceramic material indicate that their yearly needs for material do not involve large volumes, so that as little as one container a year might be sufficient to satisfy the needs of a moderate-sized antiquities shop. In short, while some form of 'social organization' might be necessary to assure a sustained and vital market of any particular form of cultural heritage material, those needs may not require the full range of organizations that might be implied in the term 'organized crime'.

There are some differences, however, between the traffic in antiquities and other major illicit markets. One of the most important is that while the movement of material from source may be illegal, the sale of cultural heritage objects in the major market centres is open and legal. We have found Khmer objects from Cambodia, and various forms of ceramic and stone material from China on sale in venues in London, New York, Paris, Amsterdam and many other western locations, objects whose absence of provenance suggests illicit origins. In fact, it is not uncommon for the dealers, when approached by naïve potential customers, to have various devices or stories which are used to convince them that the objects are plundered and illegally smuggled, in order to counter the possibility that the objects in question are fakes. While doing fieldwork out of Phimai in Thailand, we were taken by archaeologists to a burial site in a remote province which had been plundered. Some months later, in visiting a shop specializing in Thai objects in Singapore, we saw a photograph taped to a display case that bore a remarkable resemblance to the site we had seen. The picture was taken to show the 'dig' in process (which was in fact a photo of the plunderers at work). The objects on offer were distinctive bronze age ceramics of the exact size and type we had seen at the site. Once again, what the shop owners were doing is presenting evidence of plunder as a way of assuring the 'authenticity' of their merchandise, since faking is an endemic problem throughout the industry.

ILLICIT ANTIQUITIES AND ORGANIZED CRIME

Any complex criminal activity that involves a long chain of individuals linked internationally from initial plunders in supply environments, to agents, to buyers, to smugglers, and then to antiquities dealers in market states will require some degree of 'organization'. Whether that fits into traditional conceptions of organized crime is another matter. A number of issues seem important in shaping this discussion. First, there is no doubt that the type of activity we have described does in many cases match the requirements of the UN Convention against Transnational Organized Crime (UNODC, 2004; see also Bowman, 2008) to be considered as being carried out by an 'organized criminal group', namely:

> a structured group of three or more persons, existing for a period of time and acting in concert with the aim of committing one or more serious crimes or offences established in accordance with this Convention , in order to obtain , directly or indirectly, a financial or other material benefit. (Article 2)

Despite this match, unlike many other forms of illicit traffic covered by the Convention, the efforts of an established criminal enterprise are not required to keep the activities flourishing but hidden in the consuming environments, since the sale of antiquities in most market locations is legal. Most of our images of organized crime, as in the media stereotypes found in movies or TV, feature the 'mob' working in the destination market. Emphatically, the 'Sopranos' are not part of the sale of elegant Chinese antiquities in the high-end venues in London, Paris or New York.

Second, as we have already indicated, much of the traffic in antiquities is of a relatively low volume (since many of the objects are small, and not a great number are needed for a reasonable profit to be made), and does not require a large infrastructure for the support of equipment, personnel and subterfuge. Some overlap might still be expected when the need for organization in antiquities occurs in geographic proximity as it does in the Middle East with opiates (and a long history of classical antiquities), Latin America with cocaine (and Pre-Columbian objects), or perhaps sections close to the 'Golden Triangle' in Asia (with proximity to at least some cultural heritage sites). And, indeed, one does pick up some anecdotes of such overlap. In a television programme some years ago, there was a short clip of a van stopped at a customs checkpoint somewhere in the Middle East, and agents were in the process of removing a cache of both drugs and small antiquities. One of our informants in Bangkok alleged that the military authorities in Myanmar routinely sent trucks down to the border with Thailand, loaded, it was said, with 'girls, drugs and antiquities'.

Some observers have pointed out that physical items such as art and antiquities can provide objects that might prove useful as a way of 'laundering' the wealth in cash obtained from the drug traffic or other illicit activities. While authorities worldwide have sought to curb the flow of 'black money' by tightening regulations regarding banking and allied financial bodies the use of such objects for money laundering has grown. As Fidler (2003) has noted:

> Ferrying cash across borders is difficult, and carrying diamonds or bullion creates suspicion. Moving works of art or antiquities is much easier. Even big works can be moved; ancient friezes, for example, can be exported as Italian tiles. For money launderers, antiquities [also] have an advantage over prominent paintings; it is often impossible to determine if they are stolen. (Fidler, 2003, p. 1)

The lack of any documentation regarding the provenance or provenience of a particular antiquity is an issue we discuss in more detail below. But in general, unless an object has been taken from an established site or museum it is unlikely to have any verifiable identification which would reveal to a suspicious border control or customs official whether it came from a legitimate or illegitimate source. Further, most of these officials at the exporting and importing level are unlikely to have an expertise in archaeology or cultural studies which might prompt their curiosity or suspicion about the origins of an object. Thus the risk of detection for any money laundering or other related offence is usually at a minimum.

The broad conclusion that we have come to as a result of our fieldwork is that there is little evidence coming through at the present time of major involvement of traditional elements of organized crime in the illicit trade in antiquities. In fact, as we have suggested, there is for much of the trade scarce need for complex organization because of the nature of the objects being dealt with (some small, and others of moderate size and volume of trade). Large criminal organizations are quite expensive to maintain and require reasonable volumes to justify the expense. This is consistent with the observations of Mackenzie (2005), who found that for most dealers the transport problem was mundane, commenting that while drugs such as heroin are not usually trafficked by Fed Ex, '. . .this was the method of shipment recommended to me by an antiquity dealer I spoke to on Hollywood Road' (Mackenzie, 2005, p. 137).

This is not to say that there is no 'organized crime' involved in the antiquities traffic. The movement of large, bulky and heavy items involves a number of complications, and steps. Extraction of the material may require manpower and expertise at removal (especially in terms of large stone objects). Payment has to be arranged for the extraction by agents who then must work through the transit problems. The objects have to be lifted and carried from site of origin to some transit point (for example, being lifted by a crane so that they can be carried by truck to a point where they are placed in a container for shipment by sea). Papers have to be arranged which permit some form of access to both export and import procedures. Dealers who are complicitous in this process must then be found so that the items can be placed on wholesale and ultimately retail markets in destination countries. In turn, buyers must be found who are willing to purchase cultural heritage material without asking questions about provenance.

The criminal organization for antiquities in these circumstances *at the source end* likely will be surreptitious and involve individuals who know they are taking risks but for whom the financial rewards are great enough to justify taking those risks. In the less-developed regions of Asia, there is not a large range of sources that can provide the transport infrastructure that will be required for the large objects in terms of cranes, trucks, containers and ships. It is not surprising that the military often appears in accounts of traffic at this end of the market (for example, regarding the involvement of Cambodian military authorities in the traffic of Khmer objects, see Beech, 2003, p. 56; and Thosarat, 1999, p. 69 comments on a 'General' who was making 'a very lucrative profit off the sales of artefacts'), as do police (Doole, 1999, p. 7). Mackenzie (2005, p. 19) describes a situation where the looting of a Cambodian temple site involved several hundred soldiers and heavy machinery, with the objects reportedly being stolen to order by the army in response to a request by a Thai antiquities dealer operating out of Bangkok. One of Mackenzie's (2005, p. 141) informants pointed out the obvious fact that in China, '. . . the army has the lorries with which they can transport the objects'.

During our research the senior law enforcement officials within the region with whom we discussed the possible links between organized crime groups and the antiquities trade tended to share our general view of the situation. Many admitted to a lack of knowledge at large about the trafficking of cultural objects, seeing it at best as a minor law-enforcement issue and at worst as a possible distraction in the 'war against drugs'. Some acknowledged a particular interest and concern about the money laundering aspects of the antiquities marketplace.

One former crime agency head, who now spends most of his time advising governments throughout the region about anti-money laundering measures, told us recently that he suspected the 'dark figure' of cultural objects laundered by persons involved in the trafficking of drugs and humans was far greater than many believed. Further, that organised groups of traffickers were well ahead of law enforcement in recognizing the benefits of this particular ruse to wash clean the products of other illicit endeavours. The same source told us that in his view a significant weakness in the anti-money laundering arsenal was the ease with which cultural objects from the region could be trans-shipped around the globe by established air freight couriers with few questions asked at the point of shipping or receipt, usually because of the ignorance of the officials involved about the cultural significance of particular objects, or through corrupt practices such as the use of false documentation.

In the absence of detailed studies of the antiquities marketplace throughout the region views like those just expressed must remain speculative. Nonetheless, it would be misleading to give the impression that law enforcement is at a total standstill when it comes to tackling the problems of looted antiquities. For example, in Cambodia international law enforcement agencies like the FBI have been invited by the Cambodian Government to advise a new national heritage police force established to end the systematic pillaging of the country's ancient monuments (De Launey, 2007). This development was preceded by an agreement between the US, a nation which has been one of the main recipients of plundered Khmer art, and Cambodia aimed at stifling the illicit trade in cultural objects. As part of this agreement the US has placed import restrictions on ancient stone, metal and ceramic objects from Cambodia (BBC News, 2003).

ILLICIT ANTIQUITIES AND CORRUPTION

There are many forces in play to contribute to the continued vigour in the illicit traffic in antiquities. A major factor accounting for this trade is the continued demand for high-quality cultural heritage goods by consumers in the wealthier destinations. That demand will continue to put pressure upon the poorer environments that make up the supply element of the trade equation. As is true in other illicit markets, that traffic spins out its own demand for corrupt public officials who occupy the key gatekeeping roles where that supply might be interdicted.

In the case of antiquities, much of that corruption is likely to reside pretty much exclusively within the supply and transit environments. There have been no accounts that we know of corrupt officials concerned with the trade in cultural heritage material in, for example, policing or customs agencies in such developed countries as the United States, the United Kingdom, or Australia. In our view, this is to be expected because there is no need for the expense required to bring about corrupt co-operation with political figures or public servants in the demand environments, since by and large the sale of antiquities can be carried out openly, given that there are no laws defining the sale of such material as illegal. This is, of course, in sharp contrast with other illicit trafficking, such as drugs, where possession or sales is illegal in both source and demand nations, and where there are numerous instances of extensive corruption in the demand settings.

On the other hand, there are several indications of corruption, as we have noted above, involving customs, police and military figures in the supply nations. The significant problems of transport requirements in some of the poorest nations, it appears, have contributed to the involvement of military figures in providing the heavy equipment involved in moving some of the largest of the cultural objects (such as stone material from temple sites), since the price commanded by such goods results in a huge financial return for those involved. Inevitably, such figures then begin to wield their influence within governmental decisions in order to assure a continuity of their income returns.

Where there appears to be consistent evidence, impressionistic to be sure, is in the customs services at the key portals where the trade is moved onward to the ultimate supply destinations. However it might be in violation of local laws, goods manage to arrive at destinations in Australia, the United States, or the United Kingdom with what appear to be legitimate export documentation from ports such as Hong Kong or Bangkok. Certainly, in our conversations with dealers in such key portals, we are assured that there will be 'no problems' in the movement of material onward to such destinations.

Care has to be taken with such descriptions, of course. Some of the traffic in cultural heritage materials is both low volume and concerns small objects. One individual may be able to carry what amounts to a large inventory in his own personal baggage on a single airplane journey with virtually no concern about apprehension. Customs officials in Australia, the United States or the United Kingdom, for example, are simply not likely to have any training or understanding of the illicit nature of such objects. In these cases, it is ignorance on the part of customs, rather than corruption, which allows the trade to continue.

The low volume, and limited size of individual shipments, creates options for source and transit nation dealers that would be unheard of in some of the other illicit markets. As related above, we have observed directly that traders in locations such as Hong Kong are able to utilize common commercial carriers for the transport of what seem to have been smuggled antiquities, since once in the safe and 'open' transit ports, any exports, especially in what amount to small packages, are not likely to be subjected to significant scrutiny by customs officials.

Similarly, violence seems to be a rare occurrence as part of the corruption package connected with antiquities. There have been reports of violence in a few of the more notable archaeological sites, especially in Latin America where a considerable volume of gold might be involved, and there even the archaeologists at times find it necessary to carry firearms (Watson, 1999). The destination environments for antiquities, in contrast, consist of some of the most elegant addresses in locations such as New York or London, and while plush and elegance certainly are no guarantees against violence, we have heard of no stories at all of the use of violence at that end of the market chain.

This examination of corruption in the illicit traffic of cultural heritage material thereby makes an important contribution to our understanding of the interplay between prohibition, continued demand, organized crime, and corruption. A common theme that runs through much of corrupt activity is that its root resides in the attempts of moral entrepreneurs to impose their ethical standards upon a society wherein there is not the value consensus present that is consistent with those standards. Put simply, the citizenry continue to desire the goods that are now forbidden, and are willing to pay on an illicit market to obtain those goods. Some amount of organization of criminal activity then becomes required as a way of satisfying the resultant demand, since the legal prohibitions require that at least at some point in the chain of market activity the criminal actions have to be hidden.

The examples of illicit market activity involving antiquities that we have examined here help to clarify the complex possibilities that can be created by this mix. In many respects, a disservice has been done by the early examples of alcohol and drug prohibitions, since there will be many forms of illicit traffic that diverge from these models. In the case of drugs, we see one way of mixing these elements. With illicit drugs, there have been strong prohibitions imposed in source, transit, and demand environments which have not been adequate to dampen the demand that continues in the wealthy market settings, and that demand is huge. Since that demand translates into astronomical profits, it is inevitable that forms of organization would emerge to satisfy that demand, organizations that soon realize huge sums that can be translated into support for complex organizational structures and infrastructure. Further, these patterns of organized crime will seek ways to assure the continued flow of material from source to destination by using some of the resulting funds to assure co-operation of public officials and politicians in source, transit and destination environments. And, as we have seen in the tragic events that took place in Mexico, violence can become an all too common tool used by those involved in the illicit traffic (Padgett and Mascarenas, 2010).

Our examples of cultural heritage material, however, show that the mix of prohibition, organized crime, corruption and violence can take very different forms. While continued demand in response to prohibition is present, the fundamental fact that the prohibition has been imposed in the source, but not the demand, environments has a major impact on the shaping of the illicit traffic in antiquities. There is corruption, but consistent with the nature of the prohibitions imposed, our research leads us to believe that it is found exclusively in the source and transit components of the illicit market chain.

This market, it must be said, is not a static one. Consumer tastes can change over time, and that can dampen demand for a particular style of goods. Political forces in source and destination settings shift and change in terms of their support for policies regarding the traffic of cultural heritage goods. Economic conditions change within the various nations, and this can have an impact on the funds available for discretionary spending on expensive consumer goods. Educational and ethical programmes might conceivably have an impact on the stance potential consumers might take with respect to unprovenanced material. As such dynamic forces alter the demand for cultural heritage material, so then there will be some corresponding re-shaping of the terrain involving this illicit traffic, including the financial resources available for assuring the compliance of key public figures in the complex chain of corruption that can be a feature of the traffic in antiquities. In short, while some understanding of the current need for corruption in this arena might be available currently, there is no assurance that in five or more years' time these observations would still be accurate.

CONCLUSION

We have argued here that the particular forms of corruption that emerge as a part of the pattern of organized criminal activity that supports the illicit traffic in antiquities provide both an important example of how corruption results from legal prohibitions where demand is allowed to remain, yet at the same time warn us that different illicit traffic patterns will produce different forms of corruption. Certainly our observations are consistent with a view that corrupt practices are likely to flow out of organized crime, and that both of these (organized crime and corruption) result when demand for some good or service remains despite legal prohibition. It follows that any successful approach to control of corruption is likely to depend upon public policy which addresses demand. Unfortunately, much of the weight of public policy currently designed to restrict the illicit traffic in cultural heritage material is aimed at restriction in the source of environments that provide the supply side of the dynamic equation that produces this traffic. A strong lesson that emerges from our research, which is admittedly at an early stage, is that it is demand which fuels this traffic, and its resulting corruption, and that unless future policy is aimed at reduction of demand, attempts to control the illicit traffic, and the corruption, are likely to be futile.

NOTES

1. Adjunct Professor, Faculty of Law, University of Sydney.
2. Professor of Criminology, University of Melbourne.

REFERENCES

Alder, C., D. Chappell and K. Polk (2009), 'Perspectives on the organization and control of the illicit traffic in antiquities in South East Asia' in S. Manacorda (ed.), *Organised Crime in Art and Antiquities*, Milan: ISPAC, pp. 119–44.

Alder, C. and K. Polk (2005). 'The illicit traffic in plundered antiquities', in P. Reichel (ed.) *Handbook of Transnational Crime*, London: Sage Publications, 98–113.

Atwood, R. (2004), *Stealing History: Tomb Raiders, Smugglers, and the Looting of the Ancient World*, New York: St Martin's Press.

BBC News (2003), *Deal to halt looting of Khmer art*, accessed 20 October 2010 at http://news.bbc.co.uk/2/hi/asia-pacific/3286129.stm

Beech, H. (2003), 'Stealing history: Inside the illicit art trade that is destroying Asia's cultural heritage', *Time Magazine* (Australian edition), **42**, 27 October, 52–60.

Bowman, B. (2008), 'Transnational crimes against culture', *Journal of Contemporary Criminal Justice*, **24**, 225–242.

Charney, N. (2009), 'Art crime in context', in Charney (ed.), *Art and Crime. Exploring the Dark Side of the Art World*, Santa Barbara, California: Praeger, pp. xvii–xxv.

Chawla, S. and T. Pietschmann (2005), 'Drug trafficking as a transnational crime' in P. Reichel (ed.), *Handbook of Transnational Crime*. London: Sage Publications, pp. 160–80.

Debaine-Francfort, C. (1999), *The Search for Ancient China*, New York: Harry N. Abrams Publishers.

De Launey, G. (2007), 'Cambodia bid to protect treasures', story from *BBC News*, accessed 2 November 2008 at, http://newsvote.bbc.co.uk/mpapps/pagetools/print/news.bbc.co.uk/2/hi/asia-pacific/7015647.stm.

Doole, J. (1999), 'Cambodian update & Thai crackdown', *Culture Without Context*, **5**, 7.

Fidler, S. (2003), 'A black art : How the trade in stolen artifacts aids money laundering, organised crime and terrorism', *Financial Times*, 24 May, accessed 2 November 2008, at http://search.ft.com/ftArticle?queryText=stolen+artefacts&y=5&aje=true&x=11&id=030524001197&ct=0.

Fisman, R. and S. Wei (2009), 'The smuggling of art, and the art of smuggling: uncovering the

trade in cultural property and antiques, *American Economic Journal: Applied Economics*, **1**(3), 82–96.
International Foundation for Art Research (2010), *Country Summary for India*, accessed 20 October 2010, at http://www.ifar.org/country_title.php?docid=1180194265.
Kaufmann, D., A. Kraay and M. Mastruzzi (2006), 'Measuring corruption: myths and realities', *World Bank*, accessed 20 October 2010 at http://www1.worldbank.org/publicsector/anticorrupt/corecourse2007/Myths.pdf.
Keefe, P. (2007), 'Letter From Jaipur: the idol thief', *The New Yorker*, 7 May 2007, accessed 20 October 2010, at http://www.newyorker.com/reporting/2007/05/07/070507fa_fact_keefe.
Mackenzie, S. (2005), *Going, Going Gone: Regulating the Market in Illicit Antiquities*, Leicester: Institute of Art and Law.
Padgett, T. and D. Mascarenas (2010), 'Mexico's next war: against the Narcos?', *Time*, 31 August 2010, accessed 20 October 2010, at http://www.time.com/time/world/article/0,8599,2014610,00.html.
Thosarat, R. (1999), 'The destruction of the cultural heritage of Thailand and Cambodia', in *Illicit Antiquities: The Destruction of the World's Archaeological Heritage*, a collection of papers from a conference held 22–25 October 1999 at Cambridge University, McDonald Institute for Archaeological Research: Cambridge, pp. 102–112.
Transparency International (2009), 'Frequently asked questions about corruption', accessed 20 October 2010 at http://www.transparency.org/news_room/faq/corruption_faq.
United Nations Office on Drugs and Crime (UNODC) (2004), United Nations Convention Against Transnational Organized Crime and the Protocols Thereto, Vienna: UNODC.
Watson, P. (1998), *Sotheby's: The Inside Story*, London: Random House.
Watson, P. (1999), 'The lessons of Sipan: archaeologists and Huaqueros', *Culture Without Context*, **4**, Spring, 15–20.

14 Corrupt misuse of information and communications technologies

Russell G. Smith and Penny Jorna

INTRODUCTION

Computers have not only provided an efficient means of communication for individuals, businesses and government agencies alike, but have also allowed criminals to plan and execute their illegal activities more quickly and with reduced risks of detection. Since their development in the 1970s, computerized technologies have developed rapidly and in imaginative ways (Smith, 2010), not only with respect to their speed of operation and capacity for storage of information, but also in relation to the physical size of devices which are now highly portable – and even attractive as fashion accessories.

One area of criminal misuse of information and communications technology (ICT) that has been identified as of growing concern is the use of electronic devices in connection with corrupt practices – both in government and in the private sector (Heeks, 1998; Bell and Zipparo, 2001). Under the provisions of the *United Nations Convention Against Corruption* (UNCAC), which entered into force on 14 December 2005 (United Nations, 2004), corruption includes not only the conventional activities such as bribery of public officials and embezzlement of public funds, but also trading in influence and acts of concealment and laundering of the proceeds of corrupt behaviour. Corruption in connection with private sector business activities is also included. Each of these areas of risk intersects closely with modern use of ICT, both in terms of the facilitation of the commission of corrupt acts, and in relation to technology being the target of offending. In this sense, risks of corruption follow the conventional definitions of cybercrime which Choo, Smith and McCusker (2007, p. 2) described as follows:

> Primarily, a distinction can be drawn between crimes in which information and communications technologies are the object or the target of offending; and crimes in which technologies are the tool in the commission of the offence. This latter category incorporates two levels of reliance on technologies: offences which are *enabled* by technologies (i.e. in which a computer is required for the commission of the offence); and offences which are *enhanced* by technologies (i.e. in which computers make it easier to commit an offence).

In the realm of corrupt conduct, ICT can be implicated in each of these types of offending. As a *target*, corrupt conduct can entail theft and misuse of mobile devices, often for the data which they contain, or trading in digital information taken illegally from government officials or corporate personnel. Perpetrating attacks on networks, such as occur in denial of service attacks facilitated through the use of botnets, is an example of ICT being a target for offending which could then be linked with acts of bribery or extortion. As a *tool that enables* corruption to occur, computers can be compromised to allow access to confidential information or data that can be stolen or compromised as it travels across networks, often in unencrypted form. Finally, as a *tool that enhances* the commission of corruption, ICT enables personal identities to be stolen or altered with ease, unauthorised financial transactions to be facilitated across jurisdictional borders, and anonymous communications to be undertaken with little chance of detection. As with other types of cybercrime, technology has been a boon to those seeking to corrupt public officials and corporate personnel, and an impediment to law enforcement and those seeking to investigate and prosecute individuals who act corruptly themselves, or seek to corrupt others.

This chapter explores the range of opportunities that exist for corruption to occur in connection with the use of ICT and provides examples of actual cases in which such scenarios have occurred in recent years. After an introductory analysis of the drivers of corruption facilitated through ICT, this chapter considers the risks that have arisen for corruption within the ICT industry itself, within government and law enforcement agencies, in the banking and financial services sectors, and in other business contexts where ICT has been involved in acts of industrial espionage. Consideration is then given to some of the likely developments in the use of ICT which may enhance corruption in the future, and of the ways in which ICT can, itself, be used to minimize risks and assist in the prevention and control of corrupt conduct. As we shall see, ICT has not only created abundant opportunities for corruption to occur, but has also provided some useful ways in which anti-corruption agencies can prevent risks from arising and track those which do occur, thus leading to effective investigation and prosecution. We begin, however, by exploring the relationship between ICT usage and the commission of corrupt conduct.

UNDERSTANDING THE RELATIONSHIP BETWEEN ICT AND CORRUPTION

In 1979, Cohen and Felson (1979, p. 589) raised for consideration a theory to explain trends in crime rates in terms of changes in the routine activities of everyday life. They argued that the structure of ordinary daily activities influences criminal opportunities, especially for so-called 'direct-contact predatory violations'. Structural changes in routine activity patterns were said to influence crime rates by affecting the convergence in space and time of the three minimal elements of direct-contact predatory violations: the presence of motivated offenders, the availability of suitable targets, and the absence of capable guardians against a violation. Some 20 years later, Felson and Clarke (1998, p. 22) outlined 10 principles of opportunity theory, one of which argued that social and technological changes produce new crime opportunities. Although not all technological changes result in new opportunities for crime, those which correspond with people's motivations for illegality and are not subject to capable guardianship are likely to lead to new or adapted forms of crime.

Smith (2010) identified the various changes in technology that have provided new opportunities for crime and indicated the ways in which motivations of offenders and the presence of capable guardianship have correlated with the introduction of new technologies, particularly digital technologies. In the present context, new technologies have provided a rich source of tools with which individuals can perpetrate acts of corruption. The development of email, social networking sites, the use of SMS, and mobile phone services have all been used to facilitate corrupt activities by making communications more efficient and less able to be intercepted.

Technology as a Tool of Corruption

Two examples investigated by the United States Securities and Exchange Commission illustrate the problem well. In the case of *SEC* v *Oscar H. Meza* (United States District Court for the District of Columbia, 28 August 2009, Civil Action No. 1:09-CV-01648 (D.D.C.) LR-21190; AAE Rel. 3041), the accused Oscar Meza had been employed by Faro Technologies Inc., a software development and manufacturing company with headquarters located in Florida (Faro) which had a subsidiary company, Faro Shanghai Co. Ltd. (Faro-China). Mr Meza was alleged to have authorized bribes totalling US$444 492 between 2004 and 2006 to employees of Chinese state-owned companies in order to obtain contracts worth approximately US$4.5 million in sales for Faro of which, approximately US$1.4 million was net profit. Mr. Meza was able to arrange for an employee of Faro-China to authorize and negotiate bribes through the use of email which facilitated the acts of corruption across country borders. Throughout the email exchanges, Mr. Meza was aware that what he was doing was contrary to US and Chinese laws and he directed the

Faro-China to conceal the bribes for accounting purposes (Securities and Exchange Commission, 2009).

In another case, *SEC* v *American Rice, Inc., Joseph A. Schwartz, Jr., Joel R. Malebranche and Allen W. Sturdivant* (Admin. Proc. Rel. No. 34-47286/30 January, 2003), employees of a Texas company that processed and marketed rice in both international and domestic markets, American Rice Inc., were alleged to have made numerous bribery payments to Haitian customs officials between January and August 1999 to reduce American Rice's import taxes. The Rice Corporation of Haiti, was a Haitian company located in Port-au-Prince, which packaged and marketed rice for American Rice in Haiti. In January 1998, American Rice employees and agents in Haiti entered into an illicit arrangement with some Haitian customs officials. In exchange for bribery payments, customs officials permitted American Rice to declare less than the full tonnage of rice it shipped to Haiti. With respect to 12 shipments of rice to Haiti, the total amount of taxes saved by American Rice was US$1 536 731.82, while the total bribe paid was US$528 383.52. Communications between American Rice and Rice Corporation of Haiti were carried out via email and on two occasions managers of American Rice advised other employees to 'destroy the message' – meaning the email bribery payment schedules and predicted savings (Securities and Exchange Commission, 2003).

Both of these examples illustrate how email can be used to communicate between those issuing and receiving bribes across jurisdictional borders. This clearly makes the commission of the corrupt acts more efficient as international telephone calls are expensive, or may be blocked within businesses, while email is a cheap and available alternative. In addition, the anonymity associated with free email accounts can be used to ensure that communications cannot be traced, or that tracing is made all the more difficult.

In one case, for example, a global supply manager for Apple Computers was alleged to have accepted kickbacks of at least US$2.5 million over the period from February 2007 to August 2010 from a number of Asian suppliers of component parts for iPhones and iPods. It was alleged that he had supplied confidential information to the suppliers so that their bids would be successful. Apple's security protocols were circumvented by the accused using personal email accounts on Windows Live Hotmail and Gmail in order to avoid suspicion and security email checks. He specifically told his supplier contacts not to use his Apple email account as the '. . . Apple IT team will randomly scan emails for suspicious email communications on forecast, cost and new model information' (Keizer, 2010). The case illustrates how adept use of email for communications can easily facilitate acts of corruption within business. The bribery in this case was discovered when Apple personnel imaged the hard drive of the accused's company-supplied notebook, which contained the incriminating Hotmail and Gmail emails. Civil and criminal proceedings have been taken against the manager involved.

Text messaging has also been used to facilitate corruption in a case in which a Customs and Border Protection official in the United States had, over a number of years, worked on behalf of a Mexican crime syndicate, La Linea, to assist in trafficking drugs and people across the United States-Mexican border. In 2009, Martha Garnica had attempted to corrupt another customs official by establishing a relationship with him using text messages and bribes. This official was, in fact, a covert informant whose evidence led to Garnica being convicted on six counts of drug smuggling, human-trafficking and bribery and sentenced to 20 years' imprisonment (Connolly, 2010).

It is also clear that organized crime groups now make considerable use of ICT in connection with the planning and execution of their criminal activities. One of the most celebrated examples of this concerned the Colombian drug cartels, which devoted many billions of dollars building sophisticated computer infrastructures. In 1994, for example, Colombian police raided a Cali complex and found a US$1.5 million IBM AS400 mainframe computer with half-a-dozen monitors connected. The computer had a database of residential and office phone numbers of United States diplomats and agents (both known and suspected law enforcement, intelligence, and military operatives) based in Colombia. In addition, a telecommunications company was found to have supplied the Cartel with complete records of all telephone calls in the form of the originating and destination phone numbers. The Cartel's intelligence arm then used custom-designed software to cross-reference the telecommunications company records against their own list of suspected law enforcement, military, and intelligence officials or agents to find out the phone numbers that these officials were calling or the phone numbers that were used to place calls to the officials. These numbers were then correlated back to addresses and names, giving the Cartel a list of people who were possibly informing on them (McNamara, 2003, p. 14).

Although most public officers make regular use of email and text messaging for official purposes, risks can arise where the boundaries between official and personal use become blurred. Not only can it be difficult to track emails sent using anonymous personal accounts, but the attractions of convenient, instantaneous communication make the process of engaging in corrupt activities considerably more efficient.

Technology now also makes the process of economic espionage and industrial spying more efficient as data can be captured through the use of spyware, or transferred from computers using micro-storage devices (Nasheri, 2005). In the United States on 9 December, 2010, two former tyre engineers were convicted of stealing trade secrets from the Goodyear Tire and Rubber Company. The jury found them guilty of one count of conspiracy to commit trade secret theft, one count of trade secret theft, one count of unlawful photographing of trade secrets, three counts of transmittal of trade secrets, one count of possession of trade secrets, two counts of wire fraud and one count of conspiracy to commit wire fraud. According to the evidence, their company secured a US$1.2 million contract in early 2007 with a Chinese tyre manufacturing company to supply tyre building equipment for use in producing radial 'off the road' tyres, which are used on very large earth moving and mining equipment. In order to build the equipment, the offenders needed a special piece of machinery that they knew Goodyear had developed. They arranged to visit the Goodyear plant in Kansas to service their own equipment, which was located in the Goodyear plant, and then used a cell phone camera to surreptitiously take seven unauthorized photographs of the Goodyear machinery which they then emailed to employees at their subsidiary company in England. The trade secret information contained in the photographs was then used to complete a similar piece of tyre building equipment for use in the Chinese contract (United States Department of Justice, 2010).

Technology as a Target of Corruption

Information and communications technologies can also be a focus or target of corrupt conduct, owing to their desirability in restricted environments, their high commercial value, and, most importantly, the information they contain.

In 2010, the New South Wales Independent Commission Against Corruption (2010a) reported on its inquiry into the conduct of Sebastian Wade, a Senior Corrections Officer with Corrective Services New South Wales who was found to have supplied contraband, including compact discs and drugs, to inmates at the John Morony Correctional Centre (JMCC) in return for payments. It was established that on at least four occasions between mid-2009 and January 2010, Mr Wade obtained contraband from associates of two inmates and gave them to the inmates in return for payment. His attempt to smuggle contraband into JMCC on another occasion for a third inmate was aborted when he was apprehended and arrested by NSW Police.

Mr Wade admitted to supplying compact discs and clothes to inmates; however, on 27 April, 2009 the Manager of Security at the JMCC received information from an inmate that Mr Wade was being paid $500 to bring steroids and prohibited drugs into the centre for inmates as well. The corrupt conduct was organised by inmates with the use of a smuggled mobile phone to contact people outside the prison who then contacted Mr. Wade via SMS to arrange meetings and exchanges. However, telephone intercepts inferred that it is likely that the bribery was established between Mr. Wade and the inmates, and then formalized by the outside parties via SMS. A witness who was the sister of an inmate testified that her brother would call her on the mobile phone used by inmates to arrange what he wanted. She would then SMS Mr. Wade to arrange a meeting where she would hand over the contraband and money.

The extent of illegal use of ICT in prisons was discussed by the Commission, and although it was not determined how the inmates came to have the mobile phone, there is a likelihood it was smuggled by corrupt guards. The use of telephones by inmates is tightly controlled and inmates are not permitted to have mobile telephones in their cells. Accordingly, the possession and use of phones is a valuable form of currency that can be used in connection with corruption. In the transcript of evidence it was reported:

> The Commission identified that in a period of approximately three months a contraband mobile telephone used by inmates was in constant use, utilising four separate SIM cards, which must also have been trafficked into the centre. One of this uses was apparently detected by staff at the centre. A total of 17 different inmates were identified as using the contraband mobile telephone. They made 1,023 calls in that period. Of those calls, 48% related to drug related criminal activity, including a large scale and systematic trafficking of illegal drugs into the centre through contact visits. Other uses including downloading pornography from the internet as well as establishing and maintaining Facebook accounts (New South Wales Independent Commission Against Corruption, Transcript, 27 April, 2010b, p. 3).

It was also found that the use of the mobile phones made the corruption more difficult to detect as there was less suspicious physical contact between Mr. Wade and the inmates. The inmates also had more than one SIM card, which meant that it made phone tracing more difficult. Mr. Wade was aware of possible risks with mobile phone technology and a witness testified that he had asked her to delete his number from her mobile phone.

The other principal way in which ICT can be a target of corrupt conduct, is in connection with public servants being paid money in order to permit access to official databases, or for obtaining access to information themselves and supplying it, for a fee, to external parties. Once again, the information held on official databases has high commercial value, as well as value for strategic intelligence purposes.

An instance of corruption in Australia's higher education sector, involved a student liaison officer, Toto Sujanto, employed at the University of Technology, Sydney within the Graduate School of Business. An inquiry by the New South Wales Independent Commission Against Corruption (2002, p. 3) found that:

> Sujanto improperly gained access to electronic student records without authorisation. He then improperly altered certain students' academic results by substituting the notation or record 'failed' with 'cancelled' against specific subjects. On some occasions he did this in return for payment of money, other times for favours and offers of hospitality. Those students whose records were altered received the benefit of not having to pay fees when re-sitting the subject or another in substitution. They would have further benefited from being issued an academic transcript which would not have contained a notation of these failures.

Between 1 March 2000 and 20 June 2001, Mr. Sujanto altered 21 records belonging to 11 separate students and received $7900 in cash from six students, while other students invited him to parties or social occasions. At the time, the University had recently updated the way in which students' records were electronically stored on the 'Student Administration System' (SAS). Most staff working in student administration were required to have access to SAS for their normal duties and there were different levels or areas of access, known as 'pools'. The functions performed by each officer determined the pools to which they had access. Mr. Sujanto's duties required that he have access to the students' histories and certain results sheets. He was not required to have access that would have enabled him to change a student's academic record. However, during each semester certain staff, including Sujanto, were granted access in order to vary students' subject enrolments *within specified timeframes,* such as the census dates. The computer 'pool' access was controlled by the University's Technology Systems and Information Unit which also provided support to the SAS. This access was not, however, removed from the staff members when the high volume time periods had passed, thus enabling the illegality in question to be committed.

Internal audits were conducted by a different unit at the University and it was noticed that Mr. Sujanto's employee identity number was present against several changes, both for an undergraduate student and a postgraduate student. It was then determined that Mr. Sujanto worked in the Graduate School and should not have needed to have access to or alter an undergraduate student's records. After further investigation, University staff then attempted to locate the supporting documentation for these changes. No record or trace of an Authority to Vary Results

Form had been completed by the relevant academic or administrative staff and a further search failed to locate any hard copies of these forms. It was also noticed that Mr. Sujanto should not have been able to substitute 'cancelled' for 'fail' on student records long after the relevant census date, as this was limited to specified officers and based upon appropriate academic authorization (New South Wales Independent Commission Against Corruption, 2002).

On occasions, corrupt conduct can be driven by non-financial motivations. In the United States, a database administrator responsible for a very large database containing personal employee information for an insurance company became frustrated over time by what he perceived to be unfairly low pay. He took revenge by downloading over 60000 employee records to removable media and then advertised the information online in the underground economy, which he hoped would be able to abuse the information in damaging ways. He also leveraged newsgroups dedicated to credit card fraud to post employee credit card numbers and encouraged the malicious use of these credit cards and suggested that readers of the newsgroup use the information he was providing to obtain additional credit cards in the names of victim employees. He was eventually detected when an undercover agent posed as a potential buyer of the insider's stolen information (Hanley, Moore, Cappelli and Trzeciak, 2009, p. 8).

One similar Australian case involved a 27-year-old male, known as 'Optik Surfer', who was sentenced to three years' imprisonment (with 18 months' suspended) on 27 March, 1998 in Sydney, for eight counts of obtaining unlawful access to a computer and one count of unlawfully inserting data into a computer.

The offender, who was a computer networking consultant, had been refused employment with an Internet Service Provider (ISP) in January 1994, and in March 1994 took revenge by illegally obtaining access to the company's computer network using the user account and password of the company's technical director. He then gained access to the company's database of 1225 subscribers and publicized their credit card account details by disclosing them to various journalists. He also altered the company's home page on 17 April, 1994, including a message that the company's security system had been compromised. The publicity resulted in the company losing more than A$2 million in lost clients and contracts. It was required to change its business name and sold the Internet access part of its business to another ISP (R. v *Stevens* unreported decision of the NSW District Court, 27 March, 1998; appeal to the NSW Criminal Court of Appeal dismissed on 15 April, 1999 [1999] NSWCCA 69).

ICT-based Corruption Driven by Crime Displacement

In understanding the relationship between the use of ICT and risks of corruption, assistance can be found in the criminological theory of crime displacement. In 2003, Smith, Wolanin and Worthington (2003) identified a variety of ways in which developments in computer security could result in counter-productive consequences occurring. The problem arises from the traditional response to cybercrime being to devise a range of situational measures that seek to make the commission of crime less attractive to potential offenders. Such measures aim to increase the levels of effort and skill required to commit offences, to create a greater risk of apprehension of offenders, and to decrease the potential rewards that offenders seek to derive from their illegal activities. If, however, it is assumed that potential offenders act on the basis of some rational calculation to balance the likely risks against the benefits of some course of conduct, then as some crimes are seen to be more risky, other easier targets may be considered instead.

One consequence of the development of electronic security systems could be that offenders may employ different methods to achieve their ends. For example, the use of multi-factor authentication systems may cause offenders to change their *modus operandi* by bribing staff within Registration Authorities to disclose keys that have been issued or to issue duplicates for illegal purposes. This might be a much easier way in which to perpetrate on-line fraud than trying to compromise the high-level encryption used in public key systems. Smith, Wolanin and Worthington (2003, p. 3) describe specific ICT-related risks of corruption as follows:

> Hardening electronic targets, for instance through the construction of firewalls and the implementation of regimes of user authentication checks, may prevent remote unauthorised access to computers with the result that offenders will seek to gain access using internal methods. This may involve external offenders co-opting or even planting agents within the organisations they target. Employees of agencies, particularly those who work in information technology departments, may be subject to bribes or threats such as blackmail or physical coercion by offenders seeking access to computers or confidential information.

An example of this occurred in the United States in 2000 when a Mexican man resident in the United States, Fidencio Estrada, alleged to have been involved in drug trafficking, sought access to a law enforcement database, the Treasury Enforcement Communications System (TECS), which contained more than a billion records used by Customs and other law enforcement agencies (McCullagh, 2008). TECS included a watch list and was designed to identify individuals, businesses, and vehicles suspected of or involved in violation of federal laws. TECS also worked as a communications system that permitted the transmission of messages between law enforcement offices and other federal, state, and local law enforcement agencies. The database served as the principal information system supporting border management and the law enforcement mission of the Customs and Border Protection Agency and other federal law enforcement agencies. As such it provided an important source of information that could assist drug traffickers in executing their activities.

Rather than seeking to hack into the database electronically, Estrada arranged to bribe Rafael Pacheco, an agent with the US Customs Service in Florida who, in February 2000, accessed TECS to check for records on Estrada. He searched for Estrada under two aliases and looked-up records for those aliases in the NCIC database, which lists outstanding warrants against individuals. He also helped Estrada's family members in Mexico to obtain visas. In return, Estrada sent approximately US$18 000 in Western Union money transfers to Pacheco, who deposited the cash in his personal bank account and used it to pay off a vehicle loan (McCullagh, 2008).

Pacheco was convicted of receiving a bribe, hindering law enforcement, money laundering, obstruction of justice, and unlawfully accessing restricted federal computer databases and was sentenced to 87 months' imprisonment, concurrent on a further sentence of 60 months' imprisonment. Estrada was found guilty by a jury of conspiring to bribe a public official, conspiring to launder money, bribery, and money laundering and was sentenced to 41 months' imprisonment, followed by 36 months' supervised release (McCullagh, 2008).

Cyber security measures, such as firewalls, passwords and anti-virus software, may have the unintended effect of increasing the threat of corruption of insiders in businesses and government agencies (IBM, 2006). Most security measures are aimed at blocking attempts from outsiders to gain access to information being held within organizations. However, with increased levels of security, it may be easier for criminals to corrupt insiders rather than devoting the considerable resources required to breach security measures externally. The CSO *e-Crime Watch Survey* (CSO Magazine, 2007) found that social engineering techniques, such as gaining access to systems via people who have access to or who can facilitate access to systems or data, were the primary method used by insiders to perpetrate e-crimes. With more personal information of customers being gathered and stored on databases, businesses and governments must ensure that the information remains secure. The alleged information security breach by Vodafone staff illustrates the problems associated with allowing customer records to be stored on online databases to which employees have access through shared logon details (ABC News, 2011).

Having considered the various ways in which corruption can be driven by technology and its use, the present discussion now turns to the different sectors most at risk. These include the ICT industry itself, where threats arise from both within organizations and external to them, government, and law enforcement in particular, and the private sector generally in relation to risks of economic corruption, espionage and industrial spying in the financial services sector and other large organizations.

CORRUPTION CONCERNING THE ICT INDUSTRY

Corruption within the ICT industry arises both from insiders who seek to obtain some financial or other advantage by providing access to systems or information, and by persons external to organizations who seek to bribe those working in the industry to provide items of value in return for illegal payments. Those working in the industry are well-placed to act corruptly as they can often disguise their illegality by altering data trails or by embedding malicious code in systems that can be activated covertly or remotely to allow access to information or to damage the operation of systems. Corruption in connection with outsourcing and consultancies is also a lucrative source of income for those who may have lost their employment due to financial downturns.

Employees and contractors working within organizations are a high-risk group for ICT-related corruption because of the technical knowledge of systems which they possess and their ability to gain access to all parts of secure networks. Risks of this nature arise in both the public and private sectors and the impact can have significant financial and national security implications.

In one case in the United States, Sushil Bansal, President and CEO of Advanced Integrated Technology Corporation (AITC), admitted that between September 2005 and 12 March 2009, he and his company paid over US$700000 in bribes to employees of the District of Columbia Office of the Chief Technology Officer. Bansal and AITC paid the bribes in exchange for the public officials improperly favouring Bansal and his companies, AITC and Integrated IT Solutions, Inc. (IITS), for award of contracts with the Office of the Chief Technology Officer, ensuring that contractors proposed by Bansal, AITC and IITS were approved, falsely approving time sheets and invoices for AITC and IITS employees which represented overbilling, falsely approving time sheets for AITC and IITS employees which were actually ‘ghost employees’ and performed no work, and falsely certifying receipt of software purchased through Bansal and AITC (United States Attorney’s Office, 2010). Bansal was changed with bribery of a public official and engaging in monetary transactions in property derived from specified unlawful activity for his role in the bribery and kickback scheme.

In another case involving an IT Systems Administrator, authorized access was provided to sanitized databases of customer information on an FTP server hosted by one of the accused's organization's business partners, which had been contracted by financial institutions and phone companies to perform services using customer data. The accused located an unsanitized version of the customer databases on the server by overcoming passwords and encryption and located original and complete phone records, billing information, social security numbers, birthdates, and other personally-identifiable information in respect of millions of individuals (Hanley et al., 2009, p. 9). Although the information was not further disseminated, it nonetheless represented a major breach of security. In the case involving the database administrator in the insurance company, noted above, the 60000 employee records were disseminated online and sold for a fee (Hanley et al., 2009, p. 8).

Corruption within the ICT industry can also be initiated by individuals external to organizations who seek to corrupt insiders for personal gain. In the cases discussed above relating to the Apple Computers supply manager who accepted kickbacks from external Asian suppliers of component parts (Keizer, 2010), and the employees of the District of Columbia Office of the Chief Technology Officer who accepted bribes to secure contracts (United States Attorney's Office, 2010), the acts of corruption were initiated outside the organizations in question. In other instances, as we shall see, IT personnel employed within government can be targeted for bribery and kickbacks by business associates with whom they deal.

Finally, a number of large IT corporations have also alleged to have been involved in bribing both government officers and staff in other corporations to facilitate the provision of contracts for the supply of IT equipment. For example, Hewlett-Packard was investigated by the Department of Justice in the United States in connection with the payment of bribes in Russia worth approximately €8 million for a contract worth some €35 million between 2001 and 2006 (Crawford, 2010).

In 2004, 48 people were indicted for bribery and other irregularities in a corruption investigation involving a subsidiary of IBM Corporation in Korea. Officials at IBM Korea and its two sister firms – LG IBM and Winsol – were alleged to have bribed government officials or colluded with other firms to secure 66 billion won ($A73.43 million) in contracts from government departments. Those arrested included IBM Korea's executive director Jang Gyeong-ho, who allegedly took 340 million won for helping Winsol win contracts from public offices through pre-arranged bidding between 2001 and 2003. Jang and his accomplices were accused of providing kickbacks to government officials and other bidding companies (*Sydney Morning Herald*, 2004).

The telecommunications corporation, Siemens, has also allegedly been involved in corruption in connection with securing contracts in Nigeria, Argentina, Bangladesh, Iraq and Venezuela. Two former Siemens managers were found guilty in a Munich Court of using bribery to obtain telecommunications contracts in Nigeria and the company was fined US$201 million by the court. The cases against Siemens were initiated by the German and United States governments, with fines divided between the two countries. Prosecutors claimed that Siemens had a slush fund used to bribe authorities to secure contracts in a number of countries and that up to €1.3 billion may have been used to illegally win foreign contracts (Malataka, 2010).

It is apparent, therefore, that corruption in the ICT industry can involve not only those within the corporations themselves who seek to act improperly to secure new contracts, but also those outside the sector seeking to corrupt insiders.

CORRUPTION AND ICT RISKS WITHIN GOVERNMENT AND LAW ENFORCEMENT

Within government, ICT-related corruption poses particular problems in view of the extensive databases which exist, large procurements funding that is available, and the often low salaries that are paid to public servants in comparison with those performing comparable work in the ICT sector. Law enforcement personnel are particularly at risk of being persuaded to provide confidential policing intelligence that could assist offenders in evading prosecution, in return for a fee. As noted above, in the United States, a Customs and Border Protection official, Martha Garnica, provided information to members of a Mexican crime syndicate over a number of years that assisted in drug trafficking and people smuggling across the United States-Mexican border (Connolly, 2010).

In Britain, the development of 'high-policing' in recent years, a form of intelligence-led policing, relies on gathering intelligence on criminal activities and potential criminals and comparing this with either national or international sources. While this makes trans-border policing easier, it does require storing vast amounts of sensitive, private information about criminals, their families and innocent civilians on official databases to which a range of people have access, including both police officers and civilian staff. Although official policies govern access to such information, risks arise for passwords to be compromised or officers bribed to reveal passwords. In one case, for example, a Liverpool police officer, PC O'Leary, supplied information to an ex-police officer from police records for transmission to his criminal associates. On 21 February, 2006 O'Leary pleaded guilty to six counts of misconduct in public office and was sentenced to 3½ years imprisonment (*Bolt, R (on the application of)* v *Merseyside Police and Another* [2007] EWHC 2607 (Admin) (High Court, 16 November, 2007).

Also in Britain, a police constable, Mark Bohannan, was found to have supplied both sensitive and confidential intelligence held on police computers regarding police operations and confidential details of private citizens to a dealer in cocaine, ecstasy and cannabis who, in turn, provided drugs to Constable Bohannan's wife, a long-time cocaine user. The drug trafficker would also occasionally pay money to the accused for tipping him off to impending searches of his premises and for identifying areas in the locality in which police operations were in existence. This meant that the drug dealing business flourished without police interference. The corrupt behaviour occurred over a period of six years commencing in 2002. He was arrested in 2007 and convicted of conspiracy to commit misconduct in public office. On 12 March, 2010, he was sentenced to a term of three years' imprisonment, which was increased to six years on appeal (R v *Bohannan* [2010] EWCA Crim 2261, Court of Appeal, Criminal Division, 21 September, 2010).

In China, Yu Bing, the former head of Beijing's Municipal Public Security Bureau, was found guilty of accepting bribes from Rising, an antivirus firm, to frame an executive at a rival firm, Micropoint Technology. Yu was specifically targeted due to his position as the head of the Internet Supervisory Department. Yu and his fellow police officers manufactured evidence that Tian Yakui, the executive from Micropoint Technology, had spread computer viruses and had hacked computer systems to steal confidential information. Tian Yakui served 11 months in prison until the corruption was discovered and he was released without charge. Two deputies of Yu, Zhang Pengyun and Qi Kun, confessed that Yu had instructed them to push several companies to make false allegations that Micropoint had planted a virus in their computer systems. Yu had also threatened to demote the two if they did not obey his orders. Mr Yu received bribes of more than RMB 40 million (US$5.8 million) for framing Mr Tian. Yu was sentenced to death with a two-year suspended sentence (Zetter, 2009; *Beijing News*, 2010).

A comparable case occurred in Western Australia in 2008 when Stephen Alan Olsen, an Information Technology security manager at Racing and Wagering Western Australia, fabricated evidence against a colleague that indicated that his colleague had leaked information to a competitor in order to secure his own position within Racing and Wagering Western Australia. The evidence fabricated was of a technical nature, which the accused was able to create in his role as IT security manager, and led to his colleague being dismissed and being investigated by the Corruption and Crime Commission. Prosecutors submitted that Mr Olsen had been trying to ingratiate himself with his managers in order to retain his position and substantial salary. Mr Olsen was found guilty of fabricating evidence against his colleague and sentenced to 18 months' imprisonment with a non-parole period of 9 months (ABC News, 2010).

In the case of *United States* v *John Henry Weaver* (No. 05-1743, Court of Appeals, Third Circuit, 10 March, 2006), the accused was serving as director of information technology of the Harrisburg School District in Pennsylvania, which had awarded a company, EMO Communications, a contract to supply approximately 800 laptop computers. The supply was funded primarily from the Federal Communications Commission's E-rate subsidy programme. When the tender was first submitted, the computers in question cost US$7600 each. However, In the two years that it took to finalize the supply, that price had dropped to between US$1600 and US$1700 per unit. Although aware of this reduction in cost, EMO failed to inform the Department and the contract was approved for the higher amount. The accused and the contractor agreed to share the difference between the actual cost and the amount billed and in April and May 2002, Weaver received payments totalling US$1.9 million.

In another case in the United Kingdom, a computer technician had created thirty 'ghost employees' in the computerized payroll system of a public works department with the salary payments all being directed to his own account (Heeks, 1998, p. 4). This opportunity was created when a previously manual payroll system was computerized, specifically in order to reduce the possibility of employees creating 'ghost' staff and receiving salary payments dishonestly. A similar case arose in New South Wales where a Department of Defence employee used a new computer system to create 'ghost vendors' who received some 40 payments totalling almost $200 000. Each of the payments were made to a bank account that the employee had created in her maiden name. At the time, the office was short of staff which led to her performing two roles. She also had access to log-on and passwords for her colleagues, which allowed her to create the false accounts and authorize payments (Bell and Zipparo, 2001, p. 24). Each of these examples shows how those working within government are vulnerable to corruption by reason of their use or knowledge of ICT systems and processes.

CORRUPTION AND ICT WITHIN THE FINANCIAL SERVICES AND CONSULTING SECTORS

The financial services sector also provides an environment in which bribery can take place, often in order to facilitate access to secure computerized systems which are difficult to compromise remotely by hacking. Often it is simpler to corrupt insiders to provide access to account details or personal information rather than to try to hack into secure networks.

An example of how bank employees can be corrupted by organized criminal groups, was revealed in an investigation by the Identity Security Strike Force in Australia, 'Operation Hickey'. This taskforce investigated a large-scale organized criminal network engaged in fraud offences against financial institutions involving high-quality forged documents with a total exposure to the financial institutions being in excess of $1 million (CDPP, 2008, p. 17). The syndicates used forged documents to take over the identities of legitimate individuals and companies and then conduct fraudulent activities against financial institutions. Some of the syndicates also bribed officers within financial institutions to provide access to networks to obtain confidential details of customers' accounts and personal information. They also assisted with electronic funds. The two bank employees who provided access to databases were respectively sentenced to 2½ years' imprisonment to be released on a recognizance after 18 months and a fully suspended sentence of 12 months' imprisonment (CDPP, 2008, p. 17).

ICT has changed considerably the way in which financial transactions are processed with electronic transfers of funds, telephone banking and internet banking now being common. An example of how corrupt bank employees can manipulate these forms of technology is demonstrated by a case that came before the Victorian Supreme Court of Appeal ([2006] VSCA 184). The Crown alleged that a bank employee provided customer details, such as names and account details to the co-offenders who would then use the details to pass the telephone banking checks to change passwords, set up internet banking accounts and then accessed the accounts via internet banking to transfer money from the accounts (R v *Duy Duc Nguyen* [2006] VSCA 184). This case demonstrates how technology may make it easier for criminals to corrupt bank employees rather than try traditional methods of robbing banks. The use of the internet and telephone banking means that offenders do not have to physically go into the banks to steal money. All that is required is that an employee accesses the customer database to gather pertinent details and then passes them to outside offenders, who can than access the accounts anonymously.

In another case involving allegations of corruption of employees at the World Bank, it was alleged that a principal contractor of IT services for the

World Bank had bribed staff and used spyware to obtain sensitive information from the Bank. It was alleged that a keystroke logging programme had been installed on computers of employees at the World Bank in Washington allegedly by one or more contractors from Satyam Computer Services, one of India's largest IT companies. Satyam Computer Services were also accused of bribing bank officials by providing improper benefits to bank staff. The Department of Institutional Integrity (INT), the Bank's anti-corruption unit, had been investigating the relationship between the Bank's Chief Information Officer and Satyam, the Bank's strategic partner in IT systems. In 2005, The Chief Information Officer was dismissed after being accused of improperly buying preferential stock options from Satyam, just after he had awarded Satyam a major contract. As a result of its strategic partnership, Satyam became the bank's principal software contractor, building and controlling almost all of the Bank's global information network, including its accounting, finance and treasury software systems. Satyam subsequently became insolvent with criminal charges being laid against senior managers and its auditors (Edwards, 2011).

Both cases illustrate the risks of ICT-related corruption that can arise in financial institutions, both for senior management and also for lower level employees. Following the case involving Satyam Computer Services, the World Bank noted:

> In recent years, the World Bank Group has prioritized governance and anti-corruption as part of its reform agenda. Building on years of experience in investigations and sanctions, the World Bank Integrity Vice Presidency has been ramping up its investigative and preventive efforts to protect Bank Group-financed projects, while holding wrongdoers accountable for any waste of development funds. The International Corruption Hunters Alliance marks an important feature of INT's partnership portfolio, which includes co-operation agreements with OLAF, the SFO (UK), the ICC, Interpol, AusAid and USAID (World Bank, 2010).

FUTURE CORRUPTION RISKS OF DEVELOPMENTS IN ICT

Adopting an opportunity theory perspective would mean that as new technologies are developed, new opportunities for corruption will arise, unless risks of detection are enhanced or capable guardianship improved Cohen and Felson (1979, p. 589). Already predictions of criminality involving some of the latest developments in ICT have begun to emerge – often only a short time after the new technology was implemented (see Smith, 2010 for a discussion of how to quantify this time delay).

In the United Kingdom, an assessment by the Serious and Organised Crime Agency identified new ways in which technology could be used to corrupt police officers. Social networking sites, upon which police officers identify themselves as members of the police service, leave police open to approaches from criminals and the creation of inappropriate associations, while increased access by all police officers and civilian staff to confidential information in IT systems, provides important information which they can leak for financial gain (Laville, 2010). Arguably, those at risk of being targeted for corruption should refrain from disclosing their public service status on social networking sites where access is unrestricted.

At present many organisations do not have adequate policies in place to counter risks associated with social networking by staff. The results of *2011 Global State of Information Security Survey*, which is based on the responses of more than 12 840 senior managers in IT and information security from 135 countries, found that few companies were adequately prepared to counter threats associated with social networking. Most companies (60 per cent) had yet to implement security technologies supporting Web 2.0 exchanges such as social networks, blogs or wikis, and even more (77 per cent) had not established security policies that addressed the use of social networks or Web 2.0 technologies (PricewaterhouseCoopers, 2010, p. 38). Risks, from an information-security perspective, included the loss or leaking of statements or information that could damage the company's reputation, activity such as downloading pirated material with legal and liability implications, identity theft that directly and indirectly compromises the company's network and information and data aggregation in building up a picture of an individual to mount security attacks through social engineering.

One of the most recent areas of risk concerns manipulation and compromise of cloud computing systems. Cloud computing has been defined as a pool of virtualized computing resources that allows users to gain access to applications and data in a web-based environment on demand. Risks of corruption in relation to cloud platforms arise in each of the various cloud architecture and usage models that have been developed (Choo, 2010). In one study, for example, a team of computer scientists from the University of California, San Diego and Massachusetts Institute of Technology examined the widely-used Amazon EC2 services. They found that 'it is possible to map the internal cloud infrastructure, identify where a particular target VM is likely to reside, and then instantiate new VMs until one is placed co-resident with the target' (Ristenpart et al., 2009, p. 199). This enabled the research team to load eavesdropping software onto the same servers hosting targeted websites. By identifying target virtual machines, attackers could potentially monitor the cache (a small allotment of high-speed memory used to store frequently-used information) in order to steal data hosted on the same physical machine (Hardesty, 2009). This represents just one of a number of potential risks that face cloud infrastructure in the years ahead (Choo, 2010).

Increasing use of e-procurement will also create risks of corruption in connection with the identification of contractors and assessment of tenders. As we have seen (Keizer, 2010; United States Attorney's Office, 2010; Crawford, 2010), bribery has been used to secure large-scale contracts for the supply of technology, and these are likely to be expanded as more contracting is undertaken electronically.

In addition, the application of technology in connection with gambling has been identified as an area of risk of corruption, particularly concerning match-fixing in sporting events (Pierik, 2010). For example, in the case of cricket, although mobile phones are banned from locker rooms, the use of laptop computers is permitted as they are considered to be a coaching aid. This could, however, allow corrupt players to check odds and betting details online and to plan game fixing.

Corruption is no longer considered solely the domain of governments and public servants and, as such, it has led to greater scrutiny of private organizations and companies. An area which has been noted by Transparency International as an area of concern is the sporting industry. A 2009 Working Paper noted that 'the close-knit relationship between sporting officials, politicians, business people, sponsors and the media can create a high-risk context for corruption to occur' (TI, 2009, p. 1). Corruption within the sporting industry has also been affected by ICT, in particular the use of social networking sites. For example, players in the 2009 US Tennis Open were warned by the director of the Tennis Integrity Unit that their remarks on Twitter may be violating the sports anti-corruption regulations. The 'Tweets' (the online posts on the social networking forum Twitter) could have violated rules on passing insider information, such as regarding their performance or competitors (Hodgkinson, 2009). The use of Twitter in potentially facilitating corruption has also been observed by the International Cricket Council (ICC). ICC officials have banned players from posting on Twitter during World Cup matches out of fear that players may be contacted by illegal bookmaker's intent on bribing players (Hogan, 2011). An ICC spokesman commented that they preferred 'to err on the side of caution' when sensitive information may be leaked and that manager's phones should be reserved for operational reasons only (Hogan, 2011).

Developments in the sophistication of malware and spyware are also likely to facilitate acts of corruption within organizations. As we have seen, a keystroke logging programme was said to have been installed on the World Bank's computer system in order to locate sensitive commercial information concerning IT contracts (Edwards, 2011).

COUNTER-MEASURES TO ICT-RELATED CORRUPTION

Responding to risks of ICT-enabled corruption requires the implementation of the many anti-corruption measures outlined in other chapters in this volume, as well as the use of ICT itself. In 1998, Heeks (1998) identified a number of ways in which ICT could be used to minimize risks of corruption, and also, unfortunately, how computerization of procedures in the public sector could create new opportunities for bribery and illegality. He argued that public sector management needs to:

> understand the roots of corruption, not just the symptoms. It would address corruption not through individual management techniques but through strategies of institutional and contextual development. It would also see IT as having a potential role, but one which is limited and which forms only one small part of a much larger jigsaw (Heeks, 1998, p. 16).

To illustrate this, Heeks (1998) provided the example of managers in a government-owned railway system who were concerned about the efficiency of its seat/berth reservation system, and about risks of corruption within the system.

> Booking staff had access to and control over the allocation of places on trains. A few would take a bribe (either directly or via a ticket tout) to provide a passenger with a reserved place; these being at a premium since all trains were overbooked. A computerised system was introduced, one objective of which was to eliminate corruption. To achieve this, allocation of reservations was handled automatically, including the particularly 'weak link' of moving passengers on the waiting list into places vacated by cancellations. Computerisation did make it harder for the clerical staff to be corrupt because the software, not the clerk, now decided – based on booking date – which passengers would fill vacated slots (Heeks, 1998, p. 3).

However, corruption was not eliminated, owing to the fact that station managers retained manual control over a certain proportion of the train places which could still be allocated in return for cash payments. The problem of 'ticket touting' was also not solved as advance tickets could still be purchased and sold at a premium to last-minute travellers.

An obvious, although not always effective means of reducing ICT-related corruption is to impose stricter controls on the use of technology for non-work-related purposes in public and private sector organisations. This, arguably, then ensures that the data surveillance procedures undertaken as part of risk management generally, are made more effective. The activities of the US Customs officer Martha Garnica, outlined above, in texting messages during work-time to colleagues was part of the way in which the opportunities for corruption developed (Connolly, 2010). Similarly, Paul Devine, the global supply manager for Apple Computers, was able to circumvent Apple's security measures through the use of personal email accounts on Windows Live Hotmail and Gmail in order to avoid suspicion and security on his corporate email account (Keizer, 2010). Placing restrictions on the use of personal IT devices for work-related purposes or during work time might be a way in which to limit risks of abuse. Already, the United States Department of Defence has banned the use of USB's after malicious code was transferred from a USB to a Defence laptop (Hanley et al., 2009). The Australian Department of Defence also limits the amount of removable hardware that can be used in conjunction with Defence computers. The only USBs that are allowed are ones supplied and authorized by the Department.

Of course, such potential solutions may be overcome by personnel willing to take steps to avoid their effect, and so more conventional strategies such as more rigorous personnel screening, need to be employed. The difficulty arises, however, in that many cybercriminals are first-time offenders owing to the fact that levels of prosecution of cybercrime are so low internationally (Smith, Grabosky and Urbas, 2004). Criminal record checks, therefore, may not reveal any intelligence that could be useful in predicting risks of corruption.

As the above cases have demonstrated, corruption of insiders may occur when businesses only focus on external threats to their security and fail to implement internal ICT security measures. Implementing technology security systems and then making sure that employees are aware of the ramifications of breaches is the first step to limiting the damage of corruption through ICT. The CERT Insider Threat Study (Kowalski et al., 2008) found that of the 38 cases investigated, 34 of those accused faced criminal charges and that they did not anticipate the severity of the consequences of their offending.

Another way of limiting potentially corrupt behaviour of employees, is to ensure that data access is position related (IBM, 2006). In the example of the employee at the University of Technology Sydney who amended student transcripts, access should have been limited once the enrolment period was over. For the Department of Defence employee who created 'ghost' vendors, her access should have been limited either to invoice entry or to invoice approval, but not both. An alternative method of limiting corruption is for computer systems to monitor IP addresses and log in/log off times (IBM, 2006). Checks such as these may have resulted in the Apple manager's corrupt behaviour being found earlier than the three years during which it continued. The Vodafone database breach is an example of how logins and passwords should not be shared. Having employees share logins makes it difficult to determine who gained access to the data. After the breach was made public, Vodafone immediately implemented tighter information security specifically to deal with shared passwords and logins (ABC News, 2011).

What may, arguably, be the most effective solution is to ensure that staff and contractors working in ICT in organizations are not left to undertake their work without some level of supervision. Trusted and technologically-literate managers need to be aware of the work that is being done on ICT systems and be willing to monitor what employees and contractors are undertaking. Relatively simple monitoring could, for example, have detected the many 'ghost' employees created in the District of Columbia Office of the Chief Technology Officer (United States Attorney's Office, 2010), or the many 'ghost' vendors in the New South Wales Department of Defence (Bell and Zipparo, 2001, p. 24).

CONCLUSIONS

Information and communications technologies are now established features of life in industrialized societies. They have created untold benefits for education, delivery of health services, recreation, commerce, and government and changed considerably the nature of modern workplaces and patterns of employment (Smith and Grabosky, 2006). They have also created unprecedented opportunities for crime and corruption.

Smith, Wolanin and Worthington (2003) summarized the various crime-prevention measures designed to reduce cybercrime by employing the categorization of traditional crime prevention measures developed by Clarke (1995, p. 109). Table 14.1 shows some of the possible situational strategies that would be appropriate to address the principal risks of ICT-related corruption discussed in this chapter.

Applying situational measures to prevent corruption is not new (see, for example, Graycar and Felson, 2010), but in the context of ICT-related risks, it provides a useful catalogue of the wide variety of measures that are available and which could be adapted to this ever-changing environment. Often, however, new technologies create criminogenic consequences that are, in essence, not entirely new as the motivations of offenders remain the same as in the past – in the present context, invariably related to cupidity

Table 14.1 Situational cyber-corruption prevention measures

Crime prevention measure	ICT-related corruption application
Increasing the effort required to offend	
Target hardening	Firewalls, anti-spyware, hardware/data storage anti-theft devices
Access control	Passwords, tokens, biometrics and encryption
Deflecting offenders	Controlled use of ICT for personal use
Controlling facilitators	Registration of ICT hardware and software
Increasing the risks of detection	
Entry / exit screening	Monitoring use of passwords/encryption
Formal surveillance	Analysis of patterns of ICT usage
Surveillance by employees	Workplace surveillance of ICT usage
Natural surveillance	Reporting by colleagues and reporting hotlines
Reducing the rewards of offending	
Target removal	Government or industry-funded services, adequacy of salaries for public servants
Identifying property	Registration of hardware and software
Removing inducements	Restricted publicity of crimes through chat rooms and in the media
Rule setting	Codes of conduct for ICT usage

and self-promotion. Accordingly, the anti-corruption measures created in the pre-digital age should continue to have much to offer those of us living in the electronically-driven 21st century.

BIBLIOGRAPHY

[All URLs were correct at 3 March 2011]

ABC News (2010), 'IT manager jailed for fabricating evidence against colleague', *ABC News Online*, 14 January. http://www.abc.net.au/news/stories/2010/01/14/2792515.htm

ABC News (2011), 'Watchdog finds Vodafone breached Privacy Act', *ABC News Online*, 16 February, http://www.abc.net.au/news/stories/2011/02/16/3140592.htm

Behar, R. (2009), 'Exclusive: World Bank's web of ties to "India's Enron"'. *Fox News Online*, 12 January, http://www.foxnews.com/story/0,2933,479545,00.html

Beijing News (2010). 'Death sentence given to ex-police internet supervisory department head', *China Digital Times*, 22 August. http://chinadigitaltimes.net/2010/08/death-sentence-given-to-ex-police-internet-supervisory-department-head/

Bell, C. and L. Zipparo (2001), *Exploiting Emerging Technology Corruptly in the NSW Public Sector: A Strategic Assessment*, Sydney: New South Wales Independent Commission Against Corruption, http://www.icac.nsw.gov.au/index.php?zoom_query=technology&zoom_and=1&zoom_per_page=100&option=com_zoomsearch&zoom_sort=0&Itemid=2655

Choo, K-K. R. (2010), 'Cloud computing: challenges and future directions', *Trends and Issues in Crime and Criminal Justice*, **400**, Canberra: Australian Institute of Criminology.

Choo, K-K. R., R.G. Smith, and R. McCusker (2007), 'Future directions in technology-enabled crime: 2007-09', *Research and Public Policy Series*, **78**, Canberra: Australian Institute of Criminology.

Clarke, R. V. (1995), 'Situational crime prevention', in M. Tony, M. Farrington and D.P. Farrington (eds), *Building a Safer Society: Strategic Approaches to Crime Prevention*, Chicago: University of Chicago Press, pp. 91–150.

Cohen, L. E. and M. Felson (1979), Social change and crime rate trends: a routine activity approach', *American Sociological Review*, **44**, 588–608.

Commonwealth Director of Public Prosecutions (CDPP) (2008), *Annual Report 2007–08*, Canberra: CDPP, http://www.cdpp.gov.au/Publications/AnnualReports/CDPP-Annual-Report-2007-2008.pdf

Connolly, C. (2010), 'A double agent helps net corrupt immigration official', *Sydney Morning Herald*, 20 September, http://www.smh.com.au/world/a-double-agent-helps-net-corrupt-immigration-official-20100919-15hwy.html

Crawford, D. (2010), 'Probe of bribery at H-P heats up', *Wall Street Journal*, 13 August, http://online.wsj.com/article/SB10001424052748703723504575425303867402456.html?KEYWORDS=corruption+and+technology

CSO Magazine (2007), *E-Crime Watch Survey 2007*, CSO Magazine, US Secret Service, CERT Program, Microsoft Corporation, Washington DC, http://www.csoonline.com/documents/pdfs/e-crime_release_091107.pdf

Edwards, B. (2011), 'The Satyam fraud, two years later', *Government Accountability Project*, Washington, 11 January, http://www.whistleblower.org/blog/31-2010/928-the-satyam-fraud-two-years-later

Felson, M. and R.V. Clarke (1998), *Opportunity Makes the Thief: Practical Theory for Crime Prevention*, London: Home Office, Policing and Reducing Crime Unit.

Graycar, A. and M. Felson (2010), 'Situational prevention of organized timber theft and related corruption', in K. Bullock, R.V. Clarke and N. Tilley (eds) *Situational Prevention of Organized Crimes*, Cullompton, UK: Willan Publishing.

Hanley, M., A.P. Moore, D.M. Cappelli and R.F. Trzeciak (2009), 'Spotlight on malicious insiders with ties to the internet underground community', Pittsburgh: CERT Software Engineering Institute, Carnegie Mellon University, http://www.cert.org/search_pubs/search.php?sort=pub_dated

Hardesty, L. (2009), 'Secure computers aren't so secure', MIT Press Release, 30 October, http://www.physorg.com/news176107396.html

Heeks, R. (1998), 'Information systems for public sector management', *Working Paper Series*, **4**, Manchester: Information Technology and Public Sector Corruption, Institute for Development Policy and Management, University of Manchester, http://www.sed.manchester.ac.uk/idpm/research/publications/wp/igovernment/documents/igov_wp04.pdf

Hodgkinson, M. (2009), *The Telegraph*, 'US Open 2009: players warned over sharing "Inside Information" on Twitter', 28 August, http://www.telegraph.co.uk/sport/tennis/usopen/6103411/US-Open-2009-players-warned-over-sharing-inside-information-on-Twitter.html

Hogan, J. (2011), 'ICC bans Twitter use during Cup matches due to corruption fears', *Sydney Morning Herald*, 16 February, http://www.smh.com.au/technology/technology-news/icc-bans-twitter-use-during-cup-matches-due-to-corruption-fears-20110216-1avj6.html

IBM (2006), *Stopping Insider Attacks: How Organizations Can Protect their Sensitive Information*, New York: IBM Global Services, http://www-935.ibm.com/services/us/imc/pdf/gsw00316-usen-00-insider-threats-wp.pdf

Keizer, G. (2010), 'IT pros ape Apple Manager charged with bribery', *Techworld*, 19 August, http://www.techworld.com.au/article/357491/it_pros_ape_apple_manager_charged_bribery/

Kowalski, E., T. Conway, S. Keverline, M. Williams, D. Cappelli, B. Willke and A. Moore (2008), *The CERT Insider Threat Study: Illicit Cyber Activity in the Government Sector*, Pittsburgh: Joint United States Secret Service and CERT Software Engineering Institute, Carnegie Mellon University, http://www.cert.org/insider_threat/

Laville, S. (2010), 'Serious and Organised Crime Agency turns spotlight on police corruption', *Guardian*, 5 February, 7, http://www.guardian.co.uk/uk/2010/feb/14/soca-crime-agency-police-corruption
Malataka, M. (2010), 'Nigeria moves to query Siemens on bribery allegations', *Techworld*, 11 June, http://www.techworld.com.au/article/349677/nigeria_moves_query_siemens_bribery_allegations
McCullagh, D. (2008), 'Corrupt US Customs Agent sentenced for data deals', *CNet News*, 18 January, http://www.zdnet.com.au/corrupt-us-customs-agent-sentenced-for-data-deals-339285213.htm
McNamara, J. (2003), *Secrets of Computer Espionage: Tactics and Countermeasures*, New York: John Wiley & Sons.
Nasheri, H. (2005), *Economic Espionage and Industrial Spying*, Cambridge: Cambridge University Press.
New South Wales Independent Commission Against Corruption (2002), *Report of the Investigation into the Conduct of Officers and Students at University of Technology, Sydney* (Operation Tudor), Sydney: ICAC, http://www.icac.nsw.gov.au/investigations/past-investigations/investigationdetail/63
New South Wales Independent Commission Against Corruption (2010a), *Report of the Investigation into the Smuggling of Contraband into the John Morony Correctional Centre* (Operation Cicero), Sydney: ICAC, http://www.icac.nsw.gov.au/investigations/past-investigations/investigationdetail/168
New South Wales Independent Commission Against Corruption (2010b), *Transcript of Proceedings, Operation Cicero*, 27 April, Sydney: ICAC, http://www.icac.nsw.gov.au/investigations/past-investigations/article/3602
Pierik, J. (2010), 'Matches are scripted like movies: Latif', *Australian Financial Review*, 8, http://www.afr.com/p/item_p3zyYiwyIJyH8JLhKHUFSO?hl
PricewaterhouseCoopers (2010), *2011 Global State of Information Security Survey*, Washington DC: PricewaterhouseCoopers. http://www.pwc.com/gx/en/information-security-survey/pdf/giss-2011-survey-report.pdf
Ristenpart, T., E. Tromer, H. Shacham and S. Savage (2009), 'Hey, you, get off of my cloud: exploring information leakage in third-party compute clouds', in *Proceedings of the 16th ACM Conference on Computer and Communications Security*, **7**, 199–212, New York: ACM Press.
Securities and Exchange Commission (2003), *SEC v American Rice, Inc., Joseph A. Schwartz, Jr., Joel R. Malebranche and Allen W. Sturdivant* (Admin. Proc. Rel. No. 34-47286/30 January 2003), http://www.sec.gov/litigation/admin/34-47286.htm
Securities and Exchange Commission (2009), 'SEC sues former sales executive for foreign bribery', *SEC News Digest*, **167**, 31 August, Washington DC: SEC. http://www.sec.gov/news/digest/2009/dig083109.htm
Smith, R.G. (2010), 'The development of cybercrime', in R. Lincoln and S. Robinson (eds), *Crime Over Time: Temporal Perspectives on Crime and Punishment in Australia*, Newcastle upon Tyne: Cambridge Scholars Publishing, pp. 211–36.
Smith, R.G. and P.N. Grabosky (2006), 'Cyber crime', in A. Goldsmith, M. Israel and K. Daly (eds), *Crime and Justice: A Guide to Criminology* (3rd edn), Sydney: Lawbook Co, pp. 195–218.
Smith, R.G., P.N. Grabosky and G.F. Urbas (2004), *Cyber Criminals on Trial*, Cambridge: Cambridge University Press.
Smith, R.G., N. Wolanin and G. Worthington (2003), 'e-Crime solutions and crime displacement', in *Trends and Issues in Crime and Criminal Justice*, **243**, Canberra: Australian Institute of Criminology.
Sydney Morning Herald (2004), '48 Indicted in IBM Korea probe', 5 January, http://www.smh.com.au/articles/2004/01/05/1073151243606.html?from=storyrhs
Transparency International (2009), *Corruption and Sport: Building Integrity and Preventing Abuses*, Working Paper No **3/09**, Berlin: Transparency International, http://www.transparency.org/news_room/in_focus/2009/sport_and_corruption

United Nations, (2004), *United Nations Convention Against Corruption*, New York: United Nations, http://www.unodc.org/documents/treaties/UNCAC/Publications/Convention/08--50026_E.pdf

United States Attorney's Office (2010), 'President and CEO of technology company pleads guilty to bribery of a public official in DC technology office case', News Release, 27 April, United States Attorney's Office, District of Columbia, http://www.justice.gov/usao/dc/Press_Releases/2010%20Archives/April/10-079.pdf

United States Department of Justice (2010), *Two Engineers Found Guilty of Stealing Goodyear Trade Secrets*, Washington DC: Computer Crime & Intellectual Property Section, Department of Justice. http://www.cybercrime.gov/howleyPlea.pdf

World Bank (2010), Press Release, 'First "International Corruption Hunters Alliance" meets at World Bank to accelerate global enforcement action', Press Release No. 2011/216/INT, 7 December, Washington DC: World Bank, http://web.worldbank.org/WBSITE/EXTERNAL/NEWS/0,,contentMDK:22783894~menuPK:34463~pagePK:34370~piPK:34424~theSitePK:4607,00.html

Zetter, K. (2009), 'Beijing's top internet spy arrested', *Wired*, 24 February, http://www.wired.com/threatlevel/2009/02/beijings-top-in

PART III

PREVENTION AND CONTROL OF CORRUPTION

15 From information to indicators: monitoring progress in the fight against corruption in multi-project, multi-stakeholder organizations

Scott A. Fritzen and Shreya Basu

INTRODUCTION

Corruption's rise to prominence in the global discourse on governance and development can be witnessed in the high-profile legislative activity and the proliferation of organizations committed to combating it in recent years. Despite public commitments by governments and international organizations to root out corruption, many of the efforts of the last two decades have struggled to move past the rhetoric of reform. While much scrutiny is directed towards national governments, vested as they are with the responsibility of ridding their polities of corruption, pressures have also increased on private sector corporations and non-governmental actors as well. In practice, any organization that functions across multiple jurisdictions and projects, and that works with multiple partner organizations under complex accountability arrangements, has a potentially difficult task at hand: managing corruption risks *within* their organization, while managing *external* expectations, perceptions and pressures about the same (Fritzen, 2007). While large multilateral donor agencies like the World Bank fit neatly into this profile (and form the focus of this chapter), so do publicly-listed international corporations, national and bi-lateral aid agencies, international non-government organizations and even (often statutorily independent) governmental anti-corruption agencies.

A range of anti-corruption interventions have been tried and tested by these organizations over the years. Yet, practical and effective implementation of anti-corruption measures – especially in climates of systemic resistance and adversity – has often proved elusive (Bolongaita and Bhargava, 2003; Fritzen, 2006). In short, corruption continues to thrive in almost every corner of the developing world, even as public expectations of good governance are increasing. In that context, the need for a range of organizations to better augment their information management – to assess existing approaches to prevention and control of corruption, to gain understanding of what works and what does not, and to modify interventions in real time – is strong and increasing.

Effective monitoring systems are needed to facilitate such organizational learning. It is this monitoring challenge that forms the focus of this chapter. It argues that building robust monitoring systems is predicated upon the strategic use of information in all areas of anti-corruption activity. The development of robust, actionable indicators allowing the managers of complex organizations to track progress and take corrective action where required is a critical element in that challenge.

We first look at why corruption monitoring poses a daunting challenge for the large, multi-project/multi-sector organizations discussed above. We explain how the strategic use of information can help these organizations in carrying out their anti-corruption functions. Next, we put forth a framework for visualizing the various arenas in which the organizations will need to develop strong information capabilities (differently said, monitoring capabilities). Finally, we suggest ways in which organizations can make sense of the overwhelming amount of information available to them in order to build robust monitoring systems – by adopting a configurational approach in building indicators.

Throughout the chapter, we use the World Bank as an extended case study to illustrate both creative practices and limitations in indicator usage and corruption monitoring. In the fiscal year 2010, the World Bank committed an estimated US$72.9 billion in credits, loans, grants and guaranteed to over 65 developing countries, most of which are considered to be in varying degrees systemically corrupt (World Bank, 2010). It thus presents an extreme example of organizations that need to work across projects, sectors and countries with a wide range of actors, and face high levels of public scrutiny in doing so.[1] Yet the challenges we highlight are shared ones – they are to some degree generic. We draw out the implications of the World Bank's case for other organizations that fit the profile described above.

BETWEEN A ROCK AND A HARD PLACE: MULTILATERAL DONOR AGENCIES AND CORRUPTION

Corruption is a particularly sensitive and crucial issue for multilateral donor agencies for several reasons. First and foremost, misappropriated funds and 'leaked' resources directly impact organizational objectives – the higher the incidence of corruption, the longer the road to poverty reduction. Second, corruption scandals in and around donor projects have the potential to highlight internal failures of corruption control within these organizations (that are often viewed as overbearing 'preachers' of the anti-corruption gospel by partner governments) into the public spotlight. In many countries, citizen groups have mobilized to monitor and mount pressure on the World Bank (and other organizations in both the public and private sectors), in an attempt to hold them accountable to their commitments and rhetoric. The situation is made more complex by the fact that these organizations have often had a tenuous relationship with several developing countries in which they operate.

The scale of the challenge these organizations face in negotiating their complex stakeholder environment, and in living up to their own commitments, is indeed daunting. Often, these organizations oversee a large portfolio of projects dispersed throughout countries across the world, very often in areas where corruption is endemic. In order to carry out their mandates, they need to rely on local government machinery and partner organizations that may not necessarily share their standards for anti-corruption work. Political pressures, individual incentives and career paths, and tradeoffs between different organizational goals make the implementation of consistent anti-corruption efforts difficult. The tasks associated with monitoring and evaluating anti-corruption measures are formidable when an organization's portfolio of projects includes great diversity in scale, sector or location.

Let us turn to World Bank as a case in point. Since the now famous 1996 'cancer of corruption' speech given by then President James Wolfensohn, the Bank has gone on to support anti-corruption programmes around the world, recognizing that the challenge posed by corruption had to be faced both in its operating environment and in its internal operations (Wolfensohn, 1996; Fine, 2003). It has undertaken several initiatives to ensure internal organizational integrity, minimize corruption on Bank-funded projects, and assist countries in controlling corruption. Measures have included establishing a Department of Institutional Integrity, developing several tools and programmes for fighting corruption, commissioning special studies and reports and initiating collective action programmes. These initiatives have absorbed considerable investments. After years of experimenting with largely unsuccessful ad hoc approaches to dealing with corruption, the World Bank implemented a 'Governance and Anti-Corruption strategy (GAC), at the global, country and project levels. At the heart of this strategy was the recognition of the links between governance, corruption, growth and poverty reduction (World Bank, 2007a). As part of this strategy, now in its second year of implementation, the Bank has begun to routinely examine its own management systems, methodologies, and tools for its ability to mitigate the risk of corruption and has attempted to share key lessons through broad dissemination. It has also undertaken 'Detailed Implementation Reviews' which 'examine Bank-financed projects in a specific country or sector to determine their susceptibility and possible exposure to fraud, corruption, collusion, and coercion (fraud and corruption), (World Bank, 2007b, p. 1).

Despite these ongoing measures, the Bank continues to be criticized for its inability to detect and manage fraud and corruption-related vulnerabilities. An April 2009 report by the Independent Evaluation Group (an independent unit within the World Bank that reports directly to the Bank's Board of Executive Directors) found that the International Development Association (the arm of the Bank that assists the world's poorest countries through grants and interest-free loans) did not have in place adequate anti-corruption measures, citing material weaknesses in the Bank's risk management arsenal (World Bank, 2009a). A 2009 GAC progress report (World Bank, 2009b) concluded that while steady gains can be observed in the development of GAC tools and their mainstreaming in the Bank's operations – from upstream assistance strategies to downstream design and implementation of lending operations – challenges remain in terms of documentation and communication of impact, and in the 'mainstreaming' of anti-corruption work throughout World Bank operations. The absence of simple, meaningful and manageable indicators that can track progress in this area is identified as a critical weakness underlying the failure of donor agencies (including the Bank) to meet their anti-corruption objectives (Chêne, 2010).

ROLE OF INFORMATION IN THE BATTLE AGAINST CORRUPTION

The significance of the role of information in combating corruption can be situated within the discourse on learning organizations. According to David Garvin, 'a learning organization is one skilled at creating, acquiring and transferring knowledge, and at modifying its behaviour to reflect the new knowledge and insights' (Garvin, 1993). While the source of such insights could be internal or external to an organization, a learning organization is one that uses these insights to facilitate change in an organization's behaviour (Choo, 1995).

The 'learning organization' approach is particularly useful in the context of anti-corruption. Across a variety of multilateral development banks, considerable resources have been expended on the fight against corruption, with relatively modest results to show for the same. Clearly information pertaining to inputs, functions and outputs need to be constantly monitored to allow for the fine-tuning of tactics and approaches. Capturing the right information at different stages of organizational processes can allow for 'the creation of a feedback loop in which information about a later stage can be fed back into control of an earlier stage' (Heeks, 1998). Simply put, the information generated in the execution of various organizational functions may carry the nucleus of important insights that can be used to learn what works and what does not, and to trigger course corrections.

Information is not simply a basis for corrective action. According to Martha Feldman and James March, 'command of information and information sources enhances perceived competence and inspires confidence' (Feldman and March, 1981). Similarly, use of information in justifying decision-making processes can signal or (in Feldman and March's usage) 'symbolize' the rational basis of those decisions, and the competence and legitimacy of those making them. Understanding the role of information in these terms is especially useful to multilateral donor agencies given the active scrutiny and complex field of accountability they face, as described above. In a more direct sense too, the sharing and dissemination of information with a wide range of stakeholders may multiply organizational capabilities to suppress corruption via the enlisting or engagement of additional stakeholders to co-operate in the organization's efforts.

Fortunately, with the rapid technological and communication gains that have been made in recent times, the availability of information is not a concern for most organizations. In fact, many organizations suffer from 'information overload' (Edmunds and Morris, 2000), a condition also referred to as 'information fatigue syndrome' (Oppenheim, 1997). Yet for most organizations and indeed for multilateral donor agencies combating intractable problems such as corruption, proper harnessing of information resources is critical to achieving results in several areas. The manner in which information is *processed* within organizations so as to create value for managers and decision makers is therefore of utmost importance (Simpson and Prusak, 1995). Organizations will need to carefully identify their information needs, establish mechanisms to capture this information meaningfully and embed the use of such information within their decision-support systems in order to meet their objectives and facilitate learning.

In the following section we propose a framework for visualizing such strategic use of information in the context of multilateral donor agencies.

FRAMEWORK FOR STRATEGIC USE OF INFORMATION IN MULTILATERAL DONOR AGENCIES

For multilateral donor agencies to be effective in their fight against corruption, they will need to meet a wide spectrum of requirements, including:

- establishing robust systems/ controls for preventing corruption;
- designing awareness programmes for their own staff, partner organizations as well their clients;
- effectively detecting and investigating incidents of corruption;
- tracking vulnerabilities to steer the course of future anti-corruption actions.

They will also need to enhance managerial control, improve system-wide integrity and enhance accountability systems while undertaking the above tasks (Fritzen, 2007). More importantly, given the complexities of trying to reduce endemic corruption especially in field projects, they will need to facilitate organizational learning about which among their various tools and tactics are working and which are not, and to funnel corruption-related information to and from a broader network of stakeholders. Figure 15.1 is one way of visualizing the different arenas in which information will need to be strategically deployed in order to enable organizational learning.

The various elements of the framework can be distinguished in several ways. First, the *inherent linkages* between corruption prevention, detection, investigation, and anti-corruption steering which make it imperative for organizations to monitor trends by analysing, managing and disseminating information pertaining to each of these elements of anti-corruption control. The second concerns the *flow of information* between the various elements of corruption control. A robust monitoring system will be able to feed the information insights generated at each stage of corruption control into the next stage to enhance its effectiveness. For example, information pertaining to anomalies in processes (for example suspicious transactions) generated at the detection stage should trigger the investigation process. Findings from the detection and investigation stages need to be analysed in order to steer the future course of anti-corruption activities. The strategies generated in the steering activities need to be filtered down to redesign the prevention and education programmes of the organization. Pro-active detection activities then need to be focussed around testing the new preventive controls and the gaps in knowledge/skills remedied by education and awareness programmes conducted for staff and other

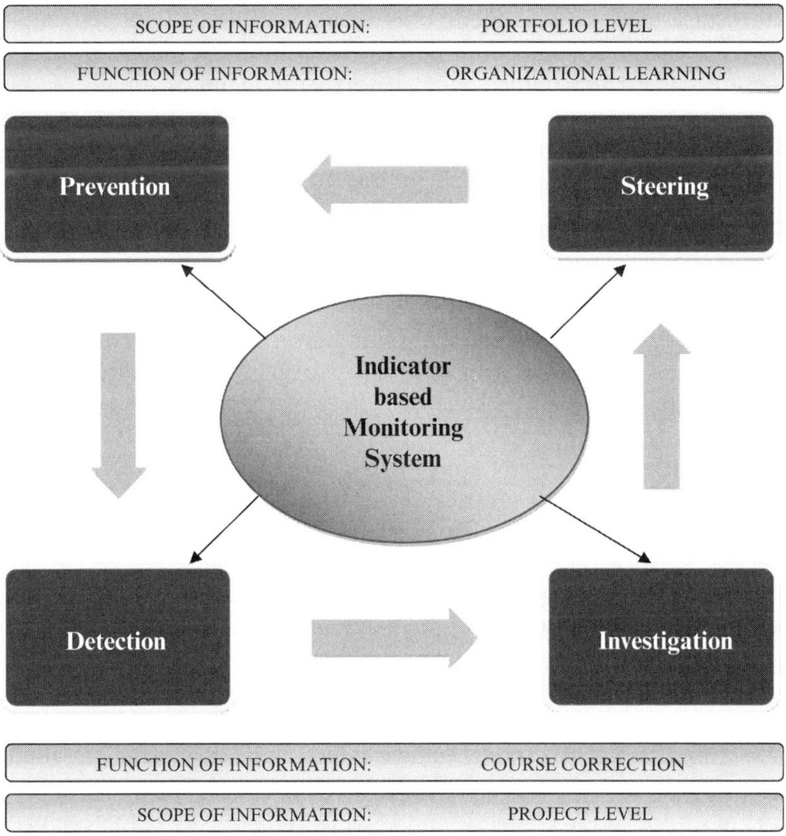

Figure 15.1 Framework for strategic use of information

stakeholders, and (often more importantly) by changes in the incentives faced by employees.

Flowing through the various stages of corruption control, *the function of information* changes from course correction (at the detection and investigation) stage to facilitating organizational learning (at the steering and prevention stages). The *scope of information* also changes from project level to portfolio level as insights generated from specific incidences of corruption within a single project can facilitate learning that is applicable across a portfolio of projects.

How does an organization make sense of the overwhelming amount of information at its disposal to build robust monitoring systems that facilitate organizational learning? The answer, we posit, lies in developing meaningful indicators from the available information. It is important at this stage to make a distinction between 'information' and 'indicators' as we use the terms. Information is the raw data that needs processing before it can be understood and contextualized. Indicators in contrast are derived from observed data and provide self-explanatory information about the state of processes and outcomes. In the next section, we turn to examining what good, actionable indicators might look like.

FROM INFORMATION TO INDICATORS

The notion of indicators as foundations of anti-corruption (or corruption) monitoring is not new. But most of the existing literature on indicators focuses on broader country level indicators of corruption and the merits and de-merits of using the various existing indicators. (Kaufmann et al., 2007; Sampford et al., 2006; Doig et al., 2006). Few works suggest meaningful ways in which indicators can be constructed at portfolio and project levels or ways in which the effectiveness of anti-corruption interventions can be monitored.

Asking the question, 'What might a set of indicators that could help multilateral donor agencies improve their monitoring and evaluation efforts look like?' is a way of benchmarking current practices (in the World Bank case), and exploring the contours of the possible. Before elaborating on such a list of indicators, it is important to note that there is and can be no single, 'magic bullet' indicator, given the multidimensional nature of the corruption problem, and the multiple functions of an indicator system. A *set* of indicators deployed jointly might improve the monitoring capabilities of an organization, as long at least as it does not lead to 'information overload' as described earlier. We argue for a configurational approach to indicator development, drawing from insights developed by Kaufman, Kray and Mastruzzi (2007) and Vlassis (2005) in the literature. The approach needs to be configurational in three senses:

1) Indicators will have to address multiple functions and needs;
2) They will have to be robust and complement each other for enhanced reliability and validity; and
3) They will need to be deployed in systems that embed appropriate incentives for their use in decision-making and steering.

Let us consider these features one at a time. First, for a monitoring system to be robust, indicators need to address multiple functions and needs Many of today's monitoring systems are built on a somewhat ad hoc basis, with over-use of indicators in some areas and inadequate indicator development in others.

Take for example the indicators used by World Bank in their Detailed Implementation Reviews (DIR).[2] The DIR uses a set of pre-defined indicators that have been classified into levels of hierarchy (level one, two and three) based on the indicator's type and its relative value as an indication of fraudulent and corrupt activities (World Bank, 2007b). The classification of the indicators, laid out in the DIR is as follows (World Bank, 2007b, p. 28):

> Level One Indicators are oral or written admissions of corrupt or fraudulent practices (e.g., admitting to paying a bribe or being solicited to do so) by winning, losing, or interested bidders, project officials or consultants, or Bank staff or consultants; and (2) objective facts demonstrating that corrupt or fraudulent practices have or very likely have occurred.
>
> Level Two Indicators are objective facts that empirically indicate with a high likelihood the presence of fraudulent and corrupt activities. Indicators at this level are sub-divided into four groups: (1) indicators of corrupt or fraudulent practices in a particular contract, such as separate bidders sharing common addresses or officials, or bidders with sequential or similar bid security serial numbers from the same bank on or about the same date; (2) objective facts that indicate the presence of a cartel (collusion among bidders); (3) objective facts or patterns that indicate bid rigging between a bidder and the Bid Evaluation Committee; and (4) suspicious practices and patterns by the project's implementation unit or related support agencies.
>
> Level Three Indicators are facts and evidence that when present represent an increased risk of possible corrupt or fraudulent practices. Level Three indicators point to factors that demonstrate increased opportunities for these activities to have occurred, such as weak controls or failure to follow strict procedures.

Most of the clearly articulated indicators in the DIR are being deployed in the area of procurement. Areas such as financial management, portfolio monitoring, and resource management, among others, are not explicitly addressed. Further, the indicators are heavily concentrated in the areas of investigation and detection of specific instances of corruption, rather than cutting across all four quadrants of anti-corruption activity presented in the earlier section. A monitoring system based on such indicators focussing narrowly on corruption detection and investigation at the project level, do not enable direct monitoring of the quality and effectiveness of interventions established by the Bank. For example, it would not shed light on questions such as: where corruption does occur, does it occur despite the existence of 'strong' anti-corruption controls? Nor does it take stock of the practical implementation of anti-corruption interventions at the project or portfolio level.

In order to be effective indicators should allow for determining progress over time, identifying good practices and allowing for the adjustment of anti-corruption policies and measures as required (Vlassis, 1995). In addition, an indicator system should be sensitive to the communication needs of an organization, and should facilitate confidence in the integrity of the system itself (since corruption risks can never be completely eliminated, particularly in systemically corrupt environments).

Second, indicators must be robust and complement each other for enhanced reliability and validity. Corruption is notoriously difficult to identify and track, and indicators do have technical characteristics as far as reliability and validity go. According to Marion Joppe (2000), validity is the ability of the indicator to chart the phenomenon it purports to cover, and reliability, its ability to measure the phenomenon consistently, present an accurate representation of the same, and be reproducible using a similar methodology. Reliability and validity can be mutually exclusive features. There are indicators that are valid but not highly reliable, and vice versa.

In addition, rules-based measures need to be complemented by and used in conjunction with outcome-based indicators (Kaufmann et al., 2007). In the context of multilateral donor agencies, rules-based indicators would measure the existence of anti-corruption interventions/plans while outcome-based indicators would measure the success or outcomes of these plans. Rules- and outcomes-based indicators should ideally be combined, given 'the inevitable role of judgment even in "objective" rules-based indicators; the complexity and lack of knowledge regarding the links from rules to outcomes of interest; and the gap between rules "on the books" and their "implementation" on the ground' (Kaufmann et al., 2007). Furthermore, linkages between outcome-based indicators and policy interventions that might influence these outcomes are not always easily inferable (Kaufmann et al., 2007).

Indicators should also allow for comparability of results across time and space (Vlassis, 1995) as well as projects. The DIR indicators come up deficient in this regard. Most indicators in use do not appear to be designed to allow for comparison *across* projects. DIR indicators that are rules-based run the risk of a 'ticking the boxes' approach, tending towards the superficial and undermining the analytical assessments that need to emerge from indicator tracking. DIR indicators that are broadly outcome-oriented, in turn, are very broadly and vaguely defined – 'level three indicators point to factors that demonstrate increased opportunities for these activities to have occurred, such as weak controls or failure to follow strict procedures' (DIR, 2007). Clearly, indicator systems will need to focus on both process/rules and outcomes, preferably in a manner that allows for cross-cutting problem analysis to take place. For example, a rules indicator measuring the percentage of projects that have anti-corruption plans might be coupled with a complementary outcome indicator tracking the percentage of projects with anti-corruption plans that actually report corruption incidence.

Finally, indicator development will need to be deployed within systems that embed appropriate incentives for their use in decision-making and steering systems. Indicators can be meaningfully used only if key performance indicators for the Bank as a whole, and for individual managers within it, go beyond the volume of lending portfolios or even the project outputs and outcomes achieved, to include also the effectiveness of integrity systems embedded within lending processes. This remains an area of concern for agencies like the World Bank where 'for an ambitious Bank employee, there are still no career rewards today for focusing on corruption at any stage in the lending process' (Winters, 2004) and where managerial incentives, political pressures and the reality of tradeoffs between different organizational goals all combine to make it organizationally painful to systematically institutionalize anti-corruption measures (Fritzen, 2007). The combination of sustained high-levels of rhetorical commitment to anti-corruption work from the leadership of these organizations combined with increasing pressures from civil society in many countries can help create an enabling environment for some managers to experiment in this area (Fritzen, 2007).

Having laid out the approach to indicator development, we now turn to exploring what an improved indicator system might look like in the multilateral donor agency context. Suggestive indicators are shown in Table 15.1, which categorizes them by organizational and anti-corruption-related function, and by scope (according to the framework presented in Figure 15.1). These indicators are aimed at enabling better monitoring systems at the project as well as the overall portfolio (or system) level, and across several organizational functions.[3] Those shown include ruled-based, outcome-based, quantitative and qualitative indicators. Many of these building blocks are already in use by several organizations (including the World Bank) in varying degrees of isolation; the important point is the possibility for adopting a 'configurational approach' to 'covering' multiple functions based on information already at the disposal of multilateral donors. The list below should be considered as an indicative list that organizations will need to build upon and adapt to meet their unique requirements, while bearing in mind time and resource constraints.

Table 15.1 Anti-corruption indicators

Organizational function	Indicator	Type of indicator	Scope of indicator (project or portfolio)	Primary anti-corruption function of indicator
Strategic planning/ resource allocation	Does planning incorporate feedback from earlier projects of a similar nature?	Yes–No, rules-based	Project and portfolio	Steering
	Share of project budget allocated to anti-corruption activity	Quantitative, rules-based	Project	Prevention
	Does the project includean anti-corruption action plan with review mechanisms?	Yes–No, rules-based	Project	Prevention
	Share of projects with anti-corruption action plans	Quantitative, rules and outcome-based	Portfolio	Prevention
	Share of earlier projects with anti-corruption plans in which corruption/ fraud occurred	Quantitative, outcome-based	Portfolio	Steering
Human resources management	Share of project team members to have undergone anti-corruption training	Quantitative, rules-based	Project	Education
	Share of employees to have undergone anti-corruption training	Quantitative, rules-based	Portfolio	Education
	No. of training sessions held for partner organizations	Quantitative, rules-based	Project and portfolio	Education
	Training sessions incorporate cases/ lessons from reported instances of corruption	Yes–No, rules-based	Project and portfolio	Steering
	Share of corruption instances detected by employees	Quantitative, outcome-based	Project and portfolio	Education and detection

Table 15.1 (continued)

Organizational function	Indicator	Type of indicator	Scope of indicator (project or portfolio)	Primary anti-corruption function of indicator
	Share of corruption instances involving employees and partner organizations	Quantitative, outcome-based	Project and portfolio	Education and detection
Procurement management	Have procurement rules been set and communicated to project officers and potential bidders?	Yes–No, rules-based	Project and portfolio	Prevention
	Do all procurement contracts include explicit clauses on corruption and collusion?	Yes–No, rules-based	Project and portfolio	Prevention
	Degree of variance between quotes provided and winning bid	Quantitative, outcome-based	Project	Detection
	No of bidders	Quantitative, outcome-based	Project	Detection
	Reduction in procurement delays	Quantitative, outcome-based	Project and portfolio	Steering
	Discrepancy between inventory received and billed amounts	Quantitative, outcome-based	Project	Detection
	Share of projects with procurement-related corruption reported	Quantitative, outcome-based	Portfolio	Detection
Financial management	No. of corruption related financial controls in place	Quantitative, rules-based	Project	Prevention
	Have financial management loopholes identified in earlier projects of similar nature been closed?	Yes–No, rules-based	Project	Steering

Table 15.1 (continued)

Organizational function	Indicator	Type of indicator	Scope of indicator (project or portfolio)	Primary anti-corruption function of indicator
	Share of total unaccounted expenditure	Quantitative, outcome-based	Project and portfolio	Detection
	Share of audit findings pertaining to fraud and corruption	Quantitative, outcome-based	Project and portfolio	Investigation
	No. of authorized expenses with no supporting documents	Quantitative, outcome-based	Project	Detection
Information systems management	Periodicity of conduction of anti-corruption reviews	Quantitative, rules-based	Project and portfolio	Detection
	Results of investigation documented and shared with relevant stakeholders	Yes–No, rules-based	Project and portfolio,	Steering
	Lessons learnt from investigation documented and made available for subsequent access	Yes–No, rules-based	Project and portfolio	Steering
	Maker–Checker controls in place for IT systems	Yes–No, rules-based	Project and portfolio	Prevention
	No. of anti-corruption and fraud specific controls	Quantitative, rules-based	Project and portfolio	Prevention
Stakeholder management	Share of projects with citizen involvement features	Quantitative, rules-based	Portfolio	Prevention and detection
	Share of projects open to external review	Quantitative, rules-based	Portfolio	Prevention and education and detection
	Share of public documents pertaining to project/portfolio made available to stakeholders	Quantitative, rules-based	Project and portfolio	Prevention and education

Table 15.1 (continued)

Organizational function	Indicator	Type of indicator	Scope of indicator (project or portfolio)	Primary anti-corruption function of indicator
	Cases of corruption highlighted in annual report	Yes–No/ qualitative, rules/ outcome-based	Portfolio	Steering
Performance management	Performance incentives established for anti-corruption related work	Yes–No, rules-based	Project and portfolio	Steering and prevention
	Course correction measures based on corruption findings taken as parameter for performance review	Yes–No/ qualitative, outcome-based	Project and portfolio	Steering
	No. of cases of corruption detected by internal staff	Quantitative, outcome-based	Project and portfolio	Detection and investigation
Complaints handling	No. of corruption complaints received	Quantitative, outcome-based	Project and portfolio	Detection
	Share of complaints pending action	Quantitative, outcome-based	Project and portfolio	Investigation
	Share of cases where significant action was taken based on complaints/ investigation	Quantitative, outcome-based	Project and portfolio	Investigation and steering

DISCUSSION

The elaborate controls and anti-corruption programmes that have been instituted in organizations attempting to curb corruption have often failed to meet expectations; some are seen mainly as further impediments to achieving organizational priorities and efficiency (Anechiarico and Jacobs, 1996). In light of the same, the manner in which corruption trends and the success of anti-corruption efforts are monitored clearly needs further improvement.

While there is no made-to-order blueprint available for the systematic monitoring of corruption trends as they affect large multi-project, multi-stakeholder and multi-sectoral organizations such as the World Bank, these organizations can use information more strategically to build meaningful indicators that can improve the efficacy of their monitoring systems.

The use of indicators outlined by us can help an organization to set baselines in its counter-corruption work. Some indicators will allow comparisons to be made across projects. Many indicators will be most useful if studied across time within individual projects. Comparing across projects will in turn allow for improved pattern identification, sectoral risk assessment and possibly even project manager performance. A central point of this chapter has been that a narrow focus on too small a set of indicators will fail to provide a balanced view of what is taking place on the ground or to serve diverse stakeholders. But clearly, monitoring and evaluation activities need to be balanced finely with other organizational priorities. They must avoid a common pitfall: the proliferation of indicators and sources of analysis to the point where focus, cost-effectiveness and managerial usefulness are all greatly reduced.

One way to resolve this dilemma may be to distinguish a set of 'leading indicators' based on organizational objectives, targets and operational contexts. The indicator list outlined by us is by no means exhaustive or universally applicable. It is meant to illustrate how a configurational and balanced approach can cover multiple steering, investigative and ultimately learning objectives.

Of course, the mere generation of indicators is not enough. How the indicators are analysed and used to redesign processes and project designs, and how in turn those improved processes come to enhance standards of accountability in anti-corruption interventions, will ultimately determine the effectiveness of this enterprise. The success of the indicator framework will depend too on the institutional environment and incentive structures within which they are embedded. Incentives for sustained managerial focus on addressing weaknesses exposed by the indicators, and for the setting of project-specific goals linked to the framework, will be vital to translate good intentions into tangible results.

NOTES

1. For a detailed discussion of the monitoring and evaluation challenge faced by the World Bank read 'Strengthening World Bank Group engagement on governance and anti-corruption: Second year progress report', http://siteresources.worldbank.org/PUBLICSECTORANDGOVERNANCE/Resources/285741-1233946247437/GACReport2.pdf

2. For the discussion on indicator usage in the World Bank, we use information that that is publicly available through the Bank's website and supplement it with the lead author's consulting experiences with the Bank in Southeast Asia. While it could well be the case that some country/project offices use more comprehensive and well documented indicators, our discussion still remains highly relevant given the lack of permeation of these efforts throughout the Bank's entire portfolio of activities. Further, there is a strong case for pushing the Bank towards sharing such practices publicly (if they exist) to promote transparency and to share learning with other organizations with similar mandates.
3. We focus on the project and country office level allows for greater engagement of the stakeholders that are directly impacted by the project (including local governments, communities, civil society organizations and project managers). For organizations that function across multiple projects in diverse political, economic and business settings, any coherent and effective anti-corruption strategy would need to include anti-corruption measures that are an intrinsic part of the design and implementation of each individual project and designed keeping the operating environment in mind. It leaves room for project managers to assess and assign priorities to different indicators based on unique project realities. Further, devolving responsibility for monitoring efforts to lower levels of management also allows for quicker detection and resolution of corruption-related concerns. Finally, indicators that can be used to assess corruption trends and effectiveness of anti-corruption measures at the project level.

REFERENCES

Anechiarico, F. and James B. Jacobs (1996), *The Pursuit of Absolute Integrity: How Corruption Control Makes Government Ineffective*, Chicago and London: The University of Chicago Press.

Bolongaita, E.P. and V.K. Bhargava (eds) (2003), *Challenging Corruption in Asia: Selected Case Studies and a Framework for Improving Anti-Corruption Effectiveness*, Washington DC: The World Bank.

Chêne, Marie (2010), 'Mainstreaming corruption within donor agencies', U4 Expert Answer, U4 Anti-Corruption Resource Centre, http://www.u4.no/helpdesk/helpdesk/query.cfm?id=23, accessed 15 October 2010.

Choo, W.C. (1995), 'Information management for the intelligent organization: roles and implications for the information professions', in *Digital Libraries Conference*, March 27–28, Singapore.

Doig, A. Stephanie McIvor, and Robin Theobald (2006), 'Numbers, nuances and moving targets: converging the use of corruption indicators or descriptors in assessing state development', *International Review of Administrative Sciences*, **72**, 239–52.

Edmunds, A. and Anne Morris (2000), 'The problem of information overload in business organisations: a review of the literature', *International Journal of Information Management*, **20**(1), 17–28.

Feldman, M. and James March (1981), 'Information in organizations as signal and symbol', *Administrative Science Quarterly*, **26** (2), 171–86.

Fine, B. (2003), 'Social capital: the World Bank's fungible friend', *Journal of Agrarian Change*, **3**(4), 586–603.

Fritzen, S. (2006), 'Beyond political will: how institutional context shapes the implementation of anti-corruption strategies', *Policy and Society*, **24**(3), 79–96.

Fritzen, S. (2007), 'Crafting performance measurement systems to reduce corruption vulnerabilities in complex, multistakeholder organizations: The case of the World Bank', *Measuring Business Excellence*, **11**(4), 23–32.

Garvin, D.A. (1993), 'Building a learning organization', *Harvard Business Review*, **71**(4), 78–9.

Heeks, R. (1998), 'Information systems for Public Sector management', Public Sector Management Information Systems Working Paper Series Paper No. 5.
Joppe, M. (2000), 'The Research Process', http://www.uoguelph.ca/htm/marion-joppe.shtml, accessed 29 November 2010.
Kaufmann, D. Art Kraay and M. Mastruzzi. (2007) 'Governance matters VI: aggregate and individual governance indicators 1996–2006', Washington DC: The World Bank .
Oppenheim, C. (1997), 'Managers' use and handling of information', *International Journal of Information Management*, **17**(4), 239–48.
Sampford, C., Arthur S., Carmel C. and Fredrik, G. (eds) (2006), *Measuring Corruption*, Aldershot, UK: Ashgate.
Simpson, C. and Prusak, L. (1995), 'Troubles with information overload: moving from quantity to quality in information provision', *International Journal of Information Management*, **15**(6), 413–25.
Vlassis, D. (1995), 'Emerging basic parameters for the measuring and monitoring of corruption and anti-corruption', in UNODC Workshop On Measuring and Monitoring Corruption and Anti-Corruption, June 17–18, Sofia, Bulgaria.
Winters, J.A. (2004), 'Criminal Debt', Written statement of evidence presenting at Hearing before the Committee on Foreign Relations, United States Senate, May 13, 2004.
Wolfensohn, J. (1996), 'Opening Address by the President of World Bank Group', in *Annual meeting of the International Monetary Fund and World Bank Group*, October 1–3, Washington DC.
World Bank (2007a) 'Implementation plan for strengthening World Bank Group engagement on governance and anti-corruption', http://web.worldbank.org/WBSITE/EXTERNAL/TOPICS/EXTGOVANTICORR/0,,contentMDK:21519459~pagePK:210058~piPK:210062~theSitePK:3035864,00.html, accessed 15 October 2010.
World Bank (2007b), 'Detailed Implementation Review: India Health Sector', http://siteresources.worldbank.org/EXTDOII/Resources/WB250_Web_Vol1_012408.pdf, accessed 15 October 2010.
World Bank (2009a), 'Review of IDA Internal Controls An Evaluation of Management's Assessment and the IAD Review', http://siteresources.worldbank.org/EXTOED/Resources/ida_controls_full.pdf, accessed 15 October 2010.
World Bank (2009b) 'Strengthening World Bank Group engagement on governance and anti-corruption: Second year progress report', http://siteresources.worldbank.org/PUBLICSECTORANDGOVERNANCE/Resources/285741-1233946247437/GACReport2.pdf, accessed 15 October 2010.
World Bank (2010) 'Annual Report 2010', http://web.worldbank.org/WBSITE/EXTERNAL/EXTABOUTUS/EXTANNREP/EXTANNREP2010/0,,contentMDK:22626599~menuPK:7115719~pagePK:64168445~piPK:64168309~theSitePK:7074179,00.html#lending, accessed 29 November 2010.

16 The United Nations Convention Against Corruption

Matti Joutsen

THE UNITED NATIONS AND INTERNATIONAL CO-OPERATION ON CRIME AND CRIMINAL JUSTICE

One of the main purposes of the UN is 'to create the conditions for stability and well-being which are necessary for peaceful and friendly international relations, based on mutual respect, equality and self-determination'.[1]

Issues related to crime and criminal justice have been on the UN agenda since the outset, and the work on them has undergone considerable evolution over the years.[2] At first, the focus was on the collection and exchange of information, research and the development of international standards and norms. This focus is understandable in the light of the membership of the UN. During the early years, the UN membership consisted predominantly of Western industrialized countries, and the persons who took part in the discussions were often practitioners, interested in trading ideas and good practice with their colleagues from other countries sharing the same immediate concerns.

This sharing of ideas and good practice resulted in a large number of UN standards and norms, beginning with the Standard Minimum Rules for the Treatment of Prisoners (1956). These standards and norms cover a broad range of criminal policy issues, from the independence of the judiciary, a code of conduct for law enforcement officials, the role of lawyers and the role of prosecutors, to the administration of juvenile justice, the treatment of victims of crime, and capital punishment.

Another aspect of this early UN focus was that the focus was on so-called traditional offences and domestic concerns: juvenile delinquency, violent crime, policing, prison administration and non-custodial sanctions, and so on. This was in keeping with the general attitude of countries, according to which crime was primarily regarded as a local, or at most national, issue.

The major exception to this domestic focus within the UN framework was drugs. Over a hundred years ago countries had realized that an effective response to drug trafficking required international agreements on the criminalization of certain drug offences. The result was among the first multilateral conventions on crime and criminal justice, the International Opium Conventions of 1912 and 1925, and the Convention for Limiting the Manufacture and Regulating the Distribution of Narcotic Drugs in 1931.[3]

When the United Nations was established, it was able to build on this earlier international work. The agreements mentioned above that had been negotiated at the beginning of the century were essentially replaced by the 1961 Single Convention on Narcotic Drugs. The 1961 Convention established new mechanisms and obligations. It assigned certain functions to new United Nations bodies, the Commission on Narcotic Drugs and the International Narcotics Control Board. The Convention also required states to provide annual estimates of drugs used for various purposes, to abide by restrictions on manufacture, production and import, to criminalize the possession, supply and transport of drugs, and make them extraditable offences.

The 1961 Single Convention was amended by a Protocol in 1972. However, this protocol did not change the substantive scope of the Convention, which continued to encompass cannabis, coca and opium, and drugs with similar effects. Developments during the 1950s and especially during the 1960s focused attention on a new form of drugs, psychotropics: perhaps first and foremost psychedelics (such as LSD), but also amphetamines and barbiturates.

Moreover, calling upon states that were parties to these agreements to criminalize drugs proved to be insufficient, without parallel agreements on various forms of procedural co-operation. When work began on a convention that would expand the substantive scope of the 1961 Single Convention to include also pyschotropics, the negotiations were for the first time extended to include procedural provisions (for example on police co-operation, and on extradition and mutual assistance). The result was the 1988 United Nations Convention against Illicit Traffic in Narcotic Drugs and Psychotropic Substances, which today remains the basic international agreement on drugs.

The 1988 Convention, the first global convention to combine substantive and procedural provisions, almost immediately became the template for further negotiation of UN conventions on crime and justice.[4] Italy, with its long experience with organized crime, began international lobbying for a corresponding UN Convention that would deal with an entirely new and far broader field, transnational organized crime. Italy hosted the World Ministerial Conference on Organized Transnational Crime in 1994,[5] only a few years after the 1988 Convention had entered into force. From that point, matters proceeded very quickly. Poland formally introduced a draft for the convention at the autumn 1996 session of the

General Assembly.[6] Only four years later, the United Nations Convention on Transnational Organized Crime (UNTOC), with separate protocols on trafficking in persons, the smuggling of migrants and trafficking in firearms, was formally opened for signature.

The dust had barely settled on the negotiating tables where the UNTOC Convention had been hammered out, when work began on a UN convention on corruption. The genesis of the United Nations Convention against Corruption (UNCAC) differs from that of UNTOC. UNTOC did not have any direct forbears, any multilateral conventions on organized crime that would have served as a model. UNCAC, in turn, had several predecessors:

- the 1996 Inter-American Convention against Corruption of the Organization of American States;
- the 1997 Convention on Combating Bribery of Foreign Public Officials in International Business Transactions of the Organization for Economic Cooperation and Development (OECD);
- the 1998 Convention on the Fight against Corruption Involving Officials of the European Communities or Officials of Member States of the European Union;
- the 1999 Criminal Law Convention on Corruption and the 1999 Civil Law Convention on Corruption of the Council of Europe;
- the 2001 Southern African Development Community Protocol against Corruption; and
- the 2003 African Union Convention on Preventing and Combating Corruption.

All of these conventions, UNCAC included, have emerged within a relatively short period of time – the seven years from 1996 to 2003. Apparently a tipping point was reached sometime during the 1990s, when states realized that international conventions were the necessary next step in dealing with the problem of corruption. It is also likely that when work began in one forum on the drafting of a convention (the Inter-American Convention and the OECD Convention), this influenced the decision to begin work elsewhere (the European Union, the Council of Europe, Southern Africa and Africa, as well as within the framework of the United Nations).

More than a hundred Member States of the United Nations took an active part in the negotiations on the United Nations Convention against Corruption (UNCAC). The General Assembly adopted the Convention on 31 October, 2003 (GA resolution 58/4). Two years later, on 14 December 2005, the Convention entered into force. In 2011, it has 148 States Parties, making it one of the most widely ratified Conventions in the world.[7]

THE IMPACT OF THE UN CONVENTION ON CORRUPTION

UNCAC (together with the 1988 Convention and UNTOC)[8] has influenced international co-operation in at least three respects:

- as a global convention it has considerably expanded the geographical scope of co-operation,
- it provides common definitions of certain key offences, and requires (or, in some cases, at least encourages) States Parties to criminalize these acts, and
- it has standardized, and contributed to, the development of procedural forms of co-operation.

The UN Convention on Corruption is specifically a *global instrument*, open to countries around the world. With the exception of the OECD convention, all the earlier agreements had a regional scope. The OECD convention, in turn, has a narrower substantive scope, since it is limited to the bribery of foreign officials in international business transactions. UNCAC provides a relatively clear basis for co-operation between countries around the globe, regardless of their legal system or the underlying principles of the operation of their criminal justice system.

UNCAC contains a number of *criminalizations*. The provisions on money laundering and obstruction of justice (arts 23 and 25) are broadly similar to those to be found in UNTOC, which was opened for signature five years earlier. Understandably, UNCAC goes into greater detail than UNTOC in requiring the criminalization of corruption offences, such as bribery, and misappropriation or other diversion of property by a public official (arts 15, 16(1) and 17). In addition, UNCAC contains definitions of some acts that States Parties are encouraged to criminalize, although there is no obligation to do so. This non-mandatory approach is the result of the fact that, during the negotiations, many states were dissatisfied with what they saw as the vagueness of such definitions of offences as trading in influence (art. 18), abuse of functions (art. 19), and illicit enrichment (art. 20). In addition, some States Parties opposed making bribery in the private sector (art. 21) a mandatory offence.

To illustrate the impact of UNCAC on procedural co-operation, it may be helpful to attempt to describe what co-operation was typically like before the three UN conventions entered into force (referred to here as 'traditional cooperation') and compare this with the 'new, improved' co-operation to which the three conventions have contributed. These two regimes are summarized in Table 16.1.

Table 16.1 Two regimes of co-operation

The traditional co-operation regime	The 'new, improved' co-operation regime
Each country uses its own 'traditional' investigative means	Introduction of various modern investigative means
Each country carries out its own criminal investigation	The possibility of joint investigations
Limited scope of mutual assistance available	Many possible forms of mutual assistance available
No provisions on confiscation of the proceeds of crime	Such provisions included, as are provisions on mutual assistance related to confiscation
Use of diplomatic channels in requesting and giving assistance	Use of a central authority, and the possibility of direct contacts between lower level authorities
Bureaucratic	'Good practice' standards followed; e.g. the possibility of consultation before possible refusal
Requested state applies solely its own laws in granting assistance	Procedures requested by the requesting state can be applied if these are not contrary to the laws of the requested state
Extradition of nationals not possible	Nationals can be extradited, although conditions may be imposed

Introduction of new investigative means. Because of the diversity of legal systems, investigative techniques that have proven useful in one country may not be allowed in another. This applies, for example, to such techniques as electronic surveillance, controlled delivery, undercover operations, the promising of immunity from prosecution or a reduced sentence in return for co-operation in investigations, and the use of anonymous witnesses. If an investigative technique is legal in one country (A) but not legal in another (B), this may result in at least two types of problems. The first is that A will be frustrated by the inability of the law enforcement authorities of B to use what A regards as an effective tool. The second is that the judicial authorities of B may not allow the use of any evidence that has been gathered through the use of what, for B, are illegal techniques, even if the evidence has been obtained in a jurisdiction where the evidence was acquired legally.

In response to this problem, UNCAC and the other two UN conventions encourage State Parties to allow the use of certain special investigative techniques. The 1988 Convention introduced controlled delivery (art. 11). Art. 20 of UNTOC and art. 50 of UNCAC refer not only to controlled delivery, but also to electronic and other forms of surveillance and undercover operations. These techniques are especially useful in dealing with sophisticated organized criminal groups because of the dangers and difficulties inherent in gaining access to their operations and gathering information and evidence for use in domestic prosecutions or in other States Parties in the context of mutual legal assistance schemes.

Possibility of joint investigations. A number of provisions in the UN instruments focus on overcoming problems that result when each country carries out their own criminal investigations. Among the innovations are the possibility of the establishment of joint investigation teams,[9] co-operation in the protection of witnesses,[10] the establishment of formal channels for the exchange of operational and general information between police agencies,[11] and the possibility of appointing liaison officers.[12]

Broader range of forms of assistance. The earliest agreements on mutual legal assistance treaties concerned merely the service of summons. Over time, the range of measures has gradually widened. For example, the 1988 Convention (art. 8), UNTOC (art. 21) and UNCAC (art. 47) include specific provisions on the transfer of criminal proceedings, whereby if a person is suspected of having committed an offence under the law of one State Party, that country may request another country to take action on its behalf in accordance with the Convention, and the latter would prosecute the alleged offender under its own law.

It has only been relatively recently that international agreements began to contain provisions on assistance in identifying, tracing and freezing or seizing proceeds of crime for the purpose of eventual confiscation (which can be regarded as a special form of mutual legal assistance). The need to come to grips with the profit motive behind the rapid growth of drug crime led the drafters of the 1988 Convention to require that States Parties criminalize money laundering. The 1988 Convention also requires States Parties to create domestic mechanisms for the tracing, restraint and confiscation of the proceeds of drug-related crime. International co-operation was recognized in that States Parties are also required to be able to respond to requests presented by other states for the tracing, restraint and confiscation of the proceeds of drug offences. The 1988 Convention was the primary point of reference in the formulation of the respective provisions in UNTOC (arts 12 and 13). Since the international return of assets is of particular concern in connection with corruption (where individuals in some cases have been alleged to have received up to hundreds of millions of dollars as the result of corrupt activity), it is not surprising that UNCAC has an entire chapter devoted to this (chapter V).

Both UNTOC and UNCAC allow several forms of assistance that were not envisaged under earlier international instruments. Examples include video conferences (art. 18(18) UNTOC and art. 32(2) UNCAC), and what is known as the 'spontaneous transmission of information', whereby the authorities are allowed, even without a prior request, to pass on information to the competent authorities of another state that they believe might be of use (article 18(4) and (5) UNTOC and art. 46(4) UNCAC).

Use of a central authority. Traditional mutual legal assistance treaties required that requests be sent through diplomatic channels. What this entails is that, for example, a request for evidence, usually originating from the prosecutor, is authenticated by the competent national court in the requesting state, and then passed on by that state's Foreign Ministry to the embassy of the requested state. The embassy sends it on to the competent judicial authorities of the requested state, generally through the Foreign Ministry in the capital. Once the request has been fulfilled, the chain is reversed.

The 1988 Convention introduced a significant innovation, the concept of a 'Central Authority' (art. 7(8)), a concept that was then incorporated into UNTOC (art. 18(13) and UNCAC (art. 46(13)).[13] Although each State Party may continue to insist on diplomatic channels, the 1988 Convention requires that they identify an authority – in practice, often the Ministry of Justice, although also for example Supreme Courts have been designated as such – to specialize in the transmission of international requests, and to provide guidance for practitioners. This has tended to shorten the chain of authorities involved, and accordingly has speeded up the process of obtaining assistance.[14]

Adoption of 'good practice' standards. One of the major problems in mutual legal assistance world-wide is that the requested state is often slow in replying, and suspects must be freed due to absence of evidence. There are many understandable reasons for the slowness: a shortage of trained staff, linguistic difficulties, differences in procedure that complicate responding, and so on. Nonetheless, it can be frustrating to find that a case must be abandoned because even a simple request is not fulfilled in time. The 1988 Convention does not make any explicit reference to an obligation on the part of the requested state to be prompt in its reply. UNTOC, however, makes the point of the importance of promptness in two separate provisions. Art. 18(13) of the TOC Convention provides that, if the central authority itself responds to the request, it should ensure speedy and prompt execution. If the central authority transmits the request to, for example, the competent court, the central authority is required to encourage the speedy and proper execution of the request. Art. 18(24) provides that the request is to be executed 'as soon as possible' and that the requested state is to take 'as full account as possible of any deadlines suggested by the requesting State Party and for which reasons are given'.[15]

Difficulties may also arise due to different legal standards. An example of this is the concept of 'prima facie evidence of guilt', which some countries require as a condition for extradition. Since different countries apply differing rules of evidence, it may be difficult for a practitioner in one country to know what evidence should be provided. Both UNTOC (art. 16(8)) and UNCAC (art. 44(9)) call upon State Parties to simplify their evidentiary requirements in this respect.[16]

Possibility to apply the law and procedures of the requesting state. Since the procedural laws of states differ considerably, the requesting state may require special procedures (such as notarized affidavits) that are not recognized under the law of the requested state. Traditionally, the almost immutable principle has been that the requested state should follow its own procedural law. This principle has led to difficulties, in particular when the requesting and the requested state represent different legal traditions. For example, the evidence transmitted from the requested state may be in the form prescribed by the laws of this state, but such evidence may be unacceptable under the procedural law of the requesting state.

The modern trend is to allow more flexibility in respect of procedures. According to art. 7(12) of the 1988 Convention, a request shall be executed in accordance with the domestic law of the requested state. However, the article goes on to say that, to the extent not contrary to the domestic law of the requested state and where possible, the request shall be executed in accordance with the procedures specified in the request. Thus, although the 1988 Convention does not go so far as to require that the requested state comply with the procedural form required by the requesting state, it does clearly exhort the requested state to do so. This same provision was taken verbatim into art. 18(17) of UNTOC and art 46(17) of UNCAC.

Extradition of nationals. One of the most cherished principles in extradition law has been that states will not extradite their own nationals and will, at most, undertake to bring them to trial in their own courts. Today, more and more states are allowing extradition of their own nationals, although some conditions may be placed, such as that the national, if convicted, should be returned to his or her own country to serve the sentence. UNTOC (art 16(11)) and UNCAC (art. 44(12)) incorporate provisions that reflects this development, by allowing for the possibility of 'temporary surrender' of the fugitive on the condition that this person will be returned to the requested State Party for the purpose of serving any sentence imposed. In cases where the requested state refuses to extradite a fugitive on the grounds that the fugitive is its own national, the state is often seen to have an obligation to bring the person to trial. Where extradition is requested for the purpose of enforcing a sentence, the requested state may also enforce the sentence that has been imposed in accordance with the requirements of its domestic law.[17]

REVIEW OF IMPLEMENTATION OF UNCAC

UNCAC is not self-executing. Each State Party has to take domestic action (legislation, policy formulation, allocation of resources) in order to implement the provisions of UNCAC. While the objectives of UNCAC are specified in the text of the convention itself, agreement could not be reached during the negotiation phase on how to review this implementation, or on how the States Parties could ascertain that implementation was on track, that implementation was in line with the objectives, and that success was in fact being achieved.

UNCAC contains only one provision on implementation. Article 63 provides for a Conference of States Parties which is to 'promote and review' implementation of UNCAC. However, the Conference meets only every second year, for five days. It does not have the capacity to collect and analyse information on implementation. It needs a supplementary review mechanism to do this work and prepare recommendations for the Conference.

The worst case scenario was that there would be no evaluation of the implementation and recalcitrant signatories would proceed as if there had been no treaty. Corruption would continue to run rife. An alternative scenario would be a massive centralized data-gathering exercise. Such an exercise would be enormously time consuming, and if it were to be comprehensive would require an army of reviewers and large volumes of data. Even so, at the end of the day the data would most likely be incomplete, and almost impossible to compare. The States Parties would find themselves with a mountain of data, indiscriminately collected, of variable quality, and probably neither valid nor reliable.

One logical way forward would be to undertake a programme of peer review where State Parties take turns reviewing one another. The review of implementation of the anti-corruption treaties prepared by the Council of Europe and the Organization for Economic Co-operation and Development has shown that direct consultations among experts doing an on-the-ground review provide very much a learning experience. Talking with experts from other systems often helps one understand one's own system better and realize that there are other – and perhaps more effective – ways to deal with an issue.

The major difficulty to this was that at the time UNCAC was being negotiated, peer review had been in use for only a few years, and primarily by industrialized countries. The many other countries were unfamiliar with the process, and many were concerned that the process could be misused for political ends.

The first conference of the State Parties to UNCAC, held in Amman, Jordan at the end of 2006, decided that a supplemental review mechanism was necessary, but did not have the time to determine what such a mechanism should look like. It was able to reach agreement only on certain characteristics that this mechanism should fulfil: it should be transparent, efficient, non-intrusive, inclusive and impartial; it should not produce any form of ranking; it should provide opportunities to share good practices and challenges; and it should complement existing international and regional review mechanisms in order to avoid duplication of effort. Other than that, the formulation of the terms of reference for the mechanism was delegated to an 'open-ended intergovernmental expert working group'.

Even in respect of these at first glance rather bland characteristics, the vigorous debate in Amman revealed that in some key respects even these were understood differently. For example, *transparency* was understood by some to mean that all the States Parties would be involved throughout the process. In effect, they understood that the review would be carried out by a plenary body, as opposed to a smaller expert body. Others understood transparency to refer to the ability of all stakeholders (including, for example, civil society) to follow and possibly even provide input to the review process. Still others understood transparency to refer to whether or not the reports that are produced as a result of the review process are available to all States Parties, or indeed are made public.

A second example was *non-intrusiveness*. The United Nations Charter stipulates that the UN may not 'intervene in matters which are essentially within the domestic jurisdiction of any state'. The concept is generally used in international law to mean that the UN has no authority in respect of disputes which are essentially within domestic jurisdiction. There appeared to be different views as to what constitutes such intervention. At various stages in the negotiations, arguments based on non-intrusiveness and the protection of sovereignty were used to counter proposals for, inter alia, the use of independent experts, the arrangement of country visits, the use of any information not provided by the Government of the State Party under review, and the publication of the full report – all elements which other negotiators regarded as essential elements of the peer review process.

In preparing for the second session of the Conference of the States Parties (COSP), in Bali at the beginning of 2008, the Secretariat had looked at existing review mechanisms, and on this basis set out what it regarded as elements that could be incorporated into the UNCAC review mechanism:[18] *self-assessment* (each State Party would fill in a questionnaire on what implementation steps it had taken), *review* (by which the Secretariat meant that the process should be carried out by groups of experts or peers), *dialogue* (a 'process of constructive dialogue' between the Secretariat and the country concerned, or between the expert / peer reviewers and the country concerned), *co-operation with existing review mechanisms, country visits* and *benchmarking and technical assistance*.

Despite the efforts of the Secretariat to stake out common ground, the discussions at the second session of COSP could be characterized as drawn-out and difficult. The elements identified by the Secretariat in its background report appeared to meet acceptance on a general level. Once the discussion entered into details, however, it was becoming clearer that two opposing positions were emerging. These two positions could be called the '*open review*' and the '*controlled review*' positions.

The open review position incorporated many elements to be found in peer review within the framework of the OECD or the Council of Europe: a team of experts collects information from a variety of sources; this team of experts then visits the country under review in order to meet a wide range of stakeholders; they then prepare a country report that contains recommendations; they submit this draft report to the country under review for comment; the amended country report together with recommendations goes to a plenary body for discussion and adoption; the report is published; and there is some mechanism for follow-up by the plenary body to see whether the recommendations have been implemented.

The proponents of the open review position tended to take a technocratic view of implementation. To them the review was a technical exercise in reporting and accountability, and the results should be transparent and available immediately for the world to see. The experts conducting the review should be free to gather information on implementation from a variety of sources in order to familiarize themselves with the situation and engage in discussions with a number of different stakeholders. Armed with this knowledge, they would be able to suggest 'best practice' to the experts of the country under review.

According to the controlled review position, a team of experts (defined by some espousing this position to include also experts representing the country under review) uses information received from the Government to prepare a country report; the report is finalized on the basis of a dialogue between the experts and the representatives of the country under review; and the Secretariat prepares a general report for the plenary body that does not contain references to individual countries. The plenary body decides by consensus on the publication of these reports; whether or not the country report is published is for the country under review to decide.

The proponents of controlled review tended to see the process as involving a number of serious political risks that had to be identified and defused. Since outside experts lacked local understanding, they might receive a distorted view of how the legal and administrative system actually operates in the country under review. Information obtained during the review process could be misused for political purposes, and thus there was a need to keep a tight Governmental control on what and how information is used. Non-governmental actors could in fact be hostile to government policy and use involvement in the review process for their own ends. If the reports produced as a result of the review process became construed as 'UN endorsed' assessments of the extent of corruption in a certain country, this could have a negative impact on foreign investments in that country. Donors might seek to attach a variety of conditions on any offers of technical assistance. There were also considerable concerns about the expense of on-site visits and other aspects of peer review, and that the necessary funds would then not be available for direct technical assistance.

Due to the deadlock between the open review and controlled review positions, very little progress could be achieved at Bali. Resolution 2/1 began by essentially repeating what had been decided two years earlier: if indeed a supplemental review mechanism was to be established, it should be transparent, efficient, non-intrusive, inclusive and impartial; it should not produce any form of ranking; it should provide opportunities to share good practices and challenges; and it should complement existing international and regional review mechanisms in order that the Conference may, as appropriate, co-operate with them and avoid duplication of effort. The resolution continued with a number of self-evident statements about effective implementation, a balanced geographical approach, non-adversarial and non-punitive, concluding that it should be of a technical nature and promote constructive collaboration.

Once the negotiations got underway in the intergovernmental working group, the two rigid positions soften. One key catalyst for this was that the apparently solid 'controlled review' group began to suffer from defections. A number of developing countries did in fact have favourable experience with peer review. Most Latin American countries were using peer review in connection with the implementation of the 1996 Inter-American Convention against Corruption. In addition, several developing countries were familiar with peer review in the context of the FATF. Those advocating controlled review began to realise that holding out against peer review was not a sustainable position, and that some workable format had to be found.

This workable format emerged in the last few weeks before the third session of the conference of States Parties, in Doha, 9–13 November 2009, and during the conference itself. The elements of the mechanism adopted at Doha are the following:[19]

- an implementation review group is set up for the review process. This body is, to use the UN parlance, intergovernmental and open, which means that any and all States Parties may participate. Intergovernmental and non-governmental groups are not accorded a seat at the table;
- each State Party is to be reviewed by two other States Parties;
- each State Party is to designate governmental experts who would actually conduct the reviews. (Disagreement arose over who is a 'governmental expert'. Those opposed to the peer review concept generally stressed that these experts must be civil servants, and that they reserve the right to refuse to accept anyone whom they regard as biased);
- the review process consists, basically, of four stages: a 'self-assessment' conducted by each State Party on the basis of a checklist prepared by the Secretariat, discussions between the experts and the representatives of the authorities of the Member State, preparation of a country report, and discussion at the implementation review group of consolidated thematic and regional reports;
- in responding to the self-assessment, each State Party should seek to engage in wide consultations with relevant individuals and groups outside the public sector;
- the experts may also use information produced by other corresponding evaluation mechanisms;
- on-site visits may be arranged with the consent of the State Party under review. However, the costs of these must come from voluntary funding, not the regular UN budget;
- in connection with on-site visits, the State Party under review is encouraged to promote discussions with all relevant national stakeholders;
- on the basis of the evaluation, the experts prepare a country report, which contains a summary. The report requires the approval of the State Party under review;
- the Secretariat prepares thematic and supplementary regional geographical reports for the implementation review group;
- these thematic and regional reports are submitted to the implementation review group for informational purposes only, and not for discussion. (Those opposed to peer review did not want the implementation review group to be able to open discussion on implementation in a specific State Party, where the authorities of that State Party would be required to respond to questions); and
- the country reports themselves are confidential, and thus for example are not submitted as such to the implementation review group. However, the States Parties in question are encouraged themselves to publish these reports. In addition, 'States parties shall, upon request, endeavour to make country review reports accessible to any other State party. The requesting State party shall fully respect the confidentiality of such reports'.

CONCLUSIONS

With the increase in international travel, the improvement in technology and communications, the greater likelihood that a crime can have an impact beyond national borders, as well as the increased profits that can be made from corruption, the need to obtain assistance from other states in bringing corrupt persons to justice, gathering necessary evidence or confiscating the proceeds of corruption has expanded rapidly. The basic modalities of international co-operation that can be used as a response – in particular extradition and mutual legal assistance in criminal matters – continue to evolve, often struggling to keep pace with developments in crime.

Increased efforts have been made over the last years to expand and deepen international co-operation as a response to transnational organized crime through the conclusion of multilateral instruments. The pace of development has clearly quickened during the 1990s and the beginning of the new millennium. The United Nations Convention against Corruption is a clear sign that multilateral instruments are assuming increasing importance. It calls upon States Parties to seek to conclude bilateral and multilateral agreements or arrangements to enhance the effectiveness of extradition and mutual legal assistance mechanisms and promote the co-operation between law enforcement agencies. Consequently, states will presumably continue to expand their treaty network in the field of international co-operation by entering into bilateral agreements or arrangements with other countries' states with which they share particular concerns and interests.

The growing number of bilateral and multilateral instruments and, thus, the availability of multiple provisions on international co-operation is not a cure-all for overcoming problems and difficulties encountered in daily practice. These international instruments may provide a satisfactory or even an autonomous and self-contained legal basis for co-operation, given that the recent UN instruments lay down a quite detailed and well-articulated framework for such co-operation. However, their provisions should be applied in a way that avoids piecemeal solutions and takes into account the need to ensure the proper administration of justice. It is therefore important to adopt and follow a holistic and flexible approach that renders the different modalities of international co-operation complementary to each other for the purpose of promoting co-operation among states and avoiding loopholes of impunity. In that sense, prosecution on the basis of the principle 'aut dedere aut judicare' where, for example, extradition of a person suspected of corruption is denied on the grounds of nationality could only be effective if mutual legal assistance or transfer of criminal proceedings mechanisms are, at the same time, available and used properly. Countries should therefore envisage adopting and implementing the appropriate legal framework that will facilitate and promote the use of the full array of available forms of co-operation.

UNCAC reflects in many ways the 'state of the art' of international co-operation in criminal justice. In particular, it includes many provisions that are new for practitioners in many countries, and may well improve the day-to-day practice of international co-operation.

Negotiation of the Convention, however, is only the first stage. The Convention must be ratified and the investigators, the prosecutors and the judges must be given the tools they need to complete the job.

NOTES

1. Article 55 of the UN Charter.
2. For a general presentation of the UN crime prevention and criminal justice programme, see Roger Clark (1994), *The United Nations Crime Prevention and Criminal Justice Program. Formulation of Standards and Efforts at their Implementation*, Philadelpia: University of Pennsylvania Press.
3. The 1925 Convention has subsequently been amended several times with protocols. Following the Second World War, this series was extended in 1953 by the Protocol Limiting and Regulating the Cultivation of the Poppy Plant, the Production of, International and Wholesale Trade in, and Use of Opium.
4. A contributing factor was that the UN crime prevention and criminal justice programme itself was overhauled at the beginning of the 1990s. The former Committee on the Prevention of Crime and the Treatment of Offenders, which had consisted of individual experts, was replaced by a Commission on Crime Prevention and Criminal Justice, which directly represented Member States. Such direct involvement of states changed the focus to finding more effective forms of international co-operation.
5. Naples, Italy, 21–23 November 1994.
6. General Assembly resolution 51/120 of 12 December 1996.
7. http://www.unodc.org/unodc/en/treaties/CAC/signatories.html
8. In the following, reference is made also to provisions in the UN Convention on Transnational Organized Crime. This is for two reasons: the provisions in UNCAC were often modelled on those of UNTOC, and UNTOC may be applicable also in cases of corruption.
9. See art. 9 para. 1 (c) of the 1988 Convention, art. 19 of UNTOC and art. 49 of UNCAC. Joint investigation teams can be set up when a criminal investigation requires close co-operation among two or more states. They consist of representatives of law enforcement agencies or other competent authorities of the states in question. The members of the team carry out their operations in accordance with the law of the host State.
10. See art. 24 of UNTOC and arts 32 and 33 of UNCAC.
11. For example, art. 27 of UNTOC Convention encourages States Parties to co-operate closely with one another by enhancing and, where necessary, establishing channels of communication between their competent authorities, agencies and services in order to facilitate the secure and rapid exchange of information concerning all aspects of the offences covered by the Convention, strengthen the co-operation in conducting inquiries, provide items for analytical and investigative purposes, exchange information on offenders' modus operandi or exchange personnel, including the posting of liaison officers. See also art. 9 of the 1988 Convention and art. 48 of UNCAC.
12. Liaison officers provide a point of direct contact with the law enforcement and government authorities of the host State, develop professional relationships, and foster mutual trust and confidence between the law enforcement agencies of the two states. Although liaison officers do not have any law enforcement powers in the host state, they can nonetheless use their contacts to gather information that may be of benefit in preventing and

detecting cross-border offences, and in identifying the offenders responsible and bringing them to justice.

13. This concept was originally developed in civil law, and introduced in the 1965 Hague Convention on the Service Abroad of Judicial and Extrajudicial Documents in Civil or Commercial Matters.
14. Art. 7(8) of the 1988 Convention, art. 18(13) of UNTOC and art. 46(13) of UNCAC also allow for the possibility that, in urgent cases and when the countries in question agree, the request can be made through the International Criminal Police Organization, if possible.
15. Other elements of 'good practice' in mutual legal assistance have also worked their way into UNTOC and UNCAC, making the life of the practitioner easier than under, for example, the 1988 Convention. According to art. 18(24) of UNTOC and art. 46(24) of UNCAC, the requested state should respond to reasonable requests by the requesting state for information on progress of its handling of the request, and the requesting state should promptly inform the requested state when the assistance sought is no longer required.
16. See also the 'Report of the Informal Expert Working Group on Effective Extradition Casework Practice' (Vienna, 12–16 July 2004), paras. 41–43 and 46.
17. Art. 6(10) of the 1988 Convention, art. 16(12) of UNTOC and art. 44(13) of UNCAC.
18. Parameters for defining the review mechanism for the United Nations Convention against Corruption. Background paper prepared by the Secretariat. CAC/COSP/2008/10.
19. http://www.unodc.org/unodc/en/treaties/CAC/CAC-COSP-session3.html

17 The global architecture of foreign bribery control: applying the OECD Bribery Convention

Cindy Davids and Grant Schubert

INTRODUCTION

The Organisation for Economic Co-Operation and Development (OECD) drew significant international attention to the behaviour of domestic companies doing business overseas with the *Convention on Combating Bribery of Foreign Public Officials in International Business Transactions* (hereafter, 'the Anti-bribery Convention', OECD, 1997). Prior to the promulgation of the Convention, although domestic bribery was generally regarded (at least formally) as a criminal offence in most countries (Deming, 2006), the issue of bribery in *international* business transactions, including those conducted entirely within the borders of another jurisdiction, was rarely considered a criminal offence under respective domestic laws. The USA was the notable exception, having introduced the Foreign Corrupt Practices Act (FCPA) 1977, largely as a response to revelations of domestic and foreign corrupt practices by US businesses (Santangelo et al., 2007). At the time the US government was bitterly criticized by its own companies who argued that the new rules disadvantaged them in the global market (Salbu, 1997). Many observers regard the eventual development of the OECD Convention as, at least in part, a response by pressure from the USA to level the playing field (Baughn et al., 2010). To 2010, 38 countries have implemented domestic legislation in accord with the Convention requirements, criminalizing the practice of pursuing commercial advantage through bribery of public officials in another jurisdiction.

Building on the philosophy and impetus of the Anti-bribery Convention, a web of related international arrangements and domestic legislative responses has been introduced. Notable amongst these is the *United Nations Convention against Corruption* (United Nations Office on Drugs and Crime, 2004), which, like the Anti-bribery Convention, requires the criminalization of bribery of foreign public officials (art 16). There is also a raft of anti-money laundering (AML) requirements, mostly building on the recommendations of the Financial Action Task Force (Financial Action Task Force on Money Laundering, 2004; Financial Action Task Force, 2005).

In addition to dealing with the specific offence of bribery, these arrangements are designed to combat criminal money flows (particularly, flows of the proceeds of crime, or flows which support the commission of crime). Associated with these efforts are a range of reporting obligations that have been placed on banks, other financial institutions and professionals.

Yet despite the rigour with which the problems of international bribery and criminal money flows have been tackled at a formal level, many governments have been criticized for lacking the will to adequately empower their integrity and governance structures and financial regulatory systems. Specific criticisms in various jurisdictions have included: the failure to adequately enforce 'due diligence' requirements; inadequacy of the AML legal regimes adopted by many countries; and definitional vagaries associated with the identification of 'politically exposed persons' (Global Witness, 2009; de Koker – Chapter 18 in this volume).

The OECD (2009, p. 16) defines bribery as a 'voluntary giving of something of value to influence performance of official duty either by doing something improper or failing to do something they should do within the authority of their position'. It is thus a *specific form* of corruption. In addition to requiring signatories to adopt national legislation making it a crime to bribe foreign public officials, the Anti-bribery Convention requires the prosecution and punishment of individuals and companies through criminal penalties similar to domestic regimes (OECD, 1997, art. 3; Osajda, 2010b). 'Public official' is broadly defined to include:

> . . . any person holding a legislative, administrative or judicial office of a foreign country, whether appointed or elected; any person exercising a public function for a foreign country, including for a public agency or public enterprise; and any official or agent of a public international organisation (art. 1(4)).

In their domestic legal frameworks, member states are also required to prohibit *accounting practices* that conceal bribery (OECD 1997 art. 8(1)).

Although the requirements of the Anti-bribery Convention seem clear, the multifaceted nature of the offence of bribery and a range of prosecution and enforcement challenges inherent in transnational criminal investigations goes some way to explaining the somewhat mixed track record on prosecution and enforcement that has been exhibited in many countries (Heimann and Dell, 2010). There is also considerable evidence that although many of the wealthiest countries in the world are signatories to the Convention, and that senior government officials in those countries are aware of their global responsibilities, this pattern is not necessarily reflected in the behaviour of senior business executives (ACCA, 2007; Carr and Outhwaite, 2009; Working Group on Bribery in International Business Transactions, 2009 [hereafter, 'Working Group']).

This chapter examines and compares the experience of the USA, UK and Australia in terms of the compliance and enforcement framework set down in the Anti-bribery Convention. In the most recent Transparency International (TI) Progress Report on the enforcement record of member states (Heimann and Dell, 2010), it is clear that very few signatory countries are effectively enforcing the Convention's provisions, with only 7 signatories regarded as 'active'. While the USA is ranked as 'active', the UK was assessed as 'moderate' but now 'active' (previously described as a 'laggard'), and Australia is still described as having 'little or no enforcement' (see also Heimann and Dell, 2006, 2009).

In light of this differential track record, key elements in the anti-bribery regimes in Australia, the USA and the UK are outlined, with illustrative examples from each country used to elucidate issues, obstacles and key investigatory and prosecutorial challenges.

BACKGROUND

Growth in bribery has accompanied significant growth in international trade and cross-border transactions in the last 50 years. Bribery takes myriad forms including payoffs for favourable treatment in winning contracts or other procurement-related services, licensing arrangements, reduction of import duties, and favourable tax treatment. In some countries, the frequency of bribery practices has reached a point where bribes are regarded as 'routine grease payments' for conducting normal business affairs (Baughn et al., 2010). TI has identified the public works and defence sectors as common targets for perpetrators of corruption and bribery, both in terms of the frequency of engagement in bribery and the level at which they undermine the public interest. However, patterns of bribery are also heavily implicated in the mineral, resources exploration, real estate, telecommunications and power sectors, particularly of developing economies (Riaño and Hodess, 2008). Of particular note are the activities of subsidiary companies of multinationals and the behaviour and role of agents and intermediaries in bribery (OECD, 2009).

Proponents of rigorous enforcement of anti-bribery provisions focus on the harms brought about by illicit payments. Arguments are often based in a concern that corruption works to undermine a 'free' global market by promoting unfair practices and operating as a type of 'tax' on foreign investment. An extension of these concerns relates to the potential infrastructure consequences in lesser developed countries, where selection of contractors based on bribes or other illicit payments rather than on merit, especially where it is commonplace, constitutes a threat to development efforts. Concerns about such practices also extend to what may be regarded as more pernicious problems arising when wealth and power is concentrated in corrupt hands, undermining the rule of law and the operation of democracy through a process of 'state capture'. This arises both through the effect on democratic representation and the pollution, potentially from the top down, of public service standards in areas such as policing, customs and immigration (see McFarlane, 2001).

The remainder of this chapter examines key elements in anti-bribery regimes, considering scope and reach, accounting provisions, the importance placed on corrupt intent, the nature of payments that constitute bribery (including the significant issue of 'facilitation payments'), the tracing of bribe recipients, the nature of the 'business purposes' test, and a range of enforcement issues including penalties.

SCOPE AND JURISDICTIONAL REACH

The FCPA, introduced in the USA in 1977 (with significant amendments in 1988 and 1998), is an influential legal model in dealing with non-domestic bribery (Carrington, 2007; Sebelius, 2008). The FCPA makes it 'unlawful' for a US person or company, certain foreign issuers of securities, and foreign firms and persons who take any act in furtherance of a corrupt payment while in the USA, to make a corrupt payment to a foreign official for the purpose of obtaining or retaining business for or with, or directing business to, any person. The key element is that the payment is made with the knowledge that it will be used to influence a public official. The relevant payment can be made to any person, including intermediaries. Amendments to the law since its introduction have resulted in a wide application of FCPA provisions; the Act now captures any individual, firm, office, director, employee or agent/stockholder including US citizens or residents acting on behalf of foreign incorporated subsidiaries. Its scope encompasses all US publicly-traded companies and foreign companies listed on a US Stock Exchange including multinationals (US parent companies are liable for the actions of their subsidiaries) (Santangelo et al., 2007; Osajda, 2010b).

Australia enacted its obligations under the Anti-bribery Convention primarily in the form of an amendment to the Commonwealth Criminal Code (Criminal Code Amendment (Bribery of Foreign Public Officials) Act 1999). Under s70.2 a person must not offer or provide a benefit to another that is not legitimately due to that person, with the intent to influence a public official in the exercise of an official discretion. The offence occurs only if the influence is designed to obtain an undue business advantage. There is a sufficient territorial nexus if the conduct of the offence is at least partly within Australia (this extends to an Australian aircraft or ship) (Criminal Code s70.5(1)(a)). The ambit of these provisions includes situations where an instruction is made from Australia to another person to offer a bribe; it is an offence under s70.2 to *cause another* to offer a bribe. The term 'partly in Australia' is dealt with in s16.2 of the Criminal Code which provides that where a person sends a thing or electronic communication outside of Australia, that conduct is regarded as having occurred partly within Australia.

Australia's initial legislative response to the OECD Convention was not nearly as broad as the USA model. For example, the initial Bill limited jurisdiction to cases where at least part of the *behaviour* had occurred in Australia. This would not have been consistent with the Convention (art 4(2)) which requires countries to exercise jurisdiction over their nationals operating abroad where their legal systems give them the capability to do so. Subsequently, and consistent with the action of most other signatories, Australia opted to include a *national* as well as *territorial* basis to the jurisdiction of the anti-bribery provisions, employing the 'active nationality' principle of jurisdiction (allowing a country to reach its citizens and residents acting abroad) in situations where the questionable conduct occurs wholly outside Australia but the perpetrator is an Australian resident, citizen or body corporate registered within Australia (Criminal Code s70.5(1)(b)).

The UK took some time to expressly give effect to the Anti-bribery Convention in the form of a separate legislative instrument focused on bribery. It ratified the Convention in 1998 and introduced Part 12 of the Anti Terrorism, Crime and Security Act (2001) to domestically implement the Convention. Whilst attention was drawn to the inadequacies of this legal regime (Law Commission 2008), it nevertheless resulted in some prosecutions against UK businesses for bribing foreign public officials.

The reach of the newly-promulgated Bribery Act (2010) in the UK is greater than its counterparts in both Australia and the USA in that it is not limited to public officials carrying out public duties (constitutional limitations in both the USA and Australia may partially explain this difference; detailed consideration of this issue is beyond the scope of the present discussion). The UK Bribery Act includes 'private to private' forms of bribery, encompassing actions which constitute bribing any person associated with or connected to a business, or carrying out functions of a public nature to act contrary to a reasonable expectation that they will perform the function in good faith or impartially (s3). The idea of improper performance is held to the standard applicable in the UK, even if the actions in question are carried out overseas. Thus, UK citizens are subject to the same standard of behaviour regardless of where particular problematic acts are performed, subject to a defence that the local *written laws* permit different standards (s5(2)).

In addition to the general bribery offences covered by the UK Act, there is a specific offence of 'bribery of foreign public officials' (s6); written in accord with implementation expectations of the Anti-bribery Convention. The definition is similar to that in the Australian and the USA legislation, with a focus on individuals exercising functions on behalf of a foreign country or individuals who are officials or agents of international organizations (s6(5)). Unlike the general bribery offences discussed above, this provision relates only to a person who 'offers, promises or gives' a bribe (s6(3)) and does not include the acceptance of bribes. The Act provides for wide extra-territorial jurisdiction such that even if the behaviour and all elements that make up the offence occur outside the UK, the law applies if the offender is a UK citizen (resident in the UK or abroad), is ordinarily resident in the UK (s12); or is a UK-incorporated body or does part of its business in the UK (s7).

On the issue of intention, the person or commercial organizations or 'associated persons' under s8 must intend to influence the recipient in the performance of their functions as a public official and, for commercial organizations, must do so in order to obtain or retain business or a business advantage (s6). The key aspect here is the fault element on the part of a commercial organization in seeking an illicit benefit. Influence must be *intended*; this covers circumstances where a recipient official fails to exercise functions of the office or purports to have authority in a position, even if they do not actually have such authority.

ACCOUNTING PROVISIONS: 'BOOKS AND RECORDS'

The regulation of accounting books and records in the FCPA model has had a widespread influence on legislation developed elsewhere and, in its narrower application, has become a key feature of most models particularly in relation to the distinction between *bribery* and *facilitation payments*. Essentially, these provisions require companies which fall within the scope of the FCPA to keep books and records that *accurately reflect* the transactions of the company. This is crucial to companies which rely on a 'facilitation payments' defence to an accusation of bribery (this issue is further discussed later in the chapter). Failure to exercise certain internal controls (in the FCPA model) itself constitutes a breach and enables the prosecution of an alternate crime of 'false accounting'. A conviction under the 'books and records' provisions does not require proof that an accused is engaged in a specific act of bribery; that false accounts were maintained or sham consulting agreements entered into is sufficient to secure a conviction.

The FCPA accounting provisions differ to other anti-bribery regimes where the prosecution may need to prove an entire chain of criminal offences leading up to the bribery of a foreign official. In such cases, the prosecution may, for example, need to first prove the existence of sham consulting agreements in connection with a specific crime (such as forgery), then prove that this led to bribing a foreign official. Some jurisdictions further require that each individual beneficiary be identified in the sequence before a conviction can stand. The use of intermediaries or agents can therefore complicate matters enormously, making it extremely difficult for investigating and prosecuting authorities to trace and prove an entire chain of events and persons involved in passing on bribes. Therefore, although under the FCPA courts can find against an accused on the basis of proof that the accused maintained false accounts or books and records, in many non-US jurisdictions such proof is, on its own, insufficient to secure a conviction (Gordon, 2009; Working Group, 2009).

The US Securities and Exchange Commission (SEC) has a relatively strong record on corruption-related enforcement based exclusively on violation of the 'books and records' provisions. Among the most recent was the successful prosecution of General Electric in relation to matters arising out of the UN Oil-for-Food scandal. It was found that GE and its subsidiaries failed to accurately record illicit surcharges and kickbacks and failed to maintain adequate internal controls to detect and prevent illicit payments. The amount paid by GE to Iraq under illicit contracts was estimated at US$7.45 million for a return of an estimated $18.2 million in contracts. The SEC extracted $23.4 million in penalties, disgorgement and interest, even though there was no Department of Justice prosecution for criminal bribery, as the illicit payments were paid to the Iraq Government rather than public officials (Wyld, 2010).

Australia struck a similar issue in dealing with the Australian Wheat Board (AWB) scandal. Allegations in this case involved the use of a Jordanian trucking firm to pay AWB kickbacks to the Iraqi regime in return for securing wheat contracts. The trucking firm channelled illicit payments back to the Iraq government, which was subject to a UN embargo (UN Resolutions 661 and 986). However, the subsequent Cole Inquiry in Australia found that the payments were made to the Iraq government as such and were not in fact unlawful in that country at the time (Cole, 2006). At the time it was a defence to an allegation of a breach of s70.2 (the bribery provisions) that the defendant would not have been guilty of a breach of a law in force in the place that governs the public official (Criminal Code s70.3(1)). Thus, AWB were able to rely on a defence of *lawful conduct*. Commissioner Cole found the payments were similar to a tax or tariff imposed by governments on imports. Subsequent to the Cole Inquiry, an amendment to the Act added an 'in writing' component to the effect that the benefit offered must be required or permitted in the *written* law of the country (Explanatory Memorandum, International Trade Integrity Bill 2007). (The Australian Securities and Investment Commission also pursued 6 AWB directors and officers for breaches of domestic statutory duties under the Corporations Act; at the time of writing, contested hearings, appeals and amended pleas have yet to produce a resolution to these matters.)

Australia, like the USA, has legislated books and records requirements; however, the authority and reach for these comes from sources spread across the Corporations Law and other legislation, rather than forming a distinct part of the Bribery of Foreign Officials Act (s70.2 of the Criminal Code (Cth)). For example, s286 of the Corporations Act 2001 (Cth) requires a company to keep financial records that, inter alia, correctly record and explain its transactions. Failure to comply is an offence (s1311(1)(b)). A director who does not take reasonable steps to secure compliance by a company contravenes s344(1). If the contravention of s286 is *dishonest* the conduct or omission is an offence (s344(2)). The maximum penalty for breach of s344(2) is 2000 penalty units (currently $220 000) and/or imprisonment for 5 years. The penalty for a non-complying corporation is 125 penalty units (currently $13 750). This is much lower than the penalties applied under the FCPA books and records provisions. However, there is also a possibility that the Proceeds of Crime Act 2002 (Cth) could be utilized to impose pecuniary penalty orders that disgorge the profits the corporation has gained directly or indirectly by keeping false records if there are resulting breaches of the Anti Money Laundering and Counter Terrorism Act (Cth) 2006.

The UK Bribery Act (2010) also contains no specific 'books and records' provision. The absence of these specific measures is, however, at least partially ameliorated by the inclusion of provisions designed to encourage corporate self-monitoring. The UK Bribery Act makes it a criminal offence for a commercial organization to *fail to prevent* those who carry out services for it committing bribery (s7). In its defence, such an organization can argue that it had 'appropriate procedures' in place designed to prevent such conduct occurring (s7(2)). The UK government is required to publish guidance on the procedures that commercial organizations can put in place to prevent bribery (s9) and a range of principles have been proposed: risk assessment, top-level commitment, due diligence, clear practical and accessible policies and procedures, effective implementation, monitoring and review (ICAEW, 2010; Ministry of Justice, 2010).

In Australia, the corporate culture provisions in s12 of the Code have a similar effect. A company that takes appropriate steps to ensure compliance by its agents with the law and maintains a corporate culture of compliance will not, in the absence of bribes authorized by the company itself, be liable for bribery on the part of its agents. Corporations can utilize Australian Standard AS3806 to construct effective compliance programmes, although such standards have no legal force and are only a guide (Clough and Mulhern, 2002).

The statutory requirement that a commercial organization has in place appropriate procedures is clearly aimed at making commercial entities responsible not just for their employees but for the actions of agents or associates operating on their behalf, thus introducing an element of strict liability. This bears an interesting contrast to the Australian principles of corporate liability contained in the Code. By making the offence one of strict liability and then providing for a corporate culture defence, the UK Bribery Act places the evidentiary burden on the corporation to show that it has appropriate procedures. In the Australian Code, the prosecution must prove the non-existence of the relevant corporate culture element beyond reasonable doubt. At least technically this leaves the burden of proof entirely with the prosecution, which may cause difficulties if insufficient evidence can be discovered.

Overall, Australia appears to have a domestic scatter-gun approach in regard to accounting provisions and could do well to further expand the criminal framework to allow for a specific 'books and records' breach along the lines of the FCPA.

CORRUPT INTENT

Under the FCPA proof is not required that the action succeeded in influencing the foreign public official; the mere promise or offer of an inducement/payment constitutes a violation. Corrupt intent is proven when a payment is made to influence any official act or decision of a foreign official; to induce a foreign official to do or omit to do any act against his/her public duties; or to use an official position to affect any decision taken by the official's government (Osajda, 2010b). The UK Bribery Act (s6) is similar in that reference is also made to the offer, promise, or giving of any financial or other advantage, but no improper performance is required on the part of the receiving official; again, an offer itself is sufficient to demonstrate corrupt intent. The effect of the Australian anti-bribery provisions is also very similar.

The use of intermediaries and agents considerably complicates the issue of the mental state of the briber. There is some evidence that such intermediaries are frequently used in public procurement and that the Anti-bribery Convention actually increased their use as companies sought to distance themselves from bribery through fear of prosecution (Working Group, 2009). In such circumstances, ignorance or lack of subjective intent on the part of the principal is crucial in determining criminal liability. The prosecution of the German engineering company, Siemens, provides a case in point. Here, it was revealed that over 7 years the company engaged in widespread and systematic practice of foreign bribery in at least 10 countries. The case involved several subsidiaries and lines of business, and thousands of payments, many of which were through intermediaries (Heimann and Dell, 2009).

Claims of ignorance (which could be wilful blindness) can often be defeated on the facts, as illustrated in a recent OECD report of actual case scenarios (Working Group, 2009). The report cites examples where consultancy fees are paid out of all proportion to the services rendered, or goods are procured at hugely inflated prices. In one case a company paid a consultant US$132 million over a period of 7 years for vaguely-described marketing and advisory services (TSKG Case). In another case (Cash for Signatures), a company paid US$2 million to a consultant with no relevant expertise. In the Baker Hughes Case, the company paid an Angolan Agent US$10.3 million in commissions over five years, purportedly for seismic data; and paid another agent US$4 million, but there was no evidence that the agent produced any work (Working Group, 2009, p. 12).

The Oil-for-Food (Iraq) prosecutions showed that corporations cannot rely on a defence that the inclusion of a no-corruption clause in contracts justifies a refusal to enquire or a failure to demonstrate appropriate due-diligence. These cases show the effectiveness of provisions to the effect that where a principal refuses to make reasonable inquiries or pays unreasonable fees or prices, a *reasonable inference* can be drawn of knowledge by the principal of the intermediary's actions of engaging in bribery.

The bite of the UK legislation in this regard is yet to be tested. There is a strict liability element in the Bribery Act, but despite the issuing of government guidelines there remains doubt as to what will constitute the 'bar' for a claim by a commercial organization that they had in place 'appropriate anti-bribery procedures' when faced with potential criminal liability for the behaviour of agents or subsidiaries. In Australia, a lack of prosecutions under the principles of corporate criminal responsibility in the Code creates a similar lack of certainty.

PAYMENT

'Payment' may take a very broad meaning and, again, the FCPA has provided a global benchmark on this element, prohibiting the payment of or making an offer of anything of value (not limited to money; with no quantification in the statute). This has been interpreted broadly to include travel, gratuities, physical gifts, and payment of an official's family obligations such as school fees or any other expenses. Because the very essence of bribery usually requires subterfuge and secrecy, attempts to disguise payments in forms such as scholarships for the children of family members, charitable contributions, creative descriptions of various 'consulting services', or the diverting of payments through intermediaries are extremely common. In the UK legislation the interpretation of 'offers, promises or gives any financial or other advantage' to a foreign public official could also be very broad. Australia, the USA and the UK all provide for a defence that the payment was lawful/required under the written laws of the country or a reasonable and bona fide expense.

FACILITATION PAYMENTS

There is one category of payment to foreign public officials that is permitted in many jurisdictions and commercial entities can often claim a legitimate tax deduction for this element: 'facilitation payments'. Although the UK is one of the few countries that prohibit facilitation payments, both the USA and Australia allow facilitation/expediting payments for 'routine governmental action'. Such 'grease payments' are regarded as a legitimate exception to the general anti-bribery framework provided that they are limited to the 'non-discretionary' acts of the official and limited to 'ordinarily and commonly-performed' actions in a number of specified circumstances (s70.4, Criminal Code).

There are several justifications given for this category of exceptions, including arguments that facilitation payments do not involve the exercise of discretion by the official and therefore do not result in the same harms (largely because the benefit obtained is not an *undue* one). A variant on this argument is the idea that because a facilitation fee is one routinely required by the official, there is less moral culpability compared with larger bribes paid voluntarily in order to influence the exercise of official discretion in specific cases (Nichols 2009).

During debate on the Australian legislation it was argued that although facilitation payments may be illegal in the jurisdiction in which they are paid, foreign enforcement of this illegality was not appropriate due to the smaller size of the payments and their frequency (Commonwealth of Australia, 1999). In the USA, commentary surrounding amendments to the FCPA included the oft-repeated claim that it was not possible to do business in some countries without making facilitation payments, and that to implement a ban would unduly disadvantage USA companies.

The official OECD Commentaries provided with the original Anti-bribery Convention suggested that 'small "facilitation" payments' did not constitute a bribery offence, explained as follows:

> Such payments, which, in some countries, are made to induce public officials to perform their functions, such as issuing licences or permits are generally illegal in the foreign country concerned. Other countries can and should address this corrosive phenomenon by such means as support for programmes of good governance. However criminalization by other countries does not seem a practical or effective complementary action (OECD, 2010, 14 ¶9).

However, in 2009 the OECD's position appears to have shifted from one of inaction or 'resigned acceptance' of facilitation payments to one of dissuasion of their use with the recommendation that:

> . . . in view of the corrosive effect of small facilitation payments, particularly on sustainable economic development and the rule of law, member countries should:
>
> 1. undertake to periodically review their policies and approach on small facilitation payments in order to effectively combat the phenomenon;
> 2. encourage companies to prohibit or discourage the use of small facilitation payments.
>
> (OECD Working Group on Bribery, 2009, p. 63)

Section 70.4 of the Australian Commonwealth Criminal Code limits payments to situations where the bribe is of minor value; is made to secure performance of minor and routine government action, and record-keeping and retention requirements are complied with. In the USA, 15 USC 78dd-1(b) on 'routine governmental action' provides that payments are permitted in the following circumstances: obtaining permits, licences, or other official documents to qualify a person to do business in a foreign country; processing governmental papers such as visas and work orders; providing police protection, mail pick-up and delivery, or scheduling inspections associated with contract performance or inspections related to transit of goods across country; providing phone service, power and water supply, loading and unloading cargo, or protecting perishable products or commodities from deterioration; or actions of a similar nature. The Australian provision mirrors the FCPA in that s70.4 (2)(b) of the Code provides the same list.

Accurate record keeping is the key to businesses being able to claim that a payment was for facilitation, as a defence to an accusation that the payment was a bribe. Typically, the following information is required by a country's respective tax regime: a description of the benefit secured and the circumstances (proof that it was in fact for a 'routine action'); date of the benefit; amount/gift/value; country in which the benefit was secured; method of payment; date of benefit to the company; identity and position of the foreign public official or other person; a signature on the record by the Company's authorizing officer or other identification (e.g. Income Tax Assessment Act 1997, s26-52).

In addition to claims that payments may have been facilitation payments rather than bribes most anti-bribery regimes also recognize that payments may not be bribes if in fact they were lawful in the recipient's own country or were for bona fide business expenses incurred by or in connection with the execution or performance of a contract with a foreign government (Osajda, 2010a). The Australian Code expressly states that the defendant bears the evidentiary onus when relying on this defence (s13.3(3)).

Significantly, both Australia and the USA expressly exclude payments for either the awarding of new business or for the continuation of existing business contracts.

RECIPIENT

The FCPA includes as a bribe 'recipient' a foreign official or party, candidate for office or a third party acting as an agent for such a person. The rank or position of the official is irrelevant and it applies to all public officials (this makes the distinction between facilitation payments and bribery crucial in many cases – Santangelo et al., 2007). As noted earlier, the UK Anti Bribery Act negates the requirement to prove that the receiver was a 'public official' as the Act is also directed at bribes to private persons carrying out a 'relevant function or activity'. Of the three countries only the UK criminalizes receiving a bribe in a foreign country under its general bribery offences. The separate offence dealing with bribery of foreign public officials relates to 'offer, promise or payment', not receipt of a bribe. As is the case in both the USA and in Australia, the focus is on individuals exercising public functions on behalf of a foreign country and individuals or officials/agents of international public bodies.

The Australian provisions provide a wide definition of 'foreign public official' and include any employee/official of a foreign government; member of the executive, judiciary or magistracy of the foreign country;

a person who performs official duties under a foreign law; member or officer of the legislature; an employee or official of a public international organization such as the United Nations.

Research indicates that recipients will sometimes go to great lengths to conceal their identity as the ultimate recipient of a bribe. The OECD has identified three common schemes of concealment that utilize intermediaries (Working Group, 2009). First, a scheme can make use of an official's family, friends or other third parties who are used as conduits for the bribe. In this scenario the principal usually knows the identity of the foreign public official; the company and the official agree on the amount to be paid and the services that are to be rendered by the official, but to avoid detection the parties agree to channel the money indirectly. There is often no money trail between the official and the company and to justify payments from the company to the intermediary false invoices are often deployed for fabricated goods or services.

The OECD (ibid.) refers to a number of cases that illustrate the use of family and friends to conceal the recipients of illicit payments. In the *Green* case (2008) the USA defendants bribed a Thai official to run the Bangkok International Film Festival. They negotiated the size of the bribe and the nature of the contracts directly with the official (inflating the value of the contract by the size of the bribe), but channelled the payments through bank accounts held in the UK, Singapore and Jersey by the official's daughter and a friend. One element in the *Siemens* case (2001–2007), referred to earlier, involved senior Nigerian officials and bribe payments routed through a USA intermediary who was the wife of a former Nigerian Vice-President.

The second scheme of concealment involves the hiring of a 'business consultant' ostensibly as an intermediary, but in practice as a 'front' for the foreign official. Sham invoices for non-existent 'services' to the company are presented and paid, and the funds are channelled to the official in the amount of the agreed-upon bribe (there may be a number of layers and other companies between the initial payment and the official). The *Siemens* case (above) is again illustrative. A Hongkong-based consultant was hired to work on a power plant contract, but no actual services were provided to the principal; the consultant was in fact a clothing company with no power industry expertise.

False invoices or other documents may actually be entered into the company's books of account, but general and vague descriptors may be used both on invoices and in the accounting records. Common examples drawn from actual cases include terms on invoices such as: *Consultancy fee for period A–B* or *Fee as agreed for Project ABC, Phase 1*. Records in accounts are similarly general: *Supporting the company's business in country X*; *Conducting market research*; *Establishing necessary contacts*; or *Information, advice and support*. Staying with the *Siemens* case, one example of bribe paying involved a Chinese train project where consultant agreements, invoices and payments used the descriptions 'identify and define sales opportunities, provide market intelligence' and 'support contract negotiations', but no services were ever actually performed. The chain of paperwork was a sham designed to hide grease or bribery payments (see also Gordon, 2009; Ahrens, 2010).

In the third major modus operandi for concealment, the intermediary may offer real goods and services mixed with illicit payments. It is not uncommon for agents to provide real services such as freight forwarding, logistics or procurement expertise, with inflated invoicing to hide the bribe. Payment may be staggered over a contract or hidden in payments associated with contract milestones. The Australian AWB case is a good example of this arrangement.

BUSINESS PURPOSE TEST

A key thrust of the Anti-bribery Convention is to promote a global level playing field for business transactions. This is reflected in the basic idea that corrupt activity may provide a payer with an unfair business advantage over competitors, but the key issue is how far this principle should extend. In the USA, a wide interpretation has been applied, covering almost anything to do with obtaining or retaining business, including payments to officials for more favourable tax treatment. However, there are some exceptions; as noted earlier, purely private bribes and grease or facilitation payments for non-discretionary or routine governmental actions do not fall within the scope of the FCPA (Osajda, 2010a).

Similar provisions apply in Australia. For example, a payment by an Australian firm to an overseas public hospital official as an inducement to purchase the company's medical equipment or supplies is likely to breach the Australian anti-bribery provisions. This is because in a number of countries public hospital officials may be regarded as 'foreign officials' and the purpose of the payment was to award the business to the particular Australian company (Ahrens, 2010).

In the UK, the wording of the legislation goes beyond the notion of obtaining a business advantage to cover 'any function of a public nature', 'any activity connected with a business' (specifically defined to include 'a trade or profession'), 'any activity performed in the course of a person's employment' and 'any activity performed by or on behalf of a body of persons (whether corporate or unincorporate' (s3(2)). However, the breadth and reach of the law is qualified by specifying that the function to which a bribe relates is expected to be carried out 'in good faith', or 'impartially', or 'in a position of trust' (s3(3)–(5)).

PENALTIES AND ENFORCEMENT

Under the FCPA, penalties can apply to the entity as well as to individual officers, directors, employees, agents and shareholders. Issuers and domestic concerns can be subject to a fine of up to US$2 million per wilful violation or twice the benefit sought to be obtained, whichever is the greater (Alternative Fines Act). Individuals can be fined up to $100 000 and face imprisonment of up to five years. There is an additional civil penalty regime of up to $10 000 for each violation, and other injunctive relief such as cease-and-desist orders. In addition, the SEC can make disgorgement orders, which may require, for example, the surrender of ill-gotten gains (based on calculations of the financial benefit received). Other sanctions include banning of companies or individuals from government contracts and declarations of ineligibility for export licences.

According to the 2010 TI Progress Report the USA has 138 concluded cases with 30 cases pending. The report outlines 'record settlements' in 2009/10 including $579 million against Halliburton and its subsidiary KBR, relating to a joint venture to build a natural gas facility in Nigeria; $800m against Siemens, relating to charges of global bribery; and $400 million against BAE Systems (Heimann and Dell, 2010). As noted earlier in this chapter, the SEC has a strong record of enforcement action against corporations which breach the FCPA 'books and records' provisions, with significant penalties yielded in cases such as the GE case in the Oil-for-Food scandal being related to findings of inaccurate records of illicit surcharges and kickbacks, and of inadequate internal controls to detect and prevent such payments.

In the UK, the first prosecution for bribing a foreign official was launched in 2008, a decade after the ratification of the Convention. To May 2010 a further 7 prosecution or enforcement actions had commenced (Heimann and Dell, 2010). The enactment of the Bribery Act (2010) provides a more structured focus for prosecutorial authorities and should make it easier to secure convictions. Penalties available upon conviction of an individual for foreign bribery differ based on whether the conviction is summary or on indictment. Where an individual or corporation receives a summary conviction, the available penalty is 12 months in prison or a fine of up to £5 000, or both. Where an individual's conviction is on indictment the available penalty is 10 years imprisonment or an unlimited fine, or both. The corporate liability offence contained in the Act can only be tried on indictment, thus exposing corporations convicted to an unlimited fine (s11).

These most recent developments must be set against the controversy surrounding the BAE bribery case. In late 2006 the UK halted an inquiry into accusations of bribery arising from a £43 billion arms deal with Saudi Arabia which commenced in 1985. The then Prime Minister Tony Blair was quoted as saying that he thought pursuing the case would have strategically damaged crucial relations with the oil-rich kingdom, and in announcing the discontinuance of the investigation, the Serious Fraud Office (SFO) said:

> This decision has been taken following representations that have been made both to the Attorney General and the Director of the SFO concerning the need to safeguard national and international security.
>
> It has been necessary to balance the need to maintain the rule of law against the wider public interest. (SFO, 2006)

Critics of the decision pointed to two significant underlying factors: threats by the Saudi Government to immediately cease relations on security and intelligence, and commercial considerations relating to the fallout from losing one of the biggest contracts of the decade to the French. Whilst the latter consideration was vehemently denied by the SFO, it was also reported that the Saudi government had become a significant partner in the intelligence war against al-Qaeda and that the threat of withdrawal of this information flow was taken seriously by the UK Government (Gibb and Evans, 2008). The UK was criticized internationally (Heimann and Dell, 2006) and faced domestic legal challenges to the action. The High Court initially ruled that the halt to the investigation was unlawful and that it did arise from pressure by the Saudi government (Gibb and Webster, 2008); however, this decision was overturned on appeal to the House of Lords (SFO, 2008).

In 2010 the SFO announced a set of settlements with BAE Systems, 'achieved collaboratively' with the USA Department of Justice. The SFO agreement resulted in a guilty plea in relation to 'failing to keep reasonably accurate accounting records [under the Companies Act 1985] in relation to [the company's] activities in Tanzania', with a penalty of '£30 million comprising a financial order to be determined by a Crown Court judge with the balance paid as an ex gratia payment for the benefit of the people of Tanzania' (SFO, 2010).

It should be noted that the issue of political willpower to pursue bribery prosecutions against certain parties may still be a factor, notwithstanding the new UK legislative framework. The 2010 Act requires the consent of specified parties (s10) to proceed with a prosecution, one of which is the Director of the SFO. Given that it was the SFO Director who made key decisions relating to the discontinuance of the BAE investigation, the independence of prosecutorial decisions from political pressure may still be an issue.

The Australian Criminal Code differentiates the penalties applicable to individuals and corporations for offending under the foreign bribery provisions of s70.2. A corporation may be sanctioned by a fine calculated in three alternative ways. First, a fine may be imposed of up to three times the benefit obtained by the corporation or its related entities as a direct or indirect consequence of the offence (Criminal Code s70.2(5)(b)). Second, should that amount prove impossible for the court to ascertain, a fine of up to 10 per cent of the annual turnover of the company is available (s70.2(5)(c)). If either of these amounts is less than the amount equivalent to 100000 penalty units (currently A$11 million), then the third option is to impose a fine not exceeding that amount (s70.2(5)(a)). An individual found guilty of the s70.2 offence is exposed to a fine of up to 10000 penalty units (currently A$1.1 million) and/or up to 10 years' imprisonment.

Despite a considerable armoury of available sanctions, Australia, in contrast to both the USA and the UK, has had no prosecutions since it ratified the Anti-bribery Convention, although the Australian Federal Police are currently pursuing at least one high-profile investigation into an Australian banknote company (Securency) involved in allegations of bribe paying to win currency printing contracts in an array of countries.

TI has identified a number of inadequacies in the Australian legal framework including a gap in its scope. Only Australian resident entities and executives (or citizens) are subject to the provisions in the Criminal Code, which means that improper payments made by subsidiaries incorporated offshore may not be covered. Considerable difficulties exist in obtaining admissible evidence from other countries or applying specialist expertise; this may reflect issues around mutual legal assistance, extradition treaties and inadequate resourcing of a specialist law enforcement unit within the Australian Federal Police. Australia also lacks strong and effective whistleblower protection (Hellman and Dell, 2010), standing in contrast to a fascinating development in the USA where payments may be made to whistleblowers who disclose violation of books and records provisions of the FCPA; these may be 10–30 per cent of any monetary penalty or monetary sanction imposed by the SEC exceeding $1 million (Wyld, 2010).

CONCLUSION

Bribery of foreign officials clearly undermines good governance and ethical decision-making by those who should be motivated solely by notions of 'public interest'. There is little doubt that issues of bribery and corruption will be prominent in the considerations of businesses when there are tangible consequences for ignoring the issue. Well-publicized and successful prosecutions do much to focus the mind (and the balance sheet) of corporate CEOs and executives. The record of the USA utilizing the FCPA to implement the OECD anti-bribery agenda has exceeded the record of both the UK and Australia with the use of the 'books and records' provisions enabling considerable success for the SEC in obtaining settlements worth billions of dollars. The ability and ease with which documentary evidence can be gathered and the lower standard of proof required for civil prosecutions are key factors in the success of these provisions. Jurisdictions elsewhere could find that enacting similar measures into their domestic legal frameworks is beneficial from an enforcement perspective.

The UK has at least attempted to give effect to the spirit of the Convention in the 2010 Bribery Act, which includes the express offence of 'failure to prevent bribery'. This is an important addition that directly addresses issues related to management failures such as lack of due diligence in hiring, the absence of education, and failures to exercise adequate supervision and control of employees, subsidiaries and agents. The extension of the idea to 'anyone who has acted on behalf' of the accused company enables the full circumstances of a particular company's operations to be examined as it is a substantive rather than a formal test. This captures situations where formal contracts would not support legal liability to be carried by the parent company, even though a public official may have sought assurances that the parent company would indeed support a payment notwithstanding the contrary indication in the paperwork.

In the Australian legal response to the Anti-bribery Convention, the scope of provisions is unclear partly due to jurisdictional questions which remain unaddressed and partly through the absence of judicial guidance, given that there has still been no testing of the legislation through prosecution. It may be the case that a more expansive reach to include the idea of negligence in failing to act and the extension of the scope of the law to include entities incorporated offshore but which are acting on behalf of a parent company in Australia, would be valuable additions. Despite the existence of corporate responsibility principles, which appear to create a similar fault standard to negligence through the use of 'corporate culture provisions', it nevertheless remains the case that Australia has had no prosecutions since it ratified and introduced the Convention into its domestic legal framework.

REFERENCES

ACCA (2007), *Bribery and Corruption: the Impact on UK SMEs*, London: ACCA.

Ahrens, M. (2010), 'Protecting your integrity abroad', *Keeping Good Companies*, **62**(10), 597–601.

Baughn, C., N. Bodie, M. Buchanan and M. Bixby (2010), 'Bribery in international business transactions', *Journal of Business Ethics*, **92**(1), 15–32.

Carr, I. and O. Outhwaite (2009), 'Corruption and business integrity: law, policy and company practices', *Manchester Journal of International Economic Law*, **6**(3), 16–64.

Carrington, P.D. (2007), 'Law and transnational corruption: the need for Lincoln's Law abroad', *Law and Contemporary Problems*, **70**(4), 109–138.

Clough, J. and C. Mulhern (2002), *The Prosecution of Corporations*, South Melbourne: Oxford University Press.

Cole, Hon T.R.H. (2006), *Report of the Inquiry into certain Australian companies in relation to the UN Oil-for-Food Programme*, Volume 1, Summary, Recommendations and background, Canberra: Commonwealth of Australia.

Commonwealth of Australia (1999), Parliamentary Debates (Hansard), House of Representatives, 3 June 1999, 6045 (Daryl Williams, Attorney-General).

Deming, S.H. (2006), 'The potent and broad ranging implications of the accounting and record keeping provisions of the Foreign Corrupt Practices Act' (2006), *Journal of Criminal Law and Criminology*, **96**(2), 465–502.

Financial Action Task Force (2005), *Money Laundering and Terrorist Financing Typologies*, Paris, OECD.

Financial Action Task Force on Money Laundering (2004), *The Forty Recommendations* (incorporating the amendments of 22 October 2004). Paris, OECD.

Gibb, F. and M. Evans (2008), 'BAE investigation: it all came down to sales, not security', *The Times*, 11 April.

Gibb, F. and P. Webster (2008), 'High Court rules that the halt to BAE investigation was "unlawful, a threat to British justice"', *The Times*, 11 April.

Global Witness (2009), *Undue Diligence: How Banks Do Business with Corrupt Regimes*, London: Global Witness, available at www.globalwitness.org/library/undue-diligence-how-banks-do-business-corrupt-regimes (accessed 30 November 2010).

Gordon, R.K. (2009), 'Laundering the proceeds of public sector corruption', *Case Research Paper Series in Legal Studies*, Working Paper 09–10.

Heimann, F. and G. Dell (2006), *2006 TI Progress Report: Enforcement of the OECD Convention on Combating Bribery of Foreign Public Officials*, Berlin: Transparency International.

Heimann, F. and G. Dell (2009), *Progress Report 2009: OECD Anti-bribery Convention*, Berlin: Transparency International.

Heimann, F. and G. Dell (2010), *Progress Report 2010: Enforcement of the OECD Anti-bribery Convention*, Berlin: Transparency International.

ICAEW (2010), *Business and Economic Crime in an International Context: A Review of International Law and Practice in Relation to Crimes Committed by or on Behalf of Business*, London: ICAEW.

Law Commission, The (2008), *Reforming Bribery*, London: HMSO, HC 928, available at www.lawcom.gov.uk/bribery.htm (accessed 30 November 2010).

McFarlane, J. (2001), 'Corruption and the financial sector: the strategic impact', *Journal of Financial Crime*, **9**(1), 8–21.

Ministry of Justice (2010), *Consultation on Guidance about Commercial Organisations Preventing Bribery (section 9 of the Bribery Act 2010)*, London: Ministry of Justice, available at www.justice.gov.uk (accessed 30 November 2010).
Nichols, P.N. (2009), 'Who allows facilitating payments?', *Agora without Frontiers*, **14**(4), 303–323.
OECD Working Group on Bribery (2009), *Annual Report 2009*, Paris: OECD.
Organisation for Economic Co-Operation and Development (OECD) (1997), *Convention on Combating Bribery of Foreign Public Officials in International Business Transactions*, Paris: OECD.
Organisation for Economic Co-Operation and Development (OECD) (2009), *OECD Bribery Awareness Handbook for Tax Examiners*, Paris: OECD Centre for Tax Policy and Administration.
Organisation for Economic Co-Operation and Development (OECD) (2010), *Convention on Combating Bribery of Foreign Public Officials in International Business Transactions and related Documents*, Paris: OECD.
Osajda, M. (2010a), 'FCPA Prosecution: Lessons from Kay', *World-Check White Papers*, available at www.world-check.com/whitepapers/2010 (accessed 30 November 2010).
Osajda, M. (2010b), 'The FCPA and why it matters', *World-Check White Papers*, available at www.world-check.com/whitepapers/2010 (accessed 30 November 2010).
Riaño, J. and R. Hodess (2008), *2008 Bribe Payers Index*, Berlin: Transparency International.
Salbu, S.R. (2007), 'Bribery in the global market: A critical analysis of the Foreign Corrupt Practices Act', *Washington and Lee Law Review*, **54**(1), 229–287.
Santangelo, B., G. Stein and M. Jacobs (2007), 'The Foreign Corrupt Practices Act': Recent cases and enforcement trends', *Journal of Investment Compliance*, **8**(3), 31–55.
Sebelius, N. (2008), 'Foreign Corrupt Practices Act', *American Criminal Law Review*, **45**(2), 597–606.
Serious Fraud Office (SFO) (2006), 'BAE Systems Plc/Saudi Arabia', Press Release, 14 December, London.
Serious Fraud Office (SFO) (2008), 'BAE/Saudi defence contract: House of Lords ruling on the discontinued investigation', Press Release, 30 July, London.
Serious Fraud Office (SFO) (2010), 'BAE Systems plc', Press Release, 5 February, London.
United Nations Office on Drugs and Crime (2004), *United Nations Convention against Corruption*, New York: United Nations.
Working Group on Bribery in International Business Transactions (2009), *Typologies on the Role of Intermediaries in International Business Transactions: Final report*, Paris: OECD.
Wyld, R. (2010), 'Anti-Corruption regulation in Australia – myth or reality?', *International Serious and Organised Crime Conference 2010*, Melbourne.

Legislation

Alternative Fines Act, 18 USC§§3571 (2006) (USA)
Anti Money Laundering and Counter Terrorism Act 2006 (Cth) (Australia)
Anti Terrorism, Crime and Security Act 2001 (UK)
Bribery Act 2010 (UK)
Corporations Act 2001 (Cth) (Australia)
Criminal Code Act 1995 (Cth) (Australia)
Foreign Corrupt Practices Act 1977, 15 USC§§78dd-1–78dd-3 (2006) (USA)
Income Tax Assessment Act 1997 (Cth) (Australia)
International Trade Integrity Bill 2007 (Cth) (Australia)
Proceeds of Crime Act 2002 (Cth) (Australia)

18 Applying anti-money laundering laws to fight corruption

Louis de Koker

INTRODUCTION

In July 1989 the G7 meeting in Paris, joined by the President of the Commission of European Communities, expressed concern about the devastating proportions of the drug problem and urged all countries to support the fight against drug trafficking and the laundering of its proceeds. To assist in that regard, they convened a financial action task force. This task force was mandated to (1) assess the results of co-operation already undertaken in order to prevent the abuse of the banking system and other financial institutions for money laundering and (2) to consider additional preventive efforts in this field, including adapting legal and regulatory systems to enhance multilateral judicial assistance (G7, 1989, par. 52–53). The task team's report (Financial Action Task Force, 1990) contained 40 recommendations on preventive steps and these were endorsed by the G7 meeting in Houston in July 1990 as part of its narcotics strategy. The participants in that meeting also committed their countries to a full implementation of all the recommendations without delay and invited other countries to do the same (G7, 1990, p. 78; Pieth, 1999, p. 531; Shams, 2001, pp. 111–112; Gilmore, 2004, pp. 89–98).

Two decades later this task force (generally known as the Financial Action Task Force or FATF) and its Forty Recommendations, since supplemented by Special Recommendations on Terrorist Financing, lie at the core of an international framework that combats the laundering of proceeds of crime and financing of terrorists. The Recommendations are recognized as the international standards for anti-money laundering (AML) and combating of financing of terrorists (CFT) and obligations to meet these standards and combat money laundering and terrorist financing are re-enforced by a number of international conventions, regional instruments and international regulatory and industry standards. More than 180 countries have either implemented laws to meet these standards or are in the process of doing so.

Although much has been written about the AML/CFT system, limited research underpins and interrogates the combating measures and their efficacy in relation to various types of criminal conduct that generate proceeds of crime. This chapter briefly considers some of the key elements of the AML framework with a view to identifying questions that should be probed as part of a research agenda. A brief overview of the current AML/CFT system is required to contextualize the analysis and observations.

THE AML/CFT FRAMEWORK

Development of the System

Law enforcement interest in tracing proceeds of crime to obtain intelligence, and evidence linking criminals, especially leaders of crime syndicates, to offences that generated the proceeds, increased in the latter part of the 20th century. The use of tax avoidance charges to convict Al Capone in the 1930s (De Feo, 1989, p. 406) and of financial investigations to trace Nazi leaders after the Second World War proved the usefulness of financial investigations in a broader criminal context. Such investigations were, however, hampered by a non-financial focus by law enforcement, a general lack of law enforcement expertise in forensic accounting, a lack of international law enforcement co-operation and by a generally hostile commercial environment. Client records were protected by strict bank secrecy rules and professional confidentiality, especially legal professional privilege, often complicated efforts to trace transactions and probe beneficial ownership. In addition, secrecy havens proliferated, making it difficult for domestic investigators to unravel an international money trail (Rider, 1993, pp. 234–237).

In the 1980s, deeply concerned about the rising power and increasing wealth of drug trafficking syndicates, a new law enforcement strategy focusing on criminal money flows was adopted. It was partially informed by early American experiences with the US Bank Secrecy Act 1970. This Act compelled US financial institutions to keep records of especially larger cash transactions, obtain specific information about clients and report large cash transactions as well as suspicious transactions that may be linked to money laundering, tax evasion or other criminal transactions (Villa, 1988, pp. 489–492; De Feo, 1989, pp. 405–415).

The new strategy recognized that drug syndicates operated as businesses. It therefore attempted to hamper their flow of funds and strip criminals of their criminal profits (Rider, 1993). The main objectives were to disrupt the business of crime and to generate evidence and intelligence to assist law enforcement. The strategy aimed to make it more difficult and dangerous for criminals to invest their proceeds of crime in the legitimate economy. Key elements of the new strategy included (1) criminalizing as money laundering any attempt to hide or disguise ill-gotten gains or any interest in it; (2) compelling the financial sector to know their customers and to report suspicious and unusual transactions; (3) confiscating criminal assets to prevent their re-investment in crime and to signal to society that crime does not pay; and (4) increasing law enforcement co-operation nationally and internationally.

This strategy underpinned new AML laws that the US and the UK adopted in 1986. In 1988 a rudimentary AML strategy was adopted as part of the 1988 United Nations Convention against Illicit Traffic in Narcotic Drugs and Psychotropic Substances. The AML framework in its current form was, however, largely shaped by the FATF Recommendations that were adopted in 1990 and revised in 1996 and 2003 and also by the associated work, especially the mutual compliance evaluations, undertaken within the FATF framework.

The FATF is continuing to function as a temporary task force whose mandate is revisited at intervals. It currently has a membership of 34 jurisdictions and 2 regional organisations. These represent most of the major financial centres internationally. Other jurisdictions are indirectly represented, mainly through associate FATF members such as the eight FATF-style regional bodies (FSRBs). Countries are periodically subjected to mutual peer reviews of their compliance with the FATF Recommendations. Mutual evaluation reports are published and adverse findings may impact negatively on commercial relationships. The key mechanism in this regard is located in Recommendation 21. This recommendation advises financial institutions to give special attention to business relationships and transactions with persons and institutions from countries which do not or insufficiently apply the FATF Recommendations. A negative report may trigger such 'special attention' which may in practice even lead to the termination of business relationships with entities linked to such a jurisdiction. The threat of such indirect economic sanctions has proved quite effective to ensure compliance. It was used in an earlier blacklisting process (Reuter and Truman, 2004, pp. 165–166) and currently supports the FATF's International Co-operation Review Group's processes that may result in the application of Recommendation 21 in respect of countries with a poor mutual evaluation report and a lack of political will to address the deficiencies effectively.

The AML framework is internationally underpinned by key United Nations Conventions, for example the 1988 United Nations Convention against Illicit Traffic in Narcotic Drugs and Psychotropic Substances, the 1999 United Nations Convention against Transnational Organized Crime and the 2003 United Nations Convention against Corruption, by various regional instruments and by the political support of the Security Council of the United Nations and the G20.

Footprint of the AML Framework

In general a national AML framework consists of a set of legal provisions criminalizing money laundering; a set of regulatory requirements compelling regulated businesses to perform specified customer due diligence measures to ensure that they identify and know their customers and report suspicious transaction reports to the authorities; and the establishment and maintenance of a national financial intelligence unit (FIU) to receive and analyse suspicious transaction reports and provide intelligence to the appropriate law enforcement agencies. The framework also includes appropriate regulation and supervision of financial activities as well as other high-risk business and professional activities; law enforcement, especially asset forfeiture, powers, procedures and capacity; as well as powers and capacity to support cross-border co-operation in criminal matters.

The application of the AML framework broadened considerably over the past two decades. The FATF's Recommendations were initially aimed at proceeds of drug trafficking and attempted to prevent these proceeds from entering banks and other financial institutions, notably bureaux de change. It was, however, realized quite early that AML controls can also be useful in respect of non-drug offences. The money laundering provisions of the 1990 Council of Europe Convention on Laundering, Search, Seizure and Confiscation of the Proceeds from Crime were therefore not restricted to proceeds of drug-related offences. FATF later followed suit and broadened the focus of money laundering to the proceeds of all serious offences, specifically including a category of serious offences designated as 'corruption and bribery'. The FATF Recommendations set a minimum standard that countries may exceed. Some countries therefore extended their money laundering offences to the proceeds of all crimes, and to laundering acts committed by persons who did not know, but negligently failed to appreciate, that these involved proceeds of crime.

In 2001 the FATF framework was employed to combat terrorist financing too and in recent years the FATF has issued guidance on the application of the framework to support action against the proliferation of weapons of mass destruction. In 2003 FATF also broadened the application of its principles to specific designated non-financial businesses and professions that it regards as particularly vulnerable to money laundering abuse, for instance casinos, real estate agents, dealers in precious stones and metals, lawyers and accountants.

AML AND CORRUPTION

In the late 1990s various cases were identified where customer due diligence controls failed and banks, especially private banks, assisted prominent foreign politicians to launder proceeds of corruption (Financial Services Authority, 2001; US Senate Permanent Subcommittee on Investigations, 1999). Concern about these failures coincided with heightened international concern about corruption. Anti-corruption initiatives, such as those of the OECD Working Group on Bribery, Transparency International and the Anti-Corruption Working Group of the Society of Advanced Legal Studies (The Society for Advanced Legal Studies, 2000) coincided with the drafting of customer due diligence guidance by the Basel Committee on Banking Supervision (Basel Committee on Banking Supervision, 2001). In 2000 leading international private banks, some of which were implicated in the handling of proceeds of corruption, drafted and published a set of voluntary AML standards for private banks, the so-called Wolfsberg AML Principles on Private Banking (Pieth and Ailofi, 2003). As a consequence of these developments Recommendation 6 that focuses on Politically Exposed Persons (PEPS) was introduced when the FATF Recommendations were revised in 2003.

PEPS

According to the glossary to the FATF Recommendations PEPs:

> . . . are individuals who are or have been entrusted with prominent public functions in a foreign country, for example Heads of State or of government, senior politicians, senior government, judicial or military officials, senior executives of state owned corporations, important political party officials. Business relationships with family members or close associates of PEPs involve reputational risks similar to those with PEPs themselves. The definition is not intended to cover middle ranking or more junior individuals in the foregoing categories.

FATF's PEP Recommendation focuses on customer due diligence measures that regulated institutions should implement. As background, it is important to note that the FATF Recommendations require regulated institutions to undertake the following standard customer due diligence measures (FATF, 2003, Recommendation 5):

a) Identifying the customer and verifying the customer's identity using reliable, independent source documents, data or information.
b) Identifying the beneficial owner, and taking reasonable measures to verify the identity of the beneficial owner such that the financial institution is

satisfied that it knows who the beneficial owner is. For legal persons and arrangements this should include financial institutions taking reasonable measures to understand the ownership and control structure of the customer.

c) Obtaining information on the purpose and intended nature of the business relationship.

d) Conducting ongoing due diligence on the business relationship and scrutiny of transactions undertaken throughout the course of that relationship to ensure that the transactions being conducted are consistent with the institution's knowledge of the customer, their business and risk profile, including, where necessary, the source of funds.

For higher risk categories or customers and transactions, financial institutions should implement enhanced due diligence measures. In this respect Recommendation 6 advises institutions to take the following PEP-related steps in addition to the standard due diligence measures:

a) Have appropriate risk management systems to determine whether the customer is a PEP.
b) Obtain senior management approval for establishing a business relationship with a PEP.
c) Take reasonable measures to establish the source of wealth and source of funds of a PEP where such a relationship is approved.
d) Conduct enhanced ongoing monitoring of the business relationship.

Designated non-financial businesses and professions are also required to implement Recommendation 6, but only in specific situations, for instance dealers in precious metals and stones are only required to do so when they engage in a cash transaction involving at least USD/EUR 15,000 (FATF, 2003, Recommendation 12(c)).

There is a measure of definitional vagueness relating to the PEP concept (Chaikin and Sharman, 2007, pp. 34–53; Wolfsberg Group, 2008; World-Check, 2008; Choo, 2008; Gilligan, 2009; United Nations Office on Drugs and Crime and the World Bank, 2009; Choo, 2010; Greenberg et al., 2010, pp. 25–32). A variety of PEP definitions are applied internationally. Although these definitions share a common focus on persons holding prominent political or civil service functions, some appear more detailed or extensive than others. The FATF definition, for example, does not explicitly extend to domestic PEPs, although such an extension is encouraged in the FATF's interpretative notes to Recommendation 6. The Basel PEP definition (Basel Committee on Banking Supervision 2001, para. 41), on the other hand, does not differentiate between foreign and domestic PEPs. Unlike the FATF and Basel definitions, the Wolfsberg Principles include in their PEP definition members of ruling royal families with governance responsibilities (Wolfsberg Group, 2008, par. 3). The Wolfsberg definition potentially extends to heads of supranational bodies (for example the United Nations, the International Monetary Fund and the World Bank) and members of parliament or national legislatures, senior members of the diplomatic corps and members of boards of central banks, unless the risk of corruption or abuse is considered to be low.

The reference to family members and close business associates increases the definitional uncertainty in practice. Corrupt leaders often use family members and associates to establish and manage their business relationships. It is therefore sensible to extend PEP controls to such persons. However, there are differences of opinion regarding the strength of the ties that should exist or the closeness of a relationship before a third party should be subjected to these controls. The FATF definition refers to family members in general terms while article 3(8) of the 2005 Third European Union Money Laundering Directive refers only to 'immediate' family members. In practice regulated institutions generally have to decide for themselves where to draw the line. The same challenge arises in relation to the question whether a person holds a 'senior' or 'junior' position in politics or the civil service. It is also unclear how long a PEP remains a PEP after vacating or relinquishing the prominent political position. Regulation 14(5) of the UK Money Laundering Regulations 2007 limits PEP status to a person who is or has at any time in the preceding year been entrusted with the relevant functions. The wisdom of using such a general period of time is, however, questionable. Former PEPs can retain their influence for much longer than a year and others will be able to avoid the PEP controls by merely postponing transactions involving proceeds of corruption for 12 months.

In practice, regulated institutions not only grapple with the confusing differences regarding the appropriate definition of a PEP, but also with determining whether a prospective customer meets the criteria of the definition that they employ. Countries do not issue comprehensive lists of their PEPs. Regulated institutions therefore depend on commercial providers of PEP data. These, in turn, must observe international standards of privacy and can therefore only rely on publicly available information. PEPs from countries with limited media coverage may not be reflected at all or in full in such a database. PEPs that are sufficiently powerful to control what is reported on them by their domestic media and those who are adept at managing the public availability of their personal and financial information can limit the impact that PEP controls can have on them.

The general compliance picture relating to PEP controls is murky. Mutual evaluation reports on country compliance with the FATF Recommendations show that countries are seriously lagging on the implementation of Recommendation 6 (Johnson, 2008; Choo, 2010). After an analysis of FATF mutual evaluation reports, Greenberg et al. came to the following conclusion (Greenberg et al., 2010, p. xv):

> The picture today is of an overall failure of effective implementation of international PEP standards. There is surprisingly low compliance with FATF requirements on PEPs, especially among FATF members. Of the 124 countries assessed by FATF or by FATF-Style Regional Bodies, 61 per cent were non-compliant and 23 per cent were partially compliant. More than 80 per cent of these jurisdictions are far behind.

These mutual evaluation reports, however, do not provide a comprehensive PEP compliance picture. They focus on the statutory provisions and formal processes that countries adopted and implemented to meet the FATF standards and do not comprehensively consider the level of compliance by regulated institutions. Many banks have implemented PEP controls, despite the absence of domestic laws compelling them to do so, or implemented more comprehensive PEP controls than required by the law (Greenberg et al., 2010, pp. 15–16). Banks would tend to overcomply with local laws to meet requirements of foreign shareholders, correspondents and business counterparts and to meet national and international corporate governance and risk management standards, especially in relation to reputational risk (De Koker and Symington, 2010). Such practices are generally not reflected in the mutual evaluation reports.

According to providers of PEP data and management systems, many banks perform PEP checks. For example, World-Check a key commercial provider of PEP data, reports on its website that its PEP data is used by more than 4500 institutions in over 160 countries, including 49 of the world's top 50 banks (http://www.world-check.com). PEP controls therefore appear more widely implemented than indicated by the mutual evaluation reports. The quality of these control measures is, however, difficult to gauge. Despite the apparent widespread use of PEP data by large financial institutions, cases still surface where banks have dealt wittingly and unwittingly with proceeds of corruption (Global Witness, 2009). Whether this is a result of a flawed PEP approach, of inherent limitations in the current system or of lax implementation of PEP controls, it requires scrutiny.

RESEARCH AGENDA

The application of the AML framework to combat corruption, provides a rich field for research. While this brief discussion does not attempt to comprehensively identify the relevant research questions, it outlines some of the key areas that require research attention. Many of the issues are cross-cutting, but for purposes of this discussion it is useful to separate questions relating to crime combating strategy, from those relating to integrity and governance challenges and the design, implementation and evaluation of the controls.

Crime Combating Strategy

The crime combating strategy that is advanced by AML should be subjected to closer analysis.

It was pointed out earlier that the AML system was originally designed to counter the abuse of banks and other financial institutions by those who launder drug money. The original recommendations to counter this abuse were not informed by detailed research. As Pieth, a key participant in the drafting of the original Recommendations, puts it (Pieth, 1999, p. 531): 'The first version of its "40 Recommendations" adopted in 1990 was written in less than half a year, with no ulterior ambition and very little academic preparation'.

In this process insufficient attention has been given to the inherent tensions between the objective to keep dirty money out of regulated institutions and the reliance on regulated institutions to monitor dirty money and provide intelligence by way of suspicious transaction reports to law enforcement. This tension recently surfaced again in the financial inclusion debate, with differing views on whether customers whose backgrounds and identities cannot be ascertained, should be allowed or even encouraged to access financial services (Bester et al., 2008; De Koker, 2009). Questions such as these have remained unresolved because the AML tools themselves (financial transparency, customer due diligence, asset confiscation etc.) are generally regarded as inherently valuable and desirable tools that deliver law enforcement value. While there is much to commend measures to ensure that criminals cannot hide or enjoy their criminal wealth, it should also be acknowledged that there is little data or evidence supporting the argument that the benefit of these tools outweighs their financial and social costs (Naylor, 2004, p. 18; Reuter and Truman, 2004), especially in relation to civil liberties of honest citizens.

The original Recommendations reflected expert opinion, especially law enforcement opinion, regarding the flow of drug money, the business structure of drug syndicates and the criminal interaction with banks and embodied a strategy to counter the operations of drug syndicates. Whether that strategy would be equally effective against non-organized, non-drug offences does not appear to have been considered comprehensively. In fact, the extension of the application of these recommendations to non-drug offences was not informed by a comprehensive analysis of the flows of proceeds of these types of offences. As a result, amendments to the Recommendations to ensure that they address the proceeds of non-drug offences effectively were not seriously considered.

The strategy to employ AML against corruption was therefore adopted without a thorough understanding of the laundering of proceeds of corruption. It is likely that this approach will lead to some inefficiencies and unintended consequences. These require careful scrutiny by researchers as the results may differ from country to country and region to region. Most of the more comprehensive studies on the laundering of proceeds of corruption were published after the adoption of the 2003 revised Recommendations. Case studies, litigation and reports mainly relating to 'grand corruption' provided valuable indications of some methodologies (Chaikin and Sharman, 2007; Levi, Dakolias and Greenberg, 2007; Gordon, 2009; Global Witness, 2009; Goredema and Madzima, 2009; Chaikin and Sharman, 2009; United States Senate Permanent Subcommittee on Investigations (Committee on Homeland Security and Governmental Affairs) 2010). However, more research is required on how the proceeds of general or petty corruption are laundered in different countries and economies (Levi 2010) and the factors at play that would influence a criminal's choice of methodology or laundering.

There are furthermore inherent limitations in using AML controls to combat corruption. Levi, Dakolias and Greenberg argue, for example, that AML controls are skewed towards corruptees rather than corruptors because they do not reach sufficiently into the business controls of non-financial companies that may be paying bribes. AML controls rely furthermore on the gatekeepers to the financial system. As a result their knowledge of corruption and of transactions laundering proceeds of corruption determines the effectiveness of the controls (Levi, Dakolias and Greenberg, 2007, p. 411). Corrupt regimes can furthermore undermine AML controls by selectively implementing laws that were adopted or by underfunding the FIU or other key law enforcement agencies (Tang and Ai, 2010). More research is required on the design of AML controls to optimally balance civil liberties and anti-corruption objectives and on ways to ensure the integration of such controls into good corporate governance principles.

As part of this enquiry, the broad anti-corruption strategy that underpins the PEP approach should also be considered. While the Recommendations provide a framework that applies to corruption in general, the PEP approach focuses much of the AML attention on grand corruption and especially the international investment of proceeds of grand corruption. While international laundering of proceeds of grand corruption certainly merits attention, it is appropriate to question whether that should be at the expense of efforts to combat systemic petty corruption or pure domestic laundering of proceeds of corruption.

The FATF PEP focus was the result of international concern about the laundering of the proceeds of grand corruption at the time when the current set of Recommendations were considered. There is little indication that serious consideration was given to the adoption of a slightly broader approach to advance a broader anti-corruption agenda (Financial Action Task Force, 2002, pp. 12–13). For example, if the PEP definition was broadened to all civil servants the PEP controls would have had a broader anti-corruption footprint. Civil servants generally have fixed remuneration levels and salaries that are paid into bank accounts on standard payment dates. It is therefore relatively easy for financial institutions to identify customers as civil servants and to monitor their accounts and detect unusual transactions. In addition, institutions would not have had to grapple with the distinction between 'senior' and 'junior' civil servants. The current PEP approach furthermore focuses primarily on public corruption. This approach is therefore not strengthening the UNCAC framework in relation to the laundering of the proceeds of commercial corruption. A broader deployment of the PEP strategy and the costs and impacts of a broader strategy should therefore also receive research attention.

Integrity and Governance Challenges

The drug history of the AML framework tends to mask some of the integrity challenges that may arise in relation to the processing of suspicious transaction data. Although FIUs and law enforcement agencies may be infiltrated or corrupted by drug syndicates, this has not happened so generally as to raise international concern. AML systems therefore often lack good governance assurance systems. This becomes problematic when an FIU and other AML parties must deal with corruption at high levels of government.

Unlike drug offences in most countries, corruption, especially at senior government levels, is often politically sensitive. Law enforcement agencies may find themselves embroiled in matters that are politically challenging. In these circumstances political pressure may be exercised, inducements, even corrupt inducements, may be offered or staff members may be intimidated to ensure a desired outcome. Even where agencies are committed to acting with integrity, they report to senior officials and ultimately politicians who may be vulnerable to these pressures. They also co-operate with other law enforcement agencies, some of which may be very vulnerable to these pressures. This creates dilemmas at all levels of the AML system, for instance where:

- An institution has to report a suspicious transaction that was concluded by the minister that oversees the FIU or the financial supervisor;
- An FIU received a report on a transaction by the Minister of Police and has to pass it to the domestic police service to investigate further; or
- A foreign FIU possesses intelligence relating to the country's president and is hesitant to share it with the domestic FIU because the information may be divulged to the president's office.

The effectiveness of the STR reporting system depends heavily on the confidentiality of the report that is filed and the protection enjoyed by the reporters. If they fear that they may be exposed as the reporters of sensitive information, they will generally be very reluctant to do so. It is therefore crucial that the FIU operates with a measure of confidentiality. Confidentiality can, however, also undermine the integrity of the FIU. It may enable it to engage in practices that it would otherwise avoid. Even where it operates with integrity, the confidentiality may give rise to perceptions that it is acting in a biased or corrupt manner or may deprive it of the ability to counter such allegations effectively. Such perceptions can be highly damaging to law enforcement agencies, as was demonstrated in the past years by the experiences of the Economic and Financial Crimes Commission of Nigeria and the Scorpions of South Africa (Byrne, Arnold and Nagano, 2010, pp. 1–2).

The Egmont Group and the World Bank undertook a survey of FIUs in 2008 to probe aspects of their governance. Sixty-five FIUs participated in the survey and the results indicate that there are grounds for concern (Egmont Group and World Bank, 2010):

- A significant number of the heads of FIUs (for example, 46 per cent of the heads of administrative FIUs) are appointed by a minister, by cabinet or by the head of state. 34 per cent are appointed to fixed terms of office while 62 per cent do not have fixed terms.
- Only 47 per cent of FIUs reported 'that membership or management of political parties or bodies are prohibited for heads of FIUs, as are other political activities as well as certain business activities or directorships'.
- FIU employees are required to periodically report their assets to a competent authority in 56 per cent of FIUs.
- Only 42 per cent of FIUs reported that they have a code of conduct tailored to the functions of FIU employees.
- 72 per cent of FIUs reported that they cannot be given instructions or

guidance from another state body concerning the conduct of the FIU's assignment.
- In more than half of the respondent FIUs some other state body or judicial authority have access to the FIU's data holdings while 62 per cent reported that they can (or must) disclose their findings or the results of their analyses to a superior authority (for example a ministry, the government or a supervisory authority).
- 60 per cent of the respondent FIUs 'are not governed by any oversight or review board or other governing body that determines policies of strategies with regard to operational matters, or strategies concerning non-operational matters'.

While many FIU seem to meet basic good governance requirements, a significant number do not. They may be very vulnerable when they deal with sensitive political matters (Chaikin and Sharman, 2007, pp. 18–33, 69–72). Appropriate governance mechanisms should be considered. These mechanisms should preserve the confidentiality of STRs but still enable an independent audit of FIU processes. The governance and oversight structures that are employed in respect of intelligence agencies may provide indications of workable solutions.

When the integrity challenges lie outside the FIU in any of its law enforcement partners, the problems are more challenging. An FIU provides law enforcement agencies with access to data and financial intelligence. If that access is abused or the FIU feels unable to entrust key agencies with the sensitive data that it controls, the AML system in relation to law enforcement can break down. These concerns will often be shared by regulated business who will be increasingly unwilling to file any but the most clear instances relating to clients that are politically of little significance. The management of such a scenario and the restoration of integrity and effectiveness to the AML law enforcement system as a whole where it is absent, require research attention.

Design of the Framework

Despite some of the questions raised by the PEP strategy, it is clear that it can strengthen the combating of grand corruption. However, it is equally clear that the design of the current framework requires improvement.

For example, greater clarity and consensus about the reach of the PEP definition is required. Who or what should be included in this definition? Should it extend to political parties themselves, instead of only senior office bearers? Should the concept be broadened to corporate entities and their office holders, especially in industries that have been shown to be prone to corruption? Or will an extension of the PEP concept complicate the current system and overburden institutions to such an extent that effectiveness will decline?

The role of non-bank institutions in PEP controls should also be considered. The FATF footprint is limited to financial institutions and specific designated non-financial institutions and professions. PEP controls can therefore be evaded by transacting with businesses that are not covered by the Recommendations, for instance auction houses, antique dealers, motor vehicle dealers. A number of designated non-financial institutions and professional institutions are only required to implement PEP controls when a customer engages in a cash transaction involving a minimum amount, for instance where a customer concludes a transaction with a dealer in precious metals or stones involving at least USD/EUR 15000. This leaves ample room for such transactions to be structured to avoid PEP controls. These gaps in the PEP system require closer attention.

While all financial institutions are required to implement PEP controls, compliance audits focus primarily on large institutions. Many countries have also failed to take active steps to ensure that designated non-financial businesses and professions actually implement adequate PEP controls. The reality is that many smaller institutions, businesses and professions lack the funds to access PEP lists and the capacity to ensure comprehensive PEP controls. Some supervisors and compliance officers believe that PEP controls do not need to extend to low-value accounts and transactions (Bester et al., 2008, p. 13). Many supervisors are happy if the controls are primarily centred on high-net worth clients and the types of bank products that they would typically employ. This approach provides PEPs with opportunities to evade PEP controls. The design and footprint of the controls, and their impact on laundering patterns of proceeds of corruption should therefore be researched. Researchers should especially consider modifications that may be required to ensure that such controls are equally effective in every country and region.

Further thought should also be given to the concept of proceeds of corruption and its incorporation into the general AML framework. Current AML efforts focus primarily on bribes and misappropriated funds and assets. Little attention is given to the benefit that a company acquires as a result of a bribe that was paid. The definition of proceeds of crime in the laws of many countries would be sufficiently broad to capture corporate proceeds resulting from contracts and rights, for instance development and mining rights, that were acquired corruptly (Alexander, 2009). Law enforcement has been reluctant to pursue this avenue because it raises complex legal questions regarding corporate and financial stability. Clarity is required regarding the best approaches to follow and appropriate ways to balance the interests of the citizens of a country that was exploited by a corrupt company and the innocent stakeholders in that company who did not know, and could not reasonably have foreseen, that the company would engage in corruption. Thought will need to be given to the legal position of the directors, management, the employees, the bankers, the auditors and professional advisors of that company. These complexities also arise where countries elect to prosecute and fine the company. The fine penalizes current stakeholders in the company while the former stakeholders may have received the lion's share of the corrupt benefit. It may even bankrupt the company, thereby injuring the current stakeholders, and enrich the state at the expense of the victims of corruption.

A broader view of the concept of 'proceeds of crime' therefore raises interesting and important research questions relating to corporate stability and corporate penalties, victim empowerment and just and equitable asset forfeiture regimes.

Implementation and Evaluation

More research is required to understand the challenges that institutions and law enforcement agencies face when applying AML to combat corruption. Important research focusing primarily on specific regions has already been done (Chaikin and Sharman, 2007; Goredema and Madzima, 2009) but far more detailed work, especially at a national level, is required. It is important to understand how institutions deal with the complexities of the current approach and why controls fail or are overridden. It is similarly important to evaluate the impact of the strategy internationally, regionally and nationally.

Research in this field often grapples with the secrecy that surrounds the AML/CFT framework. The number of suspicious transactions that are filed by a particular institution, the intelligence value of reports received and of information that the FIU shares with law enforcement are examples of questions that are generally difficult to probe outside of government. Reports that are produced in conjunction with government agencies tend to be confidential or are only released in a sanitized format. Despite these difficulties, such research is crucial to guide the development of the framework.

Greenberg et al., for example, found that a low number of PEP-related STRs are filed, relative to the total number of STRs. They also point to uneven reporting rates within jurisdictions, with a handful of banks submitting the majority of the reports (Greenberg et al., 2010, p. 63). Further research is required to interrogate findings such as these and especially to determine the reasons for such reporting patterns. Is the number of reports relatively low because the number of PEPs is low? Are the reporting rates uneven because some banks have more effective PEP controls than others? Or is the data misleading because FIUs are not comprehensively recording all PEP-related suspicious transactions? Correct answers to questions such as these are required to guide policymakers.

Banks and supervisors are concerned about the ease with which PEPs can hide their beneficial ownership in companies and transactions. The current framework puts the onus on institutions to take reasonable steps to identify and verify the identities of the beneficial owners of their customers. This approach has not proved very effective. Where customers are legal entities with complex structures, it can be very difficult to identity beneficial ownership. Greenberg et al. suggests that the burden should be shared with customers. Customers should be required to declare the identity and details of beneficial owners concerned. If they are not truthful, they can be therefore be charged with fraud (Greenberg et al., 2010, pp. 35–38). While such an approach will add a measure of effectiveness to the controls, it will not impact on those customers who believe that their structures are sufficiently complex to hide the true facts. A complementary approach may be to change laws and procedures that enable persons to obscure their beneficial ownership. There is little justification, for instance, for not ensuring that the names of directors of companies are publicly available at the relevant companies registry and that those whose names are displayed are held liable as directors. Similarly, the names of shareholders of private companies can also be made available. In some countries, shareowners in small corporations, for examples members of South African close corporations, cannot vest ownership rights without registration in a public office. This ensures that ownership of interests in these corporations is generally transparent. It is possible to amend trust laws to achieve similar objectives. Geary suggests the current approach could be strengthened by bringing government agencies that incorporate companies and register trusts into the AML framework, for example by requiring them to undertake customer due diligence measures when new entities or trusts are incorporated (Geary, 2010, pp. 104–105). Research on amendments to laws and procedures to ensure availability of such information and appropriate protection of privacy will be important to support the effectiveness of the system.

Impact assessments are required to determine the effect that the current AML strategy has on anti-corruption, good governance strategies and law enforcement in general. The controls will complicate the movement and spending of corrupt funds and may lead to more corruption being uncovered and successfully prosecuted. On the other hand, even the original 1990 FATF report acknowledged that AML may generate a measure of corruption as some criminals will be incentivized to bribe their way past the AML controls of financial institutions (FATF, 1990, p. 8). They may also change their laundering patterns, for example, by investing more proceeds domestically to avoid the current international focus on foreign PEPs. In addition, good governance strategies may still be under pressure with criminals shifting their focus from corruption to intimidation and acts of violence to reach the same goals.

Current initiatives to return stolen assets deserve to be studied. What are the challenges that are encountered (for example, Pavletic, 2009) and what was the impact on countries that received assets that were stolen? An assessment is also required of the broad framework itself, of the way in which it developed and what global policymakers can learn from it.

An evaluation of the FATF, its role within international law-making and the rise in the stature of the Recommendations is also required. The FATF remains an exclusive club representing a number of influential nations. Its decision-taking processes are largely non-transparent, even to the parliaments and citizens of its member nations. It acts as an expert group but its expertise is generally not backed by verifiable data and its experts are generally anonymous. This powerful group has the brief to combat money laundering and terrorist financing, but it does not have an equally clear brief to protect civil liberties. It is therefore not designed to ensure that an authoritarian government does not abuse its AML compliance to erode the right to financial privacy and other rights of its citizens. Much of the influence of the FATF stems from its association with politically desirable aims such as combating drug trafficking, terrorism and corruption (Reuter and Truman, 2004, pp. 139–170). The anti-corruption measures are strengthened by AML, but the FATF has also gained in stature and influence by embracing anti-corruption. The complex relationships of power and its impact on citizens around the world deserves closer attention.

CONCLUSION

Anti-corruption and AML became firmly intertwined in the past ten years. This chapter highlights some of the important research questions and themes that should be explored. Far more research, especially of a national and regional nature, is required to ensure that the AML system supports anti-corruption efforts in a proportional and effective manner. Both systems are still developing. As a consequence researchers are not only addressing a dynamic and rich subject but also a field where their research can impact by reflecting upon, and informing, the development of international AML and anti-corruption systems.

BIBLIOGRAPHY

Alexander, R. A. (2009), 'Corruption as a financial crime', *The Company Lawyer*, **30**(4), 98–104.

Basel Committee on Banking Supervision (2001), *Customer Due Diligence for Banks*, Basel: Basel Committee on Banking Supervision.

Bester, H., D. Chamberlain, L. de Koker, C. Hougaard, R. Short, A. Smith and R. Walker (2008), *Implementing FATF Standards in Developing Countries and Financial Inclusion: Findings and Guidelines*, Washington, D.C.: The FIRST Initiative, The World Bank.

Byrne, E., A.K. Arnold and F. Nagano (2010), *Building Public Support for Anti-Corruption Efforts*, Washington, D.C.: World Bank.

Chaikin, D. and J.C. Sharman (2007), *APG/FATF Anti-Corruption/AML/CFT Research Paper*, Asia/Pacific Group on Money Laundering and Financial Action Task Force, FATF/PLEN(2007)37, Sydney: Asia and Pacific Group on Money Laundering.

Chaikin, D. and J.C. Sharman (2009), *Corruption and Money Laundering: A Symbiotic Relationship*, New York: Palgrave Macmillan.

Choo, K-K. R. (2008), 'Politically exposed persons (PEPs): risk and mitigation', *Journal of Money Laundering Control*, **11**(4), 371–87.

Choo, K-K. R. (2010), 'Challenges in dealing with politically exposed persons', *Trends & Issues in Crime and Criminal Justice, no.* 386, Canberra: Australian Institute of Criminology.

De Feo, M.A. (1989), 'Depriving international narcotics traffickers and other organized criminals of illegal proceeds and combatting money laundering', *Denver Journal of International Law and Policy*, **18**, 405–415.

De Koker, L. (2009), "Identifying and managing low money laundering risk: perspectives on FATF's risk-based guidance", *Journal of Financial Crime*, **16**(4), 334–52.

De Koker, L. and J. Symington (2010), *Conservative Compliance Behaviour – Drivers of Compliance Responses to AML/CFT Laws in the Financial Services Industry in South Africa*: Bellville: Centre for Financial Regulation and Inclusion; Midrand: FinMark Trust.

Egmont Group and World Bank (2010), *Executive Summary of the Final Report on Survey of FIU Governance Arrangements*, available at http://www.egmontgroup.org/library/egmont-documents, (accessed 5 October 2010).

Financial Action Task Force (1990), *Report*, Paris: Financial Action Task Force.

Financial Action Task Force (2002), *Review of the FATF Forty Recommendations: Consultation Paper*, Paris: Financial Action Task Force.

Financial Action Task Force (2003), *FATF Forty Recommendations*, Paris: Financial Action Task Force.

Financial Services Authority (2001), 'FSA publishes results of money laundering investigation', Press release FDA/PN/029/2001, 8 March 2001, London: Financial Services Authority.

G7 (1989), *Paris Economic Declaration*, Paris: G7.

G7 (1990), *Houston Economic Declaration*, Houston: G7.

Geary, J.M. (2010), 'PEPs – let's get serious', *Journal of Money Laundering Control*, **13**(4), 103–108.

Gilligan, G. (2009), 'PEEPing at PEPs', *Journal of Financial Crime*, **16**(2), 137–43.

Gilmore, W.C. (2004), *Dirty Money: The Evolution of International Measures to Counter Money Laundering and the Financing of Terrorism*, 3rd edition, Strasbourg: Council of Europe Publishing.

Global Witness (2009), *Undue Diligence: How Banks Do Business with Corrupt Regimes*, London: Global Witness.

Gordon, R.K. (2009), 'Laundering the proceeds of public sector corruption', *Case Legal Studies*, Research 09–10, available at SSRN: http://ssrn.com/abstract=1371711 (accessed 5 October 2010).

Goredema, C. and J. Madzima (2009), *An Assessment of the Links Between Corruption and*

the Implementation of Anti-Money Laundering Strategies and Measures in the ESAAMLG Region, Nairobi: ESAAMLG.
Greenberg, T.S., L. Gray, D. Schantz, C. Gardner and M. Latham (2010), *Politically Exposed Persons: A Guide on Preventive Measures for the Banking Sector*, Washington, D.C.: The World Bank.
Johnson, J. (2008), 'Third round FATF mutual evaluations indicate declining compliance', *Journal of Money Laundering Control*, **11**(1), 47–66.
Levi, M., M. Dakolias and T.S. Greenberg (2007), 'Money laundering and corruption', in J.E. Campos and S. Pradhan (eds), *The Many Faces of Corruption – Tracking Vulnerabilities at the Sector Level*, Washington, D.C.: The World Bank, 389–426.
Levi, M. (2010), 'The impact of anti-money laundering measures within developing countries against the proceeds of crime', unpublished paper.
Naylor, R.T. (2004), *Wages of Crime: Black Markets, Illegal Finance and the Underworld Economy*, New York: Cornell University Press.
Passas, N. (2006), 'Fighting terror with error: the counter-productive regulation of informal value transfers', *Crime Law and Social Change*, **45**(4–5), 315–36.
Pavletic, I. (2009), 'The political economy of asset recovery processes', *Working Paper Series*, no. 7, Basel: International Centre for Asset Recovery, Basel Institute of Governance.
Pieth, M. (1999), 'The harmonization of law against economic crime', *European Journal of Law Reform*, **1**(4) 527–45.
Pieth, M. and G. Ailofi (2003), 'The private sector becomes active: the Wolfsberg process', *Journal of Financial Crime* **10**(4) 359–65.
Reuter, P. and E. Truman (2004), *Chasing Dirty Money: The Fight against Money Laundering*, Washington, D.C.: Institute for International Economics.
Rider, B.A.K. (1993), 'The practical and legal aspects of interdicting the flow of dirty money', *Journal of Financial Crime*, **3**(3) 234–53.
Shams, H. (2001), 'The fight against extra-territorial corruption and the use of money laundering control', *NAFTA: Law and Business Review of the Americas*, no.85, 85–133.
Tang, J. and L. Ai (2010), 'Combating money laundering in transition countries: the inherent limitations and practical issues', *Journal of Money Laundering Control*, **13**(3) 215–225.
The Society for Advanced Legal Studies (Anti-corruption Working Group) (2000), *Banking on Corruption: The Legal Responsibilities of Those Who Handle the Proceeds of Corruption*, London: The Society of Advanced Legal Studies.
United Nations Office on Drugs and Crime and the World Bank (2009), *Stolen Asset Recovery: Towards a Global Architecture for Asset Recovery*, Policy Note, Washington, D.C.: The World Bank.
United States Senate Permanent Subcommittee on Investigations (Committee on Governmental Affairs) (1999), *Private Banking and Money Laundering: A Case Study of Opportunities and Vulnerabilities*, Senate Hearing 106–428, November 9 and 10, Washington D.C.: U.S. Government Printing Office.
United States Senate Permanent Subcommittee on Investigations (Committee on Homeland Security and Governmental Affairs) (2010), *Keeping Foreign Corruption out of the United States: Four Case Histories*, Majority and Minority Staff Report, Washington D.C.: Permanent Subcommittee on Investigations.
Villa, J.K. (1988), 'A critical view of Bank Secrecy Act enforcement and the money laundering statutes', *Catholic University Law Review*, No. 37, 489–509.
Wolfsberg Group (2008), 'Wolfsberg frequently asked questions (FAQs) on politically exposed persons ('PEPs')", available at www.wolfsberg-principles.com/pdf/PEP-FAQ-052008.pdf (accessed on 5 October 2010).
World-Check (2008), '"Politically exposed person": refining the PEP definition (edition II)', available at http://www.worldcheck.com/media/d/content_whitepaper_reference/Refining_the_PEP_Definition_-_EditionII.pdf (accessed on 5 October 2010).

19 Recovering corruptly obtained assets

Larissa Gray

INTRODUCTION

Corruption is a global epidemic. Its impact can be particularly devastating on developing countries, which lose between $20 to $40 billion every year through corrupt acts such as bribery and embezzlement (Baker, 2005 cited in UNODC and The World Bank, 2007, p. 10). Assets stolen by corrupt officials are often laundered through the global financial system and find safe haven in the world's financial centres. The scale of the problem is vast and solutions are complicated by the diverse range of stakeholders involved, including law enforcement and justice officials in developing countries and financial centres, banks, private companies, development organizations, civil society and the media.

Over the past decade, international bodies have recognized that preventing and detecting the theft of public assets, and supporting attempts to recover them, is an integral part of broader development efforts to improve governance and fight corruption and an important contribution to the fight against poverty. A number of successful high-profile cases with creative international co-operation have demonstrated that asset recovery *is* possible. However, the recovery of these assets from foreign jurisdictions is estimated at only $5 billion over the past 15 years (Stolen Asset Recovery Initiative, 2009, p. 4).

The huge gap between even the lowest estimates of assets stolen and those repatriated demonstrates that a more visible, tangible progress in forcefully prosecuting corruption cases, and systematic recovery of proceeds of corruption is needed. This chapter summarizes the international commitments to date, describes the process of asset recovery, and presents the necessary legal framework for asset recovery. It will also attempt to highlight some of the barriers to the recovery of stolen assets and propose some of the critical elements of successful asset recovery efforts. See Box 19.1 for defining terms.

INTERNATIONAL COMMITMENTS

Over the past few decades, the international community has stressed the international dimensions of corruption and recognized the inadequacy of

BOX 19.1 DEFINING TERMS

Stolen assets include any money, property or other assets derived from or obtained, directly or indirectly, through the commission of corruption offences by public officials. Corruption encompasses the offences identified under the United Nations Convention against Corruption (UNCAC) such as: bribery of public officials; bribery of foreign public officials; embezzlement, misappropriation or other diversion of property by a public official; trading in influence; abuse of functions; illicit enrichment; bribery in the private sector; embezzlement of property in the private sector; abetting an accomplice. It involves participation in any capacity (e.g., as an accomplice, assistant or instigator), attempts and preparations for any such offences.

Asset recovery is the process by which stolen assets are recovered and returned to those harmed by corruption, whether a government, individual victims, or duly designated third parties.

controls to effectively detect and deter these illicit flows. As a result, the international community is progressively focusing on the associated risks that financial centres could serve as safe havens for the stolen assets of corrupt leaders. These concerns facilitated the negotiation of international agreements establishing a common international framework and standard for anti-corruption activities. Building on the Inter-American Convention against Corruption (1996) and the OECD Convention on Combating Bribery of Foreign Public Officials in International Business Transactions (1997), the United Nations Convention against Corruption (UNCAC 2003) was the first global treaty to address asset recovery as a fundamental principle.

UNCAC provides a universal, robust and comprehensive international framework for asset recovery. Chapter V of the Convention provides this framework for the return of stolen assets, requiring States Parties to take measures to prevent and detect the proceeds of corruption by implementing systems to identify and monitor politically exposed persons (PEPs) – senior government officials and their family members and close associates – and by establishing asset and income disclosure requirements for public officials (UNCAC, art. 52). UNCAC also requires States Parties to restrain, seize, confiscate and return stolen assets using a variety of mechanisms, such as:

- measures for the prevention and detection of the proceeds of crime, art. 52 of the UNCAC;
- direct enforcement of freezing or confiscation orders made by the court of another State Party (UNCAC, art. 54(1)(a) and 54(2)(a));
- non-conviction based asset (NCB) confiscation, particularly in cases of death, flight or absence of the offender or in other cases (UNCAC art. 54(1)(c));
- civil actions initiated by another State Party, allowing them to recover the proceeds as plaintiff (UNCAC, art. 53);
- confiscation of property of a foreign origin by adjudication of an offence of money laundering or other offences (UNCAC, art. 54(1)(b) and 54(2)(b));
- court orders of compensation or damages to another State Party and recognition by courts of another State Party's claim as a legitimate owner of assets acquired through corruption (UNCAC, art. 53(b) and (c));
- spontaneous disclosure of information to another State Party without prior request (UNCAC, art. 56); and
- international co-operation and asset return (UNCAC, art. 55 and 57).

In addition to this anti-corruption framework, the recovery of the proceeds of corruption has also been addressed in international agreements and standards dealing with anti-money laundering and law enforcement issues. Many of these instruments have specific provisions for the restraint, confiscation and return of the proceeds of corruption, such as the Financial Action Task Force 40+9 Recommendations and the United Nations Convention against Transnational Organized Crime.

Recent statements by the international community demonstrate continued commitment to implementation and the underlying principles (see Box 19.2).

In support of these international efforts to end safe havens for corrupt funds, the World Bank Group and the United Nations Office on Drugs and Crime launched the Stolen Asset Recovery Initiative (StAR) in 2007. StAR works with developing countries and financial centres to prevent the laundering of the proceeds of corruption and to facilitate more systematic and timely return of stolen assets.[1] StAR focuses on lowering the barriers to asset recovery through sharing of knowledge (see Box 19.3) and advocacy in global forums; building national capacity for asset recovery; and preparatory assistance in the recovery of assets. Preparatory assistance is aimed at collecting and sharing information to encourage the progress of a country's specific asset recovery efforts.

BOX 19.2 INTERNATIONAL SUPPORT FOR ASSET RECOVERY

'Donors will take steps . . . to track, freeze, and recover illegally acquired assets.' Accra Agenda for Action, September 2008.

'Additional measures should be implemented to prevent the transfer abroad of stolen assets and to assist in their recovery and return . . . we note the efforts of . . . the Stolen Asset Recovery Initiative and other relevant initiatives'. Conference on Financing for Development, Doha, December 2008.

'As we increase the flow of capital to developing countries, we also need to prevent its illicit outflow. We will work with the World Bank's Stolen Assets Recovery (StAR) program to secure the return of stolen assets to developing countries, and support other efforts to stem illicit outflows. We ask the FATF to help detect and deter the proceeds of corruption by prioritizing work to strengthen standards on customer due diligence, beneficial ownership and transparency. . . . We call for the adoption and enforcement of laws against transnational bribery, such as the OECD Anti-Bribery Convention, and the ratification by the G-20 of the UN Convention against Corruption (UNCAC) and the adoption during the third Conference of the Parties in Doha of an effective, transparent, and inclusive mechanism for the review of its implementation.' Leaders' Statement, The G20 Pittsburgh Summit, September 24–25, 2009.

'To support the recovery of proceeds of corruption stowed abroad, all G20 countries will adopt measures related to, inter alia, preventing and detecting transfers of proceeds of crime; measures for direct recovery of property; mechanisms for recovery of property through international cooperation in asset tracing, freezing and confiscation; measures for special cooperation in voluntary disclosure; and return and dispose of assets as enshrined in Chapter V of the UNCAC. To this end, G20 countries will by the time of the 2011 Summit in France, establish clear and effective channels for mutual legal assistance, and other forms of international cooperation, on corruption and asset recovery, in particular, if they have not done so already, designate an appropriate authority responsible for international mutual legal assistance requests relating to corruption and asset recovery; establish points of contact for law enforcement and international cooperation on corruption cases; and develop specialized expertise for asset recovery in an appropriate agency.' Leaders' Declaration, G20 Seoul Summit, November 11–12, 2010, Annex III – Anti-Corruption Action Plan.

BOX 19.3 THE STOLEN ASSET RECOVERY INITIATIVE (STAR)

StAR generates knowledge on the legal and technical tools used to recover the proceeds of corruption, promoting the sharing of global best practices. Publications are available at www.worldbank.org/star and include:

- *Asset Recovery Handbook: A Guide for Practitioners*
- *Politically Exposed Persons: Preventive Measures for the Banking Sector*
- *Towards a Global Architecture for Asset Recovery*
- *Income and Asset Declarations: Tools and Trade-offs*
- *Stolen Asset Recovery: A Good Practices Guide to Non-Conviction Based Asset Forfeiture*
- *Management of Returned Assets: Policy Considerations*
- Upcoming: *Lowering the Barriers to Asset Recovery; Misuse of Corporate Vehicles, Illicit Enrichment Study, Asset Recovery Watch Database.*

THE LEGAL FRAMEWORK

There are a number of legal actions for pursuing asset recovery, including criminal or non-conviction-based (NCB) confiscation, a private civil action, or a request that authorities in another jurisdiction pursue criminal or NCB confiscation.[2] Where assets have been transferred to foreign jurisdictions, international co-operation will be essential for all legal actions to succeed (see Box 19.4). These avenues are outlined below, with their advantages and disadvantages. The availability of these various actions is important because experience has demonstrated that multiple avenues are necessary (Brun, Gray, Scott, Stephenson 2011, 19). While a criminal *conviction* is always important to combat and deter corruption, criminal

BOX 19.4 TYPES OF INTERNATIONAL CO-OPERATION

The primary modes of international cooperation are 'informal assistance'[3] and mutual legal assistance (MLA) requests.

Informal assistance is used to gather *information* and *intelligence* to assist in the investigation and to align strategies and forthcoming procedures for recovery of assets (Brun, Gray, Scott, Stephenson, 2011, p. 128). Types of assistance may include the gathering of publicly available information, asset tracing, or emergency freezing of assets. Information may be shared on request or spontaneously.[4] The most common channels for informal assistance are between counterpart law enforcement authorities, prosecutors, investigating magistrates or regulatory authorities.

An **MLA request** is used to gather admissible or formal *evidence*, obtain provisional measures, and seek enforcement of domestic orders in a foreign jurisdiction. It is typically submitted in writing and must adhere to specified procedures, protocols, and conditions set out in multilateral or bilateral agreements or domestic legislation. In investigation stages, such requests can be used to gather evidence (for example, bank account documents and formal witness statements) and freeze assets. MLA requests are required for the enforcement of confiscation orders.

confiscation is not always the best option for asset recovery. Some authorities will use a combination of the avenues to pursue confiscation (see Box 19.5). Alternatively, the presence of obstacles may warrant consideration of another legal avenue. In cases involving multiple jurisdictions, a number of different avenues may be pursued – for example, domestic confiscation followed by an MLA request for enforcement in one jurisdiction and private civil recovery in another.

Criminal Prosecution and Confiscation

When authorities seeking to recover stolen assets decide to pursue a criminal case, criminal confiscation is a possible means of redress (other means of asset recovery include fines or compensation ordered after criminal trial or guilty plea). Practitioners must gather evidence, trace and secure assets, conduct a prosecution against an individual or legal entity, and obtain a conviction. After obtaining a conviction following a trial or guilty plea,

BOX 19.5 USE OF LEGAL AVENUES IN PRACTICE

Vladimiro Montesinos and his associates (Peru): In this case against Peru's chief of intelligence, over $250 million was recovered from Switzerland, the United States and from local banks in Peru. For the assets in Switzerland, the Peruvian authorities conducted domestic prosecutions (including guilty pleas) and then sought recovery of the assets through MLA requests and waivers signed by the defendants authorizing the foreign banks to transfer their assets to the Peruvian Government. Assets in the United States were recovered through NCB confiscation proceedings in California and Florida and the funds repatriated to Peru for the investment into human rights and anticorruption efforts.

Diepreye Alamieyeseigha (Nigeria): A total of $17.7 million was recovered from South Africa and the United Kingdom in this case against the former governor of Bayelsa State. Nigerian authorities brought a civil action in the United Kingdom and simultaneously pursued domestic criminal proceedings. Through the civil proceedings, they obtained evidence that had been gathered in investigations of the London Metropolitan Police and used this to obtain a worldwide restraint order over assets in Cyprus, Denmark, and the United Kingdom. Alamieyeseigha eventually pleaded guilty in Nigeria and summary judgement was obtained against him in the United Kingdom, leading to the return of the restrained assets. In South Africa, assets were recovered through NCB confiscation.

confiscation can be ordered by the court. In some jurisdictions, particularly common law jurisdictions, the standard of proof for confiscation will be lower than the standard required for obtaining the conviction. For example, 'beyond a reasonable doubt' will be required for a conviction and 'balance of probabilities' for confiscation. Other jurisdictions apply the same standard to both confiscation and conviction. International co-operation, including informal assistance and MLA requests, will be used throughout the process to trace and secure assets in foreign jurisdictions, as well as to enforce the final order of confiscation.

A benefit of criminal prosecution and confiscation is the societal recognition of the criminal nature of corruption and the accountability of the perpetrator. Further, penalties of imprisonment, fines, and confiscation serve to deter future offenders. In addition, criminal investigations generally have the most aggressive means of gathering information, including intelligence and information from law enforcement sources, financial intelligence from the financial intelligence unit (FIU) and through the Egmont Group, use of provisional measures and coercive investigative techniques (such as searches, electronic surveillance, examination of financial records or access to documents held by third parties), as well as grand juries or other means of compelling testimony or evidence. And in most jurisdictions, MLA is provided only in the context of criminal investigations. On the other hand, significant barriers may exist to obtaining a criminal conviction and confiscation, such as insufficient evidence, lack of capacity or political will, or it may be impossible to obtain a conviction by reason of death, flight or immunity. Furthermore, the conduct giving rise to the request may not be a crime in the jurisdiction where the relief is being sought (Brun et al., 2011, p. 11).

Non-conviction-based Confiscation

Another type of confiscation gaining traction throughout the world is non-conviction based (NCB) confiscation (confiscation without a conviction).[5] This approach shares at least one common objective with criminal confiscation, namely the recovery and return of the proceeds and instrumentalities of crime. Likewise, deterrence and depriving corrupt officials of their ill-gotten gains are other societal equities realized by NCB confiscation (Greenberg, Samuel, Grant and Gray, 2009, p. 13).

NCB confiscation differs in the procedure used to confiscate the assets. A criminal confiscation requires a criminal trial and conviction, whereas NCB confiscation does not. NCB confiscation is often a separate proceeding that considers whether the assets in question are the proceeds or an instrumentality of crime. In many jurisdictions, confiscation can be established on a lower standard of proof (for example, the 'balance of probabilities' or 'preponderance of the evidence' standard) which helps to ease the burden on the authorities. Other jurisdictions, mainly civil law jurisdictions, will require a higher standard of proof, specifically the same standard of proof required to obtain a criminal conviction. And similar to criminal confiscation, informal assistance, MLA, or other forms of international co-operation will be needed to enforce orders in foreign jurisdictions.

NCB confiscation is useful in a variety of contexts, particularly when criminal confiscation is impossible or unavailable, such as when the offender has died, fled the jurisdiction, or is immune from prosecution; an asset is found and the owner is unknown; or there is insufficient evidence to seek a criminal conviction, or criminal proceedings have resulted in an acquittal (applies in jurisdictions that apply a lower standard of proof). However, because NCB confiscation is not available in all jurisdictions, practitioners may have difficulty obtaining MLA to assist with investigations and enforce NCB confiscation orders (Brun et al., 2011, pp. 156–57).

Private Civil Action

Authorities seeking to recover stolen assets have the option of initiating proceedings in domestic or foreign civil courts to secure and recover the assets, and to seek damages based on torts, breach of contract, or illicit enrichment.[6] The courts of the foreign jurisdiction may be competent if a defendant is a person (individual or business entity) living or incorporated in the jurisdiction (personal jurisdiction), if the assets are within or have transited the jurisdiction (subject matter jurisdiction), or if an act of corruption or money laundering was committed within the jurisdiction. As a private litigant, the authorities seeking redress can hire lawyers to explore the potential claims and remedies. The plaintiff usually has the option to petition the court for a variety of orders against defendants and third parties, such as orders to freeze or seize assets, to disclose information on the source of assets and relevant documents, or to prevent the deterioration of the petitioner's assets or legal interests (or both).

The principal disadvantage of litigating in a foreign jurisdiction is the cost of tracing assets and legal fees entailed in obtaining relevant court orders. In addition, civil cases can be stretched out over years and private investigators do not typically have the range of investigative tools or access to intelligence that is available to law enforcement. On the other hand, the litigant has more control in pursuing civil proceedings and assets in the hands of third parties, and may have the advantage of a lower standard of proof, as civil cases are often decided on a lower standard of proof (for example, in common law jurisdictions, civil cases are usually decided on a balance of probabilities or preponderance of the evidence standard). In cases which cross borders, a civil action affords a jurisdiction seeking to recover assets, greater control of the process compared to criminal proceedings in foreign jurisdictions and may offer a more expedient route than waiting for enforcement action by the foreign jurisdiction (Brun et al., 2011, p. 159).

Actions Initiated by Foreign Jurisdictions

Authorities seeking to recover stolen assets may seek to support a criminal or NCB confiscation proceeding which has been initiated in another jurisdiction against the corrupt official, associates or identified assets. At the conclusion of the proceedings, the state or government may be able to obtain a portion of the recovered assets through orders of the foreign courts or pursuant to legislation or agreements. This will require that the foreign authority has jurisdiction, the capacity to prosecute and confiscate and, most importantly, be willing to share the proceeds. The initiation of an action may occur after the jurisdiction harmed by corruption files a complaint or shares incriminating evidence with the foreign authority. Alternatively, a foreign authority may decide independently to initiate proceedings for money laundering or foreign bribery activities undertaken within its national territory.[7]

In some civil law jurisdictions, it may also be possible for the victim – including a state or government that has been harmed by corruption offences – to participate in foreign proceedings as a private prosecutor or as a civil party to the proceedings. As a party to the proceedings, the victim will have access to disclosure and will be able to participate in the examination of witnesses and make submissions before the court.

This avenue is a possible option if the jurisdiction seeking redress does not have an adequate legal basis, capacity or evidence to pursue an international investigation on its own. Moreover, if the limitation period rules out the prosecution of the initial corruption charges, it may still be possible to investigate offences of money laundering or possession of stolen assets in other jurisdictions. On the other hand, the jurisdiction that has been harmed by corruption offences does not have control over the proceedings and success depends to a large extent on the priorities of the foreign authorities. In addition, unless the return of the assets is ordered by the court, it will be dependent on asset-sharing agreements or the ability of the authorities to return the assets on a discretionary basis (Brun et al., 2011, p. 14).

GENERAL PROCESS FOR ASSET RECOVERY

Successful asset recovery requires a comprehensive plan of action that incorporates a number of important steps and considerations. A plan or strategy will need to involve the gathering and assessment of the facts to understand the case; assembling a team; identifying key allies; communicating with foreign practitioners; grappling with the legal, practical, and operational challenges; and ensuring effective case management (Brun et al., 2011, p. 19). Each aspect will help determine the most appropriate legal avenue (as outlined above) for recovering assets.

Whatever legal avenue is selected, the fundamental process for recovery

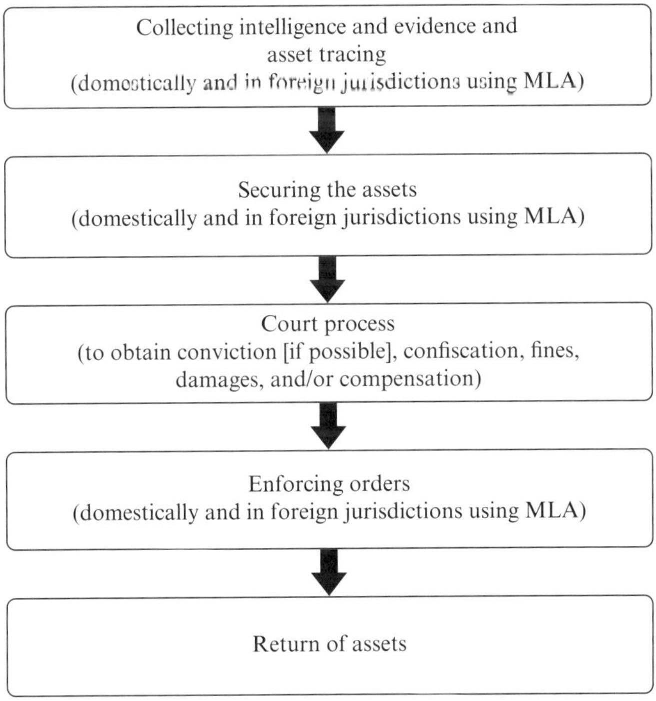

Source: Reproduced from Brun, Gray, Scott and Stephenson (2011, p. 6).

Figure 19.1 Process for recovery of stolen assets

of assets is generally the same (see Figure 19.1). In the initial phases, evidence is gathered, assets are traced, and proceeds and instrumentalities subject to confiscation are secured to avoid dissipation, movement, or destruction. Court proceedings will take place to recover the assets and may involve criminal or NCB confiscation, or private civil actions. Where enforcement of the court order results in the confiscated assets being transferred to the general treasury or confiscation fund of the requested jurisdiction (as opposed to the court ordering the direct return of stolen assets to victims, including the foreign jurisdiction), another mechanism will be needed to arrange for the return of the assets, such as UNCAC or another international convention, domestic legislation, mutual legal assistance treaties or special agreements (for example, asset sharing agreements).

Where assets have been transferred to foreign jurisdictions, international co-operation will be essential in all stages. It will be required for the gathering of evidence, the implementation of provisional measures, and the eventual confiscation of the proceeds and instrumentalities of corruption. And once the assets are confiscated, co-operation is critical for the return of the stolen assets. International co-operation is a two-way street: not only will the jurisdiction that has been victimized by corruption be requesting assistance from the financial centre where the assets are hidden, but it will likely need to provide information or evidence to this other jurisdiction to obtain the most effective recovery of assets.

BARRIERS IN ASSET RECOVERY

Despite these international commitments and various legal options for recovery of assets, a number of barriers continue to stymie the successful recovery of assets. Political will is, and will remain, the cornerstone of success for any asset recovery regime. In a study by StAR on the barriers to assets recovery, the 'lack of political will' is cited as a key impediment to the recovery of stolen assets (Stephenson et al. (in press)). The study found this to be vague terminology and an easy shortcut to avoid confronting the underlying issues. As such, the study defines 'political will' to mean a comprehensive, sustained and concerted policy to identify asset recovery as a priority and the alignment of necessary objectives, tools, and resources.

There are also legal barriers inhibiting asset recovery. Many jurisdictions lack NCB confiscation procedures, investigative tools to quickly trace assets, or are unable to enforce a foreign NCB order (or both).[8] Criminal confiscation systems may be burdened by short limitation periods, broad immunity provisions, and narrow jurisdiction. Efforts can be further complicated as the corrupt official is likely to use all avenues to delay the process through procedural or constitutional applications. In cases that require international co-operation, there are often onerous requirements to the provision of MLA which effectively disrupt and impede recovery efforts, such as obligations to disclose the MLA request to the asset holder in tracing or freezing requests (as opposed to *ex parte* proceedings that exist in many jurisdictions), strict interpretations of dual criminality, and burdensome procedural and evidentiary laws (for example, requiring that charges be instigated prior to the granting of a freezing order) (Stephenson et al. (in press)).

Even with a sound legal framework, asset recovery is blocked by operational barriers – impediments involving processes and communication between parties. Communication issues dominate: difficulties in identifying focal points or the designated competent authority to make MLA requests, challenges in maintaining contacts and co-ordinating asset recovery actions, delays in processing and responding to MLA requests, and deficiencies in the drafting of the requests all impede the provision of assistance (Stephenson et al. (in press)). Other important operational barriers include difficulties in identifying bank accounts and failure to manage and preserve assets that have been restrained during the recovery process before a formal confiscation occurs.

CRITICAL ELEMENTS OF SUCCESSFUL ASSET RECOVERY EFFORTS

There are many important elements needed to overcome these barriers and succeed in asset recovery efforts. A few of the most critical elements are outlined below.

1. Asset Recovery is a Priority

As indicated above, many jurisdictions do not sufficiently prioritize asset recovery cases or devote sufficient resources to asset recovery, resulting in a lack of competent practitioners and successful cases. Recovery efforts have been most successful when jurisdictions develop and implement a transparent and comprehensive policy for stolen asset recovery, a policy which communicates the significance of asset recovery as an integral part of broader anti-corruption efforts, assigns the relevant authorities with the appropriate resources and sufficient expertise to trace, seize and confiscate stolen assets, and effectively supports the relevant authorities in granting the widest range of international assistance (Stephenson et al. (in press)).

Some jurisdictions have established specialized investigative or prosecution teams as part of policy implementation. The United Kingdom created an International Corruption Group in the Metropolitan Police Service and City of London Police (City of London Police 2010) to strengthen capacity to investigate and prosecute corruption occurring between developed and developing countries and return stolen assets; the United States launched the Kleptocracy Initiative under the leadership of the Asset Forfeiture and Money Laundering Section (United States Department of Justice, 2010) to recover assets on behalf of countries victimized by high-level corruption; and Switzerland has launched several initiatives to promote internationally co-ordinated action to combat grand corruption (Federal Department of Foreign Affairs (Switzerland), 2011). Such units target foreign high-level leaders engaged in corruption through domestic prosecutions for money laundering and by providing assistance to the foreign jurisdiction, such as technical and capacity support in asset tracing. Similarly, the European Union countries are establishing Asset

Recovery Offices to promote co-operation in asset tracing and identification pursuant to Council Decision 2007/845/JHA (6 December, 2007).

Other jurisdictions have introduced legislation to improve the effectiveness of asset recovery efforts. During the case against Vladmiro Montesinos, chief of Peru's intelligence service, Peru adopted Law 27.738 which permitted guilty plea agreements in organized crime investigations (guilty pleas did not exist in Peru). This allowed the Government to secure convictions, avoid years of litigation, and recover over $175 million in assets (Brun et al., 2011, p. 28). Switzerland adopted the Act on Restitution of Illicit Assets (adopted by Parliament in 2010 and entered into force on 1 February 2011) to assist in the context of failed states and has been used to freeze assets of ex-dictator Jean-Claude Duvalier of Haiti (Federal Department of Foreign Affairs (Switzerland) 2011).

2. A Sufficient Legal Framework for Confiscation, Including Capacity to Rapidly Trace and Restrain Stolen Assets

As indicated above, some confiscation regimes do not have an adequate legal framework for confiscation and recovery. There may be delays in executing a tracing or restraint request, which results in the transfer or dissipation of stolen assets. MLA laws may not be sufficiently agile to allow prompt asset tracing and freezing, especially in common law countries that require a judicial order to trace or temporarily freeze assets. Asset tracing is further thwarted by banking secrecy laws and lack of publicly available property registries, as well as insufficient mechanisms for filing complaints and protecting witnesses or whistleblowers (Stephenson et al. (in press) and Stolen Asset Recovery Initiative 2010, p. 8). Finally, many jurisdictions are not able to enforce confiscation orders from foreign jurisdictions.

To overcome these problems, jurisdictions have enacted legislation or implemented policies to enable the rapid tracing and restraint of stolen assets and confiscation. Examples of legislation and policies include measures that:

- enable the rapid restraint of assets, such as temporary administrative restraint, automatic restraint upon the filing of charges or an arrest, or restraint by investigating magistrates or prosecutors;
- limit and precisely define the types of information that are protected by banking secrecy;
- implement and maintain publicly available registries (company, land, bank account) that are accessible to foreign authorities through informal or administrative channels;

- provide a system for reporting of corruption, including protection to witnesses and whistleblowers;
- adopt NCB confiscation, particularly in cases of death, flight, or absence, and allow for enforcement of foreign NCB confiscation orders;
- allow for the lowering standard of proof for confiscation in cases involving corruption offenses and shifting of the burden of proof when the prosecution has provided credible evidence that assets have no legitimate source; and
- permit substitute- or equivalent-value restraint and confiscation of legitimate assets of the same value as the stolen assets.

3. Financial Sector Due Diligence

Progress has been made in putting in place anti-money laundering regimes that meet international standards and ultimately help protect the financial system against the proceeds of corruption. Such standards require that financial institutions conduct customer due diligence measures, identify and monitor PEPs, and determine the beneficial owner (Financial Action Task Force, 2003, Recommendations 5 and 6). However, compliance with standards requiring the detection and enhanced ongoing monitoring of PEPs remains low (Greenberg, et al., 2010, pp. 7, 13, 14). Recent case studies of the United States Senate Permanent Subcommittee on Investigations (2010) also reveal how PEPs have used bankers, lawyers, real estate and escrow agents, and lobbyists to circumvent anti-money laundering and anti-corruption safeguards.

The financial sector must take action to comply with these international standards and supervisory authorities will need to ensure that standards are enforced. Potential tools adopted by financial institutions to assist in implementation include written declarations of beneficial ownership, use of asset and income disclosure systems to identify PEPs and to assist with monitoring, and periodic reviews of PEP customers by senior management (Greenberg, et al. 2010, pp. xv–xviii).[9]

4. Development of Channels for Informal Assistance and MLA

Informal assistance and MLA is often inhibited or delayed due to mistrust between jurisdictions, poor communication, and a lack of information about the process – difficulties which are augmented when jurisdictions have significantly different legal, political and judicial systems (for example, civil law vs. common law) (Stephenson et al. (in press)). Without trust, jurisdictions are hesitant to share intelligence data; to assist in gathering evidence; or to freeze, seize, confiscate, or repatriate assets. Similarly, insufficient information about informal assistance, MLA requirements and the status of requests results in poor-quality requests. Measures to cultivate trust among counterparts, improve communication and facilitate the sharing of information have included:

- creation of resource positions in foreign regions to facilitate international co-operation, such as liaison magistrates or law enforcement attachés;
- identification of primary and secondary focal points within the central authority and other relevant competent authorities;
- adoption of legislation allowing for the spontaneous sharing of information with another jurisdiction;
- implementation of programmes (by financial centres) to build capacity, provide technical support, mentor and provide other assistance to developing countries, including assistance with the drafting of MLA requests;
- participation in practitioner networks, including regional asset recovery networks, and relevant international and bilateral meetings and forums;
- publishing comprehensive information on informal assistance and MLA channels – preferably on a government Web site – such as MLA laws, explanatory guidelines, sample requests for assistance, and permitted informal assistance; and
- systems for informing on the status of a request or reasons for rejection.

5. Engagement of Informal Assistance Channels before Transmitting an MLA Request

Many practitioners immediately resort to drafting an MLA request when they determine that international co-operation is required. However, some important information can be obtained more quickly and with fewer formalities through direct contact with counterpart law enforcement agencies, financial intelligence units, prosecutors, or investigating magistrates, or from liaison magistrates or law enforcement attachés posted abroad (Brun et al., 2011, p. 124).[10] Such assistance may lead to a more rapid identification of assets; confirm the assistance needed; and, even more importantly, build trust and provide the proper foundation for an MLA request (including assistance with the drafting of requests). These contacts also offer an opportunity to learn about the procedures and system of the foreign jurisdiction and to assess strategic options. In larger cases, a face-to-face meeting among counterparts has facilitated the exchange of information, for example in cases in Peru and Brazil (Brun et al., 2011, p. 123).

CONCLUSIONS

Recent crises in several Middle Eastern countries have focused attention on both the vast amount of wealth that can be misappropriated by corrupt leaders and their families and the high-profile spending of family members in foreign jurisdictions and financial centres. Fortunately, a number of countries have responded, freezing assets held by these leaders and their family members. Yet further action is required to create an effective, global anti-corruption regime that prevents the laundering of stolen assets in the global financial system and detects and recovers the proceeds of corruption for developing countries. This chapter has described some of these critical elements for success in asset recovery. Fulfilling these elements requires participation of all stakeholders, including law enforcement and justice officials in developing countries and financial centres, banks, private companies, development organizations, civil society and the media. It demands innovative solutions and flexibility to overcome various barriers and obstacles. And it needs a proactive approach to developing necessary legislation, initiating cases, and commencing international co-operation. Conditions are set for progress in tackling the proceeds of corruption and returning stolen assets to developing countries. It is hoped the countries will take the necessary steps to make this happen.

NOTES

1. For more information on StAR visit: www.worldbank.org/star
2. Other legal avenues for recovery include administrative confiscation, abandonment, taxation of illicit profits and fines or compensation ordered in a criminal trial or guilty plea. For more information on these various avenues see Brun et al. (2011, pp. 14–15).
3. For the purposes of this chapter, 'informal assistance' is used to include any type of assistance that does not require a *formal* MLA request. Legislation permitting this informal, practitioner-to-practitioner assistance may be outlined in MLA legislation and may involve 'formal' authorities, agencies or administrations.
4. Spontaneous disclosures of information is a proactive form of assistance used by competent authorities and FIUs to alert a foreign jurisdiction to an ongoing investigation in the disclosing jurisdiction and indicates that existing evidence could be of interest. The receiving jurisdiction may use the information to further its own investigation and eventually submit an MLA request.
5. Jurisdictions include Anguilla, Antigua and Barbuda, Australia, some of the provinces of Canada (Alberta, British Columbia, Manitoba, Ontario, Quebec, Saskatchewan), Colombia, Costa Rica, Fiji, Guernsey, Ireland, Isle of Man, Israel, Jersey, Liechtenstein, New Zealand, the Philippines, Slovenia, Switzerland, Thailand, South Africa, the

United States, the United Kingdom and Zambia. International conventions and multilateral agreements have urged countries to consider NCB Confiscation: See UNCAC, Article 53(1)(c) and Recommendation 3 of the FATF 40+9 Recommendations.

6. UNCAC, Article 53(a) calls on States Parties to permit another State Party to initiate a civil action in domestic courts.
7. The foreign authority's attempt to freeze or confiscate assets suspected to be proceeds of corruption may trigger the involvement of the country harmed by corruption, in which case the process of asset recovery may be successful.
8. Some jurisdictions will enforce foreign NCB confiscation orders even in the absence of a domestic NCB confiscation system, including Hong Kong SAR, China, Jersey and EU members. In some EU countries, enforcement of foreign NCB confiscation orders is limited to other EU members.
9. These tools have also been recommended by the United States Senate Permanent Subcommittee on Investigations (2010).
10. Informal networks or contacts are often cleared with the central authority in advance to ensure that proper protocols and confidentiality agreements are followed.

REFERENCES

Brun, J.P., L. Gray, C. Scott and K.M. Stephenson (2011), *Asset Recovery Handbook: A Guide for Practitioners*, Washington, DC: The World Bank, available at http://www1.worldbank.org/publicsector/star_site/publications/ar_handbook.html (Accessed 7 March 2011).

City of London Police (2010), *Department for International Development (DfID)*, available at http://www.cityoflondon.police.uk/CityPolice/Departments/ECD/anticorruptionunit/DfID.htm (Accessed 7 March 2011).

Federal Department of Foreign Affairs (Switzerland) (2011), *Dictators' Assets (potentate funds)*, available at http://www.eda.admin.ch/eda/en/home/topics/finec/intcr/poexp.html#ContentPar_0003 (Accessed 7 March 2011).

Financial Action Task Force (2003), *The Forty Recommendations*, Paris: Financial Action Task Force.

Greenberg, T.S., L. Gray, D. Schantz, C. Gardner and M. Latham (2010), *Politically Exposed Persons: Preventive Measures for the Banking Sector*, Washington, DC: The World Bank, available at http://www1.worldbank.org/publicsector/star_site/publications/politically_exposed.html (Accessed 7 March 2011).

Greenberg, T.S., L.M. Samuel, W. Grant and L. Gray (2009), *Stolen Asset Recovery: A Good Practices Guide to Non-Conviction Based Asset Forfeiture*, Washington, DC: The World Bank, available at http://www1.worldbank.org/publicsector/star_site/publications/non_conviction.html (Accessed 7 March 2011).

Stephenson, K.M., L. Gray, R. Power, J.P. Brun, G. Dunker and M. Panjer (in press), *Barriers to Asset Recovery*, Washington, DC: The World Bank.

Stolen Asset Recovery Initiative (2009), *Towards a Global Architecture for Asset Recovery.* [online] Paper presented to the Conference of State Parties to the United Nations Convention against Corruption, Doha, 9–13 November, available at http://www1.worldbank.org/publicsector/star_site/publications/global_architecture.html?resourceurlname=GlobalArchitectureFinalwithCover.pdf (Accessed 7 March 2011).

Stolen Asset Recovery Initiative (2010), *No Safe Havens: A Global Forum on Stolen Asset Recovery and Development*, Paris, France 8–9 June, 2010, Washington, DC: Stolen Asset Recovery Initiative.

United Nations Office on Drugs and Crime (UNODC) and the World Bank (2007), *Stolen Asset Recovery (StAR) Initiative: Challenges, Opportunities, and Action Plan*, Washington, DC: World Bank, available at http://siteresources.worldbank.org/NEWS/Resources/Star-rep-full.pdf (Accessed 7 March 2011).

United States Department of Justice (2010), *Attorney General Holder at the African Union Summit, Kampala, Uganda, July 25, 2010*, available at http://www.justice.gov/ag/speeches/2010/ag-speech-100725.html (Accessed 7 March 2011).

United States Senate Permanent Subcommittee on Investigations (2010), *Keeping Foreign Corruption Out of the United States: Four Case Histories, February 4, 2010*, available at http://hsgac.senate.gov/public/index.cfm?FuseAction=Hearings.Hearing&Hearing_id=dd873712-eb12-4ff7-ae1a-cbbc99b19b52 (Accessed 7 March 2011).

20 Activist regulatory practices in corruption prevention: a case study from Montenegro

Bryane Michael

INTRODUCTION

Anti-corruption agencies are mushrooming across Central Europe and the Former Soviet Union. In 2009, over 40 per cent of the countries in the region had some form of anti-corruption agency. As shown by de Sousa (2006), many of these agencies are preventive – rather than repressive. Namely, they serve to co-ordinate policy (often serving as the international contact point for international co-operation), help educate the public about the harms of corruption and conduct research on corruption-related issues. The legislation devolving these competencies to such agencies often consists of highly abstract language, riddled with ambiguities, and often provides the same competencies to other agencies (such as preventive departments in repressive agencies in police, customs and sometimes even a special office in the prosecutor's office charged with finding and chasing large bribe takers and receivers).

The design of preventive anti-corruption agencies is of interest to legal scholars for three reasons. First, the anti-corruption law – and particularly questions related to the organizations needed to enforce such law – represents a burgeoning field of public law and international law. As argued below, the UN Convention Against Corruption imposes obligations on signatory states, which make the issue of preventive anti-corruption policy necessary and timely. Second, the question brings legal scholars into the realm of organizational theory – hitherto the preserve of management scholars, economists and scholars of public administration. Legislation which sets out the organizational design and function of an anti-corruption agency touches on all the classic issues tackled by both classical and post-modern organizational theorists.[1] Third, practically everyone – except legal scholars (the people who are supposed to draft and implement anti-corruption agencies) – has written about the optimal structure of an anti-corruption agency. The issue has provoked debate in the international development, political science, and economics literatures. As the design of a preventive anti-corruption agency represents a legal problem, legal scholars should – and probably will – devote more energy to the issue (Charron, 2008).

This chapter argues that preventive agencies – especially like Montenegro's Directorate for Anti-Corruption Initiatives (DACI) – have a key role to play in supporting the work of repressive law enforcement agencies if regulatory (rather than legislative) instruments clearly define their role in anti-corruption work. The first part of the chapter reviews the legal issues involved in creating a preventive anti-corruption agency. The second part provides an overview of Montenegro's anti-corruption legal framework – showing the relevant law related to the function of the Montenegrin preventive anti-corruption agency – the DACI. The third part of the chapter discusses legal weaknesses which prevent the DACI from operating as an effective preventive anti-corruption agency. The fourth part describes the issues involved in the adoption of an activist regulation which would correct the flaws in Montenegro's anti-corruption law. An activist regulation (for our purposes) comprises a regulation which interprets existing legislation as providing the DACI with competencies (unless prohibited by law). The section also provides the basis for such as activist regulation – explaining the major provisions and the way such a regulation would improve DACI performance. The final section concludes by presenting further issues of legal scholars to research. I most emphatically do not argue for a Montenegrin executive 'run amok'; or one which takes power for itself. Instead, I simply focus on one particular area of Montenegrin law, and make observations about the way in which the executive can increase performance without denying Montenegrin citizens of any positive or negative liberties.

THE ROLE OF PREVENTATIVE ANTI-CORRUPTION AGENCIES IN ANTI-CORRUPTION LAW

The preventive anti-corruption agency emerged as a construct of the 1990s work by donor agencies (like the World Bank) with an eye of the Hong Kong experience. Such work relied heavily on analysis such as Meagher (2008), who in a study of anti-corruption agencies in the early 1990s, finds that the main – and most important role – of an anti-corruption agency is to centralize information and co-ordinate activities across disparate government agencies. However, little consensus – in both donor agencies and in the member countries they serve – has emerged on exact legal competencies these agencies should have. The UN Convention Against Corruption creates the obligation for each signatory to establish a preventive anti-corruption agency (United Nations, 2005). Namely, the Convention's provisions require preventive anti-corruption bodies – like the DACI – to

Table 20.1 Weaknesses of Article 5 of the UN Convention Against Corruption

Provision from UN Convention	Weaknesses for legislative/regulatory adoption
Article 5(1): 'develop and implement or maintain effective, coordinated anti-corruption policies that promote the participation of society and reflect the principles of the rule of law, proper management of public affairs and public property, integrity, transparency and accountability'.	1. No litmus test for determining if policy is 'effective' or 'co-ordinated'. 2. No litmus test to establish an adequate level of 'reflect[ion]'. 3. No definition of 'rule of law,' 'proper management of public affairs and public property,' 'integrity,' 'transparency' and 'accountability'.
Article 5(2): 'establish and promote effective practices aimed at the prevention of corruption'.	1. No definition of 'practices aimed at the prevention of corruption'. 2. No definition of 'effective'. 3. The article is tautological – the section requires preventive agencies to engage in policies aimed at preventing corruption! 4. Substantively repeats article 5(1). 5. Does repression constitute an effective preventive practice (through deterrence)?
Article 5(3):'shall endeavour to establish and promote effective practices aimed at the prevention of corruption'.	1. The phrasing 'shall endeavour' is tantamount to 'should' – imposing no definitive legal obligation. 2. Repeats article 5(2).
Article 5(4): 'collaborate with each other and with relevant international and regional organizations in promoting and developing the measures referred to in this article'.	1. No definition of 'collaboration'. 2. Requires 'promoting and developing the measures referred to in this article' (which are in themselves ambiguous).

Source: Authors.

'ensure the existence of a body or bodies, as appropriate, that prevent corruption' (ibid., art. 6). Specifically, the Convention requires the preventive body to 'implement [ ] the policies . . . and, where appropriate, oversee [ ] and coordinat[e] the implementation of those policies' (ibid.). Yet, as shown in Table 20.1, those policies are extremely problematic. For example, while article 6.1(b) requires 'increasing and disseminating knowledge about the prevention of corruption', however, no textbook exists summarising knowledge about preventing corruption – or even defined what constitutes such knowledge.[2]

The Convention requires that 'each State Party shall grant the body or bodies . . . the necessary independence . . . to enable the body or bodies to carry out its or their functions effectively and free from any undue influence. The necessary material resources and specialized staff, as well as the training that such staff may require to carry out their functions, should be provided' (ibid., art. 5.2). Such a provision runs into four problems. First, independence in corruption cases often proves difficult or impossible to define and establish (and is not even desirable) – as the prosecution service, judiciary, and other bodies must act as advocates for policies recommended by the preventive anti-corruption agency. Such a problem has seriously (and negatively) affected the ability of anti-corruption commissions around the world from effectively co-ordinating anti-corruption policy.[3] Second, as will be shown in the DACI's case, a preventive anti-corruption agency still requires support from a ministry or other part of government – to militate for policies in cabinet as well as to ensure internal audit provides sufficient accountability for the way the agency uses government funds. Third, as numerous anti-corruption commissions show, the inclusion of non-governmental organizations does not promote the commission's (or agency's) independence. In some cases, the commission can serve business or special interests to represent special interests' views in government anti-corruption policy. In other cases, the commission can serve as a vector to coerce business or NGOs to accept government policy.[4] These three examples show the difficulties and ambiguities inherent in interpreting the Convention.

Such difficulties and ambiguities have resulted in rather different approaches being chosen for legislation establishing these 'article 5 anti-corruption agencies'. Indeed, a number of countries – particularly in Central and Eastern Europe – have taken very different legal approaches to implementing the policy of establishing a preventive anti-corruption agency. Most authors – like Klemencic and Stusek (2007) – divide anti-corruption agencies into three categories: multi-purpose, law enforcement and preventive agencies. In brief, preventive agencies – like the Albanian Anti-corruption Monitoring Group – engage in (or encourage) trainings, speeches and research. They tend to be organizationally structured as either independent research centres or as committees/commissions. Human resources and staff tend to draw from different government agencies. Law enforcement agencies – like Romania's National Anti-Corruption Directorate – focus on investigating and prosecuting corruption. These agencies tend to be part of the prosecutor's office (in order to have the competence to conduct law enforcement activities). Human resources tend to be investigators and prosecutors from law enforcement agencies like police, military (in limited extents) customs and the prosecutor's office. Multi-purpose agencies – such as those in the Baltic – can conduct both educational activities and engage in some investigatory and prosecutorial functions.

In practice, most non-repressive agencies tend to have repressive elements as well. First, the preventive agency must work with law enforcement agencies – necessitating in-depth knowledge (and even experience with) law enforcement and other repressive methods of fighting corruption. As Hussman et al. (2009) note, 'as the UNCAC requires such bodies to be in place not only for coordinating and supervising preventive anti-corruption policies, but also for their implementation [of these preventive bodies], it is unavoidable that this implies the involvement of a variety of institutions'. Such involvement necessarily implies a closer overlap in functions between the multi-purpose, repressive and preventive agencies so neatly delineated above. Second, many of these preventive agencies have recently been given the competency for controlling asset declarations and conflict of interest declarations. These new competencies force these preventive agencies to bump up against rules of evidence, reasonable doubt and other legal concepts required in law enforcement. In other cases (as in the case of Montenegro), national action plans require these preventive agencies to either train law enforcement agencies, oversee such training, or evaluate their work. Clearly, the preventive anti-corruption agency needs to know repressive measures as well as the law enforcement agencies they are training or evaluating. The UN Convention requires signatories to 'establish and promote effective practices aimed at the prevention of corruption' (United Nations, 2005, art. 5.2). However, the Convention does not take a position on whether deterrence through repressive measures consist of a preventive anti-corruption practice. Indeed, as Anechiarico (2006) shows in his historical studies of anti-corruption agencies – agencies with law enforcement powers have been the norm. Thus, the line separating a preventive and repressive agency is far from clear.

Recent evidence also questions the effectiveness of preventive agencies on the grounds that they simply do not work. Charron (2008), looking at 18 anti-corruption agencies world-wide fails to find any statistically significant effects of these preventive agencies on the incidence of corruption in places like Montenegro. Such findings echo authors, such as Steves and Rousso (2003), who also fail to find any significant effect on corruption of work in educating citizens on the harms of corruption or co-ordinating anti-corruption policies across agencies. Indeed, they quite explicitly state 'omnibus anticorruption activity [having an action plan and anti-corruption commission or agency] and membership in international anti-corruption conventions have not resulted in reductions in the level of administrative corruption' [in Eastern Europe and the Former Soviet region] (28).

MONTENEGRO'S LEGAL FRAMEWORK RELATED TO THE PREVENTION OF CORRUPTION

Unlike many other countries in the region, Montenegro has a highly disarticulated set of laws and institutions governing anti-corruption work.[5] Figure 20.1 shows a schema of Montenegro's anti-corruption law and the organizations which such law spawned. Unlike other countries, such as Macedonia, Montenegro has no single, consolidated law on fighting corruption.[6] The 2007 Decision on the Establishment of the Anti-Corruption Commission creates the competence for a commission of 11 people to take decisions about national anti-corruption strategy (Government of Montenegro, 2007a). The Commission clearly looks temporary as specific individuals are specifically nominated (instead of general posts) – necessitating the amendment of the Decision every time specific individuals need to be changed. The 2008 Conflict of Interest Law establishes competencies for the Commission to monitor conflict of interest declarations (Government of Montenegro, 2008). The Law on Civil Servants prohibits civil servants from taking bribes.

These laws – along with an Anti-Corruption Action Plan (discussed below) create and define the competencies of the Anti-Corruption

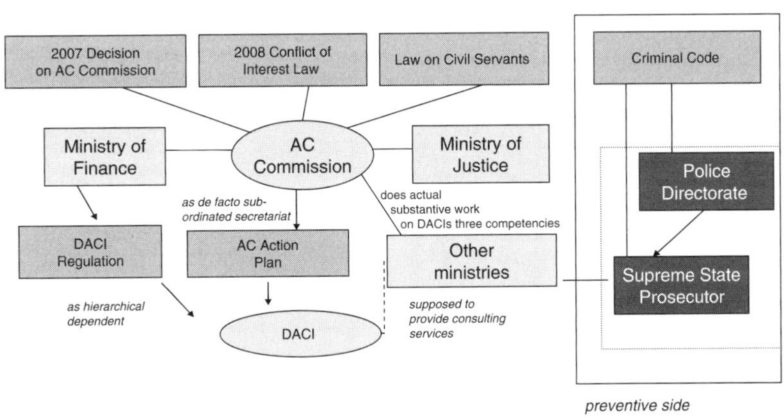

Note: The AC Action Plan does not represent hard law per se. See text for more.

Figure 20.1 Montenegro's anti-corruption institutional framework

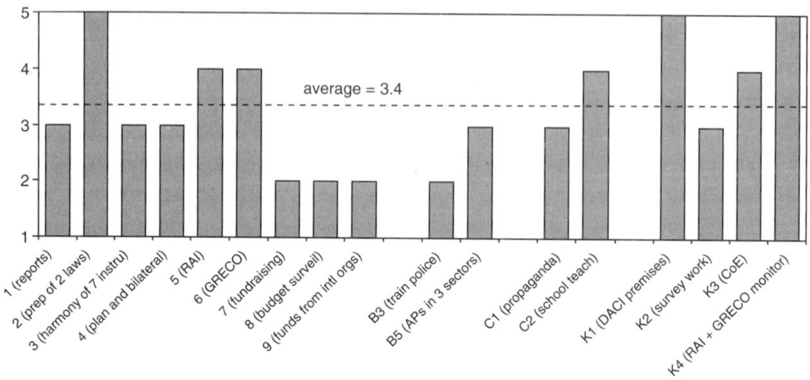

Figure 20.2 Specificity rankings of DACI Action Plan obligations

Commission). The Commission – like most of its kin – must (in relation to the Action Plan): a) manage, organize and harmonize the activities of governmental and other relevant institutions, b) manage funds allocated for implementation, c) set priorities, dynamics and deadlines for implementation, as well as assess results achieved and d) submit reports to the Government, at least twice a year, reviewing progress on measures taken and remaining to be taken.

One of the chief obligations of the Anti-Corruption Commission lies in monitoring the Anti-Corruption Action Plan. To date, action plan reports have been issued for 2007 and 2008. The Action Plan calls for a staggering 280 activities to be implemented by various government and non-government actors covering a wide-range of governmental bodies. The Action Plan holds a confusing place in Montenegrin law. On the one hand, the Montenegrin Parliament has adopted the Action Plan – giving it at least the cachet of law. The Action Plan also creates on-going obligations on the Anti-Corruption Committee and invests particular organizations with both obligations and competencies.

Nevertheless, from an outside perspective, the Action Plan fails to constitute a solid basis for binding administrative law for three reasons. First, the Action Plan does not create well-defined competencies and obligations expected of pieces of legislation. As shown above in Figure 20.2, many of the admonitions of the Action Plan are too vague to be considered legally binding administrative law per se.[7] As such, the Action Plan represents an expression of parliamentary intent or a resolution instead of a sound statutory basis for administrative rulemaking. As I argue below, the Action Plan 'law' provides no tests for compliance with the Action Plan (which an administrative judge could use to rule for or against the agency charged

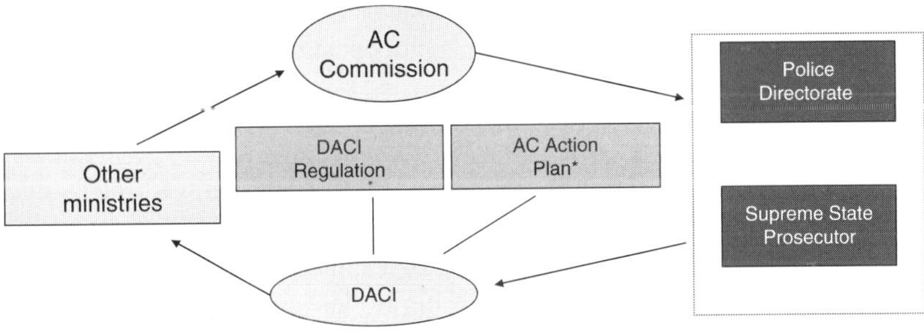

Note: The AC Action Plan does not represent hard law per se. See text for more.

Figure 20.3 Regulatory reforms making up for legislative deficiencies

with implementing a particular provision). Indeed, in several cases, the Action Plan assigns tasks to agencies outside of the executive's jurisdiction – such as NGOs. The tasking of agencies outside governmental jurisdiction clearly signals a role for the action plan as a political instrument instead of the basis for hard law.

In this rather muddled legal framework, the Government established the Montenegrin Directorate for Anticorruption Initiatives (the DACI). The DACI Competencies Decree (and other subordinate regulations and possibly various items in the Action Plan which are tasked to the Directorate) regulate the Directorate's work (Government of Montenegro, 2007b). Figure 20.3 shows the DACI's competencies arising from these various legal instruments. As shown, these competencies (and quasi-competencies in the case of Action Plan obligations) may be divided into three categories – promotional and preventive activities, international co-operation activities and 'co-ordinative' activities. Promotional competencies include printing flyers about the harms of corruption (and other educational activities), preparing reports on anti-corruption actions undertaken by the government, and the preparation of reports, surveys and other analyses. Competencies relating to international co-operation give the DACI the mandate to make proposals for legislative changes – particularly with regard to the SPAI (Stability Pact Anti-Corruption Initiative) and the GRECO (Council of Europe's Group of States Against Corruption). The DACI also has the mandate to draft bills on the protection of whistleblowers, a new law on Integrity in Public Sector, and the ratification of various Council of Europe Conventions. Co-ordinative activities comprise fundraising for anti-corruption activities and substantive training of police in receiving complaints about corruption from the public.

However, the legal framework governing the DACI's work severely weakens the Directorate's ability to play an effective part in Montenegro's anti-corruption policy. Perhaps the most striking flaw relates to the lack of specificity of the authorities and obligations given to the Directorate. Figure 20.2 shows the specificity of the various legal provisions from the Action Plan governing the DACI's work. Less specific provisions (represented by a score closer to 1) signify that the provision defines a relatively abstract and non-specific obligation. For example, Action Plan point 7 requires the DACI to define priorities in the fight against corruption and organized crime, draft projects and propose them for budgetary financing or financing from international organizations and institutions as well as ensure financial support from the budget for the government bodies implementing these projects. Clearly, the point provides no guidance on the types of projects which the DACI can propose, nor sets the terms under which the DACI can contract with donors or third-parties in such fundraising.[8]

The disarticulated nature of the legal framework governing the DACI's work has severely restricted the Directorate's ability to tackle the more hard-hitting aspects of anti-corruption work. So far the DACI has been unable to exercise its authority and has mostly been conducting speeches, often labelled as trainings. Namely, of the 48 activities mentioned on the DACI website, over a quarter of those activities consist of giving public lectures, the announcement of the adoption of various legislative acts, and other speeches, round-tables and memoranda of understanding.

WEAKNESSES IN EXISTING MONTENEGRIN ANTI-CORRUPTION LAW AND POTENTIAL REMEDIAL STRATEGIES

A number of factors explain the failure to invest the DACI with the needed competencies and training in order to serve as an effective preventive anti-corruption agency. By all indications, the Government of Montenegro created the DACI to comply with international donors' advice and the obligations imposed by the UN Convention. However, Heibrunn (2004) notes, in his review of anti-corruption commission performance, that 'anti-corruption commissions are especially problematic when political leaders are only responding to demands from international donors' (p. 1).[9] In the most recent Council of Europe report – of the Group of States Against Corruption – the report only mentions the DACI four times (GRECO, 2008). Each of those mentions relates to a speech or other relatively minor event. A possible – through wrong – explanation for the

DACI's lack of hard-nosed wins would see the lack of DACI's competence as a strategic choice. Messick (2001) has argued that a legislature should craft laws around enforcement capacity.[10] Such a view suggests that the parliament (and people) have given the DACI all the authority it can reasonably handle. Yet with a staff of roughly 22 people and a multi-million dollar budget, the DACI hardly seems a dilapidated organisation. Clearly, the DACI's inability to exercise its authority stems from deeper-rooted problems in the DACI's legal framework.

Perhaps the most important problem with the DACI's legal structure lies in its lack of independence. According to the UN Convention, the preventive anti-corruption agency (or agencies) should be independent. However, neither the DACI Competencies Decree nor the subsequent DACI Regulation provides direction related to the relationship between the Ministry of Finance and the DACI (as a subordinated entity).[11] Such a lack of independence means the Director cannot safely make denouncements or critical reviews of the government's anti-corruption work (as required by Montenegrin law). Indeed, to date, the DACI has served as a government cheerleader – announcing successes while overlooking failures. For example, the DACI's website still reads like the government announcements of yester-year, announcing that 'Montenegro Made Success in the Process of Implementation of GRECO Recommendations' (DACI 2010). More critical reports, such as the recent UNDP financed report carried out by independent consultants working for the U4 Centre in Bergen, Norway do not appear on their website.[12]

Another implication of the DACI's lack of independence relates to ambiguity in the DACI's rights to procure for services. In all likelihood, the DACI does not have the skills required to carry out more technical aspects of its work – from the conduct of sophisticated statistical studies to the analysis of international law. As such, the DACI will need to contract with independent experts, businesses and NGOs. In theory, as the DACI is subordinate to the Ministry of Finance, the Minister would decide the DACI's expenditure priorities – clearly a violation of the principle of independence. The 2008–2009 Anti-Corruption Action Plan gives the DACI the obligation to obtain funds for anti-corruption projects. However, the DACI clearly does not have the equal authority as other ministries or agencies to negotiate with the Ministry of Finance as part of the annual budget cycle or to submit independent proposals for funding.

The DACI also does not have sufficient authority to collect the vast range of anti-corruption-related information required by the Action Plan. Good government lawmaking sets off each obligation with a corresponding competence (or authority). The Action Plan charges the DACI with a number of obligations related to the co-ordination of information

– for final submission to the National Anti-Corruption Commission. For example, Action Plan point 5 notes that the DACI must collect reports from institutions, which are mentioned in the Stability Pact Declaration and GRECO Recommendations – including the Ministry of Justice, political parties, customs, 'all government agencies' and so forth (Stability Pact, 2005). However, no remedies are in place for agencies who fail to provide the DACI with information. Indeed, technically, while the DACI has the obligation to collect such information, its counterpart organizations do not have the administration obligation to provide such information!

The DACI's unclear relationship with the Ministry of Justice will likely create significant problems in the Directorate's ability to submit proposals for legislative amendments to anti-corruption related bills. The DACI Regulation clearly gives the DACI the competency to work on legislation related to international conventions. However, the 2009 Anti-Corruption Action Plan omits the DACI as a body responsible for 'continu[ing] with the harmonization of legislation with the UN Conventions against corruption (Palermo, UNTOC Convention), and other conventions in field of fight against organized crime' (Government of Montenegro, 2009). In practice, the Ministry of Justice currently does the 'real' work on legal drafting – leaving the DACI to continue giving speeches in schools.

Another significant reason for the DACI's resort to 'safe' activities – like giving speeches at schools – stems from unclear job functions and insufficient specification of skills required. Unclear specification of job functions derives from Montenegro's continued use of the former Yugoslav method of 'systematisation'. In the systematization exercise, government agencies create enormous tables where they place the number of staff they want in the next budget cycle. The job specifications for each post must fit into the row in the systematization table.

Moreover, and more importantly, the 2009 Anti-Corruption Action Plan requires DACI staff to work extensively in law enforcement areas (assessing laws, providing legal advice to citizens and government agencies, and assessing action plans). For example, the DACI has the obligation to provide 'training of police officers and employees for the implementation of the instructions on reporting corruption to the police', assistance in drafting an anti-corruption action plan for the health sector, education and 'spatial planning'. Publicity campaigns require skills in marketing, poster design, internet page design, the organisation of focus groups (to check how messages are received) and other skills. Survey work requires a basic knowledge in statistics (knowledge about efficient estimators, survey instrument design, objective versus subjective indicators, sample sizes, stratification and blocking . . . among other issues) in order to create valid results. Such work requires extensive law-enforcement experience (and even persons doing studies on laws should have served as practicing law enforcement officers). The systematization (as per article 6 of the DACI Regulation) does not require any law enforcement experience – making DACI staff unqualified to provide advice based on practical law enforcement work.

At the heart of each of these problems lies the vagueness of the present DACI Regulation. At less than one page, the regulation defines in very broad terms the obligations incumbent on the Directorate. In a Western European administrative law context, such a regulation may be sufficient – as administrative jurisprudence in most EU member states and in the Anglo-Saxon jurisdictions across the Atlantic allow civil servants to work in the way they think will result in the most efficient outcomes. However, in the post-Yugoslav context, public officials view law as providing instructions on actions which they are allowed to take. Such a restrictive view of law requires lawmakers (at both the legislative and regulatory levels) to define very precise drafts.[13]

ACTIVIST REGULATORY REMEDIES FOR WEAK LEGISLATIVE PROVISIONS IN MONTENEGRO'S ANTI-CORRUPTION LEGAL FRAMEWORK

A more activist DACI regulation could provide the DACI with clarification about the competencies required to fulfil the mandates given by the DACI regulation itself and the Action Plan. Trivunovic et al. (2007) note that the Montenegrin Parliament has been rather antithetical toward passing effective anti-corruption legislation – noting floundering on the draft law on conflict of interest in July 2006, changes to the Criminal Procedure Code, providing for the use of special investigative measures, changes in the Law on the State Audit Institution (which reduced the institution's independence), and parliament's refusal to lift immunity for several members under investigation for corruption. Moreover, the provisions already in place (as shown in part in Figure 20.2) provide the DACI with extremely ill-defined competencies. So the most effective legal strategy lies in a liberal – or activist – interpretation of the existing legislation already adopted.

In order to pass such an activist regulation – namely one which interprets existing legislation as providing the DACI with competencies (unless prohibited under existing law) – two conditions must be (and are) present. The first condition requires that the executive possesses sufficient authority to use legal ambiguities in existing legislation in order to engage in activist regulation. As far as black letter law is concerned, article 5 of the

Administrative Procedure Law allows Montenegrin executive agencies to regulate '[not] opposite to . . . legally established public interests' in order that 'such measures are sufficient for the achievement of the objective of the law' (Government of Montenegro, 2003). As long as no substantive rights are removed from Montenegrin citizens – and the conduct of surveys and teaching can hardly impinge on such liberties – executive agencies should take a teleological view of rule-making.

Established legal practice also militates for an activist view of regulating the DACI. Over the past two years, the Government of Montenegro has passed a number of government decrees which have no direct basis in legislation. The decree on the establishment of the Anti-Corruption Commission and the establishment of monitoring mechanisms for GRECO and SPAI recommendations are two notable examples where the executive has used its prerogative to engage in activist administrative law-making. While the Parliament has not adopted a piece of legislation as active as the US Administrative Procedure Act, precedents for activist rulemaking in Montenegro clearly exist.

The second condition requires Montenegrin courts to uphold provisions – or at least fail to sanction executive agencies like the DACI – contained in such activist regulation. More simply put, would activist regulation expose the executive to averse administrative court decisions which would revoke its authority? Article 38 of the State Administration Law clearly allows the Ministry of Finance – and thus the DACI – to 'pass bylaws, orders and instructions for the enforcement of laws and other regulations', whereas article 39 requires that such 'instructions shall prescribe the manner of work and performance of affairs of administrative authorities . . . in performing delegated, respectively entrusted affairs' (Government of Montenegro, 2003). As the Law on Administrative Disputes provides no over-arching principles upon which administrative judges would adjudicate cases, the principles previously mentioned from the State Administration Law and Administrative Procedure Law seem to form a reasonable basis for activist rulemaking. Such an activist regulation, satisfying both conditions, would therefore need to be crafted 'close to' the legislation. Through such a crafting, the regulation would retain the substantive rights (and obligations) already available to the DACI – and perhaps clarifying those already inherent rights – while only changing the procedural rights.

Such a regulation would need to 'rearrange' already existing authority in order to simplify the law related to the fight against corruption. Figure 20.3 presents such an approach. A revised DACI regulation – which explicitly gives the DACI the mandate as the Anti-Corruption Commission's secretariat and empowers the staff to learn about – and train in – particular methods of policy analysis and law enforcement would eliminate much of the confusion in Montenegro's anti-corruption legal framework. The quasi-competencies enshrined in the Action Plan would need to be incorporated in the revised DACI regulation. Independence from the Ministry of Finance would ensure the DACI can play the neutral role which the members of parliament clearly intended for the Directorate.[14]

Given parliament's likely reluctance to engage in activist legislation to promote the DACI's interests, can the Ministry of Finance unilaterally grant the DACI independence? Can the Ministry of Finance 'cut away' (grant independence) to a dependent entity? The answer is yes and no. The Ministry must still – as required by the Law on State Administration – be responsible for the functioning of the DACI. The Ministry of Finance must still control the legality of the DACI's acts. However, the Minister can agree to give the DACI director freedom by agreeing not to interfere in the Directorate's activities. Unless prohibited by the Law on State Administration, the Ministry of Finance can outline the DACI's operational independence in a Memorandum of Understanding between the DACI and its parent organization (the Ministry of Finance). Such a Memorandum of Understanding would also define the responsibilities of the Ministry of Finance to request budgetary support for DACI initiatives as well as the responsibilities of the Ministry of Finance to bring DACI-led policy initiatives before the Cabinet of Ministers.

In order to make such independence operational in practice, a provision should be put in place for the defense of those rights. Should the DACI Director deem that the DACI's independence has been politically or operationally compromised – or if any other state agency tried to exercise undue pressure on the DACI Director – he or she shall, in the first instance, file a petition with the body of administrative disputes (as defined in the Law on Administrative Disputes). Failing satisfactory remedy, the DACI Director could publicize any interference with the DACI's activities in the media, in annual reports, and to the parliament.

Once (and only when) the DACI obtains operational and political independence, the Directorate can serve as an effective Secretariat for the Anti-Corruption Commission. Point 1.2.1 of the Anti-Corruption Action Plan charges the DACI with 'delivering periodic reports based on the Innovated Instruction on preparation of the reports on implementation of the Action Plan, and delivering of other analysis and reports relating to corruption and organized crime'.[15] However, the ambiguity of section II of the National Commission Decision (listing the specific names of people rather than institutions as members) as well as the failure of the decision to nominate a Secretariat clearly hinder the DACI from playing that role.

Naturally, a provision should be put in place in such an activist regulation in case a dispute arises about the DACI's powers or responsibilities. An activist regulation should require the DACI Director to summarize the dispute in writing (and provide a copy of the dispute to the agency making the dispute), send the dispute to the Anti-Corruption National Commission seeking clarification from its members, await a decision (which the DACI shall consider legally binding) by the Anti-Corruption National Commission members either taking an opinion outside of officially planning meetings, or during a planned meeting. Failing satisfactory recourse, the DACI Director should be allowed to appeal to an administrative instance without interference from the Ministry of Finance.

Procedures should also be put in place to task the DACI (and the DACI in turn should have the right to refuse tasking). Any member of the Anti-Corruption National Commission should have the right – by virtue of the authority in the revised regulation – to task the DACI with preparing things such as agendas and issues papers for Anti-Corruption National Commission meetings. The DACI may have the right to refuse if the tasks fall outside the DACI's competence or if the task represents bureaucratic work which is unlikely to have a significant impact on corruption in Montenegro, among other things.

Another major area for activist regulation involves the extent to which the DACI – rather than the Ministry of Justice – drafts bills and amendments to existing laws. The DACI must have the right, as defined by point 2 of the DACI Competencies Regulation, to draft new bills or legal projects for first reading by the parliament in co-operation with the Ministry of Justice. However, the DACI cannot do this unless its experts are as qualified – or more qualified – than Ministry of Justice staff. In order to ensure they are capable of such legal drafting, four provisions should be in place. First, DACI staff should have very liberal rights to attend trainings and engage in self-study. Second, a formal 'division of labour' should be in place; contact persons should be nominated in each agency, and the DACI must have consultative rights on drafts produced by the Ministry of Justice (and visa versa of course). Again, a Protocol or Memorandum of Understanding would be required as the DACI cannot unilaterally engage in rule-making on elements which involve the Ministry of Justice. Moreover, provisions for resolving disputes should be included in the Memorandum of Understanding – as anti-corruption lawmaking tends to be a contentious activity.

A fourth element which would need to be included in a revised DACI regulation involves the definition of consulting and assurance services offered by the Directorate. As previously discussed, the Action Plan clearly requires the DACI to engage in consulting (particularly the police) and in assurance (in evaluating progress of work on the Action Plan and

GRECO/SPAI recommendations). Provisions in a revised DACI regulation would need to define liberal terms for the acceptance and conduct of such training. In other words, if other Montenegrin institutions are to trust and use the DACI's services, the revised DACI regulation should enable staff to informally receive requests and respond to them without the heavy handed bureaucracy of filling in forms or getting approvals from the DACI Director. However, in order for DACI staff to obtain the qualifications needed to respond to such training needs, staff should be granted liberal rights to attend lectures by local and international experts, encouraged (through promotion prospects) for engaging in independent study and allowed to 'shadow' staff in other agencies, or undertake study visits to other Montenegrin agencies.[16]

As for assurance services related to anti-corruption activities carried out across the public sector, a revised regulation would define clearly the role of the DACI (as opposed to internal audit) in carrying out anti-corruption assessments – though allowing for both parties to be involved in audits as needed. Ideally, the assessment methodology would follow the Law on Public Internal Financial Control System. Namely, the DACI would apply the same standards of quality for anti-corruption related audits and research as those used by any internal auditor acting under the law – interpreting those standards as comprising the standards defined by the International Framework of Professional Practices set forth by the International Audit and Assurance Standards Board.[17] The DACI should also assess its own performance – with independent assurance of that report being undertaken by the internal auditor of the Ministry of Justice.

If the present DACI Competencies Regulation spans only one page, an activist regulation might span 20 or 25 pages and look roughly as presented in Table 20.2. Antecedent provisions would deal with the legal basis for establishing such an activist regulation. One chapter would delineate (in some detail) the way the DACI interacts with the Anti-Corruption Commission, the Ministry of Finance and the Ministry of Justice. A clear division of responsibilities for representing the republic abroad in anti-corruption co-ordination and consultation meetings would need to be specified. The Directorate's rights for assembling and using information – particularly information related to corruption-related cases – would need to be scrupulously defined, as issues such as privacy, confidentiality and even state secrets are involved.[18] Another chapter would need to deal with the division of labour in legal drafting between the DACI and the Ministry of Justice. A further section would define the terms under which the DACI provides consulting and assurance services. A final section would tackle training and skills issues through the creation

Table 20.2 Table of contents for potentially revised activist regulation on the functioning of the DACI

ANTECEDENTS
Chapter 1: Antecedents

RELATIONS WITH OTHER ORGANIZATIONS
Chapter 2: Competencies Related to Secretariat Functions for the Anti-Corruption National Commission
Chapter 3: Relations Guaranteeing the Independence and Accountability of the DACI
Chapter 4: Relations with Other Domestic, Foreign and International Organizations

INFORMATION USE, PROCESSING AND MANAGEMENT
Chapter 5: Rights and Obligations of Using Information from Other Agencies
Chapter 6: Procedures for Obtaining, Processing and Using Statistical Information about Corruption
Chapter 7: Rights and Obligations for Posting Information on Agency's Website
Chapter 8: Procedures in Cases of Public Complaints about Specific Cases of Corruption
Chapter 9: Rules and Recommendations Related to Press Contacts

CO-OPERATION ON LEGAL DRAFTING AND RULEMAKING
Chapter 10: Work on Draft Laws and Legal Advising
Chapter 11: Procedures for Working with the Ministry of Justice on Anti-Corruption Legal Reform
Chapter 12: Opinions and Advisories Issued by the DACI to other State Bodies

CONSULTING AND ASSURANCE SERVICES
Chapter 13: Provision of Consulting and Training Services
Chapter 14: Provision of Anti-Corruption Assurance Services

INTERNAL PROCEDURES
Chapter 15: Procedures to Implement ISO 9001:2001 (Knowledge Management)
Chapter 16: Performance Appraisal and Management
Chapter 17: Training Requirements for DACI Recruits and Retraining Existing Staff

FINAL DISPOSITIONS
Chapter 18: Final and Executing Dispositions

APPENDIX 1: MEMORANDUM OF UNDERSTANDING BETWEEN THE DACI AND THE MINISTRY OF FINANCE

of knowledge management systems and a liberal performance assessment and improvement system. Memoranda of Understanding with the Ministry of Finance and Ministry of Justice would need to be appended to the regulation.

CONCLUSIONS AND DIRECTIONS FOR FUTURE RESEARCH

Montenegro's anti-corruption laws require significant amendment if the DACI wishes to play an effective role in preventing corruption in Montenegro. However, the parliament is unlikely to amend legislation anytime soon – and legal scholars as well as international conventions provide no guidance on ways of bolstering Montenegro's preventive anti-corruption efforts. As such, the legal strategy should be to engage in an activist regulatory approach. Such an approach would encourage the DACI to take a proactive role in anti-corruption legislative work and consulting. Such a regulation would also clear up significant organizational design issues, which would allow the DACI to collect information on (and objectively) assess Montenegro's anti-corruption work.

Making generalizations on the basis of only one country's experience always represents a perilous adventure. However, some generalizable lessons may be possible – as Smilov (2009) notes:

> institutions with preventive and coordinative functions, whose prerogatives are limited to creating anticorruption strategies and plans, monitoring their implementation, advising the government . . . became very popular in Southeast

Europe during 2000-2004: in Albania, there was the so-called Anticorruption Monitoring Group; in the Former Yugoslav Republic of Macedonia, the State Commission against Corruption; etc.

The countries in the region, to some extent, are following a similar mould. The primordial research question arising from this chapter asks about the extent to which the Montenegrin (and other executive agencies in developing countries) should use their regulatory discretion in order to promote the goals and aims of the anti-corruption legislation which provides their mandate. In many former Socialist countries, public officials cast a very wary eye on the exercise of administrative and regulatory discretion. I assume regulation-writers and rule-makers will craft regulatory provisions of their secondary legislation close to the substantive rights they are granted in the primary legislation – and in the interest of citizens. However, the difference between our liberal approach and the conservative approach actually taken by anti-corruption regulators probably masks a series of interesting research questions which explain the relative failure of these transition economies to adopt proactive anti-corruption laws.

Further research can also shed light on more anti-corruption specific questions. First, given the obvious problems related to clearly defining the mandate of a preventive anti-corruption agency, how should article 5 of the UN Convention Against Corruption evolve? Tellingly, few if any Western European or North American countries have created the same types of (donor financed) commissions and agencies which became popular in Eastern Europe and the Former Soviet Union. Second, how does variation in the type of preventive anti-corruption commission or agency across countries reflect the legal tradition of those countries? The UN Convention takes great pains to impose obligations only 'in accordance with the fundamental principles of its legal system'. Such a conditional clause opens up enormous room for legislative and regulatory differences between signatory states. Such variation may tell scholars something about the effects of 'legal origins' on anti-corruption performance.[19] Does variation in preventive anti-corruption agencies shed light on the deeper questions related to the basic effects of a legal system on law enforcement outcomes? While answering the main question which I posed in this chapter from a normative perspective, a definitive answer will require a positive (empirical) analysis. In other words, can an activist regulatory stance overcome legislative problems in preventive anti-corruption agencies like Montenegro's? Only time – and data – can tell.

NOTES

1. No single author has yet provided a single overview of research in the field of organizational theory as applied to anti corruption work. See Huang and Wu (1994) for a highly stylised view and Cheng (2000) for an example of the 'location problem' in the specific context of China.
2. A number of scholars have tacked the epistemological problem of trying to define what constitutes 'anticorruption knowledge.' Mathisen and Duncan (2006) provide a comprehensive overview.
3. If the anti-corruption agency or commission remains overly insulated from administrative political pressures from other parts of government, the organization becomes sidelined (as in the case of the Latvian anti-corruption agency). If, as in the Polish case, the anti-corruption agency becomes beholden to bureaucratic interests, the agency or commission becomes ineffective.
4. Lamour (2007) provides several examples of such two-way coercion (transmitted through organizational design of anti-corruption policy).
5. A number of other authors – such as Trivunovic et al. (2007) find similarly. These authors note that, 'with such a deficient regulatory framework in place, it is perhaps no surprise that compliance with the rules is low. In its 2006 report, the Montenegrin Anti-Corruption Commission noted that 6 per cent of state-level and 38 per cent of local/municipal level officials are in violation of the conflict of interest rules, and these are almost exclusively elected [vs appointed] officials', 16.
6. In this way, Montenegro reflects a Western European approach to legislating on anti-corruption issues. In such Western European model countries, anti-corruption provisions are scattered across a number of laws. In contrast, the Eastern European model relies on a single anti-corruption act (Michael and Mishyna, 2009).
7. Head (2008) discusses the conditions required in many jurisdictions for properly formed administrative law. Specifically, three factors militate against Action Plan items comprising a solid basis for rulemaking. First, Action Plan items are assigned to multiple agencies – sometimes as many as 14 – without any precision about how derived authority should be allocated among them. Second, the items in the Action Plan are sometimes so vague that no parliamentary intent can be deduced. Third, no sanctions (and no resources) are provided to ensure execution – suggesting weak parliamentary interest in actual enforcement.
8. As discussed below, the DACI is subordinated to the Ministry of Finance. Its lack of independence would mean the Ministry of Finance would determine the cost of overheads (such as office space, staff time and so forth) the DACI can charge for projects. The potential for the Ministry of Finance to 'capture' these projects also impacts on the DACI staff's incentives to request funding – as they benefit less.
9. Doig et al. (2006) find enough support for the assertion that donor assistance cripples anti-corruption agencies that they make the assertion one of their three broad hypotheses for future empirical research.
10. He cogently argues that anti-corruption laws should be drafted with the enforcement capabilities of the executive in mind. Such an approach clearly ignores the liberal view of legislation as seeking to stretch the state's capacities.
11. The data on the DACI's independence are somewhat mixed. De Sousa (2006) categorises the DACI as independent – finding for the DACI's independence on the grounds that the head cannot be removed. However, the DACI Competencies Decree does not guarantee the head such immunity from removal (the de Sousa data relied on surveys filled in by agency staff themselves).
12. The only study available on the website consists of a study on Governance in Education from the International Institute for Educational Planning in Paris (Hallak and Poisson, 2006). The study does not refer to Montenegro. Available at: http://www.gov.me/files/1187007034.pdf
13. New Institutional Economics also predicts that Montenegrin law-makers should prefer

more specific to less specific drafts. Given uncertainty about rights (both within and outside of the state) and large enforcement costs (due to a weak judiciary), more specific drafts would help the lower transaction costs of enforcing anti-corruption law. For more background on this type of analysis see Stephen and van Hemmen 2008.

14. All the pieces of legislation (and derived regulations) referring to the DACI require the Directorate to engage in assessments of anti-corruption compliance and performance across the executive. Clearly, the members of parliament wanted the DACI to play the role of independent assessor instead of cheerleader. As such, the obligations imposed on the DACI clearly create an implicit requirement for the DACI's political and operational independence from the rest of government.
15. Other provisions can be cited in defence of the DACI's right to serve as the Commission's Secretariat. Point (b) of the DACI Competencies Regulation mandating DACI 'cooperation with relevant state bodies aimed at drafting and implementing of the legislative and programmatic documents that are important for prevention and combating corruption'. Article 3A of the Systematisation Regulation provides for 'expert assistance in the elaboration of reports submitted by competent state authorities and preparing draft report on realization of measures defined in the Action Plan for the implementation of the Programme of fight against corruption and organized crime'.
16. Such provisions, while legal in Montenegro, would encounter deep cultural resistance. For more, see Erakovich et al. (2008).
17. As previously mentioned, the DACI has an ambitious assessment schedule – being legally required to assess the Ministry of Justice, political parties, customs, all government agencies, work of the SECI Centre, Europol and Eurojust, government audit organization, local government, public procurement, energy, education, health, infrastructure, tax administration, customs, business registration and licensing, banking, insurance and pensions. The IAASB standards would provide a comparable and internationally recognized standard for conducting those assessments.
18. In many former Yugoslav countries, the issue of state secrets continues to arise as much government information comprises a state secret (partly as a way for civil servants to circumvent new freedom of information laws being adopted by parliaments across the region). Hopefully, private information about citizens will cease to become a state secret once collected by a state agency.
19. The legal origins literature (or more formally, the law and development literature) seeks to explain everything from the development of capital markets to enforcement powers of the tax authorities as the result of historical differences in the way legal systems developed across countries. The law and development literature has developed sufficiently to find some good reviews. See Siems (2007).

REFERENCES

Anechiarico, Frank (2006), 'Prosecution as corruption control: paradigms of public integrity in context', *Wayne Law Review*, **52**, 1415–33.

Charron, Nicholas (2008), 'Mapping and measuring the impact of anti-corruption agencies: A new dataset for 18 countries', *New Public Management and the Quality of Government Conference, November 13–15 2008*. Göteborg, Sweden.

Cheng, Joseph (2000), 'Guangdong's challenges: streamlining, economic restructuring and anticorruption', *Pacific Affairs*, **73**(1), 9–35.

De Sousa, Luis (2006), *European Anti-Corruption Agencies: protecting the Community's financial interests in a knowledge-based, innovative and integrated manner*. Available online at http://www.ancorage-net.org/content/comparative/national%20assessment%20survey%20on%20acas%20a%20comparative%20perspective.pdf

Doig, Alan, David Watt and Robert Williams (2006), 'Hands-on or hands-off? Anti-corruption

agencies in action, donor expectations, and a good enough reality', *Public Administration and Development* **26**(2), 163–72.
Erakovich Rodney, Emile Kolthoff, Wyman Sherman Wyman and Dragoljub Kavran (2008), 'Comparative analysis of ethical leadership and integrity development in local government: US, Netherlands, Montenegro and Serbia', *Living Law*, **57**(7–8), 7–25.
GRECO (2008), 'Joint first and second evaluation rounds: compliance report on Montenegro'. *GRECO RC-I/II (2008) 5E.*
Hallak, Jacques and Muriel Poisson (2006), *Governance in Education: Transparency and Accountability*. Paris: UNESCO, available online, http://www.gov.me/files/1187007034.pdf
Head, Michael (2008), *Administrative Law: Context and Critique*, New York: Federation Press.
Heilbrunn, John (2004), *Anti-Corruption Commissions: Panacea or Real Medicine to Fight Corruption?*, Washington DC: World Bank Institute.
Huang, Peter and Ho-Mou Wu (1994), 'More order without more law: a theory of social norms and cultures', *Journal of Law, Economics, and Organisation*, **10**(2), 390–406.
Hussmann, Karen, Hannes Hechler and Miguel Penailillo (2009), 'Institutional arrangements for corruption prevention: considerations for the implementation of the United Nations Convention Against Corruption', Article 6, *U4 Issue 4*.
Klemencic, Goran and Janez Stusek (2007), *Specialised Anti-Corruption Institutions*, Paris: Organisation for Economic Co-operation and Development.
Lamour, Peter (2007), 'International action against corruption in the Pacific Islands: policy transfer, coercion and effectiveness', *Asian Journal of Political Science*, **15**(1), 1–16.
Mathisen, Harald and Nick Duncan (2006), 'Knowledge management for anti-corruption: problems, perspectives and prospects', *U4 Issue 2*.
Meagher, Patrick (2004), 'Anti-corruption agencies: rhetoric verses reality', *Journal of Political Reform*, **8**(1), 69–103.
Messick, Richard (2001), 'Writing an effective anticorruption law', *PREM Notes 58*, Washington DC: World Bank.
Michael, Bryane and Natalya Mishyna (2009), 'A review and critique of Azerbaijan's Anti-Corruption Law', *Journal of Eurasian Law*, **1**(2).
Siems, Mathias (2007), 'Legal origins: reconciling law & finance and comparative law', *McGill Law Review*, **52**(1).
Smilov, Daniel (2009), 'Designing anticorruption institutions in Central and Eastern Europe', *Development and Transition*, **12**, 2009, *available at* http://www.developmentandtransition.net/index.cfm?module=ActiveWeb&page=WebPage&DocumentID=710
Stability Pact (2005), *Declaration on 10 joint measures to curb corruption in South Eastern Europe*, Brussels: Stability Pact Initiative. Regional Secretariat Liaison Office.
Stephen, Frank and Stefan van Hemmen (2008), 'Laws, enforcement, legality, and economic development', *Washington University Journal of Law and Policy*, **26**(37).
Steves, Franklin and Alan Rousso (2003), 'Anti-Corruption programmes in post-communist transition countries and changes in the business environment 1999–2002', *EBRD Working Paper 85*.
Trivunovic, Marijana, Vera Devine and Harald Mathisen (2007), 'Corruption in Montenegro 2007: overview over main problems and status of reforms', *CMI Report 9*.

Legislation

Government of Montenegro (2003), Decree on the Proclamation of the Law on General Administrative Procedure (*Official Gazette of the Republic of Montenegro, no. 60/03*, 28.10).
Government of Montenegro (2007a), Decision On Establishing the National Commission for Monitoring the Action Plan for implementation of the Programme for the Fight against Corruption and Organized Crime (*Official Gazette of the Republic of Montenegro,*

no. 15/07 of March 14 2007), available at: http://www.rai-see.org/montenegro/index.php?option=com_docman&task=doc_download&gid=28&Itemid=61.
Government of Montenegro (2007b), 'Competencies of the Directorate for Anti-Corruption Initiative' (*Official Gazette of the Republic of Montenegro*, no. 16/07).
Government of Montenegro (2008), Conflict of Interest Law.
Government of Montenegro (2009), 2009 Anti-Corruption Action Plan.
United Nations (2005), UN Convention Against Corruption.

21 The Hong Kong ICAC's approach to corruption control

Ian Scott

Hong Kong's Independent Commission Against Corruption (ICAC) is often regarded as a model of the way in which efforts to prevent and control corruption should be organized and implemented. Its achievement in transforming Hong Kong from a place where corrupt practices were accepted to a place in which they are the exception has been widely admired and studied (Lethbridge, 1985; Huberts, 2000; Quah, 2003, pp. 129–45; Manion, 2004, pp. 27–83; Scott, 2010, pp. 112–116, 267–70; de Speville, 2010). In those studies, the ICAC's success is attributed to its distinctive characteristics, which may be said to form a syndrome in the sense that each of its features is thought to be necessary for the organization to work well. The principal features of this model of corruption control include:

- a single organization with a *de facto* monopoly over corruption control rather than multiple anti-corruption organizations performing the same function;
- independence from government;
- a strategy of prevention, education and sanction that is reflected organizationally in the division of the ICAC into Corruption Prevention, Community Relations and Operations Departments;
- extensive powers that include the right of arrest and detention;
- secure funding even in the face of major cutbacks in public expenditure;
- personnel of the highest moral calibre;
- the political will to combat corruption; and
- public support of sufficient strength that the ICAC has repeatedly been found to be the most trusted organization in Hong Kong.

Although features of the ICAC model have been adopted elsewhere, it is difficult to replicate the entire syndrome of characteristics because they are underpinned in Hong Kong by unique political and cultural factors. The ICAC, by providing clean government, has been important in reducing the legitimacy deficit from which both the present regime and its colonial predecessor have suffered. Political support for the ICAC has been unequivocal because it is seen to have symbolic as well as practical value. Similarly, public support is of a kind which anti-corruption agencies seldom enjoy. Hong Kong citizens, prior to the creation of the ICAC in 1974, were subject to widespread and syndicated police corruption. The payment of bribes for many other government services was common practice. The support for the ICAC is support for the maintenance of a corruption-free relationship between the people and their government and the consequence is that it enables the ICAC to exercise powers that might not be acceptable, for example, to citizens in more democratic countries.

Because the ICAC is seen to be functionally useful by both government and people and because any departures from its current practices would spark public concern, it sometimes appears that the model is set in stone, a 'one best way' of dealing with corruption problems. In reality, the ICAC, like any other organization, has had to adapt to a rapidly changing political and economic environment. The resumption of Chinese sovereignty over Hong Kong in 1997 brought with it greater integration with mainland China and fears that corruption would once more become rampant. New and more sophisticated forms of corruption began to emerge after 1997 which required fresh thinking on how the government and the ICAC could best deal with integrity issues in the civil service. There was also a need to supplement *The Prevention of Bribery Ordinance,* which had been the ICAC's principal weapon for prosecuting offences with other legal means of covering potential loopholes in the legislation. Organizationally, the ICAC began to collaborate even more than it had done in the past with other government departments and with many private sector bodies. In this chapter, the model and its impact on Hong Kong is first considered, followed by a discussion of the adaptations that have been made to counter new forms of corruption and challenges posed by a changing environment.

THE CREATION OF THE ICAC

Corruption was an endemic feature of colonial rule in Hong Kong for well over a hundred years. In government, it was concentrated principally in the police and in those departments which provided services, sold licences or carried out inspections. The administrative grade, however, from which the most senior civil servants were drawn, was generally not corrupt. Beginning in 1858, various attempts were made to counter corruption in the civil service, but it was difficult to change a culture in which the payment of 'tea money' to officials had become accepted and expected

(Munn, 2001, pp. 290–308; McWalters, 2010, pp. 3–18). Police corruption eventually became syndicated in the sense that a percentage of the payments made to the constables on the beat was siphoned up through the hierarchy to middle level and senior officers. Within the civil service, as Sir Alastair Blair-Kerr was later to report, corruption was likened to a bus which an officer could board (accepting corruption) or run alongside (not interfering with it) but should never try to stand in front of (preventing it) (Blair-Kerr, 1973, p. 24). In 1966, there were riots in Hong Kong in which police corruption was probably one of the underlying causes. Certainly in the submission to the Commission of Inquiry into the riots, there was evidence of major resentment of the police among hawkers, taxi-drivers, prostitutes and factory workers, all of whom were subject to 'squeeze' (Scott, 1989, pp. 89–92; Tu, 2003, pp. 49–56, 67–83).

From 1898 onwards, Hong Kong had specific laws and ordinances which dealt with corrupt offences. In 1956, an advisory committee was set up to try to identify the departments most susceptible to corruption. But after a period of some activity in which it made recommendations for changes to the laws and considered, but ultimately rejected, the idea of an independent investigatory body, it seems to have lapsed into inaction (McWalters, 2010, pp. 13–14). The investigation of corruption was carried out by a branch of the police force. It did charge and convict some officers but it did not have public confidence; a large number of complaints about corruption were anonymous and were not investigated (Blair-Kerr, 1973, pp. 11–18). After the 1966 riots and further disturbances in 1967 arising from a spillover of the Cultural Revolution in China, the government decided to look again at the legislation and set up a working party to make recommendations. The working party advised that new legislation was required and, in 1970, *The Prevention of Bribery Ordinance* was passed. The differences from the previous legislation were that there was a much more comprehensive treatment of corruption offence and much stronger powers were given to the Attorney-General to authorize the police to investigate cases. A critical difference from previous legislation was that neither corruption nor the word 'bribe', which had created problems of definition, were mentioned in the text of the Ordinance; rather, the offence was to 'offer, solicit or accept' an advantage. It was also an offence to be in possession of unexplained assets in excess of earnings. The new legislation was a considerable improvement over past legislation, but it still left the investigation of corruption cases in the hands of the police.

In June 1973, Peter Godber, at the time a Deputy District Commander in the Police Force, was advised by the Acting Attorney-General that he would be prosecuted under Section 10 of the Ordinance for having 'pecuniary resources or property disproportionate to your present or past official emoluments' (quoted in McWalters, 2010, pp. 26). Godber fled Hong Kong and in response to strong public reactions and suspicions of a conspiracy within the police, the Governor appointed Sir Alastair Blair-Kerr, a judge, to report on the circumstances surrounding Godber's escape and on the effectiveness of *The Prevention of Bribery Ordinance.* Blair-Kerr found that there was no conspiracy to assist Godber (Blair-Kerr, 1973). However, he reported that there was widespread corruption within the civil service, much of it of a syndicated nature. He made some recommendations for strengthening the Ordinance, including that suspects should surrender their travel documents, but left open the question of whether there should be a separate and independent body to investigate corruption. The decision then rested with a reforming Governor, Sir Murray MacLehose, who felt that the key issue was public confidence and that 'the public would have more confidence in a unit that was entirely independent and separate from any department of Government, including the police' (Hong Kong Hansard, 1973, p. 17). The creation of the ICAC was given the highest of priorities and it was able to start work in February 1974. Godber was eventually extradited from Britain in 1975 and tried, convicted and sentenced to four years in jail.

THE MODEL AT WORK

Despite the haste with which it was established, the basic principles underpinning the work of the ICAC were remarkably clear from the outset. The Colonial Secretary in introducing the bill to create the ICAC in the Legislative Council spoke of its roles in investigating and preventing corruption and in civic education and of how these were reflected in its organization, outlined its powers of arrest and detention, and noted that to ensure high moral probity the Commissioner would have the right to dismiss officers in whom he had lost confidence without giving reasons (Hong Kong Hansard 1973/74, pp. 400–404). The ICAC was well-funded with an establishment of 600 officers, who were concerned initially with the investigation of public sector corruption in a civil service which at the time had less than 100 000 officers. Although this focus was inevitably coloured by the Godber case and by the prevalence of police corruption, the Commissioner soon made it clear that the private sector would be investigated with equal vigour.

The principal task for the ICAC at the outset was to build public confidence in the institution. It did so by prosecuting corrupt police officers in a number of well-publicized, high-profile cases. The Godber case was understandably one of great public interest. But there were also other police cases which destroyed the syndicates and increased public support for the organization. In one case alone – the 'Tsim Sha Tsui Conspiracy case' – 22 policemen were charged with conspiring to obstruct the course of justice by accepting bribes from illegal establishments (ICAC, 1977, p. 19). In the 20 years after its creation, the ICAC went on to investigate 22 828 cases of alleged corruption of which 6261 were successfully prosecuted. Of those cases, 1355 concerned civil servants, 218 involved public corporations with private sector cases making up the balance (Lo, 2001).

The period between 1974 and 1994 might be regarded as the classical period of the model at work. Only two incidents over that period challenged the dominance of the ICAC and the way in which it went about its work. The first occurred in October 1977, a month in which 140 policemen had been arrested by the ICAC. On 28 October, about 2000 junior police officers staged a demonstration and marched on the office of the Commissioner of Police. Following a meeting with him, a splinter group of 40 to 100 policemen stormed the ICAC headquarters, injuring some staff members (Lethbridge, 1985, p. 14). They wanted all corruption charges to be dropped. The Governor, MacLehose, evidently felt that he had little option but to allow a partial amnesty in which it was announced that the ICAC would not normally act on complaints or offences committed before 1 January, 1977 except in cases involving officers who had already been dismissed from the Police Force, persons against whom warrants had been issued and persons outside Hong Kong (Hong Kong Hansard, 7 November, 1977, p. 157).

As MacLehose was well aware, there was strong public feeling that the amnesty should not have been granted or that its provisions went too far (Hong Kong Hansard, 7 November, 1977, p. 1957). The immediate result was that corruption reports dropped by nearly one-third in the year following the amnesty. However by 1979 reports were again rising and public confidence was increasing. The major reasons for the change in public sentiment appear to be that, after the demonstration, the ICAC continued to prosecute corrupt policemen and that, in April 1978, 100 policemen who had participated in the demonstration were summarily dismissed (Lethbridge, 1985, p. 155). There was also continuing support for the work of the ICAC from the government and a boost from the courts which found that unexplained assets acquired before 1 January 1977 were still germane to the prosecution's case (ICAC, 1978, pp. 20–21).

The police demonstration and the subsequent amnesty illustrate how dependent the colonial state was on a police force which had seriously abused its powers. In the transition to the resumption of Chinese sovereignty in 1997, the need to gain public confidence in a clean police force and in the ability of the ICAC to prosecute corrupt officers was critical to the maintenance of stability. Consequently, the ICAC was able to implement its preferred model backed by unequivocal political support while the police force underwent significant reform immediately after the amnesty but, even more extensively, in the 1990s when its para-military role was modified in favour of a more community-based approach to policing. With a government in need of short-term support and legitimacy, the political circumstances were congruent with the major principles underlying the ICAC model.

A second event that called into question the way in which the ICAC worked was the dismissal in November 1993 of Alex Tsui Ka-kit, then Senior Assistant Director in the Operations Department. The Commissioner terminated Tsui's employment summarily, as he was entitled to do under the ICAC Ordinance, simply saying that he had lost confidence in him. His decision was subsequently backed by the Governor. In the terms of his normal career path, Tsui, who was the most senior Chinese ICAC official at the time, would have expected to succeed to the position of Director of Operations and his summary dismissal raised public concerns. Legislative Council members noted that the 'legislation does not excuse the ICAC from public accountability' and they voted against the government to set up an investigation by the Council's Security Panel (Hong Kong Hansard, 1 December 1993, p. 1195).

The Panel then questioned the Commissioner who said that the principal reasons for Tsui's dismissal had been that he was friendly with people of dubious moral character, and that he had in effect diverted an investigation away from an individual who was financially supporting a boxing tournament run by an organization of which Tsui was the Chairman (Legislative Council 1994: 4-8). A further allegation was that Tsui had tried to bribe a foreign consulate official to obtain a forged letter of support for a licence for the boxing tournament. Tsui denied the charges and alleged that he had been the victim of racism and of his opposition to the politicization of the ICAC and the vetting of civil servants (Legislative Council, 1994, pp. 10–12). Although the Security Panel did not accept all the reasons that the Commissioner provided for the termination of Tsui's employment, it found that overall 'it was not unreasonable for the Commissioner to . . . come to the conclusion that he had lost faith in Mr Tsui's trustworthiness and integrity' (Legislative Council, 1994, p. 23).

Legislative Councillors were still uneasy about the powers that the ICAC and its Commissioner possessed (Legislative Council, 1994, pp. 24–5). At a time of rising concern about civil liberties and the rule of law in Hong Kong, when the government was intent on introducing new legislation and establishing statutory bodies to protect those liberties, the ICAC with its virtually untrammelled powers seemed to be in an anomalous position. 'The ICAC's powers', as one Legislative Councillor put it, 'are . . . regarded as anachronistic' (Hong Kong Hansard, 26 January 1994, p. 2128). Under pressure in the Legislative Council in the wake of the Tsui affair, the government announced that it would set up an independent committee to review the powers of the ICAC and to determine whether its systems of accountability needed to be modified (Hong Kong Hansard, 26 January, 1994, p. 2151).

Potentially, the Independent Review Committee might have recommended a widespread revision to the legislation and rules under which the ICAC operated. While the ICAC was widely commended for the work that it had done in reducing corruption, there were clearly growing public concerns about its powers. About one-third of the 100 responses to the Committee raised issues relating to its powers and about half referred to problems of accountability (Independent Review Committee, 1994, pp. 20–21). The Committee felt that the appropriate way to move forward was not to make sweeping changes to the powers of the ICAC which were left largely unchanged, but rather to ensure that existing rules and practices were circumscribed to some extent by advisory bodies and external authorities such as the judiciary and the Director of Administration. It recommended that liaison with government should be strengthened and that the power of the Commissioner to dismiss staff without giving reasons should be modified to require him/her to seek the advice of the Advisory Committee on Corruption before making a decision on termination (Independent Review Committee, 1994, p. 7). It did not make any changes to the ICAC's powers of arrest, detention and bail although it sought to introduce a reporting mechanism for suspects on bail for over six months (Independent Review Committee 1994: 4).

Although there was increasing concern over the powers of the ICAC, the extent of that concern needs to be put into perspective. In 1990, the ICAC commissioner reported that only 2.5 per cent of respondents to a survey felt that the ICAC's powers were excessive (Hong Kong Hansard, 1994, p. 2121). By 1994, the percentage of respondents who thought that its powers were too great had risen to 9.2 per cent but thereafter the percentage dropped, remaining steady at just over 4 per cent after 2000 until it dropped again to 3.2 per cent in 2008 (Market Behaviour Hong Kong, 1994, p. 15; Cimigo, 2008, p. 76). By comparison, the percentage of respondents who thought that the powers were not large enough has risen from 10.5 per cent in 1996 to 13.8 per cent in 2008 (IRAHK, 1996, p. 19; Cimigo, 2008, p. 76).[1] Contrasting with the public perception of its powers is the degree to which the public feels that external supervision over the ICAC should be increased. Perhaps as a consequence of the Tsui case, the percentage of respondents who felt that the ICAC should be subject to increased external supervision stood at a high of 63.5 per cent in 1994 but thereafter it has dropped (Market Behaviour Hong Kong, 1994, p. 16). In 2008, the percentage of respondents who thought that external supervision should be increased was 34.4 per cent (Cimigo, 2008, p. 88).

The Independent Review Committee represents something of a watershed for the ICAC. Although it re-affirmed the traditional model as the approach to combatting corruption, it also identified some of the factors which were to bring about a changing environment and which would require the ICAC to refine its approach to corruption control. It is to these factors that we now turn.

THE CHANGING ENVIRONMENT

In the years immediately before the transition to Chinese sovereignty, there was a marked change in public attitudes towards the ICAC and in perceptions that it would be able to continue its work in the same way after the handover. These perceptions were reinforced by statistics that showed that corruption reports were increasing significantly in both the public and private sectors (Independent Review Committee, 1994, p. 27). There were fears that Hong Kong would revert to the bad old days before the establishment of the Commission and that it might become an instrument in the hands of a future government which would require it to use its powers in substantially different ways. The dropping of the word 'Independent' in describing the Commission in the Basic Law, Hong Kong's constitution after 1997, was widely interpreted to be a sign that the Commission would lose its impartiality and ability to act on its own after the handover (Basic Law, 1990, Article 57). A second concern, which was to become even more apparent after 1997, was that the nature of corruption itself was changing. As Hong Kong became more economically sophisticated, so the traditional forms of corruption such as bribes were giving way to advantages that were deferred and less easy to prosecute under *The Prevention of Bribery Ordinance*. Finally, there were concerns that the nature of public support for the ICAC was changing. Surveys reported greater toleration of corruption among youth and there were signs, arising from the Tsui case, that 'public support for the Commission is not unqualified' and that the special powers which the Commission had been granted should be 'used in a responsible way and for the purpose for which they were intended' (Independent Review Committee, 1994, p. 28).

In the following sections we examine the ways in which the model has been refined to try to meet these new challenges.

Strategic Changes

Quah (2003, p. 145) has identified political will as a critical element in the ICAC's success and, as 1997 approached, the question was whether there was sufficient political will to allow it to pursue its anti-corruption policies with the same vigour that it had done in the past. In his first major policy address, the new Chief Executive stressed that there would be no change in the government's attitude towards corruption and that the ICAC would be provided with additional resources (Chief Executive, 1997, para. 143). Four years later, the then Commissioner was able to report an increase in the number of prosecutions and a drop in the number of corruption reports (Chief Executive, 1997; Lai, 2001). Although this might be regarded as an affirmation of the traditional model, there was at the same time a change of emphasis in approaches to corruption control in both the private and public sectors. The new approach acknowledged the success of the ICAC in dealing with traditional forms of corruption but sought to deal with new forms of corruption by seeking greater collaboration with relevant organizations, both within Hong Kong and across the border in China. This represented a shift from the previous stress on a rule-based approach, in which sanctions were the principal deterrent, to a value-based approach in which, although the rules remained important, more attention was paid to enhancing integrity and strengthening the role of personal values in preventing corrupt practices.

In the private sector, during the transition, major challenges had been posed by the greater integration of Hong Kong with the Pearl River Delta. In the period between 1992 and 1996, for example, the number of reports of cross-border corruption increased four-fold (Legislative Council, 1996). The Delta was a major attraction to Hong Kong small and medium-size enterprises looking for cheaper land and labour. By 2007, there were 80000 of these Hong Kong companies operating in the Delta employing some 11 million people (ICAC and Guangdong Provincial People's Procurate, 2007, p. 5). Paying bribes to officials was seen as a necessary way of obtaining permission to do business and there was little effective control over corruption in the Delta. The anomaly was that a Hong Kong businessman who would never be involved in corrupt practices at home might find them necessary to remain competitive in the Delta. The ICAC has responded to this problem by trying to work with its counterpart in Guangdong Province to specify what is and is not legally permissible (ICAC and Guangdong Provincial People's Procurate, 2007) and by seeking to identify the processes in which corrupt practices might be prevalent in the registration of businesses, the granting of environmental protection permits and in customs clearance. Nonetheless, the problem of this cross-border corruption is a continuing one and can probably only be dealt with through more effective action by the mainland Chinese authorities.

Within Hong Kong, the ICAC has also made efforts to improve integrity and corporate governance in local business. In 1995, it established the Hong Kong Ethics Development Centre, which operates within the Commission and which seeks to improve integrity through collaboration with the Chambers of Commerce and professional organizations such as the Hong Kong Institute of Certified Public Accountants and the Institute of Directors. The Centre offers services to business organizations to help them prevent corruption and produces booklets and leaflets to enable them to develop codes of conduct and best practices. While it is difficult to assess the success of these efforts, they do ensure that the ICAC engages in collaborative work with major business and professional organizations and that a consistent message is being relayed to the private sector on the values to which businesses are expected to adhere. The change in emphasis has been from a reliance on the threat of prosecution to achieve anti-corruption goals to one in which sanctions and collaborative value approaches to corruption control work hand-in-hand.

In the public sector, the shift from rule-based corruption control to value-based integrity management has been even more pronounced. In 1998, the Chief Secretary for Administration met with 300 top-level civil servants in a conference on integrity management. The aim appears to have been to address public concern about corruption at the time of the transition, but it may also be seen as marking the beginning of integrity management programmes in the civil service which sought to cover wider issues than traditional forms. By the 1990s, bribery was no longer a serious problem in the public sector and there was a continuing trend for both corruption reports and prosecutions of public servants to drop. In 2009, for example, of the 342 persons prosecuted on corruption charges only 21 were public servants and of those only 14 were convicted (ICAC, 2009, p. 37, Appendix 10). A further 66 cases were found not to warrant prosecution but were referred to the Civil Service Bureau for possible disciplinary action (ICAC, 2009, p. 38).

A more serious concern which has been reflected in the integrity management initiatives adopted by the ICAC and the Civil Service Bureau after 1998 is that the nature of corruption itself has been changing. Instead of an immediate payment for a service, civil servants might take deferred advantages or pass the advantage on to relatives. They are also more likely to find themselves in conflict of interest situations arising from the greatly increased amount of contracting-out or from post-public employment positions which impinge on areas for which they have previously been responsible. Two high-profile cases aroused public concern. In 2005 a former senior civil servant was in effect accused of lobbying for a multi-million government contract for the parent company of the subsidiary for which she worked. She defended herself vigorously, pointing out that it had been many years since she had worked in the area for which the contract was being awarded, and that her actions had not been in violation of the rules under which she had been permitted to take up employment. The Secretary for the Civil Service conceded that she had been engaged in a conflict of interest but warned that she should discontinue any lobbying activities. In 2008, a former Director of Housing was offered a position with a developer with whom he had previously had dealings while in government. Although he had served a 'sanitization' period of two years which fulfilled the government's requirement, the public outcry was such that he was forced to resign his position (Scott and Leung, 2008).

The problem that faced the government was that it could not tighten the rules sufficiently to appease public outrage. After both cases, it made some effort to increase controls over post- public employment but there were two major difficulties. First, senior civil servants were opposed to major changes, noting that the Basic Law guaranteed the right to work. Second, there was no guarantee that more rules would resolve the problem; in both cases, the former civil servants had complied with most of the rules, although the government claimed that they had not provided it with enough information about what they planned to do. The answer probably lay in creating more awareness of potential conflicts of interest and to move from rule-based to more value-based integrity management. The government has in fact been moving in that direction since the 1998 conference. For the first time, the personal values that civil servants are expected to hold have been spelled out in a published guide to good practice (Civil Service Bureau, 2005). In 2006 integrity management programmes, which are run by the Civil Service Bureau and the ICAC, were institutionalized. An Ethics Officer, of senior rank, was appointed in each department or bureau to chair the Corruption Prevention Group and to devise annual integrity management programmes for the department or bureau. The content of the programme still relies heavily on a rule-based approach, especially in departments with large numbers of junior staff, but there was a much greater emphasis than in the past on potential conflicts of interest with which more senior officers would have to deal in areas such as outsourcing, working with contractors and post-public employment. Finally, in 2009 a Civil Service Code was promulgated which outlines the personal responsibilities of civil servants and provides guidance on potential conflicts of interest (Civil Service Bureau, 2009).

Legal Responses

The changing nature of public sector corruption also required a reconsideration of ways of supplementing *The Prevention of Bribery Ordinance*. The ordinance had been drafted at a time when the most common form of corruption was bribery and when an immediate advantage would be received by the person providing the service. If the advantage was deferred or received by another person, there was less certainty that prosecution would be successful under the Ordinance. In 2002, the landmark case of *Shum Kwok Sher v HKSAR* reached the Court of Final Appeal. Shum, who had been the Chief Property Manager of the Government Property Agency, was found to have awarded large contracts to companies which were unqualified to tender and which were controlled by relatives by marriage (McWalters, 2010, p. 678). He was not charged, however, under *The Prevention of Bribery Ordinance* but rather with the common law offence of misconduct in public office, presumably because the prosecutors thought they might not be able to prove that an advantage had been received by the defendant. The issue for the Court of Final Appeal was whether the offence of misconduct in public office was too broad to provide certainty in prosecution. The Court found that it was not, if it was used in respect of offences in which a public official who in the course of or in relation to his public office wilfully and intentionally culpably misconducts himself (*Shum Kwok Sher v HKSAR; Sin Kam Wah v HKSAR*). The Court distinguished further between acts of omission (non-feasance) and acts of commission (misfeasance and malfeasance). In addition, it said that the offence must be serious. Armed with this new power, between 2003 and 2008 the ICAC initiated the prosecution of a further 33 cases under the misconduct in public office charge.

The potentially wide applicability of the misconduct in public office charge and the difficulty in defining 'serious' has been shown in two 2009 cases in which defendants were charged under the offence with improperly copying public records which might have been useful to them when they took up employment in the private sector (*HKSAR v Chan Tak Ming; HKSAR v Chu King Kwok;* Lai, 2010). In both cases – one involving a doctor who copied medical records; the other concerning tax records – the Court eventually held that the offence was sufficiently serious to warrant conviction under the misconduct in public office charge. The use of the offence to prosecute such cases broadens the concept of corruption and takes it some way beyond the narrower definition of accepting an advantage provided in *The Prevention of Bribery Ordinance.*

Public Support and Collaborative Governance

One of the striking features of the ICAC's work since 1997 has been its clear intent to establish and maintain contact with public servants, with the community and with the private sector. While the ICAC has always been conscious of the need to work with the public, the community and the private sector, this intensification of its efforts could only be achieved by working with partners in those sectors and by becoming much more collaborative than it had previously been. In the public sector, an analysis of its annual reports shows that there has been a steady and very substantial rise in its direct contact with civil servants through seminars and training programmes. In 1993, for example, the ICAC directly contacted 12 378 civil servants in a civil service with a strength of 182000, while in 2009 it had contact with 23 347 civil servants in a civil service with a strength of 157000 (ICAC, 1993, 2009). In addition, the ICAC has its material delivered to every department and bureau through the integrity management programmes, which are presented in part by the departments or bureaus themselves. There are similar broad-based contacts with businesses and business groups, district organizations, youth organizations, housing estates and housing owners' corporations. In 2003, a territory-wide parenting programme which was jointly organized by the ICAC's Community Relations Department, various youth bodies, parent-teacher associations and Radio Television Hong Kong successfully contacted over one million people, about one-seventh of Hong Kong's population (ICAC, 2003). The effects of this intense effort to relate to the society, coupled with continuing publicity through the media and its own television programmes, mean that it is now virtually impossible to avoid the ICAC's anti-corruption, pro-integrity message.

CONCLUSION

While the major features of the ICAC's traditional model remain in place, it has been modified in three important respects to deal with the changing nature of corruption in Hong Kong. First, there has been an increasing emphasis on the need to promote value-based integrity management to deal with conflicts of interest, particularly those relating to post-public employment and contracting-out. Second, legal means have been found to cover offences in those new areas of corruption or unethical behaviour, especially by supplementing *The Prevention of Bribery Ordinance* with the common law offence of misconduct in public office. Finally, the ICAC has become much more collaborative in its approach to corruption prevention, seeking to penetrate deeply into the departments and bureaus through the integrity management programmes and actively looking for partners in the private sector. There is no doubt that the organization has outlived its original mission, which was focused on cleaning up corruption in the public sector, particularly the police. New challenges in fields where neither the problem nor the solution is as evident as in the past will require innovative responses and continuing adaptation of the original model.

ACKNOWLEDGEMENT

I am grateful for the assistance of the Centre of Anti-Corruption Studies, ICAC in writing this chapter. The views expressed, however, are my own.

NOTE

1. The Cimigo report was a random sample of 1543 persons aged between 15 and 64 who were successfully interviewed in November 2008.

REFERENCES

Basic Law of the Hong Kong Special Administrative Region of The People's Republic of China (1990), Hong Kong: The Consultative Committee for the Basic Law of the Hong Kong Special Administrative Region of The People's Republic of China.

Blair-Kerr, Sir Alastair (July 1973), *First Report of the Commission of Inquiry under Sir Alastair Blair-Kerr*, Hong Kong: Government Printer.

Blair-Kerr, Sir Alastair (September 1973), *Second Report of the Commission of Inquiry under Sir Alastair Blair-Kerr*, Hong Kong: Government Printer.

Chief Executive (1997), *Building Hong Kong for a New Era*, Hong Kong: Printing Department.

Cimigo (2008), *ICAC Annual Survey 2008 –Report*, Hong Kong: mimeo.

Civil Service Bureau (2005), *Civil Servants' Guide to Good Practices*, 2nd edition, www.csb.gov.hk.

Civil Service Bureau (2009) *Civil Service Code*, www.csb.gov.hk.

de Speville, Bertrand (2010), 'Anticorruption commissions: The "Hong Kong Model" revisited' *Asia Pacific Review* **17**(1), 47–71.

Hong Kong Hansard Session 1973/1974, 17 October 1973; 30 January 1974, available at: http://onlinebooks.library.upenn.edu/webbin/serial?id=hklchansard.

Hong Kong Hansard Session 1977/1978, 7 November 1977, available at: http://onlinebooks.library.upenn.edu/webbin/serial?id=hklchansard.

Hong Kong Hansard Session 1993/1994, 1 December 1993; 26 January 1994, available at: http://onlinebooks.library.upenn.edu/webbin/serial?id=hklchansard.

Huberts, Leo (2000), 'Anticorruption strategies: The Hong Kong model in international context', *Public Integrity* **2**, 211–228.

ICAC Review Committee (1994), *Report of the ICAC Review Committee*, Hong Kong: Government Printer.

Independent Commission Against Corruption (ICAC) (1974–2009), *Annual Reports of the Commissioner of the independent Commission Against Corruption*, Hong Kong: Government Printer.

Independent Commission Against Corruption Ordinance, Cap 204 available at: http://www.hklii.org/hk/legis/en/ord/204/

Independent Commission Against Corruption (ICAC) and Guangdong Provincial People's Procurate (2007), *Integrity and Compliance with the Law: A Guide for the Prevention of Corruption for SME Investors in Guangdong and Hong Kong*, www.icac.org.hk.

International Research Associates (HK) (1996), *Annual ICAC Survey*, Hong Kong: mimeo.

Lai, Alan N. (2001), 'Keeping Hong Kong clean: experiences of fighting corruption post 1997', *Harvard Asia Pacific Review* **5**(2), (Fall), 51–54.

Lai, Louisa N.M. (2010), 'Facing the challenges of corruption in the 21st century – are laws on corruption effective?', Paper presented to the conference 'Collaborative Governance and Integrity Management', Hong Kong, 16–18 September.

Legislative Council, Panel on Security (1994), *Enquiry into the circumstances surrounding the termination of the employment of Mr. Alex Tsui Ka-kit, former Senior Assistant Director of the Independent Commission Against Corruption*, Hong Kong: mimeo.

Legislative Council, Panel on Security (1996), *Minutes*, Legislative Council Paper No CB (20 329/96-97.

Lethbridge, Henry J. (1985), *Hard Graft in Hong Kong*, Hong Kong: Oxford University Press.

Lo, Jack M.K. (2001), 'Controlling corruption in Hong Kong: from colony to special administrative region', *Journal of Contingencies and Crisis Management*, **9**(1), 21–8.

McWalters, Ian (2010), *Bribery and Corruption Law in Hong Kong*, 2nd edition, Hong Kong: Lexis Nexis.

Manion, Melanie (2004), *Corruption By Design: Building Clean Government in China and Hong Kong*, Cambridge, Mass.: Harvard University Press.

Market Behaviour Hong Kong (1994), *Annual ICAC Survey*, Hong Kong: mimeo.

Munn, Christopher (2001), *Anglo-China: Chinese People and British Rule in Hong Kong 1841–1880*, Richmond, Surrey: Curzon.

Quah, Jon S.T. (2003), *Curbing Corruption in Asia: A Comparative Study of Six Countries*, Singapore: Eastern Universities Press.

Scott, Ian (1989), *Political Change and the Crisis of Legitimacy in Hong Kong*, Hong Kong: Oxford University Press.

Scott, Ian (2010), *The Public Sector in Hong Kong*, Hong Kong: Hong Kong University Press.

Scott, Ian and Joan Leung (2008), 'Managing integrity: the regulation of post public employment in Britain and Hong Kong' *Public Organization Review*, **8**, 365–80.

Tu, Elsie (2003), *Colonial Hong Kong in the Eyes of Elsie Tu*, Hong Kong: Hong Kong University Press.

22 Developing cultures of integrity in the public and private sectors

Richard Mulgan and John Wanna

Anti-corruption strategies place considerable emphasis on the importance of developing appropriate cultures which encourage integrity in those entrusted with positions of responsibility (and more broadly within the wider community). Integrity cultures, in this sense, may be broadly understood as the set of endorsed social understandings, behaviours and practices that affect how people think and act. Cultures are commonly distinguished from the formal organizational structures, such as institutions and legal rules. While such institutions and rules provide the background context and can help to frame social action, it is the living-breathing culture that determines how they operate in practice and how people act in the many situations not covered by formal rules. Accordingly, while the quality of legal regulation is certainly an important factor in affecting the extent of malfeasance or corruption, research has repeatedly shown that underlying cultural values and informal expectations among the actors involved are equally, if not more, influential (Dobel, 2005; Heintzman, 2006). For this reason, much of the emphasis in building ethical environments and in combating corruption has moved from legal enforcement of ethical rules towards trying to change cultural attitudes in the direction of greater support for integrity and greater intolerance of corrupt behaviour.

The contrast and interplay between culture and legal enforcement in anti-corruption strategies reflects more general philosophical tensions between two approaches to professional ethics in both the private and public sectors. One, a more legalistic or codified approach concentrates on following rules and procedures that specify standards of appropriate practice, where breaches can be clearly identified and, if necessary, penalized. The emphasis is usually on formal regulatory regimes, stimulating common or minimal thresholds of acceptable behaviour and relying primarily on disincentives, such as the fear of detection and punishment, to encourage compliance (for example rules for company directors or heads of government agencies). The other approach is more aspirational in tone and informal in practice, highlighting ideal or desired values, such as public service or corporate commitment, rather than rules and regulations. A values-oriented approach appeals to people's sense of individual responsibility and their commitment to the collective good as a motive for action. It is motivational rather than compliance driven; and also emphasizes the importance of values as a major foundation of organizational culture that underpins individual and collective responsibility and commitment. Values may be shaped and recalibrated by societal, ideological or religious views, organizational aspirations, as well as by professional and personal ethics.

Neither approach is sufficient on its own to guarantee sound ethical and professional practice. A purely legalistic strategy has obvious deficiencies in that rules-based codes can be perfunctory and disregarded, and much of the behaviour associated with ethically appropriate action cannot be stipulated in explicit pro-forma rules. Latitude must always be allowed for the exercise of personal discretion in facing particular situations. Moreover, rules tend to concentrate on specifying prohibitions (suppressing or outlawing transgressions or corrupt behaviour) or setting minimal standards of good behaviour, whereas ethical values often call for positive initiatives well beyond negative avoidance of malpractice. Recent thinking about management in general, in both the public and the private sectors, has absorbed many of these lessons. Management theory has moved beyond the detailed, quasi-contractual specification of objectives and now emphasizes the role of goal-driven action and individual discretion on the part of managers, placing common purpose and shared values at the core of organizational performance (Dobel, 2005). Values are a powerful driving force behind both culture and performance.

On the other hand, culture and values, though vital to integrity, cannot be maintained alone without the back-up of rules and enforcement. Laws need to be clearly articulated and breaches need to be detected and penalized as an inducement encouraging a threshold of minimal compliance within which a culture of ethical practice can flourish. A combination of incentives grounded in self-interest and other-regarding motives derived from collective values (sticks as well as carrots) is essential to any strategy of integrity. Indeed, the formal promulgation of rules and of procedures for enforcing compliance, like all legal codes, have their own wider ethical purpose through transparency as a public affirmation of the values they incorporate. If culture is now the focus of anti-corruption policies, it is as a previously neglected supplement to legal enforcement, not as a direct replacement of it.

The greatest responsibility for promoting a culture of integrity lies with those placed in charge of an organization who cannot only institute relevant policies to encourage ethical standards but also, through their own personal actions, set high ethical standards for their subordinates. Such 'demonstration effects' operate at all levels in organizations where members or employees will be either encouraged, or discouraged, by the practice of their immediate superiors. Indeed, a culture of integrity is the responsibility of all members of an organization, whatever their position in the organizational hierarchy (a point neatly captured by Uhr's 'lattice of leadership', which extends concepts of moral leadership to the more dispersed, informal networks found in all organizations (Uhr, 2005)).

Integrity cultures are found in different settings and at different levels of particularity, for instance across whole societies or in specific institutions or organizations. Culture is also seamless and cannot be neatly separated into distinct sub-divisions. The culture of an organization is iterative and developmental; it is clearly affected by the national civic cultures of a society, social groups or professions while its members will, in turn, also contribute to those civic values. Similarly, national cultures themselves are not wholly independent and self-sufficient but are increasingly affected by outside norms and influences, including international cultural attitudes. Indeed, the current worldwide drive against corruption can be seen as an expression of global culture, as articulated, for instance by the opinion-leading think tank, Transparency International, and by international aid donors such as the World Bank and the International Monetary Fund (Pope, 2010).

If we wish to reduce corruption, the interplay between national and organizational cultures is highly relevant. National culture, for example, affects general social attitudes towards acceptable or unacceptable behaviour, including what 'counts' as corrupt behaviour in that society. Organizational culture is also important insofar as it can either encourage or discourage general attitudes of honesty and fair dealing within particular organizations, which are the main site of corrupt behaviour.

Anti-corruption strategies of cultural change therefore operate at both the national and the organizational level. Transparency International, for instance, has centered its corruption perceptions index (CPI) on individual nations taken as a whole and its concept of a National Integrity System adopts a society-wide focus, including changes to national attitudes. At the same time, as part of this holistic approach, Transparency International has also developed a series of policy positions aimed at controlling corruption within particular organizations, including government departments, accountability agencies and private-sector corporations. Anti-corruption strategies at the organizational level are seen as essential building blocks for increasing wider social support for government integrity.

The main focus of the rest of this chapter is on how individual organizations can develop their own internal cultures of greater integrity with less tolerance of corruption. The influence of the wider society cannot be ignored, both the general cultural attitudes towards corruption and the effectiveness of external accountability agencies including the judicial system. But the emphasis is on organizations themselves and on their distinctive values and internal practices which are within the control of the organization and its members.

Building organizational cultures of integrity (and reducing the incidence of corruption) is of concern to both public and private sector organizations. Traditionally, much analysis of integrity shortcomings centered on the public sector and on government officials who had contravened the public interest for private gain, but private corporations can also be undermined by the illegitimate pursuit of private interests. The collective good in a private company may be more narrowly circumscribed than in a public organization, referring more to the pursuit of the company's particular objectives, such as shareholder benefit, than to the common good of society as a whole. But members of a private organization can clearly act corruptly to pervert the company's objectives by preferring their own advantage, as when company executives enrich themselves at the shareholders' expense, when rank-and-file employees improperly siphon off company assets, or when managers engage in nepotistic activity. Encouraging a culture of integrity is therefore a management function common to both sectors, involving common approaches and strategies.

The extent of such commonalities arguably reflects a growing convergence between management practices in the two sectors. In the last quarter century, public sector management has adopted many of the concepts and strategies of business management (including the generic term 'management' itself), leading to a greater emphasis on managerial autonomy and accountability in terms of measurable results. The notion of the values-based, mission-driven organization, now central to public management, is largely derived from business management. More recently, in turn, the world of business management itself has been shaken by a number of systemic failures brought on by executives more interested in their own enrichment than in sustaining the long-term value of their companies, notably the collapse of ENRON in 2002, Parmalat in 2003–04 and Lehman Brothers in the sub-prime and financial crisis dating from 2008 (Beggs and Dean, 2007; Hamilton and Micklethwait, 2006; McDonald and Robinson, 2010). It can also include greedy executives taking massive severance or termination packages from failing or underperforming companies, or adopting government bail-outs as personal bonuses. These collapses and executive practices have led many commentators on corporate ethics to expound a wider, social role for commercial companies beyond the narrow pursuit of profit (for example Corporate Social Responsibility (CSR) or sustainable responsible businesses), bringing private corporations somewhat closer to public institutions in their scope and values.

Against such a background, it is not surprising to find considerable common ground between the sectors over both the need to develop strong ethical cultures and the measures that should be adopted for this purpose. At the same time, relevant differences between the sectors should not be overlooked. For instance, public institutions are still enmeshed in a more extensive panoply of public accountabilities and retain a greater professional commitment to due process and impartiality in the conduct of their business, both in their treatment of the citizenry and in their own internal organizations. Such process pre-occupations, though sometimes disparaged by managerialist reformers critical of bureaucratic red tape, stem from widespread public expectations about the value of a rule-based government system with demonstrable public accountabilities. These expectations, in turn, feed a greater intolerance of corruption in government agencies than in commercial companies. The bar for institutional and professional integrity is set significantly higher in the public sector than in the private sector, as is the corresponding threshold for types of nominated corruption (for example nepotism or patronage, inducements, sponsorships). Transparency and disclosure is also far greater in the public sector context.

Moreover, it is misleading to equate a concern for ethical integrity in commercial companies as equivalent to a broadening of their goals to encompass social responsibility as well as the pursuit of profit, a simplistic conflation of objectives commonly assumed in the business ethics literature. Even when companies focus narrowly on maximizing profit and returns to shareholders, important ethical dilemmas can still arise. For instance, anti-trust behaviour between firms in the marketplace is illegal and unethical – and constantly policed by trade commissions and competition watchdogs. Similarly, bribes and other inducements given to officials in overseas countries to secure international contracts is a common but ethically dubious practice. So too is self-interested behaviour by executives who receive performance bonuses according to the movements in the share price of public companies and who can 'inflate' the price in the short-term to the detriment of the interests of the company. In this way, executives and managers can pit their own interests against those of the company and leave well before the repercussions are felt.

The ethical failure of executives in such instances was not an *excessive* focus on corporate profit, as some critics have maintained, but rather a neglect of long-term shareholders' financial interests brought on by the selfish pursuit of personal interests. Similarly, workers who steal from the companies that employ them are behaving unethically, even if the companies' owners are concerned only with making a profit. Ethics in the private sector should be seen as primarily focused on the stewardship of the enterprise as a going concern (the owners' financial investments and employee entitlements) and not necessarily combined with the quite separate campaign for Corporate Social Responsibility

Important differences, relevant to the development of cultures of integrity, can also be found within each sector. The private sector, for example, involves both commercial for- profit companies and non-profit organizations (NGOs) such as charitable organizations and public-interest advocacy groups. Compared with for-profit companies, non-profit organizations have typically operated with lower levels of accountability, both to external agencies and internally within their own ranks. They have preferred to rely more on trusting the personal commitment and values of their members (see Goodin, 2003; Mulgan, 2003, ch. 4), though this trust can sometimes be abused.

Significant institutional and professional differences are also found within the public sector. For instance, the concept of 'a public service', with its own particular ethical values and responsibilities, usually applies only to government departments and related agencies and excludes many other government employees working for publicly-owned organizations and employed out of public funds (for instance staff in public hospitals and public schools or universities, employees in state-owned utilities, political advisers working directly for politicians, and so on). These latter groups typically have their own professional standards and codes, but they tend to be slightly different from those covering the core public service.

Integrity cultures in the public sector cover corrupt or improper behaviours ranging far and wide, such as not leaking confidential information or using confidential information for private gain, avoiding conflicts of interest (or properly declaring them), not accepting bribes or inducements, maintaining the accuracy of the public record, dealing fairly and promptly with members of the public, avoiding partisan political activity. Public officials have to abide by tougher laws and procedures, such as freedom of information regimes, statutory requirements under public service acts, judicial review of decisions, investigations of behaviour by various public sector commissioners, ombudsmen and legislators, as well as the more generally applied crimes acts. They are more liable to be routinely investigated by congressional or parliamentary committees and at public hearings.

In addition, elected members of legislatures have their own distinct ethical issues and their own methods for dealing with them (Allen, 2009). Their ethical standards tend to concentrate on issues such as their pecuniary interests and any perceived conflicts of interest, accepting bribes or even misleading the legislature in statements; but they are generally less strict on matters of impartiality than those applying to professional public servants. Politicians operate in the political realm of public dialogue and are subject to the more variable and flexible standards of political accountability. As elected members of the supreme law-making body, they are usually jealous of their own prerogatives and reluctant to make themselves accountable to strict codes or to other authorities (although many countries have seen the growth of parliamentary commissioners and integrity commissioners for members of parliament – see Woodhouse 1998). Similarly, members of the judiciary, under the standard separation of powers, maintain their own distinct standards and enforcement structures, and in some jurisdictions can even decree statutory provisions that apply to the community but do not apply to them as the judiciary.

Thus, although a culture of integrity is important across all types of organizations, and many of the measures used in cultivating such a culture have relevance in different environments, allowance must always be made for the particular nature of the organization in question as well as for the wider cultural context in which it operates.

A strategy for inculcating a culture of integrity within an organization is generally recognized to incorporate the following elements:

(i) defining corporate values and norms through codes of conduct;
(ii) modelling ethical practice by the leadership and members of an organization;
(iii) establishing governance structures that encourage compliance with the values and norms; and
(iv) ethical training as a part of professional development.

In addition, large organizations operating in areas highly vulnerable to ethical jeopardy or where the risk of corruption is higher (such as the police and enforcement agencies, security services, the gaming and liquor industries, procurement agencies, elite sports leagues, some key regulators such as competition and commerce commissions) may also need be monitored and investigated by specialist standing anti-corruption commissions (for example crime and misconduct commissions, special anti-corruption investigative agencies, royal commissions, international misconduct investigatory bodies). For some of these bodies, entrapment and integrity testing is a means of gauging the integrity of organizational cultures and the honesty of individual officials.

(i) Codes of conduct and statements of ethical values have long been a feature of modern organizations and public services, although they were not always labelled as such. Codes are articulations of a combination of values and rules proscribed for the organization. They sit under the

mission statement of an organization that sets out the core objectives and values of that organization. Codes are positive inducements to members or staff (and perhaps clients) to behave ethically and be aware of ethical obligations/expectations. Moreover, such codes of conduct are usually produced through some process of deliberation in or across the organization, meaning the entire process of developing such a code can in itself be an exercise in ethics education for the organization (Messikomer and Cirka, 2010). As sanctioned documents, these codes should be made widely available through the organization and should be regularly referred to by leaders and in relevant personnel or contexts or in interactions with outsiders.

Codes usually specify requirements for the members of the organization, and sometimes for those who might have interaction with the organization (for example clients or customers). They require staff to observe legal obligations (in the spirit as well as in the letter) and often to some professional ethics or standards. They also tend to include desired personal qualities such as employees must display honesty and integrity, dedication, respect, courtesy, respect for others and property. Such codes can be short pithy lists – able to be conveyed in a handbook or displayed publicly in a poster (say on the wall of a bank or government department); these codes are typically aspirational in character – expressing an organizational commitment to promote desired behaviour. Alternatively, they may be lengthy legalistic statements infused with professional standards and legal obligations. Professional codes for lawyers, financiers and accountants tend to be of this type. Both types of codes have advantages and disadvantages in terms of culture and compliance (see Benson 1989).

In the public sector, many civil service cultures have expressed service-wide values and codes which apply to the constituent organizations as a whole. Comparatively speaking, we find that US governments have preferred lengthy legalistic codes governing public ethics (able to be investigated by the Office of Government Ethics), whereas more recent European practice has been for shorter, principle-based codes. In some cases, national public service codes are stipulated in statutory form and have legal enforcement (for example Canada, Australia and New Zealand, each of which has a dedicated public service or state sector Act, as well as regularly updated accountability Acts covering resources and behaviours – for example the *Canadian Federal Accountability Act 2006*). These codes often reiterate that support for traditional public service, values of merit appointment and promotion, and independence from political pressure, helps build and retain a culture of integrity (OECD, 2009). It is not unusual for generic codes to apply across a public service, while specific agencies within the service have articulated complementary codes for their own purposes. Often these codes derived from earlier guidelines of official conduct which stipulated dimensions of illegality and misconduct but generally only in a negative fashion. Other government agencies not covered by these generic codes have tended to adopt their own version of a code that is suitable to their activities (for example public universities, public broadcasters, utilities providers), and these may have special provisions for their operatives (for example on plagiarism, service standards, attention to bias, confidentiality, animal or human experimentation or research).

Moreover, at the international level the United Nations and other professional bodies have produced similar codes for public officials, such as the1996 UN *International Code for Public Officials* and the OECD's principles for managing ethics (1998), its survey of ethical measures in OECD nations (2000), and its principles-based codes of good governance and good corporate governance (Dobel, 2005, p. 156; OECD, 1998, 2000 and 2004). The OECD also issued an ethics checklist for the public service in 1997 to assist member countries in designing and undertaking reviews of their ethics regimes – and this checklist has been used for public assessments of ethical standards (see Briggs, 2009).

One of the potential sticking points with public service codes is whether they apply equally to ministers as well as officials, and whether other co-producers (consultants and lobbyists, NGOs, other partners, public employees from other levels of government) are bound by them. Most governments have adopted separate codes for ministers (sometimes executively issued, sometimes tabled in legislatures), as well as more minimalist codes for other politicians (pecuniary interests registers, parliamentary codes of conduct), and registers for lobbyists and consultants. Codes applying to politicians of whatever rank tend to be politically enforced (discretionary – usually the chief minister or cabinet or more formally the legislature – see Williams, 2002), although serious breaches of the law can be enforced and formal charges pressed by enforcement agencies and independent crime and misconduct commissions. There have long been arguments for the need for dedicated parliamentary integrity commissioners to oversee politicians as a discrete cohort (Woodhouse, 1998; Uhr, 2002; Preston, 2002). Following the ground-breaking report from Lord Nolan (1997) into parliamentary standards (called as a result of the cash-for-questions affair), the UK parliament has established a Parliamentary Commissioner for Standards to monitor MPs' behaviour, but it is not clear whether that office has really improved behaviour given the later expenses scandals. Woodhouse (1998) has also criticized the commissioner's office as having insufficient independence from the legislature and its privileges committee.

Typically, the most frequent breaches of public service codes are usually improper use of the internet, diverse misconduct matters, harassment and bullying, and improper influence in recruitment and selection processes. Breaches of misconduct in the public sector are largely policed internally: with public service commissions, central agencies, employment agencies, controller-general (auditors) and organizational executives in the front line (the police and courts are less frequently involved unless breaches are relatively serious breaches – criminal acts, assaults). Enforcement requires reporting mechanisms, complaints procedures, and support for whistle-blowing agents. Sanctions or punishments include termination of employment, counselling, reprimand, demotion, reduction in salary and re-assignment.

In the private sector, too, codes of conduct are very common; they were previously known as 'Credos' in US corporations combining desired codes of ethics with intended corporate ambitions or strategies. As Stevens (2008) argues, when codes are embedded in a sympathetic corporate culture they can help to reinforce that culture. Formal requirements for public companies to have a code of ethics have also risen; for instance, since 2004 the New York Stock Exchange and NASDAQ have required that all listed companies operate from and disclose a code of ethics (Svensson, Wood and Callaghan, 2010). In Europe, including the UK, company codes of conduct are still less common than in US, but are more likely to be focused on the firm's Corporate Social Responsibility (CSR) (Stohl, Stohl and Popova, 2009). Many large corporations have corporate-wide codes applying to their various divisions, and franchised businesses often require their franchisees to accept to operate within an umbrella code of conduct across all their outlets.

Private sector codes are variably enforced by company executives and boards internally, with the range of sanctions paralleling those for the public sector mentioned above. Serious breaches may be investigated by competition commissions, securities commissions, trade commissions, and other corporate enforcement bodies. The legal system is able to be used for specific offences (for example sexual harassment or fraud).

Debates around codes of conduct centre on whether they are of practical value or are merely cosmetic window dressing. The issue is how much notice does the organization (and its members) take of such formal statements and does it affect day-to-day behaviour (instil good values and behaviour and prevent lapses). Some organizations that have committed illegal behaviour and displayed reprehensible ethical lapses have nevertheless possessed a code of conduct (Enron had a code of conduct). In and of themselves, codes are not sufficient to guarantee ethical practice. Rather the consensus of opinion is that codes are important statements of integrity intent but that organizational commitment is still needed (Svensson, Wood and Callaghan, 2010).

(ii) When *modelling ethical practice* in organizations, leaders concerned about inculcating a culture of integrity should ensure their own behaviour clearly reflects the organization's core values and approved ethical principles, both in their dealings with the wider public and when interacting with their own staff or members. Other organizational members naturally take their lead from their superiors and from their perception of whether honest practice will help or hinder their own personal advancement in the organization. No amount of specific ethical policies can compensate for poor ethical values in everyday conduct. At the same time, leaders need to recognize that responsibility for the ethical health of an organization lies with all of its members and that the role of leaders, though crucial, is not sufficient on its own.

(iii) Organizations should *establish governance structures* that encourage and impose compliance with ethical values and codes of conduct. Explicit responsibility for upholding and promoting these values, as well as overseeing compliance, should immediately rest with senior executives and, where applicable, with boards of directors (including external appointees and community representatives). In larger organizations, specialist compliance officers can also be appointed within the organization, for instance, integrity or ethics officers, inspector generals and internal auditors, who are clearly responsible to senior management. Even public ombudsmen can play a monitoring and educative role here after following up complaints. Internal whistle-blowing procedures should be established, with special provisions for the protection of whistle-blowers. Also of value are 'ethics hotlines', web-based 'chat-rooms' and commentary boxes designed to illicit queries, suggestions and complaints from staff or members. Regular reports should be published on aspects of the organization's ethical culture, demonstrating compliance in the interests of transparency and accountability, including, for example, reports on how the organization inculcates and expresses its values and norms, progress or achievement reports, reviews of internal procedures, reports admitting problems or lapses, such as ethical dilemmas or incidents, or other complaints.

(iv) All professional development should include provision for *formal ethical training* including mentoring and providing assistance with negotiating ethical dilemmas in situ. In the public sector, ethics training is often a component of induction programmes and specialist training modules (from short courses to residential programs). Many central agencies and public service commissions routinely deliver integrity training specially adapted to the needs and requirements of that jurisdiction. And on the basis of cross-country experience, the OECD (2009) has declared dedicated ethical training to be a key part of an integrity policy for government. In the private sector, there have been calls for business schools to teach professional ethics within their curricula to counter the perception that business schools inculcate a cut-throat 'anything does' attitude. But there are doubts about whether isolated classroom teaching of ethics is successful when compared with internal, on-the-spot acculturation. It has been claimed that there are limitations and problems with internal ethics courses conducted within companies because they typically focus on compliance with rules and sanctions rather than encouraging positive values (Beggs and Dean, 2007). There are also risks in relying too heavily on external professional ethics experts who have little direct experience with the organization and its particular challenges. The best approach appears to be to base the training on actual case studies of ethical dilemmas faced by members of the organization and to draw directly on the experience of senior staff in helping resolve them satisfactorily. In addition, some business theorists support the adoption of wider views of corporate responsibility (for example triple bottom line, stakeholder responsiveness) as ways of inserting an ethical compass into organizations (Beggs and Dean, 2007, p. 31).

Finally, in conclusion, as we have shown, a culture of integrity has many causes and is not easily cultivated by any single approach. A combination of the above measures outlined in the 'strategy for inculcating a culture of integrity' will therefore be required. Moreover, because ethical practice is the responsibility of all members of an organization, as Uhr's 'lattice' metaphor underlines, it cannot be imposed solely by top-down direction. Ethical leadership is necessary but by no means sufficient for an ethical organization. Any ethical 'strategy', understood simply as a plan for leaders to implement, can therefore never be wholly successful on its own.

BIBLIOGRAPHY

Allen, N. (2009), 'Voices from the shop floor: MPs and the domestic effects of ethic reforms', *Parliamentary Affairs*, **62**(1), 88–107.

Beggs, J. M. and K.L. Dean (2007), 'Legislated ethics or ethics education? Faculty views in the post-Enron era', *Journal of Business Ethics*, **71**, 15–37.

Benson, G. (1989), 'Codes of ethics', *Journal of Business Ethics*, **8**(5), 305–19.

Briggs, L. (2009), Testing APS Ethics: where's the integrity?', *Australian Journal of Public Administration*, **68**(2), June, 119–136.

Dobel, J. P. (2005), 'Public management as ethics' in E. Ferlie, L. E. Lynn and C. Pollitt (eds), *The Oxford Handbook of Public Management*, New York: Oxford University Press, 156–81.

Goodin, R. (2003), 'Democratic Accountability: the distinctiveness of the third sector', *Archives Europeennes de Sociologie*, **44**(3), 359–96.

Hamilton, S. and A. Micklethwait (2006), *Greed and Corporate Failure: the Lessons from Recent Disasters*, Basingstoke: Palgrave Macmillan.

Heintzman, R. (2006), 'Public Service values and ethics: from principles to results', *Canadian Government Executive*, Ottawa, February.

Kaptein, M. (2009), 'Ethics programs and ethical culture: a next step in unraveling their multi-faceted relationship', *Journal of Business Ethics*, **89**(2), 261–81.

McDonald, L. and P. Robinson (2010), *A Colossal Failure of Common Sense: the Inside Story of the Collapse of Lehman Brothers*, New York: Crown.

Messikomer, C. M. and C.C. Cirka (2010), 'Constructing a Code of Ethics: an experiential case of a national professional organization', *Journal of Business Ethics*, **95**, 55–71.

Mulgan, R. (2003), *Holding Power to Account*, Basingstoke: Palgrave Macmillan.

OECD (1998), *Principles for Managing Ethics in the Public Service PUMA Policy Brief* http://www.oecd.org/dataoecd/60/13/1899138.pdf

OECD (2000), *Trust in Government: Ethics Measures in OECD Countries*, Paris: OECD.

OECD (2004), *Policy Brief: The OECD Principles of Corporate Governance*, http://www.oecd.org/dataoecd/41/32/33647763.pdf

OECD (2009), *Towards a Sound Integrity Framework: Instruments, Processes, Structures and Conditions for Implementation*, http://www.oecd.org/officialdocuments/displaydocument pdf?cote=GOV/PGC/GF%282009%291&doclanguage=en

Pope, J. (2007), 'The third phase in the fight against corruption: implementation and comparative administrative ethics', *Public Integrity*, **10**(1), 75–83.

Pope, J. (2010), 'Getting integrity reforms adopted: lessons from experience with Transparency International', ANZSOG Conference 2010, Delivering Policy Reform, Melbourne, 11–12th August.

Preston, N. (2002), 'Conduct unbecoming: Independent Commissioners and Ministerial Office, in J. Fleming and I. Holland (eds), *Motivating Ministers to Morality*, Dartmouth: Ashgate.

Stevens, B. (2008), 'Corporate ethical codes: effective instruments for influencing ' *Journal of Business Ethics*, **78**(4), 601–609.

Stohl, C., M. Stohl and L. Popova (2009), 'A new generation of corporate codes', *Journal of Business Ethics*, **90**, 607–622.

Svensson, G., G. Wood and M. Callaghan (2010), 'A comparison of business ethics commitment in private and public sector organizations in Sweden', *Business Ethics: A European Review I*, **19**(2), 213–232.

Uhr, J. (2002), *Reforming the Parliament* (Democratic Audit of Australia), http://arts.anu.edu.au/democraticaudit/categories/accountabfrm.htm

Uhr, J. (2005), *Terms of Trust*, Sydney: University of New South Wales Press.

Uhr, J. (2010) 'Modernised modes of government ethics', in R. Koch, P. Conrad and W. H. Horig (eds), *New Public Service*, Wiesbaden: Gabler Verlag, pp. 2–16.

Williams, R. (2002), 'Conduct unbecoming: the regulation of legislative ethics in Britain and the United States', *Parliamentary Affairs* **55**(4), 611–625.

Woodhouse, D. (1998), 'The Parliamentary Commissioner for Standards: lessons from the "cash for questions" inquiry', *Parliamentary Affairs* **51**(1), 51–71.

23 Reporting corrupt practices in the public interest: innovative approaches to whistleblowing

Inez Dussuyer, Stephen Mumford and Glenn Sullivan

> Secrecy is no longer acceptable; too many lives and livelihoods have been lost or destroyed because a whistle could not be blown. But too often the voice of the honest worker or citizen has been drowned out by abusive, unaccountable bosses. Invariably, staying silent was the only option. Creating a safe alternative to silence represents a difficult challenge, legally and culturally; separating the message from the messenger is still obstructed by vested interests, deeply ingrained sociological habits and attitudes, and by the limitations of the law.[1]

INTRODUCTION – WHISTLEBLOWING IN THE PUBLIC INTEREST

Whistleblowing, or public interest disclosure, is integral to tackling corruption and misconduct. It is essential to democratic accountability and should be encouraged. How whistleblowing is handled is also a means of demonstrating commitment to integrity in government and to good public administration.

The media has widely reported on many hidden forms of corruption and misconduct exposed by whistleblowers across the public and private sectors. The list world-wide is long – dramatic examples include the 1971 'Pentagon papers' regarding the involvement of the United States of America in the Viet Nam war; fraudulent accounting practices at Enron; and prisoner abuse at Abu Ghraib. In Australia examples are: 'Dr Death' at Bundaberg Hospital Queensland and security breaches at Sydney airport in 2003.[2]

The media also frequently reports on the outcome of official investigations into corruption and misconduct, following allegations by whistleblowers. Recent examples are public reports of investigations triggered by whistleblowers conducted by the Victorian Ombudsman; including allegations of bribery at a university which had the potential to impact on public safety (July, 2010) and another about the integrity and accountability of police drug exhibits and mistreatment of a whistleblower in relation to the Victoria Police Forensic Services Centre (December, 2009).[3]

This chapter discusses responses to whistleblowing in the public interest,[4] about misconduct and corruption in areas such as education, transport, health and other public authorities, as well as by members of parliament, ministers and judicial office holders, local government councillors and employees, government departments and related organizations. Key themes in responding to whistleblowing in different countries are identified, and ways of managing whistleblowing which assist in strengthening the confidence of whistleblowers to come forward and ensure they are protected and their concerns effectively handled are described. The example of the Victorian Ombudsman's approach and practical experience in dealing with whistleblowing complaints is also addressed. Improvements are also identified for managing whistleblowing within public sector organizations and for developing good practice.

There are considerable obstacles for any employee who brings corruption and misconduct to light from within an organization. Individuals who have blown the whistle on corrupt conduct are reported to experience serious, adverse consequences and reprisals in the workplace; and they may incur personal and financial costs. They may also believe little action is taken as a result of their disclosures. It is not surprising therefore that those persons with knowledge of corruption and misconduct have often remained silent (Miceli & Near, 1992; De Maria & Jan, 1994; De Maria, 1999; Brown, 2008).

However, the price of keeping quiet about corruption and misconduct is high. As Calland and Dehn (2004) note, there are damaging effects to workplace culture when corruption and misconduct are ignored. Opportunities to deal with corruption and serious misconduct before it is too late are missed, potentially causing more problems and perhaps leaving the public at risk and may include long-term consequences for the integrity of an organization. This impacts on the public's trust and confidence in government and signals that accountability processes are not working effectively. In the past, the media has often been the main outlet for reporting on corruption and misconduct, in the absence of whistleblower laws. While it has a role to play in reporting on corruption, the media does not provide a course of action for formal investigation or redress, nor protection for the whistleblower.

It is clear that whistleblowing performs an important role in public sector organizations and is integral to good public administration. Whistleblowing should be seen as providing a valuable service in the public interest rather than a form of betrayal or disloyalty. It is essential then to have effective responses within a protective framework, to enable reporting on corruption and misconduct to take place whereby persons observing corruption and misconduct can report it safely through clearly designated and trusted channels within an organization, and/or to external authorities, without fear of suffering reprisal. This is important not only for the whistleblower, but also for those who may be at risk of false allegations. The responses to whistleblowing should also facilitate the formal investigation of whistleblower allegations so that action can be taken where necessary on the findings. They should also allow for the exoneration of the innocent.[5]

In the 1980s and 1990s there was increasing recognition of the need for effective responses to whistleblowing and systems have now been established in many countries for the official recognition and management of public interest whistleblowing (Calland & Dehn, 2004; Vandekerckhove, 2006). These include whistleblower protection legislation, processes for receiving and investigating whistleblower complaints and allegations. Other initiatives within organizations include whistleblowing policies and guidelines, codes of conduct and training programmes all designed to promote change to a positive, open workplace culture, where corruption and misconduct are effectively reported and dealt with.

What is Whistleblowing and Who Are the Whistleblowers?

The term whistleblower is widely credited to consumer advocate Ralph Nader (1972), who contrasted whistleblowing to organizational loyalty. Nader described the whistleblower as a person who believes 'the public interest overrides the interest of the organization which he serves' and publicly 'blows the whistle'[6] if the activity is corrupt, fraudulent or harmful.

A commonly accepted and widely used definition of whistleblowing is 'the disclosure by organization members (former or current) of illegal, immoral or illegitimate practices under the control of their employers to persons or organizations that may be able to effect action'.[7] Brown (2008) notes that this definition allows for many types of wrongdoing to be disclosed and many forms of whistleblowing. Another definition focuses on the motivation for making a public interest disclosure, where a whistleblower '. . . is a concerned citizen totally or predominantly motivated by notions of public interest, who initiates of their own free will an open disclosure about significant wrongdoing in a particular occupational role to a person or organization capable of investigating the complaint and facilitating the correction of the wrongdoing' (De Maria, 1999). Although, according to Brown (2008), the question of motive[8] is irrelevant and may indeed be unhelpful. These authors further note that 'there is confusion and inconsistency in the ways in which whistleblowing is defined and labelled' and that the definition of whistleblowing is complex in practice. These authors in their research prefer the term 'wrongdoing' as it is less constraining. The Victorian Ombudsman in his role in managing whistleblowing, also considers misconduct or corruption within an organization not as narrowly defined discrete categories, but rather as being located along a continuum of organizational wrongdoing which can range from serious corruption to varying degrees of lesser misconduct, all able to be managed within the Ombudsman's jurisdiction, which includes both the *Whistleblowers Protection Act 2001* and the *Ombudsman Act 1973*.

It is notable that whistleblowing protection legislation seldom defines the term 'whistleblowing' or 'whistleblower', but rather sets out the requirements for disclosure of conduct which is corrupt or improper, and the circumstances and matters about which persons who report may receive protection. Thus, for example, in relation to the type of conduct covered, under section 3 of the Victorian Whistleblowers Protection Act, 'corrupt conduct' is defined as:

> (a) conduct of a person (whether or not a public officer) that adversely affects, or could adversely affect, either directly or indirectly, the honest performance of a public officer's or public body's functions; or
> (b) conduct of a public officer that amounts to the performance of any of his or her functions as a public officer dishonestly or with inappropriate partiality; or
> (c) conduct of a public officer, a former public officer or a public body that amounts to a breach of public trust; or
> (d) conduct of a public officer, a former public officer or a public body that amounts to the misuse of information or material acquired in the course of the performance of their functions as such (whether for the benefit of that person or body or otherwise); or
> (e) a conspiracy or attempt to engage in conduct referred to in paragraphs (a) to (d).

While in the 1980s, the type of conduct reported by a whistleblower was predominantly limited to criminal activities, increasingly a broader range of wrongdoing, such as unsafe work practices, environmental pollution and other practices putting the health or safety of the public at risk, is now included as part of the conduct about which public interest disclosures can be made (Brown, 2006; Calland & Dehn, 2004).

Positive and Negative Perceptions of the Whistleblower

The term whistleblower is emotive; it conjures up a variety of images and stereotypes[9] which can impact on its usefulness.

On the positive side, whistleblowers are often described as showing moral courage, wanting truth to come out and for justice to prevail. They can be further described as . . . highly moral, heroic, courageous, honoured, pro-social, and respected for their refusal to remain silent.[10] On the negative side, descriptions of whistleblowers can include . . . naïve, idealistic, feared, loathed, vengeful, troublemakers, malcontents, betrayers (or colloquially as 'dobbers' and 'rats'). Whistleblowers have also been labelled as psychologically disturbed, unbalanced, unstable and vindictive, and by their actions deserve or provoke reprisals (Calland & Dehn, 2004; Vandekerckhove, 2006). The negative labelling may be associated with reprisals or attempts to discredit the whistleblower, and can be part of the complex reactions which reflect broader socio-cultural values about loyalty, not upsetting the status quo, as well as about dissent and freedom of speech.[11] It is not surprising that whistleblowers can arouse strong reactions and unease, which can hinder the development of a robust supportive whistleblower culture within organizations and counter the establishment of effective protective mechanisms.

In this context, it may be desirable to minimize the use of the term whistleblower and use instead the term 'public interest disclosure' (Brown, 2008), as much legislation already does, as a more neutral, less emotive term.[12] Use of the term 'public interest disclosure' could also encourage the perception that a person reporting on corruption and misconduct in an organization is simply a witness, like other types of witnesses, acting in the public interest and not to be considered so different from other forms of disclosure, such as reporting illegal or sexual misconduct, terrorist activity, or malpractice by professionals.

Research into whistleblowing has grown significantly in recent years and much has focused on the experience of individual whistleblowers, their motivations, characteristics and decision-making processes (Near and Miceli, 1986; De Maria & Jan, 1997a; Brown, 2008). Studies have examined to what extent the negative connotations or consequences have impacted on the decision to make a disclosure or to remain silent; and whether the perceived ineffectiveness of the responses to whistleblowing also plays a role (Gundlach, Martinko & Douglas, 2008; Lewis, 2006; Rehg et al., 2008; Stansbury & Bart, 2009).

Although employees of an organization are best placed to raise concerns, research has found that they have the most to lose when they do. The experience has often been reported as 'shooting the messenger', 'professional suicide' and 'being treated as if you have committed a crime'. These widely reported experiences (Miceli & Near, 1992, 2005; De Maria, 1999; De Maria & Jan, 1997b) do little to encourage others to follow suit. Some research has shown that between half and two-thirds of those who make public interest disclosures lose their jobs, and many are unable to find work in their area of expertise again (Alford, 2001). It has also been reported by De Maria and Jan (1994) that whistleblowers and their families are often harassed and suffer emotional and financial consequences; 71 per cent of whistleblowers surveyed reported official reprisals while 94 per cent were subject to unofficial reprisals. The New South Wales Independent Commission Against Corruption (1994) reported on a survey showing the Australian public was fearful of the consequences of blowing the whistle; 74 per cent of people surveyed agreed with the statement 'people who report corruption are likely to suffer for it'. The survey also showed, however, that 'dobbing in' could be perceived as a force for good, as 96 per cent of people surveyed disagreed with the statement that 'people who report corruption are just troublemakers'.

However, important research by Brown et al. (Australian Research Council Linkage Project, 2007) showed that it is inaccurate to describe whistleblowing as a 'bleak picture'. According to this research, whistleblowing is relatively frequent and is well recognised and accepted in many organizations in the public sector.[13] Brown (2008) also found that many whistleblowers did not experience 'deliberately inflicted negative outcomes' and were not treated differently. Less research has been conducted on the whistleblowing process itself and the consequences for the organization when the whistleblowing is dealt with either internally,[14] or externally (Faunce & Bolson, 2004; MacNab & Worthley, 2007; Lewis, 2006). Further research in this area is clearly needed (Brown, 2008).

Regardless of the motives of the whistleblower – scrupulous honesty, good intentions, a strong sense of right and wrong, acting in the public interest, or, by desire for personal reasons, they are confronted by significant decisions in what is a complex process. Options for the person with knowledge of corruption and misconduct are: stay silent or not; when and whether to report internally to the organization, which can be problematic, or externally to an independent integrity body, or to the media; and whether to do so anonymously. Research has found the decision to report was related to many complex individual and organizational factors (Micelli et al., 1991; MacNab & Worthley, 2007; Gundlach, Martinko & Douglas, 2008; De Maria, 2008).

To facilitate such multi-faceted complex decision-making about what to do when misconduct and corruption is observed, it is of critical importance that there are effective systems in place for managing the whistleblower which, under defined circumstances, provide protection, enable investigation of the allegations or complaint and ensure there is effective follow-up action to address any corruption or misconduct found.

What is Being Done – Key Themes and Approaches

Within the public sector attempts are being made to develop a more positive culture toward whistleblowing, facilitated by the introduction of legislation to protect whistleblowers and through comprehensive public interest disclosure policies, procedures and guidelines, as well as training and education programmes (Australia House of Representative Standing Committee on Legal and Constitutional Affairs, 2009; Lewis, 2006; Kaptein, 2002). These measures have legitimized at an official level the act of speaking out about corruption and misconduct; and are intended to encourage and empower the individual employee to speak up, although denigration of whistleblowers remains prevalent (Martin, 2003; Vandekerckhove, 2006).

There has also been recognition that in a democratically accountable society the public should have access to as much information on the workings and activities of government and its servants, as is compatible with the effective functioning of that government.[15]

Many countries have now introduced initiatives for responding to and managing whistleblowing in the public sector, often as a result of government enquiries into major corruption scandals.[16] Many of these initiatives appear to be leading to greater public acceptance and support for whistleblowing, although questions regarding their effectiveness have been raised (Brown, 2008).

The private sector too is addressing whistleblowing. For example, in the United States of America the *Sarbanes-Oxley Act 2002* includes mandatory whistleblowing provisions requiring listed companies to have whistleblower procedures for employees in relation to accounting, financial control and auditing. The Australian Standard AS 8004-2003: Corporate Governance, provides for whistleblower-protection programmes and sets out elements for establishing, implementing and managing an effective whistleblower programme to be applied within companies, government organizations and non-governmental organizations. These initiatives are assisted by changes of legislative provisions relating to companies, such as the *Australian Corporations Act 2001*. Many professional regulatory bodies, such as those for medical practitioners, are also developing and mandating whistleblowing policies for their members. In addition, there are a number of civil society initiatives, some of which offer advice to employees on whether to and how to speak out and provide support to those who do blow the whistle (Calland and Dehn, 2004). These diverse organizations include Wikileaks,[17] an international publishing service for whistleblowers; Open Democracy Advice Centre (ODAC),[18] Public Concern at Work,[19] Whistleblowers Australia,[20] Information Clearinghouse Japan[21] and Transparency International,[22] a non-government organization based in Berlin aimed at combating corruption by collecting and disseminating information and governance from around the world.

Opportunities for 'leaking' in the public domain have also increased significantly with access to modern information technology. Email alerts and Twitter postings regularly emanate from concerned or outraged employees who want to speak out, usually anonymously, about perceived corruption and misconduct and other unacceptable 'goings on' in their workplace. Whistleblowing hotlines for private sector companies are also common,[23] although erroneous or slanderous workplace denunciations may be challenged in court.

Responding to Whistleblowing Across Different Jurisdictions

Some studies have examined how different countries respond to whistleblowing and show a range of differing approaches but with some common elements.

Vandekerckhove (2006), as part of a theoretical approach to whistleblowing, reviewed developments in a number of countries with whistleblowing legislation in place.[24] He also examined the policies recommended by intergovernmental bodies, including the Organization for Economic Co-operation and Development (OECD), the European Commission, and the Council of Europe where the focus has been on enhancing information about corruption and bribery.

Transparency International conducted a major study, co-funded by the European Commission, to assess whistleblowing policies and practices in public and private sectors in 2009[25] in ten European countries (most are from the Eastern bloc where negative connotations against whistleblowers are reported to be strong). The report found that across the countries surveyed, legislation was generally fragmented with no comprehensive framework in place for whistleblowing. A recurrent theme in a number of European countries was 'a general lack of will to pass and effectively enforce whistleblowing legislation'. Another theme identified by Transparency International (2009) is that whistleblowing laws can contradict other laws that prohibit the release of information and libel and defamation regulations which may further deter a whistleblower from making a disclosure. While in many countries there is a legal duty to disclose corruption, fraud and other criminal acts, there is often insufficient legal provision for the protection of whistleblowers[26] and this can further deter persons from making disclosures.

Common across the countries' whistleblowing policies surveyed by transparency International, was the general lack of information available outlining the disclosure process; what the appropriate and designated channels are for disclosure; how protection is provided and enforced; and what the follow-up procedures are. With this comes a low level of awareness and familiarity with whistleblower rights and requirements. A further theme noted in the Transparency International (2009) report is the general weak enforcement of whistleblowing laws, including action to prevent reprisals against whistleblowers, and failure to ensure effective sanctioning of the reported wrongdoing. It was also found that anonymous whistleblower complaints are rarely followed up. A general lack of systemic data collection on whistleblowing responses, such as on the number of whistleblower disclosures or what percentage result in legal action was also found. The absence of statistical information means that it is impossible to assess the extent of whistleblowing, as well as the public benefit of disclosure or the damage to the public interest where wrongdoing is not disclosed (Transparency International, 2009).

In some countries, cultural issues may heighten the reluctance of employees to access formal whistleblowing reporting mechanisms. In France, for example, employees[27] prefer to report wrongdoing through their line managers. Although in the context of French personal data protection and privacy laws this can be problematic and 'could result in an organized scheme for denunciations in the workplace, and the right of whistleblowers to remain anonymous only heightened the risk of slanderous denunciations which may unduly damage reputations' (Baumgartner, 2007).

Calland and Dehn (2004) cover the legal and civil society responses to whistleblowing in the United States of America, the United Kingdom, South Africa, Japan, Australia and New Zealand. However, the authors stress caution in assuming that the way one country has handled whistleblowing can readily be adapted to another. As they state 'the role of the law differs so greatly between countries, not only in the protection it offers [to whistleblowers], the balance it strikes and how accessible it is, but also in the culture it reflects' (Calland & Dehn, 2004, p. 15). A brief look at several countries from their overview is presented below:

United States of America

The United States of America pioneered whistleblowing legislation with its *Civil Service Reform Act* of 1978 (US) to protect whistleblowers by prohibiting reprisals against federal employees who lawfully disclose information which they reasonably believe involves illegality, mismanagement, gross waste of funds, abuse of authority or substantial danger to public health or safety. The *Whistleblower Protection Act* of 1989 (US) provided further protection. Devine (in Calland & Dehn, 2004) reports that there have been many positives in support of whistleblowing laws in the United States of America; he perceives them to be 'effective catalysts for exposure of bureaucratic corruption and misconduct where in spite of frustrations through the courts some major victories have been achieved by whistleblowers for the public interest'. However, he also identifies the negative side, where the Unites States of America whistleblower laws are 'saturated with arbitrary inconsistencies and contradictions', and notes the 'chaos with a plethora of different and conflicting provisions that now apply to its whistleblowers'.

United Kingdom

The United Kingdom designed its whistleblower laws, introduced in 1989 and driven by civil society pressures, with a focus on organizational accountability and individual responsibility (Myers (2004)). The intent according to Myers (2004) was to communicate a change in cultural values and perceptions following a number of major disasters and scandals where whistleblowers played key roles. According to Myers (2004) the legislation attempts to 'address the message rather than the messenger' and there has been a degree of success in achieving change. However, it has been questioned whether the heavy reliance on internal procedures in the United Kingdom may be less effective for the public interest than a more externally focused system (Lewis 2008). The United Kingdom model has also influenced developments in New Zealand and in South Africa (Trott in Calland & Dehn, 2004).

New Zealand

In New Zealand the *Whistleblowers Protection Act 1994* represents a regime where whistleblowers must first 'blow the whistle' in accordance with internal policies and procedures which are mandatory for the public sector; with some exceptions, concerns can only be raised externally and under certain conditions with the Ombudsman. The New Zealand approach includes a Whistleblowers Protection Authority to advise and counsel whistleblowers, investigate and monitor disclosures and provide protection by giving the whistleblower immunity from civil and criminal proceedings and rights of compensations (Trott in Calland & Dehn, 2004).

Australia

In Australia, a number of major inquiries into corruption scandals were held in the late 1980s and early 1990s.[28] The common law was found to be ill-adapted and unable to provide employees with the right to disclose confidential or even non-confidential information about their workplace, because of a duty of trust implied in the contractual employment relationship under common law. This increased the risk that disclosure could be perceived as an undermining of this duty, leading an employer to take legal action against them.

Since the 1990s there has been significant legislation in all Australian states and Commonwealth territories aimed at protecting whistleblowers or public interest disclosures. At the state level the specific legislation has mostly been directed at the public sector and does not apply to the corporate or non-government sectors. There are also significant differences in measures for protecting whistleblowers. The Commonwealth, following the recommendations of the Senate Select Committee on Public Interest Whistleblowing 1994, introduced the *Public Interest Disclosure (Protection of Whistleblowers) Bill 2002*.

The Australian developments have been comprehensively reviewed by Brown (2006) who noted that the comparative analysis raises a number of fundamental questions about the 'tapestry' of Australian whistleblowing laws. He also found there was little empirical evidence of their performance.

Responding to whistleblowing in the public interest – common elements

In spite of the variety of legislative provisions and administrative arrangements that exist for managing whistleblowers, not only between countries, but also, as is the case in federal jurisdictions, such as Australia and Canada, there are a number of common elements that can be found in many systems for responding to whistleblowing. In examining these, the useful review of international best practice regarding whistleblower laws by Latimer and Brown (2008) is acknowledged.

Latimer and Brown (2008) identify a number of improvements in the way the laws could better operate, including the need for greater consistency in legal thresholds and operational requirements imposed by whistleblower legislation, common tests and processes covering both public and private sectors. They also report on a number of potential improvements for responding to whistleblowing, as exemplified by best practice internationally. However, they view the 'transition towards a more effective, less "symbolic" regime as dependent on a "clearer" consensus regarding the public importance of employee disclosure and the organizational advantages of open, proactive approaches to disclosure management'.

Also useful in considering improvements to responding to whistleblowing are the recommended principles for guiding whistleblowing legislation developed by Transparency International (2009), in conjunction with experts and practitioners from a number of countries.

Who can make a public interest disclosure?

Not everyone can make a public interest disclosure. It is usually limited to employees of an organization and, depending on the legislation in the jurisdiction, can be further limited in a number of ways: to some or all categories of public sector employees, or extended to include employees from the private sector. If limited only to public employees, (and depending on the nature of their employment, for example, part-time or contract), this has been criticized as too narrow. Latimer and Brown (2008) argue that more comprehensive and uniform coverage of who can make a public interest disclosure appears desirable to avoid 'loopholes', so that former employees, the unemployed as well as non-employee members of charitable organizations, non-governmental organizations, political parties and trade unions also be included. Although there may be obstacles, such as constitutional constraints and client/professional relations with this broadening, many public sector tasks are increasingly outsourced to contractors and non-government organizations whose employees provide public services; these too should be eligible for protection if they make whistleblower disclosures. Nevertheless, as Latimer and Brown (2008) note, it is internal whistleblowers that are most likely to have the most valuable public interest information and because of their employment are most vulnerable to reprisals and need special legal and management protection.

Many countries exclude anonymous whistleblowers from whistleblower protection laws; arguing they may not be perceived as 'genuine' and as a result often do not act on such disclosures. According to Latimer and Brown (2008) anonymous whistleblowers are rarely protected and should be seen as a last resort. However, when the whistleblower is required to identify themselves, it may discourage disclosure, unless effective ways of keeping the identity of the whistleblower confidential are established.

What type of conduct is covered by a public interest disclosure?

The types of conduct and under which circumstances disclosure may be justified are defined in the various legislative provisions. They must be in the public interest, not for private or personal interest. They may include forms of illegality and corrupt conduct, improper conduct, maladministration, waste, substantial mismanagement and improper use of public funds, potential environmental damage and substantial risk to public health and safety such as a health officer who conceals illegal dumping of toxic waste; or an agricultural officer who delays destruction of infected animals; or a building inspector who ignores poor building practices. If proved, these forms of conduct must constitute a criminal offence or reasonable grounds for dismissal.

Corrupt conduct in particular has been the focus of considerable definitional debate. It generally covers, as in the Victorian legislation, conduct affecting the honest performance of a public officer's functions; performing those functions dishonestly or with inappropriate partiality; conduct involving a breach of trust, misuse of information or material acquired in the official functions and conspiring or attempting to conspire with any of the above. The more serious the corruption and misconduct exposed, the more likely the disclosure will be in the public interest.

To whom and how can a public interest disclosure be made?

For whistleblowers to be protected, most of the legislative measures require that the information the whistleblower has should be disclosed internally or to an external investigative authority. Depending on the jurisdiction, external avenues can include the Ombudsman, police and anti-corruption bodies, and Auditors General, which are all independent from the organization employing the whistleblower. These bodies can investigate as well as protect the whistleblower from any detrimental action. In some jurisdictions and under some circumstances, members of parliament or the media may also receive whistleblower disclosures. Who to report to and how concerns should be raised, can depend on the seriousness and sensitivity of the issue.

The general approach has been for public sector organizations to establish formal policies and procedures to allow for the reporting of misconduct by whistleblowers through designated internal or external channels. Issues covered include whether a whistleblower should first be required to report internally or go direct to an independent body that will assess whether the disclosure is in the public interest and protection is required, and who will investigate the disclosure. The public interest disclosure may be made by a person either in writing or orally; it may also be made anonymously in some jurisdictions. It needs to be made in the belief (more than a mere suspicion) that there are reasonable grounds that a public officer or public body has engaged in improper conduct (including corrupt conduct), in their official capacity; and must be made in good faith. Other elements usually included are the need to deal with the complaint within certain time frames; provision of welfare support and advice to the whistleblower; including feedback on what actions have been taken; as well as procedures for oversight and monitoring of the investigation and follow-up actions.

What protection is available to a whistleblower?

A major concern addressed by the legislation is that whistleblowers can be subjected to reprisals and retaliatory actions and that they should be protected. Provisions for the protection of whistleblowers may include the right to sue for damages or to stop the action when there are reprisals; immunity from liability for breaching confidential provisions of other Acts; immunity from civil and criminal liability and disciplinary action for making a disclosure.

Confidentiality and anonymity are important safeguards to protect whistleblowers. A duty to not reveal the identity of the whistleblower is often imposed on the recipient of the disclosed information, although there will always be risks and no guarantee of absolute anonymity. Immunity from legal action or disciplinary or defamation proceedings and protection against reprisals and malicious allegations can be persuasive factors in a whistleblower coming forward. Such safeguards can take the form of making it a criminal offence for anyone to take detrimental action against the whistleblower and/or that such action is deemed to be victimization which may give rise to legal action, for example under equal opportunity legislation. Compensation measures for whistleblowers vary, although in some jurisdictions, there are rewards for disclosure of wrongdoing.[29] It should be noted that whistleblower management systems also usually ensure that those against whom allegations are made have a natural justice process when findings of the investigations are complete.

There are also extensive administrative responses directly linked to or required to be established by the whistleblowing legislation. These include the development and implementation of internal whistleblowing policies and procedural guidelines, and are important safeguards to ensure legislation is implemented into effective practice in the workplace. The guidelines, such as those published by the Victorian Ombudsman (at www.ombudsman.vic.gov.au), are an example.

The Victorian Ombudsman Approach

The practical experience of the Victorian Ombudsman in handling whistleblower matters provides a valuable insight into how whistleblowing is responded to, as well as identifying where improvements can be made. The strengths of the Victorian Ombudsman approach to successfully respond to whistleblowing are also identified within the context of a legislative framework which has been found to be frustrating and problematic and which is currently under consideration for reform.

The Whistleblowers Protection Act entrusts the Victorian Ombudsman with the responsibility for addressing most[30] disclosures of improper and corrupt conduct by public officers and public bodies in Victoria, including elected local councillors. It also provides protections for whistleblowers. The Ombudsman Act under which the office operates confers wide powers on the Ombudsman in relation to conducting investigations on matters relating to public administration, either upon receipt of a complaint (or by referral from Parliament) or on his 'own motion' where systemic or other public interest issues arise.

The juxtaposition of the two Acts – the Ombudsman Act and the Whistleblowers Protection Act – has, apart from some gaps, given the Ombudsman the broad powers and extensive coverage required to investigate allegations about maladministration, misconduct and corruption across the Victorian public sector. It also provides significant intelligence about organizations, their culture, attitudes and performance, and the opportunity to compare and contrast how organizations undertake their statutory responsibilities, thereby promoting good practice.

A key strength of the Ombudsman in responding to whistleblowers is the power to investigate all administrative actions of wrongdoing, from minor errors, maladministration, and misconduct, to serious malfeasance and corruption.[31] The Victorian Ombudsman is not hampered, as are some anti-corruption bodies dealing with whistleblowers in other Australian jurisdictions, by having to meet strict definitional thresholds that require actions to be criminal or grounds for dismissal before investigations can commence. Such threshold issues do not restrict the Victorian Ombudsman in being able to investigate a broad range of issues and to report as comprehensively as he considers appropriate whether the allegation meets the threshold of a public interest disclosure or not. Allegations which at face value appear minor, may reveal significant corruption elements during the course of an enquiry or investigation. On occasion that situation is reversed when serious corruption matters reveal less serious misconduct relating to poor administrative practices. The flexibility inherent in the Ombudsman Act set alongside the Whistleblowers Protection Act, together with the broad definition of 'administrative action', has enabled handling of matters including misconduct and corruption across a wide range of issues and complexity and is a significant strength.

Crucial to any legislation to maintain public sector integrity and investigate allegations is the definition of wrongdoing. Too narrow a definition can hamper and restrict investigators by limiting the scope of an investigation or necessitating closure of an investigation, where issues are subsequently found not to meet the defined threshold.

In the absence to date of an anti-corruption body in Victoria (although the new Victorian Liberal-national coalition government in December 2010 had as a key priority to establish an independent broad-based anti-corruption commission), the Ombudsman in a de facto way has over the past six years undertaken this role successfully despite some limitations in powers and the gaps in coverage.

In Victoria the Whistleblowers Protection Act has been an important component of the integrity framework and by complementing the jurisdiction of the Ombudsman, has proven to be highly beneficial in identifying allegations and disclosures of corruption and improper conduct by public officials and public bodies in the Victorian public sector. It is another strength of the Ombudsman's role that when individuals raise allegations about issues in the public sector which, while not meeting the strict threshold definition of a public interest disclosure, have been able to be examined under the provisions of the Ombudsman Act. This flexibility to manage matters has enabled a wide range of allegations, from minor maladministration to serious corrupt conduct, to be investigated and providing a systemic approach to issues of organizational integrity.

The outcome of whistleblowing investigations may only be publicly reported if it is in the public interest to do so. As a result, a number of reports of investigations initiated by whistleblowers have received wide coverage when tabled in Parliament.[32]

The Review of Victoria's integrity and anti-corruption system (2010) found the public perception of the effectiveness of Victorian integrity arrangements to be comparable to those in New South Wales and Queensland, both of which have anti-corruption commissions in place. Indeed, in terms of appearing to meet public need for an effective avenue for whistleblowing, there has been a significant increase in the number of whistleblowers approaching the Victorian Ombudsman. As shown in Table 23.1, in 2008–09 there were 96 whistleblower matters received and 174 in 2009–10 (an increase of 81 per cent). This suggests a greater level of public awareness and confidence about the Ombudsman's role in managing whistleblower disclosures.

A further strength of the Victorian approach is that it gives the Ombudsman the flexibility to investigate matters that have been determined to be a public interest disclosure or to refer them to the Chief Commissioner of Police or the Auditor-General to investigate, if appropriate to do so; or, where the matter is not a public interest disclosure, the Ombudsman may deal with it as a complaint under the Ombudsman Act.

Thus within the broader role of the Ombudsman and his general focus on improving public administration, any concerns including misconduct or corruption arising as a result of complaints can be examined flexibly. If warranted, they can be investigated through normal Ombudsman procedures or through the specific jurisdiction provided by the Whistleblowers Protection Act. It also means that issues relating to definitions – what is and is not improper or corrupt conduct, are subsumed within the general concept of maladministration – thus corruption and misconduct are not qualitatively different, and often cannot, nor should be considered in isolation of wider systemic issues or from other instances of

Table 23.1 Whistleblower matters received by the Victorian Ombudsman 2006–2010

	2006–07	2007–08	2008–09	2009–10
Total disclosures received	84	114	96	174
Public Interest Disclosure (PID)	21	18	28	28
Protected Disclosure (PD)	9	18	20	15
By Ombudsman	14	10	12	14
By Public Body	6	8	13	14
By Auditor–General	1	0	1	0
By Chief Commissioner Victoria Police	0	0	1	0
Not investigated	0	0	1	0
Under Ombudsman Act	14	7	8	28
Police Regulation Act	2	3	3	2
No jurisdiction	0	0	0	14
Under Review	0	0	0	1
Withdrawn	0	0	0	2

Source: Victorian Ombudsman Annual Reports 2006–07 to 2009–10.

maladministration in the organization. As a result, there is no need for the Victorian Ombudsman to artificially separate the investigation of public interest disclosures from consideration of other concerns within which they are embedded in the organization.

Within the context of limited resources, an increasing number of whistleblower disclosures received by the Victorian Ombudsman have been referred back to organizations for internal investigation. Unfortunately, the quality of some of the investigations undertaken by these organizations has been frequently inadequate and the Ombudsman is required to either request further investigation to address the deficiencies, or to take back the carriage of the investigation. This is both inefficient and time-consuming, resulting in unnecessary delay and uncertainty for persons making disclosures.

Across Australian jurisdictions, the responsibility for whistleblowing legislation sits with different bodies, indicating important differences in how whistleblowing is dealt with. Detailed analysis by Brown (2006) has shown how marked these differences are in relation to the respective legislation. In an attempt to illustrate the diversity in arrangements for responding to whistleblowing across Australia, the figures contained in annual reports of the relevant bodies have been compiled by the Victorian Ombudsman (Table 23.2) in relation to the number of annual whistleblower complaints/public interest disclosures reported. Considerable

Table 23.2 Reported Whistleblower/Public interest disclosures across Australian jurisdictions, 2006–2010

Jurisdiction Act/Bill	Integrity body	2006–07	2007–08	2008–09	2009–10
Act Public Interest Disclosure Act 1994	Chief Minister's Department[1]	1	0	0	0
Commonwealth Public Service Act 1999;	Australian Public Service Commission[2]	21	22	15	NA
Public Interest Disclosure Bill	Commonwealth Ombudsman	–	–	–	–
New South Wales Public Interest Disclosure Act 1994	Independent Commission Against Corruption[3]	194	282	262	253
	Ombudsman NSW[4]	76	96	89	78
Northern Territory Public Interest Disclosure Act 2005	Commissioner for Public Interest Disclosures[5]	–	–	–	78
Queensland Whistleblowers	Ombudsman Queensland[6]	33	17	15	14
Protection Act 1994	Office of the Public Service Commissioner[7]	0	0	0	0
	Crime and Misconduct Commission[8]	110	251	456	515
South Australia Whistleblowers Protection Act 1993	Ombudsman South Australia	101	86	82	NA
	Anti-Corruption Branch (SA Police)[9]				
Tasmania Public Interest Disclosures Act 2002	Ombudsman Tasmania[10]	0	3	2	NA
Victoria Whistleblowers Protection Act 2001	Victorian Ombudsman[11]	84	114	96	174
Western Australia Public Interest Disclosure Act 2003	Office of the Public Sector Standards Commissioner[12]	14	4	13	NA

Notes:
NA = Not available

1. Chief Minister's Department Annual Reports, Canberra: ACT Government: 2008–2009 Vol 1, 72; 2007–2008 Vol 1, 71; & 2006–2007, 114.
2. Australian Public Service Commissioner Annual Report 2008–2009, 39 Canberra: Australian Public Service Commissioner.

Table 23.2 (continued)

3. Independent Commission Against Corruption (ICAC) Annual Reports, Sydney: Independent Commission Against Corruption: 2008–2009, 7; 2007–2008, p22; and 2006–2007, 19.
4. New South Wales Ombudsman Annual Reports, Sydney: New South Wales Ombudsman: 2008–2009, 105; 2007–2008, 156; and 2006–2007, 129.
5. This office commenced operations in August 2009.
6. Queensland Ombudsman Annual Reports, Brisbane: Queensland Ombudsman: 2008–2009, 70; 2007–2008, 68; and 2006–2007, 18.
7. Public Service Commission Annual Reports Canberra: Australian Public Service Commission 2008–2009, 32; 2007–2008, 13; and 2006–2007, 23.
8. Crime and Misconduct Commission Annual Reports Brisbane: Crime and Misconduct Commission 2008–2009, 59; 2007–2008, 66; and 2006–2007, 78.
9. South Australia Annual report 2008-2009, Adelaide: Ombudsman South Australia; note that these figures cover reports of alleged corruption from a variety of sources, including whistleblowers pursuant to the *Whistleblowers Protection Act 1993*
10. Ombudsman Tasmania Annual Reports, Hobart: Ombudsman Tasmania: 2008–2009, 30; 2007–2008, 25; and 2006–2007, 17.
11. Victorian Ombudsman Annual Report 2010 – Part 1, 66 Melbourne: Victorian Ombudsman.
12. Office of the Public Sector Standards Commissioner State of the Service Report 2009, 83, Perth: Office of the Public Sector Standards Commissioner.

caution is advised in comparing the figures between jurisdictions, as definitions and counting rules used were not available. Nevertheless, taking the figures at face value, they show an almost doubling of disclosures in Victoria between 2008–09 and 2009–10, in contrast to other jurisdictions.

IMPROVING RESPONSES TO PUBLIC INTEREST WHISTLEBLOWING

Since the implementation of whistleblower legislation, many concerns have been widely raised about the effectiveness of such legislation.

Some have criticized the legislative approach as being inadequate; that it has become obtuse with vexed legal questions and overly complex; that the protection in practice is limited and needs strengthening, especially when there is increased use of secrecy clauses in employee contracts (Brown, 2007). An individual who has breached secrecy provisions, risks legal action, even when there is demonstrated public benefit from disclosure (Marr, 2007; Wilkie, 2007). Above all, according to Brown (2007) there is a perception that the legislation generally may not offer the best protection for whistleblowers and will reduce the likelihood of disclosures by directly impacting on the confidence of whistleblowers to come forward. Other concerns about the effectiveness of whistleblowing laws relate to high thresholds for acceptance of public interest disclosures and that the protection for a whistleblower can apply only within strict criteria (e.g. some are rejected for 'technical' reasons).

Review of whistleblower legislation is taking place in a number of jurisdictions, including Australia. In Victoria, such a review commenced in 2007, with the Victorian Ombudsman participating on an interdepartmental committee with representatives from the Department of Justice and the Department of Premier and Cabinet.[33] The challenges created by existing Victorian legislation have been identified indicating a need for change. These include:

- simplifying the day-to-day operation of the Act
- improving the protections for whistleblowers and those involved with their management
- ensuring the management framework provided fulfils the aims of the Act and encourage public interest disclosures.

In Australia, the Commonwealth House of Representatives Standing Committee on Legal and Constitutional Affairs in its report *Whistleblower protection: a comprehensive scheme for the Commonwealth public sector* (2009) sets out a preferred model for new legislation to protect public interest disclosures within the Commonwealth public sector. The proposed federal model places responsibility for administration of the Act with the Commonwealth Ombudsman. It has no threshold of corrupt conduct; it includes maladministration in its broad definition and protects disclosures made to the media. However, unlike the existing Victorian legislation, the federal model limits whistleblowers to 'insiders', that is, from within the public sector only. The Victorian Ombudsman maintains that there should be unrestricted access for all whistleblowers, so as to encourage the wider reporting of wrongdoing.

The federal proposal to include maladministration in its whistleblower legislation is in line with the Victorian Ombudsman's views that corrupt conduct can include administrative action. However, the Ombudsman has recommended that the investigative provisions of the Whistleblowers Protection Act be rationalized into those of the Ombudsman Act, leaving the Whistleblowers Protection Act provisions to provide protection for whistleblowers. The result of these proposed changes would see all investigations, from those arising from allegations of minor maladministration to those of serious corruption, being undertaken under the provisions of a single Act, the Ombudsman Act. This would provide a seamless and flexible capacity to undertake comprehensive investigations and to adapt quickly and effectively to changes in the nature and scope of the issues which arise from time to time during the course of an investigation, without the need to change the legislative basis or to cease an investigation. The Whistleblowers Protection Act would contain only those provisions necessary to provide protection to whistleblowers.

The federal model advocates an education function. Such a function would also be beneficial if added to the Victorian legislation as it would provide additional impetus and resources, and ensure better outcomes from those organizations to which allegations are referred for investigation.

Developments in other countries have been or are also underway to review and reform the whistleblower legislation and consider improved ways of handling public interest disclosures (Vandekerckhove, 2006; Calland & Dehn, 2004; Latimer & Brown, 2008) and include many proposed improvements to whistleblowing legislative and management systems. The comprehensive review of international best practice regarding whistleblowing laws previously referred to (Latimer and Brown, 2008) identifies a number of improvements that could be made in the way the laws are formulated and how related processes operate.

While until recently there has been little research to show how effective whistleblowing laws are in practice and to what extent employees are encouraged to blow the whistle (Trott, 2004), significant research into public sector whistleblowing in Australia was conducted by Brown (2008). This project 'Whistle while they work' was conducted in conjunction with partner organizations (including the Victorian Ombudsman) with responsibility for integrity functions, from around Australia. The project collected data from 304 federal state and local government organizations and surveyed 7600 public employees from 118 organizations. The findings showed that many public sector organizations manage their whistleblower matters well and that at least 70 per cent of all whistleblowers are treated no differently by management and co-workers as a result of making a disclosure. When organizations conducted investigations themselves into the disclosures, some led to disciplinary action against the staff involved in corruption or misconduct; others to improved procedures and to changes in workplace culture. Many of the internal investigations were reported to be conducted in a professional and timely manner; the whistleblower was supported during the investigation with their confidentiality maintained and no reprisals taking place.

In practice, significant difficulties have been found in implementing whistleblower management systems which undermine the confidence of whistleblowers to come forward and prevent action being taken to address corruption and misconduct. Through its role and extensive experience in applying the Whistleblowers Protection Act, the Victorian Ombudsman has found some public sector organizations fail to meet their statutory responsibilities under the Whistleblowers Protection Act, even though all public sector organizations in Victoria are required to have implemented policies and procedures for whistleblowing. A number of improvements have been identified based on the Victorian Ombudsman's experience and focus on the way whistleblower systems are implemented in practice, and in particular, how whistleblowers are dealt with internally when they raise concerns in the workplace:

Improving Awareness of Whistleblowers Legislation Through Training

Although the Victorian Ombudsman publishes whistleblower guidelines (www.ombudsman.vic.gov.au) to assist public sector organizations, it has been found there is limited knowledge across the public sector of the Whistleblowers Protection Act and its obligations. Some public sector organizations do not understand or are not adequately aware of the Act and its requirements, including how to handle whistleblower disclosures when they are received. Some organizations treat a whistleblower's disclosure in a similar manner to any other complaint, although clearly it is not.

In the Ombudsman's experience, some officers only find out they are the designated disclosure officer with responsibility for managing whistleblower matters when they are asked to receive a whistleblower disclosure. This is simply too late.

A survey conducted in 2009 by the Victorian Ombudsman of 20 of the 79 municipal councils in Victoria assessed understanding of the Whistleblowers Protection Act and what information about whistleblowing is available to staff. Two-thirds of the councils surveyed did not fully meet their obligations under the Act. Some council officers reported they had never heard of the Whistleblowers Protection Act, while others misunderstood its provisions. Several councils reported they did not train their staff in receiving whistleblower disclosures or in conducting investigations. One respondent stated 'we don't do whistleblowing here'. Council websites and annual reports did not make adequate reference to the Whistleblowers Protection Act. If the survey results from local councils are indicative of the low level of awareness across the public sector, there is cause for serious concern about the effectiveness of the whistleblowing legislation in practice.

As part of its role under the Act, the Victorian Ombudsman has been proactive in providing education, training and support to public sector organizations about the Whistleblowers Protection Act. This includes:

- providing Fact Sheets and Guidelines
- conducting workshops to public sector organizations on how whistleblowers should be handled

- communicating and monitoring the whistleblower investigations
- ensuring agencies provide support for whistleblowers
- providing feedback to whistleblowers.

However, much of this has been done on an ad hoc basis due to limited resources.

Clearly more needs to be done. Adequate training in handling whistleblower reports should lead to greater awareness and facilitate a change in culture and attitude towards whistleblowers.

Stronger Leadership by Public Sector Managers

Management and senior management in particular, have a critical role to play in promoting a culture which actively encourages whistleblowers to speak up when they observe corruption and misconduct, and to support them. Managers should themselves set the standard for ethical conduct and make it clear to staff that whistleblowers will not be ostracized or criticized, but rather supported and protected from detrimental action. Robust systems for the effective investigation of whistleblower disclosures should also be put in place.

Proactive Management

The need for management to be proactive in dealing with whistleblowing was highlighted in the following:

Case study 1
A disclosure from a whistleblower was received about how drug exhibits were managed by the Victorian Police Forensic Services Centre. A further disclosure was received that detrimental action had been taken against the whistleblower for having made the original disclosure. The investigation identified many issues, including:

- no fully independent audit of drug holdings for at least 15 years
- over the past 16 years concerns had been raised about drug exhibit management on numerous occasions but had not been addressed
- reluctance by senior managers to improve processes and procedures
- senior management failed to provide appropriate leadership and direction which led to grievances, occupational health and safety complaints, and Federal Court action
- mismanagement and a lack of accountability created an environment in which corruption could occur and go unnoticed.

Recommendations were made to improve accountability, processes and procedures and were all accepted by the Chief Commissioner of Police.

Improving the Treatment of Whistleblowers

Protecting whistleblowers against reprisals is essential to ensure the effective operation of the Act, which provides that whistleblowers can make disclosures about detrimental action taken (or to be taken) against them in reprisal for making a public interest disclosure.

While it is a serious offence under the Act to take (or propose to take) detrimental action against a whistleblower, (such as disadvantage, intimidation, harassment, injury, or loss of employment opportunities) some organizations are not taking adequate or proactive measures to protect whistleblowers against such detrimental action.

Preventing Adverse Consequences for the Whistleblower

Ensuring that the whistleblower does not suffer negative consequences in the workplace, including protection of identity:

Case study 2

The Ombudsman investigated allegations of detrimental action against a whistleblower in a major government department when it was disclosed that two employees were alleged to have been involved in unethical and unprofessional conduct involving the provision of professional services to family members and altering official records. The line manager was possibly biased in failing to document, report and investigate critical incidents which involved the two employees.

It was also alleged that a manager had distributed material which identified the whistleblower. In response to the whistleblower's allegations, the two employees complained that the whistleblower had in turn breached their privacy and had bullied and harassed them. The investigation identified deficiencies and procedural flaws in the department's grievance processes as well as significant problems with the way the whistleblower allegations were managed and investigated by senior managers.

The Ombudsman concluded that three senior departmental officers did not act with the integrity, impartiality or respect as prescribed by the *Public Administration Act 2004*, the *Code of Conduct for Victorian Public Sector Employees*, and the department's own disciplinary policies. The Ombudsman made a number of recommendations, all of which were accepted by the department, including:

- review the conduct of the senior officers involved in the investigation
- ensure conflict of interest issues are resolved before starting any investigation
- review the way disciplinary matters are managed and delegated to ensure officers are accountable and processes are transparent
- apologise to the whistleblower
- consider taking disciplinary action against the manager for circulating material which identified the whistleblower
- consider paying the whistleblower compensation for the unfair treatment.

Strengthening Welfare Support

The lack of welfare support provided to whistleblowers is a major area of weakness for many organizations and may lead to whistleblowers feeling vulnerable and unsupported, as well as exposed to the risk of reprisal action against them. Public sector organizations need to be more proactive in addressing welfare support for whistleblowers to help prevent stress-related health problems.

Addressing Conflicts of Interest

Corrupt conduct investigated by the Victorian Ombudsman demonstrates the importance of taking steps which can prevent corruption from arising in the first place. In particular, where there are conflicts of interest in an organization which are not addressed there is an opportunity for corrupt conduct to occur.[34]

While a conflict of interest is not in itself corruption, failing to recognize it or manage it appropriately is at best improper or, at worst, criminal. When it is not addressed corrupt conduct can easily emerge. Specific attention in this context should be paid by public sector organizations to:

- outside/secondary employment and private business interests
- employment and business activities after leaving public sector employment
- employment and private business interests of family members, friends, and associates membership of community groups and organizations
- inappropriate or personal relationships.

Maintaining an Ethical Culture

Maintaining an ethical culture is the single most important factor that ensures the public sector retains the degree of public trust required in a modern democracy. A commitment to ethical conduct must be espoused at every level of an organization and in every task performed. Strong leadership by senior managers is critical to the development of an ethical culture, and where they fail to act ethically there is a higher likelihood of corrupt conduct occurring throughout an organization affecting the understanding of staff as to what constitutes ethical practices. While the establishment of an ethical culture takes time, the development of a sound internal code of conduct assists in reducing the likelihood of corrupt conduct.

Improving Governance Processes

Governance processes in place have been found to be deficient enabling misconduct to occur. For example:

Case study 3

A public interest disclosure was referred to the Victorian Ombudsman by the train operators V/Line for investigation. The disclosure related to allegations that V/Line employees received cash for scrap metal, which was not recorded in the V/Line accounting system and was used for staff related expenses. The investigation concluded that cash payments from the sale of scrap metal were not part of the formal accounts receivable process and instead the money received was kept in a safe under the names of two V/Line employees.

When interviewed the employees stated that they used the money for staff-related matters such as Christmas functions, flowers and leaving gifts. Other employees who were interviewed during the investigation also confirmed that they had received gifts in the forms of cash and lottery tickets and had attended subsidized Christmas functions. The investigation concluded that $4713.20 in cash and one cheque to the value of $880.35 were not processed via V/Line's accounts receivable system during the period 1 July, 2007 to 31 July, 2009. As a result of the investigation, a number of changes were made. V/Line's cash-handling procedures have since been improved; staff were counselled; and payments for scrap metal are to be paid and received only by cheque.

Improving Investigation of Public Interest Disclosures

The Victorian Ombudsman can and does refer many public interest disclosures to relevant public bodies for initial investigation; and it monitors these referrals in accordance with the whistleblower legislation and guidelines.

Many shortcomings have been identified regarding internal investigations into public interest disclosures. The poor quality of some investigation reports is of concern: conclusions are asserted without sufficient substantiating evidence; important lines of enquiry are not pursued; investigations are not conducted in a timely manner; and investigators having little, and at times no, prior investigative experience.

Reducing Delay in Completing Investigations

Delays, up to 12 months in some cases, in finalizing investigations into public interest disclosures and in providing the Victorian Ombudsman a completed investigation report are common. Such delays impact on the wellbeing of the whistleblower and do not reflect the significance and priority that should be given to a whistleblower investigation.

Greater Compliance with the Ombudsman's Guidelines[35]

The Ombudsman's guidelines are a statutory requirement under the Whistleblowers Protection Act and are published on the Victorian Ombudsman website. They outline the procedure to be followed by public bodies in relation to disclosures and investigations. Despite this, organizations often overlook advice contained in the guidelines.

Preventing Breaches of Confidentiality

There appears to be a lack of understanding about confidentiality and its importance for the protection of whistleblowers. Breaches have been found where the identity of the whistleblower has been disclosed, whether intentionally or through a lack of knowledge of the confidentiality requirements and protections to be given to the whistleblower.

Preventing Collusion of Witnesses

Several examples have been identified where confidentiality provisions have not been properly explained by organizations to witnesses. As a result, witnesses may have the opportunity to collude prior to being interviewed; this subsequently affects the reliability of evidence.

To minimise the risk of collusion between witnesses, the Victorian Ombudsman investigators will generally:

- contact witnesses prior to their being required to attend an interview
- provide an information sheet outlining the confidentiality requirements which apply to the interview and the rights of witnesses
- refer witnesses to the public interest disclosure co-ordinator in the agency if they have questions.

Improving Public Interest Disclosure Reporting Practices

Annual reports are an integral part of an organization's accountability to the public. Failure to report on the number and type of whistleblower disclosures in an organization's annual report contravenes its legal obligations. Public bodies are required to report on public interest disclosures. This includes:

- the number and types of disclosures made to the public body during the year
- the number of disclosures referred to the Ombudsman for determination and whether they are public interest disclosures
- the number and types of disclosed matters referred to the public body by the Ombudsman for investigation
- the number and types of disclosed matters referred by the public body to the Ombudsman for investigation
- the number and types of investigations taken over from the public body by the Ombudsman
- the number of requests made by a whistleblower to the Ombudsman to take over an investigation by the public body
- the number and types of disclosed matters that the public body has declined to investigate
- the number and types of disclosed matters that were substantiated upon investigation and the action taken on completion of the investigation
- any recommendation made by the Ombudsman under the Act that relates to the public body.

It has been noted that the level and frequency of whistleblowing tends to be under-reported (Brown, 2008; Transparency International, 2009). Improved data on public interest disclosures which are publicly reported enhances transparency and assists in gauging the nature and extent of whistleblowing. This would require greater attention to reporting processes to enable comparisons over time and between sectors.

In summary, there are many practical improvements to be made for responding more effectively to public interest disclosures. These include:

- Making clear, up-to-date whistleblower policies and procedures available in all public sector organizations (including on websites and in annual reports). These policies and procedures must specify how to make a public interest disclosure and who to make the disclosure to.
- Strong commitment to the value of whistleblowing in the workplace and support to encourage whistleblowers to report improper conduct wherever it is observed. This should include commitment by senior management to leadership and responsibility for ensuring that whistleblowers are protected from direct and indirect detrimental action.
- The provision of whistleblower training to ensure an adequate level of awareness among staff about whistleblowing. This training should be incorporated into induction programmes for all new staff and include regular whistleblower refresher training.
- Specific training for staff involved in conducting investigations and/or responsible for receiving whistleblower disclosures or providing welfare support.

CONCLUDING COMMENTS

Corruption and misconduct are difficult to fight when they are concealed. Whistleblowing is a powerful tool for uncovering such conduct but, as Brown (2008) notes, whistleblowing 'remains a complex and challenging process'. It requires social acceptance, an appropriate legislative framework and an organizational commitment. But the benefits are clear: whistleblowing reinforces good corporate governance, promotes ethical standards and integrity in democratic government. Above all, when used effectively it can make significant inroads on corruption and misconduct.

A number of ways of responding to whistleblowing have been outlined in this chapter. It shows through the practical experience of the Victorian Ombudsman in dealing with whistleblower protection legislation that many public sector organizations are still unaware of the legislative requirements and do not recognize the value of whistleblowing or facilitate its reporting. Failure to comply with the procedural requirements of the Whistleblowers Protection Act is of serious concern, as it erodes confidence in government and undermines the effectiveness of the whistleblowing legislation. Potential whistleblowers are also deterred from raising allegations.

Whistleblowers play a vital role in exposing and preventing corruption and misconduct, and thereby contribute significantly to the wellbeing of organizations and in so doing contribute to good public administration. The challenge is getting the right balance between a legislative framework for whistleblowing and flexible effective arrangements for its implementation in practice. Encouraging the whistleblower to come forward is dependent not only on a good legislative framework, but also on suitable arrangements on the ground. These include a conducive workplace culture where whistleblowers are perceived as conscientious employees rather than as troublemakers. Whistleblowers need confidence in an internal scheme where they are not discouraged by inaction when raising concerns. At the same time there should be an external monitoring and integrity body to which disclosures can be made in a flexible and appropriate manner and which has a broad holistic role for improving public administration. The strengths of the Victorian Ombudsman approach provides such a comprehensive model.

NOTES

1. Kennedy, Helena (2004), in foreword Calland, R. & Dehn, G. (eds), *Whistleblowing around the World: Law, Culture and Practice*, xv.
2. For examples, see http://www.pcaw.co.uk/aboutus/whistleblowers/htm
3. www.ombudsman.vic.gov.au
4. Suspected or alleged 'public interest' wrongdoing involves more than personal or private interests of the person making the disclosure and includes wrongdoing that threatens public integrity.
5. An example of this is the Victorian Ombudsman's Report, (June 2002) *An Investigation Into A Complaint About Preferential Treatment Of A Student By The University Of Melbourne* Melbourne, Victoria: Victorian Government Printer, where the Ombudsman identified innocent parties to a matter in his report because the allegations against them had been widely reported in the media.
6. The expression 'to blow the whistle' conjures up colourful images . . . of a policeman blowing his whistle to summon help to catch an offender escaping; . . . of a referee blowing the whistle on the football field, . . . of a canary in a coal mine (Lennane, 1995).
7. Near and Micelle (1984), 89; cited by Brown (2008).
8. Most legislation currently excludes consideration of motive, as it presents evidentiary difficulties. Instead, there is reliance on the notion of 'good faith' and/or having 'reasonable grounds to believe the information provided is true' and that 'knowing or reckless provision of false information is deemed to be an offence'.
9. Lennane (1995); Near & Miceli (1986).
10. Whistleblowers have been portrayed in film and print as being dramatically involved in a struggle between conscience and the omnipotent organization.
11. Vandekerckhove (2006); Hamilton & Maddison (2007); Clemmons (2007); Davis & Konishi (2007).

12. Whistleblowing is translated in French as '*droit d'alerte*', meaning the 'right to raise the alarm', avoiding the pejorative connotations in English.
13. The research found that 12 per cent of all public servants had reported some form of public interest wrongdoing in their organization in a two-year period . . . the number prepared to [blow the whistle] was also high.
14. Prenzler (2010) reported that the 'more matters are dealt with in-house, the more likely it is the corruption and misconduct will be ignored or down-graded, complainants will be dissatisfied and the public will be distrustful; and the issue of public integrity will be ongoing, highly contentious and politicized'.
15. Review of Commonwealth Criminal Law, Final report, Australia, 1991, p. 315.
16. Queensland Electoral and Administrative Review Commission 1991, Report on protection of whistleblowers. Brisbane, Australia.
17. www.wikileaks.org; see also Paul Barratt, *How Wikileaks changed the world*; presentation to the Australian Institute of International Affairs, Melbourne, 23 February 2011.
18. www.opendemocracy.org.za
19. www.whistleblowing.org.uk
20. www.whistleblowers.org.au
21. www.foi-asia.org
22. www.transparency.org
23. See The Ernst & Young 11th Global Fraud Survey, May 2010; KPMG Revisiting the role of the corporate whistleblower December 2009, Adelaide: KPMG Forensic Accounting available at http://www.kpmg.com/AU/en/IssuesAndInsights/ArticalesPublications/ForensicUpdate/Documents/Revisiting-the-role-of-the-corporate-whistleblower.pdf; Deloitte Forensic Corporate Counsel Survey 2010, Melbourne: Deloitte Touche Tohmatsu, available at http://www.deloitte.com/assets/Dcom-Australia/Local%20Assets/Documents/Services/Forensic/Coporate%20Counsel%20Survey%202010%20v2.0.pdf.
24. The United States of America, Australia, New Zealand, the United Kingdom, South Africa, Japan, the Netherlands, Ireland, Canada and Belgium, as well as Germany, India and Switzerland.
25. Transparency International reported no or no comprehensive whistleblower legislation in many countries and correlates this with its Corruption Perception Index for 2006 http://www.transparency.org/policy_research/nis
26. Protection mechanisms often rely on labour laws which exclude many persons working in an organization according to Transparency International.
27. *Commission National de l'Informatique et des Libertes* (28e Rapport d'Activite 2007).
28. For example Queensland's Fitzgerald Inquiry into corruption (1987–1989) found that police had observed corruption but felt powerless to act, and exposed the difficulties that whistleblowers faced as a result of disclosing information.
29. In some United States of America jurisdictions whistleblowers are provided protection from financial impact that the disclosure may have on their lives and can receive a proportion of any recovered funds. Although compensation payments to whistleblowers has been criticized (Lewis, 2003) as being too difficult and going against the notion that whistleblowing is done in the public interest, not for personal gain or private interest.
30. If the disclosure is made to an agency and they determine it is a protected disclosure, but not a public interest disclosure, and if the complainant does not seek to have the decision not to make it reviewed by the Victorian Ombudsman, the Ombudsman would not get to hear about it.
31. Serious corruption matters are also directed to Victoria Police where prosecutorial action may arise.
32. The Ombudsman's 'Investigation into the handling of drug exhibits at the Victoria Police Forensic Services Centre', December 2009; and 'Investigation into the disclosure of information by a councillor of the City of Casey', March 2010.
33. Unfortunately, the review of whistleblower legislation in Victoria has been delayed by the Victorian Government's acceptance of the recommendation that the whistleblowing

function be transferred to the (yet to be established) Victorian Integrity and Anti-corruption Commission.
34. Victorian Ombudsman, Conflict of interest in local government, March, 2008.
35. *Whistleblowers Protection Act 2001*, Ombudsman's Guidelines, August, 2009.

BIBLIOGRAPHY

Australia House of Representatives Standing Committee on Legal and Constitutional Affairs (2009), *Whistleblower protection: a comprehensive scheme for the Commonwealth Public Sector*, Canberra: Australian Government Publishing Service.

Australian Research Council Linkage Project (2007), *Whistling While They Work: Enhancing the Theory and Practice on Internal Witness Management in Public Service Organizations*, 2005–2008, available at http://www.griffith.edu.au/centre/slrc/whistleblowing/content_research.html (accessed August 2010).

Alford, C. (2001), *Whistleblowers: Broken Lives and Organizational Power*, Ithaca: Cornell University Press.

Baumgartner, F. (2007), 'Whistleblower procedures and personal data protection in France', *The Corporate Governance Law Review* **3**(2), 206–224.

Brown, A. J. (2006), *Public Interest Disclosure Legislation in Australia: Towards the Next Generation*, Canberra: Commonwealth Ombudsman.

Brown, A. J. (ed.) (2007), *Whistleblowing in the Australian Public Sector*, Draft Report: Griffith University.

Brown, A. J. (ed.) (2008), *Whistleblowing in the Australian Public Sector: Enhancing the Theory and Practice of Internal Witness Management in Public Sector Organizations*, Australia: The Australian National University E Press.

Calland, R. and C. Dehn (eds) (2004), *Whistleblowing Around the World: Law, Culture and Practice* ODAC and PCaW in Partnership with the British Council: Southern Africa, South Africa: Idasa Publishing.

Clemmons, D. (2007), 'Europeans Reluctant to Blow the Whistle', *Internal Auditor*, **64**(4), 16.

Commonwealth House of Representatives Standing Committee on Legal and Constitutional Affairs (2009), *Whistleblower protection: a comprehensive scheme for the Commonwealth public sector*, Canberra: Australian Government Publishing Service.

Davis, A. J. and E. Konishi, (2007), 'Whistleblowing in Japan', *Nursing Ethics*, **14**(2), 194–202.

De Maria, W. (1999), *Deadly Disclosures: Whistleblowing and the Ethical Meltdown of Australia*, Kent Town, SA: Wakefield Press.

De Maria, W. (2008), 'Whistleblowers and organizational protesters: Crossing Imaginary Border', *Current Sociology*, **56**(6), 865–83.

De Maria, W. and C. Jan (1994) 'Wounded workers: Queensland whistleblower study, Result release two', Brisbane: University of Queeensland.

De Maria, W. and C. Jan, (1997a), 'Eating its own: the Whistleblower's organization in vendetta mode', *Australian Journal of Social Issues*, **31**(1), 45.

De Maria, W. and C. Jan, (1997b) *Wounded Workers*, University of Queensland, Dept. of Social Work and Social Policy, Brisbane: University of Queensland.

Devine, T. (2004), 'Whistleblowing in the Unites States: the gap between vision and lessons learned', in Calland, R. and C. Dehn, (eds), *Whistleblowing Around the World: Law, Culture and Practice*, ODAC and PCaW in Partnership with the British Council: Southern Africa. South Africa: Idasa Publishing, pp. 74–100.

Ernst & Young 11th Global Fraud Survey on bribery and corrupt business practices, 25 May 2010, (www.ey.com)

Faunce, T. and S. Bolson, (2004), 'Three Australian whistleblowing sagas: lessons for internal and external regulation', *The Medical Journal of Australia*, **181**(1), 44–7.

Glazer, M.P. and P.M. Glazer (1989), *The Whistleblowers: Exposing Corruption in Government and Industry.* New York, NY: Basic Books.

Gundlach, M., M. Martinko and S. Douglas, (2008), 'A new approach to examining whistle-blowing: the influence of cognitions and anger, Society for Advancement of Management (SAM)', *Advanced Management Journal*, **73**(4) 40–50.

Hamilton, C. and S. Maddison, (2007), *Silencing Dissent: How the Australian Government is Controlling Public Opinion and Stifling Debate*, Crows Nest, NSW: Allen and Unwin.

Kaptein, M. (2002), 'Guidelines for developing an ethics safety net' *Journal of Business Ethics*, **41**(3), 217–235.

Latimer, P. and J. Brown (2008), 'Whistleblower laws: international best practice', *University of New South Wales Law Journal*, **31**(3), 766–94.

Lennane, J. (1995), 'The canary down the mine: what whistleblowers' health tells us about their environment'. Paper given at the Department of Criminology, Melbourne University conference 'Whistleblowers: protecting the nation's conscience?' 17 November, 1995.

Lewis, D. (1996), 'Employment protection for whistleblowers: on what principles should Australian legislation be based?', *Australian Journal of Social Issues*, **31**(1), 1997, 37–59.

Lewis, D. (2003), 'Whistleblowing statutes in Australia', *Deakin Law Review*, 319.

Lewis, D. (2006), 'The contents of whistleblowing/confidential reporting procedures in the UK: some lessons from empirical research', *Employee Relations*, **28**(1), 76–86.

Lewis, D. (2008), 'Ten years of public interest disclosure legislation in the UK: are the whistleblowers adequately protected?' *Journal of Business Ethics*, October, 497–507.

MacNab, B.R. and R. Worthley, (2007), 'Self efficacy as an intrapersonal predictor for internal whistleblowing: A US and Canada examination', *Journal of Business Ethics*, **79**, 407–421.

Marr, D. (2007) 'His Master's Voice: The Corruption of Public Debate Under Howard', Quarterly Essay, Number 26, Melbourne, Victoria: Black Inc.

Martin, B. (2003), 'Illusions of whistleblower protection' *University of Technology, Sydney, Law Review*, **5**, 120–125.

Miceli, M.P., and J.P. Near, (1992), *Blowing the Whistle*, New York: Lexington Books.

Miceli, M. and J. Near, (2005), 'Standing up or standing by: what predicts blowing the whistle on organizational wrongdoing', *Research in Personnel and Human Resources Management*, **24.**

Micelli, M.P., J.P. Near and C.R. Schwenck, (1991), 'Who blows the whistle and why?', *Industrial & Labor Relations Review*, **45**(1), 113–130.

Moore, L. (1996), 'Will the law in Australia protect the whistleblower?' Monash University, Economics and Business Faculty, School of Business and Electronic Commerce. Working Paper Series, Law, 1/96.

Myers, A. (2004) 'Whistleblowing – the UK Experience', in R. Calland & G. Dehn (eds), *Whistleblowing Around the World: Law, Culture and Practice*, ODAC and PCaW in Partnership with the British Council: Southern Africa, South Africa: Idasa Publishing, pp. 100–111.

Nader, R. (1972), 'Whistle blowing: the report of the Conference on Professional Responsibility', New York: Grossman Publishers.

Near, J.P. and M.P. Miceli, (1986), 'Retaliation against whistle-blowers: predictors and effect', *Journal of Applied Psychology*, **71**, 137–45.

New South Wales Independent Commission Against Corruption, *Unravelling corruption: a public sector perspective.* April 1994, Sydney, Australia.

Parliament of Australia, Department of Parliamentary Services (2005), 'Whistleblowing in Australia – Transparency, Accountability. . .But Above All, the Truth', Parliamentary Library Research Note, 14 February 2005, **31**, 2004–05.

Prenzler, T. (2010), Submission to the Victorian Integrity Review. available at http://www.apo.org.au/node/21530

Rehg, M. T., M. P. Miceli, J. P. Near, and J. R. Van Scotter, (2008), 'Antecedents and outcomes of retaliation against whistler-blowers: gender differences and power relationships' *Organization Science*, **19**(2), 221–40.

Security Executive Council (2007), 'Corporate Governance and Compliance Hotline Benchmarking Report', retrieved from www.securityexecutivecouncil.com/login.html

Stansbury, J. and V. Bart, (2009), 'Whistle-blowing among young employees: a life-course perspective', *Journal of Business Ethics*, **85**(3), 281–99.

Transparency International (2009), *Alternative to Silence: Whistleblower Protection in 10 European Countries*, Berlin: Transparency International.

Trott, K. (2004), in R. Calland and C. Dehn (eds), *Whistleblowing Around the World: Law, Culture and Practice* ODAC and PCaW in Partnership with the British Council: Southern Africa, South Africa: Idasa Publishing, pp. 119–142.

Tsahuridu, E. E., and W. Vandekerckhove, (2008), 'Organizational whistleblowing policies: making employees responsible or liable?' *Journal of Business Ethics*. **82**(1), 107–118

Vandekerckhove, W. (2006), *Whistleblowing and Organizational Social Responsibility: A Global Assessment*, Great Britain: Ashgate Publishing Company.

Wilkie, A. (2007) 'The Military and Intelligence Services', in C. Hamilton and S. Maddison, *Silencing Dissent: How the Australian Government is Controlling Public Opinion and Debate*, Crows Nest, NSW: Allen and Unwin, pp. 175–98.

24 The role of education in changing corrupt practices

Rose Gill Hearn

INTRODUCTION: KEY ISSUES

The New York City Department of Investigation (DOI) is the City's anti-corruption agency and one of the oldest law enforcement agencies in the country. We approach our mission by attacking corruption on many fronts – corruption prevention training, arrests, and recommendations for procedural changes when internal vulnerabilities in City agencies are exposed by our investigations. We often work closely with prosecutors and City agencies in these endeavours. The goal is to prevent or stop corruption in its tracks, effect positive change, and deliver a definitive and influential message of deterrence. The agency's strategy incorporates an array of educational outreach and press announcements to ensure that DOI's mission and purpose resonate within City government and externally to the public. This comprehensive approach DOI believes is good government. The lasting impact of DOI's reach for taxpayers is to prevent recurrence of fraud.

DOI's mandate is supported by a host of statutes that strengthen our investigatory powers. Our jurisdiction includes all City agencies, employees, elected City officials, any vendor who does business with the City, and anyone who receives benefits from the City. The agency has three principal functions: conduct background investigations on people hired or promoted into any managerial positions in City government to ensure that people of integrity work in those positions; conduct checks on vendors awarded most contracts with City government, thus ensuring that only vendors of integrity are receiving the City's many valuable taxpayer-funded contracts; and, of course, investigations.

Investigators routinely investigate and make arrests in cases such as housing fraud, theft of City funds and bribery, while also 'sinking their teeth into' long-term probes that have exposed and stopped large-scale official corruption by City and elected officials. DOI addresses corruption not only in the form of fraud and swindles, but corruption that impacts public safety. This expansive docket has resulted in a record number of complaints, arrests, and policy changes. In 2009, DOI received more than

13 700 tips and complaints as a result of our outreach efforts, through a variety of means.[1] People call us with allegations and information, file complaints on our website, write us letters, or visit our offices to report on problems and issues. In the past 20 years, DOI has made more than 6500 arrests, about 4000 of them have been made since 2002. Through a programme formalized in 2006, DOI has issued more than 2200 policy and procedure recommendations to City agencies, most of which have been implemented.

These accomplishments are due in large part to raising the Department's profile and accessibility. The Inspectors General with DOI maintain a constant physical presence at City agencies and have established other ways of communicating to keep up with evolving technology. Since 2002, DOI's agency website is interactive, enabling people to file complaints online; our background forms and annual financial disclosure forms can be prepared and filed online; and the public can follow DOI matters through our press releases and reports on DOI's website and Twitter account.

A STORIED HISTORY

DOI understands the significant impact that fraud and corruption have on City government since our Department was created as a result of a wide-ranging scandal that hit New York City in the late 1870s. William Boss Tweed was a corrupt politician who conspired with those who held the power and the purse strings in City government to cleverly manipulate the checks and balances in place. His schemes included getting contractors to present excessive bills for work performed on City contracts and City development projects, including the construction of the Brooklyn Bridge. All told, Tweed and his cronies skimmed an estimated $200 million dollars from the City's coffers. There was no mechanism in City government to stop them.

Tweed's ring began to unravel after a City employee from the Comptroller's Office, who felt betrayed by Tweed and his men, stepped forward and provided several newspapers with the phony set of books maintained by the Tweed ring that covered up their graft. A newspaper published what the Comptroller's employee dug up, and Tweed's power ended. In the wake of that scandal, the public was outraged and people in City government realized they needed to create a robust and independent agency empowered to investigate corruption anywhere in government without fear or favour. Thus, in 1873 the City established the Office of the Commissioners of Accounts, the precursor to DOI. The new department was given subpoena power and the power to take testimony under oath.

So today's Department of Investigation owes its existence as the City's watchdog to Tweed and his unscrupulous colleagues.

Things today are certainly much better than they were in the 1870s. But in a City with more than 300,000 employees and an annual budget of $63.1 billion, the need for DOI hasn't diminished. Our mission is much the same as it was at our inception more than 135 years ago: DOI remains the City's watchdog when it comes to corruption and fraud.

At DOI, we have a budget of just over $19.3 million and a staff of approximately 210 people comprising investigators, attorneys, auditors, computer forensics specialists and administrative personnel. Many investigators have peace officer status. We also have a squad of New York City Police Department detectives assigned to DOI. Within DOI we are divided into a network of Inspectors General overseeing each of the City's 45 agencies.

In addition to the 210 people for whom we are funded, over the years we have added another nearly 200 people to our investigative cadre by entering into memoranda of understanding (MOUs) with various agencies to increase the size of DOI so that we can provide more oversight of those agencies. Typically, these MOUs have come about in the wake of arrests or some type of problem within the agency; but several agencies have also provided us with additional funding for lines proactively.

DOI has created several inspector general offices over the years for several City-related entities that have a direct connection to City activities. For example, we oversee the large offices of inspectors general for our school system, housing authority, and economic development agency. These extra funding and oversight arrangements have been extremely successful and have helped us to expose corruption on a broader scale.

DOI'S STRENGTH ROOTED IN LEGAL AUTHORITY

DOI's success is based on the legal foundation that imbues DOI with many of its powers. Since the corruption of the Tweed Ring occurred at the very top echelon of New York City government, it was necessary to create a watchdog agency that was statutorily independent, nonpartisan and effective. A toothless watchdog, one that lacked the statutory powers to be meaningful, or a watchdog too close to the executive branch of City government, or one unable to root out Tweed-style corruption, would not have been acceptable to New Yorkers in the 1870s. DOI was thus empowered to address these concerns and protect the public from corruption.

The New York City Charter is the City's principal source of structure and governance. Chapter 34 of the Charter establishes DOI as a law enforcement agency within City government, and sets forth its powers and jurisdiction. Thus, DOI is a 'Charter' agency, which means it cannot be eliminated on the whim, fear, or desire of the leaders in City government who may be nervous about any given DOI investigation.[2]

The Charter provides DOI with its independence. First, while the DOI Commissioner is appointed by the Mayor, that appointment must be confirmed by a vote of the full City Council. This feature, unique to the DOI Commissioner, is intended to impart a check and balance against the appointment of a DOI Commissioner who may lack independence. Second, with regard to dismissal of a DOI Commissioner by the Mayor, the Mayor would have to file his reasons for doing so publicly. This statutory feature is intended to fortify DOI's ability to investigate anyone in City government, all the way to the top echelons.

The Charter jurisdiction of DOI empowers the Department to investigate anything that might be fraudulent, corrupt, or wasteful in City government – a broad mandate. The Charter also provides DOI with the necessary investigative tools; for example, DOI may examine and remove any books and records of City agencies, confer immunity, and issue subpoenas for witness testimony and for books and records.

DOI refers cases for criminal prosecution to New York City's five District Attorneys, the State Attorney General, and the two US Attorneys that cover our region. DOI can also issue written reports to the public of findings and recommendations – a powerful and effective tool for exposing problems in any given sector of City government and for mandating reform.

DOI's statutory authority is also bolstered by Mayoral Executive Orders, which over the years have given additional powers to DOI. For example, an Executive Order signed by former Mayor Edward I. Koch in 1986 removed the internal inspectors general from the City agencies and put them under DOI's supervision. Up until that point, agencies each had an internal inspector general. These internal inspectors general were part of the agency and reported to the agency head, their investigative docket was known to the agency, and their budget came from the agency. In the 1980s, a series of municipal corruption scandals at several City agencies were thought to have flourished unchecked, in part, because of this arrangement, prompting Mayor Koch to sign the Executive Order (EO) that established DOI as the overall Inspector General for New York City government. The EO also reiterates that the DOI Commissioner has the discretion to conduct investigations in a confidential matter.[3]

There are several other important statutory features stemming from other Executive Orders that help DOI carry out its mission. As it was in Boss Tweed's time, we rely heavily on the many honest City employees to come forward and blow the whistle on corrupt schemes. And, in fact, that is the law. By Executive Order, employees of the City must cooperate with a DOI investigation upon penalty of termination for failure to do so. That Executive Order also mandates that every City employee has an affirmative obligation to report to DOI, without delay, any potentially corrupt activity taking place within City government, subject to penalty, including termination. That 'must report' obligation was also the result of corruption scandals where it was determined that various employees knew that wrongdoing was taking place, but did nothing or said nothing about it. Thus, the inclination to 'not get involved' was eliminated by law for City employees and the mandatory report obligation is one that DOI wields on a daily basis, yielding a tremendous flow of information about matters that should be investigated.[4]

At the same time the City requires employees to come forward, the City has a strong Whistleblower statute that protects City employees from retaliation for reporting wrongdoing. DOI is charged with investigating any allegation made by a City employee who has reported some wrongdoing, and then feels that he or she has been penalized for doing so. If DOI finds that an agency took such retaliatory action, DOI can request that the agency undo the action. If there is a refusal to do so, the DOI Commissioner can go to the Mayor to have him direct the agency to undo the retaliation.[5]

What facilitates DOI's mission is the fact that City employees are obligated to report possible wrongdoing to DOI, and the law provides them with protection for doing so.

EDUCATION: MAKING AN IMPACT BEYOND THE ARREST

Criminal arrests are a core function of DOI. But thanks to the agency's unique role within City government, DOI's authority to effect lasting change goes beyond putting an individual in handcuffs. The following pages outline the four strategies the agency uses to accomplish that goal. Each has the common theme of educating others about DOI's purpose.

1. Corruption Prevention Lectures

Since 2002, DOI's inspectors general have waged a consistent and targeted educational campaign, conducting nearly 4000 corruption prevention lectures for tens of thousands of City employees and contractors.[6] These lectures have become a key way for DOI to publicize its mission and alert people of their obligation to report wrongdoing to us, and the

Whistleblower law that protects them when they do. These lectures are vibrant opportunities to connect with City participants on a one-to-one basis. Inspectors general know these lectures make a difference from attending employees' comments and from the tips received.

At one lecture, a City employee from our housing agency came forward at the end of the lecture and told us about suspicious activity within the employee's agency. That information led to a DOI undercover operation that ultimately resulted in corruption charges against a New York State Assemblywoman. The public official marketed herself as a corrupt legislator ready to use her position to help a private builder unlawfully acquire City-owned land in her district if, in exchange, he would build her a half-million-dollar house in a gated community in Queens for practically no money. A DOI investigation led to criminal charges against the legislator who was convicted, stripped of her elected office, and sentenced to between two and six years in prison.[7]

Another lecture delivered an unforgettable message to the participants. The background is as follows: a corrupt City housing employee had been arrested by an arbitrator. This chain of events was well known in the agency, and it was poor for morale. Once gainfully re-employed at the agency, the corrupt City housing employee again came under investigation by DOI for taking a bribe to refrain from reporting housing code violations. DOI made the case, and as we were preparing to arrest him we discovered that he had signed up for a DOI anti-corruption lecture. The deterrent value was too much to pass up, and so DOI arrested the recidivist at the end of the lecture.

In another instance, DOI arrested City environmental agency employees for participating in an illegal gun sale on City property and then conspiring to cover it up – all based on a tip from a corruption prevention lecture. The tip alleged that there was favourable treatment between a City Department of Environmental Protection supervisor and his subordinate as a result of an illegal gun sale. DOI's investigation substantiated that a supervisor, who did not have a valid pistol permit in New York State, purchased a Colt .45 magnum semi-automatic pistol from a subordinate for $650, and the illegal transfer of the gun was conducted in the parking lot of a City facility. In addition, the investigation found that the defendants conspired to cover up the illegal gun sale by falsely filing documents to make it appear that the gun was legally transferred.

2. Reforming City Government in Real Time

DOI shares its knowledge of the problems it exposes with the relevant City agencies by recommending remedies to the corruption vulnerabilities uncovered in our investigations. The function of effecting change within City operations is so important to DOI that we appointed a senior analyst to track all recommendations made by inspectors general to City agencies, as well as how and when the recommendations are implemented. The programme has been a patent success, with inspectors general issuing more than 2200 policy and procedure recommendations since 2002 on a wide variety of topics. Agencies that do not take corrective action will hear from DOI again. Being able to measure the change that results from our investigations illustrates the significant impact DOI has in attacking corruption.

These recommendations are powerful tools toward agency improvement. For instance, in January 2007, DOI issued a public report regarding 14 members of the Fire Department who had submitted bogus educational degrees in an attempt to obtain promotions or appointments. DOI's report included recommendations to strengthen the agency's degree verification process. Later that same year, because DOI's recommendations had been implemented, the Fire Department knew what to look for and became suspicious of educational degrees submitted by six job applicants. The Fire Department notified DOI, which arrested the six applicants on charges of submitting phony educational degrees.[8]

In another case, when the media captured video of rats scurrying around the dining room of a fast-food restaurant in Manhattan, only a day after a City inspector gave it a passing grade, DOI stepped in to investigate. In the spring of 2007, we issued a public report and recommended a host of improvements, including the termination of the Health Inspector who gave the restaurant a passing grade, the simplification of the system used by City Health Inspectors to grade food establishments, and public notification if an establishment failed an inspection. The Health Inspector no longer works at the agency, and the Health Department incorporated our recommendations as part of a new food-safety programme.[9]

In August 2007, DOI issued findings on its investigation into the deaths of 11 children who were under the care of the City's child welfare agency, issuing a series of recommendations in a 129-page public report. DOI's key finding and recommendation to the agency was the need to strengthen its investigations by hiring more experienced investigators into their ranks.[10] The City's child welfare agency responded by adding law enforcement personnel to its ranks, and, two years after the report, the recommendation took root by enhancing the child welfare agency's ability to investigate child abuse cases effectively. Hearing some of the particular case-related anecdotes where issues relating to fragile children were identified and then addressed due to the expertise of these investigators was a rewarding and poignant testament to DOI's comprehensive work on this case.[11]

These examples show that DOI's investigations and recommendations have real and enduring impact.

A case study: DOI's unique role[12]

DOI's strength is its unique combination of law enforcement expertise and insight into City practices and procedures. These distinctive skills are highlighted in criminal cases where specific City functions, such as procurement and regulatory processes play a role in fraud or malfeasance. This was particularly apparent in a rapidly unfolding case from the summer of 2010 in which DOI and its federal partners worked around the clock to expose a prolific criminal network exploiting the City's publicly-funded and regulated day-care programme that touched at least three City agencies and more than 30 day-care centres.

The investigation exposed a criminal scheme in which children's interests were sacrificed for greed. The defendants – seven City employees and four day-care directors – held various jobs that were supposed to protect and enrich children's lives, but instead their focus became about money.

The investigation was a full-court press and is continuing. But even as the criminal probe advanced, DOI was there to close the fraud gaps it found at the various City agencies immediately, that is, recommending unannounced site visits at the day-care centres to confirm that the children for which the City was paying were actually in attendance, rotating work locations of City employees to reduce the risk of fraternization between staff and clients, and conducting audits of files.

In addition, DOI alerted the appropriate Health Department officials to the need for prompt and thorough inspections of the day-care facilities associated with the investigation. More than 20 day-care centres were closed due to violations that were part of the fraud exposed by the investigation. DOI's access and keen understanding of City processes allows it to step in quickly and safeguard the public. The agency deftly balances the momentum of the criminal investigation with sharing what it has learned to correct problems in real time and prevent the same type of fraud from recurring.

3. Working with City Agencies

DOI, unlike other law enforcement agencies, will share lessons learned from an investigation with the affected City agency, and suggest changes for successfully changing vulnerable practices. DOI has also worked very closely with some agencies to overcome cultures of corruption. This type of outreach builds a better understanding between DOI and City agencies and gives DOI a greater, more effective ability to attack unique problems at specific agencies.

Addressing Entrenched Corruption at the Buildings Department in 2002, DOI arrested 19 current and former employees of the Department of Buildings (DOB) in a large-scale bribery case, which nearly wiped out the entire plumbing-inspector unit. Two of those 19 employees had been arrested previously by DOI and had got their jobs back at the DOB. Following those arrests, scores of re-inspections had to be done at tremendous cost to the Buildings Department. For decades, DOI arrested a double-digit number of Buildings employees approximately every two years.

Corruption was a definite problem at the DOB. But DOI had an opportunity. DOI could not on its own change what had become a culture of corruption at the Buildings Department. Indeed, it needed to work with DOB to effect lasting change. DOB became a full partner with DOI in a forceful, concentrated, and intelligent push-back. For example, DOI arrested not only the DOB inspectors who accepted bribes, but also the contractors, owners, and others who paid the bribes, and DOI conducted anti-corruption lectures throughout DOB to engage employees in discussions about their legal obligation to report corruption to DOI and that they may do so confidentially and with whistleblower protection.

When it came to the sentencing of the plumbing inspectors arrested in 2002, at DOI's suggestion, the Mayor wrote a victim-impact letter to the Judge. Such a letter is certainly not something a judge receives every day, and it explained that the effect of this corruption was very real and very costly to the City. At sentencing, the Judge commented on the letter he received from the Mayor, and sentenced the inspectors to jail, which was exactly the deterrent message that DOI wanted to be sent.

In addition, in 2004, DOI combined forces with the DOB to create the Buildings Special Investigations Unit (BSIU), a sizeable unit that is supervised by DOI and includes staff from DOB. This unit was formed to identify, investigate, and suspend or revoke the DOB licences of individuals and companies that deliberately violate the City's construction codes.

BSIU exposes licenced professionals and other individuals who try to circumvent the building and construction codes to file jobs faster and cheaply, illegal behaviour that can lead to potentially dangerous conditions. And because DOI supervises the Unit, it can easily initiate criminal investigations where warranted, such as the August 2010 arrest of a City sewage treatment worker who applied at DOB for a site safety manager's licence, and to meet licence requirements, used a forged letter purportedly from his City-agency supervisor, which falsely reported his experience. BSIU investigators check backgrounds of applicants and questioned the experience this individual reported to obtain the licence. DOI investigators were immediately notified and, working with the BSIU investigator, DOI arrested the applicant whose licence application was rejected by DOB. Other arrests DOI has made as a result of BSIU actions include engineers, general contractors, and expeditors charged with filing false documents and engaging in 'plan stamping' schemes. Together, the agencies are sending the message that criminal conduct that undercuts DOB's authority and puts the safety of workers and the public at risk will not be tolerated.

Since 2004, BSIU has investigated and administratively prosecuted more than 350 cases, resulting in more than 192 revocations or suspensions of licences and certification privileges of professionals, including architects and engineers, and fines totalling approximately $1.2 million.

The results of DOI's targeted efforts with DOB have been profound. Since 2002, DOI has arrested 38 DOB employees and 247 members of the construction trades on charges relating to DOB matters. In addition, more DOB employees report bribe offers made to them than ever before. The evidence: DOI has arrested more than 75 individuals in investigations originating from tips from DOB personnel.

In short, as a result of our combined efforts, over an eight-year period, DOI has seen a sustained improvement at DOB in reducing corruption and, in particular, changing from a culture of turning-a-blind-eye to corruption to one of reporting corruption. Buildings' employees recognize that they are the City's frontline when it comes to guarding against potential wrongdoing and uncovering potential safety hazards in construction. The relationship between DOI and DOB is a model of how it should work.[13] It is an example of cooperation that continues.[14]

A case study: DOI's comprehensive approach

In 2007 and 2008, New York City experienced several fatal construction-related incidents that starkly showed the tragic connection between integrity issues and safety. DOI's knowledge about construction crimes, its access and relationship to the DOB, and its partnership with prosecutors meant that DOI became the investigative hub for criminal probes into wrongdoing and administrative examinations that resulted in changing troubled or unsafe construction practices. This strategy sent a definitive message that wrongdoing would bring a coordinated and swift response from the City.

DOI conducted a top-to-bottom review of DOB's Cranes and Derricks division, resulting in the arrests of two veteran DOB employees – a crane inspector charged with falsifying Cranes and Derricks inspection records, and an assistant chief inspector who was charged and convicted of receiving bribes from a crane company, falsifying mobile crane inspection reports and tampering with licensing exams. DOI also worked with the Manhattan District Attorney in an investigation that resulted in the indictment and conviction of the crane company and its principal in connection with that bribery scheme.

In the summer of 2008, DOI also worked with DOB to conduct a proactive inspectional sweep of nearly 50 construction sites in Manhattan, Brooklyn, Queens and the Bronx to determine if crane operators at these sites were properly licenced. The positive news was that investigators found the operators all in compliance. However, they also found an expired permit for operation of a tower crane at a Manhattan site, issuing a violation and stop work order for operation of that crane.

Based on the corruption uncovered by DOI, and as the result of a DOI recommendation, DOB overhauled the testing process it administered for one of the crane operator's licences it issues, designating an experienced organization to create and administer the test.

DOI's investigation of a fire at the demolition of a building near Ground Zero that killed two City firefighters resulted in indictments of the company that was demolishing the building, the site safety manager, the director of abatement and a foreman on the site. DOI also closely examined the practices of the Fire and Buildings Departments as it related to this incident, issuing a public report of its investigation, findings, and recommendations.[15]

Vendor/corrupt elected official

DOI's role as the City's anti-corruption agency includes offering solutions to difficult dilemmas that occur as a result of exposing corruption.

In 2006, a lengthy and complicated investigation by federal authorities and DOI of a State legislator, who was also the leader of the union whose members execute the multi-hundred-million-dollar contracts for maintaining New York City's street lights, culminated in the official's indictment on corruption charges. The City was faced with the challenge of re-bidding these crucial City contracts while also ensuring that the City's street lights continued to burn. In coordination with the City Department of Transportation, DOI employed its integrity monitor programme.

An integrity monitor provides a contractor with an expert team of attorneys, forensic accountants and investigators with special training and experience to establish and enforce good business practices and a code of ethical conduct for the contractor. This integrity monitor, in turn, reports to DOI, and works closely with DOI to ensure the City's interests are protected.

Specifically, DOI put in place integrity monitors that oversaw the relevant vendors to guard against corruption and misconduct. The situation was evaluated on a day-to-day basis in light of the then-ongoing criminal investigation. The cost of the monitors was incurred by the electrical vendors. At the end of the limited period prescribed in these monitoring agreements, one of the contractors withdrew its bid for new City contracts, while the other entered into an appropriately tailored monitoring agreement with DOI.

In 2008, the now former state legislator and labour leader pleaded guilty to a federal racketeering and fraud charge involving the theft of money from the union's bank account, accepting payments from union contractors, and maintaining a secret interest in a company doing business with the union. As part of his guilty plea, he agreed to forfeit $2.2 million that he derived from his crimes and to forfeit an expensive property on Long Island, N.Y. The defendant is now serving a 10-year federal prison sentence.[16]

DOI has a long history of utilizing monitors and an established procedure for selecting them, which includes a public posting soliciting expressions of interest from any firm that seeks consideration for an appointment as a monitor. When a situation arises that calls for the appointment of a monitor, a committee evaluates and decides which firm from among those that have expressed interest is best suited for the project. DOI does not allow companies to select their own monitors so that monitors will be truly independent of the companies' interests.

Significantly, DOI's integrity monitor programme has received national and international attention for its success in helping to ensure the proper expenditure of funds in connection with the recovery project at Ground Zero. DOI even testified about its monitor programme before a Congressional Committee that examined ways the federal government could avoid fraud and waste when it is called upon to respond with emergency services in the wake of disasters such as Hurricanes Katrina and Rita.[17]

Proactive monitor of a massive public infrastructure project

DOI utilized integrity monitors again when DEP (Department of Environmental Protection) embarked on the multi-billion-dollar building of a water filtration project in the Bronx. Due to the scope, scale and significance of the project, the City took the additional proactive step of placing a private monitor on the project, which reports directly to DOI and serves as DOI's on-site eyes and ears at the project. The monitor has a fulltime presence at the site and its goal is to ensure accountability as well as compliance with legal, regulatory and contractual requirements, including proper billing on the project. DOI oversees the monitor's work by regularly meeting with the monitor to discuss issues. When warranted, DOI requests that the monitor conduct investigations, which DOI directs.

DOI and DEP took a similar route on another water filtration project in Brooklyn. DOI used DEP funds to hire additional investigative engineering audit resources to ensure that City funds have been and will continue to be properly spent.

These two undertakings were in keeping with DOI's and New York City's goal to prevent corruption and avoid taxpayer money from sluicing out the door.[18]

DOI has several integrity monitors reviewing the work of contractors engaged in City projects that include construction and electrical work.

DOI has seen tangible results from its integrity monitor programme. In fact, a tip received by an integrity monitor on a City capital project led to a DOI-federal undercover investigation and the March 2010 arrest of a Queens man on charges that he sold numerous fraudulent safety training certifications to undercover investigators, construction workers, and companies. The tip received by the monitor and passed on to DOI was a validation of the wisdom and effectiveness in building into capital projects ways to prevent and/or detect fraud.

Exposing theft of public dollars

A DOI investigation that uncovered adoption-subsidy and fictitious services schemes operating within the City's child welfare agency not only resulted in the arrests and convictions of two City employees and five other individuals, but also revealed a need to tighten the financial controls that involved these City processes.[19] DOI worked closely with the City's Administration for Children's Services (ACS) and as a result the ACS Commissioner appointed an integrity taskforce consisting of several leaders from within the child welfare agency, expert analytical staff from various divisions within the agency, and consultants with knowledge of ACS operations and business processes to target areas for change.

DOI's investigation found that the criminal schemes continued undetected because the arrested City employees were allowed unfettered access to the system, with little or no oversight. DOI and ACS discussed this finding and ACS took the adoption-subsidy function, which was previously housed in one division, and spread it across three divisions. Currently, no sole unit has full access to all the systems involved in the process.

In addition, ACS is in the process of establishing clear and written operating policies where previously there were none. The expected outcome is that each programme area under adoption subsidies and services will have a definite operating manual, outlining staff members' functions. In the interim, ACS has created a workflow chart to clarify staff members' roles and responsibilities.

In consultation with DOI, ACS is moving forward on establishing an internal audit unit that will review the financials of the various programmes that ACS controls.

Investigations as opportunity

DOI constantly looks for particularly problematic areas to focus its resources to make a significant impact. After DOI investigators uncovered several embezzlement cases at City-funded nonprofits, the agency recognized the need for increased scrutiny of these organizations that receive millions of City-taxpayer dollars. As a result, DOI created a special nonprofit-vendor fraud unit about three years ago, to respond to that need.

Two key DOI investigations that led to the formation of the unit were:

- DOI exposed fraud and mismanagement at a City-funded nonprofit, in which executives fraudulently siphoned hundreds of thousands of dollars and routinely falsified records, regarding how public funds were spent and medical records of preschool children. As a result of this investigation, DOI issued a public report and a series of recommendations demonstrating ways that City agencies and not-for-profits can help protect themselves against fraud and abuse. Two of the organization's executives were charged, and each pleaded guilty.
- The prosecution of a now former State Senator and three co-defendants originated from a referral to DOI from another City agency regarding financial impropriety at a City-funded Bronx nonprofit, which DOI auditors and investigators meticulously examined, exposing the trail and extent of the fraud that involved the State Senator, three of his associates and ultimately four Bronx nonprofits. DOI investigators did what they do best; they followed the money, uncovering hundreds of thousands of dollars in public funds that paid for personal luxuries, such as the Senator's membership in a vacation club, a luxury villa in the Dominican Republic, and even costs related to the Senator's private cigar manufacturing and distribution company. DOI worked with federal authorities to stop the corruption, and ultimately each of the four co-defendants was held accountable, including the former state Senator who was sentenced to seven years in prison.[20]

The results of the Not-for-Profit/Vendor Fraud Unit have been prolific: more than 35 arrests, almost all ending in convictions, have resulted from DOI's forensic auditors' success in following the money stolen by unscrupulous insiders, City employees, public officials, and others. One investigation resulted in the 30-month prison sentence of a former deputy director of two non-profits who embezzled hundreds of thousands of dollars in public funds intended for the City's neediest children. At another non-profit, DOI's investigation led to the arrest of two executives for embezzling more than $100,000 and spending it on clothing, restaurants, travel, campaign contributions, and other personal expenses. Both were convicted and sentenced to prison terms.[21]

DOI investigators are experts in this area and, as a result, bored into how these unscrupulous non-profits are funded. DOI joined with the US Attorney's Office for the Southern District of New York and began to examine the way that the City Council dispersed millions of dollars in discretionary funds to non-profits, with little oversight. That probe has yielded a series of criminal cases, including the arrest of two former City Councilmen and one current City Councilman on corruption charges, one of whom is serving a five-year prison sentence after pleading guilty to diverting funds from non-profits that earned him more than $100,000. It also brought to light the so-called 'holding codes' in which the names of nonexistent organizations were used to hold sums of discretionary money each year when the budget was adopted. That practice was stopped due to DOI's probe.

Because DOI's investigations revealed that discretionary funds were a source of temptation for individuals to engage in corruption or conflicts of interest, DOI worked with the Speaker of the City Council, who controls the discretionary funding process, to establish reforms that would safeguard integrity. DOI shared its observations and recommendations stemming from our ongoing examination into this complicated discretionary funding arena. In the spring of 2010, as a result of DOI's discussions with the Speaker, a series of reforms were announced, including new restrictions on funded organizations' use of consultants and on Council members' sub-letting office space, practices DOI found in its investigations to have been abused.

4. The Importance of Public Outreach

DOI promotes its mission in the media through press releases and public reports and makes information about the agency available on its website and through Twitter feeds Making sure the public knows about our arrests, what the cases are about, and that DOI's mission is active, productive, and continuing is a key component of the agency's message of deterrence.[22] Building a robust relationship with the press is important because it raises the public's awareness of the cost of corruption and DOI's success in curtailing it.

Over the past several years, DOI has issued hundreds of releases and in

Fiscal Year 2010 it netted over 1 million views of the pages on its website. Visitors to DOI's homepage can find out more about the agency, the cases we investigate, our history, and they can also file a complaint, or directly email the Commissioner. DOI's public website also holds an archive of the annual reports we issue, which catalogue DOI's accomplishments and a variety of statistics about the agency, such as the number of arrests, complaints handled, and corruption prevention lectures presented. DOI's record high numbers reflect the agency's significant influence in stopping corruption and transforming deficient and flawed practices.

One of DOI's greatest strengths is that we issue public reports of our findings and recommendations – a compelling way to expose problems and recommend reform. These are authoritative, detailed publications that offer a window into our investigative findings and recommendations for improvements.

Since 2002, DOI has issued 17 public reports[23] on an array of investigations, including drinking and fighting at a firehouse where a firefighter was severely injured and the subsequent cover-up; an examination of the circumstances surrounding the death of a woman in the psychiatric emergency room at a City hospital; and the findings from an investigation into the improper disposal of scrap metal and environmentally hazardous materials by City Sanitation Workers. Making our findings public in the form of a report creates transparency and instills confidence that the system isn't afraid to bare all and make improvements where necessary.

In addition, DOI seeks out opportunities to speak at relevant conferences to present DOI's mission to a global audience. DOI has represented the New York City perspective and spoken at integrity conferences in Amsterdam, Turkey, and California; provided training to fledgling anti-corruption agencies in Tanzania, Africa, Chicago, and Philadelphia. Furthermore, in October 2008, DOI hosted the first New York City National Watchdog Conference, bringing together 11 Inspectors General from other municipalities and states in the country, the US Navy and scholars and experts on integrity to discuss and debate the issues that anti-corruption agencies face. Those conference findings are the subject of a special issue of Public Integrity, a renowned journal on ethics and leadership.

The DOI effect

DOI's vital and visible role has dealt a decisive blow to corruption in New York City. The agency dead-ends corruption by arresting individuals who perpetrate it and stays behind to recommend ways to strengthen controls and prevent fraud in the future. The agency's impact reflects how education in its many forms through outreach and partnerships results in eliminating and changing corrupt practices. One of the City agencies where

DOI has made a significant impact is at the DOB, not only in ferreting out corruption from within the ranks but also stopping contractors and others from committing fraud against the DOB.

DOI embraces a comprehensive strategy to attack corruption, one that encompasses making arrests, changing government policy and procedures, and reaching out to City employees, contractors and the public. The agency is a testament to good government principles, stemming corruption's corrosive effects, safeguarding taxpayers' dollars, and making government more effective.

A case study: the benefits of outreach

As part of its mission and message of deterrence, DOI regularly educates a variety of groups of the agency's mission, findings and needs, including:

- City employees and contractors about their obligation to report corruption;
- the public about DOI's work and its impact on corruption;
- fellow City agencies about corruption vulnerabilities DOI has uncovered and changes it has recommended; and
- prosecutors, with whom DOI works closely to maximize the City's recovery of stolen public funds. As a result of those efforts, since fiscal year 2002, DOI cases have resulted in the City recouping $35 million in restitution.

DOI always looks for new educational opportunities to further our message of deterrence and root out corruption. A case in point occurred in 2010 when DOI worked with a vendor providing the agency access to an array of online informational databases to streamline and strengthen review of the approximately 5400 financial disclosure forms electronically filed with DOI annually. The discussion with the vendor was fruitful, and the outcome resulted in the vendor creating a unique computer programme that will cross-reference these forms with a variety of records, identifying discrepancies and potential red flags. Any concerns will then be followed up by DOI investigators. DOI seized an opportunity to meet face-to-face and inform the vendor of DOI's mission and the many roles it has, which had beneficial results.

NOTES

1. DOI Release #55-2010, 'DOI Arrests 877 in 2009, Continuing the Agency's Record-High Trend of Arrests' (2009), New York City Department of Investigation.

2. New York City Charter Chapter 34, §§ 801-807 (Lexis 2010).
3. New York City Mayoral Executive Orders 16 (July 1978), 78 (October 1984, amending EO16), 105 (December 1986, amending EO16), 'The Commissioner of Investigation, Inspectors General and Standards of Public Service'.
4. Mayoral Executive Order No. 16, 'The Commissioner of Investigation, Inspectors General and Standards of Public Service,' § 4(d).
5. New York City Administrative Code § 12-113 (2001), 'Protection of sources of information'.
6. DOI Press Release #55-2010: 'DOI Closes Out Fiscal Year 2010 with 822 Arrests, a 12% Increase from Last Fiscal Year' (2010), New York City Department of Investigation.
7. DOI Press Release #48-2008: 'Statement by Department of Investigation (DOI) Commissioner Rose Gill Hearn on Prison Sentence of Former New York State Assemblywoman Diane Gordon' (2008), New York City Department of Investigation.
8. DOI Press Release #69-2007: 'DOI Arrests Six Fire Department Job Applicants for Allegedly Submitting Phony Educational Degrees' (2007), New York City Department of Investigation.
9. DOI Press Release #23-2007: 'DOI Recommends Termination of DOHMH Inspector Who Gave Passing Grade to Greenwich Village Restaurant, Despite Indications of Rat Infestation' (2007), New York City Department of Investigation.
10. DOI Press Release #59-2007: 'DOI Examination of Eleven Child Fatalities and One Near Fatality Finds Serious Deficiencies in How the City's Child Welfare Agency Conducted Investigations' (2007), New York City Department of Investigation.
11. DOI Press Release #133-2009, 'DOI Arrests 877 in 2009, Continuing the Agency's Record- High Trend of Arrests' (2010), New York City Department of Investigation.
12. United States Attorney Southern District of New York Press Release: 'Manhattan U.S. Attorney Charges 11 with Operating Massive Day Care Fraud and Bribery Scheme' (2010), US Attorney Southern District of New York, and DOI Release #60-2010: 'Remarks of DOI Commissioner Rose Gill Hearn Regarding Arrests in Day Care Fraud' (2010), New York City Department of Investigation.
13. Anechiarico, Frank and Smith, Dennis (2008), 'Evaluation of the New York City Integrity System', in Leo Huberts, Frank Anechiarico, Frederique Six (eds), *Local Integrity Systems: World Cities Fighting Corruption and Safeguarding Integrity*, The Hague: BJu Legal Publishers; p. 72.
14. DOI Press Release #108-2009: 'Spotlight on the Office of Inspector General for the New York City Department of Buildings (DOB)' (2009), New York City Department of Investigation.
15 DOI Release #55-2009, 'DOI Issues Report on Inspectional Issues Relating to Fatal Fire at 130 Liberty Street' (2009), New York City Department of Investigation.
16. United States Attorney Southern District of New York Press Release: 'Former New York State Assemblyman and Labor Leader Brian McLaughlin Sentenced to Ten Years in Prison for Racketeering and False Statement Crimes' (2009), U.S. Attorney Southern District of New York, and DOI Press Release #44-2009, 'DOI Statement on the Sentencing of Brian McLaughlin to 10 Years in Federal Prison' (2009), New York City Department of Investigation.
17. DOI Press Release #79-2006, 'Commissioner Rose Gill Hearn Testifies at the House Committee on Homeland Security's Subcommittee on Management, Integration and Oversight' (2006), New York City Department of Investigation.
18. Anechiarico, Frank and Smith, Dennis (2008), 'Evaluation of the New York City Integrity System', in Leo Huberts, Frank Anechiarico, Frederique Six (eds), *Local Integrity Systems: World Cities Fighting Corruption and Safeguarding Integrity*, The Hague: BJu Legal Publishers; p. 72.
19. United States Attorney Southern District of New York Press Release: 'Former Fiscal Officer at Foster Care Agency Sentenced in Manhattan Federal Court to 51 Months in Prison for Adoption Subsidy Scheme' (2010), U.S. Attorney Southern District of New York.

20. United States Southern District of New York Press Release: 'Former New York State Senator Sentenced in Manhattan Federal Court to Seven Years in Prison' (2010), US Attorney Southern District of New York.
21. United States Southern District of New York Press Release: 'Chief of Staff to NYS Assemblywoman Sentenced to One Year in Prison for Embezzling $115 000 in Federal Funds from Low-Income Tenants in the Bronx' (2010), U.S. Attorney Southern District of New York.
22. New York City Department of Investigation website, http://www.nyc.gov/html/doi/html/home/home.shtml.
23. New York City Department of Investigation website, http://www.nyc.gov/html/doi/html/pr/public.shtml.

Index